LATIN AMERICA AND CANADA

Latin America and Canada are fascinating places with people of
many cultures. This stone carving is from the Temple of Quetzalcoatl
in Mexico. It was built over 1,000 years ago by people who lived in
ancient Mexico.

JAMES A. BANKS   JEAN CRAVEN

BARRY K. BEYER   GLORIA LADSON-BILLINGS

GLORIA CONTRERAS   MARY A. McFARLAND

WALTER C. PARKER

MACMILLAN/McGRAW-HILL SCHOOL PUBLISHING COMPANY

NEW YORK   CHICAGO   COLUMBUS

PROGRAM AUTHORS

Dr. James A. Banks
Professor of Education and Director of
 the Center for Multicultural Education
University of Washington
Seattle, Washington

Dr. Barry K. Beyer
Professor of Education and American Studies
George Mason University
Fairfax, Virginia

Dr. Gloria Contreras
Professor of Education and Director of
 the Office of Multicultural Affairs
University of North Texas
Denton, Texas

Jean Craven
District Coordinator of Curriculum
 Development
Albuquerque Public Schools
Albuquerque, New Mexico

Dr. Gloria Ladson-Billings
Assistant Professor of Education
University of Wisconsin
Madison, Wisconsin

Dr. Mary McFarland
Director of Staff Development and
 Instructional Coordinator of
 Social Studies, K-12
Parkway School District
Chesterfield, Missouri

Dr. Walter C. Parker
Associate Professor of Social
 Studies Education and Director
 of the Center for the Study of
 Civic Intelligence
University of Washington
Seattle, Washington

CONTENT CONSULTANTS

Virginia Arnold
Adjunct Professor of Reading, Language Arts,
 and Children's Literature
Virginia Commonwealth University
Richmond, Virginia

Yvonne Beamer
Resource Specialist
Native American Education Program
New York, New York

Joyce Buckner
Director of Elementary Education
Omaha Public Schools
Omaha, Nebraska

Patricia J. Dye
Social Studies Coordinator
Plymouth-Carver Regional Schools District
Plymouth, Massachusetts

Walter Enloe
Director of Global Education
University of Minnesota
Minneapolis, Minnesota

Ted Scott Henson
Outreach Coordinator,
 Canadian Study Center, Duke University
Sixth Grade Teacher
Middleburg, North Carolina

Héctor Lindo-Fuentes
Associate Professor of History
Fordham University
Bronx, New York

Narcita Medina
Reading Specialist
Middle School 135
New York, New York

Harlan Rimmerman
Director of Elementary Education
Kansas City Public Schools
Kansas City, Kansas

Joseph B. Rubin
Director of Reading and Language Arts
Fort Worth Independent School District
Fort Worth, Texas

Clifford E. Trafzer
Professor of Ethnic Studies and Director
 of Native American Studies
University of California
Riverside, California

Nancy Winter
Former Member of the Executive Board of the
 National Council for Geographic Education
Social Studies Consultant
Clark University
Worcester, Massachusetts

GRADE-LEVEL CONSULTANTS

Ronnie Adams
Sixth Grade Teacher
Jackson Middle School
Jackson, Alabama

Gary Colonna
Sixth Grade Teacher
Hopewell Memorial Junior High School
Aliquippa, Pennsylvania

Diane Gralinski
Sixth Grade Teacher
Hoover Elementary School
West Berlin, Wisconsin

Nancy Harper
Sixth Grade Teacher
Cascade Junior High School
Bend, Oregon

Terry Heeter
Sixth Grade Teacher
Durkee School
Kenosha, Wisconsin

Billie Madux
Curriculum Specialist
De Soto County Schools
Hernando, Mississippi

Karen Tryda
Sixth Grade Teacher
Cleveland School of Science
Cleveland, Ohio

Theresa Zielsdorf
Sixth Grade Teacher
Whittier School
Kenosha, Wisconsin

CONTRIBUTING WRITERS

Peter Cipkowski
New York, New York

Diane Hart
Menlo Park, California

Eric Kimmel
Portland, Oregon

ACKNOWLEDGMENTS

The publisher gratefully acknowledges permission to reprint the following copyrighted material: "Owl" from THE MAGIC ORANGE TREE AND OTHER HAITIAN FOLKTALES collected by Diane Wolkstein. Text Copyright © 1978 by Diane Wolkstein. Reprinted by permission of Alfred A. Knopf, Inc. Excerpt from ARCTIC DREAMS by Barry Lopez. Copyright © 1986 by Barry Holstun Lopez. Reprinted with permission

continued on page 613

Macmillan/McGraw-Hill School Division
10 Union Square East
New York, New York 10003

Printed in the United States of America
ISBN 0-02-146009-4
1 2 3 4 5 6 7 8 9 RRW 99 98 97 96 95 94 93 92

CONTENTS

UNIT 4   Latin America   180

UNIT 5   Mexico   258

REFERENCE SECTION   561

Building Citizenship

PEOPLE WHO MAKE A DIFFERENCE

POINT/COUNTERPOINT

Traditions

Building Skills

THINKING/READING

GEOGRAPHY

STUDY/TIME

Songs

Charts, Graphs, Diagrams, and Time Lines

Maps

USING YOUR TEXTBOOK

TABLE OF CONTENTS
Lists all parts of your book and tells you where to find them

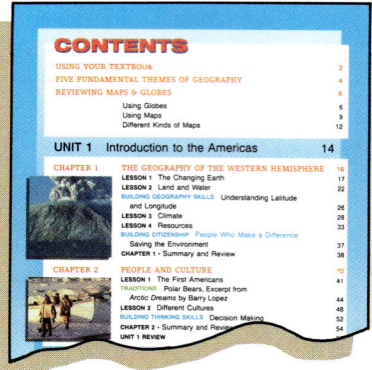

Your textbook contains many special features that will help you read, understand, and remember the people, geography, and history of Latin America and Canada.

TRADITIONS
Lessons which give you a deeper insight into the literature and cultures of the regions you are studying

REVIEWING MAPS & GLOBES

Using Globes   can also help you to make comparisons between places.

REVIEWING MAPS AND GLOBES
Reviews skills that will help you use the maps in your book

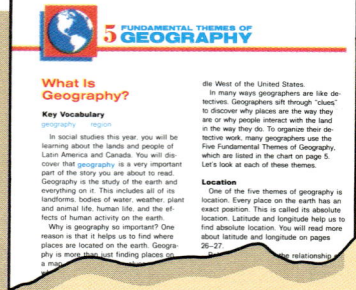

5 FUNDAMENTAL THEMES OF GEOGRAPHY

What Is Geography?

Key Vocabulary
geography   region

In social studies this year, you will be learning about the lands and people of Latin America and Canada. You will discover that geography is a very important part of the story you are about to read. Geography is the study of the earth and everything on it. This includes all of its landforms, bodies of water, weather, plant and animal life, human life, and the effects of human activity on the earth.

Why is geography so important? One reason is that it helps us to find where places are located on the earth. Geography is more than just finding places on a map...

...the West of the United States.

In many ways geographers are like detectives. Geographers sift through "clues" to discover why places are the way they are or why people interact with the land in the way they do. To organize their detective work, many geographers use the Five Fundamental Themes of Geography, which are listed in the chart on page 5. Let's look at each of these themes.

Location
One of the five themes of geography is location. Every place on the earth has an exact position. This is called its absolute location. Latitude and longitude help us to find absolute location. You will read more about latitude and longitude on pages 26–27.

...the relationship...

FIVE FUNDAMENTAL THEMES OF GEOGRAPHY
Introduces important themes of geography that will help you to compare, to contrast, and to understand the regions and people you will be studying

LESSON OPENER
Important vocabulary, people, and places introduced in the lesson

Lesson introduction

Asks you to think about what you already know from previous lessons or your own experience

Questions you should keep in mind as you read the lesson

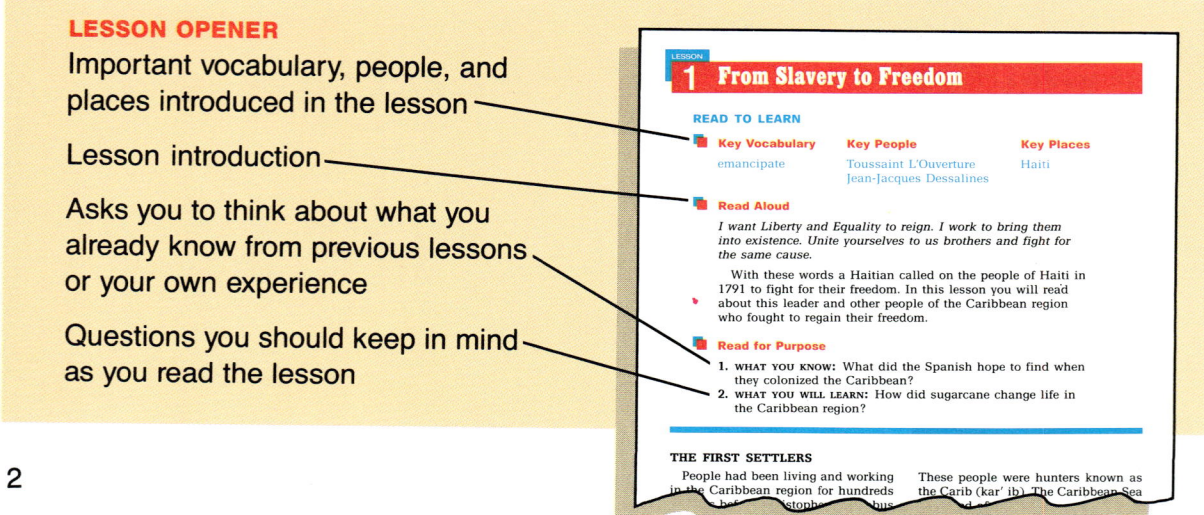

LESSON
1 From Slavery to Freedom

READ TO LEARN

Key Vocabulary	Key People	Key Places
emancipate	Toussaint L'Ouverture	Haiti
	Jean-Jacques Dessalines	

Read Aloud

I want Liberty and Equality to reign. I work to bring them into existence. Unite yourselves to us brothers and fight for the same cause.

With these words a Haitian called on the people of Haiti in 1791 to fight for their freedom. In this lesson you will read about this leader and other people of the Caribbean region who fought to regain their freedom.

Read for Purpose

1. **WHAT YOU KNOW:** What did the Spanish hope to find when they colonized the Caribbean?
2. **WHAT YOU WILL LEARN:** How did sugarcane change life in the Caribbean region?

THE FIRST SETTLERS

People had been living and working in the Caribbean region for hundreds...before...thus...

These people were hunters known as the Carib (kar' ib). The Caribbean Sea...

REFERENCE SECTION

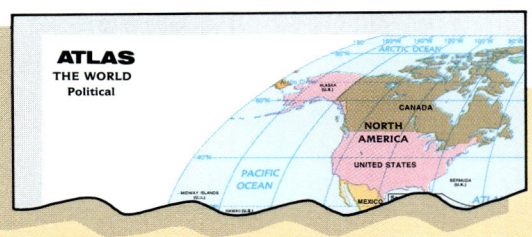

ATLAS

Maps of Latin America, Canada, and the world

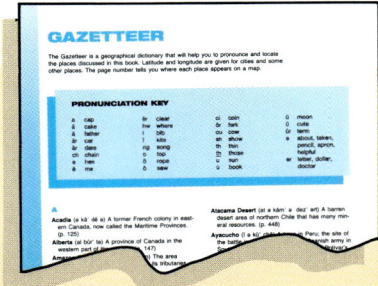

GAZETTEER

Location and pronunciation of major places discussed in your book and page where each is shown on a map

DICTIONARY OF GEOGRAPHIC TERMS

Definition and pronunciation of major geographic features

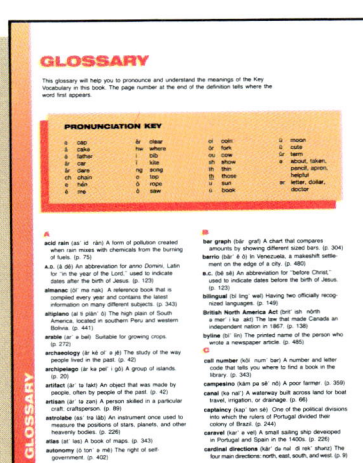

GLOSSARY

Definition and pronunciation of all Key Vocabulary and page where each is introduced

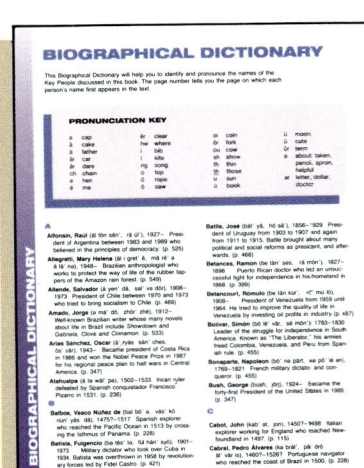

BIOGRAPHICAL DICTIONARY

Identification and pronunciation of important people discussed in your book and page where each is introduced

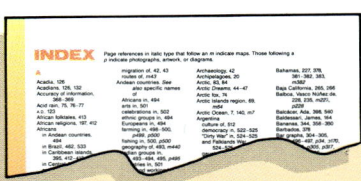

INDEX

Alphabetical list of important people, places, events, and subjects in your book and pages where information is found

What Is Geography?

Key Vocabulary

geography   region

In social studies this year, you will be learning about the lands and people of Latin America and Canada. You will discover that **geography** is a very important part of the story you are about to read. Geography is the study of the earth and everything on it. This includes all of its landforms, bodies of water, weather, plant and animal life, human life, and the effects of human activity on the earth.

Why is geography so important? One reason is that it helps us to find where places are located on the earth. Geography is more than just finding places on a map, though. It also involves studying what places are like. People play a big role in geography, too, for we affect—and are affected by—the land on which we live. The photo below, for example, shows how farming has affected land in the Mid-dle West of the United States.

In many ways geographers are like detectives. Geographers sift through "clues" to discover why places are the way they are or why people interact with the land in the way they do. To organize their detective work, many geographers use the Five Fundamental Themes of Geography, which are listed in the chart on page 5. Let's look at each of these themes.

Location

One of the five themes of geography is location. Every place on the earth has an exact position. This is called its absolute location. Latitude and longitude help us to find absolute location. You will read more about latitude and longitude on pages 26–27.

Relative location, or the relationship of one place to other places, is also very important to geographers. It helps them to understand the characteristics of places. For example, Florida is farther south than Vermont. This helps to explain why Florida is much warmer year-round than Vermont.

FIVE FUNDAMENTAL THEMES OF GEOGRAPHY

THEME	
Location	• Where is a place located? What is it near? What direction is it from another place?
Place	• What is a place like? What characteristics does it have?
Human-environment interaction	• How are people's lives shaped by the place where they live? How has a place been shaped by human activity?
Movement	• How do people and things move from one place to another? Why do they make these movements?
Regions	• Why are some places similar to others? Why are some places thought of as "belonging" together?

Place

Another theme of geography is place. A place is a particular site or spot on earth or in space. Each place has its own features, its own special feel. Geographers try to show what makes each place unique. They also compare places to see how they are similar and different.

Human-Environment Interaction

Human-environment interaction, or the relationship between people and the land on which they live is another theme of geography.

Think about how the environment helps to determine what people do to earn a living. For example, many people in the state of Iowa earn their living by farming, because Iowa contains vast amounts of good soil. Understanding connections between people and the land is an important part of geography.

Movement

Another theme of geography is the movement of people, goods, and ideas around the world.

Individuals and families move to new places for many reasons. Just as individuals and families move, so do large groups of people. For example, large numbers of people have moved to the United States from all over the world. Geographers study how patterns of movement affect people and the way in which communities develop.

Regions

Regions is another of the Five Fundamental Themes of Geography. A region is an area with common features that set it apart from other areas. Regions can vary in size. One example of a region is the Northeast of the United States. What is another example of a region? Geographers divide the world into regions in order to study different parts of the earth more closely.

1. What is geography?
2. Use the Five Fundamental Themes of Geography to describe the community in which you live.
3. Why does it help geographers to divide the world into regions?

Using Globes

Key Vocabulary

continent   equator

hemisphere   prime meridian

Before you begin to read this book, you will need to review the basic tools used by geographers. These tools are maps and globes. They will help you to understand connections between the lands and the people of Latin America and Canada.

Maps and globes can help you find out information about countries and cities, oceans and rivers, and mountains and deserts. They illustrate the geographic theme of location by showing the absolute and relative locations of places. They can also help you to make comparisons between places.

Comparing Maps and Globes

Look at your classroom globe. Globes are especially valuable tools for learning about the earth. Globes are models, or small copies, of the earth that provide very accurate information. Looking at a globe is much like looking at the earth from a point in outer space. On a globe, shapes and sizes are shown correctly in relation to each other. Directions and distances between places are also shown correctly.

Maps are drawings on flat surfaces of all or part of the earth. Maps have some advantages that globes do not. They can

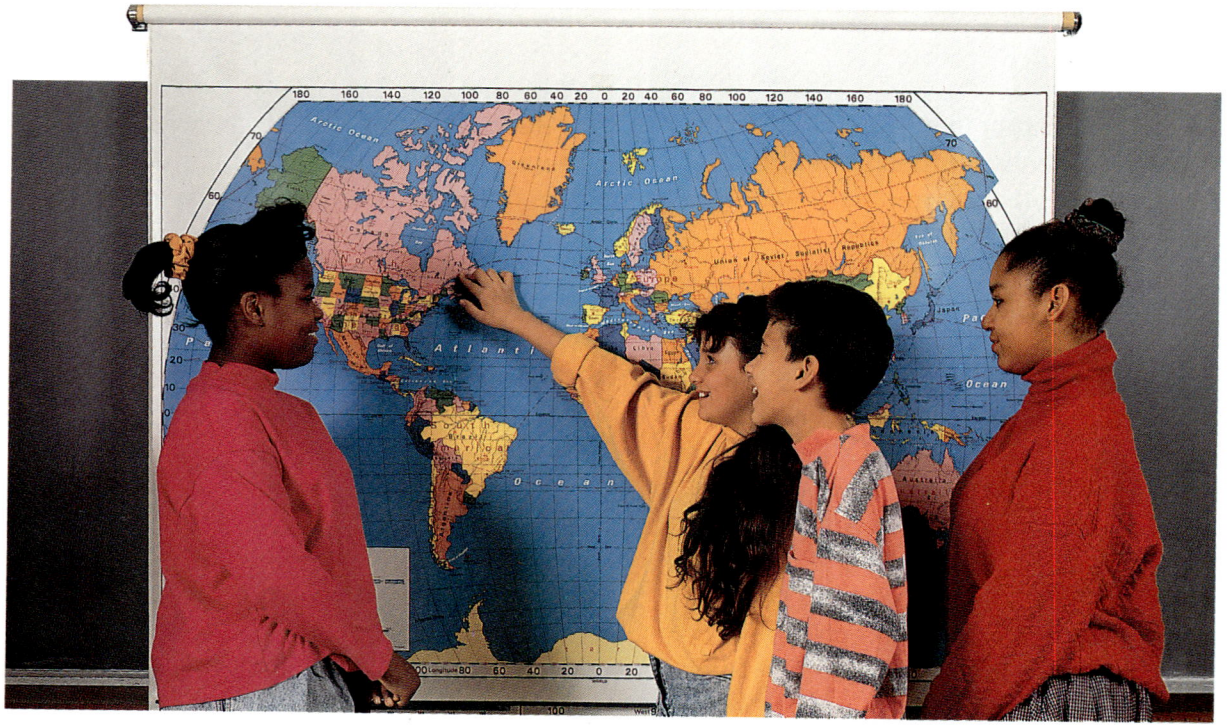

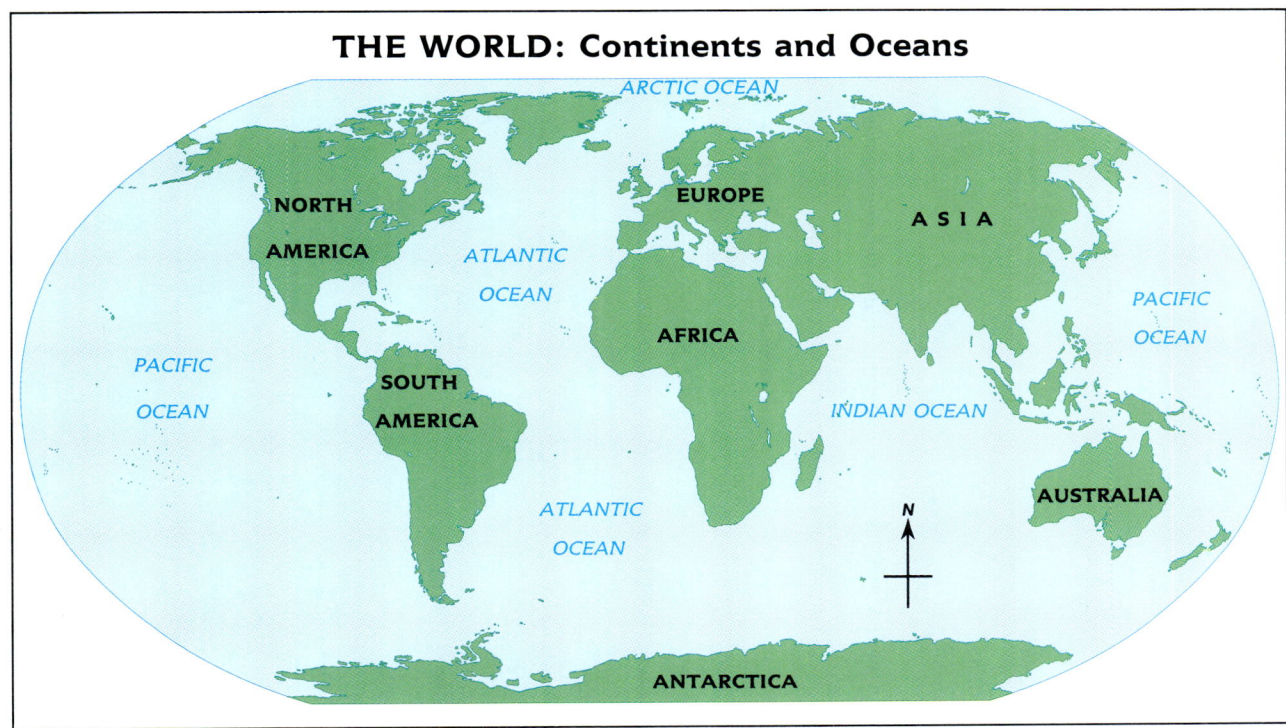

THE WORLD: Continents and Oceans

ARCTIC OCEAN

NORTH AMERICA

EUROPE

ASIA

ATLANTIC OCEAN

PACIFIC OCEAN

AFRICA

PACIFIC OCEAN

SOUTH AMERICA

INDIAN OCEAN

AUSTRALIA

ATLANTIC OCEAN

N

ANTARCTICA

be folded or rolled. They can be carried and stored easily. A map can show all of the world at once. On a globe, only half of the world can be seen at a time. You will be using maps as you read this book.

Continents and Oceans

The surface of the earth is made up of land and water. Globes show which parts of the earth's surface are land and which parts are water. Large bodies of land are called **continents**. There are seven continents: North America, South America, Europe, Asia, Africa, Australia, and Antarctica.

As the map on this page shows, the continents are separated, or nearly separated, from one another by water. If you look carefully at a globe, you will see that all the water on the earth's surface is part of a single large body of water. This body of water, which covers more than half the earth, is divided into smaller parts called

oceans. The earth has four oceans: the Atlantic, the Pacific, the Indian, and the Arctic. Find these oceans on the map above.

Hemispheres

Do you know what a **hemisphere** is? A sphere is a round object, such as the earth. *Hemi* is a Greek word that means "half." Thus, the word *hemisphere* means "half a sphere." Geographers use the term *hemisphere* to refer to half of the earth.

By turning a globe or moving around it, you can see that the earth can be divided into an almost endless number of hemispheres. In order to make studying the earth easier, geographers divide the earth in two ways.

One division is made along an imaginary line called the **equator**. The equator circles the earth halfway between the North Pole and the South Pole. It divides the earth into the Northern Hemisphere and the Southern Hemisphere.

7

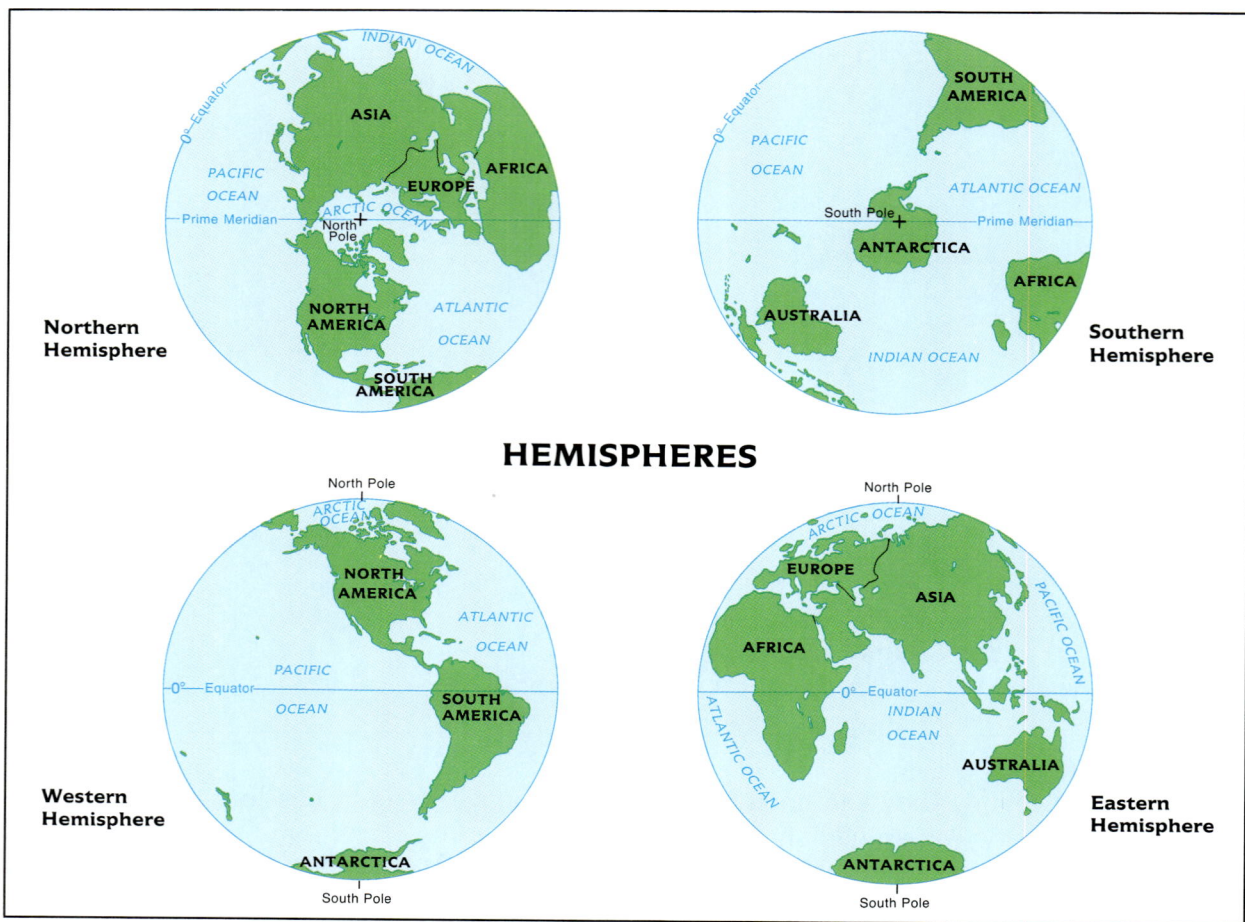

HEMISPHERES

The Northern Hemisphere is the part of the earth we would see if we were to look at the earth from a point in space directly above the North Pole. The Southern Hemisphere is the part of the earth we would see if we were to look at it from a point in space directly above the South Pole.

The earth can also be divided into the Eastern Hemisphere and the Western Hemisphere. These hemispheres are separated by another imaginary line around the earth. This line is known as the **prime meridian**. You will learn more about the prime meridian on pages 26–27.

One way in which you can identify the hemispheres is by learning the names of the continents they contain. As you can see from the maps of the hemispheres on this page, most of the earth's land is found in the Northern Hemisphere. Use the four hemisphere maps above to name the continents located in the Western Hemisphere.

1. What is a continent? Name the continents that border the Atlantic Ocean.
2. What is a hemisphere?
3. Which imaginary line separates the Northern Hemisphere and the Southern Hemisphere?
4. Which imaginary line separates the Eastern Hemisphere and the Western Hemisphere?
5. How can using globes help you to learn about the earth?

Using Maps

Key Vocabulary

cardinal directions   symbol
intermediate directions   map key
scale

While globes are the most accurate representations of the earth, maps are usually much more useful. This book includes more than 100 maps. Some show the entire world, and others show only a part of the world.

In order to use maps effectively, you must know how to "read" them. Information on maps is presented in a special "language." The language of maps allows mapmakers to show a great deal of information in a small space. In this section you will review the language of maps.

Directions

You already know that there are four **cardinal directions**—north, east, south, and west. North is the direction toward the North Pole. When you face north, south is directly behind you, east is to your right, and west is to your left. The letters *N*, *E*, *S*, and *W* are used to stand for the cardinal directions.

There are four **intermediate directions** as well. *Intermediate* means "between." The intermediate directions are the directions halfway between the cardinal directions. For example, northeast (*NE*) is the intermediate direction halfway between north and east. The other intermediate directions are northwest (*NW*), southeast (*SE*), and southwest (*SW*).

Most maps are drawn so that north is toward the top of the map. Many maps have a north pointer that shows which way is north on the map. If you know where north is, you can easily find all the other directions.

BRAZIL

✹ National capital
• Other city

Directions help you to determine the relative locations of places. Look at the map of Brazil on this page. In which direction is Brasília (brə zēl′ yə) from São Paulo (sou pou′ lō)? As you can see from the map, Brasília lies north of São Paulo. In which direction would you travel going from Manaus (mə nous′) to Fortaleza (fôr tə lā′ zə)?

Scale

All maps are smaller than the part of the earth they show. For this reason, a short distance on a map stands for a much greater real distance on the earth. Suppose that you are studying a people's movement from one place to another. How can a map help you to find out the actual distance between places?

The **scale**, or relative size, of a map will tell you how much smaller map distances are than real distances. The scale

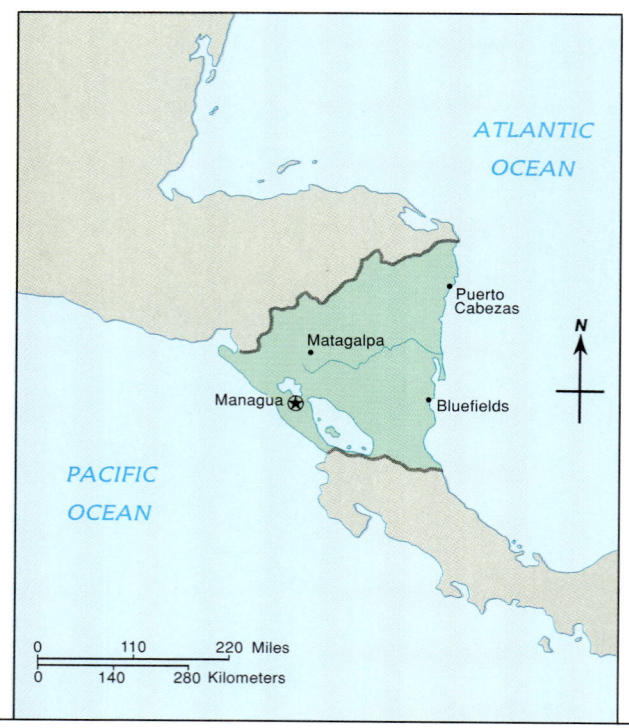

MAP A: NICARAGUA

⊛ National capital   • Other city

MAP B: NICARAGUA

⊛ National capital   • Other city

of a map can be shown in several ways. On the maps in this book, scale is shown by lines, which are called line scales. Each map has two line scales—one for miles, and the other for kilometers.

Find the line scales on **Map A** of Nicaragua on this page. The top line shows how many miles on the earth are represented by 1 inch on the map. The bottom line shows how many kilometers on the earth are represented by 2 centimeters on the map. How many miles on the earth does 1 inch on the map represent? How many kilometers do 2 centimeters on the map represent?

Suppose that you wanted to know the distance between the cities of Managua (mə nä′ gwə) and Puerto Cabezas. Use a ruler to measure the map distance in inches between the two cities. Then multiply the number of inches by 220 to find

the real distance in miles. To learn the number of kilometers between Managua and Puerto Cabezas, multiply the number of centimeters by 140 to find the real distance in kilometers. What is the real distance between Managua and Puerto Cabezas in miles? What is the real distance between the cities in kilometers?

Now look at **Map B**. It shows the same area that **Map A** shows. The shape of Nicaragua is the same on both maps, but Nicaragua appears to be larger on **Map B**. You know, of course, that Nicaragua has not changed in size. What has changed is the scale of the map. One inch on **Map B** stands for fewer miles than 1 inch on **Map A**. How many miles does 1 inch stand for on **Map B**?

Use the line scale and a ruler to determine the distance between Managua and Puerto Cabezas on **Map B**, just as you did

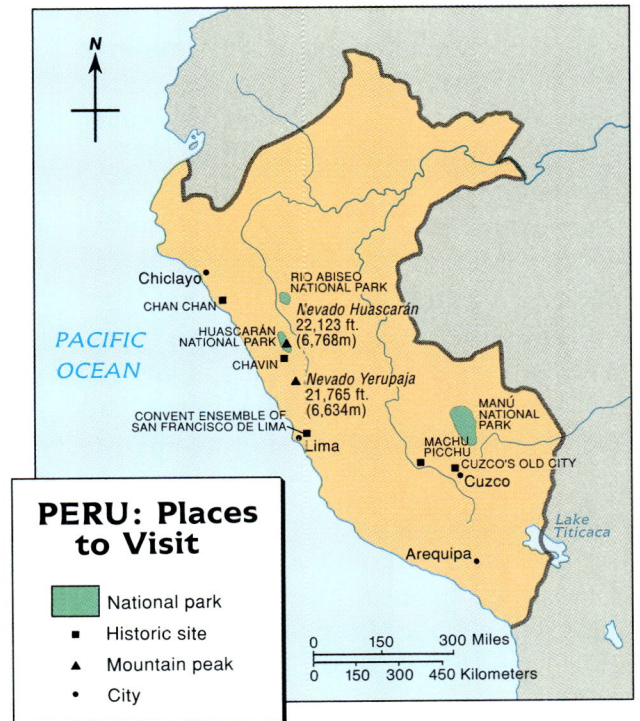

PERU: Places to Visit

- ▮ National park
- ■ Historic site
- ▲ Mountain peak
- • City

Chiclayo

CHAN CHAN

RIO ABISEO NATIONAL PARK

Nevado Huascarán 22,123 ft. (6,768m)

HUASCARÁN NATIONAL PARK

CHAVIN

PACIFIC OCEAN

Nevado Yerupaja 21,765 ft. (6,634m)

CONVENT ENSEMBLE OF SAN FRANCISCO DE LIMA

Lima

MANÚ NATIONAL PARK

MACHU PICCHU

CUZCO'S OLD CITY

Cuzco

Lake Titicaca

Arequipa

0   150   300 Miles
0   150   300   450 Kilometers

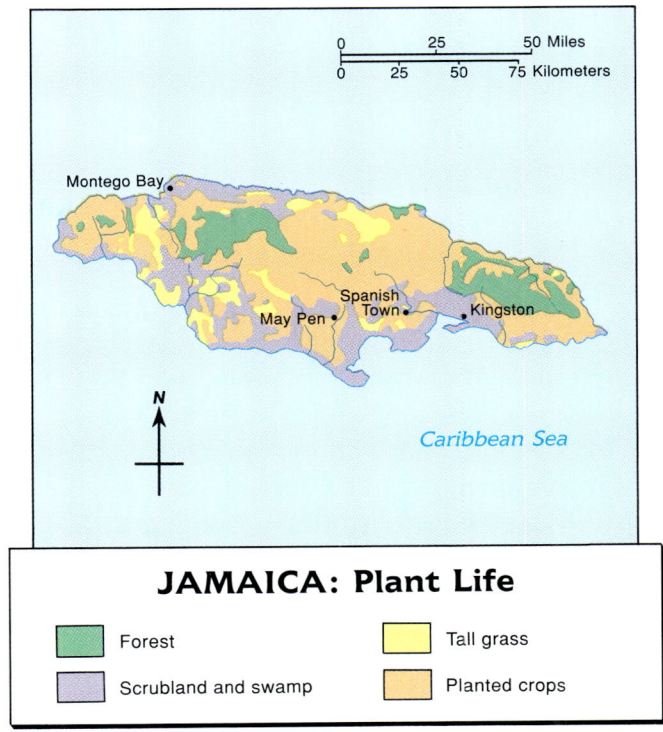

JAMAICA: Plant Life

- ▮ Forest
- ▮ Scrubland and swamp
- ▮ Tall grass
- ▮ Planted crops

Montego Bay

Spanish Town

May Pen

Kingston

Caribbean Sea

0   25   50 Miles
0   25   50   75 Kilometers

on **Map A**. What is the distance in miles and in kilometers? If you measured and figured correctly, your answers will be the same as they were before.

The scale of **Map B** is larger than that of **Map A**. More details can be shown on large-scale maps than on small-scale maps. Which things shown on **Map B** are *not* shown on **Map A**?

Symbols

Information on maps can be shown by **symbols**. A symbol is anything that stands for something else. Common map symbols are dots, stars, squares, triangles, and lines. Color is a special symbol on maps. It is often used to stand for rainfall, weather patterns, plant life, and height above sea level. Colors are often used to distinguish states or countries from one another. Blue is commonly used as a symbol for water.

Some symbols look like the things they stand for. Others suggest the things they

stand for. For example, a tiny drawing of an airplane may be the symbol for an airport. A small drawing of a tree may be the symbol for a forest.

To find out what the symbols used on a map mean, you must look at the **map key**. The map key explains what each symbol stands for. It is important to check the map key on each map you use. A symbol that stands for one thing on one map may stand for a completely different thing on another map.

Look at the two maps on this page. What does the color green stand for on the map of Peru? What does it stand for on the map of Jamaica?

1. Name the cardinal and intermediate directions.
2. How can line scales help you to determine distances on maps?
3. Why do you think it is important to understand what the symbols on maps stand for?

Different Kinds of Maps

Key Vocabulary

political map   elevation map
physical map   distribution map

People study maps in order to understand the earth and the way in which people live. The variety of information that can be shown on a map is endless. In order to present information clearly, most maps have a special purpose.

Maps can be grouped according to the kind of information they provide. For example, **political maps** show countries, capitals, and political boundaries. **Physical maps** show landforms and bodies of water such as mountains, deserts, plains, rivers, and oceans.

Special-purpose maps provide information about particular subjects. No matter what you want to know about the world, there is sure to be a map that suits your purpose.

For example, the focus of a special-purpose map may be on land use, the movement of people and ideas, or the features of a region. Think back to the Five Fundamental Themes of Geography. Which themes would the maps listed above help you to learn more about?

Political Maps

In every unit of this book, you will find at least one political map. These political maps will help you to understand both the absolute and relative locations of places.

The political map on this page shows relative locations of the United States and

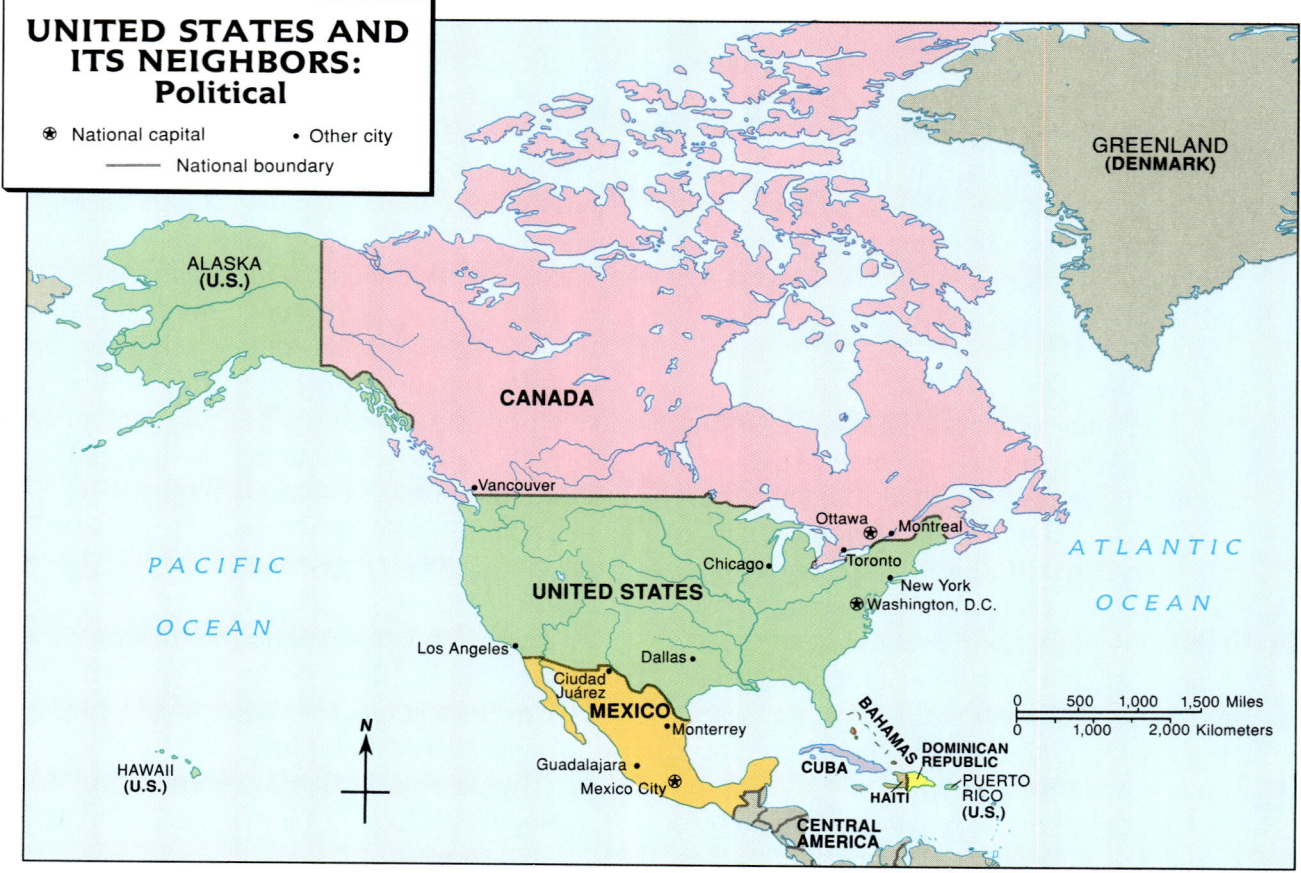

UNITED STATES AND ITS NEIGHBORS: Political

✸ National capital   • Other city
⎯⎯ National boundary

GREENLAND (DENMARK)

ALASKA (U.S.)

CANADA

Vancouver

Ottawa Montreal

Chicago Toronto

UNITED STATES New York Washington, D.C.

PACIFIC OCEAN

ATLANTIC OCEAN

Los Angeles Dallas

Ciudad Juárez

MEXICO Monterrey

BAHAMAS

DOMINICAN REPUBLIC

CUBA

HAITI

PUERTO RICO (U.S.)

Guadalajara

Mexico City

HAWAII (U.S.)

N

CENTRAL AMERICA

0 500 1,000 1,500 Miles
0 1,000 2,000 Kilometers

its neighbors. Which country is south of the United States?

This map also shows such political features as national boundaries, capitals, and other cities. Note that each country is shown in a different color to set it apart from its neighbors.

Physical Maps

Physical maps point out the natural features of the earth. The earth's physical features include oceans, islands, lakes, rivers, mountains, plains, and deserts.

Elevation maps are physical maps that use different colors to show how high or low the land is. Look at the map below. Which color is used to show land that is above 14,000 feet (4,000 m)?

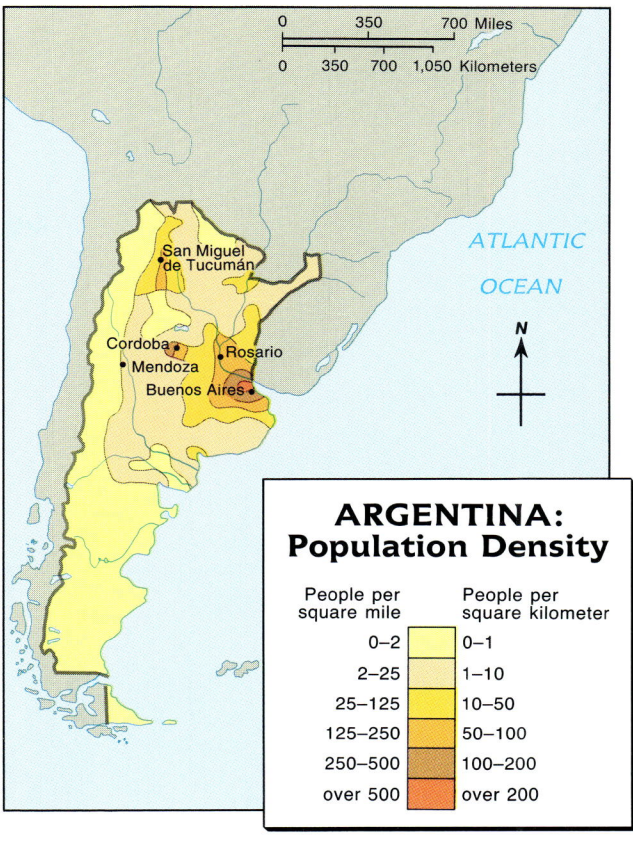

ARGENTINA: Population Density

People per square mile		People per square kilometer
0–2		0–1
2–25		1–10
25–125		10–50
125–250		50–100
250–500		100–200
over 500		over 200

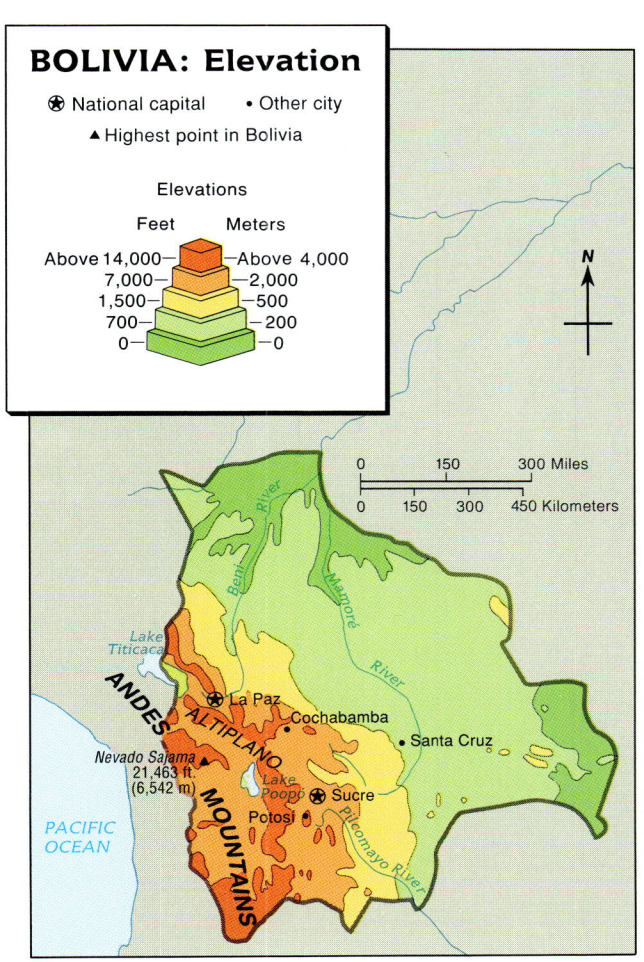

BOLIVIA: Elevation

⊛ National capital • Other city
▲ Highest point in Bolivia

Elevations

Feet	Meters
Above 14,000	Above 4,000
7,000	2,000
1,500	500
700	200
0	0

Distribution Maps

Some maps, called distribution maps, show how particular things are spread out throughout parts of the world. The subject of these maps may be anything from population, to rainfall, to language.

The map above is a population-density map of Argentina. It shows that some places are crowded with people, while other places have few people. The map key shows four different ranges of population in Argentina. Which color shows areas where there are more than 500 people per square mile?

1. What are some of the things that are commonly shown on political maps?
2. What are some of the things that are commonly shown on physical maps?
3. What is a distribution map? How is the distribution of population shown on the map above?

13

ARCTIC OCEAN

75°N

Baffin
Bay

60°N

Gulf of Alaska

Hudson
Bay

NORTH

AMERICA

75°W

60°W

Tropic of Cancer

Gulf of Mexico

CARIBBEAN
ISLANDS

PACIFIC

Gulf of California

OCEAN

Caribbean   Sea

CENTRAL
AMERICA

165°W

150°W

135°W

120°W

105°W

90°W

SOUTH

AMERICA

Tropic of Capricorn

PACIFIC   OCEAN

60°S

14

ATLANTIC

OCEAN

45°N

30°N
30°W
15°W

45°W

15°N

Equator—0°

15°S

30°S

UNIT

1

INTRODUCTION TO THE AMERICAS

WHERE WE ARE

Many, many millions of years ago, all of the earth's continents formed one giant landmass. Over long periods of time, this giant supercontinent broke apart, and separate continents drifted away from one another.

You are about to begin an adventure that will take you through the lands that form the continents of the Western Hemisphere today. As you read about the land and people of North America, Central America, the Caribbean, and South America, think about what these areas share, and the ways in which they are different from one another.

CHAPTER 1

THE GEOGRAPHY OF THE WESTERN HEMISPHERE

FOCUS

For many years the volcano slept. It was silent and still, big and beautiful. Then the volcano . . . was shaken by a strong earthquake. The quake was a sign of movement inside . . . it was a sign of a waking volcano that might soon erupt.

Patricia Lauber, a geographer, wrote this passage about Mount St. Helens. "Volcanoes remind us that the earth has not always been the same," she also wrote. In this chapter you will read about how the earth has changed, and about the Western Hemisphere's geography today.

1 The Changing Earth

Key Vocabulary

plate tectonics
isthmus
archipelago

Key Places

Central America
Greenland
Caribbean islands
Middle America

Read Aloud

Like adolescents, the Himalaya Mountains are young . . . and their bodies just will not stop growing.

A *New York Times* article in 1990 revealed new information about the world's largest, fastest-growing mountain range. "News" is discovered all the time about the earth's history and geography as scientists continue to explore the forces that shape our land. In this lesson you will read about how the history of the land, like the history of people, is one of constant change.

Read for Purpose

1. **WHAT YOU KNOW:** What are the earth's four hemispheres?
2. **WHAT YOU WILL LEARN:** Which forces helped form the continents of the Western Hemisphere?

STUDYING THE EARTH

The earth is always changing. A volcano erupts under the sea and its lava rises to form an island. Strong ocean waves lash against the coast, breaking away tiny pieces of the land. Winds push desert sands over grasslands. Icy glaciers carve huge canyons into the land. Some of these geographical changes happen in moments. Others take place extremely slowly, over millions of years.

As strange as it may seem, even the seven continents are constantly moving. Scientists now believe that the continents move at the rate of about 2 inches (5 cm) a year.

PLATE TECTONICS

The idea that the continents are moving was first developed hundreds of years ago. An English philosopher named Francis Bacon came up with the theory by making a simple observation that you can make yourself. Look at the map of the continents on page 18. What do you notice about the shapes of the landmasses?

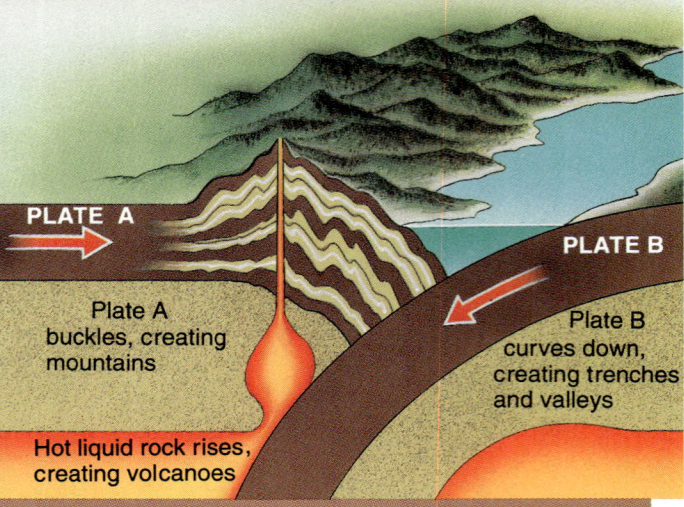

HOW MOUNTAINS ARE FORMED

PLATE A

PLATE B

Plate A buckles, creating mountains

Plate B curves down, creating trenches and valleys

Hot liquid rock rises, creating volcanoes

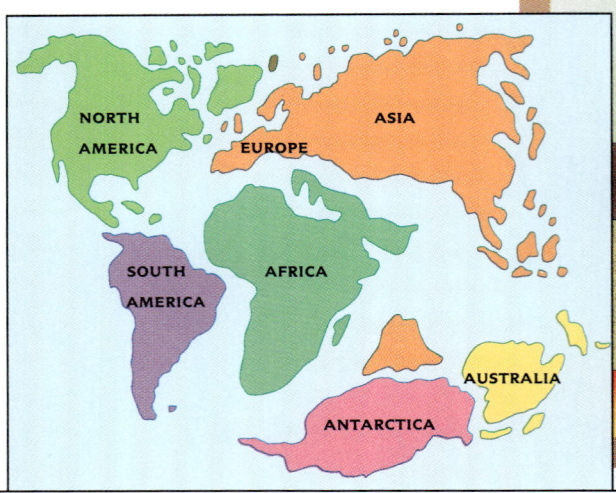

NORTH AMERICA

EUROPE

ASIA

SOUTH AMERICA

AFRICA

AUSTRALIA

ANTARCTICA

CONTINENTAL DRIFT
65 Million Years Ago

MAP/DIAGRAM SKILL: The theory of **plate tectonics** explains how there may once have been one giant continent. How does the diagram (*above, right*) show that mountains can be formed?

Many of the landmasses look as if they could fit together, like pieces of a jigsaw puzzle. Perhaps all seven continents once formed one giant continent. Scientists have developed a theory called **plate tectonics** (tek ton′ iks) that explains how the continents may rest on large plates of the earth's crust. Tectonics is the science of the structure of the earth.

The earth is made up of several different layers, including the outermost layer of rock, called the crust. Most scientists now believe that the crust is made up of eight large tectonic plates, or pieces of the earth's structure. These plates move, carrying the continents and ocean floors with them. The theory that the seven continents slowly drifted apart is called continental drift.

The tectonic plates push and pull and grind against each other. The diagram above, right, shows how two plates that collide can sometimes form mountains. Two colliding plates can also create valleys. At other times, even the small movement of one plate against another can cause a major earthquake.

THE WESTERN HEMISPHERE

As you know, the earth contains seven continents. Two continents— North America and South America— make up more than 90 percent of the land in the Western Hemisphere. That is why the land of the Western Hemisphere is often called the Americas.

Look at the map of the Western Hemisphere on page 19. As you can see, North America and South America are connected by a narrow piece of land. This land stretches between southern Mexico and northern Colombia and is divided into seven countries. Actually, this piece of land is part of the continent of North America. However, because of its central position

ARCTIC OCEAN

120°W 90°W 60°W 30°W

GREENLAND
(DEN.)

Baffin Bay

Davis Strait

Arctic Circle

Nuuk

Iqaluit

Beaufort Sea

Yukon River

ALASKA
(U.S.)

Fairbanks

Anchorage

Juneau

60°N

Hudson
Bay

Labrador Sea

60°N

Mackenzie River

Yellowknife

CANADA

NORTH AMERICA

Edmonton

Vancouver

Winnipeg

Seattle

Portland

Missouri River

Minneapolis

UNITED

Salt Lake
City

Great Salt
Lake

Denver

Chicago

Detroit

STATES

St. Louis

San
Francisco

Quebec

Ottawa

St. John's

Gulf of
St. Lawrence

Montreal

Toronto

Boston

Halifax

New York City

Washington, D.C.

Great Lakes

ATLANTIC
OCEAN

30°N

Los
Angeles

Colorado River

Phoenix

Houston

Atlanta

BERMUDA
(U.K.)

Rio Grande

New
Orleans

Gulf of
California

30°N

Miami

see inset

Tropic of Cancer

HAWAII
(U.S.)

PACIFIC
OCEAN

MEXICO

Guadalajara

Mexico
City

Belmopan

BELIZE

GUATEMALA

HONDURAS

Tegucigalpa

Guatemala City

San Salvador

NICARAGUA

Caribbean
Sea

EL SALVADOR

Managua

Maracaibo

CENTRAL AMERICA

COSTA RICA

San José

Panama

Caracas

PANAMA

City

VENEZUELA

SURINAME

150°W 120°W

Bogotá

Georgetown

Paramaribo

Cayenne

West Indies

COLOMBIA

GUYANA

FRENCH
GUIANA (FR.)

Equator—0°

ECUADOR

Quito

Guayaquil

Manaus

Belém

Amazon River

PERU

Recife

Callao

Lima

BRAZIL

SOUTH AMERICA

Brasília

Bahia

La Paz

BOLIVIA

Sucre

Santa
Cruz

Rio de
Janeiro

Tropic of
Capricorn

PARAGUAY

São
Paulo

Antofagasta

Asunción

Pôrto
Alegre

Tucumán

30°S

CHILE

Rosario

URUGUAY

Santiago

Buenos
Aires

Montevideo

La Plata

Concepción

ARGENTINA

Mar del
Plata

Comodoro
Rivadavia

Strait of
Magellan

FALKLAND
ISLANDS
(U.K.)

SOUTH
GEORGIA
(U.K.)

Punta
Arenas

90°W 60°W 30°W

N

500 1,000 1,500 Miles
0
0
1,000 2,000 Kilometers

80°W 70°W

Nassau

BAHAMAS

N

Tropic of Cancer

Havana

20°N

CUBA

TURKS AND
CAICOS IS. (U.K.)

PUERTO
RICO
(U.S.)

VIRGIN ISLANDS
(U.S.)/(U.K.)

CAYMAN
ISLANDS
(U.K.)

DOMINICAN
REPUBLIC

San
Juan

ANTIGUA AND
BARBUDA

HAITI

Port-au-Prince

Santo
Domingo

Basseterre

JAMAICA

ST. KITTS AND NEVIS

St. John's

GUADELOUPE (FR.)

Kingston

MONTSERRAT
(U.K.)

DOMINICA

Roseau

Caribbean Sea

MARTINIQUE (FR.)

Castries

ST. LUCIA

Kingstown

BARBADOS

Bridgetown

NETHERLANDS ANTILLES
(NETH.)

GRENADA

ST. VINCENT AND
THE GRENADINES

ARUBA (NETH.)

St. George's

TRINIDAD AND
TOBAGO

0 250 500 Miles
0 250 500 750 Kilometers

Port-of-Spain

10°N

10°N

70°W 60°W

WESTERN HEMISPHERE:
Political

⊛ National capital   • Other city

MAP SKILL: The Western Hemisphere is made up of two continents as well as many islands. Which is the larger of the two continents?

These photographs were taken from space with special telescopic lenses. They provide some amazing views of the different landforms that make up our hemisphere.

between two large landmasses, this region is called **Central America**. As you read on page 5, a region is an area with common features that set it apart from other areas.

LOOKING CLOSER

Who knows how much longer that skinny neck of land will resist the tectonic forces and keep us united.

In the passage above, the astronaut Michael Collins describes his thoughts as he gazed through space toward the earth. "*Apollo 11* took me to the moon," he wrote, "but it's this magnificent earth that really makes me think."

Look again at the map of the Western Hemisphere on page 19. Can you find the "skinny neck of land" to which the astronaut refers?

That narrow strip is called the Isthmus of Panama. You may know that an **isthmus** (is′ məs) is a narrow strip of land bordered by water that connects two larger areas of land. The Isthmus of Panama is the narrowest part of Central America. At one point the isthmus is only 40 miles (64 km) wide.

Collins also saw many islands from his window in space. North America includes many large islands. The world's largest island, **Greenland**, lies off the northeastern coast of North America. Further south he saw countless **archipelagoes** (är kə pel′ i gōz), or groups of islands, located between

MIDDLE AMERICA

North America and South America. These archipelagoes are together known as the **Caribbean** (kar ə bē′ ən) **islands**. Many of the Caribbean islands were once volcanoes. The Caribbean islands, together with Central America and Mexico, form a region known as **Middle America**.

A VARIED GEOGRAPHY

As you have read, the earth's surface is constantly changing. So, too, is our knowledge of geography and the history of the land. The Western Hemisphere contains two continents and many islands. The hemisphere can be divided into different regions, making it easier to study. As you explore the Western Hemisphere, you will look more closely at its different regions.

MAP SKILL: The Caribbean islands are in the region of Middle America. How many countries are found in the other parts of this region?

Check Your Reading

1. Name three ways in which the earth's surface can change.
2. How can the movement of tectonic plates create a mountain?
3. Which continents make up the Western Hemisphere?
4. **GEOGRAPHY SKILL:** Use the map of Middle America on this page to name the three areas that make up the region.
5. **THINKING SKILL:** What questions would you like to ask a scientist about the different ways in which the earth has changed?

21

2 Land and Water

READ TO LEARN

Key Vocabulary

tributary
elevation

Key Places

Amazon River   Andes Mountains
Great Lakes   Mount Aconcagua

Read Aloud

I think I shall paint the Andes forever. Their colors dazzle the eye so greatly that I cannot recall a more glorious subject. I adore them. I will never go home.

Frederick Church, a United States painter, made two trips to the Andes Mountains in the 1850s. In a letter home, the painter tried to explain why the Andes delighted him. In this lesson you will read about the magnificent land and water that colors the landscape of the Western Hemisphere.

Read for Purpose

1. **WHAT YOU KNOW:** Which geographical features does your community have?
2. **WHAT YOU WILL LEARN:** What are some of the major landforms and waterways of the Western Hemisphere?

ACROSS THE HEMISPHERE

Imagine that you are at the northern tip of the Western Hemisphere, in Canada. A friend of yours is at the southern tip of the Western Hemisphere, in Chile (chil´ ē). You are about as far away from each other as two people can possibly be. The land of the Western Hemisphere extends almost from the North Pole to the South Pole. No two points on earth are farther apart.

Separating you from your friend is one long, continuous stretch of land. Every geographical feature that exists, from forests to deserts, can be found between you and your friend.

THE VIEW FROM SPACE

Imagine now that you are an astronaut looking at the earth from outer space. From this great distance the planet looks very small and very fragile. Its beautiful colors contrast with the inky blackness of space.

One of the first things you would probably notice is that there is surprisingly little land. In fact, almost 75 percent of the earth's surface is covered by water. Huge oceans completely surround each of the continents. The Pacific Ocean, the world's largest ocean, lies to the west of the Americas. The Atlantic Ocean lies to the east.

You might notice that there are several smaller bodies of water that are a part of the Atlantic Ocean. One is the Gulf of Mexico, which is just south of the United States. Another is the Caribbean Sea, whose warm waters flow between North America and South America. Still another is Hudson Bay, whose chilly waters extend into the northern part of Canada.

GREAT RIVERS AND LAKES

Two of the earth's longest rivers are found in the Western Hemisphere. One of them, the **Amazon River** in South America, is the second-longest river in the world. Only the Nile River in Africa is longer. The Amazon River and its many **tributaries** (trib′ yə ter ēz) drain half of South America! A tributary is a river or stream that flows into a larger body of water.

The Mississippi River is the second-longest river in the Western Hemisphere and the longest river in North America. This mighty river flows from the northern part of the United States south to the Gulf of Mexico. Like the Amazon River, the Mississippi River has many tributaries.

North America also has some of the largest freshwater lakes in the world. A group of five freshwater lakes, called the **Great Lakes**, is located on the border between the United States and Canada. These lakes cover an area about the size of Texas.

LOOKING AT THE LAND

Looking down from your window in outer space, you can also see huge masses of land. These are the continents of the Western Hemisphere. The different surfaces and plant life have a great variety of colors. As you descend toward earth, you begin to keep a record of what you see. You might write:

I can't take my eyes off this amazing view of the Western Hemisphere. The oceans are so huge and so blue. But it's the land that's really incredible. Brown and green, it looks so wild and dense; I can even make out the great mountain chains—ridges and hidden valleys covered with long stretches of green and brown and yellow. Of course, I can't see national borders from up here. All I see is one big world!

Geographers divide the earth's varied land into four main types of landforms: mountains, hills, plateaus, and

A family paddles in a dugout canoe along one of the world's longest rivers, the Amazon.

plains. Each type of landform is identified and labeled based on how rugged it is and how far it is above sea level, the level of the surface of the ocean. As you can see on the map on the next page, height above sea level, or **elevation**, varies greatly in the Western Hemisphere.

Some mountains have such a high elevation that their peaks are always capped with snow. Looking down at the **Andes Mountains** in South America,

WESTERN HEMISPHERE: Elevation

Elevations

Feet	Meters
Above 14,000	Above 4,000
7,000	2,000
3,500	1,000
700	200
0	0

Below sea level

⊛ National capital

• Other city

▲ Mountain peak

Ice cap

MAP SKILL: What is the name of the highest peak in North America? In which mountain range is this peak located? What is the **elevation** of the area to the north of this mountain range?

The land in the Western Hemisphere varies in elevation, from tall mountain ranges to low-lying plains.

you see the tallest mountain in the Americas. This is Mount Aconcagua (ak ən kä′ gwə), which rises 22,834 feet (6,960 m). You will read more about these majestic mountains and the people who live there in Unit 8.

PLAINS AND PLATEAUS

You know that a plain is a large area with either level or gently rolling land. Many plains are located along coasts, such as the land that borders the eastern coasts of North America and South America. There are also vast inland plains. According to Canadian writer Andrew H. Malcolm, parts of the Canadian plains are extremely flat.

> *Under certain conditions a child on a wintry walk to school can see on the horizon recognizable buildings of a town 40 miles away.*

The largest plain in the Americas stretches for 2,500 miles (4,000 km) from northern Canada through the United States to southern Texas.

Plateaus, like plains, have mostly level land surfaces. Plateaus are usually located at higher elevations than plains. A plateau may also have one or more steeply dropping edges that, from above, look like steps.

LANDFORMS TO REMEMBER

In this lesson you have read about some of the great varieties of land and water that stretch across the Western Hemisphere. You may already know a lot about the geography of the United States. In this book you will continue to explore the geography of our neighbors in the Western Hemisphere.

Check Your Reading

1. What is a tributary?
2. What is the longest river in North America? In South America?
3. GEOGRAPHY SKILL: Use the elevation map on page 24 to find the highest mountains in the Western Hemisphere. What are they?
4. THINKING SKILL: List the landforms you have read about in this lesson. Arrange them in order of elevation from highest to lowest.

Understanding Latitude and Longitude

Key Vocabulary

latitude
longitude
degree
parallel

meridian
prime meridian
grid

In Lesson 2 you read about the majestic Mt. Aconcagua. You know it is located somewhere in South America, but if you wanted to know the absolute location of Mt. Aconcagua, you would look for its **latitude** and **longitude**. Latitude and longitude are imaginary lines that are shown on many maps and globes. As you read in the Five Fundamental Themes of Geography, latitude and longitude can help you to find the absolute location of a place.

Latitude and Longitude

Lines of latitude and lines of longitude are measured in **degrees**. A degree, written °, is a unit of measurement for latitude and longitude. The starting point for measuring latitude is the equator. The equator is the imaginary line that circles the globe halfway between the North Pole and the South Pole. The latitude of the equator is 0°. The latitudes of places north of the equator are labeled *N*, for "north." Places to the south of the equator are labeled *S*, for "south." Find the line on **Map A** that is marked 30°N, which means 30 degrees north. Now find the line that is labeled 30°S, or 30 degrees south.

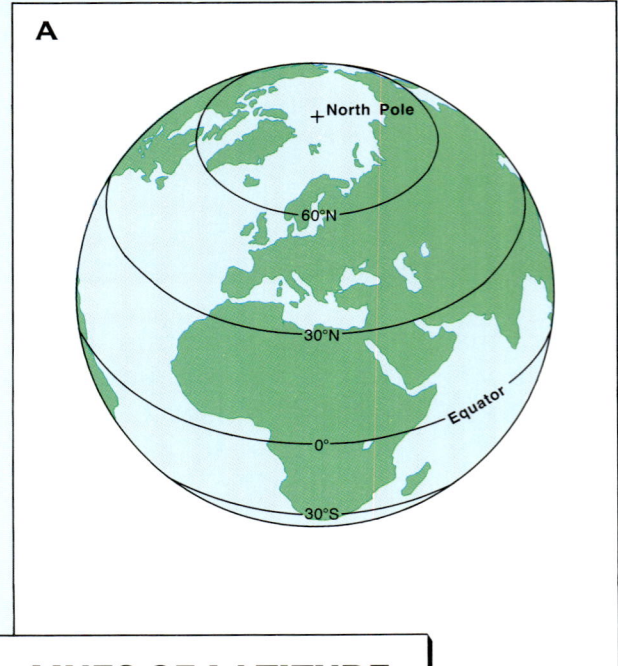

A

LINES OF LATITUDE

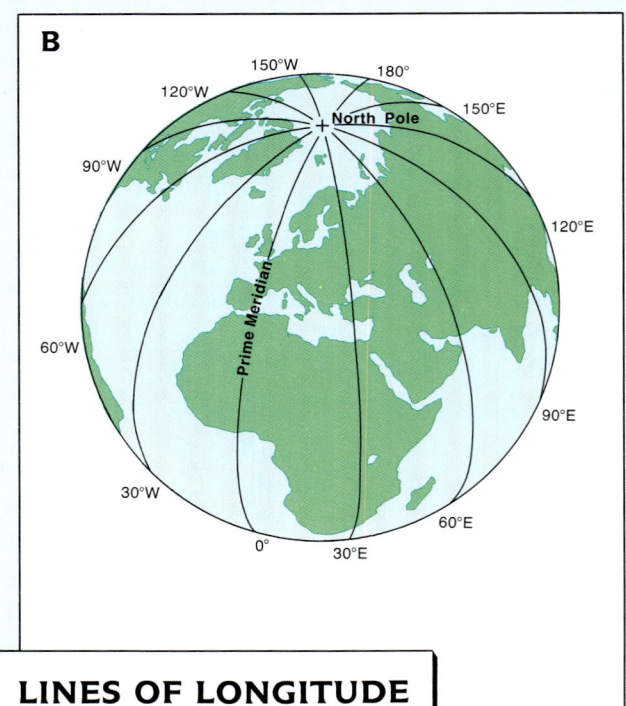

B

LINES OF LONGITUDE

26

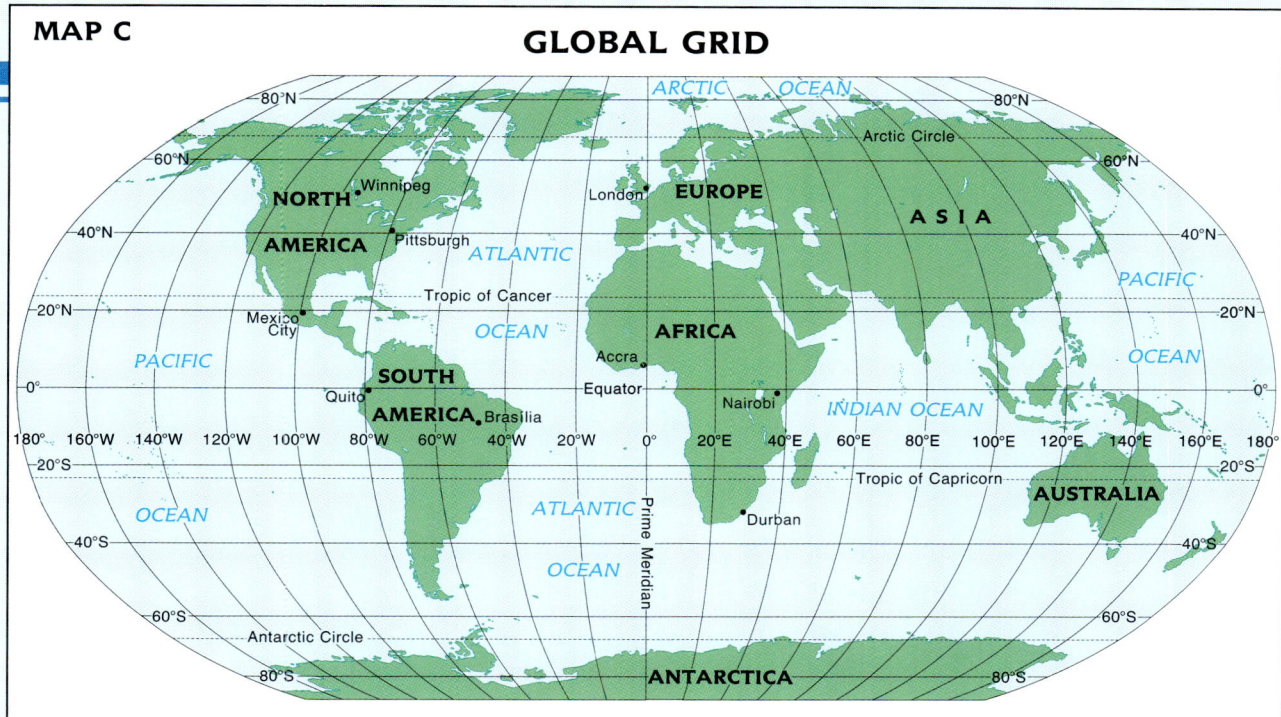

MAP C

GLOBAL GRID

Lines of latitude are called **parallels**. Each line of latitude is parallel to the equator, which means that it always circles the earth at the same distance from the equator.

Most maps and globes also have lines that run north and south. These lines are called lines of longitude or **meridians**. Meridians meet one another at the North Pole and the South Pole.

The starting place for measuring longitude is the **prime meridian**. Find the prime meridian on **Map B**. Notice that this meridian is labeled 0°. Lines of longitude measure distances east or west of the prime meridian. Lines of longitude east of the prime meridian are labeled *E*, for "east." Those that are west of the prime meridian are labeled *W*, for "west."

Using a Global Grid

Notice on **Map C** how the lines of latitude and longitude cross each other to form a **grid**. You can use this grid to find the exact location of a place.

Suppose that you want to give the latitude and longitude of Mexico City. Begin by placing your finger on the spot where the equator and the prime meridian meet. Then move your finger north along the prime meridian until you come to the parallel on which Mexico City is located. It is labeled 20°N, which means that it is located 20 degrees north of the equator.

To find Mexico City's longitude, move your finger west along the 20°N line until you come to Mexico City. This meridian is labeled 100°W. Mexico City is located 100 degrees west of the prime meridian. By using the global grid you have found that the exact location of Mexico City is 20°N, 100°W.

Reviewing the Skill

1. What are lines of latitude and longitude? What do they help you to do?
2. Is the line 20°W a parallel or a meridian? Explain how you know this.
3. What is the longitude of Quito?
4. At which latitude is Winnipeg located?

READ TO LEARN

Key Vocabulary

environment
climate
precipitation
tropical climate

polar climate
temperate climate
current

Read Aloud

. . . two pairs of long underwear, wool trousers, three layers of socks, a scarf, and a parka . . .

The Canadian writer Andrew H. Malcolm wrote these words to describe what people need to wear in order to stay outdoors for even a short time on a winter day in northern Canada. On the same day, people on an island in the Caribbean Sea might be wearing shorts and T-shirts outdoors. As you will read, the weather makes a big difference in what a place is like and how its people live.

Read for Purpose

1. **WHAT YOU KNOW:** What is the weather like on a typical January day in the area where you live?
2. **WHAT YOU WILL LEARN:** Why do climates vary?

LIVING ENVIRONMENTS

If you could live anywhere in the world, where would you most like to live? Why would you like to live there? The chances are that your choice had something to do with the **environment** (en vī′ rən mənt). The environment includes all the land, water, plants, and animals found in an area.

You might choose to live in a particular place because it's near an ocean. Or you might choose to live high on a mountaintop because of the view. You might want to live near a park with a good baseball field. The ocean, the mountain, and the park are all parts of the environment.

Perhaps you answered that you want to live where you could swim all year long. Or where you could go skiing in the winter. Weather is another important part of the environment. As you can see on the map on the opposite page, weather patterns vary greatly in the Western Hemisphere. How does the map describe the weather patterns where you live?

WESTERN HEMISPHERE: Climate

Map key:

- Very cold winter, cold summer, dry
- Very cold winter, cool summer, wet
- Warm and wet all year
- Cold winter, hot or warm summer, wet
- Mild or warm winter, hot summer, wet
- Warm all year, wet with one dry season
- Mild winter, cool summer, wet
- Mild, wet winter; hot, dry summer
- Semidry, temperature varies with latitude
- Dry, temperature varies with latitude
- Highlands, temperature and precipitation vary with elevation
- Ice cap

MAP SKILL: Use the map key to describe the **climate** of French Guiana. How does this climate differ from Venezuela's climate?

29

WHAT IS CLIMATE?

"We get so much snow here that I usually don't see the ground from January to March!"

"It's so humid today that I don't even want to leave the house."

One of these two statements is about weather. The other refers to climate (klī′ mit), or the weather patterns of an area over a long period of time. Which statement is about climate?

The temperature and precipitation (pri sip i tā′ shən) are two of the most important parts of an area's climate. Precipitation is any form of water, such as rain, hail, or snow, that falls to the earth. Wind and air pressure are two other important parts of climate.

Have you ever noticed that there is more snow in the mountains, or that it rains more near the sea? Let's examine why these general conditions exist.

LATITUDE AND CLIMATE

There are three major factors that affect climate. The first is latitude—how far north or south of the equator a place is located. As you can see on the diagram below, places near the equator tend to have hot climates.

As the diagram shows, geographers have divided the earth into five climate zones. The places that are closest to the equator have the warmest climates because they receive the sun's most direct rays. Because the low latitudes reach from the Tropic of Cancer to the Tropic of Capricorn, their climates are called tropical climates. Temperatures in the tropics are very warm and do not change much throughout the year.

The closer a place is to either the North Pole or the South Pole, the cooler it is. The reason is that these parts of the earth receive fewer direct rays from the sun than places close to the equator. Most of the world's coldest climates are found in the high latitudes.

DIAGRAM SKILL: In how many climate zones is North America located? In which zone is most of North America located?

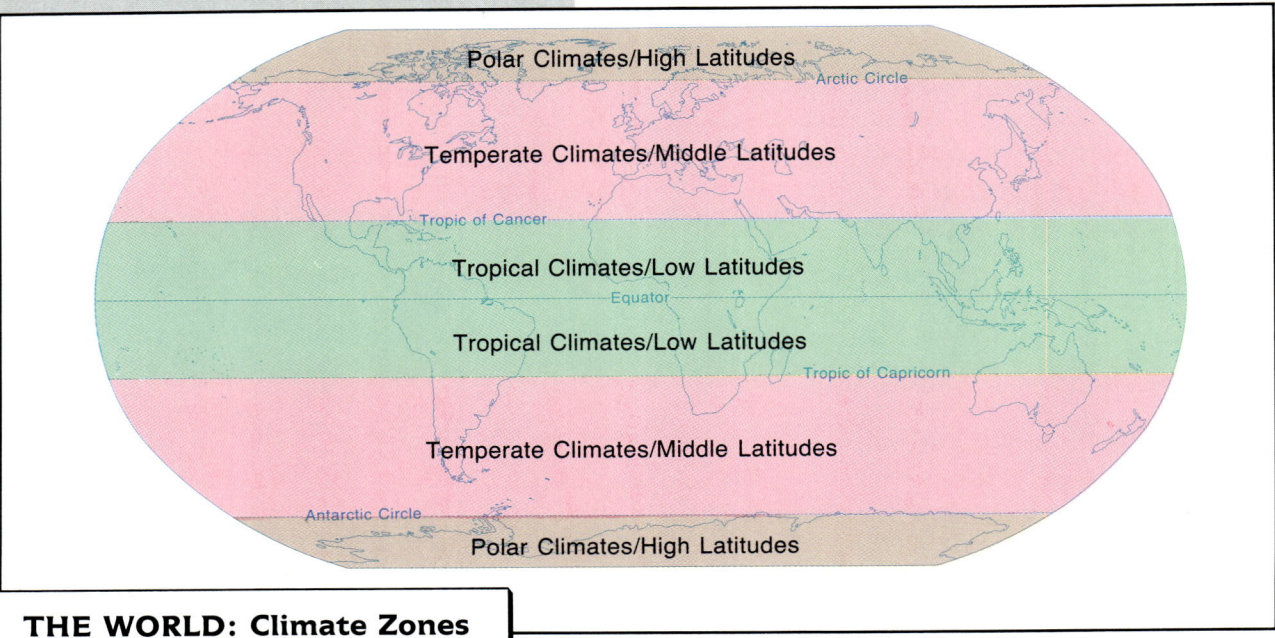

Polar Climates/High Latitudes
Arctic Circle
Temperate Climates/Middle Latitudes
Tropic of Cancer
Tropical Climates/Low Latitudes
Equator
Tropical Climates/Low Latitudes
Tropic of Capricorn
Temperate Climates/Middle Latitudes
Antarctic Circle
Polar Climates/High Latitudes

THE WORLD: Climate Zones

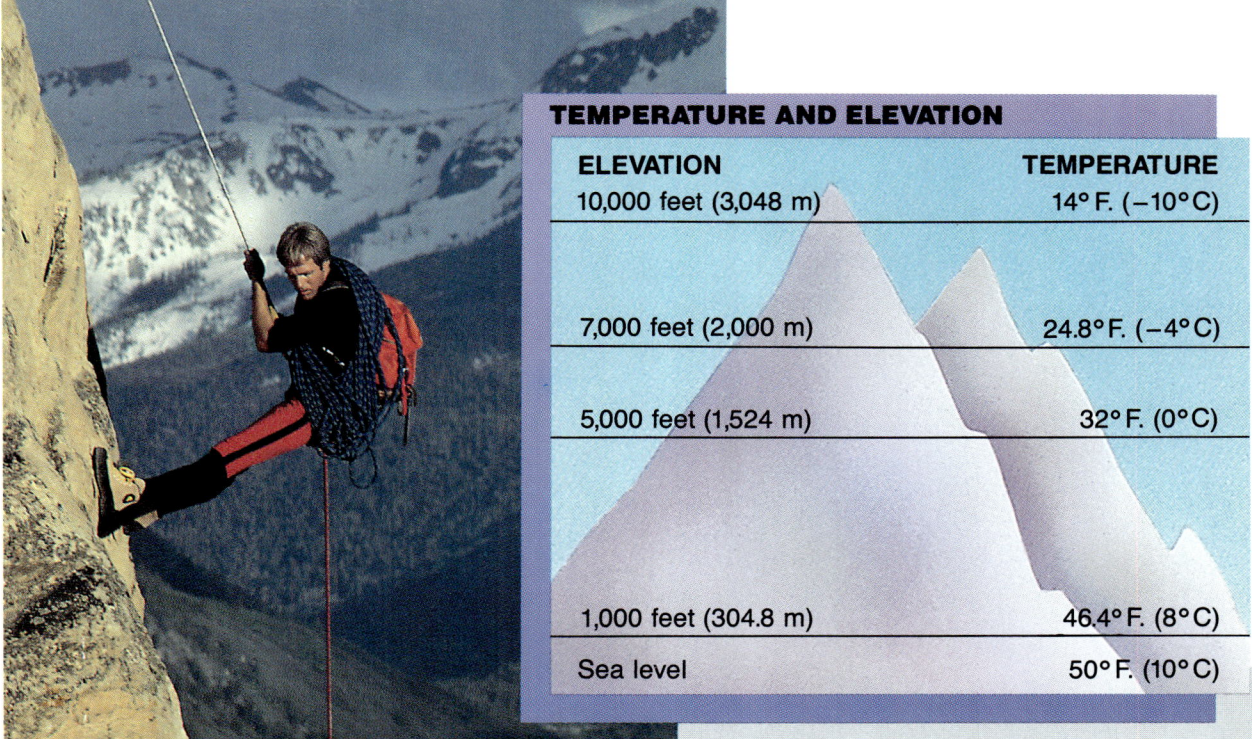

TEMPERATURE AND ELEVATION

ELEVATION	TEMPERATURE
10,000 feet (3,048 m)	14° F. (−10°C)
7,000 feet (2,000 m)	24.8° F. (−4°C)
5,000 feet (1,524 m)	32° F. (0°C)
1,000 feet (304.8 m)	46.4° F. (8°C)
Sea level	50° F. (10°C)

CHART SKILL: Mountain climbers notice the effect of elevation on temperature. When it is 50°F. (10°C) at sea level, what is the temperature at 7,000 feet (2,000 m)?

They are called **polar climates** because these cold climates are found near the poles.

The middle latitudes fall between the low and the high latitudes. Most of North America lies in the middle latitudes. The middle latitudes are generally cool in the winter and warm in the summer. Because they are temperate, or mild, climates in this zone are called **temperate climates**.

ELEVATION AND CLIMATE

Elevation, or height above sea level, is the second major factor that affects climate. Both North America and South America have high mountain ranges. As the elevation of these mountain ranges increases, temperatures become lower because the air is thinner—it has less oxygen. The temperature drops about 3.6°F. (2°C) for each increase of 1,000 feet (304 m) in elevation. Use the chart above to see how elevation affects temperature.

Imagine that you are at the beach in the spring. There at sea level you are enjoying a temperature of about 60°F. (15.6°C). It's a nice day, so you decide to go hiking in the nearby mountains, which are 10,000 feet (3,048 m) high. After walking a while you begin to feel chilly and you turn back. When you check a guidebook that lists the temperature at the top of the mountains, you discover that it is only 24°F. (−4.4°C). This change in temperature at high elevations helps you to understand why some mountain peaks in tropical climates are snowcapped.

OCEAN CURRENTS

The third major factor that affects climate is nearness to bodies of water. Winds that blow over water onto land affect the land temperatures. Land temperature changes faster than water

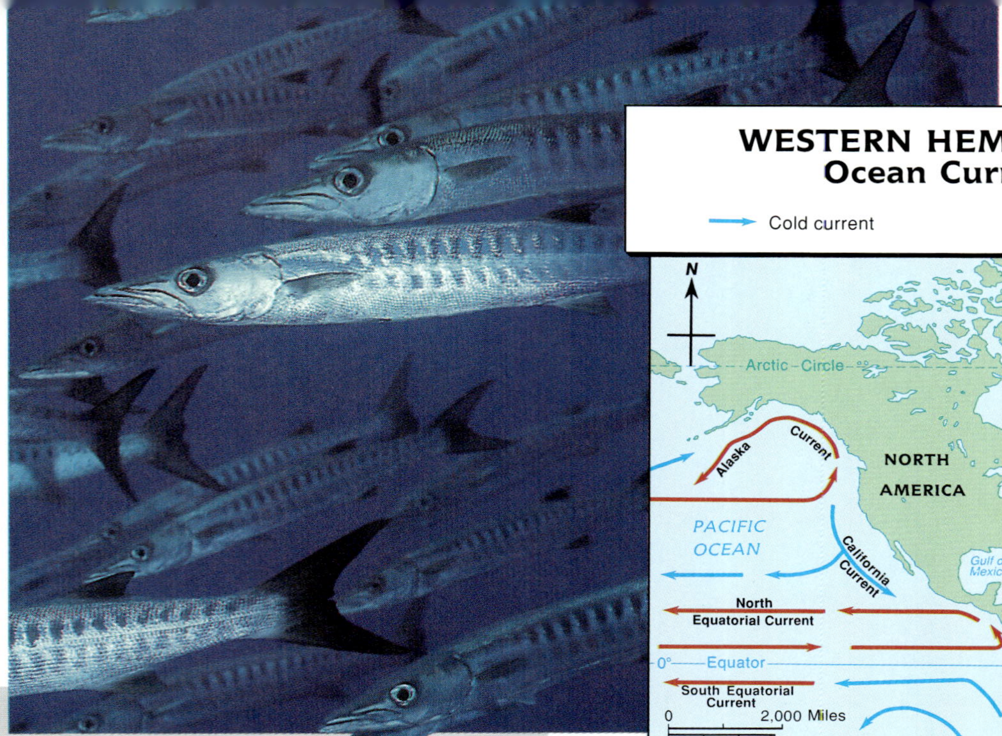

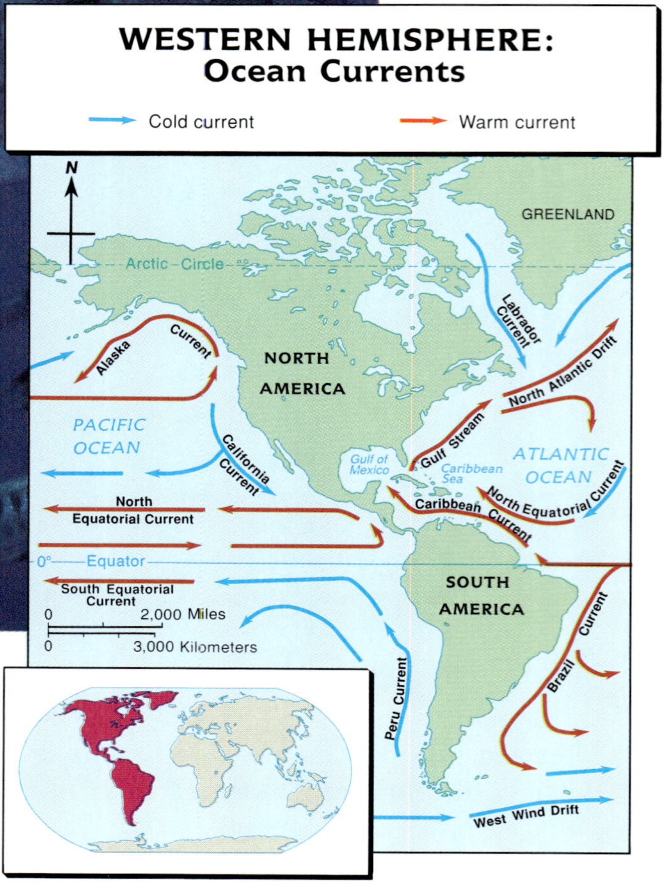

WESTERN HEMISPHERE: Ocean Currents

→ Cold current   → Warm current

GREENLAND

Arctic Circle

Alaska Current

Labrador Current

NORTH AMERICA

North Atlantic Drift

PACIFIC OCEAN

California Current

Gulf of Mexico

Gulf Stream

Caribbean Sea

ATLANTIC OCEAN

North Equatorial Current

North Equatorial Current

Caribbean Current

0°— Equator

South Equatorial Current

SOUTH AMERICA

0   2,000 Miles

0   3,000 Kilometers

Peru Current

Brazil Current

West Wind Drift

MAP SKILL: Currents affect the temperature of the ocean, which in turn affects the temperature of nearby land. Is the Brazil Current warm or cold?

temperature. Winds that blow over warm waters warm the land. If winds blow over cool waters, they cool the land. Why do you think the water temperature varies?

As the map on this page shows, the oceans are filled with currents. A current is a portion of a body of water or air that flows continuously in approximately the same path. Cold currents flow from the high latitudes near the poles toward the equator. Warm currents flow in the opposite direction, from the low latitudes toward the poles.

CLIMATE MAKES A DIFFERENCE

You have read that an important part of an area's environment is its climate— its weather patterns over a long period of time. There are three major factors

that affect an area's climate. The many different landforms in the Western Hemisphere help to create the wide variety of climates found there. These climates help to shape the lives of the people who live in a particular place.

Check Your Reading

1. What is the difference between weather and climate?
2. Why does latitude cause climate to vary?
3. **GEOGRAPHY SKILL:** Look at the map on page 29. Describe the climates of Haiti and Greenland.
4. **THINKING SKILL:** Describe the characteristics of the environment that you see in the photograph on page 31.

4 Resources

Key Vocabulary

natural resource   pollution
mineral   extinct
vegetation   nonrenewable resource
renewable resource

Read Aloud

I speak for the trees, for the trees have no tongues.

Do you recognize the line above? If it sounds familiar, it may be because you read it years ago in a book by Dr. Seuss. None of the many useful things we find in nature can speak for themselves. As you will read, it is up to us to protect them.

Read for Purpose

1. **WHAT YOU KNOW:** What are some things found in nature that you enjoy?
2. **WHAT YOU WILL LEARN:** Why are natural resources important?

NATURAL TREASURES

What do the following things have in common: a rock, a river, an acorn, a worm, a piece of coal, and a handful of dirt? They are all natural resources— things found in nature that are useful to people. Almost anything can be a resource. It just depends on how you use it.

Let's look at the different ways a tree can be a natural resource. Did you know that one large tree can provide a day's oxygen for four people? Trees can be used to clean a city's air of carbon dioxide better than any available air cleaner. A tree can provide shade for other plants to grow in and for people and animals to rest in. And last but not least, a tree can be fun to climb. That, too, makes a tree a natural resource.

SHARING THE WEALTH

Without natural resources, we would not be able to survive. All of our basic needs—water, air, food, clothing, and shelter—are met by natural resources.

The Western Hemisphere is incredibly rich in natural resources. Some of its areas, however, have more useful resources than others. For instance, Canada has more oil than Central America. Therefore, it is fortunate that precious natural resources can often be transported to places where they are needed. Pipelines and oil tankers can carry oil to areas that have none.

MINERALS

Some of the most important natural resources are **minerals**. Minerals are natural substances that are reached by mining, or digging into the earth. Canada is one of the earth's most mineral-rich areas. Many of its minerals are mined from the area around the Hudson Bay. Mineral deposits such as nickel, zinc, oil, gold, copper, iron, coal, and uranium are found throughout the Western Hemisphere. Often, though, they are located in hard-to-reach areas.

For instance, oil, silver, and tin are mined in large quantities in South America. However, these resources are often located in the mountains or offshore, at a distance from the coast. The graph below shows that some of the world's leading copper-producing countries are in South America. What the graph does not show is that the largest deposits of South American copper are in the rugged Andes Mountains. As you can imagine, the location of this copper makes it difficult to mine and transport to other areas. You will read more about how South America uses its resources in Unit 8.

VEGETATION

Another important natural resource of the Western Hemisphere is its plant life, or **vegetation**. Every environment has its own unique vegetation. The different kinds of plants found in an area are affected by that area's temperature, precipitation, and kind of soil. Suppose that an area is fairly warm, receives a lot of rainfall, and has good

GRAPH SKILL: Many important **minerals** can be found in South America. In which country is the most copper found?

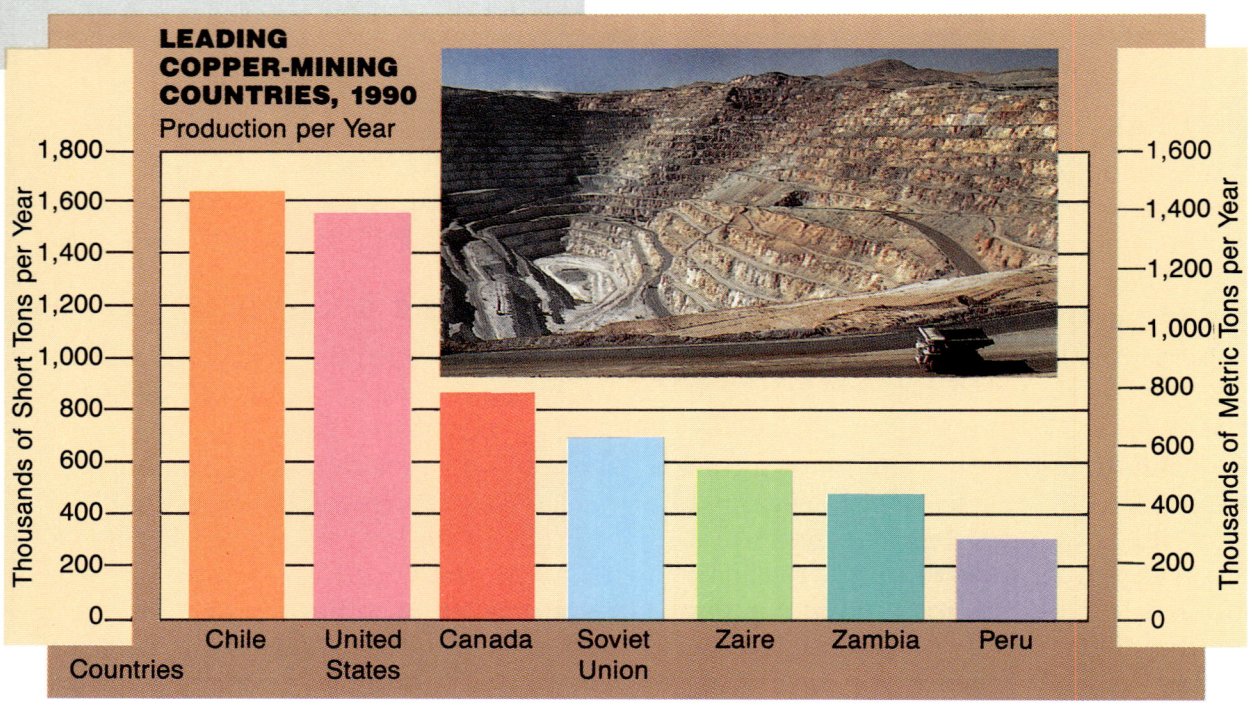

LEADING COPPER-MINING COUNTRIES, 1990
Production per Year

Thousands of Short Tons per Year

Thousands of Metric Tons per Year

Countries: Chile, United States, Canada, Soviet Union, Zaire, Zambia, Peru

soil. As you might expect, trees and many different kinds of plants grow well under these conditions.

The map on this page shows the great variety of vegetation found in the Western Hemisphere. Use the map key to identify the main types of vegetation in North America and South America. What is the natural vegetation of the area in which you live?

PRESERVING THE EARTH'S RESOURCES

All resources are valuable. Some of them are renewable resources, or those that can replace or rebuild themselves. For example, plants and trees are renewable because they can be replanted. Animals are also renewable because they can reproduce. Air, soil, and water are other renewable resources. If used correctly, renewable resources will always be available.

Even though renewable resources can be replaced, they must be used wisely. Water, air, and other resources can be damaged or made dirty by substances. Such pollution has reduced many of the earth's resources.

Did you know that zoos in the United States attract more visitors each year than do major league baseball, football, and hockey games combined? Despite this evidence that people love wildlife, they have not always kept the well-being of animals in mind. You will read about how some people are trying to protect our resources in the Building Citizenship feature that follows this lesson.

The building of dams and shopping centers has destroyed the environments of many plants and animals. People around the world have also hunted animals that threaten their

MAP SKILL: Vegetation, such as the forest shown above, is an important natural resource. What kind of vegetation is found in most of Canada?

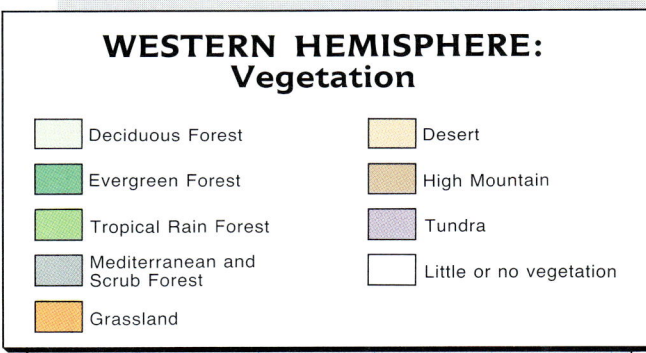

WESTERN HEMISPHERE: Vegetation

- Deciduous Forest
- Evergreen Forest
- Tropical Rain Forest
- Mediterranean and Scrub Forest
- Grassland
- Desert
- High Mountain
- Tundra
- Little or no vegetation

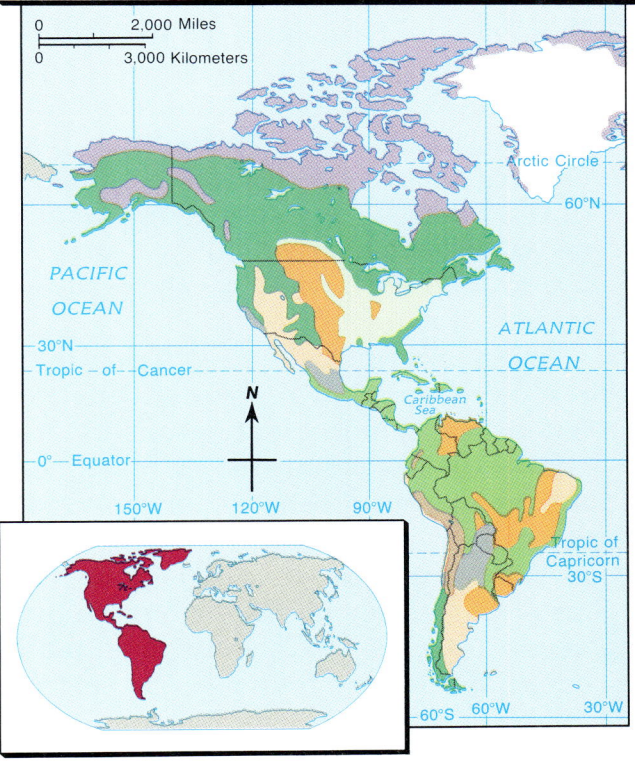

ENDANGERED ANIMALS

Major Causes of Extinction	Destruction of Animal's Environment	Overhunting	Both
North America	caribou	gray whale	bobcat / condor
South America	vicuña / howler monkey	tapir	macaw / golden parakeet

Source: National Wildlife Federation

CHART SKILL: Many animals are in danger of becoming **extinct**. Why is the gray whale endangered? The howler monkey?

livestock, or have used animal skins and fur to make luxury items. Thus, some kinds of plants and animals have become **extinct**, or have died out. Use the chart above to learn which animals of the Western Hemisphere are endangered, or have nearly died out. According to the chart, what are the leading causes of extinction?

In modern times the need for natural resources has grown greatly. Unfortunately, many important resources are **nonrenewable resources**, or resources that can never be renewed or replaced. Once a nonrenewable resource, such as coal or iron, is gone, it is gone forever. Therefore, if the world's future needs are to be met, people must plan carefully the way they use our earth's natural resources.

OUR GREATEST RESOURCE

The Western Hemisphere has many natural resources—water, soil, minerals, vegetation, and animals. Perhaps the most important resource of all, however, is our people. It is people who mine the coal, dam the streams, build the houses—who put our resources to good use. But the most productive thing we can do with our resources is to protect them.

Check Your Reading

1. What are natural resources?
2. Why must natural resources be used carefully?
3. Look at the graph on page 34. Which of the countries shown are in the Western Hemisphere?
4. **THINKING SKILL:** Classify six objects in your classroom according to whether they are made from renewable or nonrenewable resources.

Saving the ENVIRONMENT

In 1987 Jeff Gibbs, an eleventh grader from Vancouver, Canada, gained a new view of rain forests when he camped on Moresby Island, off the western coast of British Columbia. The unique climate found in a rain forest makes it one of the Western Hemisphere's most important resources. On Moresby Island, Jeff saw a world filled with 1,000-year-old trees and a wonderful variety of plant and animal life. This was a world untouched by human beings and unlike any Jeff had ever seen.

Later that year, Jeff started an environmental club at his school. The club's first project was to join the already existing national campaign to protect southern Moresby. The students named their group the TREE Club, or Teenagers' Response to Endangered Ecosystems. An endangered ecosystem is a community of plants and animals that is in danger. Usually, people want to build on its land. The TREE Club wrote to elected officials, raised money to print 50,000 newsletters about southern Moresby, and went door-to-door to talk to voters about protecting the rain forest. "Just doing a small part was satisfying," said Jeff, "because other people were also doing small parts." The students shared the thrill of success when southern Moresby was declared a national preserve in 1987. A preserve is an area set aside for the protection of plant and animal life.

Jeff's work for southern Moresby led to an invitation to tour the Brazilian rain forest. After he returned to Vancouver, Jeff presented a slide show about the Amazon River to some students. The show was so popular that Jeff took it to high schools across British Columbia. You will read more about the Amazon River in Chapter 8.

In a speech at a youth conference in 1989, Jeff suggested that environmental clubs at high schools and universities across Canada form an information network. Students responded by forming the Environmental Youth Alliance, with Jeff Gibbs as director.

In addition to local projects, the student-run EYA holds national environmental conferences, sponsors wilderness outings, and publishes a newspaper. The EYA has also introduced the network idea in other countries, including the United States. Jeff plans to have an international network in place before he retires from the Environmental Youth Alliance at age 25. No one doubts that he will succeed.

IDEAS TO REMEMBER

- The earth's surface is always changing.
- The Western Hemisphere extends in length almost from the North Pole to the South Pole. It contains four of the major types of landforms and some of the world's largest freshwater lakes and longest rivers.
- The three major climates in the Western Hemisphere are affected by latitude, elevation, and nearness to bodies of water.
- Natural resources are plentiful in the Western Hemisphere. However, both renewable and nonrenewable resources must be used wisely if the needs of future generations are to be met.

REVIEWING VOCABULARY

climate   pollution
environment   precipitation
natural resource

Number a sheet of paper from 1 to 5. Beside each number write the word or term from the list above that best matches each statement.

1. Everything that makes up a place, including its water, land, plants, and animals
2. Materials found in nature that are useful to or needed by people
3. Moisture that falls from the sky, such as rain or snow
4. The weather patterns of an area over a long period of time
5. The harming of resources by misusing them

REVIEWING FACTS

1. What is one way that the earth's surface changes quickly? What is one way that it changes very slowly?
2. What are tectonic plates?
3. Which archipelago is located in the Western Hemisphere? Where is it located?
4. What is the tallest mountain in the Western Hemisphere? Name two important rivers that are located in the Western Hemisphere.
5. What is the difference between a plateau and a plain?
6. How are temperature and precipitation related to climate?
7. What are three factors that affect the temperature and precipitation of a place?
8. Describe tropical climates, polar climates, and temperate climates.
9. Give an example of a renewable and a nonrenewable resource. Explain why each is renewable or nonrenewable.
10. What could happen if people do not use natural resources wisely?

WRITING ABOUT MAIN IDEAS

1. **Writing Journal Entries:** Imagine that you are a passenger on a ship in the Atlantic Ocean. The ship is sailing from the east coast of South America near the equator north to Hudson Bay. How does the environment change as you travel? Write at least three journal entries—at the beginnning, the middle, and the end of the trip—describing the changes you observe.

2. **Writing About Local Climate:** Write a description of the climate in your area. Explain what factors, such as elevation and latitude, affect the climate in your area. Give one reason why you like or dislike your area's climate.

3. **Writing a Paragraph:** Write a paragraph with this topic sentence: Water is a very important natural resource throughout the Western Hemisphere.

4. **Writing a Persuasive Paragraph:** Identify one natural resource that you think is important in the daily life of people in Canada. Write a paragraph describing a plan for protecting that resource. You might discuss how to keep the resource from becoming polluted or being used up altogether. In your paragraph describe a plan and try to convince others to follow it.

5. **Writing a Song:** Choose a melody that you like. Then make up words to go with the melody that will describe a place you enjoy visiting.

6. **Writing About Perspectives:** Imagine that you work for an organization whose purpose is to solve environmental problems. Your organization plans to mail a fund-raising letter to raise the money to carry out its goals. Write a letter that could be mailed throughout the country. Your letter should describe the need for the organization. Also, based on what you have read about environmental problems in the chapter, describe some of the projects your organization hopes to start.

SOUTH AMERICA: Political

BUILDING SKILLS: UNDERSTANDING LATITUDE AND LONGITUDE

Use the map on this page to answer these questions.

1. What are latitude and longitude?
2. Which city is located at 10°N, 67°W?
3. Locate Montevideo, the capital of Uruguay, by giving both its latitude and longitude.
4. Which city is in the low latitudes—Bogotá, Colombia, or Santiago, Chile?
5. Why is it useful to understand latitude and longitude?

CHAPTER 2

PEOPLE AND CULTURE

FOCUS

*Indian boats, particularly the canoe and kayak, spread . . .
around the world. . . . No better boats have ever been developed for traveling over white water [rapids], into unexplored
territory, [or] into shallow waters. . . .*

In his book *Indian Givers: How the Indians of the Americas
Transformed the World*, Jack Weatherford tells us about many
of the contributions that the American Indians have made
to the world. How did the first people reach the Americas?
This chapter will discuss how the Indians of the Western
Hemisphere lived.

1 The First Americans

READ TO LEARN

Key Vocabulary

history
prehistory
artifact
archaeology

Ice Age
glacier
migration
nomad

Key Places

Beringia

Read Aloud

"Oh, look," she cried. . . . "Mammoths! I see a herd of mammoths!" . . . No time was lost. The mammoths could decide to move away, or the weather could change again. The hunters . . . gathered to devise a plan to drive the huge woolly animals into a trap. Fire was the answer.

Jean Auel's novel, *The Mammoth Hunters*, tells us that life was very different thousands of years ago. In this lesson you will learn about the first people who lived in the Western Hemisphere. As you are about to see, their story is a fascinating one.

Read for Purpose

1. **WHAT YOU KNOW:** How does geography help to determine where people live?
2. **WHAT YOU WILL LEARN:** Who were the first Americans, and where did they come from?

STUDYING THE PAST

Have you ever wondered what your neighborhood was like 100 years ago? If you were to go to the library, you probably could read about your area's history, or the record of what happened in the past. You probably would find journals that were written by the people who lived there at that time.

But how would you learn about the people who lived in your neighborhood thousands of years ago, before a system for writing things down had been developed? The study of the period before the development of written records is known as **prehistory**.

Today we have a lot of information about prehistoric times. We know what the land looked like, what the climate was like, and how people lived thousands of years ago. How can we know these things without written records?

Scientists, working like detectives, have pieced together different clues about life long ago. They have found these clues by digging into the earth to examine ancient objects that were made and left behind by the people who lived there. Such objects are called **artifacts**. The study of the way in which people lived in the past, known as **archaeology**, has led to many discoveries. Thanks to the work of archaeologists, you are able to read about life in the Western Hemisphere thousands of years ago!

THE ICE AGE

The **Ice Age** was a long, cold period that began more than 70,000 years ago. During the Ice Age, thick sheets of ice known as **glaciers** (glā′ shərz) covered much of the earth. The glaciers moved slowly southward from the North Pole, spreading across the northern parts of North America, Europe, and Asia. At the peak of the Ice Age, glaciers covered almost one fourth of the earth.

The first inhabitants of the Western Hemisphere probably arrived from Asia some time during this cold, harsh

Ancient **artifacts** such as this have helped archaeologists to piece together the past.

Courtesy of the Smithsonian Institute

period. How they reached North America and how they survived once they were here is a fascinating mystery.

The study of artifacts such as weapons and tools has led archaeologists to conclude that the first Americans were part of a huge **migration** of people. A migration is the movement of a group of people or animals from one place to another. This migration of people from Asia to North America, which took place over thousands of years, is believed to have been one of the largest migrations in history.

LAND BRIDGE

Many people believe that the people who migrated to North America during the Ice Age were the ancestors of today's Native Americans. They came during one of the coldest periods of the Ice Age. Because so much ocean water had been frozen to form glaciers, the water levels of the oceans had dropped more than 300 feet (91 m). In addition, once-shallow seas became dry land.

As the map on the opposite page shows, a land bridge once connected North America to Asia. This land bridge, called **Beringia** (ber ən′ gē ə), may have provided the route for the first migrants to reach the Western Hemisphere. According to archaeologists, migrants also may have made their way to North America by boat.

HUNTING FOR FOOD

Whichever way they reached North America, these migrants were **nomads**, or wandering hunters and gatherers who had no permanent homes. Some may have crossed the land bridge to follow the herds of wild animals that grazed on the grasses and other plants of Beringia. Some of these nomads also fished for food or gathered plants in order to survive during the Ice Age.

Food was not hard to find. Indian legends tell of coming to a land "full of game," with animals "as tall as the high branches of a cottonwood tree." The biggest were mammoths, huge prehistoric elephants with shaggy black hair. The largest mammoths were more than 14 feet (4 m) tall. Archaeologists have found arrowheads stuck in the ancient mammoth skeletons. In *The Mammoth Hunters*, Jean Auel imagines hunters in the Ice Age.

> The hunters moved in quickly when they saw the hairy beast approach. They raced toward the giant animal . . . and throwing their spears . . . attacked. . . . In the quiet that followed, they cut off the meat from the dead animal and cleaned the skin.

Today northern Canada is still extremely cold. In the Traditions lesson on pages 44–47, you will read more about an animal that lives in the cold arctic environment today.

THE FIRST AMERICANS

Whether by land or by sea, the first Americans migrated slowly. By the time they had reached the southern tip

ROUTES OF THE FIRST AMERICANS

Land areas during Ice Age

Glaciers

Present-day shoreline

Routes of first Americans

MAP SKILL: The first Americans wore disguises to hunt. Why do you think that they took a southern route through North America?

of South America about 10,000 years ago, the Ice Age was ending. Rising ocean waters were covering the land bridge. By the time the arctic waters again covered Beringia and formed the Bering Strait, people had settled in areas throughout the Western Hemisphere's two continents.

Check Your Reading

1. What is the difference between history and prehistory?
2. How did the first Americans arrive in the Western Hemisphere?
3. GEOGRAPHY SKILL: Compare the map above with the Atlas map on pages 562–563. How close is the Bering Sea to the Arctic Circle?
4. THINKING SKILL: In what ways do you think climate can affect a people's way of life?

43

P O L A R
BEARS

Excerpt from *Arctic Dreams* by Barry Lopez

A tradition is a custom or belief that is handed down from generation to generation. Traditions are an important part of culture. Often they are very old, and help remind people of the past. Traditions also help people express their beliefs about how to live in the present.

One such tradition is the observation of wildlife. In Lesson 1 you read that many people of the Ice Age survived by hunting herds of wild animals. Because they depended on these animals for food and clothing, they watched them carefully. Sometimes hunters recorded their observations by carving pictures on pieces of stone or ivory.

Today people continue this tradition. Some people observe wildlife for scientific purposes, or because they feel that a deeper knowledge of animal life can teach humans more about themselves. Others do so for the sheer enjoyment of sharing animal stories. In this lesson you will read about how female polar bears teach their cubs to live in the Arctic environment. As you read, think about the animals you might enjoy studying and describing.

den a place where a wild animal lives; lair

consistency the degree of thickness

conserve protect from loss, harm, or waste

metabolism (mə tab′ ə liz əm) the total of all the biological and chemical processes that occur in a living thing

Cubs, usually two but sometimes one or three, and very rarely four, are born sometime in December or early January. They are blind, deaf, poorly insulated, and unable to walk or smell. In their first weeks they are dependent on three things for survival: the protection of the **den**, the warm crevices of their mother's body, and her rich milk. (Polar bear milk has the **consistency** of cream. Those who have tasted it say it tastes like cod liver oil and smells of seals or fish. It is richer than whale milk and higher in protein than seal milk.) Again, it is only with the protection of a well-made den that a female can **conserve** and direct her **metabolism** to produce the heat and milk that her cubs need.

44

The cubs are so small at birth, barely a pound, that the female can hide one in the rolled toes of her front paw. At about twenty-four days they can hear, and a week later they are able to see. It is several more weeks before they can walk and smell. By late March or early April the cubs weigh about 25 pounds, and the female, depending on the weather and the cubs' condition, breaks out of her den. For the first days she might just sit drowsily in the sun at the den entrance. Or roll in the snow to **revive** her coat. Or nose about in a **desultory** way, looking for grasses and **lichens** to nibble.

A well-placed den entrance will be protected from the wind and directed in some measure to the south and west to take advantage of the sun's afternoon warmth. Cubs venture forth onto this sheltered sun porch a few days after their mother and for the next few weeks do not travel far at all. Their mother often nurses them here in a sitting position in the sunshine, with her back against a snowbank. The cubs lie on her belly. While they nurse she may put her head back and stare at the sky, or roll her head slowly from side to side, or rock her cubs gently in the cradle of her forelegs.

revive to give new freshness to

desultory (des' əl tôr ē) without plan

lichens (lī kənz) plants without flowers, usually growing on tree trunks, rocks, or the ground

These first few weeks are a critical time for all three animals. The female balances her desire to leave in order to hunt to feed herself against an investment in the cubs' learning, exercise, and preparation for travel. For most bears the sea is no more than a day away. For others, like those denning on the southern coast of Hudson Bay, the journey is much longer and requires making temporary dens along the way.

Svalbard (sväl′ bärd) a group of Arctic Ocean islands that belong to Norway

Retzius (ret sē′ us) a mountain in Svalbard on the island Kong Karlsband

density quantity per unit of area

Rasmus Hansson and Jørn Thomassen, who have watched more bears emerge from their dens than probably anyone else, studied bears for several years at a traditional denning area called Bogen Valley, in **Svalbard**. Most of the bears there den in a long line just below the ridge of **Retzius** Mountain. (In spite of this **density** it is very rare to see two families outside their dens at the same time. How the females manage periods of exercise so as not to interfere with each other is not known.)

Since portions of the southwest face of Retzius Mountain slope at an angle of 70°, the first problem cubs face there is getting down to the floor of Bogen Valley. They learn to imitate their mothers, who slide down rump first, looking over their shoulders and breaking with their claws; or on their sides, leading with all four feet; or headfirst on their bellies. Mothers at the bottom catch cubs veering out of control.

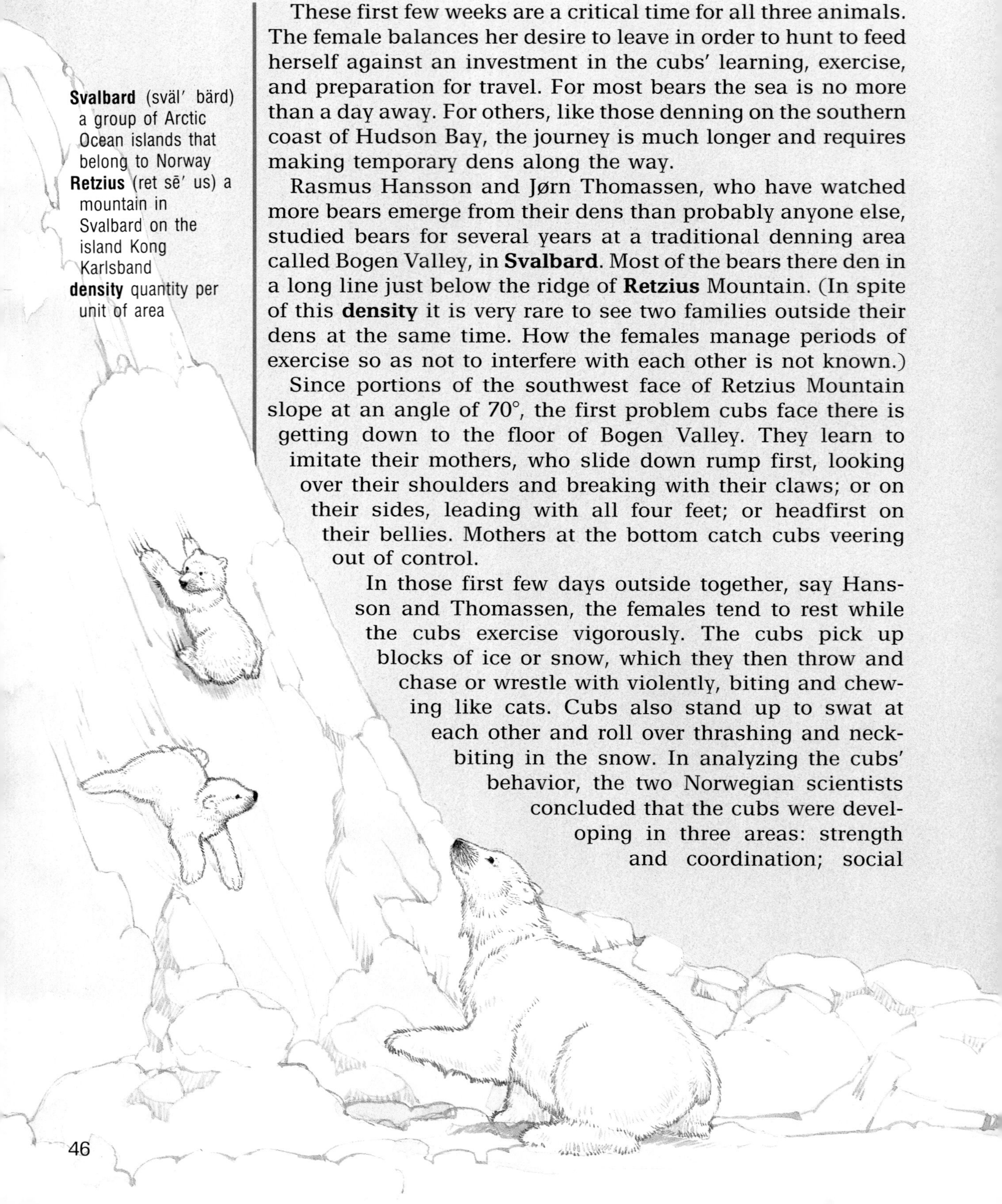

In those first few days outside together, say Hansson and Thomassen, the females tend to rest while the cubs exercise vigorously. The cubs pick up blocks of ice or snow, which they then throw and chase or wrestle with violently, biting and chewing like cats. Cubs also stand up to swat at each other and roll over thrashing and neck-biting in the snow. In analyzing the cubs' behavior, the two Norwegian scientists concluded that the cubs were developing in three areas: strength and coordination; social

habits and communication skills, which would permit the female and her cubs to live and hunt together efficiently during the next two years; and fighting techniques. In the future the latter would serve males in their battles with each other during the breeding season, and females in the defense of their own cubs. (Male bears, according to some researchers, will try to kill any cub they encounter, especially if the female offers a weak defense.)

When cubs reach some **threshold** level of strength and coordination, when they are able to walk well and are responsive to their mother's instructions to "stay" and "come," the bears depart from the den. The time of all three having to live solely on the stored fat of the female is nearly over.

How does the tradition of observing wildlife enrich many people's lives?

2 Different Cultures

Key Vocabulary

culture   value
custom   religion
society

Key Places

Latin America
Anglo-America

Read Aloud

Everything I know about surviving in the jungle was taught to me by the elders. . . . I can recognize every smell and sound. . . . The jungle provides us with wood, clay, and other materials for our home. It also provides us with fresh meat, plenty of fruit, and water. There are even plants that heal wounds and cure fevers.

Kin, a Mayan Indian, is describing how he lives off the land. His method of survival might remind you of the first Americans you read about in Lesson 1. People throughout the ages have discovered different ways to meet their needs.

Read for Purpose

1. **WHAT YOU KNOW:** How did the first Americans get their food?
2. **WHAT YOU WILL LEARN:** What is culture? What are the culture regions of the Western Hemisphere?

WAYS OF LIFE

As the first Americans migrated throughout the Western Hemisphere, different groups settled in different places. One group may have found a small lake that was surrounded by plant and animal life. A large mountain or a river might have prevented another group from continuing its journey. As you read in Chapter 1, geography and the environment have a great effect on the places in which people choose to live.

Some people settled down in one area, had children, and their population slowly grew. They formed a community and used the area's resources to meet their needs. When people work together as a group, they develop a special way of life. The way of life of a group of people is called its culture.

Throughout this book you will read about the different ways of life in the Western Hemisphere. As you will read, there are hundreds of different culture groups, from the Inuit in northern Canada to the cattle herders of Argentina. Despite the enormous variety of culture groups in the Western Hemisphere today, they can be grouped into two major culture regions.

CULTURE REGIONS

These two culture regions are Latin America and Anglo-America. *Latin America* is the term used to describe the culture region of the Western Hemisphere that was strongly influenced by the European countries of Spain, Portugal, and France. As the map on this page shows, Latin America includes all of the land of Middle America and South America—the entire area south of the United States.

Anglo-America is the term used to describe the culture region of the Western Hemisphere that was strongly influenced by the country of England. The map shows that Anglo-America includes both the United States and Canada. English culture has remained strong in the lands in which English people have settled. What are some of the cultural differences between the two regions? Continue to read and you will be able to answer this question.

SOCIAL GROUPS

A culture is shaped as a group of people work together to meet their basic needs. The kinds of food people eat and the types of homes they live in are affected by climate and geography. For example, in the tropical areas of Latin America people build open, breezy homes to keep cool. What kind of shelter do you think the people of the Ice Age had?

The way in which people meet their needs also depends on the customs, or social habits of their culture. In some

cultures, for example, it is the custom not to eat meat. As people worked together in order to survive, they organized into social groups. In most cultures the main social group is the family. Clubs and sports teams are other kinds of social groups.

Social groups such as the family are part of a larger group called a society (sə sī′ i tē). A society is a group of people who are bound together by the same culture and purposes. An entire country may be a society. So may smaller groups of people who share the

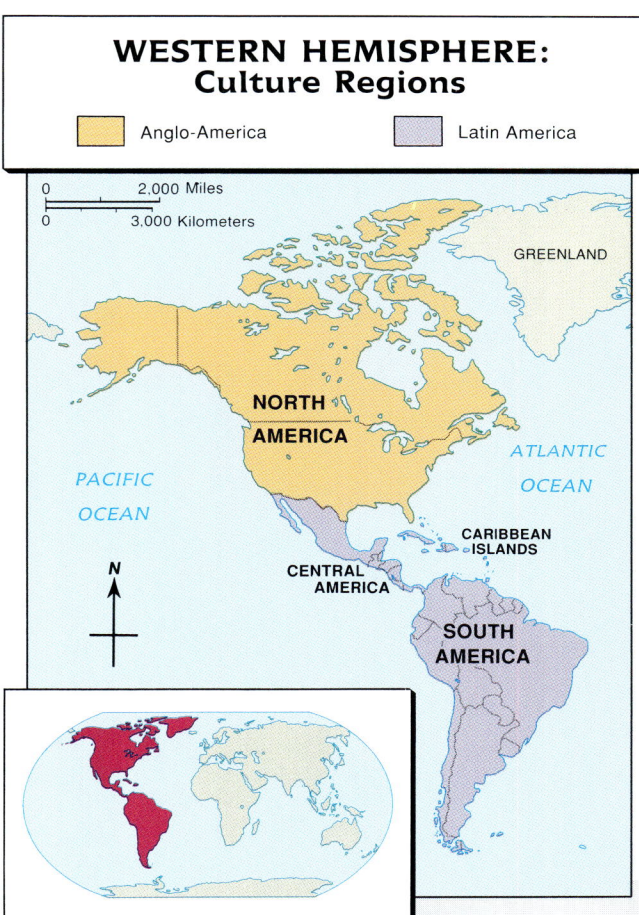

WESTERN HEMISPHERE: Culture Regions

Anglo-America   Latin America

MAP SKILL: Which parts of the Western Hemisphere are in the Latin America culture region?

49

same interests and goals. For example, the pioneers on the American frontier formed a pioneer society. Name a society to which you belong.

LANGUAGE AND CULTURE

The chart below shows some of the aspects of a culture. One of the most noticeable differences between Latin America and Anglo-America is language. The major languages in Latin America are Spanish, Portuguese, and French. These languages are called Latin languages because they are derived from Latin, the language of the ancient Roman Empire.

English is the major language spoken in Anglo-America. However, many other languages are spoken in both regions. For example, Canada has a large French-speaking population because of the many French people who settled there. What are some of the languages spoken in the United States?

VALUES AND RELIGION

Members of a culture also share the same beliefs. People of all cultures have felt the need to find the answers to the basic questions in life. How should people act toward one another? What is right and what is wrong? What is the purpose of life?

The way in which people answer such questions often depends on their **values** (val' ūz). Values are the principles, standards, or ideals of a person or group.

Values are an important aspect of culture. The works of writers, painters, and other artists often deal with

CHART SKILL: Give an example of each of the features in the chart.

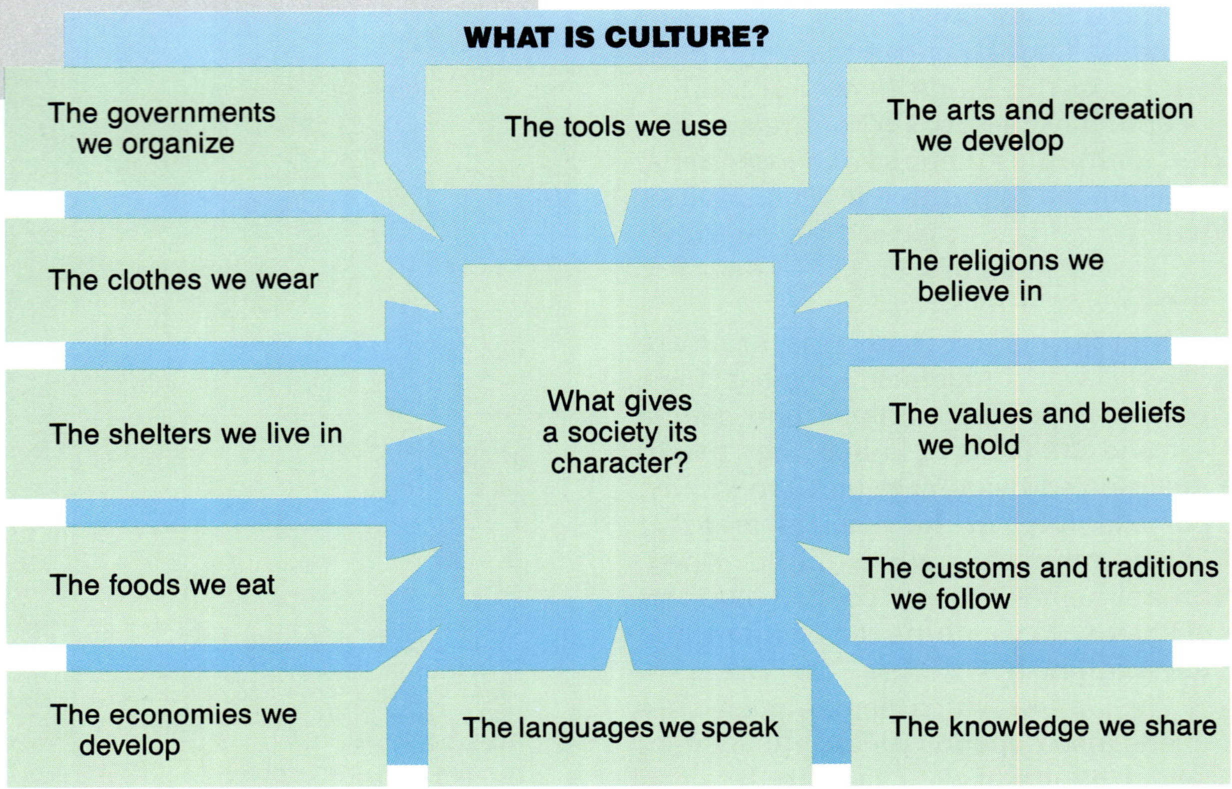

WHAT IS CULTURE?

The governments we organize

The tools we use

The arts and recreation we develop

The clothes we wear

The religions we believe in

The shelters we live in

What gives a society its character?

The values and beliefs we hold

The foods we eat

The customs and traditions we follow

The economies we develop

The languages we speak

The knowledge we share

50

The Mexican dance and the Inuit play pictured above are two examples of the diverse cultures found throughout the Western Hemisphere.

values. Even the way in which people relax tells us something about the values of a culture. For example, the Indians of the northwest coast of Canada developed a custom called the *potlatch* (pot' lach). A potlatch was a kind of party held to show how important the hosts were. You will read about this custom in Chapter 3.

Values are also expressed through **religion**. Religion is the way in which people worship the God or gods they believe in. Members of a religious group share a common form of worship. Christianity is the major religion in both Latin America and Anglo-America. Roman Catholicism is the form of Christianity practiced by most Latin Americans. In both regions other religions are also practiced, including Judaism, Islam, and Indian religions.

Values also affect how people are governed and the type of economy a society has. In the chapters that follow you will read about the different values of the countries that make up the Western Hemisphere.

VARIED CULTURES

You have read that a people's culture is its way of life—its language, society, religion, arts, and recreation. People who share a culture have many similar beliefs and values. As you continue to read about the people and places of the Western Hemisphere, you will learn about the features that make each of the cultures of Latin America and Anglo-America special.

Check Your Reading

1. Name four aspects of a culture.
2. What are the two cultural regions of the Western Hemisphere?
3. Which religion is most common in Latin America?
4. **THINKING SKILL:** Compare Latin America and Anglo-America. How are the two regions alike? How are they different?

Decision Making

Every day you choose what to do during your free time. On some days you might decide to play soccer with your friends. On other days you might decide to stay home and finish your homework. Decision making means selecting from a number of alternatives, or options, the one option that will help you to achieve your goal. In this lesson you will learn how to make good decisions.

Trying the Skill

In the last lesson you read about some of the values that influence the way people live. The following story is about a person who makes a decision in which traditions and values play an important part.

Bill Karim wants to eat only fruits and vegetables. He thinks that changing his eating habits will improve his health and well-being. Bill has to decide how to adapt his new, vegetarian diet to the meals served at home. He knows that eating meat is customary in his home, especially during religious feasts.

Bill considers his options. He can stick to his new diet except at dinner and religious feasts, when eating meat is an important family tradition. He can eat selectively at those meals, leaving the food he does not want on his plate. He can ask for special foods, or he can try to change the eating habits of his entire family. Or he can ask his mother to cook extra vegetables for him.

If Bill joins his family for their usual meal, he will be continuing an important tradition. However, he will not enjoy the benefits of eating only fruits and vegetables. If he leaves some food on his plate, he will be wasteful. He also may not get enough to eat. If Bill asks for special foods or asks his family to change their eating habits, he may offend his parents and create extra work and expense. Asking his mother to prepare extra vegetables for him will require a little extra effort and expense.

1. What is Bill's goal?
2. Which options does he consider?
3. What do you think Bill should do?

52

HELPING YOURSELF

The steps on the left can help you to make better decisions. The example on the right shows how to apply these steps to Bill's decision.

One Way to Make a Decision	Example
1. Identify and clearly define the goal you wish to achieve.	Bill's goal is to improve his health by changing his diet.
2. Identify all possible alternatives, or options, by which you can achieve your goal.	Bill has five alternatives: ignore his diet, eat selectively, request special foods, request that his mother cook extra vegetables, or ask his family to be vegetarians.
3. Predict the likely outcomes, or consequences, both immediate and long-range, of each alternative.	Bill considered the likely outcomes of each alternative. For instance, if he decided to eat the traditional family meals, he would not enjoy the benefits of a vegetarian diet.
4. Evaluate each outcome by determining whether it will benefit or harm you or others and whether or not it will help in achieving the goal.	After examining each alternative, Bill decides that following a vegetarian diet by asking his mother to cook extra vegetables for him is best for everyone.
5. Choose the best alternative.	Bill's choice will enable him to follow his diet and eat with his family, without causing much extra work or expense.

Applying the Skill

Now apply what you have learned to identify the decision-making process in the following story.

The student council wants to help protect the environment. Members want the cafeteria to stop using Styrofoam trays, which are not biodegradable, or do not decay naturally, and could create a waste problem. Metal trays, which would need washing, and cardboard trays which, though biodegradable, are flimsy, were suggested.

Members learn that the only way to pay for the new trays is by raising lunch prices. They must decide whether to buy new trays, and if so, what kind.

1. What was the student council's goal?
   a. to buy metal trays
   b. to protect the environment
   c. to hold down the cost of lunches
2. Which alternative was not considered?
   a. using cardboard trays
   b. raising the price of cafeteria food
   c. asking the students to bring lunch
3. What do you think the student council should do? Explain your answer.

Reviewing the Skill

1. Explain what *decision making* means.
2. What are some steps you can take to make good decisions?

IDEAS TO REMEMBER

■ According to archaeologists, the first Americans were nomads who traveled from Asia during the Ice Age and who, over thousands of years, spread out across the Americas.

■ The culture of a people includes their customs, beliefs, languages, arts, values, and recreation.

■ All of the Western Hemisphere can be divided into two cultural regions: Anglo-America and Latin America.

REVIEWING VOCABULARY

archaeology	migration
artifacts	nomad
culture	religion
custom	society
history	values

Number a sheet of paper from 1 to 10. Beside each number write the word from the list above that best completes the sentence.

1. _____ are the principles and standards of a person or group.
2. You read about the _____ of people who first lived hundreds of years ago.
3. A _____ wanders from place to place in search of food.
4. American _____ includes rock 'n' roll, belief in democracy, and the English language.
5. Judaism is a _____ that teaches a belief in one God.
6. Because of the science of _____, we know something about the way people lived thousands of years ago.
7. A _____ is a group of people who are joined together by the same culture and purposes.
8. Scientists believe that the _____ of people from Asia brought the first people to the Americas.
9. Among the _____ left behind by prehistoric people were arrowheads and simple tools.
10. One American _____ is to eat turkey on Thanksgiving.

REVIEWING FACTS

Number a sheet of paper from 1 to 10. Beside each number write whether the following statements are true or false. If the statement is true, write **T**. If it is false, rewrite it to make it true.

1. We have learned about the first people who came to the Americas from their writings.
2. The first people came to the Americas during a period that is called the Land Years.
3. The first people who came to the Americas almost certainly traveled by boat.
4. A mammoth looks like a large, hairy elephant.
5. A group's way of life is called its customs.
6. The United States is a part of Latin America.
7. Social groups and societies are the same thing.

8. The belief in the importance of education is an example of a value.
9. In Latin America the main language is Latin.
10. These things are part of a group's culture: the clothes they wear, the foods they eat, and the natural resources available in the area in which they live.

WRITING ABOUT MAIN IDEAS

1. **Writing a Paragraph:** Write a paragraph exploring this question: Why don't we know for sure how the first Americans came to North America?
2. **Writing a Letter:** Review the ideas about culture shown in the chart on page 50. Then write a letter to a pen pal in another country describing at least three aspects of your culture.
3. **Writing About Culture:** Study the pictures on page 51. Name the features of the cultures that are shown in these pictures.
4. **Writing About Perspectives:** You have read about the first Americans, who archaeologists believe came from Asia thousands of years ago. How was their way of life similar to your life today? How was it different?

BUILDING SKILLS: DECISION MAKING

Read the following. Then make a decision based on the information given: You are the head of a family living in Asia near the Bering Strait thousands of years ago. You must find food to feed your family. You have learned that abundant fish and herds of animals exist in a land to the east. Other people are now hunting in the area where you now hunt. Your people are complaining about the newcomers. What should you do?

1. What is the problem that you face?
2. What would you like to achieve?
3. What alternatives do you have?
4. How can the results of each alternative be helpful or harmful to your people?
5. Which alternative will you choose? Why is your choice the best decision?

REVIEWING VOCABULARY

archaeology	history
climate	migration
culture	natural resource
custom	society
environment	value

Number a sheet of paper from 1 to 10. Beside each number write the word or term from the list above that best matches the statement.

1. A material found in nature that is useful to people
2. The pattern of weather in a place over a period of time
3. Social habit; something commonly done by the people of a culture
4. A group of people who are bound together by their culture and a common purpose
5. The scientific study of the way in which people lived in the past
6. The way of life of a group of people
7. The movement of a large group of people from one place to another
8. The record of what happened in the past
9. Everything that makes up a place, including the water, land, plants, and animals
10. One of the principles, standards, or ideals of a person or group

✏ WRITING ABOUT THE UNIT

1. **Writing a List:** Review the information about the people of the Ice Age. List the tools and any other new developments that they made during this prehistoric period.

2. **Writing a Paragraph:** How does the climate in which you live affect your way of life? Write a paragraph describing at least two ways in which your culture is affected by climate.

3. **Making a Puzzle:** Make up a crossword puzzle, using at least ten words or terms from Unit 1. Write a clue for each *Across* word and each *Down* word.

4. **Writing About Perspectives:** Choose one of the geographic features that were discussed in this unit, such as a mountain, river, or plain. Write a poem from the point of view of the first Americans, seeing the geographic feature for the first time.

ACTIVITIES

1. **Researching Careers in Archaeology:** Find out how a person can become an archaeologist. Also, try to find out details about the work of an archaeologist. Present the information to the class in an oral report or on a poster.

2. **Making a Chart:** Look at the chart on page 50, and then think about aspects of your culture. Following the style of the chart in the book, make a chart of your culture, including drawings to illustrate it.

3. **Working Together to Make a Scrapbook:** Read the local newspaper to find articles about people who are working to protect the environment or who are using natural resources wisely. Clip out interesting articles and, with a partner, assemble them into a scrapbook. Prepare a table of contents and a short introduction for the scrapbook.

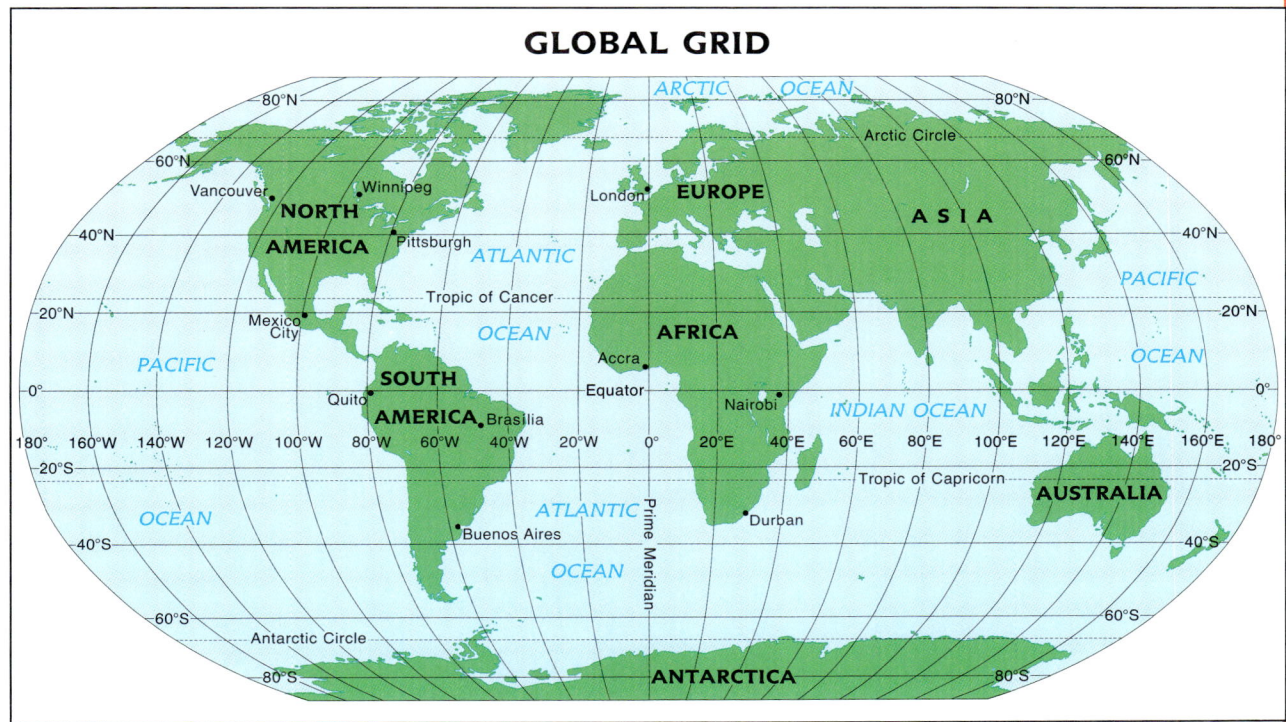

GLOBAL GRID

BUILDING SKILLS: UNDERSTANDING LATITUDE AND LONGITUDE

Use the map above to answer the following questions.

1. If you knew the latitude and longitude of a place, how would you locate that place on a map?

2. Which line of longitude is the closest to Buenos Aires, Argentina?

3. Give the location of Quito, Ecuador, in terms of its latitude and longitude.

4. Which city is located at about 20°N, 100°W?

5. Why is it helpful to understand latitude and longitude?

 **LINKING PAST, PRESENT, AND FUTURE**

You have just begun to study the lands and peoples of North America and South America. Why do you think it might be worthwhile to learn about this hemisphere and its people? Do you think that it will be worthwhile for people to study about this area in the future? Why or why not?

ASIA

EUROPE

+North Pole

ARCTIC
OCEAN

International Date Line

Bering
Strait

Bering
Sea

Beaufort
Sea

75°N

Arctic Circle

0°

Baffin
Bay

Davis Strait

60°N

180°

165°W

Gulf
of
Alaska

Labrador
Sea

Hudson
Bay

CANADA

150°W

PACIFIC
OCEAN

45°N

NORTH
AMERICA

Gulf of St. Lawrence

Ottawa

135°W

30°N

Great Lakes

120°W

60°W

Tropic of Cancer

75°W

15°N

90°W

105°W

Gulf of Mexico

0° Equator

PACIFIC OCEAN

Caribbean
Sea

15°S

SOUTH
AMERICA

UNIT 2

LEARNING ABOUT CANADA

WHERE WE ARE

Your journey through the Western Hemisphere starts in Canada. This vast country is a land of snow-covered mountains, gently rolling farmlands, thick forests, and busy cities. The people of Canada represent many cultures, and their roots extend to all parts of the world.

In this unit, you will read about the first inhabitants of Canada, where they came from, and their ways of life. You will discover the distinct cultures that developed in different parts of Canada, and you will explore how people in different places adapted to their environment. As you learn about Canada and the first people who lived there, think about the ways in which their cultures may resemble your own.

AFRICA

ATLANTIC

OCEAN

15°W

30°W

45°W

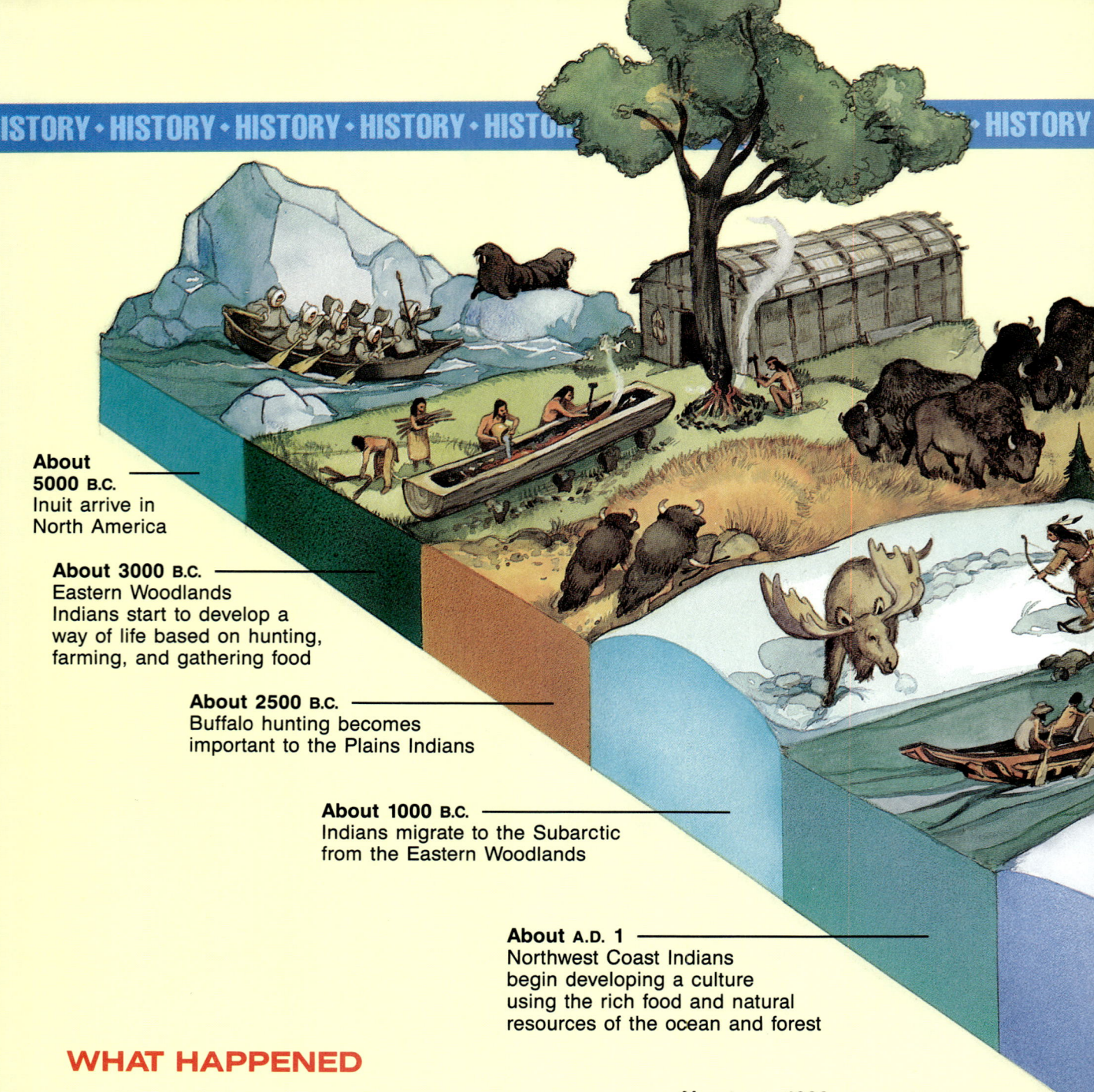

About 5000 B.C.
Inuit arrive in North America

About 3000 B.C.
Eastern Woodlands Indians start to develop a way of life based on hunting, farming, and gathering food

About 2500 B.C.
Buffalo hunting becomes important to the Plains Indians

About 1000 B.C.
Indians migrate to the Subarctic from the Eastern Woodlands

About A.D. 1
Northwest Coast Indians begin developing a culture using the rich food and natural resources of the ocean and forest

About A.D. 1000
Inuit migrate to northern Canada from Alaska

A.D. 1492
Christopher Columbus arrives in the Americas

WHAT HAPPENED

Many thousands of years ago, people began coming from Asia to North America perhaps across a land bridge or by boat. These people and their descendants settled throughout the Western Hemisphere. The beliefs and ways of life they brought with them changed over time, gradually developing into distinct cultures. The arrival of Christopher Columbus brought great changes to the Americas.

60

CHAPTER 3

THE GEOGRAPHY OF CANADA

FOCUS

*Few Canadians live more than an afternoon's drive from
wilderness. Beyond the towns are woods and lakes, . . . and
ice that stretches to the top of the world.*

In the passage above, Canadian writer June Callwood
describes some of the many beautiful landforms found in
Canada. However, Canada is much more than beautiful. Its
variety of land provides the natural resources that help to
make Canada one of the world's richest countries.

1 A Varied Land

READ TO LEARN

Key Vocabulary

rapids
canal
lock
fjord

Key Places

Newfoundland
Bay of Fundy
St. Lawrence River
Canadian Shield

Interior Plains
Rocky Mountains
Coast Ranges

Read Aloud

There were many great moments and there were a lot of hard times.

These words were spoken in May 1985 by a 19-year-old runner named Steve Fonyo. He had just finished a remarkable 14-month run across Canada. From a beach in Newfoundland in southeastern Canada, he had jogged steadily westward until he reached Vancouver Island on the west coast. What made Steve's journey so special, however, was that having lost his left leg to cancer, he had run wearing an artificial limb. As you will read, Steve saw a variety of landforms on his run.

Read for Purpose

1. **WHAT YOU KNOW:** Where is Canada located in relation to the United States?
2. **WHAT YOU WILL LEARN:** What are the six physical regions of Canada?

A GIGANTIC COUNTRY

Steve Fonyo's run across Canada was remarkable for another reason besides his handicap. He had jogged a great distance in order to cross Canada. Canada is the largest country in the Western Hemisphere and the second-largest country in the world. In fact, this vast country is second in size only to Russia. Like its southern neighbor, the United States, Canada stretches over 3,200 miles (5,149 km) from east to west. Both the United States and Canada are bordered on the east by the Atlantic Ocean and on the west by the Pacific Ocean.

During his run Steve Fonyo followed the route of the Trans-Canada Highway. Since the route of the highway is not always straight, Steve actually ran 4,968 miles (8,000 km)! This distance is about 1,700 miles (2,735 km) greater than the width of Canada.

What did Steve see as he was running? As you might imagine, a country as large as Canada has many physical regions. Physical regions are large areas that have similar landforms, climates, and resources. During his run across Canada, Steve passed through several of Canada's physical regions.

When Steve Fonyo set out from eastern Newfoundland in March 1984, the island was experiencing a severe spring snowstorm. The snow made the run difficult. Find Newfoundland Island on the map below.

THE APPALACHIAN HIGHLANDS

As you see on the map, Newfoundland Island is in the Appalachian Highlands region. This is the easternmost region of Canada. As Steve Fonyo discovered, this region has many low hills. The elevation map on page 65 shows the height of these hills.

One of the most interesting features of this region is the Bay of Fundy, which is located between the mainland of Canada and the peninsula of Nova Scotia. The tides in the Bay of Fundy are among the highest in the world— about 50 feet (15 m). Tides are the regular rising and falling of the ocean and connected bodies of water, caused by the gravitational pull of the moon and the sun.

The powerful tides of the Bay of Fundy cause some unusual natural occurrences. For example, at high tide walls of water rushing into the bay from the Atlantic Ocean force the water in the St. John River in New Brunswick to flow backward. The tides are so strong that they cause the water to flow up and over a low falls near the river's mouth. For this reason, these falls are called the Reversing Falls.

MAP SKILL: In which region are the Bay of Fundy's Reversing Falls (right) located?

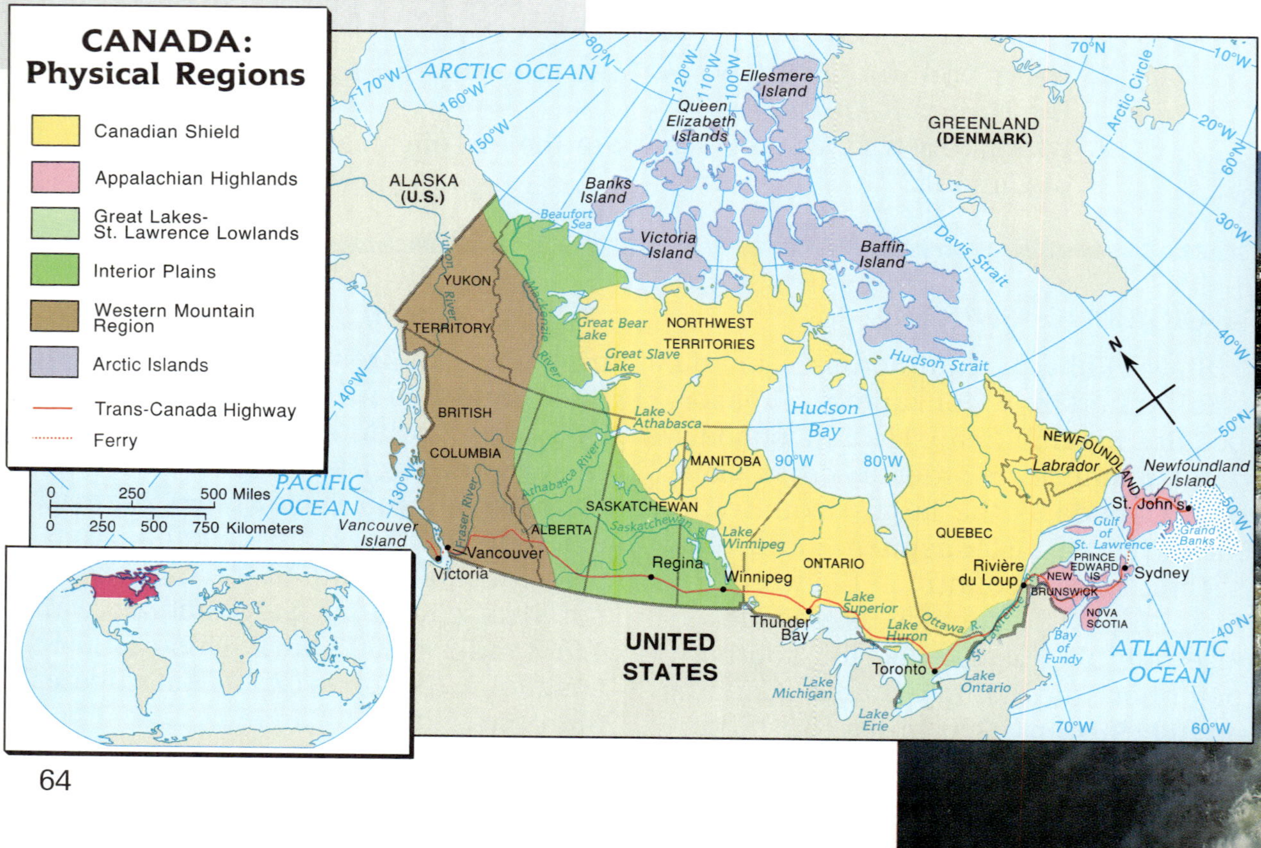

CANADA: Physical Regions

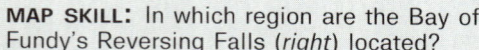

- Canadian Shield
- Appalachian Highlands
- Great Lakes-St. Lawrence Lowlands
- Interior Plains
- Western Mountain Region
- Arctic Islands
- Trans-Canada Highway
- Ferry

0   250   500 Miles
0   250   500   750 Kilometers

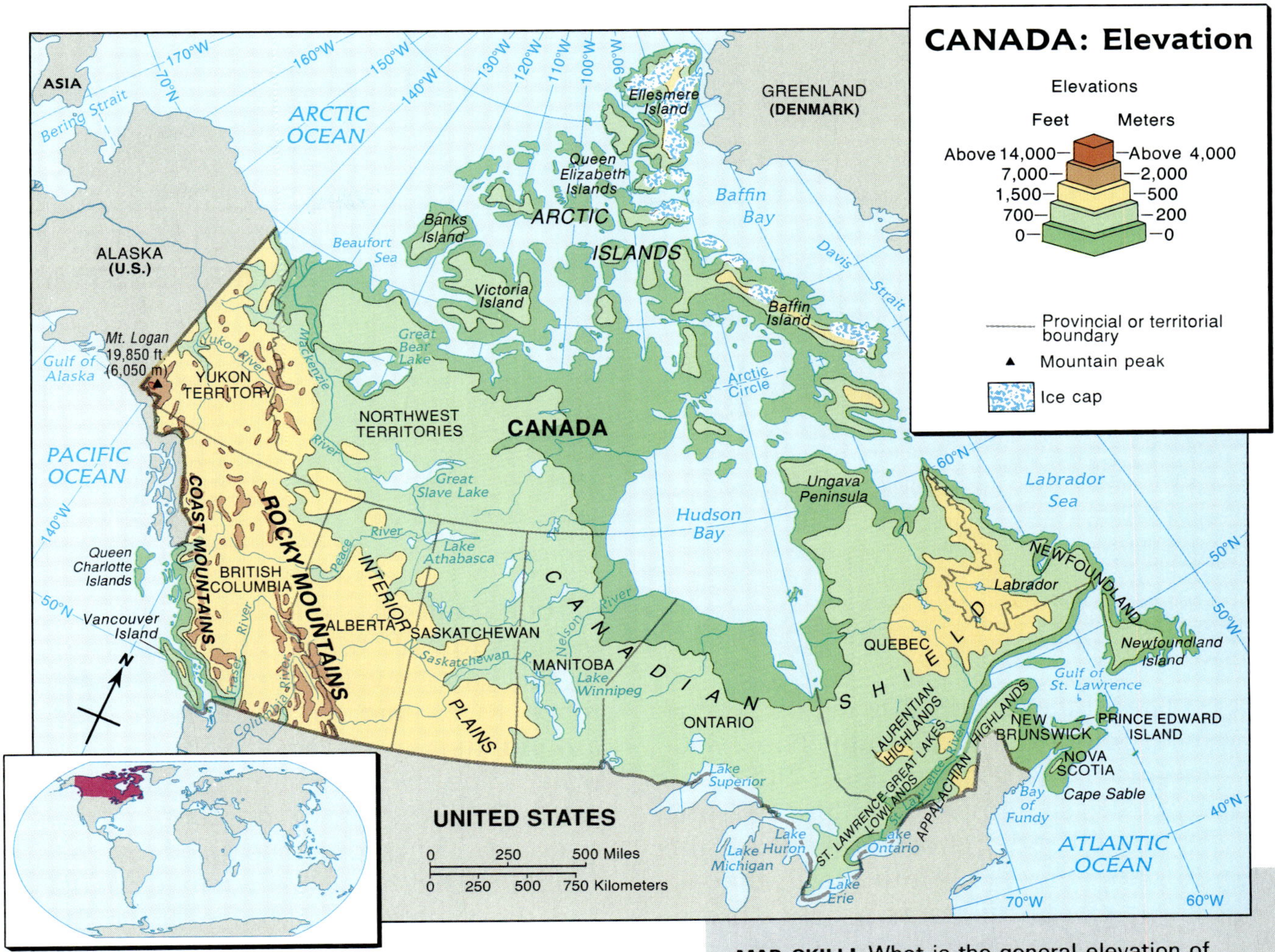
CANADA: Elevation
Elevations
Feet
Meters
Above 14,000
Above 4,000
7,000
2,000
1,500
500
700
200
0
0
Provincial or territorial boundary
Mountain peak
Ice cap
ASIA
Bering Strait
ARCTIC OCEAN
GREENLAND (DENMARK)
Ellesmere Island
Queen Elizabeth Islands
Banks Island
ARCTIC ISLANDS
Baffin Bay
Beaufort Sea
Victoria Island
Davis Strait
Baffin Island
ALASKA (U.S.)
Mt. Logan 19,850 ft. (6,050 m)
Gulf of Alaska
YUKON TERRITORY
Yukon River
Mackenzie River
Great Bear Lake
Arctic Circle
NORTHWEST TERRITORIES
CANADA
PACIFIC OCEAN
Great Slave Lake
Ungava Peninsula
Labrador Sea
Hudson Bay
COAST MOUNTAINS
ROCKY MOUNTAINS
Queen Charlotte Islands
BRITISH COLUMBIA
Peace River
INTERIOR PLAINS
Lake Athabasca
CANADIAN SHIELD
NEWFOUNDLAND
Labrador
Vancouver Island
ALBERTA
SASKATCHEWAN
Saskatchewan River
Nelson River
MANITOBA
Lake Winnipeg
QUEBEC
Newfoundland Island
Gulf of St. Lawrence
Fraser River
Columbia River
ONTARIO
LAURENTIAN HIGHLANDS
APPALACHIAN HIGHLANDS
NEW BRUNSWICK
PRINCE EDWARD ISLAND
NOVA SCOTIA
Cape Sable
Bay of Fundy
Lake Superior
UNITED STATES
ST. LAWRENCE GREAT LAKES LOWLANDS
St. Lawrence River
Lake Michigan
Lake Huron
Lake Ontario
Lake Erie
ATLANTIC OCEAN
0 250 500 Miles
0 250 500 750 Kilometers
170°W
160°W
150°W
140°W
130°W
120°W
110°W
100°W
90°W
70°N
60°N
50°N
40°N
70°W
60°W
50°W
N

MAP SKILL: What is the general elevation of the land that surrounds almost all of Canada's Hudson Bay?

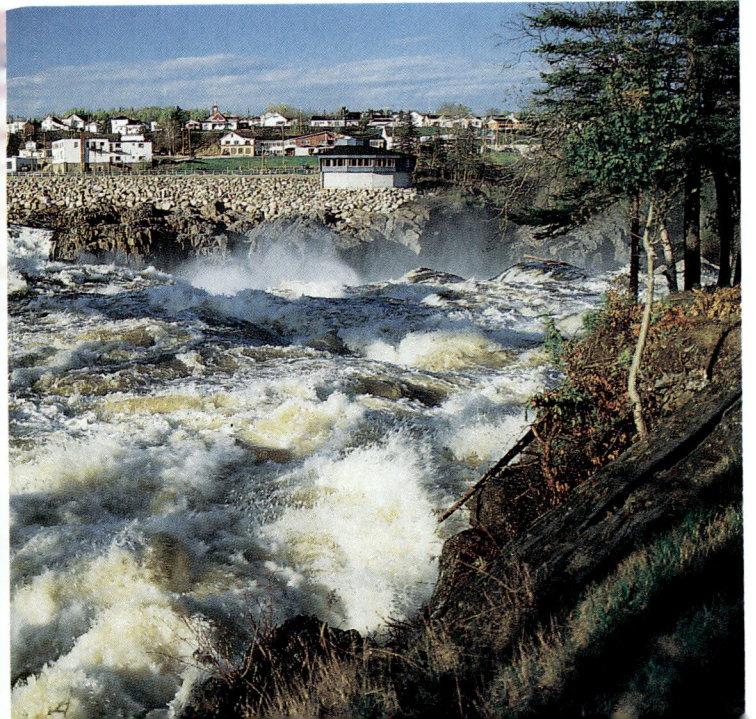

THE GREAT LAKES-ST. LAWRENCE LOWLANDS

By the time Steve reached the Great Lakes-St. Lawrence Lowlands, summer had arrived. Thousands of people gathered to cheer him on his way.

As Steve crossed the area, he saw many plowed fields and busy rivers. The region is named for its major bodies of water—the Great Lakes and the **St. Lawrence River**. You can see them on the map on this page. About 60 percent of all Canadians live in this southern region.

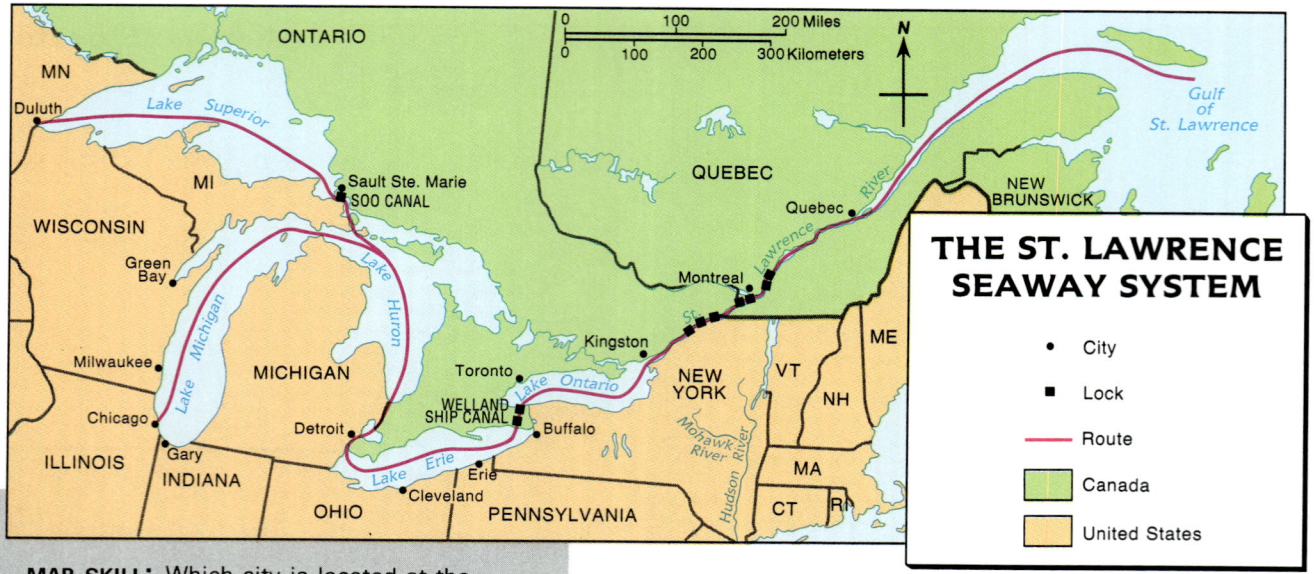

THE ST. LAWRENCE
SEAWAY SYSTEM

- • City
- ■ Lock
- — Route
- Canada
- United States

MAP SKILL: Which city is located at the western end of the St. Lawrence Seaway System? In which country is it located?

The waterways in this region are the most important in Canada. The 2,300-mile-long (4,000-km-long) St. Lawrence River empties into the Atlantic Ocean. Canadians sometimes call the St. Lawrence the "Mother of Canada." It was given this name because it was part of a waterway that was important to the Indians and later to the European explorers and settlers long before modern Canada existed. This waterway flows between the Atlantic Ocean and the center of the continent and is still used to reach inland Canada.

The St. Lawrence is not Canada's longest river system. Actually, the 2,635-mile-long (4,241-km-long) Mackenzie River system is the longest in Canada. However, the St. Lawrence is Canada's major transportation route for shipping. Also, the rivers flowing into the St. Lawrence flow through an important farming area. Dams and power plants on these rivers supply water and power for the farmers, the businesses, and the nearby cities.

Today it is easy to sail from one end of the waterway to the other. However, in the past travelers on the St. Lawrence River had to make their way around its rapids, or swiftly flowing water. The swiftness of the water is caused by the steep descent of the riverbed. The problem caused by the rapids ended in 1959 when Canada and the United States opened the St. Lawrence Seaway. You can see the route of the St. Lawrence Seaway on the map above.

Now look at the cross section diagram of the seaway on page 67. Notice that along its route are several canals and locks. A canal is a waterway that is built across land for boat travel, irrigation, or drainage. A lock is a kind of water elevator that moves boats to higher or lower levels as needed. The canals and locks on the St. Lawrence Seaway make it possible for oceangoing ships to sail all the way from the Atlantic Ocean to the Great Lakes.

THE CANADIAN SHIELD

By the time the fall had arrived, Steve began to see a change in the scenery.

66

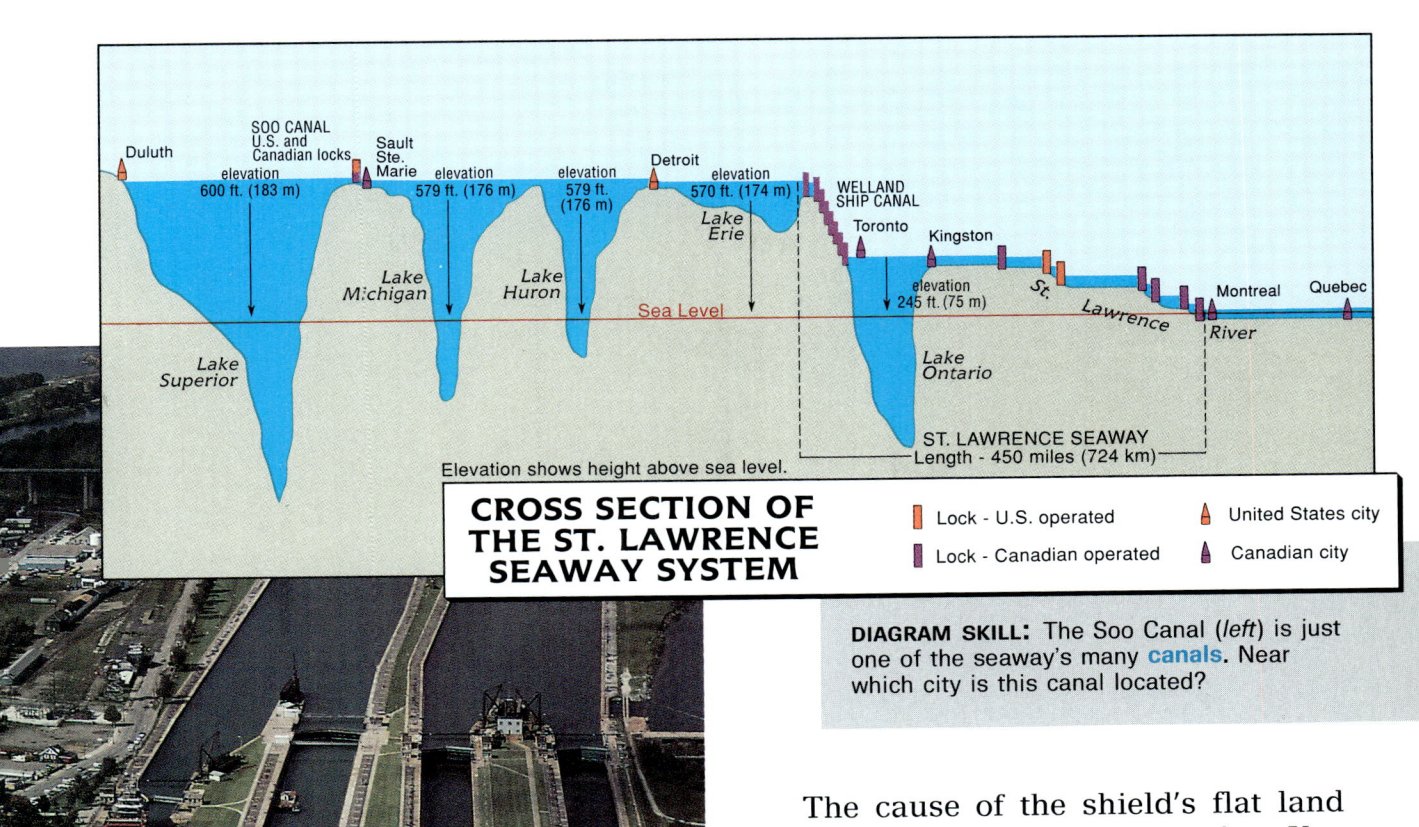

CROSS SECTION OF THE ST. LAWRENCE SEAWAY SYSTEM

Duluth
SOO CANAL U.S. and Canadian locks
Sault Ste. Marie
elevation 600 ft. (183 m)
elevation 579 ft. (176 m)
elevation 579 ft. (176 m)
Detroit
elevation 570 ft. (174 m)
Lake Erie
WELLAND SHIP CANAL
Toronto
Kingston
Montreal
Quebec
Sea Level
Lake Superior
Lake Michigan
Lake Huron
elevation 245 ft. (75 m)
St. Lawrence
River
Lake Ontario
ST. LAWRENCE SEAWAY
Length - 450 miles (724 km)
Elevation shows height above sea level.

Lock - U.S. operated
Lock - Canadian operated
United States city
Canadian city

DIAGRAM SKILL: The Soo Canal (*left*) is just one of the seaway's many **canals**. Near which city is this canal located?

The cause of the shield's flat land can be traced back to the Ice Age. You read in Chapter 2 that glaciers covered much of northern North America during that time. As they moved southward across what is now the Canadian Shield, these thick sheets of ice wore down the mountains and scraped away soil from the surface of the land. In some places the glaciers scooped up so much soil that they created riverbeds and the basins of future lakes. When the earth warmed thousands of years later, water from the melting ice filled the basins and riverbeds.

Today many rivers flow across the Canadian Shield into Hudson Bay. Around these rivers are flat, swampy areas called muskegs (mǝs' kegz). *Muskeg* is an Indian word that means "wet, spongy ground." This land is too wet for farming or for the construction of many tall buildings. As a result, the Canadian Shield has few large population centers.

Instead of plowed fields and crowded cities, he saw many pine forests. He had reached the Canadian Shield, Canada's largest region. The Canadian Shield is a vast plain that forms a huge horseshoe around Hudson Bay. Although the Canadian Shield covers about half of Canada, its surface does not change much from place to place. The land rarely rises more than 2,000 feet (610 m) above sea level.

INTERIOR PLAINS

The **Interior Plains** are located west of the Canadian Shield. This broad, flat region stretches from the Arctic Ocean all the way south to the Great Plains in the United States. Steve crossed this region in winter, when the roads were often slippery with ice.

Along the highway Steve saw hundreds of miles of fields covered with snow. The Interior Plains have some of the most fertile farmland in North America. The region's deep, rich soil was formed when the glaciers moved southward. They stripped soil off the hills and carried it down onto the plains. When the ice melted, mounds of fertile soil were left behind.

THE WESTERN MOUNTAIN REGION

One of the most beautiful regions of Canada is the Western Mountain region. This region has deep glacial lakes, hot springs, and majestic snow-capped mountains. Among the mountains in this region are the **Rocky Mountains** and the **Coast Ranges**. Their generally high elevation made Steve's run difficult. His father offered to drive him across the mountains, but Steve said, "If I have to crawl or get a skateboard, I'll do it."

By the spring of 1985 Steve had passed the highest point of the Canadian Rockies and had entered British Columbia. The weather grew hotter and more humid. During a severe rainstorm in May 1985, Steve limped onto a rocky cliff overlooking the Pacific Ocean. The city of Vancouver lay below. He made his way down to the ocean on a ramp that was covered with a red carpet for the occasion. Steve dipped his

During his run across Canada, Steve Fonyo (*above*) saw much of the country's variety, including Atlantic coast fishing villages, vast plains, and mountain lakes.

artificial leg into the water. Then he hugged his family and shouted to the crowd, "Yahoo! It's finally over."

THE ARCTIC ISLANDS

The only physical region of Canada that Steve Fonyo did not cross was the Arctic Islands region. Located in northern Canada, it is one of the world's least populated regions. It has hundreds of ice-covered islands.

The Ice Age never seems to have ended in this region. Glaciers still blanket the land, and mountain peaks rise high above the glaciers. Along the islands' coasts are also many **fjords** (fyôrdz). A fjord is a deep, narrow inlet of the sea that is bordered by steep cliffs. The water that flows through these fjords is always icy cold.

A LAND OF CONTRAST

As you have read, Canada is a land of contrast. Each of its six physical regions is different. If, like courageous Steve Fonyo, you could travel from one end of the country to the other, you would see low, rounded hills, vast plains, snow-covered mountains, rushing rivers, and thousands of crystal clear lakes. Canada is truly a land of breathtaking beauty.

 ## Check Your Reading

1. Name the six physical regions of Canada.
2. Why does the Canadian Shield have many lakes and rivers?
3. Why do so few people live in the Canadian Shield region? In the Arctic Islands?
4. **THINKING SKILL:** Imagine that you want to spend your spring vacation in Canada. What region would you choose? What alternative did you consider, and why did you decide on this region?

Comparing Maps

In Lesson 1 you looked at several kinds of maps. Each one helped you to learn something different about the geography of Canada.

As you have seen in this book, maps provide a variety of information. A political map shows where cities and boundaries are located. Other maps can show travel routes, where people live, or the kinds of crops that can be grown in a certain place. Each kind of map has its own purpose. But sometimes it is helpful to look at different kinds of maps of the same place. By doing this you can learn things that you cannot learn from any one of the maps alone. You can put facts together so that they mean something new.

Comparing Temperature Maps

Look at the two maps on this page. How are they the same and how do they differ? Each map shows the average temperature in the Canadian province of Alberta. A province is like a state. **Map A** shows the average temperature for January. **Map B** shows the average temperature for July. Notice that the average temperatures are not the same in all parts of Alberta. You have to use the map keys to see which temperature range is shown by each color on the maps.

You can see from the maps that it is generally much colder in Alberta in January than it is in July. There is also a wider variety of temperatures in January than in July. Locate Calgary on each of the maps. What is the average temperature there in January? What is the average temperature in July?

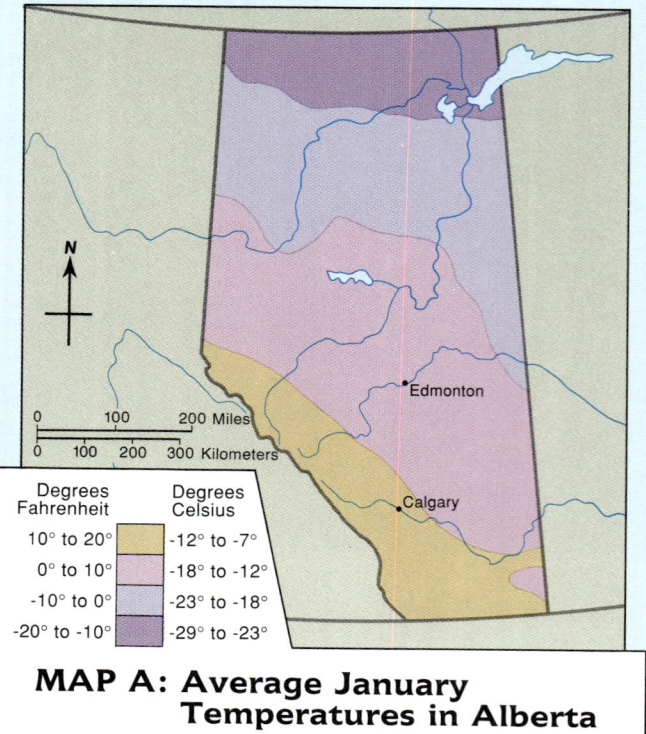

MAP A: Average January Temperatures in Alberta

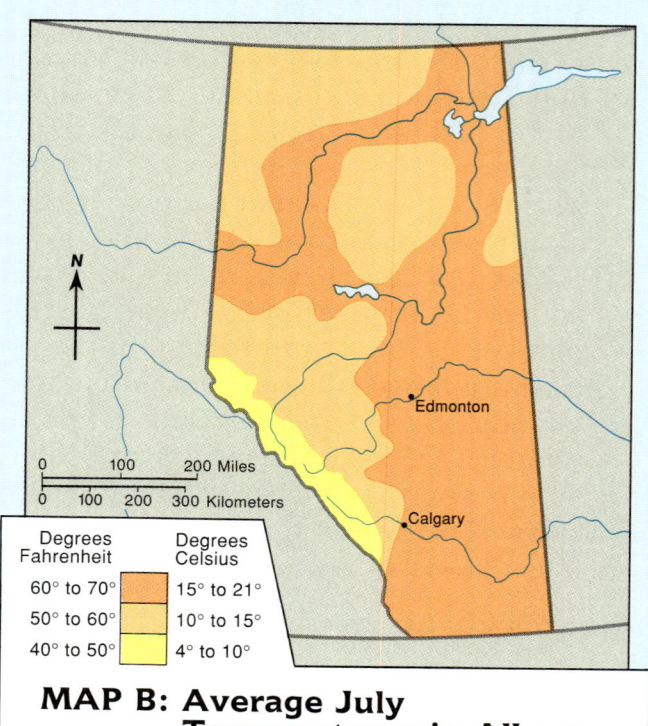

MAP B: Average July Temperatures in Alberta

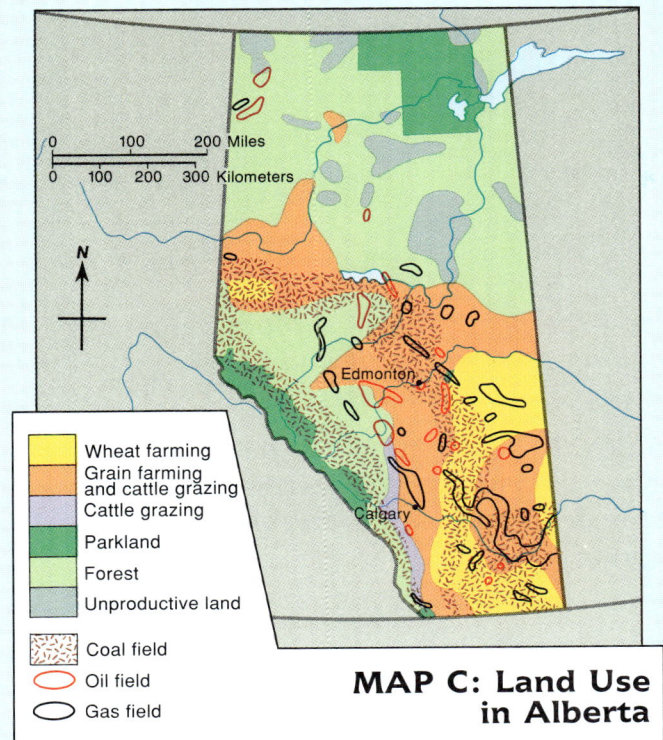

MAP C: Land Use in Alberta

Legend:
- Wheat farming
- Grain farming and cattle grazing
- Cattle grazing
- Parkland
- Forest
- Unproductive land
- Coal field
- Oil field
- Gas field

Scale: 0 100 200 Miles / 0 100 200 300 Kilometers

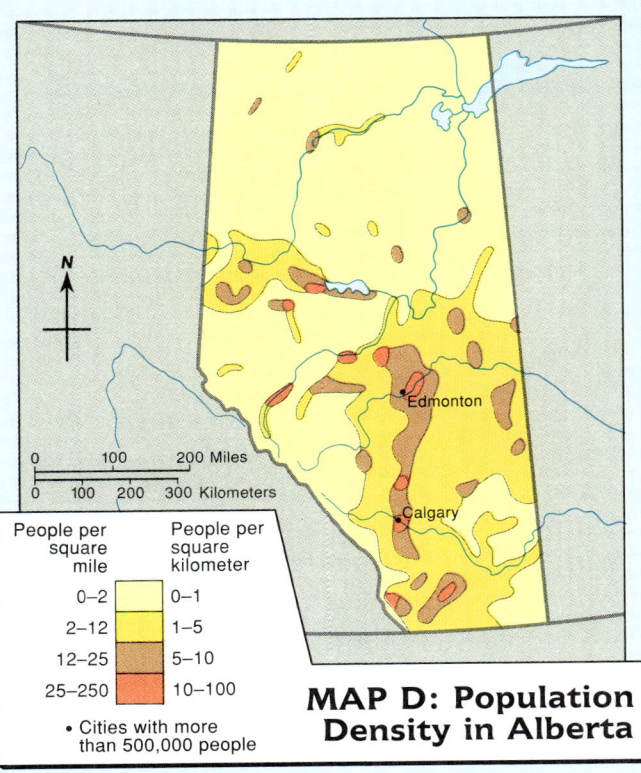

MAP D: Population Density in Alberta

Scale: 0 100 200 Miles / 0 100 200 300 Kilometers

People per square mile	People per square kilometer
0–2	0–1
2–12	1–5
12–25	5–10
25–250	10–100

• Cities with more than 500,000 people

Comparing Other Maps

Map C is a land-use map. It shows which products and resources are found in Alberta. You can see from the map that a large part of the province is forest. Which minerals are found in Alberta?

Now look at **Map D**. What is the subject of the map? The color red shows the areas with the most people per square mile and square kilometer. Which color shows the areas that have 12 to 25 people per square mile?

Now you are ready to compare the maps on both these pages. Use the population density map to learn which areas of Alberta have the fewest people per square mile and which have the most people. What are the average temperatures of those areas in January? Compare them with July. Do people in Alberta tend to live where the temperatures are more moderate or more extreme?

As you can see from these maps, you can learn more about a place when you look at two or more different kinds of maps of that place and compare them. Comparing maps can help you to understand relationships and changes in a place over time.

Reviewing the Skill

1. Why might you wish to compare two or more kinds of maps?
2. What is the average temperature in Edmonton in July?
3. How is the land around Edmonton used? Is this area densely populated?
4. Which area of Alberta is the least densely populated? How is the land in that area used?
5. What did you learn by comparing these four maps?

READreda TO LEARN

Key Vocabulary

timberline   permafrost
tundra   acid rain

Read Aloud

Spring had come to Green Gables—the beautiful, . . . reluctant Canadian spring, lingering along through April and May in a succession of fresh, chilly days, with pink sunsets. . . .

In her book *Anne of Green Gables*, L. M. Montgomery describes the weather on Prince Edward Island in southeastern Canada. As you will read, Montgomery's book is describing only one of Canada's climate regions.

Read for Purpose

1. **WHAT YOU KNOW:** What kind of seasons does the area in which you live have?
2. **WHAT YOU WILL LEARN:** What are the climate regions and the major natural resources of Canada?

CANADIAN CLIMATES

Are the spring days where you live like those on Prince Edward Island? Many places in the United States have spring weather similar to that of Prince Edward Island—as well as summer, fall, and winter weather. Look at the climate map on page 73. You can see that Prince Edward Island has cold winters, hot or warm summers, and precipitation all year. In this area the winter is cold but not harsh.

You can see from the map that not all of Canada has the same kind of temperate climate as that of Prince Edward Island. You have read in Chapter 1 that many factors determine the climate of a place. They include a place's latitude, distance from the ocean, the nearby currents, and wind patterns.

Prince Edward Island's climate is greatly affected by winds. These winds make the island's winters colder and its summers hotter than might be expected in a place near the ocean. When cold winds from the center of North America blow across the island, the temperatures there drop. When warm winds blow in from the Atlantic Ocean, where there are warm currents, temperatures on the island rise.

Look at the climate map again. It shows that Vancouver Island and all of the western coast of Canada have mild winters, cool summers, and precipitation all year. The mild temperatures of this area are caused by the winds that blow across the Pacific Ocean. As the air passes over warm ocean currents, it becomes warmer. This warm air creates a mild, wet climate all year. Look at the climate map again. What other climates are found in Canada?

A WEALTH OF RESOURCES

Prince Edward Island not only has a temperate climate, but it also has fertile soil. This combination of climate and soil makes it possible for many kinds of plants and crops to grow there. For example, in *Anne of Green Gables*, L. M. Montgomery describes the trees and flowers that Anne saw outside of her window.

> *On both sides of the house was a big orchard, one of apple trees and one of cherry trees, also showered over with blossoms. . . . In the garden below were lilac trees. . . .*

The Interior Plains also have a temperate climate and fertile soil. This climate and soil have enabled Canadians to turn these plains into some of the best farmland in the world.

MAP SKILL: What kind of climate does Toronto have? Iqaluit?

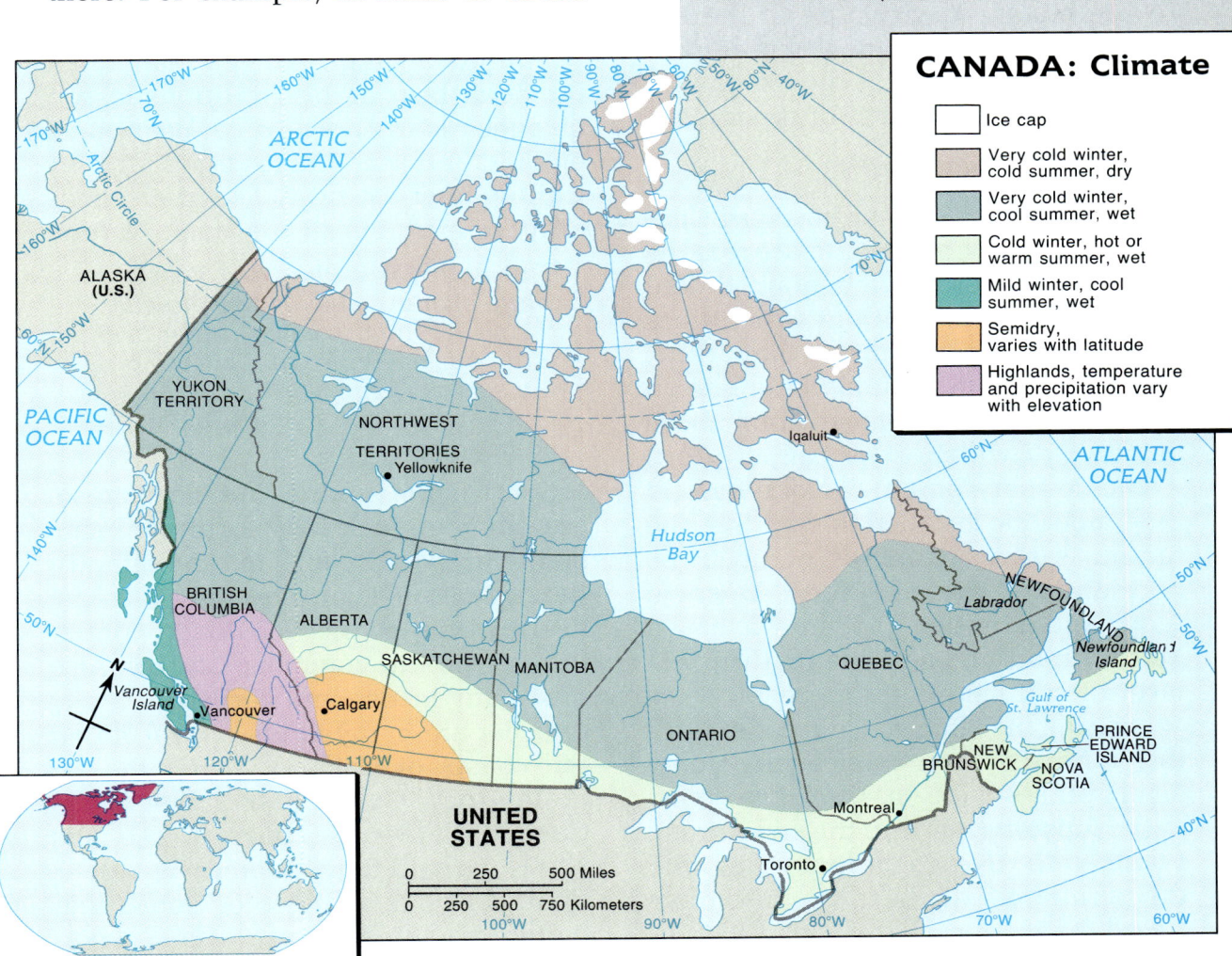

CANADA: Climate

- Ice cap
- Very cold winter, cold summer, dry
- Very cold winter, cool summer, wet
- Cold winter, hot or warm summer, wet
- Mild winter, cool summer, wet
- Semidry, varies with latitude
- Highlands, temperature and precipitation vary with elevation

FORESTS

As you read in Lesson 1, the Canadian Shield is also a plain. However, the Canadian Shield does not have fertile soil, and most of the region has cold winters and cool summers.

If you were to drive through the Canadian Shield, you would see trucks carrying loads of gigantic logs. Today much of Canada is still covered with forests. These forests are among Canada's most important resources. Their trees supply lumber for building, for paper, and for other purposes.

Canadians have long been concerned about preserving their forests. To prevent the destruction of the forests, Canadian laws now require foresters to replant trees. Loggers may cut down only certain parts of the forests.

THE TREELESS PLAIN

If you were to look at northern Canada from the air, you would see that the northern part of the Canadian Shield has no trees. The point at which trees cannot grow is called the **timberline**. The timberline is an imaginary line on mountains and in polar regions above or north of which trees cannot grow.

The northern part of Canada beyond the timberline is called the **tundra**. The tundra is a vast, treeless plain in the northernmost parts of North America, Asia, and Europe. The tundra has a polar climate and a permanently frozen layer of soil called **permafrost**.

Look at the diagram on page 75 of the tundra's soil. Notice that only small plants with shallow roots grow in the topsoil. Now find the permafrost. Plants with deep roots that reach into the permafrost die because their roots freeze there.

ANIMAL RESOURCES

Although the tundra has little vegetation, it is rich in other resources. For example, among the interesting animals that live there are the white polar bear and the arctic fox. You read about the polar bear in the Traditions lesson on pages 44 to 47. The polar bear hunts on land and sea. The fox stays alive by trailing after the bear. As writer James Shreeve explains in his book *Nature*:

> *The arctic fox is the polar bear's white shadow. One or two attach themselves to a bear in winter, trailing at a [safe] distance and cleaning up the scraps from each kill. If the bear is a good hunter, the shadow will not go hungry. . . .*

South of the tundra, Canada's forests are home to such fur-bearing animals as the beaver, the fox, and the otter. In the mountains of western Canada, deer, grizzly bears, and Rocky Mountain sheep are common. Canada also has many moose and caribou.

There are many kinds of sea life off the coasts of Canada. When the explorer John Cabot first sailed along Canada's Atlantic coast in the late 1400s, he said that "so great [were] the numbers of fish that they sometimes halted the ships."

TUNDRA SOIL

Small, low-growing plants

Soil that freezes in the winter and thaws in the summer

Permafrost

DIAGRAM SKILL: Describe the tundra soil on which the arctic fox (*far left*), polar bears, and many small plants live.

Canada's supply of fish is not as great as it once was. However, the coastal waters still contain a large number of cod and other fish.

OTHER NATURAL RESOURCES

Canada also has many mineral resources. For example, not far below its surface the Canadian Shield is made of solid rock. Some of the rock contains valuable minerals, such as copper, iron, gold, nickel, and uranium. In fact, the shield supplies Canada with so many different minerals that it is often called "Canada's Storehouse."

Among Canada's other resources are its rivers and lakes. They provide the Canadians with water power to meet a very important need—energy.

ACID RAIN

The chopping down of forests, the mining of minerals, and the building of dams have all helped Canada's industries to grow. However, some practices have also harmed wildlife and caused pollution. As a result, the Canadian government has taken steps to preserve its resources.

One step has been to pass laws that limit forms of pollution, such as acid rain. Acid rain is rain mixed with chemicals from the burning of coal, natural gas, and other fuels. Acid rain damages vegetation and pollutes bodies of water. This pollution kills the fish that live there. You will read more about acid rain in the Point/Counterpoint on pages 76 and 77.

A RICH AND VARIED LAND

Canada, as you have read, is a land of many climates and resources. Like the United States, Canada has areas with temperate climates and fertile soil for farming. It also has dense forests, plentiful fishing grounds, a variety of animals, and valuable minerals. Together these resources have made Canada a rich and varied land.

 Check Your Reading

1. Describe three Canadian climates.
2. Why does western Canada have milder temperatures than other parts of the country?
3. What is the timberline?
4. **THINKING SKILL:** Classify the resources mentioned in this lesson into at least three groups.

Are Canada's Clean-Air Regulations Too Tough?

In the last lesson, you read that some natural resources, such as plants and animals, are renewable. Over time animals replace themselves by having offspring, and plants reseed or rebuild themselves. Even though this is so, renewable resources should be used wisely and protected from damage. For example, many trees already have been destroyed by acid rain.

Acid rain is formed when the water vapor in clouds becomes polluted by certain gases. Most of these gases form when factories burn coal, oil, and natural gas. As these gases are released into the air, they mix with water vapor to form strong acids. An example of a strong acid is the fluid found in the battery of a car. Weak acids include vinegar and lemon juice.

In Canada, as in other parts of the world, acid rain is a major concern. In fact, several countries have passed laws to help control it. Some businesses say that these laws actually have benefited them. However, other businesses have argued that these laws are too strict and need to be changed.

POINT

Clean-Air Regulations Benefit Industry

Environment Canada is the department of the Canadian government responsible for planning programs to control acid rain. In 1988 it published its views in a report called "Stopping Acid Rain: The Canadian Program."

The experience gained over the past three years has demonstrated that major clean-up measures are both technically and economically [possible]. Cleaning up does not have to cripple an industry's competitiveness. In fact, environmental clean-up can be part of an industry's future strategy.

Each company must decide how to [reduce pollutants] in the context of its own competitive requirements. Their decisions have led to technological innovations [changes] with plant modernization that has helped improve air [quality] while improving . . . productivity.

● Why does Environment Canada feel Canada's clean-air regulations are not too tough?

COUNTERPOINT

Canada's Regulations Are Too Tough

Ontario Hydro is a company that produces over 20 percent of the gas emissions that cause acid rain in Canada. In 1989 a newspaper article reported on Ontario Hydro's reaction to the clean-air regulations.

The president of Ontario Hydro [Robert Franklin] says he will have a tough time meeting the Ministry of the Environment's new guidelines [to reduce pollutants]. . . .

Mr. Franklin said the ministry's new guidelines will cost $2.5 billion in capital and operating costs. . . . "It will take extraordinary measures to try and meet those emissions levels," he said.

"There is no question that [the new guidelines] are an extreme challenge for the corporation . . ." Franklin said, adding that it would mean cutting exports of power and increasing imports.

● Why does Robert Franklin feel Canada's clean-air regulations are too tough?

UNDERSTANDING THE POINT/COUNTERPOINT

1. Which side do you think presents the stronger argument? Explain your answer.
2. What other opinions might people have on Canada's clean-air regulations?
3. Do you think people might reach a compromise on this issue? Explain your answer.

IDEAS TO REMEMBER

■ Canada is the largest country in the Western Hemisphere and the second-largest country in the world. It is made up of six different physical regions, each of which has similar landforms, climates, and natural resources.

■ Canada has a wide range of climates and many natural resources, including metals and minerals such as iron, copper, gold, oil, and coal; rich farmland; water; forests; and animals.

REVIEWING VOCABULARY

Each of the following sentences contains an underlined vocabulary word or term. Number a sheet of paper from 1 to 10. Beside each number write whether each of the following statements is true or false. If the statement is true, write **T**. If it is false, rewrite the sentence using the vocabulary word or term correctly.

1. The <u>timberline</u> is a kind of wolf that lives in the Arctic islands.
2. The <u>fjord</u> helped raise the boat so that it could pass through the canal.
3. In a place with a <u>temperate climate</u> the winters and summers are the same.
4. A <u>lock</u> is a mountain so high that few people are able to cross it.
5. The <u>acid rain</u> helped the crops to grow.
6. The <u>rapids</u> blew so hard they knocked down some trees and bushes.
7. A <u>canal</u> connects two rivers so that boats can travel from one to the other.
8. Many types of trees and bushes grow on the <u>tundra</u>.
9. The <u>muskeg</u> is a treeless plain.
10. Because the <u>permafrost</u> thaws each spring, people can grow wheat on it.

REVIEWING FACTS

Number a sheet of paper from 1 to 10. Beside each number write the name of the physical region in Canada that is associated with the following. The six regions are:

Appalachian Highlands
Great Lakes-St. Lawrence Lowlands
Canadian Shield
Interior Plains
Western Mountain Region
Arctic Islands

1. "Canada's Storehouse"
2. Rocky Mountains
3. many peninsulas and islands
4. where most Canadians live
5. glaciers
6. broad and flat
7. polar bears
8. largest region
9. fertile farmland
10. hot springs

WRITING ABOUT MAIN IDEAS

1. **Making a Comparison:** Which physical region of Canada is most like the area in which you live? Consider landforms, climate, and other features to help you decide. Write a paragraph explaining how that region is like the area where you live. For each feature, include as many details as you think are necessary to make a good comparison.

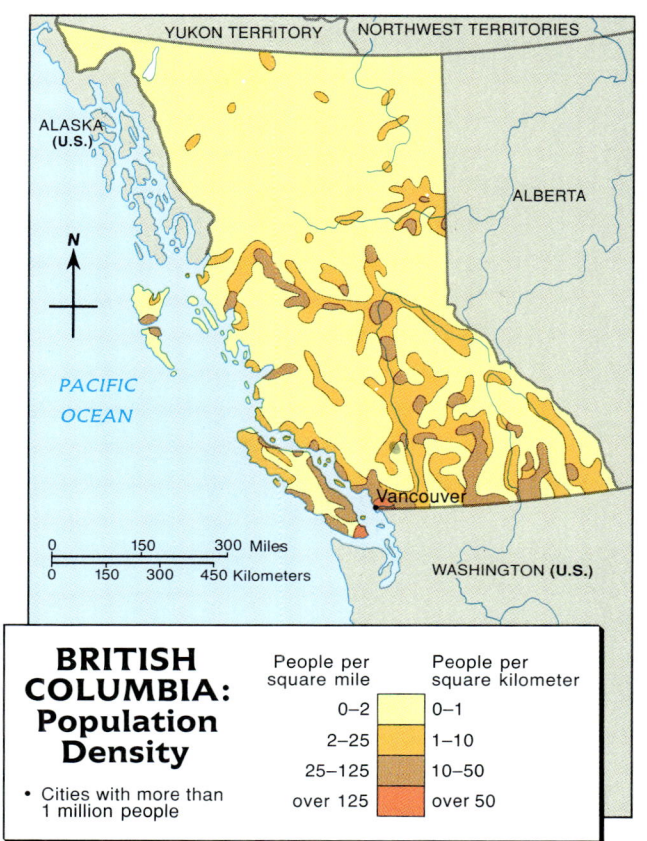

BRITISH COLUMBIA: Population Density

• Cities with more than 1 million people

People per square mile	People per square kilometer
0–2	0–1
2–25	1–10
25–125	10–50
over 125	over 50

BRITISH COLUMBIA: Elevation

▲ Mountain peak

Elevations

Feet	Meters
Above 7,000	Above 2,000
1,500	500
700	200
0	0

2. **Writing a Newspaper Article:** Choose one natural resource of Canada that you think is important and should be developed further. Based on what you have read in this chapter, write a newspaper article that expresses your point of view. Write the article in a way that will persuade others to agree with your point of view.

3. **Writing About Perspectives:** Imagine that you want to be one of the following when you are older: a fisher, a national parks guide, a farmer, an actor. In which region of Canada could you pursue your career best? Write a paragraph telling which career that you would choose and explaining why you should live in the region that you have chosen.

BUILDING SKILLS: COMPARING MAPS

Use the population density and elevation maps of British Columbia on this page to answer these questions.

1. Which parts of British Columbia have the greatest population densities? Which parts are least dense?

2. What is the highest elevation in British Columbia? In which part of the province is this elevation located?

3. What is the elevation of the areas of British Columbia where the highest population densities are located? The least densely populated areas?

4. What did you find out by comparing these two maps of British Columbia?

CHAPTER 4

THE FIRST CANADIANS

FOCUS

*The great sea has sent me adrift.
It moves me as the weed in a great river.
Earth and the great weather move me. . . .*

This song has long been sung by the people of the Arctic Islands region. It was one of many songs that their religious leaders sang to express their belief in the power of nature. Like other early Canadians, the people of the Arctic believed that nature influenced all parts of life.

1 People of the Arctic

READ TO LEARN

 **Key Vocabulary**

igloo   shaman
kayak

 **Read Aloud**

> *And yet, there is only*
> *One great thing,*
> *The only thing:*
> *To live to see, in hunts and on journeys*
> *The great day that dawns*
> *And the light that fills the world.*

These words were written by an early American hunter who lived in Canada's tundra. There in the Arctic, many days during the long winter are filled with darkness. Whenever the sun appeared, the people of this area greeted the light with joy.

 **Read for Purpose**

1. **WHAT YOU KNOW:** Which kind of climate does Canada's Arctic Islands region have?
2. **WHAT YOU WILL LEARN:** Which resources did the people of the Arctic use in order to survive in the Canadian tundra?

AMERICA'S ANCESTORS

You read in Chapter 2 that some scientists believe the first Canadians came from Asia many thousands of years ago. They believe that the hunters and gatherers who made this long journey were the ancestors of the people who today are called Native Americans, or American Indians.

You may remember that it was Christopher Columbus who first called the Native Americans "Indians." When Columbus landed on an island in the Caribbean Sea in 1492, he mistakenly thought that he had reached the Indies and that the people he saw on shore were Indians. Despite Columbus's error, the name Indians is still used to refer to the Native Americans.

Today scientists believe that as many as 2,000 different Indian groups were living in the Western Hemisphere when Columbus arrived there. Each one of these groups called itself by a different name. The Indians also had developed a variety of cultures. The map on page 82 shows that the major groups in Canada were those of the

Arctic, the Subarctic, the Eastern Woodlands, the Plains, and the Northwest Coast. You will read about these groups in this chapter.

ARRIVAL OF THE INUIT

The Inuit (in' ü it), who are often called Eskimos, were among the most remarkable early groups of the Arctic. The word *Inuit* means "the people" and is the name that these people use to refer to themselves. *Eskimo* comes from a Canadian Indian term meaning "eaters of raw meat."

The Inuit have lived in what is now the state of Alaska for about 7,000 years. However, it was not until about 1,000 years ago that the ancestors of the Canadian Inuit migrated to what is now Canada.

The Inuit who migrated to Canada chose to remain in the tundra. How did they survive in this harsh environment? According to one Indian expert:

> The secret of the Arctic peoples' success lay in their . . . adaptation to the circumstances they found.

Their ability to survive on the tundra earned the Inuit the name "Conquerors of the Arctic North."

MAP SKILL: Which of the five Indian groups of Canada lived near what is now Canada's southern border?

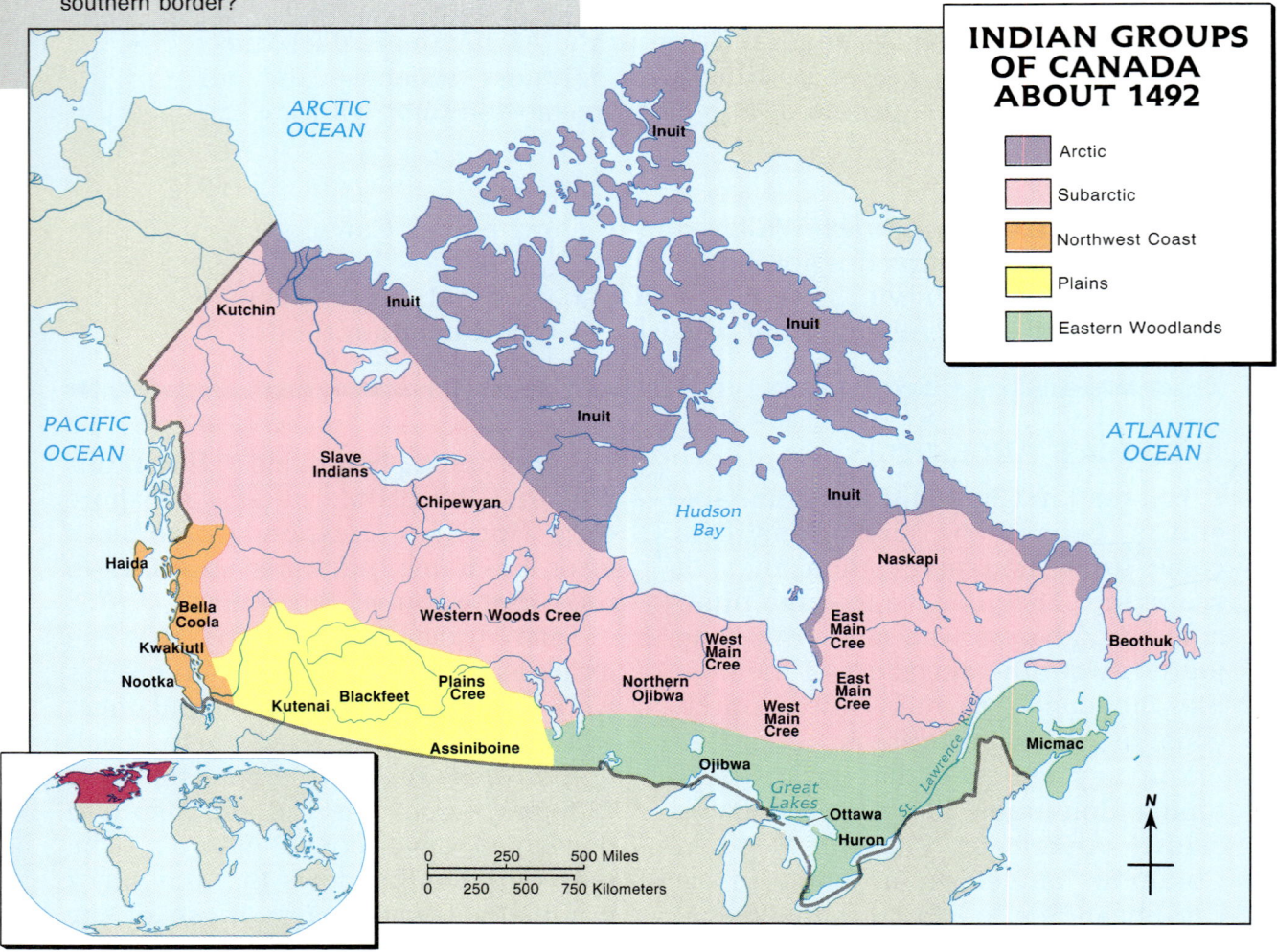

INDIAN GROUPS OF CANADA ABOUT 1492

- Arctic
- Subarctic
- Northwest Coast
- Plains
- Eastern Woodlands

CONQUERING THE ARCTIC

The Inuit met the challenge of living in the Arctic tundra by making use of the resources they found there—ice, snow, stone, soil, and animals. Inuit homes are an example of the clever way in which the Inuit used their environment. In summer when the tundra topsoil melted a little, the Inuit would build their houses partly underground. This type of house is warmer than one built above ground. They used flat pieces of rock and stone to make the walls and the roofs of their houses. They piled sod, or clumps of earth containing grass and plants, against the walls to keep out the wind and cold.

During the winter months, when food supplies were low, the Inuit traveled long distances to find food. Often these winter journeys took the Inuit hunters away from home for long periods of time. The Inuit discovered that they could keep warm while traveling by building a temporary shelter called an **igloo**. *Igloo* is the Inuit word for any kind of house. But to most people, an igloo is a dome-shaped house made of ice and snow.

When snow covered the ground, the Inuit traveled by dogsled. Arctic dogs, called huskies, with their thick fur and great strength, are able to survive in the cold temperatures of the Arctic. The Inuit trained the wild huskies of the Arctic to pull sleds, to hunt, and to guard their homes. They taught the lead dogs of their dogsled teams to respond to commands. The other dogs would then follow the lead dogs.

RESOURCES FROM THE SEA

Let's go back in time to see what life was like for the Inuit hunters in winter.

Arctic huskies are strong enough to carry heavy loads across great distances.

The Inuit hunter Oonu and his family usually travel north in winter to the Arctic coast, where the sea life is plentiful. There they hunt and fish. During the coldest winter months Oonu cuts holes in the ice. Then he fishes or waits for the sea animals—seals, walruses, and sea otters—to come to the surface for air.

Later, when the ice along the coast melts, Oonu and the other hunters use **kayaks** (kī′ aks), or small, one-person boats made of sealskin. A hunter in a lightweight kayak can paddle quickly and quietly between chunks of ice to a spot where a polar bear, a seal, or a walrus is resting. The hunters carry harpoons, which are spearlike weapons with a rope attached.

When they set forth on longer expeditions in the Arctic waters, Oonu's group travels in umiaks (ü′ mē aks),

The Inuit used the resources of their harsh environment to satisfy their basic needs and to create objects of beauty.

which are large, open boats that can hold as many as 12 people. Umiaks are made of animal skins.

Over the centuries Inuit people like Oonu discovered ways to use seals, sea otters, walruses, whales, fish, and other kinds of Arctic wildlife to provide for their needs. For example, animal skins were used to make tents, clothing, and boats. Blubber, or fat from whales, was burned for heat and light. Even the bones of animals were not wasted but were used to make needles for sewing. Animal bones and teeth were also used to make jewelry, sculptures, and other objects of beauty.

INUIT LEADERS

As you might expect, successful hunters were greatly respected leaders in Inuit communities. Another type of Inuit leader was the religious leader, or

shaman (shä′ mən). Shamans are common among people who worship many gods and nature spirits. These leaders are believed to be able to talk to the spirits that control the world.

SURVIVAL IN THE ARCTIC

As you have read, the Arctic environment presented the Inuit with a challenge to their survival. In addition to the cold climate, the tundra lacks trees, food plants, and other resources that are commonly used for survival. Yet the Inuit have developed ways to live there. While they adapted to the Arctic, the Inuit also created a special culture.

 Check Your Reading

1. What is another name for the Inuit people?
2. Why are the Inuit often called "Conquerors of the Arctic North"?
3. List three ways in which the Inuit used their environment to survive.
4. THINKING SKILL: Imagine that you are an Inuit. Predict what would happen to your way of life if the Arctic climate became milder.

READ TO LEARN

■ Key Vocabulary

wigwam   long house   artisan

■ Read Aloud

We love quiet; we [allow] the mouse to play; when the woods are rustled by the wind, we fear not.

These words were spoken by a great chief who lived in the Eastern Woodlands long ago. Like the people of the Arctic, the Indians to the south of the Inuit lived in harmony with nature.

■ Read for Purpose

1. **WHAT YOU KNOW:** What kind of products are made from the natural resources found in forests?
2. **WHAT YOU WILL LEARN:** How did the early people of the Subarctic and the Eastern Woodlands live?

A LAND OF FORESTS

You read in Chapter 3 that much of Canada is covered with forests. Imagine that you are traveling through these forests today. You notice that the forests are very quiet. Few people live there, and you see only a few homes. You wonder how the lives of people today differ from those of the Indians who lived in the forests long ago.

For thousands of years two large groups of Indians lived in Canada's forests. Both groups used the resources of the forests to survive. However, one group lived in a much colder climate than the other.

INDIANS OF THE CANADIAN SHIELD

South of the tundra, in the Canadian Shield, Canada is covered with pine, birch, and spruce forests. Caribou, moose, and other animals roam these forests. There are also many fish in the area's rivers and lakes. However, the winters are long and snowy, and the winds that blow through the forests are bitterly cold.

The Indians who lived in this region long ago are called the Subarctic Indians. For about 3,000 years groups such as the Cree, Chippewa, Slave, and Beaver lived in the northern forests, working hard just to survive.

As you just read, the forests of the north have many animals. However, most of these animals move from place to place with the changing seasons. To provide for their basic needs, the Subarctic Indians followed the animal herds as they moved. The Subarctic Indians did not farm because the soil in almost all of the Canadian Shield is thin and lacking in nutrients.

The Subarctic Indians traveled on foot and by canoe. When it snowed in winter, they used snowshoes or lightweight flat-bottomed sleds called toboggans. As they traveled, the Indians built **wigwams**, which are small, domed houses covered with strips of bark. Wigwams can be put up and taken down very quickly.

The Indians of the Canadian Shield had to spend most of their time hunting for food. Therefore, they lived in small groups and seldom gathered together in large groups.

THE EASTERN WOODLANDS

The second large group of forest Indians lived south of the Canadian Shield, in the Eastern Woodlands. These woodlands are located in southeastern Canada and extend into the northeastern United States.

In winter the Subarctic Indians often wore snowshoes to move through the snow easily.

The Indians of the Eastern Woodlands lived mostly by hunting and fishing for about 5,000 years. Unlike the Inuit and the Subarctic Indians, they did not have to struggle with a very cold climate. The Eastern Woodlands was a land of plenty. The warmer climate there made it possible for Indians in the southern part to farm.

One advantage of living in the Eastern Woodlands was the abundance of trees with usable bark. The Indians used both the bark and wood from the trees to build their homes and canoes.

The most common forms of shelter among the Woodland Indians were wigwams and **long houses**. A long house is a barrel-shaped building that is divided into sections. Sometimes several families shared one house.

The Indians built their long houses out of saplings, or young trees. They placed two rows of saplings in the ground, then bent their tops toward the center and tied them together. They covered the long houses with tree bark.

TRAVEL BY CANOE

Birch trees were used to make canoes. These canoes were the most important means of transportation for the Woodlands Indians. As they paddled, the Indians sang songs such as "My Bark Canoe," which you can see on the opposite page. This song was popular among the Ojibwa of Ontario.

To make a birchbark canoe, the Indians soaked the bark until they could bend it. Then they fastened the wet bark to the frame of a canoe made from branches. The whole canoe was held together by tightly woven vines or straps made from animal skins. The Indians also made dugout canoes by hollowing out large logs.

The canoes were made to be light enough for a few hunters to carry for long distances. Yet they were strong enough to glide easily through the rough waters and rapids that are found in many rivers of the Eastern Woodlands. The canoes were also made to move rapidly through the water. Scientist Jack Weatherford gives one reason that speed was needed.

> Speed was very important in order to [canoe into] an area and get out again before all of the water routes froze [in winter] and trapped the traveler.

With these canoes, the Indians were able not only to hunt but to trade across large areas of Canada.

VISITING A VILLAGE

Imagine that you can travel back in time more than 1,000 years to an Eastern Woodlands village called Kopake (kə päk′ ē). The small village stands beside a narrow river. An Indian guide tells you that *kopake* is an Indian word meaning "upstream." The village of Kopake is upstream from a beautiful saltwater bay.

From outside the village you can see that trees grow very close to the village walls. Pointed logs and poles placed in a large circle form a wall around the village. Your guide explains that the wall serves as protection against other Indians. The Indian groups have been fighting over possession of nearby lakes and land.

Your guide takes you inside the walls of the village, where you see long houses and wigwams. Outside one of the wigwams, a young boy, Swift Deer, is listening to his uncle. Swift Deer's uncle is preparing him for the hunts that he will take part in when he is several years older.

His uncle reminds Swift Deer that he must respect the animals that he will hunt. His uncle also tells him that the moose, the deer, the elk, and all the other creatures have living spirits. He says that after the animals die, their spirits protect the village. For this reason the heads of the animals may be placed on the poles of the village walls.

WORKING TOGETHER

Your guide tells you that in the spring the children of Kopake are sent to the woods to gather a liquid called sap from the trees. The woods are filled with a great variety of trees. However, the children are looking only for maple trees, which produce a sweet sap.

Using the sharp edges of stones, the children cut deep gashes in the trunks of the maple trees. They place boxes made of birch bark under the gashes to collect sap. Later they boil the sap until it turns into a syrup. Mixed with water, the syrup makes a favorite drink.

The inside of a **long house** was spacious. Around the village, fences protected the Indians from enemies.

WOODLAND ARTISANS

In the village a woman is grinding corn. Your guide tells you that the corn, as well as beans, squash, and pumpkins, is grown in a nearby field. Inside the long house a man is making arrows. He and other craftsworkers are **artisans**. An artisan is a person who is skilled in a particular craft. Artisans make all the objects used by the people of Kopake.

SUBARCTIC AND EASTERN WOODLANDS WAYS OF LIFE

In this lesson you have read about the two Indian groups of the Canadian forests, the Subarctic Indians and the Eastern Woodlands Indians. During the thousands of years in which they inhabited the woodlands, these groups of people developed special ways of life. They invented canoes, toboggans,

snowshoes, and maple syrup. As you can see, many of the products developed by the Indians of the forests are used by people today.

 Check Your Reading

1. Name at least three items used by the Subarctic Indians that helped them to survive.
2. What advantages did the environment of the Eastern Woodlands provide that the environment of the Subarctic did not?
3. How did the Indians of the Eastern Woodlands use their natural resources to defend themselves?
4. THINKING SKILL: Compare the way of life of the Subarctic Indians with that of the Eastern Woodlands Indians. How were the two ways of life alike? How were they different?

3 People of the Plains

READ TO LEARN

🔲 **Key Vocabulary**

  stampede   tepee

🔲 **Read Aloud**

If the Great Spirit wanted people to stay in one place, He would make the world stand still; but He made it to always change, so birds and animals can move and always have green grass and ripe berries, sun to work, and night to sleep . . . always changing.

In this passage from one of their legends, the people of the Canadian plains explained why, like the people of the Subarctic, they traveled from place to place. They followed the herds of the mighty buffalo.

🔲 **Read for Purpose**

1. **WHAT YOU KNOW:** How did the Subarctic Indians live?
2. **WHAT YOU WILL LEARN:** Why did the people of the plains depend on the buffalo?

THE VAST PLAINS

Unlike the Eastern Woodlands, Canada's Interior Plains have few trees. According to writer George Woodcock, a painter traveling through the plains in the 1800s noted that he saw meadows stretching "as far as the eye can see and thought can travel." Another writer, Lewis Spence, explained:

Of all North America's regions, few have boundaries as easily defined as the Plains.

You read about the Canadian plains in Chapter 3. They are located between the Rocky Mountains and the Great Lakes. They are part of a vast plain that extends into the central part of the United States.

Today the plains are among the world's richest farmland. Only 100 years ago, however, the plains were an open grassland upon which millions of shaggy buffalo roamed. They traveled in huge herds, migrating with the changing temperatures of the seasons.

THE BUFFALO PEOPLE

For about 4,500 years, the people of the Canadian Plains have moved from place to place. Groups such as the Blackfeet and the Assiniboine (ə sin' ə boin) hunted there to meet their needs. They followed the herds of buffalo and other animals that grazed on the plains. Before the Europeans brought horses to the Americas, the

90

Indians hunted on foot. The Indians mainly **stampeded** herds of buffalo off cliffs. A stampede is a headlong flight of a herd of frightened animals.

Imagine that you could travel back in time to observe a buffalo hunt. This is what you would see. The leader of the hunt, disguised by a buffalo skin, creeps close to a herd of buffalo. He sways from side to side, imitating a sick buffalo. As the curious herd moves toward the disguised leader, he creeps slowly toward the cliff.

At this point the other hunters appear, waving blankets and shouting. The buffalo are so frightened that they start to stampede. They rush toward the edge of the cliff, just as the Indians had planned.

AFTER THE HUNT

After the hunt the Indians work quickly. They skin the dead animals, then cook and eat much of the meat immediately. The remaining meat is placed on high racks to dry.

The Plains Indians use almost every part of the buffalo. Artisans carve the horns into tools. The Indians make warm robes from the buffalo hides. Even the rough ends of buffalo tongues are used as hairbrushes!

Buffalo skins are used to make cone-shaped tents called **tepees**. A tepee is

The people of the plains used many methods to frighten the buffalo into **stampeding**. After the hunt artisans used buffalo skins to make many objects, such as this shield.

held up by tall poles. A hole at the top of the tepee allows smoke from a fire inside to escape. According to one Plains Indian:

The tepee is much better [than other shelters] to live in; always clean, warm in winter, cool in summer; easy to move.

THE INDIANS OF THE PLAINS

The Plains Indians developed a way of life that lasted for thousands of years. On the open grassland they followed the buffalo wherever the herds led them. Products from the buffalo provided these Indians with food, clothing, and shelter.

 Check Your Reading

1. Why did the Plains Indians travel a lot?
2. Name three ways in which the Plains Indians used the buffalo to meet their needs.
3. Why was the tepee a practical shelter for the Plains Indians?
4. **THINKING SKILL:** Identify everything that you see in the picture above.

Asking Questions

Suppose that your social studies class has just seen a program about the Blackfeet. After a short discussion, your teacher asks "Does the class have any questions?"

Have you ever wanted to ask a question but then decided not to? Perhaps you were unable to think of a good question or were unable to phrase it clearly.

Asking good questions is an important part of learning. If you ask good questions about what you see, hear, or read, you will be able to learn about things that are important to you. If you do not ask questions, you might learn only what someone else wants you to know.

Trying the Skill

In Lesson 3 you read about the Indians who settled on the Interior Plains. List three questions you could ask to learn more about these Indians.

- What did you do to come up with your questions?
- Are they "good" questions?
- How do you know?

HELPING YOURSELF

The steps on the left will help you to ask questions on any topic. The example on the right shows how these steps can help you to learn more about the Plains Indians.

One Way to Ask Good Questions	Example
1. Identify and clarify the topic or subject that you want to learn more about.	The topic is the Plains Indians. To clarify the topic, you might ask, "What are the special features of their culture?"
2. Use question words such as *who, what, when, where, why,* and *how* to create questions about the topic.	Ask *who* are the Plains Indians? *Where* do they live? *How* do they meet their basic needs? *What* are some of their traditions? Use other question words such as *when* and *why* to create questions.
3. Determine whether each of your questions focuses on the topic or whether the question asks for additional information beyond the topic.	The question "What are some of their traditions?" focuses on the topic. A question such as "What effect has the Plains Indian culture had on other northern Indian groups?" asks for additional information.
4. Review each question to decide what information it will give you about the topic.	The questions will help you learn about the origins of the Plains Indians, their daily activities, their culture, and history.
5. Choose those questions that will help you learn what you want to know and cross out those that will not. Replace the crossed-out questions with ones that focus on what you want to learn.	The question "What is it like to live in Canada's Interior Plains Region?" does not focus on the topic of the Plains Indians. A better question would be "How have the Plains Indians adapted to their environment?"

Applying the Skill

In this chapter you also read about the Inuit.

1. Which of the following questions would help you to learn more about the people who lived on the tundra?
   a. How do you build a tepee?
   b. Why were canoes made to be light in weight?
   c. Why were sea animals so important to the Inuit?
2. What are three questions that you could ask to learn more about the ways in which the culture of the Inuit has changed in the 1900s?
3. Which of the three questions would help you to learn the most about the topic? Explain your answer.

Reviewing the Skill

1. What are the features of a "good" question?
2. What are some steps you can take to come up with good questions?
3. Why is it important to ask questions about what you see, hear, or read?

LESSON 4 People of the Northwest Coast

READ TO LEARN

Key Vocabulary

totem pole   myth   potlatch

Read Aloud

In the beginning, Raven made us, and everything, and totem poles, too.

The chiefs of the Northwest Coast Indian communities used the words above to begin their story of creation. The people believed that the raven, a shiny black bird, had provided them with a land rich in resources.

Read for Purpose

1. WHAT YOU KNOW: How do ocean currents affect climate?
2. WHAT YOU WILL LEARN: Which natural resources were available to the Northwest Coast Indians?

THE NORTHWEST COAST

The Indians of the Northwest Coast have lived in their humid, mountainous land since about A.D. 1. This is Canada's mildest environment, mainly because of the warm Japanese Current. You may recall that ocean currents have an important effect on the climates of regions.

The damp, mild climate of the Northwest Coast provides ideal growing conditions for the tall trees that grow along the coast. Among the giant trees are redwoods, firs, and cedars.

The Indians also had resources from the ocean. The waters along the coast are filled with salmon, cod, halibut, seals, and whales. Sea life was so plentiful that the Indians did not need to grow food.

SKILLED ARTISANS

Impressively carved details decorate the houses. Animals, birds, and all manner of wild beasts are carved into long poles. Many of these are trees which support the rooftops and make our ships look small. . . .

As this sailor noted when Captain James Cook's ship reached the Northwest Coast in 1788, the people of this part of Canada were skilled artisans. The Kwakiutl (kwä kē ü′ təl), the Nootka (nût′ kə), the Bella Coola, and other Indians of the area used cedar trees from the forest to build large houses, canoes, and fishing and other tools. Many of the masks that the people of the Northwest Coast used during celebrations and religious ceremonies were also made of wood.

94

Unlike many of the trees of the Eastern Woodlands, cedar trees can be split into straight, even planks, or boards. When they built their houses, the Indians arranged the planks in a way that created openings for smoke vents and for light.

In front of their houses stood large totem poles carved from tree trunks. A totem pole is a sort of family picture album, showing the animals and other objects that have a special meaning for the family. An animal, plant, or object that is used by a family to represent it is called a totem. Totem poles usually have several totems carved or painted on them. You will read more about totem poles in the Traditions lesson on pages 98–101.

The Indians also made their fishing tools, furniture, and other objects from the huge cedar and redwood trees of the area. Almost all of their wooden objects were not only carved but also painted by artisans to make them even more beautiful.

THE GIVING EARTH

Many of the carvings were of gods and heroes that appeared in stories of the Northwest Coast Indians. Such stories of gods and heroes are called myths. Myths are created by cultures around the world and are retold from generation to generation. Some American Indian myths contained ideas about the world that all Indians held in common. For example, they all celebrated the earth in their myths. One group in the Northwest even called themselves "Haida" (hī' də), meaning "People of the Giving Earth."

However, Indian groups had different beliefs about which god was the Great Spirit, or the most important god. To some groups, this god was the sun. To many Northwest Coast Indians, the Great Spirit lived in the sea.

Among the many beautiful objects made by the Northwest Coast Indians were this whale mask, box with a bear carved on it, and blanket woven of mountain-goat wool.

Courtesy Department of Library Services American Museum of Natural History

Museum of the American Indian

Like most other Indian groups, the Northwest Coast hunters respected the bodies of the animals they killed. They believed that animals were sacred and worked closely with the Great Spirit to help human beings.

For example, one Northwest Coast myth taught that salmon left the ocean and came ashore in order to feed the people. Each year the first catch of the season was marked by a ceremony. The fish were placed on an altar, or a table used for religious ceremonies. Later, after the fish were cooked, each villager was given a taste until only the skeletons remained. The skeletons were returned to the river, from which the Indians believed that the skeletons would return again as salmon.

THE VALUE OF THE SEA

Fish were especially important to the people of the Northwest Coast. Salmon were so numerous that with just a few weeks' work a community of Indians could supply themselves with fish for many months. In addition to salmon, the Indians caught halibut and cod.

The Northwest Coast Indians used several methods for catching fish. In deep water the Indians used hand-made wooden hooks to catch halibut and cod. They caught other kinds of fish by harpooning or netting them. The Indians smoked the fish over fires to preserve them. They also caught the valuable candlefish—fish that were so oily they could be, and were, lighted like a candle.

The waters along the coast were also well supplied with seals and whales. Like the Inuit, the people of the Northwest Coast made good use of these natural resources. As writer George Woodcock noted:

There are few places in the world where land and sea combine to offer such a rich and regular bounty for human [use], and the Indians of the Northwest Coast [developed] it to the full.

This painting by Arthur Jansson shows how the people of the Northwest Coast worked, traveled, and decorated their objects.

The American Museum of Natural History/Macmillan/McGraw-Hill School Division

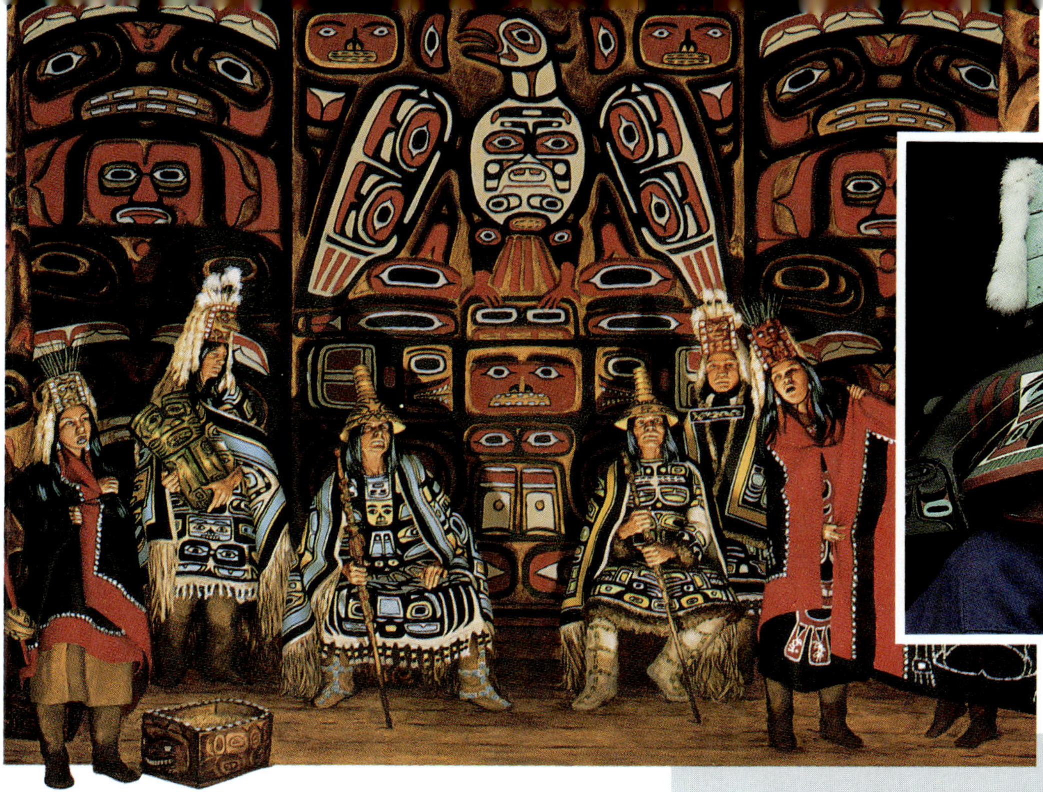

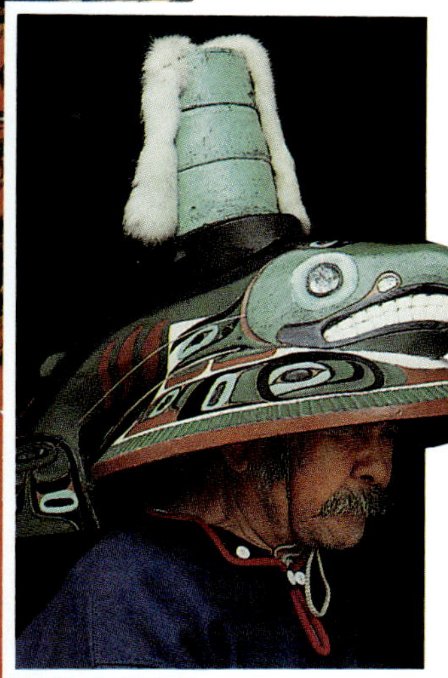

Potlatches were given to impress people. The bands on the potlatch hat (*right*) show its wearer gave three potlatches.

AN INDIAN CUSTOM

The Northwest Coast Indians appreciated the gifts that they received from the land and the sea. When a villager, usually a chief or a male of high standing in the community, felt especially grateful for all that he had, he invited other villagers to a **potlatch** (pot′ lach). A potlatch was a special feast at which a person who had plenty of food and goods would give it all away!

According to a visitor to the Northwest Coast, one chief once gave away 30,000 blankets. Another chief, who favored jewelry, gave away thousands of silver and brass bracelets. Within the community the potlatch was a kind of contest. The person who gave away the most was the winner. The prize was the respect of the other villagers.

ABUNDANCE FROM THE SEA AND FORESTS

The Indians of the Northwest Coast were fortunate because their environment provided them with the resources to meet most of their needs. In fact, the pleasant climate, rich woodlands, and teeming sea life provided the Indians of the area with more than they needed to live well. Some Northwest Coast Indians shared their wealth by holding potlatches in which they gave away many possessions.

Check Your Reading

1. Describe the environment of the Northwest Coast.
2. What is a myth?
3. Why did the Northwest Coast Indians use totem poles?
4. **THINKING SKILL:** Imagine that you are a Northwest Coast Indian. What factors might you consider to help you to decide on the size of the potlatch you wish to hold?

Totem Poles

by Eric Kimmel

In Lesson 4 you read about the totem poles carved by the Northwest Coast Indians. The Indians usually placed these majestic carvings in front of their houses. Today, however, you can see brand-new totem poles in many parks and public places throughout Canada. As their ancestors did, Northwest Coast Indians continue to use this traditional art to celebrate their myths and history. As you read, think about why people might want to keep alive the tradition of carving totem poles.

Imagine that you are walking through Victoria Park. First you notice a large wooden building. The walls of the building are painted with the traditional designs of the Northwest Coast Indians. You stop to admire them. Inside you can hear the thunk, thunk of steel hitting wood. The smell of freshly cut wood fills the air. You peep through the open door to see what is going on. A friendly voice says, "Come in!"

You go inside. There you meet several young people hard at work. They are all Northwest Coast Indians. You can't believe your eyes. These artists are carving totem poles from the trunks of tall, majestic trees, just as their ancestors had carved hundreds of years ago.

DIFFERENT KINDS OF TOTEM POLES

Exactly what are totem poles? Who made them, and why? Only a small number of Native American groups carved totem poles. These groups lived along Canada's Pacific

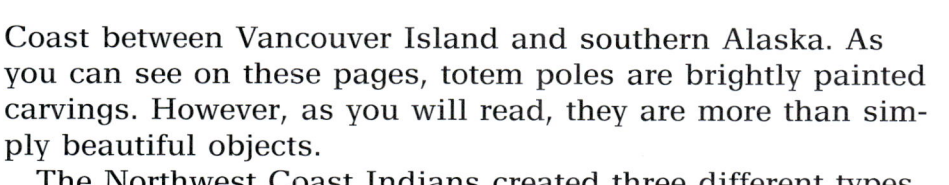

Coast between Vancouver Island and southern Alaska. As you can see on these pages, totem poles are brightly painted carvings. However, as you will read, they are more than simply beautiful objects.

The Northwest Coast Indians created three different types of totem poles. The first type was a memorial pole that celebrated a special event. For example, totem poles were often carved after the defeat of a powerful enemy or after a successful hunt. Personal events were important, too. If an animal spirit appeared to someone in a dream, that person might put up a pole with that spirit's image on it.

The second kind of totem pole was known as a house pole. The typical house of a Northwest Coast Indian had an emblem carved on the tall front pole that formed part of the doorway. An emblem is a sign or figure that stands for something. House poles served as street addresses, just as the numbers on houses do today. If you knew a family's emblem, you could easily find its home.

The third type of totem pole was the mortuary, or death, pole. This pole not only marked where a grave was located but also served as the grave itself. A box at the top of the pole held the dead person's remains. Figures carved below the box described the person's rank and accomplishments.

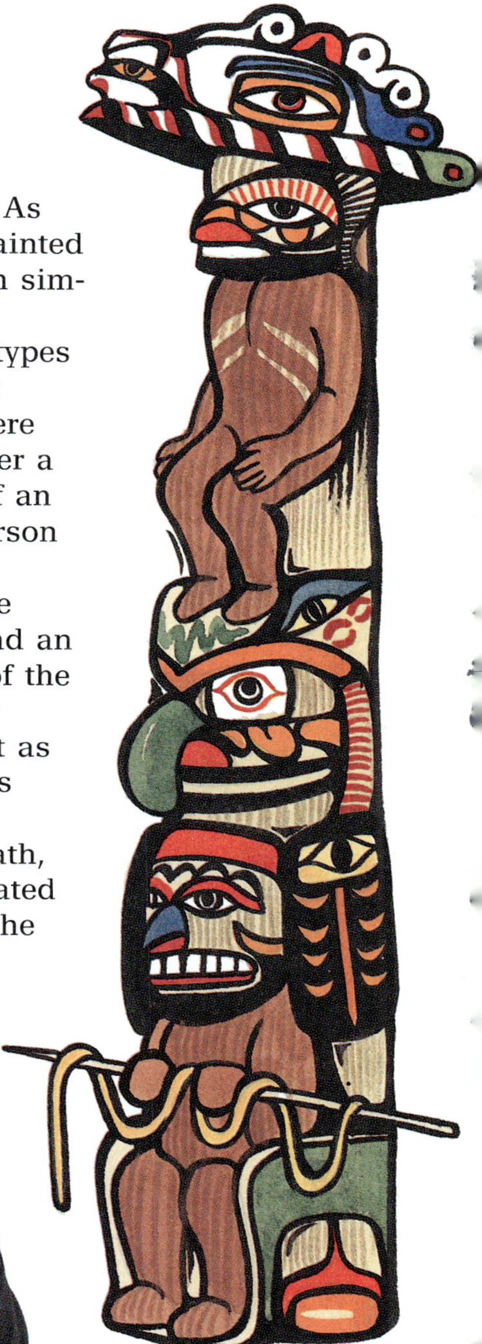

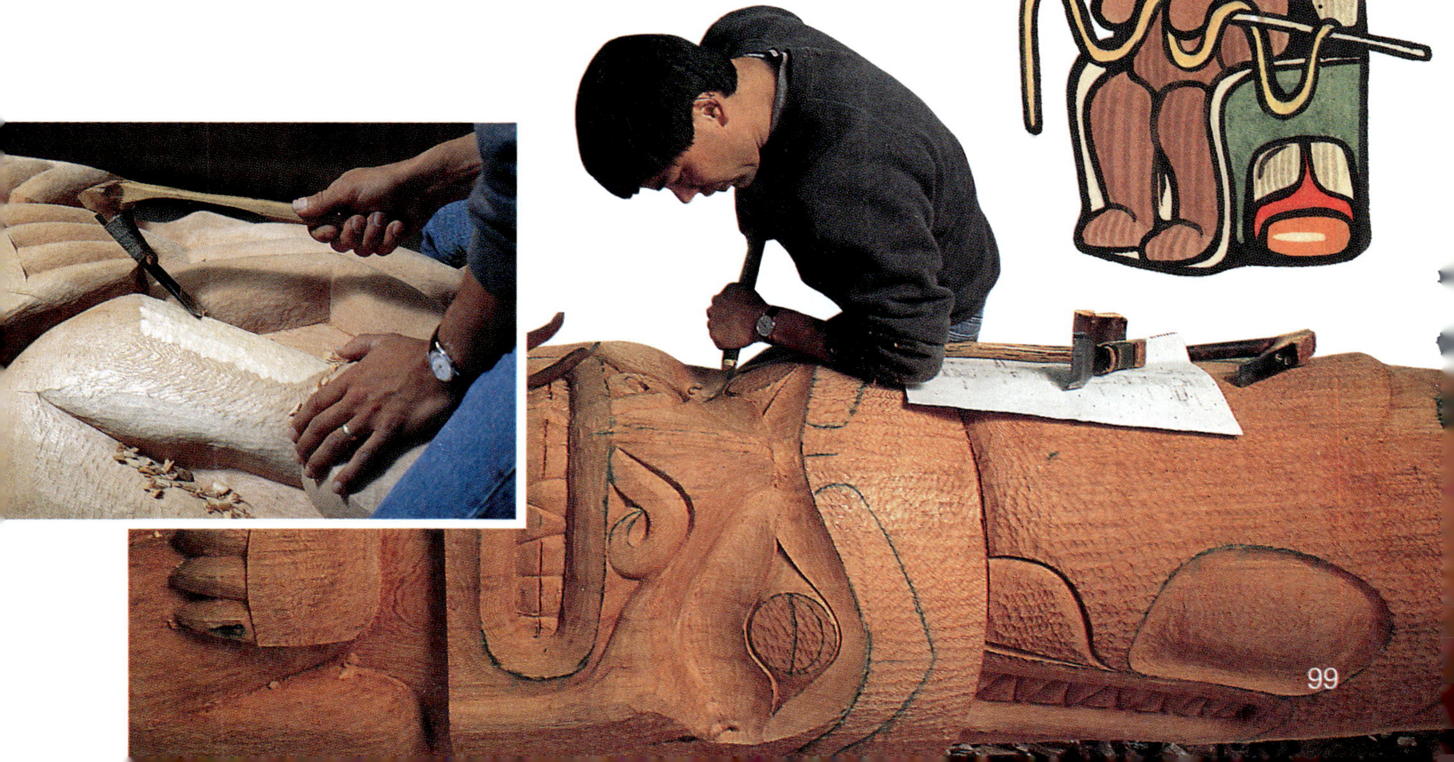

UNDERSTANDING TOTEM POLES

Today, if you were to look at most totem poles, you wouldn't be able to tell what many of the figures on them stand for. That's because the nature spirits or gods in which the Indians believe are often carved in the form of animals. The secret lies in knowing what to look for.

For instance, Beaver would have prominent front teeth and a crosshatched tail, and might be holding a chewing stick. Northwest Coast Indians believed that the first beaver was a woman who loved to swim. A long, long time ago, they say, the woman blocked a stream in order to make a lake. Then she spent endless hours swimming and floating in it. In time her body became covered with soft fur and her wide leather apron grew into a tail. According to legend, beavers have looked and acted the way they now do ever since that time.

Raven is found on many totem poles. He can be recognized by his long, straight beak, and he may be holding a round disk that represents the sun. The Northwest Coast Indians believed that Raven used his magic to create the world. However, the world was dark because a selfish chief kept the sun locked up in a box. Raven rescued the sun and threw it into the sky to light the world.

The Northwest Coast Indians believed that of all the spirits, Thunderbird was the most powerful. Only the greatest chiefs could use his emblem. Thunderbird is shown with his wings outstretched. According to storytellers, he lived in the mountains and fed on whales. Every day, when he was hungry, Thunderbird flew over the ocean. As soon as he saw a whale, he threw down the two Lightning Serpents that lived under his wings. After the serpents struck the whale with their jagged tongues and killed it, Thunderbird carried its body to his nest high in the mountains. Whenever the Northwest Coast Indians saw lightning, they said it was Thunderbird hunting whales.

A TRADITION CONTINUES

The Canadian government recognizes that the arts of the Northwest Coast Indians are part of the cultural heritage of all Canadians. As a result of government support, artists of the Northwest Coast Indian group are kept busy trying to meet the great demand for genuine totem poles throughout Canada. The poles are found in parks and shopping centers as well as in Indian villages. On these poles, Thunderbird and other spirits live on.

What do the totem poles of the Northwest Coast Indians tell about their culture?

IMPORTANT EVENTS

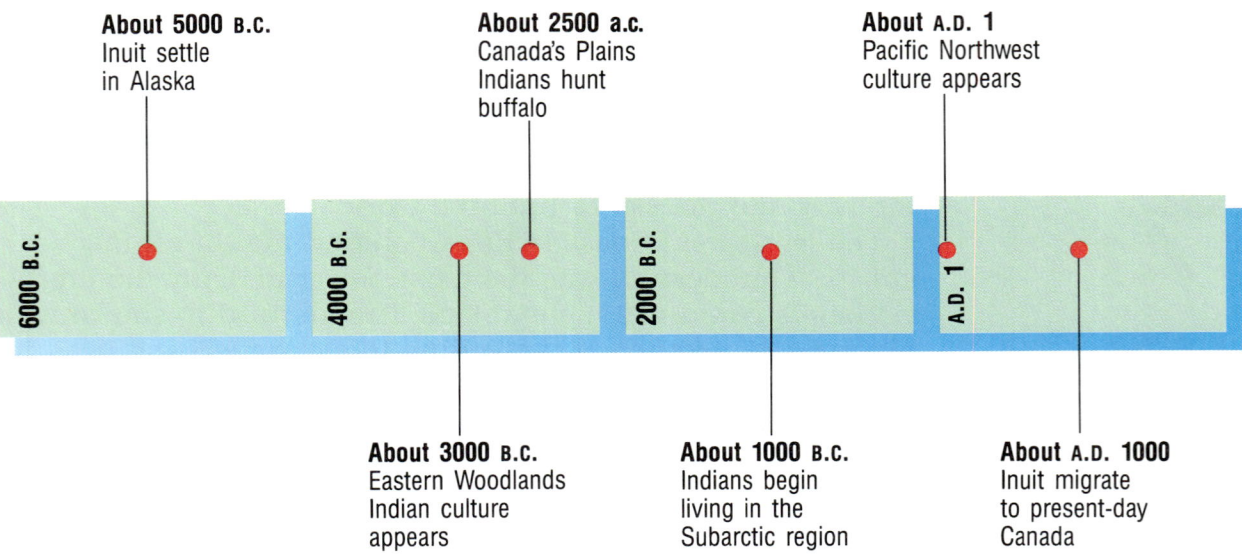

About 5000 B.C.
Inuit settle
in Alaska

About 2500 a.c.
Canada's Plains
Indians hunt
buffalo

About A.D. 1
Pacific Northwest
culture appears

6000 B.C.

4000 B.C.

2000 B.C.

A.D. 1

About 3000 B.C.
Eastern Woodlands
Indian culture
appears

About 1000 B.C.
Indians begin
living in the
Subarctic region

About A.D. 1000
Inuit migrate
to present-day
Canada

IDEAS TO REMEMBER

■ The Inuit survived the harsh environment of the Arctic region by adapting to
their surroundings. They used the resources that were available in their environment—all parts of animals, stone,
wood, soil, and snow and ice.

■ The Subarctic Indians and the Eastern
Woodlands Indians lived in the forests
of Canada where they hunted and
fished to meet their basic needs. The
Eastern Woodlands Indians of Southeastern Canada also farmed.

■ The Plains Indians depended on the
buffalo for their food, clothing, and
shelter.

■ The Northwest Coast Indians benefited
from plentiful food, many forests, and
the mild climate of their region.

REVIEWING VOCABULARY

artisan	potlatch
igloo	stampede
kayak	tepee
long house	totem pole
myth	wigwam

Number a sheet of paper from 1 to 10.
Beside each number write the word or
term from the above list that best matches
the definition.

1. A person skilled in a craft
2. A special feast celebrated among the
   Indians of the Northwest Coast, during
   which the host gives away valuable
   objects
3. An Inuit house made of snow and ice
4. A small, domed house built by the Eastern Woodlands Indians
5. A painted carving that usually showed
   the history of a family

6. A cone-shaped house used by the Plains Indians
7. A one-person boat used by the Inuit
8. A story that expresses a group's beliefs about gods and heroes
9. A barrel-shaped house used by the Eastern Woodlands Indians in which several families lived together
10. A sudden, uncontrolled flight of a herd of frightened animals

REVIEWING FACTS

1. What kinds of houses did the Inuit build in summer? In winter?
2. How did the Inuit use dogs? Seals?
3. What is a shaman?
4. Why did the Subarctic Indians move frequently?
5. Among the Eastern Woodlands Indians, what was one job done by children? By artisans?
6. Why were the Plains Indians called "the Buffalo People"?
7. What materials did the Plains Indians use to build a house?
8. Why didn't the Northwest Coast Indians need to grow their own food?
9. Name two natural resources important to the Northwest Coast Indians.
10. With which custom did the Northwest Coast Indians show their appreciation for their good fortune?

WRITING ABOUT MAIN IDEAS

1. **Comparing:** Write two paragraphs to compare the ways of life of the Inuit and the Plains Indians. Consider such things as their ways of getting food,

their igloos, canoes, and long houses, and their use of natural resources in the environment.
2. **Writing a Paragraph:** Choose one photograph in this chapter. Study it closely and read the caption. Then write a paragraph telling how the photograph you chose adds to your understanding of the information in the chapter.
3. **Writing About Perspectives:** Imagine that you are a Kwakiutl leader. You want to teach children about the importance of trees in the life of your people. Write a myth that would teach this important lesson.

BUILDING SKILLS: ASKING QUESTIONS

1. What steps can you follow to ask good questions?
2. Suppose you were doing a report about potlatches. Which of these questions would you ask to learn more about the subject?
   a. What types of gifts were given?
   b. What is a totem pole?
   c. How long did a potlatch last?
   d. How did Northwest Coast Indians prepare salmon to eat?
   e. Which was more valued—jewelry or animal skins?
3. Why are the questions you chose the best questions?
4. Write two additional questions that you could ask to learn more about potlatches.
5. What are some times in school or outside of school when it is necessary for you to ask good questions?

REVIEWING VOCABULARY

acid rain	rapids
artisan	tepee
canal	timberline
kayak	totem pole
long house	tundra

Number a sheet of paper from 1 to 10. Beside each number write the word or term from the list above that best completes the sentence.

1. No trees grow above the _____.
2. Several Eastern Woodlands families lived together in a _____.
3. The _____ had been carved with certain birds and animals that were the emblems of an Indian family.
4. The _____ connected two rivers so that boats could pass from one to the other.
5. A basket weaver, a jewelry maker, or a canoe builder is an example of _____.
6. _____ has killed many plants in the United States and Canada.
7. The Plains Indians built a cone-shaped home called a _____.
8. The canoe is a good boat to use when traveling down the _____ of a river.
9. The Inuit built a one-person boat called a _____.
10. In northern Canada there is a vast treeless plain, or _____.

◀═▶ WRITING ABOUT THE UNIT

1. **Writing a Travel Brochure:** Choose one physical region that is described in this unit. Write a travel brochure that would encourage a person to visit this region on vacation. Include a clear description of the region and an explanation of why it might be interesting or fun to visit.
2. **Completing a Chart:** Create a chart about the resources of Canada. In the first column list at least five important resources. In the second column list the ways in which the early Indians used each resource. Finally, in the third column list the ways in which each resource is important today.
3. **Writing About Perspectives:** Imagine that you are a Northwest Coast Indian who has been invited to attend a potlatch. Write a story in which you provide a vivid description of this event based on the information in this unit.

ACTIVITIES

1. **Making a Diorama:** Choose one of the early Indian groups that are discussed in this unit. Make a three-dimensional scene that shows the daily life of the group. You might show the homes or the activities of the group.
2. **Retelling a Legend:** Find a book of Indian legends and myths in your school library. Retell a legend or myth in your own words. You might write down your legend or tell it in class.
3. **Working Together to Write Letters:** Work with a partner and choose one early Indian group. One partner should pretend to be a member of that group and should write a letter to the other, telling about the group's life. Then the other partner should write a reply, telling about how life today is similar to or different from the life described by the Indian writer.

BUILDING SKILLS: ASKING QUESTIONS

1. What does it mean to ask good questions?

2. Suppose that you wanted to learn more about the Eastern Woodland Indians and their way of life. What are five questions that you might ask?

3. Look at the scene of Indian life above. What questions can you ask about it?

4. Why is it important to come up with your own questions?

5. Would the following questions help you to find out more about the natural resources of Canada? Why or why not?
   a. Does Canada have any oil resources?
   b. Where can coal be found in Canada?
   c. Which is the largest copper-producing country in the world?
   d. Why can trees be considered a natural resource?
   e. Are there any forests in Canada?

LINKING PAST, PRESENT, AND FUTURE

Early Indian peoples built homes suited to their environment and their types of family groups. What are some of the types of homes that people build today? Do they reflect the environment in which they are located? What kinds of homes do you think people might build in the future? Why might they build these kinds of homes?

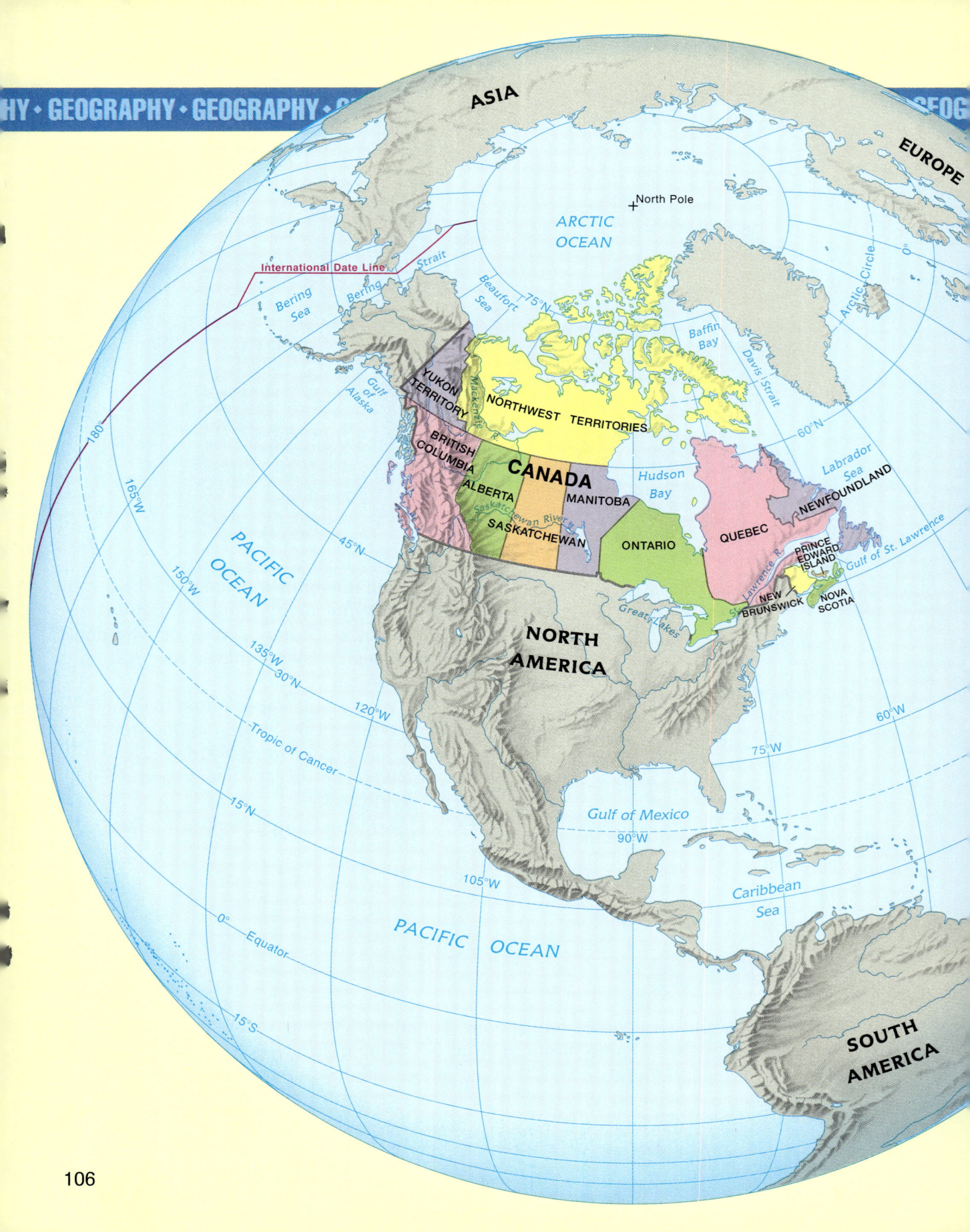

ASIA

EUROPE

North Pole

ARCTIC
OCEAN

International Date Line

Bering
Strait

Bering
Sea

Beaufort
Sea

75°N

Baffin
Bay

Arctic Circle

180°

Gulf
of
Alaska

YUKON
TERRITORY

NORTHWEST   TERRITORIES

Mackenzie R.

Davis Strait

60°N

165°W

BRITISH
COLUMBIA

CANADA

Hudson
Bay

Labrador
Sea

NEWFOUNDLAND

PACIFIC

ALBERTA

MANITOBA

150°W

Saskatchewan River

SASKATCHEWAN

ONTARIO

QUEBEC

PRINCE
EDWARD
ISLAND

Gulf of St. Lawrence

OCEAN

45°N

St. Lawrence R.

NEW
BRUNSWICK

NOVA
SCOTIA

Great Lakes

135°W

30°N

NORTH
AMERICA

120°W

60°W

Tropic of Cancer

75°W

15°N

Gulf of Mexico

90°W

105°W

Caribbean
Sea

0°   Equator

PACIFIC   OCEAN

15°S

SOUTH
AMERICA

UNIT
3

CANADA PAST AND PRESENT

WHERE WE ARE

In this unit, your Canadian journey continues. You will learn about how Canada has changed in the time between the arrival of the first European explorers and today. You will visit some of Canada's modern cities where many Canadians now live.

You will read about where people from different countries settled, and about their relations with one another and with Canada's Indians. As you read, think about which parts of Canada today are most similar to the place where you live. Which parts are most different?

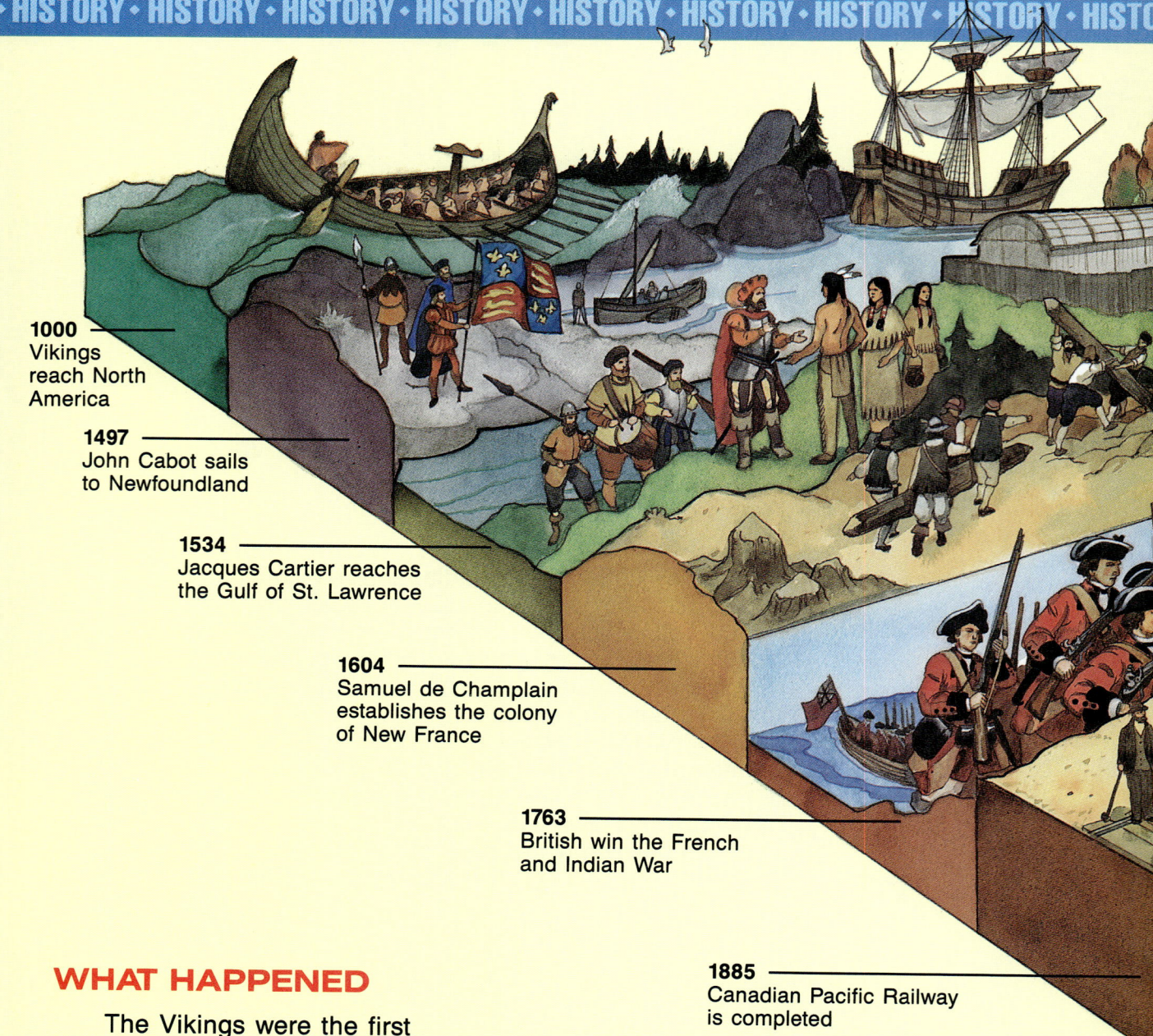

1000
Vikings
reach North
America

1497
John Cabot sails
to Newfoundland

1534
Jacques Cartier reaches
the Gulf of St. Lawrence

1604
Samuel de Champlain
establishes the colony
of New France

1763
British win the French
and Indian War

1885
Canadian Pacific Railway
is completed

1988
Winter Olympics
are held in
Calgary, Alberta

WHAT HAPPENED

The Vikings were the first
Europeans to settle in what is now
Canada. However, they established no
lasting colonies there. Centuries later,
the French built a vast colony along the
St. Lawrence River. The British gained
control of this land after they defeated the
French in the French and Indian War. During
the next 200 years Canada grew and developed
into a successful and powerful country.

108

Calgary

CANADA

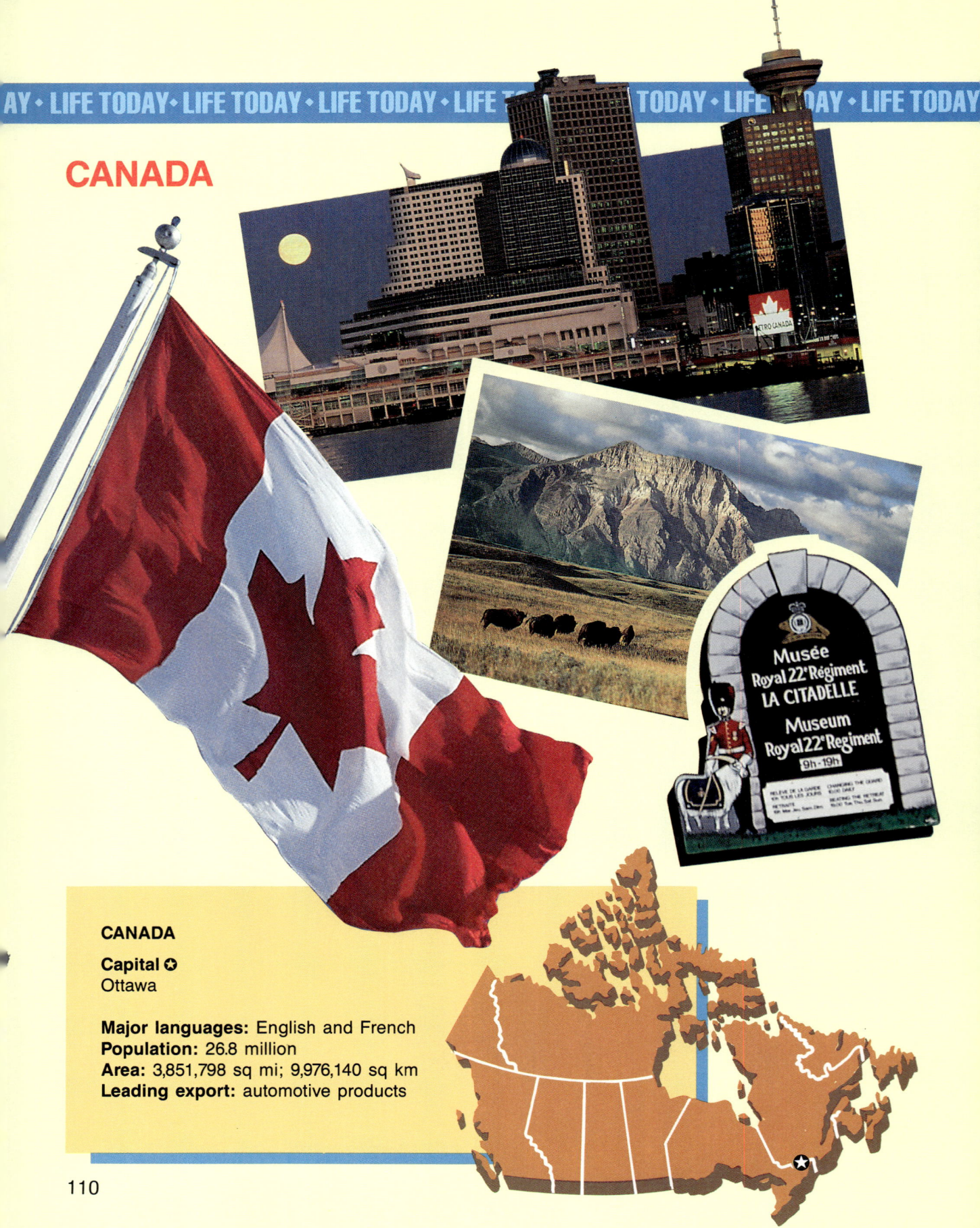

Musée
Royal 22ᵉ Régiment
LA CITADELLE

Museum
Royal 22ᵉ Regiment
9h - 19h

CANADA

Capital ✪
Ottawa

Major languages: English and French
Population: 26.8 million
Area: 3,851,798 sq mi; 9,976,140 sq km
Leading export: automotive products

ALBERTA

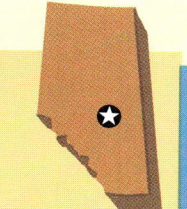

Provincial capital
★ Edmonton

Major language: English
Population: 2.4 million
Area: 255,285 sq mi; 661,185 sq km
Joined Canada: September 1, 1905

BRITISH COLUMBIA

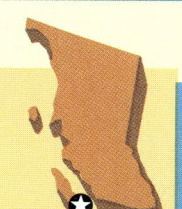

Provincial capital
★ Victoria

Major language: English
Population: 3.0 million
Area: 365,950 sq mi; 947,800 sq km
Joined Canada: July 20, 1871

MANITOBA

Provincial capital
★ Winnipeg

Major language: English
Population: 1.1 million
Area: 250,950 sq mi; 649,950 sq km
Joined Canada: July 15, 1870

NEW BRUNSWICK

Provincial capital
★ Fredericton

Major languages: English and French
Population: 0.7 million
Area: 28,354 sq mi; 74,437 sq km
Joined Canada: July 1, 1867

NEWFOUNDLAND

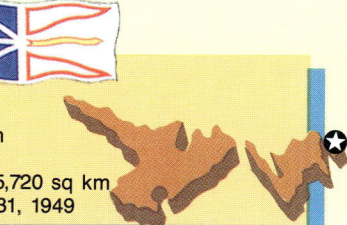

Provincial capital
★ St. John's

Major language: English
Population: 0.6 million
Area: 156,649 sq mi; 405,720 sq km
Joined Canada: March 31, 1949

NOVA SCOTIA

Provincial capital
★ Halifax

Major language: English
Population: 0.9 million
Area: 21,425 sq mi; 55,490 sq km
Joined Canada: July 1, 1867

ONTARIO

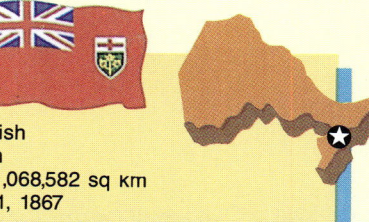

Provincial capital
★ Toronto

Major language: English
Population: 9.7 million
Area: 412,582 sq mi; 1,068,582 sq km
Joined Canada: July 1, 1867

PRINCE EDWARD ISLAND

Provincial capital
★ Charlottetown

Major language: English
Population: 0.1 million
Area: 2,184 sq mi; 5,657 sq km
Joined Canada: July 1, 1873

QUEBEC

Provincial capital
★ Quebec

Major languages: French and English
Population: 6.7 million
Area: 594,860 sq mi; 1,540,680 sq km
Joined Canada: July 1, 1867

SASKATCHEWAN

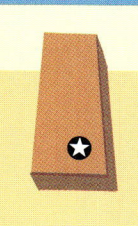

Provincial capital
★ Regina

Major language: English
Population: 1.0 million
Area: 251,866 sq mi; 652,330 sq km
Joined Canada: September 1, 1905

NORTHWEST TERRITORIES

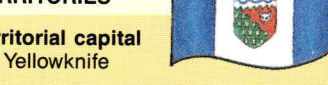

Territorial capital
★ Yellowknife

Major languages: English and Inuktitut
Population: 53,000
Area: 1,322,910 sq mi; 3,426,322 sq km
Joined Canada: July 15, 1870

YUKON TERRITORY

Territorial capital
★ Whitehorse

Major language: English
Population: 26,000
Area: 186,661 sq mi; 438,450 sq km
Joined Canada: June 13, 1898

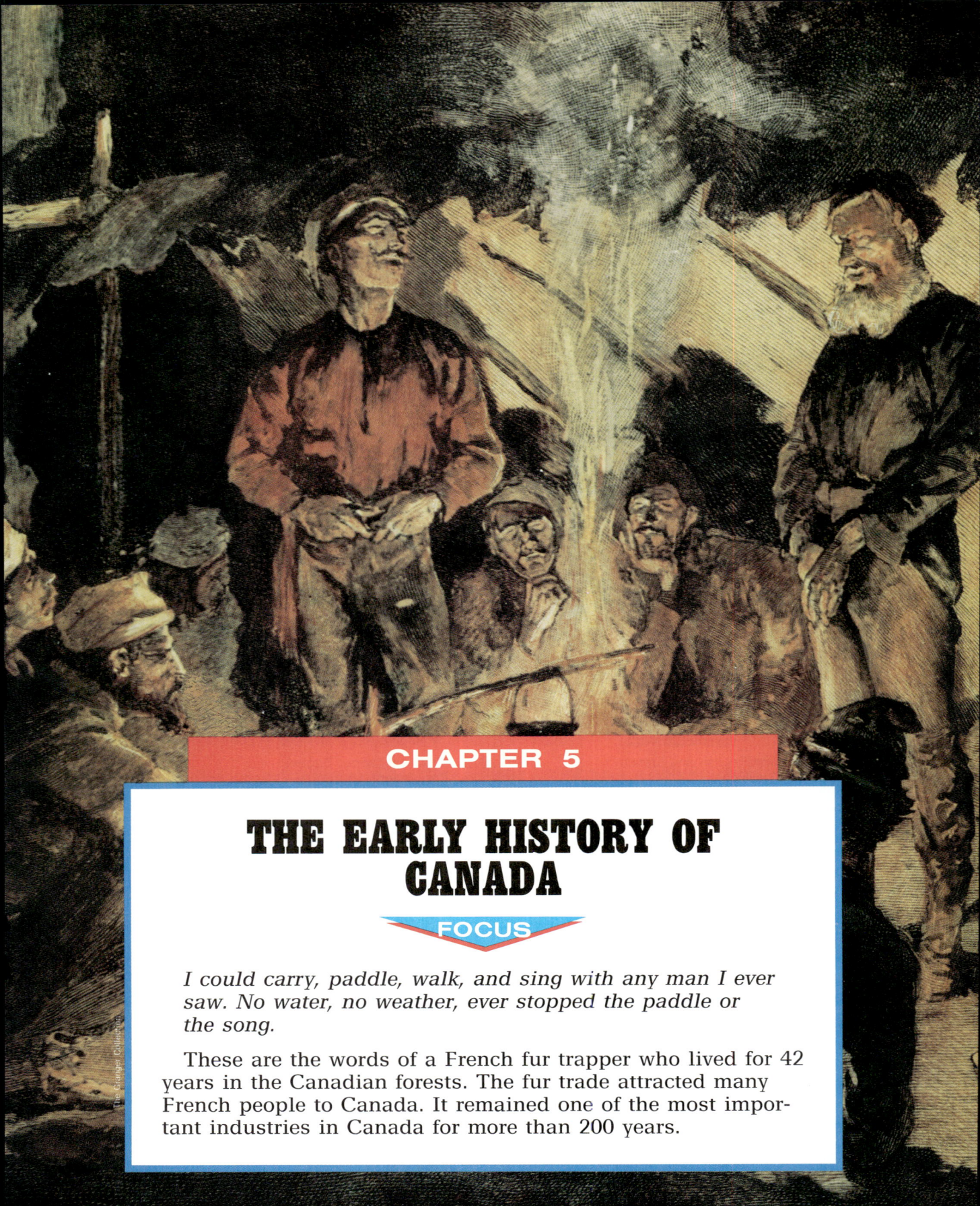

CHAPTER 5

THE EARLY HISTORY OF CANADA

FOCUS

I could carry, paddle, walk, and sing with any man I ever saw. No water, no weather, ever stopped the paddle or the song.

These are the words of a French fur trapper who lived for 42 years in the Canadian forests. The fur trade attracted many French people to Canada. It remained one of the most important industries in Canada for more than 200 years.

1 Early Exploration

READ TO LEARN

Key Vocabulary

saga
Northwest
    Passage

Key People

Eric the Red
Leif Ericson
John Cabot

Giovanni da
    Verrazano
Jacques Cartier

Key Places

Newfoundland

Read Aloud

Behind that snowcapped range must be the Great River which led to the Sea of the West [the Pacific Ocean]. *Across the sea was China, and it held more wealth than could be counted.*

The writer Robert Carse was describing the search for a sea route across North America to Asia. In this lesson you will read about the results of that search.

Read for Purpose

1. **WHAT YOU KNOW:** Why would you want to explore an unknown part of the world?
2. **WHAT YOU WILL LEARN:** Which parts of northern North America did Europeans first explore?

BEYOND THE ATLANTIC

Even if you have not traveled very much, you probably know a great deal about the world. Books such as this one describe life in other countries. Photographs, movies, television, and school have probably opened up new worlds to you.

One thousand years ago, however, people who lived in one area knew very little about the rest of the world. The Indians living in the Americas knew nothing about the people who lived on the other side of the world. And the Europeans who sailed west across the Atlantic Ocean had no idea of what they were about to find.

THE VIKINGS

The earliest European explorers were the Vikings. They lived in the part of Europe that is today called Scandinavia. The Vikings were known throughout northern Europe as great warriors and sailors. They were also excellent storytellers. Much of what we know today about their adventures comes from **sagas**. Sagas are tales that originated in Iceland and have been passed down through the years. By studying these sagas and through archaeological discoveries, historians have come to believe that the Vikings were the first Europeans to reach the Americas, about 1,000 years ago.

As the map below shows, a Viking named **Eric the Red** and his crew set sail from Iceland and landed on an island that he named Greenland. The Vikings' delight was recorded in a saga.

Salmon were plentiful both in the lake and in the river—bigger salmon than they had ever seen before.

Twenty years later, Eric the Red's son, **Leif Ericson**, reached another part of North America, the island now called **Newfoundland**. In their sagas the Vikings called the island Vinland because of the green vines they found there.

Vinland, where green fields became a home for the wanderer. Vinland, where the grass never withers in the winter.

The Indians who already lived there were angered by Viking attempts to claim their land. Fierce battles took place between the Indians and the Vikings as a result of this dispute. The Vikings eventually abandoned their settlements in North America.

THE NORTHWEST PASSAGE

Almost 500 years passed before any other European explorers sailed across the Atlantic Ocean to the Americas. During this time Europeans lived in small, isolated communities, and they had little interest in the rest of the world. By the 1400s, however, Europe had begun to change. Better ships and sailing instruments were making their long journeys safer and easier.

In the 1400s European traders had discovered that Asia was a storehouse

MAP SKILL: Which three bodies of water on this map were named after the same explorer?

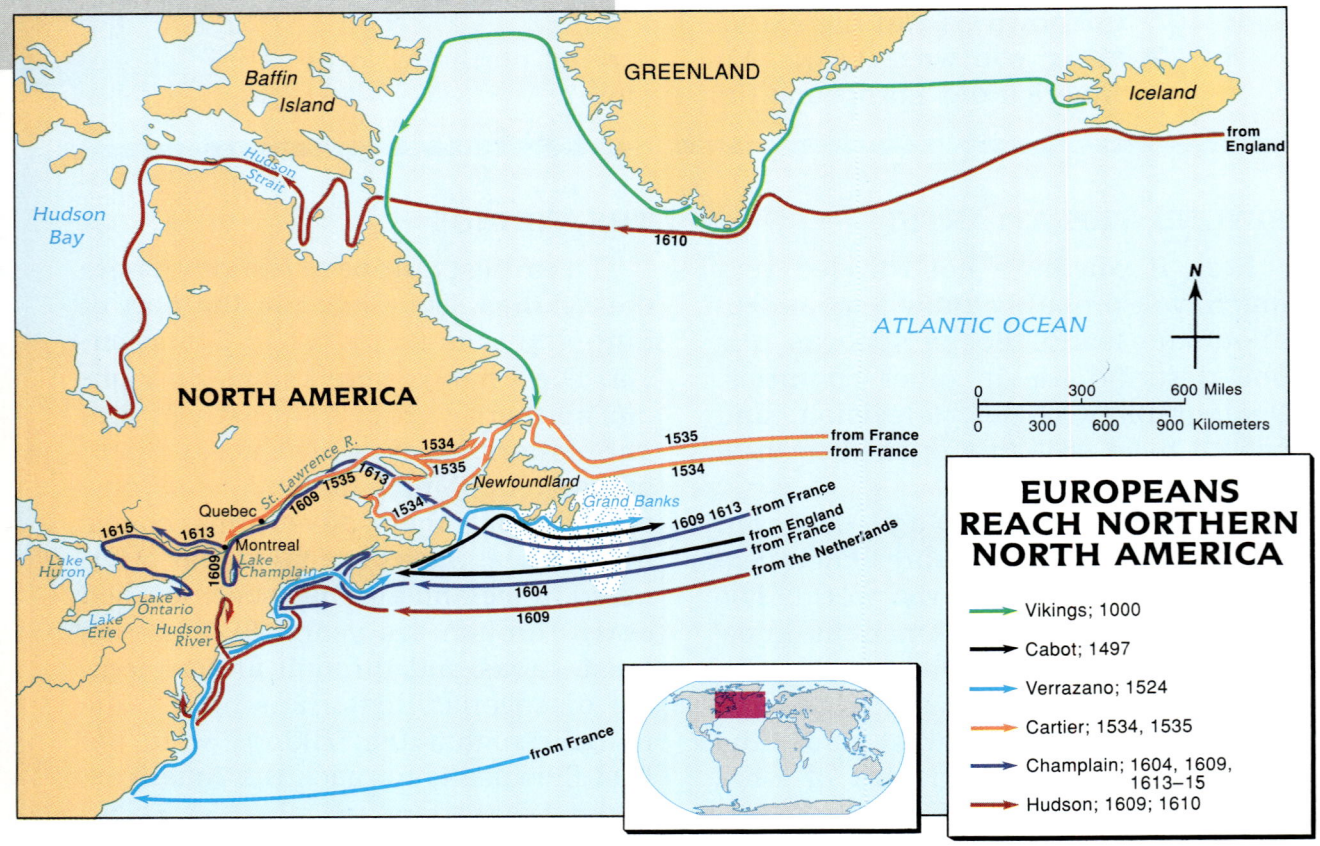

EUROPEANS REACH NORTHERN NORTH AMERICA

- Vikings; 1000
- Cabot; 1497
- Verrazano; 1524
- Cartier; 1534, 1535
- Champlain; 1604, 1609, 1613–15
- Hudson; 1609; 1610

of treasures. There was silk, perfume, diamonds, rubies, pearls, and spices like pepper, nutmeg, cloves, and cinnamon. Spices were in great demand for cooking and preserving food. Traders quickly realized that they could get rich by selling Asian goods in Europe.

However, traders knew of only two routes to Asia. They could sail thousands of miles around the southern tip of Africa—a long, dangerous route. Or they could travel east by land, across vast plains and rugged mountains.

Some people began to wonder if there was a faster, better route to Asia. They thought that if they sailed west, instead of east, they could also reach Asia. The first European to attempt this route was Christopher Columbus. But as you will read in Chapter 10, he reached the Americas instead of Asia.

Later, other explorers began to hope that they could find an all-water route to the treasures of Asia by traveling along the north coast of North America. Although none of them ever found this Northwest Passage, their voyages were valuable because they were the beginning of the European exploration of Canada.

FRENCH AND ENGLISH EXPLORERS

The king of England sent an Italian navigator named Giovanni Caboto to search for the Northwest Passage in 1497. Caboto, called John Cabot by the English, reached an island off the east coast of Canada. It was the same island that the Vikings had called Vinland 500 years earlier. He named it "New Founde Land." Although Cabot never found a passage to Asia, his explorations did lead England to claim land in Canada.

The Granger Collection

Better sailing instruments helped John Cabot's crew survive the trip to "New Founde Land" in 1497.

Fishing crews from England, France, and Portugal were drawn to Canada by reports of teeming schools of fish. But the explorers' main goal remained the search for a quick sailing route to Asia. In 1524 the king of France sent the Italian navigator Giovanni da Verrazano (dä ver ə zän′ ō) to seek the Northwest Passage. Like Cabot, Verrazano did not find a route to Asia. However, he did establish French claims to land in Canada. Find the routes of Cabot, Verrazano, and other European explorers on the map on page 114.

THE HURON AND CARTIER

In 1534 a group of Huron gathered on the shore of the Gulf of St. Lawrence. Someone had reported that a tall object, unlike anything they had ever seen before, was moving across the water. When the "great canoe" reached shore, strange-looking people climbed out. The Huron welcomed the strangers, who were French explorers.

The Huron welcomed Jacques Cartier during his explorations of the St. Lawrence River.

When the French asked the name of their country, the Huron replied *kanata*, the Indian word for "village."

The leader of the explorers was **Jacques Cartier** (zhäk kär′ tyā). Cartier explored the St. Lawrence River and reached a Huron town called Hochelaga (häsh ə lag′ ə). A mountain behind Hochelaga was ablaze with brilliant autumn colors. Cartier named it *Mont Réal* (mō rā al′), French for "royal mountain." What is the present-day name of Hochelaga?

From Mont Réal, Cartier could see upriver to some rapids. No boat could navigate those swirling, tumbling waters. Once again, no Northwest Passage had been found. Cartier and his crew spent the winter camping near Mont Réal. During this time many of the men became ill from their poor diet. Their gums became so rotten that their "teeth all fell out." The Huron showed Cartier how to cure the men by having them drink a bitter-tasting tea made of ground tree bark.

IMPORTANT EXPLORATIONS

For more than 100 years European explorers sailed the shores of North America in search of a Northwest Passage to Asia. Although they did not find the route that they were looking for, explorers like Cabot, Verrazano, and Cartier succeeded in mapping and claiming huge areas of North America for the countries for which they sailed. The Huron, who had long lived in Canada, were helpful to the explorers.

Check Your Reading

1. Who were the Vikings?
2. Why were the European explorers seeking another route to Asia?
3. What was the name of the route that they sought? Did they ever find it?
4. **GEOGRAPHY SKILL:** Look at the map on page 114. In which direction did the European explorers travel?
5. **THINKING SKILL:** Classify the explorers from this lesson according to the countries for which they sailed.

2 Settlements and Colonies

READ TO LEARN

Key Vocabulary

colony
Hudson's Bay
  Company
coureurs de bois

voyageurs
portage
missionary

Key People

Samuel de
  Champlain

Key Places

Grand Banks
Quebec
New France
Montreal

Read Aloud

The Air in Newfoundland is wholesome good;
The Fire, as Sweet as any made of wood;
The Waters, very rich, both salt and fresh;
The Earth, more rich, you know it is no less.
Where all are good, Fire, Water, Earth, and Air,
What man made of these four would not live there?

These lines are from a poem written by Robert Hayman in 1628. The promise of land and wealth brought many French and English settlers to Canada's shores. In this lesson you will read about these settlers' activities in early Canada and their effect on the Indians already living there.

Read for Purpose

1. **WHAT YOU KNOW:** Why do you think that a person might want to move to a new place?
2. **WHAT YOU WILL LEARN:** What were some of the activities of Canada's early European settlers?

FISHING IN CANADA

John Cabot wrote in his journal that the sea around Newfoundland was "swimming with fish, which can be taken not with the net but in baskets." After the Europeans learned about the rich sea life of North America, their fishing boats sailed westward from England and France each spring. Their goal was to reach the **Grand Banks**, which are located about 75 miles (120 km) south of Newfoundland. The Grand Banks still offer some of the finest fishing in the world. The English established permanent fishing villages on Newfoundland in the 1500s.

TRADING BEGINS

During the time that the French and English were very active in Canada, they began to trade with the Indians. The settlers traded copper kettles, steel

117

Fur trading and fishing were the two most important industries in early Canada. Today the Grand Banks still offer some of the finest fishing in the world.

knives, and fishhooks for the furs of the animals that the Indians had trapped. The Indians used the knives and kettles to skin and boil rabbits. The settlers then shipped the pelts back to Europe, where the demand for them grew quickly.

By 1600 many Europeans wanted to wear fur. They especially liked the fur of the beaver, which made fine hats and trimmings for coats. In the early days of Canada, the fur trade became the most important activity of the French settlers.

THE FATHER OF NEW FRANCE

As the fur trade grew, the king of France decided to start a colony in Canada. A colony is a territory that is under the control of another, usually distant, country. The king thought that establishing a colony in Canada was the best way to protect French interests in North America. Among the people whom the king sent to Canada in the early 1600s was Samuel de Champlain (də sham plān′).

Samuel de Champlain was a well-known mapmaker, explorer, and soldier. In 1608 Champlain established the settlement of Quebec in Canada. Quebec was the beginning of the first French colony in North America, which was called New France. Because of his strong leadership and hard work, Champlain became known as the "Father of New France."

Although Champlain was an effective leader, Quebec grew slowly. The French would not allow anyone who was not a Roman Catholic to settle in New France. In addition, the settlers were not used to Canada's harsh winters and found farming there difficult. When Champlain died in 1635, Quebec had only about 100 people. Nearly all of them were fur traders.

While he was in Canada, Samuel de Champlain explored deeper and deeper into the forests, creating new maps of the rivers, lakes, and land that he came upon. Champlain was the first European to see what we now call the Great Lakes. Lake Champlain, which lies in New York and Canada, was named after this explorer.

Champlain was friendly with the Hurons who lived near Quebec. He understood that it was important for the French to get along with the Indians in order for New France to grow.

THE FUR TRADE

As you read in Chapter 4, the Indians of the Subarctic and the Eastern Woodlands were hunters and trappers. They lived in or near forests in which animals were plentiful. They trapped beavers, minks, otters, foxes, muskrats, and other fur-bearing animals. After the arrival of the French, the Hurons traded the fur pelts for goods or money. The diagram on page 120 shows what a trading post looked like.

Most of the traders who ran the Canadian trading posts were French. But soon the British trade began to cut into the market. The British formed the **Hudson's Bay Company**, which quickly spread, establishing trading posts all along Hudson Bay. The bay and the company were named after the British explorer, Henry Hudson.

The traders bought furs from the Indian and European trappers and sent the furs to the larger settlements on the St. Lawrence River. From there the furs were shipped to Europe.

Some of the trappers were Europeans who lived in the forests with the Indians. They were called **coureurs de bois** (ku rûr′ də bwä), a French term that means "woods runners" or "scouts." These scouts both trapped animals and traded in furs.

One reason that the coureurs de bois prospered in the forests was that they were willing to learn from the Indians. They learned how to use the Indians' birchbark canoes. These light and portable canoes made it possible for the coureurs de bois to travel very quickly along Canada's rivers and lakes. A vast network of waterways stretches far west from the St. Lawrence River.

ABITATION. DE QVEBECQ

Champlain's house in Quebec was the center of the settlement known as New France.

The Granger Collection

FRENCH FORT AND TRADING POST

Traders

Dwellings

Smokehouse

Dairy

Store

Stable

Palisade

Voyageurs

Trapper

DIAGRAM SKILL: Who transported the furs to and from the trading post?

Landing wharf

The French **voyageurs** (voi ə zhûrz′) carried the traders' goods from the forests. They loaded hundreds of pelts into birchbark canoes and carried men, as well as the pelts, from the trading posts eastward to Quebec. The strong voyageurs paddled down Canada's swift rivers, carrying their canoes and cargo over each **portage** (pôr′ tij). A portage is a land route from one body of water to another.

One voyageur recalled spending many years in the forests.

I have now . . . been 42 years in this country [Canada]. For 22 I was a light canoeman. No portage was too long for me; all portages were alike. Fifty songs a day were nothing to me. . . . There is no life so happy as a voyageur's life; none so independent; no place where a man enjoys so much variety and freedom as in the Indian country.

MONTREAL IS FOUNDED

In 1642 France established a second colony in New France at Montreal, the site of the Huron town, Hochelaga. Find Montreal on the map on this page. Montreal became the center for a new group of settlers from France—the missionaries. A missionary is a person who is sent by a church to spread its religion among nonbelievers. The French missionaries hoped to convert the Indians to Christianity.

From Montreal the missionaries traveled throughout the Canadian forests. Often they traveled with the coureurs de bois and lived among the Indians in order to teach them about Christianity.

Montreal served as a missionary center for many years. It also became an important base for fur traders and explorers on their way to the forests. By 1760 Montreal had a population of 4,000.

The fur trade soon became the most important industry in Montreal. Many Frenchmen in the town had come hoping to make their fortunes and then to return home. One French traveler who visited Montreal in 1782 wrote:

Most of the merchants and young men of Montreal spend the greatest part of their time trading with the Indians at an amazing distance from Montreal; and it often happens that they are three years together absent from their homes.

THE GROWTH OF NEW FRANCE

As you have read, the wealth of natural resources in Canada encouraged both the English and the French to start colonies there. The plentiful fish in the Grand Banks led the English to

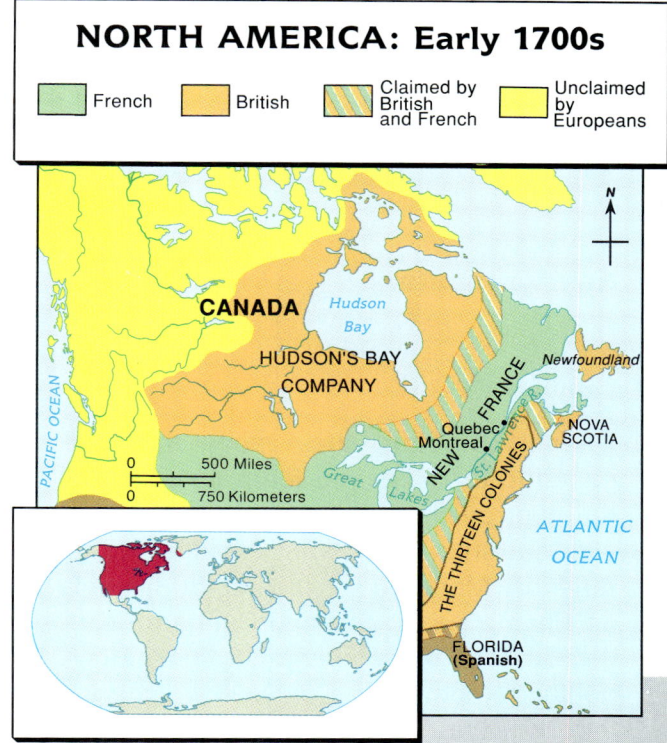

NORTH AMERICA: Early 1700s

Legend:
- French
- British
- Claimed by British and French
- Unclaimed by Europeans

MAP SKILL: Which country claimed the most land in Canada in the early 1700s?

settle Newfoundland. The fur trade drew the French inland, where Samuel de Champlain started the colony of New France. In the next lesson you will read about the difficulties that the French and English faced as they raced to colonize Canada.

Check Your Reading

1. Why were some Europeans interested in the Grand Banks?
2. Why was Samuel de Champlain called the "Father of New France"?
3. How did the Indians help the French to prosper in New France?
4. **THINKING SKILL:** List the sequence of events by which an animal pelt was transported from the forests to market in Quebec.

Reading Time Lines

Key Vocabulary

time line   B.C.
decade   A.D.
century

When you study about things that happened in the past, you learn about many different events. In the last two lessons, you read that John Cabot explored North America. Montreal was founded. Samuel de Champlain established Quebec. How do you keep these events straight? How do you remember the order in which these events occurred? One way to keep track of past events is by using a **time line**.

A time line is a diagram that shows when and the order in which important events took place. It also tells how much time passed between each event. You will find a number of time lines in this textbook, especially in the Unit Openers and the Chapter Summary and Review.

Understanding Time Lines

Time lines are divided into equal parts. Each part stands for a certain time period, such as 10, 50, or 500 years. Events are entered on the time line in the order in which they took place. Look at the time line on this page. As you can see, the earliest dates are on the left, while the more recent dates are toward the right. Into which time periods is the time line divided? Which event happened first?

Decades and Centuries

In some cases it is convenient to divide a time line into ten-year periods. A ten-year period is called a **decade**. The decade of the 1990s began on January 1, 1990 and will end on December 31, 1999. Which decade began on January 1, 1970?

Other time lines are divided into 100-year periods. A 100-year period is called a **century**. The first century was the period that included the year 1 to the year 99.

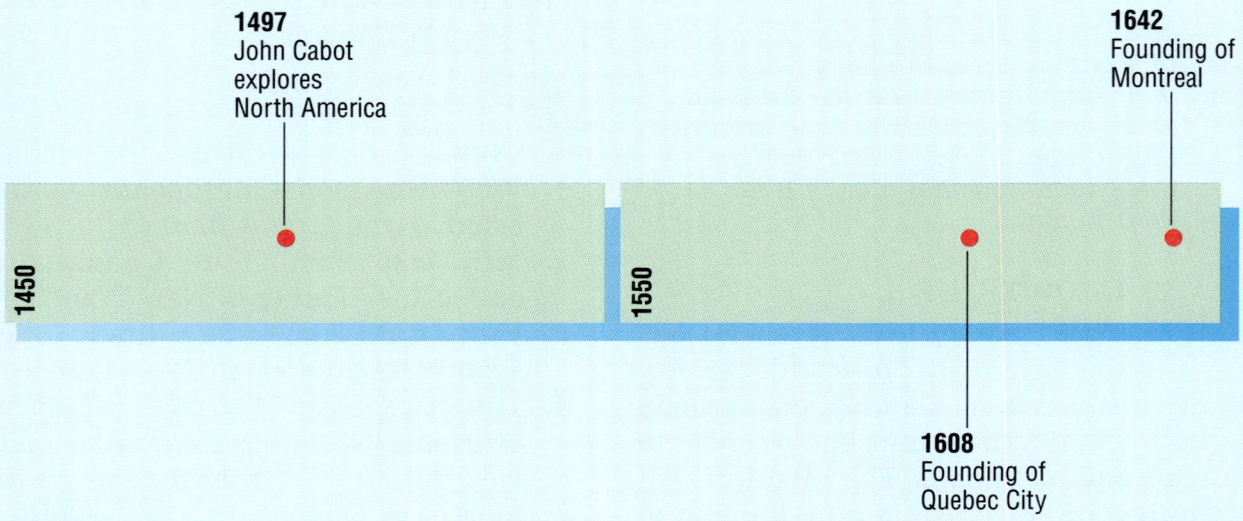

1497 John Cabot explores North America

1642 Founding of Montreal

1450

1550

1608 Founding of Quebec City

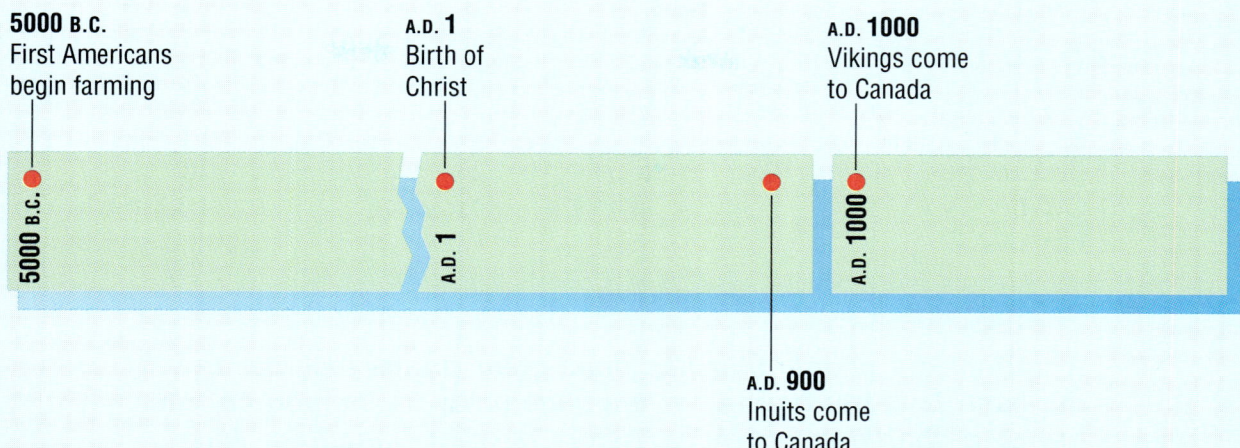

5000 B.C.
First Americans
begin farming

5000 B.C.

A.D. 1
Birth of
Christ

A.D. 1

A.D. 1000
Vikings come
to Canada

A.D. 1000

A.D. 900
Inuits come
to Canada

The second century began in the year 100 and ended at the end of the year 199. We live in the twentieth century, which began in the year 1900 and will end in the year 1999.

Sometimes a time line covers a long period of time by leaving out years between time periods. Notice the jagged line on the time line on this page. It shows that some years have been left out.

Understanding B.C. and A.D.

Most people today use a system that divides time into B.C. and A.D. Look again at the time line above. Notice that the first Americans began farming in about 5000 B.C. The abbreviation B.C. stands for "before Christ." So, 5000 B.C. means 5,000 years before the birth of Jesus Christ. Events that took place after the birth of Jesus Christ are labeled A.D., which means *anno Domini* (an′ ō dom′ ə nī). These words are Latin for "in the year of the Lord." Thus, for example, the Inuit came to Canada about 900 years after the birth of Jesus Christ, or A.D. 900.

To read B.C. dates, you must count backward from the year 1. The larger the

number, the earlier the date. For example, the year 4000 B.C. came before the year 3000 B.C. Remember that the earliest date on the time line is on the left.

To read A.D. dates, you count forward from the year 1. On the time line above you can see that the Inuit came to Canada in A.D. 900. This was earlier than the year A.D. 1000, which is the year in which the Vikings came. Again, remember that the latest date on a time line is on the right.

Reviewing the Skill

1. What is a time line?
2. Was Quebec founded before or after Montreal?
3. Which is the most recent event shown on the time line on this page?
4. Which is the earliest event shown on the time line on page 122?
5. Compare the two time lines. How many years after the Vikings did John Cabot explore North America?
6. On which time line would you put Henry Hudson's exploration of the Atlantic coast, which took place in 1610?
7. What does a time line help you to do?

3 Colonies in Conflict

 Key Vocabulary

French and Indian War
Quebec Act
Loyalist

Key People

James Wolfe
Louis de Montcalm

Key Places

Acadia
Lower Canada
Upper Canada

 Read Aloud

A nation is a people that has done great things together in the past. It is not bound by language or by a common culture but by a shared experience. History is what Canadians have in common.

In his writings about the difficulties faced by Canada, historian Ernest Renan notes the importance of shared experience. The people who live in this vast land have very different cultures. In this lesson you will read about some of the struggles that they have faced together.

 Read for Purpose

1. **WHAT YOU KNOW:** How did people make a living in New France?
2. **WHAT YOU WILL LEARN:** How did France lose its North American colonies to Great Britain?

CULTURES CLASH

By the 1700s Canada was a land of many cultures. French and British settlers lived side by side. The Huron, the Iroquois (ir′ ə kwoi), and other Indian groups lived nearby. The fact that conflicts developed among these different groups was not surprising.

In the late 1600s and early 1700s the French and British frequently fought over land and competed for the fur trade. The Huron and the Iroquois were historically enemies. As you have read in Lesson 2, Champlain and the French became friendly with the Huron. Champlain had sided with the Huron in battle, attacking the Iroquois and killing three of their chiefs. As a result, the Iroquois and the British united to drive the French colonists out of Canada. The peoples of Canada were on the brink of war.

THE GREAT RIVALRY

Events that were taking place outside of Canada also played a large role in the growing tensions. In Europe,

France and England had been enemies for hundreds of years. Each wanted to be the most powerful country in Europe, and the two powers raced to establish the largest colonies in North America. Although they had fought many battles in Europe, their fiercest conflict took place in North America.

In 1754 war broke out in the Ohio River Valley, an area claimed by both France and Britain. Find this area on the map on this page. The war spread rapidly. At first the French seemed to have an advantage. Their troops were much better trained than the disorganized British troops, and they had most of the Indians on their side. The Huron were seeking revenge against the British, who had pushed them off their land as the British colonies expanded. The war became known as the **French and Indian War** because the French and the Huron banded together against the British.

However, despite the help from the Huron, the French were badly outnumbered. There were a mere 60,000 French settlers to defend their vast land holdings. The British had over 2 million settlers, 2 new officers, and a new strategy. They surrounded New France, using a blockade to keep food and other supplies from entering the colony. Although many of the French forts began to fall to the British in 1758, the French in Quebec, the capital of New France, refused to surrender.

A DECISIVE BATTLE

One of the new British officers was General **James Wolfe**. He was determined to capture Quebec. On September 9, 1759, Wolfe's troops landed near the capital. Although the steep cliff walls of the city appeared to be impos-

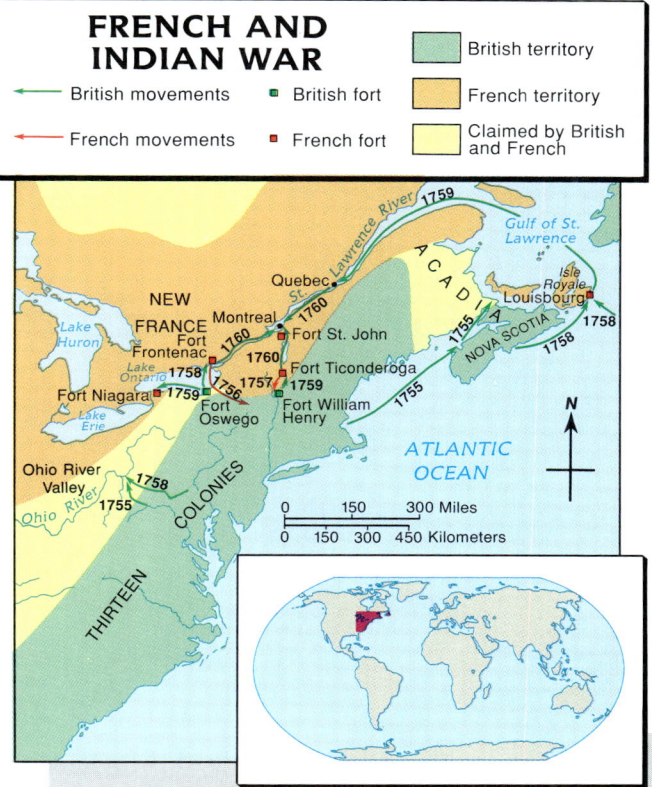

FRENCH AND INDIAN WAR

→ British movements
→ French movements
■ British fort
■ French fort
British territory
French territory
Claimed by British and French

MAP SKILL: During the **French and Indian War**, fighting broke out between the French and British. Where were the most forts located?

sible to climb, some of Wolfe's brave troops refused to give up. They studied the land carefully and found a dry streambed to climb. Quickly and quietly, they scaled the cliff's steep walls. Soon they were ready for battle.

Under General **Louis de Montcalm** (lwē' də mänt kä:m'), the French army advanced. Determined to hold on to Quebec, Montcalm declared:

I shall do everything to maintain a foothold in New France, or else die in its defense.

However, the French troops in Quebec were unprepared and disorganized. When the two armies were only 40 feet (12 m) apart, the British charged, firing shots. The French fled to the safety of

Although Montcalm (*left*) and his men fought with determination, Wolfe's forces won the decisive Battle of the Plains of Abraham at Quebec.

their fort. Both Wolfe and Montcalm died as a result of their wounds. This conflict became known as the Battle of the Plains of Abraham. Although the actual fighting lasted only ten minutes, this battle is considered the most decisive in Canadian history.

The British captured Montreal in the following year, 1760. By 1763 France had given up all of its claims to land in North America. Conflicts, however, remained. The French settlers did not want to give up their unique culture, nor did they want to be ruled by the British. In 1774 the British tried to deal with the concerns of the French settlers. They passed the Quebec Act, which guaranteed the French the right to maintain their own religion, language, and customs within Quebec.

THE ACADIANS

The French and Indian War had taken a sad toll on the lives of many people. Thousands of French-speaking people had been forced to leave Nova Scotia, then called Acadia. During the war Acadia had been captured by the British, who wanted the Acadians to swear an oath of loyalty to the British king. The Acadians, however, had refused to pledge their loyalty.

Without warning, in 1755 the British ordered the Acadians to leave their farms and then forced them onto ships. The ships took the Acadians to other British colonies. Some Acadians went to the area around present-day Louisiana, where many French people were already living.

THE AMERICAN REVOLUTION

In the 1770s a new group of people moved to Canada. As you know, the American Revolution in 1776 led to the independence of the United States. The Revolution also had a great effect on Canada. All during the war, many colonists had remained loyal to Britain. These people, known as Loyalists, had often been forced by the rebels to leave their homes. A great many of them had migrated to Canada during and after the American Revolution.

CANADA IN 1791

British colony

Hudson's Bay Company (Br.)

ARCTIC OCEAN

GREENLAND (DENMARK)

ALASKA (RUSSIA)

NORTHWEST TERRITORY

Hudson Bay

NEWFOUNDLAND

LOWER CANADA

ST. JOHN'S I. (P.E.I.)

CAPE BRETON I.

OREGON COUNTRY

NOVA SCOTIA

UPPER CANADA

NEW BRUNSWICK

PACIFIC OCEAN

UNITED STATES

ATLANTIC OCEAN

500 Miles

750 Kilometers

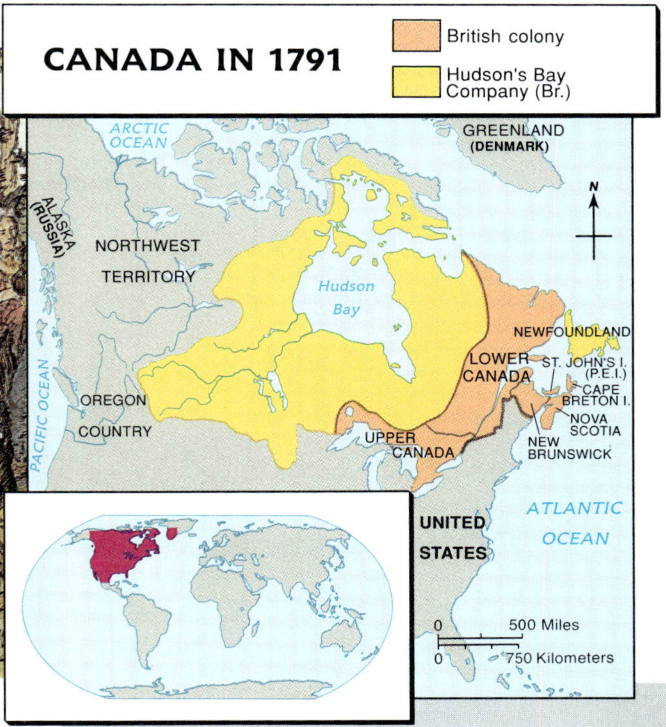

MAP SKILL: After the arrival of thousands of Loyalists, New France was divided into two colonies. What were they named?

The migration of Loyalists brought yet another culture to the land of Canada. Many Loyalists did not want to live among French-speaking Canadians. As a result, in 1791 Britain divided the former colony of New France into two colonies, **Lower Canada** and **Upper Canada**. Find these colonies on the map on this page. Most English-speaking settlers lived in the western part of Upper Canada, the colony that is present-day Ontario. Lower Canada, now Quebec, was home to many French-speaking settlers. The naming of these colonies marked the first official use of the name Canada.

ONE NATION

In the 1700s Britain gained control over the vast area of Canada. However, the British soon discovered that ruling this land would not be easy. The Indians would not willingly give up their claims to the land. The French were unhappy with the British rule. There was no single language, religion, or set of customs within Canada. How Canada would survive as one nation remained to be seen.

Check Your Reading

1. What were two causes of the French and Indian War?
2. On which side of the French and Indian War did the Huron fight? The Iroquois?
3. Which important battle was fought in Quebec?
4. THINKING SKILL: Imagine that it is the end of the American Revolution and that you are a Loyalist. Which questions would you ask about Canada before deciding whether or not to move there? Why?

127

IMPORTANT EVENTS

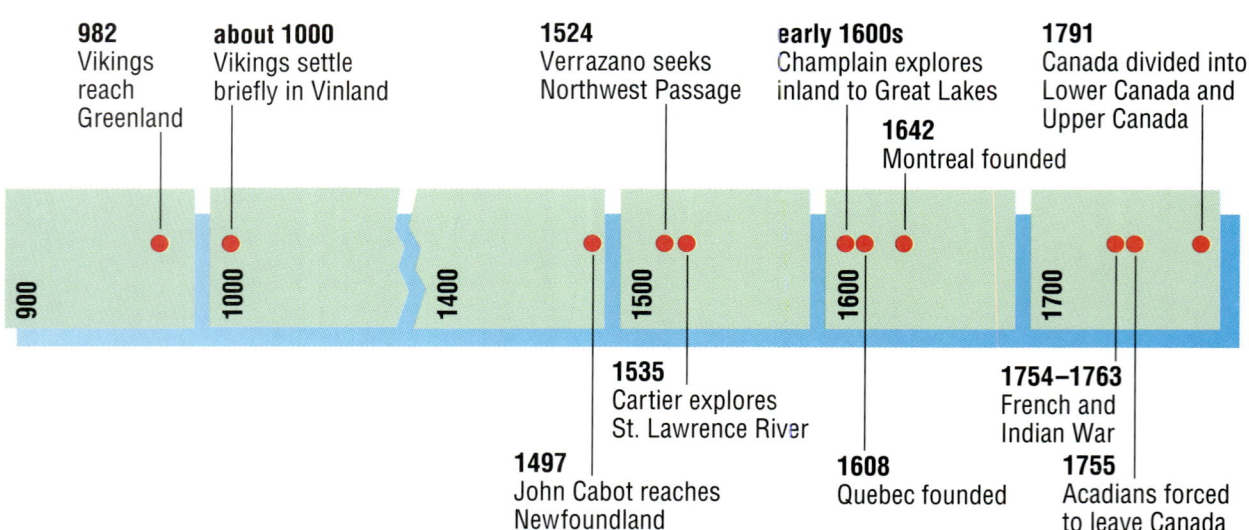

982
Vikings reach Greenland

about 1000
Vikings settle briefly in Vinland

1524
Verrazano seeks Northwest Passage

early 1600s
Champlain explores inland to Great Lakes

1642
Montreal founded

1791
Canada divided into Lower Canada and Upper Canada

1535
Cartier explores St. Lawrence River

1497
John Cabot reaches Newfoundland

1608
Quebec founded

1754–1763
French and Indian War

1755
Acadians forced to leave Canada

900 1000 1400 1500 1600 1700

PEOPLE TO KNOW

John Cabot 1450?–1498

Eric the Red 950?–1000?

Jacques Cartier 1491–1557

Leif Ericson died 1020?

Giovanni da Verrazano 1485?–1528

Louis de Montcalm 1712–1759

Samuel de Champlain 1567–1635

IDEAS TO REMEMBER

- Europeans first came to Canada as explorers, searching for the Northwest Passage.
- British and French fishers, fur traders, and missionaries populated the early settlements of Newfoundland, Quebec, and Montreal.
- Canada came under British rule after the French and Indian War, and by 1763 France had given up all its claim to land in North America.

REVIEWING VOCABULARY

colony	missionary
coureur de bois	portage
French and Indian War	Quebec Act
Hudson's Bay Company	saga
Loyalists	voyageur

Number a sheet of paper from 1 to 10. Beside each number write the word or term from the list above that best completes the sentence.

1. Voyageurs carried pelts and canoes from one river to the next over a _____.
2. A _____ is a tale that the Vikings brought with them from Iceland.
3. The _____ left the United States during the American Revolution and moved to Canada.
4. In 1791 the former _____ of New France was divided into Lower Canada and Upper Canada.
5. The _____ transported furs from the woods to trading posts.
6. The _____ guaranteed the French in Canada the right to maintain their own language, customs, and religion.
7. The British formed the _____ to establish trading posts in Canada.
8. The _____ hoped to convert Indians to his religion.
9. The _____ broke out in 1754 in the Ohio River Valley.
10. A _____ was a French fur trapper.

REVIEWING FACTS

Number a sheet of paper from 1 to 5. Beside each number write **T** if the statement is true. If it is false, rewrite the sentence to make it true.

1. The Vikings traveled to Canada just a few years before Columbus reached America.
2. The Northwest Passage was a hoped-for water route through North America to Asia.
3. The most important economic activity in New France was farming.
4. Samuel de Champlain is known as the "Father of Canada."
5. When they first arrived, the explorers called the land Canada because of the Huron word *kanata*.

WRITING ABOUT MAIN IDEAS

1. **Writing a Paragraph:** Why did the French and Indian War take place? What were some of its results? Write a paragraph describing at least one cause and one result of the French and Indian War.
2. **Writing About Perspectives:** Fur trapping continues today. Some people oppose fur trapping. Write a paragraph in which you tell who might oppose fur trapping, and why.

BUILDING SKILLS: READING TIME LINES

Study the time line on page 128 and answer the questions below.

1. What is a time line?
2. Who came to Canada first—Verrazano or Champlain?
3. Where on the time line would you add the Quebec Act of 1774?
4. Why are time lines useful?

CHAPTER 6

BUILDING A NATION

FOCUS

As I see Canada, it is a house with many rooms under a single roof that sometimes leaks. . . . They are rooms full of history, inhabited by people of many origins and traditions.

The Canadian writer, George Woodcock, used this comparison to describe Canada's history. The "rooms" he mentions are Canada's different regions. As you read this chapter, think about how Canada's "single roof" has provided shelter for all Canadians.

1 A Divided Canada

READ TO LEARN

Key Vocabulary

province
immigrant
War of 1812

Key Places

New Brunswick

Read Aloud

While I was there the Governor gave a ball—the room held two country dances. Nine tenths of the company in the one dance was French—in the other English.

Thomas Selkirk, who had traveled from England to visit Nova Scotia, wrote the above entry in his diary in 1804. In this lesson you will read more about how the different groups of Canadians lived together in the early days of British rule.

Read for Purpose

1. **WHAT YOU KNOW:** Which different groups of people were living in Canada by the end of the 1700s?
2. **WHAT YOU WILL LEARN:** What were some of the problems faced by the various groups of Canadians living in the early 1800s?

LIVING TOGETHER

Overlooking the St. Lawrence River in Quebec City is a very unusual monument. Carved into the stone is the name of General James Wolfe, who led the British to victory over the French in 1759. What makes the monument so unusual is the name engraved on the other side—Louis de Montcalm. As you read in Chapter 5, these two generals died fighting against each other. Despite this fact the French and the British Canadians built the monument together in 1823 as a tribute to their shared history.

That history was not free of problems. Although the first 75 years following the French and Indian War were mostly peaceful, Canada was not yet one single nation. It was a group of **provinces**, each ruled separately by the British government. At that time a province was any land under British rule that was not actually a part of Great Britain. In these provinces lived many different groups of people. It was not yet known how these different people would manage to live together and how they would be governed.

THE FRENCH IN CANADA

After 1763 most of the French nobility and other wealthy French settlers returned to France. The Acadians, as you read in Chapter 5, had been driven from their homes in Nova Scotia by the British troops during the war. Only around 60,000 French-speaking people remained in Canada, and they were mostly poor farmers.

Although their population was smaller, the remaining French settlers survived remarkably well at first. The Quebec Act of 1774 gave them confidence that their rights would be protected. As you have read, this act gave them the right to continue speaking French, to practice Roman Catholicism, and to preserve their customs. At that time, it was rare for a group of people to be granted such freedoms when they were ruled by a government other than their own.

LIFE IN QUEBEC

Most of the French settlers were poor. However, many enjoyed a peaceful, comfortable way of life. A favorite pastime on winter evenings was for farming families to gather at someone's home. From 7 to 11 o'clock they would feast. Then the storyteller would light his pipe, and the fiddler would begin to play on his homemade fiddle. Their stories and songs told of Canada's challenges—its wild animals and fierce winters.

Yet it was becoming harder for the French colonists to maintain their way of life. More and more English-speaking immigrants were moving to Canada and settling in French-speaking areas. An immigrant is someone who moves to a new country. The French were afraid that their culture and rights would soon be lost.

LOYALISTS IN CANADA

The American Revolution brought a great wave of Loyalist immigrants to

Immigrants, like those shown below, packed up their belongings and headed for Canada.

Canada. As you read in Chapter 5, it was their arrival that led to the division of Canada into Upper and Lower Canada in 1791. Nova Scotia was also flooded with Loyalist immigrants. Western Nova Scotia became the separate province of New Brunswick.

Most Loyalists had been more recent immigrants to the 13 English colonies that became the United States. Their ties to Great Britain were still very strong. They were pleased with British rule and with their way of life, and had not supported the American Revolution. Not all of the Loyalists were British. Many Native Americans, French, German, and Dutch people also moved to Canada because they preferred to remain under British rule. They were afraid that the United States would ignore their needs while forming a new government.

Some of the Loyalists were people of African descent who were seeking freedom from slavery. For example, in Nova Scotia there were about 4,000 Loyalists of African descent by the end of the American Revolution.

Great Britain wanted to increase Canada's population, especially with English-speaking settlers who were loyal to the British flag. The Loyalists were promised free land, horses, and food in Canada. However, the Loyalists of African descent were given the worst land. Birchtown, a black community near Nova Scotia, was described in 1790 as:

. . . beyond description, wretched, situated in the middle of barren rocks . . . their huts [were] miserable to guard against . . . a Nova Scotia winter.

Despite the hardships, many stayed in Canada, preferring their poor "miserable" huts to slavery.

Canadian Indians tried to maintain their way of life despite the growing numbers of European settlers.

THE INDIANS IN CANADA

Some of the Loyalists who moved to Canada were Mohawk Indians. The British government ordered the officials in Canada to allow these Indians to choose good land. However, other Canadian Indians did not want the Mohawk to settle in their territory and to hunt on their land.

Some Mohawk settled near Lake Ontario and Lake Erie. One group of Mohawk was given land that was bought from another Indian group. The amount of land was described in the grant as starting at the lake front and stretching "as far back as a man can travel in a day."

The Indian groups in Canada often fought over land because good farmland was rare. The European settlers, who were mostly farmers, often forced the Indians off their land. Because the Indians were divided, they were not successful in fighting back. The Indians grew to dislike most of the European settlers, although they still traded peacefully with the French.

In the **War of 1812**, French, British, and Indian Canadians fought together against the United States.

THE BRITISH IN CANADA

The British settlers formed the majority in Canada. Because many of them had grown wealthy trading with Great Britain, they were the most successful colonists in Canada.

However, like all Canadians, they were being governed by faraway rulers. They felt that decisions about their lives were being made by people who did not understand their needs.

THE WAR OF 1812

In 1812 one event brought all of the different Canadians together. War broke out between Great Britain and the United States. During the **War of 1812**, United States forces tried to conquer Canada. The United States hoped that some of the Canadians who were unhappy with British rule would support the United States troops. However, Canadians fought with British troops against the United States. For the first time all Canadians—including French, British, and Indian—united to defend their country.

The Canadians were successful. The United States agreed to remove all of their troops and forts from the Canadian border and to keep no naval ships in the Great Lakes. Today the Canada-United States border is the longest unarmed national border in the world.

A LONG ROAD AHEAD

The sense of unity among the Canadian people, however, was not to last long. Canada was still a group of provinces filled with people who were unhappy with colonial rule. The road to an independent, unified nation remained long and difficult.

 Check Your Reading

1. Which French-speaking people remained in Canada after the French and Indian War?
2. What was life like in Nova Scotia for some black Loyalists?
3. What problems did the Indians face in Canada in the 1800s?
4. **THINKING SKILL:** Predict what might have happened if the British had not passed the Quebec Act of 1774. Give your reasons.

READ TO LEARN

Key Vocabulary

legislature   British North
rebellion   America Act
confederation   dominion

Key People

Louis Papineau   Earl of Durham
William Lyon
   Mackenzie

Read Aloud

The prize is a splendid one . . . a country larger than France or England; natural resources equal to our most boundless wishes—a government of equal laws. . . . Up then, Brave Canadians!

William Lyon Mackenzie wrote these words in his *Handbill for Rebellion* in 1837. In this lesson you will read about how he and other Canadians gained their "splendid prize"—an independent Canada.

Read for Purpose

1. **WHAT YOU KNOW:** How did the United States gain its independence from Great Britain?
2. **WHAT YOU WILL LEARN:** How did Canadians gain control of their own government?

EVOLUTION, NOT REVOLUTION

Both the United States and Canada were once British colonies. The United States won its independence after the dramatic battles of the American Revolution. Canada became an independent nation through evolution, not revolution. Independence came slowly over years of small changes, instead of after a single, major war.

GOVERNMENT IN THE PROVINCES

In the early 1800s the Canadian provinces were headed by a governor and a **legislature** (lej' is lā chər). A leg-islature is a group of people who have the power to create laws. The governor and the legislature were appointed by the British king, usually for life.

The people of each province elected an assembly to represent them. However, their elected representatives did not have much power. Any laws passed by the assemblies could be vetoed by either the governor or the legislature.

REBELLION IN LOWER CANADA

In Lower Canada the French-speaking people were facing hard times. While they were struggling to

135

get by, their legislature was being run by English-speaking businesspeople. The French Canadians felt that they were being led by a government that was not representing its citizens. Calling for "responsible government," some French Canadians decided to fight back. In 1837 **Louis Papineau** (lwē pä′ pē nō), a member of the Lower Canada Assembly, declared:

The descendants of the French have no equal rights with their masters of British origin.

Papineau and his followers wanted Lower Canada to become an independent country with a government similar to the government of the United States. They translated the United States Declaration of Independence into French. They also refused to buy British goods, as many people in the 13 colonies had once done.

In 1837 Papineau led a **rebellion**, or an armed uprising against the government. Several hundred rebels gathered in the streets of Montreal with weapons, demanding to take over the government. The British troops who tried to restore order were stoned by an angry French crowd. The British troops fired on the crowd, killing three people and wounding two others.

The next day a group of French Canadians gathered to demand their freedom. "The time has come to melt our spoons into bullets," said one of Papineau's followers. However, the British put down the rebellion. Papineau escaped to the United States.

REBELLION IN UPPER CANADA

At the same time as the French rebellion, unrest was also growing in Upper Canada. **William Lyon Mackenzie**, a newspaper editor, had for years criticized the "small group of men" who ruled the province. Mackenzie was a Scottish immigrant who had been elected to the Assembly of Upper Canada in 1828.

Mackenzie led the Assembly in demanding reforms, or changes. His calls for reform caused the governor to remove him from the Assembly. The people of Upper Canada elected Mackenzie five times, only to have the British government remove him from power each time. Mackenzie and his

Growing dissatisfaction with colonial rule in Canada sparked **rebellions** in 1837.

McCord Museum of Canadian History

136

*C*ANADIANS! Do you love freedom? I know you do. Do you hate oppression? Who dare deny it? Do you wish perpetual peace, and...a government bound to enforce the law to do to each other as you would be done by? Then buckle on your armour, and put down the villains who oppress and enslave our country....One short hour will deliver our country from the oppressor; and freedom in religion, peace and tranquility, equal laws and an improved country will be the prize....

Up then, brave Canadians! Get ready your rifles, and make short work of it....

William Lyon Mackenzie called on Canadians to rise against British rule in his *Handbill for Rebellion*. What did he promise that their reward would be?

followers soon came to believe that rebellion was the only solution to the province's problems.

As you read in the Read Aloud, Mackenzie published a pamphlet called the *Handbill for Rebellion*. In it he called for Canadians to band together to fight British rule. You can read more of his stirring words in the box above.

Mackenzie and a few hundred followers set out to capture Toronto in 1837. However, they were poorly organized, and that rebellion was also quickly put down. Like Papineau, Mackenzie escaped to the United States.

DURHAM'S REPORT

Both the rebellions of Upper Canada and Lower Canada were crushed. However, these efforts had an important effect. The British government was now worried that it might lose control over Canada. John Lambton, known as the Earl of Durham, was sent to Canada in 1838 to investigate the causes of the rebellions.

In 1838 Lord Durham spent five months in Canada. He traveled widely and listened to the French Canadians and the British Canadians. In 1839 he returned to Great Britain and wrote the *Report on the Affairs of British North America*. In it he noted:

I expected to find a conflict between government and people; I found two nations at war within the same state [country]. . . . The French Canadians cannot be punished . . . for having dreamt of preserving their culture for future generations.

Lord Durham's report reminded the British government that French Canadians placed a great value on their culture. He urged Great Britain to allow the provinces greater control over their own government. Durham's report called for a union of Upper Canada and Lower Canada.

Within a few years Great Britain had enacted most of Durham's suggestions. The provinces gained greater control of their governments, and Upper and Lower Canada were united to form the Province of Canada.

CANADA BECOMES A NATION

Only Upper Canada and Lower Canada formed this united government.

CANADA'S STEPS TO INDEPENDENCE

- 1774 Quebec Act passed

- 1791 Canada divided into Upper and Lower Canada

- 1812 War of 1812 unites Canadians

- 1837 Rebellions against British rule in Canada

- 1839 Durham's report to Great Britain

- 1864 Confederation of provinces formed

- 1867 The British North America Act passed

CHART SKILL: Canada's independence came through a series of small steps. Which event led to the union of Upper and Lower Canada?

Canada's other provinces at that time —Nova Scotia, Newfoundland, Prince Edward Island, and New Brunswick— remained separate. Lord Durham's report had suggested uniting all of the Canadian provinces. Great Britain ignored this suggestion, believing that a united Canada would have too much power. It would be safer to keep the provinces separate.

Many Canadians felt that Canada needed a strong central government in order to make important decisions. In October 1864, leaders from all the provinces met in Quebec City. Nova Scotia, New Brunswick, and the Province of Canada united to form a **confederation**. A confederation is a group of states or countries that join together for a common purpose. Although these leaders faced many dis-

agreements, they managed to work out a plan to form a union.

They sent their plan to the British Parliament, which passed the **British North America Act**. Canada was now basically independent. The provinces were united as "one **Dominion** under the name of Canada." A Dominion is a self-governing country under British rule. The act became law on July 1, 1867. Canadians today celebrate July 1 as Canada Day.

Most Canadians recognize this date as their country's birthday. As you can see on the chart on this page, independence came after many steps. However, the Dominion of Canada was still part of Great Britain. Many more years would pass before Canada became completely independent.

TOWARD SELF-GOVERNMENT

In the early 1800s Canadians grew unhappy with British rule. Rebellions were crushed, but these rebellions led to greater self-government. In 1867 the British North America Act was passed. Canada was still part of Great Britain, but Canadians had greater freedom to select their own leaders and make their own laws.

Check Your Reading

1. Who were Louis Papineau and William Lyon Mackenzie? Why were they important?

2. Why did the rebels want to reform the government?

3. What kind of government did Durham's report recommend?

4. **THINKING SKILL:** Compare and contrast the concepts of reform and rebellion. When do you think each one might be necessary?

HELPING NEW CANADIANS

Throughout its history, Canada has attracted people from all over the world. Even today, refugees arrive in Canada hoping to find a home, work, and freedom. A refugee is a person who has to leave his or her country for reasons of safety.

Today many of the refugees arrive in Canada hoping to find "Mama Nancy." They carry a slip of paper that has her name and phone number written on it. They've heard that she will help them make a new life in Canada—a life finally free of fear and danger.

"Mama Nancy" is Nancy Pocock, who lives in Toronto, in the province of Ontario. Nearly 80 years old, she has been helping new immigrants for the past 30 years.

Over the years Nancy has helped refugees from countries in Southeast Asia,

Central America, South America, Africa, and the Middle East. Some people had been jailed or threatened because of their political or religious beliefs. Others were escaping the horrors of war in their home countries. These refugees often risk their lives to reach freedom and safety in Canada.

Most refugees find life in Canada very different from life in the countries they left. Nancy explains her country and its ways to people from Vietnam, El Salvador, and Iran. She finds each family a home—often they live with her for a time—and arranges for them to have English lessons. She helps them to find jobs. She introduces them to Toronto, and points out where to buy foods that are familiar to them. She finds them furniture and warm clothing. She is their first friend and protector in their new country.

Many of the refugees come from warm climates, so the cold Canadian winters are a new experience for them. The children are often excited when they see snow for the first time. Nancy loves teaching them how to make snowballs and how to ice-skate. She treats them like her grandchildren. To many children, separated from their families, she is the only grandparent they will ever know.

Over the years, "Mama Nancy" has helped hundreds of refugees. She listens to their stories, helping them ease the nightmares of the past. She takes pleasure in knowing she has helped them find a better life in her country. As she says, "When you see that you can make a difference in peoples' lives, you just have to do it."

READ TO LEARN

Key Vocabulary

métis
Mountie
transcontinental
   railroad

Key People

Alexander
   Mackenzie
Louis Riel

Key Places

Northwest
   Territories
Red River
Manitoba

Oregon
   Country
British
   Columbia

Read Aloud

I would be quite willing to leave that whole land a wilderness for the next century, but I fear that if Englishmen do not go there, Yankees [people from the United States] *will.*

In the statement above, John Macdonald, Canada's first prime minister, explained why it was important for Canada to claim the lands to its west. He was one of the many Canadians who were eager to extend the country's western border as far as the Pacific Ocean.

Read for Purpose

1. WHAT YOU KNOW: Why did people in the United States want to settle the western parts of the country?
2. WHAT YOU WILL LEARN: How did the Dominion of Canada gain its western lands?

EXPLORING THE NORTHWEST TERRITORIES

By the early 1800s both Canada and the United States had begun to explore the vast lands of the North American West. The Canadians called their western lands the Northwest Territories. Canadians thought that these territories could be used to expand the fur trade. They also hoped to find the Northwest Passage.

The land immediately west of Canada was controlled by the Hudson's Bay Company, the British fur-trading company. To acquire land farther west, Canadians formed a new company, the North West Company, in 1784.

Alexander Mackenzie was one of the explorers who worked for this company. In 1789 Mackenzie decided to follow a river that flowed out of Great Slave Lake in the Northwest Territories. He thought it might lead to the Pacific Ocean. More than 1,100 miles (1,760 km) later, he found the river's outlet. It was the Arctic Ocean, not the Pacific. Mackenzie named this river the "River of Disappointment." Little did

140

Alexander Mackenzie (*left*) and exploration companies led expeditions over land and by rivers to reach the western coast of Canada.

he realize that he had found Canada's longest river, which is known today as the Mackenzie.

In 1793 Mackenzie set out on another expedition. This time he found what he was looking for—a route to the Pacific Ocean over the Rocky Mountains. Alexander Mackenzie was the first Canadian explorer to reach the western boundary of North America by land. The words that he carved into the rocks at the ocean's edge can still be seen there today.

Alex. Mackenzie, from Canada, by land, the 22nd of July 1793.

Other explorers of the west included Simon Fraser, whose journey in 1808 took him down a dangerous river that was later named after him. You can trace the routes taken by these explorers on the map on page 142.

RED RIVER

One of the earliest settlements in the Northwest Territories was established in 1811 by a group of Scottish settlers. Called Red River, it was located at the junction of the Red and Assiniboine (ə sin′ ə boin) rivers. By the 1860s the majority of Red River's 12,000 settlers were métis (mā′ tēs), or descendants of French voyageurs and Indian women. The métis lived mainly by farming and by hunting buffalo.

In 1869 the Canadian government bought the vast territories controlled by the Hudson's Bay Company, including Red River. This purchase worried the métis of Red River, because they thought of themselves as a country independent of Canada.

Trouble began when Prime Minister John MacDonald appointed a governor to take over the Red River settlement. The métis rebelled in 1869, led by Louis Riel (rē el′). Under his leadership, the métis captured Fort Garry, an important center of the Red River fur trade.

However, the rebellion, called the "Red River Rising," was easily put down. In 1870 the government of Canada created a new province called Manitoba, centered in the Red River Valley. During the next few years many English-speaking settlers moved there, driving the métis farther west. Riel led a second uprising in 1885.

BRITISH COLUMBIA

Like the United States frontier, the Canadian frontier moved steadily west.

In the early 1800s the area between California and Alaska was known as the Oregon Country. As you can see on the map below, the Oregon Country was claimed by both the United States and Great Britain. The United States and Great Britain met to try to agree on a boundary.

The United States wanted the boundary to be set near the 54th parallel, or line of latitude. Great Britain wanted it to be set along the 45th parallel. In 1846 the two countries reached a compromise. They agreed to divide Oregon, setting the boundary at the 49th parallel. In 1871 the land north of this boundary became the province of British Columbia.

MAP SKILL: Canada's movement west led to disagreement about borders with the United States. What compromise did the two countries reach?

EXPLORING WESTERN CANADA

→ Mackenzie
→ Fraser
■ British forts and trading posts

THE MOUNTIES

The Canadians who were settling the vast western territories feared the dangers that they might find there. As one traveler reported:

This region is without law. Robbery and murder for years have gone unpunished . . . and courts are unknown.

To make the western territories safer, Prime Minister John Macdonald created the Northwest Mounted Police in 1873. This force is now called the Royal Canadian Mounted Police or, more popularly, the Mounties.

One goal of the Mounties was to protect the Indians already living in the West. The Mounties worked hard to maintain peace between the Indians and the new settlers. Their efforts helped to prevent destructive wars between the Indians and the government, such as those that had taken place in the United States. A Blackfeet leader named Crowfoot said:

The Mounted Police have protected us as the feathers of the bird protect it from the frosts of winter.

"ALL ABOARD FOR THE PACIFIC!"

Even before they began to settle the western territories, many Canadians had dreamed of building a railroad to unite their wide country. However, building a transcontinental railroad, one that crossed the continent, was an expensive and difficult task. One challenge was laying track across the Rocky Mountains. You can see the final route on the map on page 143.

In 1881 work finally began on the transcontinental railroad that would run across Canada between the Atlantic and Pacific coasts. Among the workers who built the railroad were

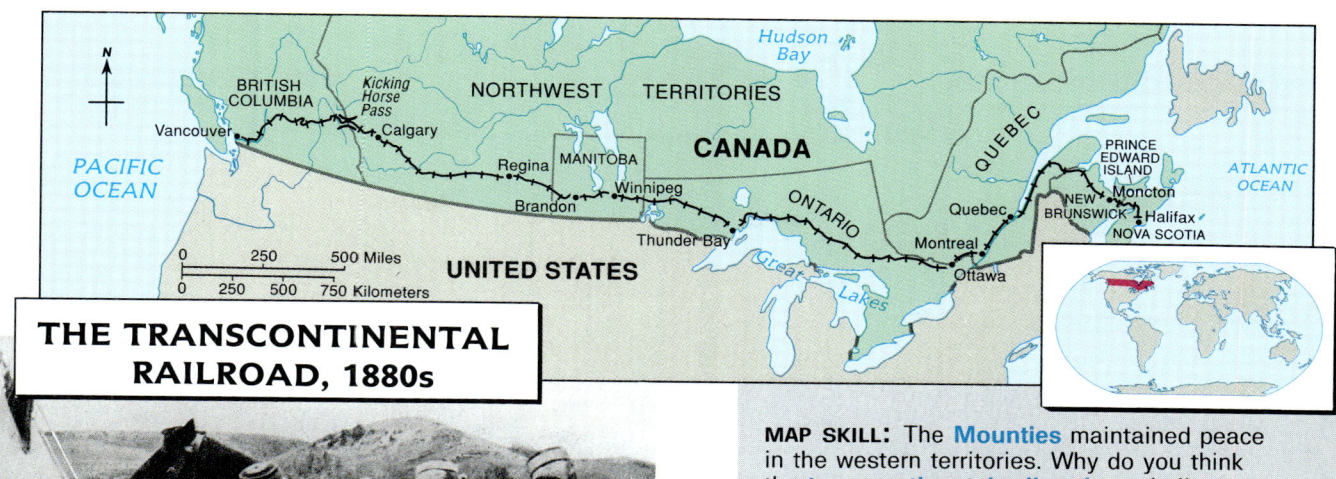

THE TRANSCONTINENTAL RAILROAD, 1880s

thousands of immigrants from China, Ireland, and other countries. The Chinese helped to lay track across the rugged western mountains. Working conditions were difficult and workers were treated unfairly. According to one writer, they worked for:

> . . . 1 dollar for a 12-hour day, and tolerated high-risk jobs blasting tunnels in solid rock and building 600 . . . bridges over gorges. . . . Unlike the prairies where track was laid at the speed a man could walk, progress in British Columbia was measured in inches.

When the transcontinental railroad was completed in 1885, many Canadians celebrated. However, the coming of the railroad resulted in the slaughter of millions of buffalo. The Indians of the plains had depended on the buffalo herds for survival. The Indians had no cause for celebration.

COAST TO COAST

As you have read, the 1800s were a time of great change in Canada. The country's boundaries were extended westward to the Pacific Ocean. However, the move west was not without conflict, and the Mounties were formed to bring law and order to the western territories. By the time the transcontinental railroad reached the Pacific Coast in 1885, two new provinces and one territory had joined the Dominion.

Check Your Reading

1. Why were Canadians exploring their western lands?
2. Who were the métis? Why did they feel threatened when the Canadian government bought their land from the Hudson's Bay Company?
3. About which land did the United States and Canada disagree?
4. **THINKING SKILL:** What effect did the westward movement have on the Indians of Canada?

Reading Historical Maps

Key Vocabulary

historical map

You have been using many maps in this textbook. Maps are important tools that allow you to understand things about places on the earth. Some maps show information about places today. For example, the map on page 73 shows Canada's climate.

Other maps show information about the past. For example, the map on page 142 shows where and in which years some explorers traveled in Canada. The map on page 82 shows which Indian groups lived in Canada about 1492. Other maps might show battles that took place in a war or the boundaries of a country in a certain year. Maps that show information about the past or where past events took place are called **historical maps**.

Historical maps are important tools in understanding history. In this chapter, you have read many interesting things about Canada's history. You can learn about how Canada changed during the 1800s by reading. But you can get an even clearer picture of those same changes by looking at historical maps.

Understanding the Map

The map on this page is a historical map. Read the title of the map. What does the map show? How does the title tell you that it is a historical map?

Now look at the map key. It shows that different colors are used to show how eastern Canada was organized in the 1790s. Which color is used to show the provinces?

EASTERN CANADA IN THE 1790s

Province   Territory

The labels on the map also help you to see how eastern Canada was organized in the 1790s. You can see that the two largest provinces were called Lower Canada and Upper Canada. This is because of the elevation of the land along the St. Lawrence River. The land around Lake Ontario, which was called Upper Canada, has a higher elevation than the land farther north, which was called Lower Canada.

Comparing Historical Maps

In the skills lesson on pages 70–71, you learned how to compare maps. You also learned that comparing maps can help you to make connections between pieces of information. Comparing maps can help you to see how things have changed or how one thing affects another. You can use your skill in comparing maps to compare historical maps, too.

EASTERN CANADA IN 1871

🟩 Province   🟪 Territory

0   200   400 Miles
0   200 400 600 Kilometers

Now look at both maps on these pages. What are two ways in which eastern Canada changed between the 1790s and 1871? In what way was Canada the same in both the 1790s and 1871?

Reviewing the Skill

1. What is a historical map?
2. How many provinces were there in eastern Canada in 1871?
3. In the 1790s old Quebec province was divided into two parts—Lower Canada and Upper Canada. Which of the two provinces was farther north?
4. York was the capital of Upper Canada in the 1790s. What was this city called in 1871?
5. What was the area known as the Northwest Territories in 1871 called in the 1790s?
6. Why is it useful to be able to read historical maps?

4 Entering the Twentieth Century

READ TO LEARN

Key Vocabulary

suffrage   bilingual
separatist

Key People

Nellie McClung

Key Places

Saskatchewan
Alberta

Read Aloud

Thought outruns the steam car, and hope outflies the telegraph. . . . I look to the future of my adopted country with hope. . . . I see one great nationality, bound . . . by the blue rim of Ocean.

Thomas D'Arcy McGee is known as one of the "Fathers of the Confederation." In 1860 he expressed this vision of Canada's future. In this lesson you will read about how McGee's hopes were fulfilled.

Read for Purpose

1. WHAT YOU KNOW: What are some of the changes that Canada experienced in the 1800s?
2. WHAT YOU WILL LEARN: Which events of the 1900s have helped to make Canada a strong, modern nation?

IMMIGRANTS HELP CANADA GROW

As you have read, Canada gradually gained greater independence during the 1800s. But even after the British North America Act of 1867, Great Britain still made many decisions for Canada. It wasn't until this century that Canadians really began to control their own government. In this lesson you will read about some changes that led Canada to become a strong nation.

One of the first important changes that took place in Canada in the twentieth century was an increase in its population. Prime Minister John Mac-Donald had developed a program to encourage immigration. He had a plan to settle people throughout the vast plains of western Canada. Hundreds of thousands of Europeans immigrated to Canada seeking political freedom and wealth. For many of the newcomers, the unsettled territory of western Canada offered great promise.

Most of the new immigrants were people from Europe, including Russians, Hungarians, Poles, Czechs, and Slovaks. Many of them were skilled farmers who were prepared to face the challenge of farming in a new land. These immigrants succeeded in making Canada more productive. They also brought new cultures to Canada.

In 1900 Canada had a population of 5.3 million people. By 1920 that number had increased to more than 8.5 million people. Many of the immigrants traveled across Canada to settle on the plains. In 1905 two new provinces were formed there. These provinces were **Saskatchewan** (sas kach′ ə won) and **Alberta**. You can find them on the map on this page.

GOLD IN THE KLONDIKE

Most of the new settlers moved west on the transcontinental railroad. In 1896, however, an event happened that led thousands of people to blaze a trail into a remote area. That event was the discovery of gold in the Klondike area of the Yukon Territory.

As word of the discovery spread, 80,000 people stampeded across the plains and mountains with hopes of striking it rich. The 600-mile (960-km) trail was dangerous, but the prospect of gold glistened in the distance. Almost overnight, the town of Dawson grew into a city of 25,000 people.

Life in the Yukon was wild and bustling for a few years. But the gold soon ran out, and all but a few thousand people left Dawson City. However, some of the disappointed gold miners went on to explore nearby areas for other minerals. They found lead, silver, zinc, copper, and coal. These minerals created more wealth for Canada. The population of the Yukon began to increase again.

WORLD WARS

Its new-found wealth helped Canada to face two major challenges—the world wars that involved many of the

CANADA: Provinces and Territories

MAP SKILL: Use the table on pages 110–111. In which part of Canada were the latest provinces formed? Why?

world's countries. In 1914 World War I broke out. Great Britain joined the war against Germany and other countries. Since Canada was still part of Great Britain, it, too, entered the war on the side of the British. The United States also fought on the same side.

Over 600,000 Canadians fought and 60,000 died. Canadian army divisions and their leaders won medals of distinction. Since no battles were fought on Canadian soil, the country's natural resources were safe. Canadians worked hard to produce food and war materials to send overseas to their troops.

Because of these contributions to World War I, Canada became known as a powerful nation. Great Britain, which now recognized Canada's strength, began to give the country greater rights of self-government. When World War II began in 1939, Canadians were able to make the decision to enter the war for themselves.

147

During World War II Canada again sent air, land, and naval forces abroad. This time over 1 million Canadians served and 40,000 died. By the end of World War II in 1945, Canada had one of the world's strongest military forces.

WOMEN WIN THE VOTE

World War I had another important and lasting effect. It helped Canadian women to win suffrage, or the right to vote. Women had been trying to win this right for many years. When thousands of Canadian men left their jobs during World War I to serve in the armed forces, women took their places.

Outspoken leaders such as Nellie McClung pointed out that women had worked as equals during the war. Now women demanded that they be consid-ered equal enough to vote. McClung made speeches and led protests and marches to gain suffrage for women. Finally, in 1918, Canadian women won the right to vote.

THE GROWTH OF INDUSTRY

Another effect of the wars was Canada's industrial development. In order to provide war materials to the troops overseas, factories and businesses ran constantly. Because goods such as clothes and shoes that Canada had imported from Europe in the past were not available during the wars, Canada began to produce more of its own goods. By the end of World War II, Canada was the world's fourth-largest industrial country.

The end of World War II brought more immigrants to Canada. Between 1945 and 1965, 1 million new immigrants came from Asia, Europe, Africa, and the Caribbean. These new arrivals filled many new positions in factories, mines, and offices.

THE SEPARATIST MOVEMENT

A political force that helped to shape modern Canada had its roots in the nation's early history. This force is the separatist movement. A separatist is a person who favors separating from a country or religious group.

As you have read, French Canadians have been determined to preserve their heritage in Canada since the 1700s. The present separatist movement began after World War II, when Quebec became known as the industrialized "New Quebec." You may recall that the majority of French Canadians live in the province of Quebec. They became increasingly concerned about their future when many large new industries

Nellie McClung helped women to win suffrage in Canada.

These **bilingual** traffic signs are just one example of the French influence in Canada.

were started in the province by British Canadians.

Since 1976 separatists have tried to convince other French-speaking Canadians that Quebec should separate from the rest of the country. The Canadian government did not want the country to be divided.

The government finally agreed to protect the French language and French customs in Quebec. As a result, in 1980 the citizens of Quebec voted to remain a province of Canada. However, as you will read in Chapter 7, many Quebec citizens continue to support the separatist movement.

THE CONSTITUTION OF 1982

In 1982 Canada drafted a new constitution. The new constitution declared that Canada was a **bilingual** country. A bilingual country is one in which two languages are officially recognized. In Canada the two official languages are English and French.

The new constitution had another very important feature. It gave Canada the right to amend, or change, its constitution without approval from Great Britain. Queen Elizabeth II signed the new constitution and Canada was no longer under British rule. With that act, Canada became truly independent.

A STRONG AND UNITED NATION

In the twentieth century Canada gained a new kind of independence. This was the strength it derived from being a strong nation respected by other countries throughout the world. Immigration from other countries, participation in two world wars, and the growth of industry have all shaped modern Canada. Finally, a new constitution made Canada a completely independent and bilingual nation.

Check Your Reading

1. What event in 1896 led thousands to journey to western Canada?
2. How did World War I affect the struggle of Canadian women for the right to vote?
3. What is the separatist movement?
4. **THINKING SKILL:** What are some of the questions that you could ask to help you determine whether or not Canada is a completely independent country?

IMPORTANT EVENTS

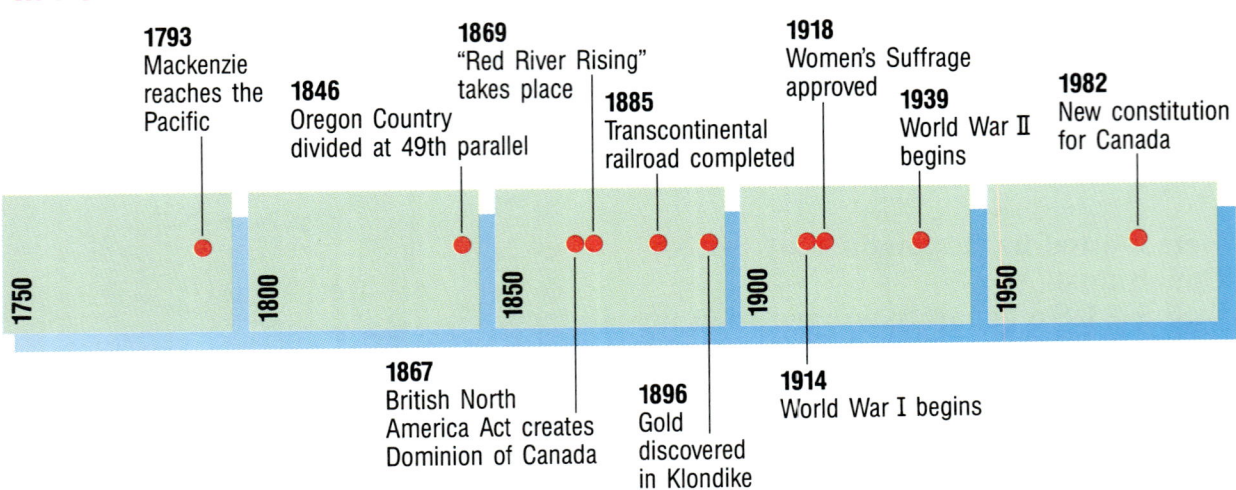

1793
Mackenzie reaches the Pacific

1846
Oregon Country divided at 49th parallel

1869
"Red River Rising" takes place

1885
Transcontinental railroad completed

1918
Women's Suffrage approved

1939
World War II begins

1982
New constitution for Canada

1750   1800   1850   1900   1950

1867
British North America Act creates Dominion of Canada

1896
Gold discovered in Klondike

1914
World War I begins

PEOPLE TO KNOW

Earl of Durham 1792–1840

Louis Papineau 1786–1871

Alexander Mackenzie 1764?–1820

Louis Riel 1844–1885

William Lyon Mackenzie 1795–1861

Nellie McClung 1873–1951

IDEAS TO REMEMBER

■ A critical issue facing Canada in the early years was how the French, British, and Indians could get along and share their country peacefully.

■ Following a period of tension and unrest, the provinces of Canada were united in 1867 to form the Dominion of Canada.

■ By 1885 Canada had pushed west to the Pacific and had added two new provinces and a territory.

■ Both immigration and industrialization helped Canada to grow and develop, and changes in its constitution brought greater recognition of the diverse ethnic makeup of its population.

REVIEWING VOCABULARY

bilingual   métis
confederation   Mountie
dominion   rebellion
immigrant   separatist
legislature   suffrage

Number a sheet of paper from 1 to 10. Beside each number write the word or term from the list above that best matches each statement.

1. The name given the descendants of French voyageurs and Indian women
2. A group of states or countries that join together for a common purpose
3. The right to vote
4. Someone who moves to a new country
5. A self-governing country under British rule
6. A lawmaking body
7. Having to do with two languages
8. A person who favors separation from a political or religious unit
9. A member of a force to maintain peace between the Indians and new settlers
10. An armed uprising carried out against the government

REVIEWING FACTS

1. Use these words in a sentence to explain how Britain governed its Canadian colonies: *province*, *governor*.
2. Between 1763 and 1840, why did Canada's population shift from mainly French to mainly British?
3. What did Louis Papineau and William Lyon Mackenzie try to accomplish?
4. Why was the Earl of Durham important to Canadian history?
5. What was the main result of the British North America Act of 1867?
6. Describe the events leading to the creation of Manitoba. Which events led to the creation of British Columbia?
7. Why was the Northwest Mounted Police formed?
8. Name two reasons that Canadians and immigrants traveled west in the late 1800s.
9. Who was Nellie McClung?
10. Name two provisions of the Constitution of 1982.

WRITING ABOUT MAIN IDEAS

1. **Writing a Comparing Paragraph:** Review the careers of Louis Joseph Papineau and Louis Riel. Write a paragraph comparing and contrasting their goals, actions, and results.
2. **Writing About Perspectives:** Imagine that you are either French Canadian or British Canadian at the time Lord Durham issued his *Report on the Affairs of British North America.* Write a journal entry expressing your reaction to the report. Explain why you feel the way you do.

BUILDING SKILLS: READING HISTORICAL MAPS

1. Identify three historical maps included in this chapter.
2. Study the map on page 142. What is the map about?
3. How is Mackenzie's route shown?
4. Name three forts shown on the map.
5. Why are historical maps useful?

CHAPTER 7

CANADA TODAY

FOCUS

Like so many really large countries, Canada has a diverse population. . . . Every year it seems like there are more and more beautiful faces from all around the world.

Rana Shaskin is proud to be a Canadian. She grew up in a little town called Lethbridge, in the province of Alberta. Her parents moved there in 1955 from Ukraine. In this chapter you will read about the many fascinating and "beautiful faces from all around the world" which make up Canada today.

READ TO LEARN

■ Key Vocabulary

mosaic	reserve
immigration	legacy
ethnic group	population density

■ Read Aloud

I'd like to learn some French, but first I'd learn Ukrainian and Cree, which are the largest other languages in my [area].

Deborah Grey, who said the above, is an English-speaking teacher in Edmonton, Alberta. Like many Canadians, she is proud of living in a country where different groups of people live close together in friendship. As you will read, Ukrainians and the Cree Indians are only a few of Canada's many different peoples.

■ Read for Purpose

1. **WHAT YOU KNOW:** What are some of the different groups of people that live in the United States?
2. **WHAT YOU WILL LEARN:** Which different groups of people live in Canada today?

A MOSAIC OF PEOPLES

Many people in Canada use the word **mosaic** (mō zā´ ik) to describe their country's mix of peoples. A mosaic is a colorful pattern or picture made up of many small pieces of stone or glass. Each piece in a mosaic is a separate color. When you stand back and look at the mosaic, you see that a wonderfully varied collection of beautiful pieces make up a whole picture.

Think about what you know of **immigration** in the United States. Immigration is the movement of people to another country in order to make a permanent home there. You will recall that immigration to the United States greatly increased in the late 1800s and early 1900s. Gradually, most of the immigrants became part of the culture of the United States.

Like the United States, Canada has welcomed many immigrant families to its shores over the centuries. These families have kept many of the beliefs and customs of their homelands. This has made Canadian society a combination of many separate cultures. Canadian journalist Andrew Malcolm

MAP SKILL: Study the map to find out how many provinces Canada has. How many territories does it have? What is the capital of the province of Alberta?

explained the difference between Canada's mosaic of peoples and the cultural blend that many believe is true of the United States.

> *The United States believes . . .*
> *in many influences coming together,*
> *each making its own contribution*
> *and each adding its own distinctive*
> *flavor to the larger whole. But*
> *Canadians believe . . . in a mosaic*
> *of separate pieces with each*
> *chunk becoming part of the whole*
> *physically, but retaining its own*
> *separate color and identity.*

MANY ETHNIC GROUPS

As Rana Shaskin mentioned in the Focus on page 152, Canada is a large country. A look at the political map of Canada on this page will show you how large Canada is. In fact, Canada is second in size only to Russia. Within this vast land are dozens of ethnic groups. An ethnic group is a group of people who usually have the same language, history, religion, and customs. The ethnic groups of Canada are the pieces of the Canadian mosaic. Each ethnic group has its own identity. However, together the pieces form a unique pattern.

Look at the chart on page 155. It shows that the British Canadians form

MAJOR ETHNIC GROUPS OF CANADA	
Ethnic Group	**Percentage of Population**
British	64.6%
French	23.2%
Mediterranean	1.7%
Asian	1.2%
African	.7%
German	.4%
Inuit and Indian	.4%
Ukrainian	.2%
Other	8.3%
Source: *Canada Year Book*	

CHART SKILL: Among Canada's **ethnic groups** are people of Polish, French, African, and Vietnamese descent. What percentage of the population is Asian?

the largest ethnic group in Canada. They make up about 65 percent of Canada's population of about 26 million people. What percentage of Canada's people are French Canadians?

In addition to millions of immigrants from Europe, Canada is home to thousands of immigrants from other continents. For example, Canada's Asian immigrants include people from Hong Kong, India, Pakistan, and China. Among the immigrants from Africa are people from Egypt, South Africa, and Tanzania.

CANADA'S INDIANS

As you know, the Indians were the first Canadians. Look again at the chart. It shows you that very few Indians live in Canada today. These descendants of the first Canadians are members of many different groups and live throughout Canada.

Most of the Indians live on **reserves**. A reserve is an area of land in Canada set aside for Indians. Such areas are called reservations in the United States. If you were to visit one of Canada's approximately 2,200 reserves, you would find that many Indians living there continue to follow traditional ways of life.

Sitting Lake is one of the Arapaho (ə rap′ ə hō) Indians who live on the Canadian Plains. He teaches the children on his reserve how to build tepees. Though today the Arapaho live in houses that were built by the Canadian government, Sitting Lake does not want the young people to forget how their ancestors lived.

In addition to the Arapaho, other Indian peoples work to preserve their traditional ways. Many of the Inuit, whom you read about in Chapter 4, hunt, fish, and follow other traditional customs. Many also speak an Inuit language. Today about 20,000 Inuit live in northern Canada.

LASTING LEGACIES

Most Canadians have European ancestors. Among the European groups that first settled in Canada, the French and the British both have left lasting legacies. A legacy is something that is handed down from earlier generations. You read about the French settlers in Chapters 5 and 6. Today their legacy can be seen most clearly in Quebec. Quebec is the largest and one of the oldest provinces in Canada.

The influence of French culture can be seen throughout Quebec province. In many cities and towns the buildings are French in style, and the street signs are written in French. About 85 percent of the people of Quebec speak French. Most French Canadians are Roman Catholics, as their ancestors were. Moreover, the French in Quebec think of themselves as a distinct society, or one that is different from any other. Alessandra Stanley, a journalist, wrote that the French Canadians "have their own national holidays, their own music videos, their own literature."

The British Canadians also have inherited a rich legacy. First of all, they speak English, the language spoken by most Canadians. British Canadian writers often describe the lives of the English-speaking Canadians. An example from *Mine for Keeps* by Jean Little is in the Traditions lesson on pages 158–161. Secondly, most British Canadians are Protestants. Canada's government is part of the British Canadian legacy, too. The government of Canada is like that of Great Britain.

LIVING NEAR THE BORDER

You read in Chapter 2 that Canada is part of the Anglo-America culture region. That means that if you were to visit most places in Canada, you would be able to speak English with the people who live there. You would also see ways of life that are like those in the United States.

The two countries share some traditions because they were both British colonies. Many Canadians also live close to the United States. Look at the map on page 157. It shows population density in Canada. Population density is the number of people who live within a square mile (or square kilometer) in a given area. The map shows that most of Canada's heavily populated areas are in southern Canada.

This teahouse on James Bay follows the British custom of serving tea with cake and sandwiches. The knitted cover on the teapot keeps the tea warm.

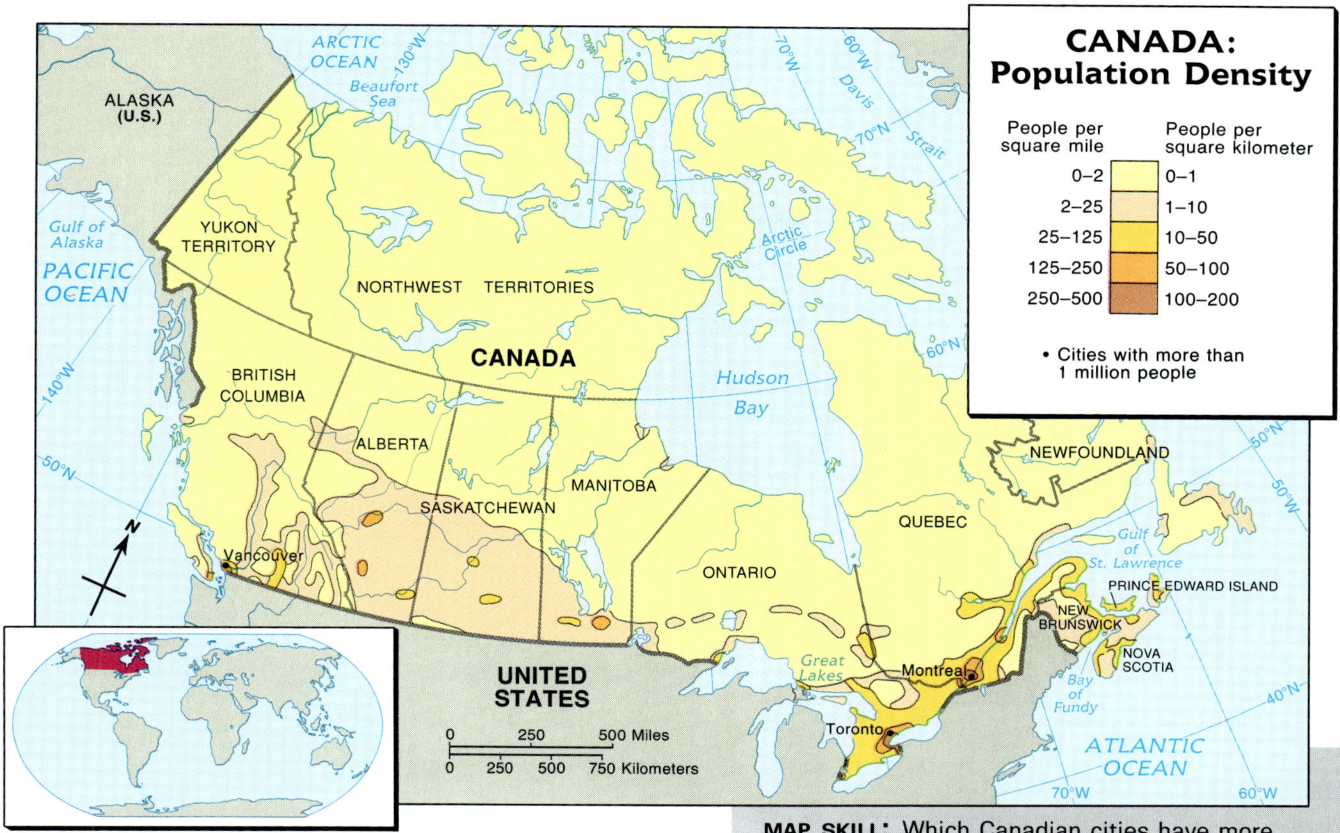

CANADA: Population Density

People per square mile	People per square kilometer
0–2	0–1
2–25	1–10
25–125	10–50
125–250	50–100
250–500	100–200

• Cities with more than 1 million people

ALASKA (U.S.)

ARCTIC OCEAN

Beaufort Sea

Gulf of Alaska

PACIFIC OCEAN

YUKON TERRITORY

NORTHWEST TERRITORIES

CANADA

BRITISH COLUMBIA

ALBERTA

SASKATCHEWAN

MANITOBA

Vancouver

ONTARIO

Hudson Bay

Arctic Circle

NEWFOUNDLAND

QUEBEC

Gulf of St. Lawrence

PRINCE EDWARD ISLAND

NEW BRUNSWICK

NOVA SCOTIA

Great Lakes

Montreal

Bay of Fundy

Toronto

ATLANTIC OCEAN

Davis Strait

UNITED STATES

0   250   500 Miles
0   250   500   750 Kilometers

MAP SKILL: Which Canadian cities have more than 1 million people? Which part of Canada has the lowest population density?

This is one of the warmest parts of Canada. About 85 percent of the country's population lives within 200 miles (320 km) of Canada's border with the United States.

Their closeness to the southern border means that many Canadians watch United States television and read United States newspapers and magazines. Some Canadians worry about this United States influence. Canadian professor Harry Hiller explains that "it is important that Canadians should see themselves and others through their own eyes" rather than through those of people in a different society.

A LAND OF MANY PEOPLES

You have read that Canada's mosaic of peoples includes many Asian, African, Indian, and European ethnic groups. The two largest groups, the British Canadians and the French Canadians, have given important legacies to the country. Their legacies include the English and French languages and the government of Canada.

Check Your Reading

1. What is an ethnic group?
2. Which are the two largest ethnic groups in Canada?
3. **GEOGRAPHY SKILL:** Look at the map on this page. Between which latitudes do most Canadians live?
4. **THINKING SKILL:** What are three questions that you could ask to find out which ethnic group has the greatest effect on the way of life in a Canadian city?

157

Excerpt from

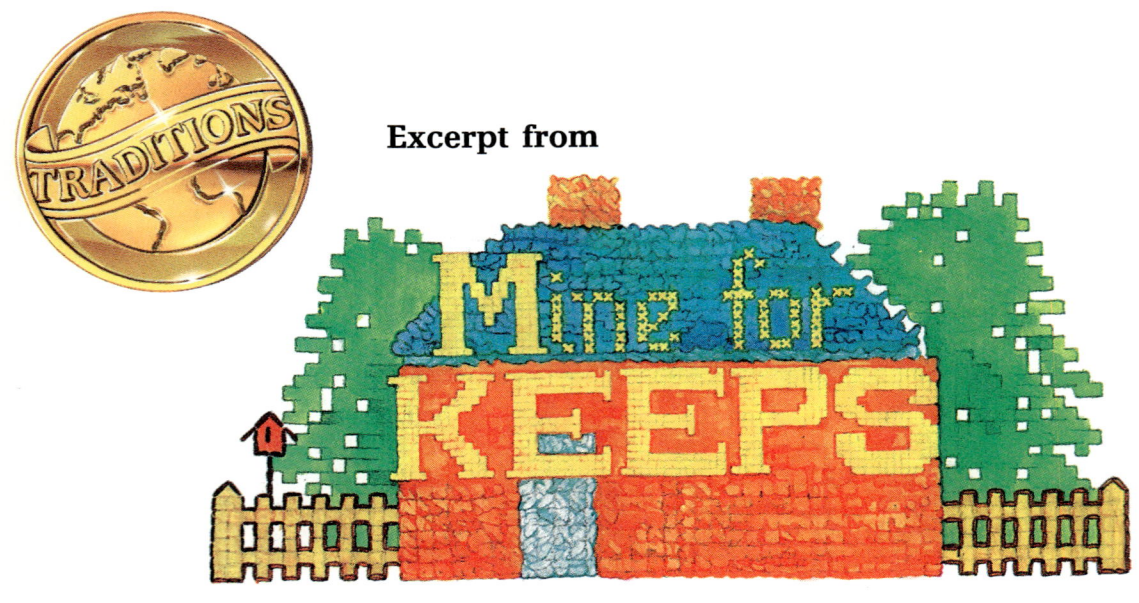

Mine for KEEPS

by Jean Little

*You have just read about the mosaic of different groups
that makes up the people of Canada. How do people learn
about the culture and life of groups other than their own?
One important way is by reading literature, such as
biographies, novels, or stories. In this lesson you will read
an excerpt from a story entitled "Mine for Keeps." It
describes the life of an English-speaking Canadian girl who
has cerebral palsy—an illness that causes people to lose
control over their muscles. As you read, think about how the
tradition of literature can help you to learn about lives that
are very different from your own.*

SAL COPELAND was scared.

When she watched the cottony clouds brush under the
wing of the plane or caught a glimpse of the earth far
below, she forgot and felt all right for a moment. Then she
would remember.

"I am going home to stay," she would say to herself—and
the queer cold feeling would come back.

She had been living at the Allendale School for Handicapped Children for over five years. During those years she
had often gone home. There had been two holidays every
year, one at Christmas and one in the summer. Sal had always spent these with her family. But this time, going home
was different. This time, nobody would be taking her back

158

to school in three weeks. Right now—this very minute—Dad was bringing her home for good! The closer she got, the queerer she felt.

Sal could not understand it. Almost ever since she could remember, she had longed, more than anything, to live at home. Whenever she had seen a first star through a window at school, she had rhymed off "Star light, star bright . . ." as fast as she could—and every time, her wish was the same, Let me live at home. It had been her wish before blowing out her birthday candles for as far back as she could remember, and it was the last bit in her prayers every night.

So what could be wrong? Her wish was coming true. Dad was beside her. They were on an airplane, on their way at last. Sal glared at the seat in front of her as though her mixed-up feeling were all its fault.

"Are you crazy?" she asked herself fiercely. "You couldn't be scared of HOME!"

She twisted around to look at her father, but he was no help. He had fallen asleep. Leaning back in the seat, with his eyes closed, he seemed almost like a stranger. Sal shivered. Then with a sigh of relief, she thought of the picture Mother had sent to her.

She burrowed into her coat pocket and dug out her wallet at once. She had looked at the snapshot so often that, once she got the wallet unfastened, it flipped open to the right place immediately. There they were—her family—Mother, Dad, Melinda, Kent and Meg. . . .

Slowly she started to put the wallet away, but just before it closed, she caught sight of the card on which she had printed her name and her home address when this wallet had been new:

Name: SARAH JANE COPELAND
Address: 43 VICTORIA STREET,
RIVERSIDE, ONTARIO, CANADA

As she saw it, Sal's stomach lurched. She was scared, after all. It was no use scolding herself. She even began to see what was making her feel so strange and cold inside. It was all very well to wish and wish and wish to go home to live, when you were sure you really wouldn't have to do it. But once such a wish came true, it meant leaving the life you were used to and beginning a new one full of unfamiliar places and people.

Even home itself would be strange. A month ago, the Copelands had left that old two-storied brick house on Victoria Street and moved to a new house she had never even seen. They had moved for her sake. Their new house was close to the Riverside Treatment Center for Children with Motor Handicaps, where she would be going for her therapy, or treatments which helped her walk easier. But it wouldn't seem like home sleeping there tonight. Without everyone running around and getting in each other's way, it wouldn't seem like home at all!

Why, she was remembering school, not the other house! Even though she had admitted to herself that she was afraid home would be different, she had not seen till now how much school had grown to seem like a home to her.

It wasn't just the girls either. Room 9 itself had become more Sally's home than the place where she spent her holidays. She knew exactly how it looked early in the morning when the other three girls were asleep and everything was still. What with 60 children and nearly as many people on the staff, school was only quiet when almost everyone was asleep. . . .

The thought of getting ready for bed in a strange house, the thought of facing days without a bell to tell her when to do things, the thought of not having the other girls around, suddenly piled up into what looked like a mountain of troubles to Sally. Not one of those girls had been the special friend she had always longed to have, but just the same she would miss them terribly. . . .

They were the last ones to leave the plane. The stewardess took Sal's crutches while Dad reached in and got Sally

herself. . . . It seemed a long way to the car, but Dad strolled along as though he did not notice that Sal was slowing him down; and when she tried to go faster, he put his hand on her shoulder and said teasingly, "What's the rush? Don't you like taking a walk with a good-looking man?"

For the first 20 miles [32 km], she sat upright beside him watching the ribbon of road unrolling ahead of them. She thought of school, but switched her thoughts away when she realized that there, everybody would be in bed by now and her bed was standing empty. Once more, she tried to imagine the new house, but it was no use. She still kept seeing the old brick house she had always known.

Finally she drifted off to sleep, her head lolling over onto Dad's shoulder. She stayed that way until the car stopped, wakening her. Before she could get herself collected enough to remember where she was, the door beside her was flung open and her mother's arms closed about her in a long tight hug.

"Oh, Sal honey, I'm so happy you're home!" her mother's voice half-sang right into her ear.

Sal blinked, and then hugged Mother back hard, as though she planned to hold on to her forever.

"Me too," she said—and the queer feeling was gone.

How does the tradition of literature help us to learn about other people?

2 Living and Working

Key Vocabulary

export
hydroelectric power

developed economy
service industry

Key Places

Ontario
Toronto

Read Aloud

I grew up in Montreal. I think some of my happiest days and nights were spent on the Lachine (lə shēn') Canal. We had incredible fun in the winter when the canal was frozen over. We would play ice hockey or just skate until our parents came looking for us.

In the passage above, Martin Blais, a university professor in Montreal, explains that when he was a child, ice hockey was his favorite sport. "It still is," he is quick to add. In this lesson you will read about some of the ways in which the people of Canada work and play.

Read for Purpose

1. **WHAT YOU KNOW:** What are the most popular sports in the United States?
2. **WHAT YOU WILL LEARN:** What are some of the popular sports and important industries of Canada?

CANADA'S FAVORITE SPORT

If you were to visit Canada, you might find many things that remind you of home. For example, you might see students eating pizza, playing baseball, or ice-skating.

People in Canada and the United States also share an interest in a favorite Canadian sport, ice hockey. Ice hockey was invented by soldiers in Ontario in 1855. Today ice hockey teams from the United States and Canada compete in the same professional ice hockey league. Each year the team

that wins receives a prize named for a Canadian leader.

Nearly 100 years ago, Lord Stanley of Preston, Ontario, was the leader of Canada's government. Lord Stanley bought a silver cup to be given to the best ice hockey team of the year. The prize soon came to be known as the Stanley Cup.

In 1988 the Winter Olympic Games were held in Calgary, Alberta. There were many exciting sports to watch, and audiences cheered the athletes who came from many countries to compete. However, one of the most popular

events was ice hockey—the sport that Canada gave to the world.

USING RESOURCES

On your visit to Canada you might also see other things that are similar to things in the United States. In the late 1980s Michigan high school student Lynn Ezell visited Canada with her family. In the cities, Lynn saw subways that connected all parts of the cities and large shopping malls. She also noticed that "the buildings looked like many of those at home."

One of the reasons for this similarity is that the United States and Canada both have strong economies and enough natural resources to produce a great variety of goods. Among these goods are food crops such as wheat. Today Canada is second only to the United States in wheat **exports**. An export is any item that is sent to another country for sale or trade.

If you were to drive across the plains of Saskatchewan and Manitoba today, you might drive for hours without seeing any cities or towns. Stretching before you would be seemingly endless wheat fields. You might see huge machines planting seed or harvesting wheat. The plains are ideal for growing wheat because of their fertile soil and flat land. Also, the plains have very few trees on them.

FOREST PRODUCTS

If you were to drive north of the plains into the Canadian Shield, you would begin to see more trees. But according to Canadian writer Margaret Atwood, the trees gradually "become smaller, there are more pines, the air cools, the sky turns an icier blue."

The forests of the Canadian Shield and elsewhere in the country provide work for many Canadian loggers. Like wheat, forest products are among Canada's major exports. Trees are used to make lumber, paper, and paper products. Canada is the world's leading producer of newsprint, which is the inexpensive paper on which newspapers are printed.

163

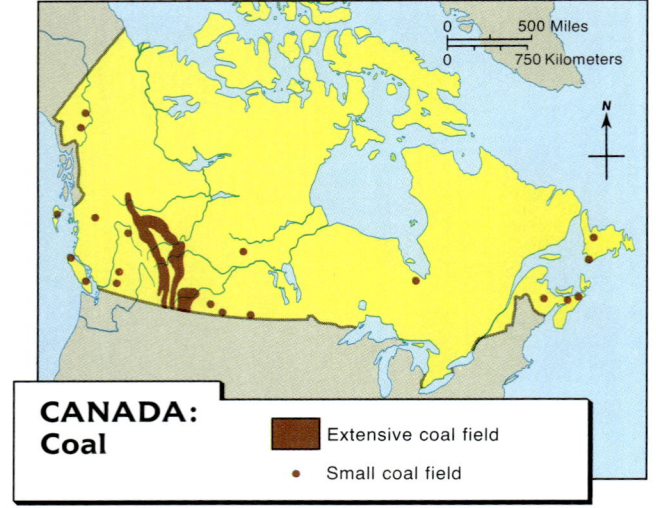

**CANADA:
Coal**

■ Extensive coal field
● Small coal field

**CANADA:
Lead, Zinc,
and Silver**

● Lead
△ Zinc
▲ Silver

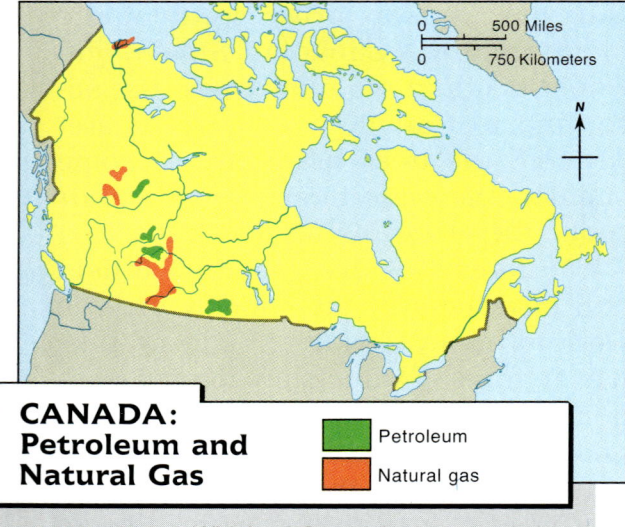

**CANADA:
Petroleum and
Natural Gas**

■ Petroleum
■ Natural gas

MAP SKILL: Which of Canada's resources are found near the Pacific Coast?

MINING

In addition to forests, Canada has zinc, lead, silver, oil, coal, and natural gas. These natural resources have helped to make Canada one of the world's largest exporters of minerals.

Look at the maps on this page to see where some of these minerals are found. Even on the Arctic Islands, miners obtain precious resources by drilling through the permafrost.

HYDROELECTRIC POWER

Water experts gaze at all that water flowing north in Canada with longing; it simply disappears untapped into the ocean. . . . Canadians have 20 percent of the world's fresh water, so . . . why not sell some of it?

As water expert James Baldessari noted, Canada has abundant water resources. By using energy from the country's many rivers and waterfalls, Canada has become an important producer of hydroelectric power. Hydroelectric power is electricity that is made by the force of rapidly moving water. Hydroelectricity supplies about 75 percent of Canada's electric power.

A DEVELOPED ECONOMY

People in Canada make a living in many different ways. You have read about Canada's farmers, loggers, and miners. Other Canadians work in factories, hospitals, or schools. Look at the circle graph on page 165 to see how Canadians make a living.

A country that has a wide range of jobs has a developed economy. A developed economy includes many different economic activities, methods of production, and advanced tools.

Many workers in a developed economy are in service industries. Perhaps

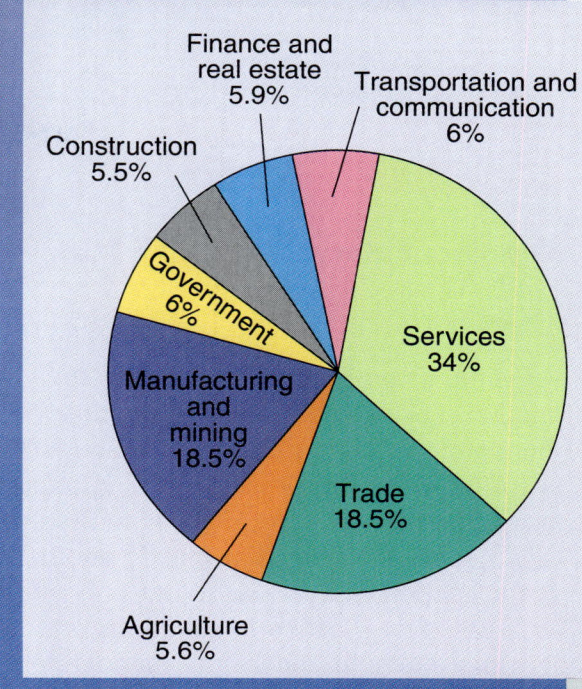

Finance and real estate 5.9%

Transportation and communication 6%

Construction 5.5%

Government 6%

Services 34%

Manufacturing and mining 18.5%

Trade 18.5%

Agriculture 5.6%

GRAPH SKILL: Loggers and wheat farmers are important to Canada's economy. In which three industries do most Canadians work?

the best way to describe workers in service industries is to say that they "serve people." For example, service workers teach, put out fires, and deliver mail. According to the graph on this page, what percentage of Canada's workers are in service industries?

MANUFACTURING

The graph also shows that many Canadians work in manufacturing. Most of these workers live in Ontario, where most of Canada's manufacturing takes place. In fact, the factories in Ontario produce as much as all the factories in the rest of Canada combined. Because of the great value of southern Ontario's automobile, iron, steel, food, and paper products, the area around Lake Ontario is called the "Golden Horseshoe." This horseshoe-shaped area is like a gold mine because of the great value of the goods produced there. Most of Ontario's factories are located around Toronto, which is Canada's largest city.

ECONOMIC GROWTH

You have read how Canada's people work and play. They invented ice hockey and enjoy many of the same sports as people in the United States. Canadians have created a developed economy. They use the country's natural resources to make products that are exported throughout the world.

Check Your Reading

1. What is a favorite Canadian sport?
2. What is a developed economy?
3. Why do so many Canadians work in the Golden Horseshoe?
4. **THINKING SKILL:** Where in Canada would you like to live? How did you arrive at this decision?

Understanding Cause and Effect

Key Vocabulary
cause
effect

Events often cause other events to happen. For example, an unexpected thunderstorm during rush hour may result in traffic jams. As a result of being stuck in traffic, many people arrive home later than usual. An event that makes another event happen is a **cause**. What happens as a result of a cause is called an **effect**.

In the example above, the thunderstorm is a cause and traffic jams are an effect. In turn, traffic jams are the cause of people being late. Many events or actions have several causes and produce several effects.

Finding cause-and-effect relationships helps you to solve everyday problems. This skill is also important in the study of geography and history. In this lesson you will learn how to identify cause-and-effect relationships.

Trying the Skill
Read the following paragraphs about the Interior Plains. You read in Chapter 3 that this region is broad and flat and stretches from the Arctic Ocean to the Great Plains in the United States. As you read, try to identify the cause-and-effect relationships being described.

Most of Canada's best farmlands are in the Interior Plains. Here the soil is rich and thick as a result of the movement of glaciers in the past. Because the fertile soil is ideal for growing wheat, this crop has become one of Canada's major exports.

However, since the discovery of coal, oil, and natural gas, the economy in this region has grown and changed. One consequence of the economic growth is that most workers in the Interior Plains no longer farm but work in service industries.

1. Which effects are described?
2. Which causes are described?
3. What did you do to identify the cause-and-effect connections?

HELPING YOURSELF

The steps on the left will help you to identify the causes and effects of an event or action. The examples on the right show how these steps can be used to identify the cause-and-effect connections described in the paragraphs about the Interior Plains.

One Way to Identify Cause and Effect	Example
1. Recall the definition of cause and effect.	A cause makes something else happen. What happens is called the effect.
2. Recall some words or phrases that are clues for causes and effects.	Language clues include: • words or phrases that signal causes, such as *because*, *since*, *as a result of* • words or phrases that signal effects, such as *therefore*, *consequently*, *as a result*
3. Examine each sentence to find these language clues.	Did you find *as a result of* and *because* in the first paragraph? Did you notice *since* and *one consequence of* in the second paragraph?
4. If you cannot find any word clues, arrange the events in the order in which they happened. Then try to find connections among them. Think: "What did one event have to do with another?"	The soil became fertile *after* glaciers moved through the region. Many workers were farmers *before* minerals were discovered in the Interior Plains. Economic growth came *after* the discovery of minerals.
5. State the causes and effects you find. An effect can have several causes. A cause can result in several effects.	Economic growth resulted from the discovery of oil, natural gas, and coal. People found different kinds of work as a result of the growing economy.

Applying the Skill

Now use what you have learned about cause and effect to help you understand the paragraph below.

Toronto's location was a natural reason for the city's role as a transportation center. Manufacturing industries were established in the Toronto area in part because of the availability of cheap and plentiful hydroelectric power. Increased industry led to population growth which, in turn, resulted in the need for additional goods and services.

1. Which came first?
    a. Toronto's population grew.
    b. Industries were established.
    c. Hydroelectric power was produced.
2. What were two results of the industrial development of Toronto?

Reviewing the Skill

1. What are some word clues that signal causes? What are some word clues that signal effects?
2. What is one way for you to identify cause-and-effect relationships in information you hear or read?
3. When might finding cause-and-effect connections help you to solve problems in everyday life?

3 Canada's Place in the World

READ TO LEARN

Key Vocabulary

democracy   Commonwealth of Nations   import
representative   tariff
federal system   free trade

Read Aloud

Canada is now an old country [when compared with other countries], older than most members of the United Nations, older even than great European countries like Germany and Italy.

Some people think of Canada as a young country struggling to define its place in the world. However, as Canadian historian George Woodcock reminds us above, Canada has existed for a long time. As you will read, some of the problems it faces today are old ones.

Read for Purpose

1. **WHAT YOU KNOW:** How can a country's people help to keep its society united?
2. **WHAT YOU WILL LEARN:** What challenges face Canada as it seeks to remain a strong and united society?

GRADUAL INDEPENDENCE

Canada is thought of as a young country because it was a British colony for hundreds of years. As you read in Chapter 6, Canada won its independence gradually. It gained almost complete independence from Great Britain in 1867. However, it did not become fully independent until 1982.

Canada inherited a rich legacy from Great Britain. For example, like the government of Great Britain, the government of Canada is a democracy. A democracy is a system of government that is ruled by the people. In almost all democratic countries, the people choose a small group of people, called representatives, to act for them in the government. The representatives in Canada make up a lawmaking body called Parliament (pär′ lə mənt).

In addition to being a democracy, Canada's government is organized as a federal system. This means that power is divided between the national government and provincial governments. Canada's national government is based in Ottawa, Ontario, the country's

168

capital city. As in the federal system of the United States, Canada's national government is in charge of matters that concern the entire country, such as foreign affairs. Provincial governments handle provincial matters, such as education.

COMMONWEALTH OF NATIONS

The Canadians still recognize the British monarch, or the king or queen of the United Kingdom of Great Britain and Northern Ireland, as the head of their country. However, the monarch has little power in Canada. When Canada gained full independence, it decided to remain a member of the Commonwealth of Nations. This organization includes the United Kingdom and a number of independent nations that were once its colonies. Most of the Commonwealth countries accept the British monarch as their head.

You may wonder why Canada decided to stay within the Commonwealth of Nations. As you have read, Canada has long had strong ties with the British. Canada has inherited many British customs and traditions. The British also help the members of the Commonwealth with financial aid,

advice, and military support when it is needed. People in the Commonwealth countries may also travel easily to other countries in the group.

Although Canada is a member of the Commonwealth, it has strong economic and friendship ties with other world powers. Among these countries are the United States, some Asian countries, and many Western European countries that are not in the Commonwealth of Nations.

TRADE WITH THE UNITED STATES

Canada and the United States have had friendly relations since the middle 1800s. The border between the two countries is the longest unguarded border in the world. During the past 40 years economic ties between the two countries have grown closer. For example, the two countries jointly control the St. Lawrence Seaway. Canada and the United States are each other's largest trading partner. The graph on page 170 shows how important this trade is.

The members of the British royal family represent the unity of the Commonwealth of Nations. Here Princess Margaret (center) makes an official visit to Canada.

169

Neither Canada nor the United States charges tariffs on trade with the other. Tariffs are fees that the government places on goods brought into the country. The trading of all goods without tariffs is called free trade.

Before 1988 there was little free trade between the United States and Canada. When it was suggested that the two countries start to trade freely, some Canadians rejected this idea. They pointed back to the 1970s, when there were no tariffs on cars brought from the United States. At that time Canadian automakers had a hard time competing with United States automakers.

Now many Canadians worried that without tariffs on imports from the United States, more goods from that country would enter Canada to compete with Canadian goods. An import is a good that is brought into a country for sale. United States business leaders pointed out that with free trade more Canadian goods would also enter the United States. One of these products is oil. Look at the graph on page 171. It shows that oil is an important product in both the United States and Canada. However, the United States imports much of Canada's oil.

Many Canadians favored free trade. For example, the Canadian business leader Valentine O'Donovan said that free trade would create new jobs for Canadians.

Looking to the future of Canada, where are the jobs going to be created? There's a limit to the number of jobs we can create by digging iron and gold out of the ground. They'll have to come from industries that rely on [new methods and inventions], and companies like that can only prosper if they can compete on equal terms in a worldwide market, especially in the United States.

After many years of public debate, Canada and the United States signed a

GRAPH SKILL: Canada exports many goods to the United States. What was the value of Canada's exports to the United States in 1986? Of imports from the United States?

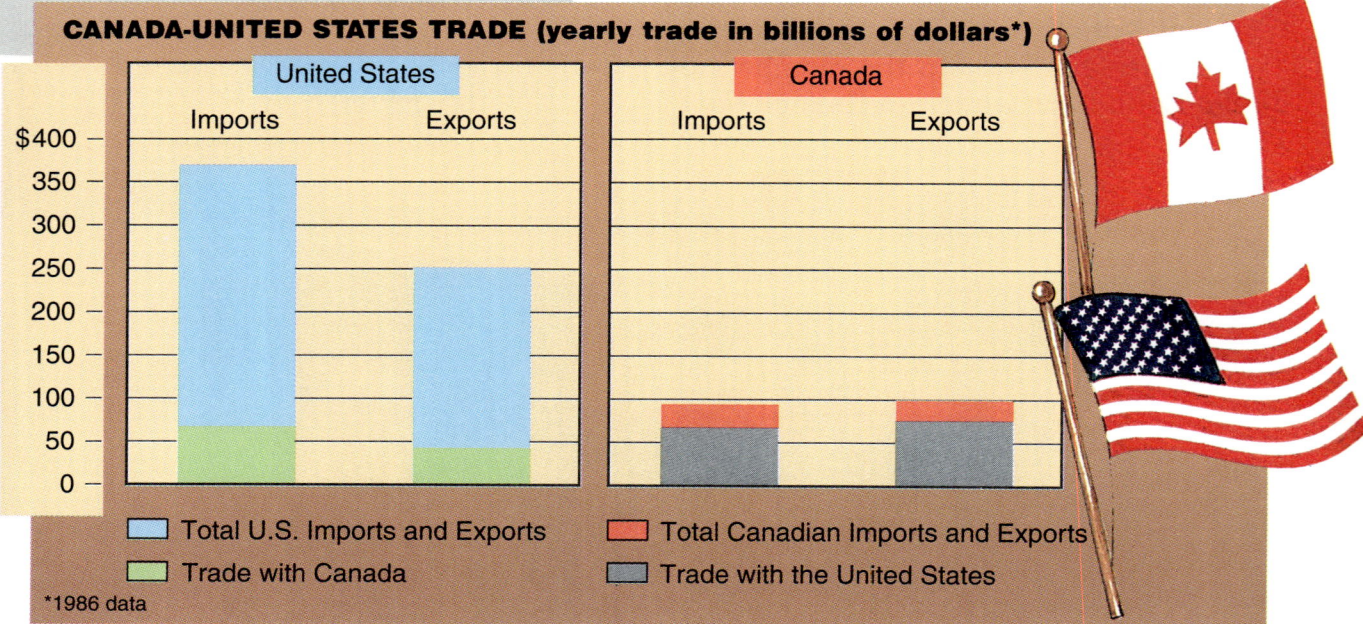

CANADA-UNITED STATES TRADE (yearly trade in billions of dollars*)

United States — Imports, Exports

Canada — Imports, Exports

$400
350
300
250
200
150
100
50
0

☐ Total U.S. Imports and Exports
☐ Trade with Canada
☐ Total Canadian Imports and Exports
☐ Trade with the United States

*1986 data

GRAPH SKILL: The United States produces five times the amount of oil a year that Canada does. How much does Canada produce?

WORLD'S LARGEST OIL PRODUCERS
(yearly production in millions of barrels*)

Country		Production
Venezuela	▤	.57 million
Canada	▤	.58 million
Iran	▤	.66 million
United Kingdom	▤	.92 million
Mexico	▤	.95 million
Iraq	▤	.97 million
China	▤	.98 million
Saudi Arabia	▤ ▤	1.5 million
United States	▤ ▤ ▤	3.0 million
Soviet Union	▤ ▤ ▤ ▤ ▤	4.5 million

▤ equals 1 million barrels   *1988 data

free-trade agreement in 1988. One successful Canadian business owner later said that he thought that "free trade has yielded benefits for both sides. This way we can be more efficient and sell to the rest of the world."

SEPARATISM

As Canada's major trading partner, the United States worries about anything that might weaken the Canadian economy. One of the leading causes of worry is the issue of Quebec separatism, or forming a separate country, which you read about in Chapter 6.

You have read that Canada's provinces have power over their provincial affairs. French Canadians, though, want even more control in the province of Quebec. Many people in Quebec want to form a separate country. You will read more about the debate over separatism in the Point/Counterpoint on pages 174–175.

As you have read, the British Canadians and French Canadians are the two largest ethnic groups in Canada. The French Canadians have long worked hard to preserve their way of life. The national government has helped by ruling that Canada is a bilingual country, or one that has two official languages. Government documents, for example, are written in

O CANADA

Music by C. Lavalée · Words by A. Routhier · Translated by R. Weir

O Ca - na - da! Ter - re de nos aï - eux,
O Can - a - da! Our home and na - tive land,

Ton front est ceint de fleu - rons glo - ri - eux!
True pa - triot love in all our sons com - mand.

Car ton bras sait por - ter l'é - pé - e,
With ____ glow - ing hearts we ____ see thee rise,

Il ____ sait por - ter la croix! Ton his - toire est une
The ___ True North strong and free! From __ far and wide,

é - po - pé - e des plus bril - lants _ ex - ploits.
O ____ Can - a - da, we stand on guard _ for ___ thee.

Et ta va - leur, de foi trem - pée,
God keep our land glo - rious and free!

Pro - té - ge - ra nos foy - ers et nos droits.
O Can - a - da, we stand on guard for thee.

Pro - té - ge - ra nos foy - ers et nos droits.
O Can - a - da, we stand on guard for thee.

Many French Canadians in Quebec held demonstrations in 1990. They were angered when a constitutional agreement to allow Quebec a special identity was refused.

French and English. Canada's national anthem, or song, is sung in both English and French. You can read the words to the anthem on page 172.

The movement for French separatism has led other ethnic groups in Canada, such as the Inuit and other Indian peoples, to ask for similar rights. For example, they have begun to ask that Inuit and other Indian languages be used in local schools and on local street signs. Such demands have made many Canadians unwilling to give special rights to the French Canadians. They say that giving many ethnic groups such rights would weaken Canada.

A UNIQUE PLACE IN THE WORLD

In this chapter you have read about Canada's unique place in the world. Canada is an independent democracy.

Yet it has chosen to keep close ties with the United Kingdom because of the many traditions they share. Canada has also chosen to strengthen its ties with its neighbor, the United States. One of the challenges that continue to face Canada is separatism.

Check Your Reading

1. What kind of government does Canada have?
2. Why did Canada choose to join the Commonwealth of Nations?
3. Why has separatism remained an important issue in Canada?
4. THINKING SKILL: Predict three effects of the free-trade agreement between Canada and the United States. Give the reasons for your predictions.

Should Quebec Seek Independence?

For many years people in Quebec have debated the question of independence. Should Quebec remain a province of Canada or become a separate country? As you have read, Canadian leaders agreed in 1989 to an amendment to their constitution that would have recognized Quebec as a distinct society within Canada. However, before the amendment became official, it had to be approved by all ten of Canada's provinces. In 1990 three provinces, Manitoba, New Brunswick, and Newfoundland, withdrew support for the amendment. And so Quebec's hopes to have special status under the Canadian constitution were dashed. What does the future hold for the people of Quebec?

Today some people in Quebec want it to remain part of Canada. Others want Quebec to become an independent country within an economic union made up of the other Canadian provinces. Finally, still others in Quebec want their province to be a completely separate country.

Quebec Should Become Independent

The political party called the Parti Quebecois (pär tē′ kwi bek wä′), or PQ, has always wanted Quebec to become a separate country. In a recent pamphlet, it described its beliefs and its goals.

> The Parti Quebecois has as its fundamental objective the sovereignty [independence] of Quebec. . . .
>
> Why do we want sovereignty? Here are some of the reasons:
>
> *To end our minority status.* In 1840 half the population of Canada was French-speaking. Today they account for barely one quarter, with the majority living in the province of Quebec. . . . Quebec must deal with a federal government and nine provincial governments, all controlled by an English-speaking majority.
>
> *To allow Quebec to take its place on the world scene.* In international forums, the only government that has the right to defend our interests, to speak in the name of the people of Quebec, is the government of Quebec. We should not permit the national government in Ottawa the power to assume this responsibility. Canadian federalism imposes barriers on us, cuts us off from the world. We must get rid of it.

● Why does the Parti Quebecois believe that Quebec should become independent?

Quebec Should Remain Part of Canada

Robert Bourassa was prime minister of Quebec during the late 1980s and the early 1990s. In a television interview with U.S. reporter Robert MacNeil, Prime Minister Bourassa described his views on the relationship between the province of Quebec and the rest of Canada.

> *Mr. MacNeil:* Are you one of those who believes that Quebec would prosper and grow as an independent nation in the world economy, if it came to that?
>
> *Prime Minister Bourassa:* Many experts will say that Quebec has a relatively strong economy. But I believe that a Canadian common market is an asset for Quebec, and my first choice is to stay within Canada. I believe that most Canadians, including those who live in Quebec, would not like to compromise the economic stability of Canada.
>
> *Mr. MacNeil:* What is the spiritual value to you as a Quebecer in being Canadian?
>
> *Prime Minister Bourassa:* I always said that Canada is one of the greatest countries in the world, because it's a country of tolerance, it's a country of social progress, it's a country of cultural diversity. . . . That's why a majority of people in Quebec would like to stay and prosper within that country.

● Why does Prime Minister Bourassa believe that Quebec should stay?

UNDERSTANDING THE POINT/COUNTERPOINT

1. Which side presents a more convincing argument? Why?
2. What other people might have opinions about separatism?
3. How might the two sides reach a compromise? Explain your answer.

IDEAS TO REMEMBER

- The population of Canada is made up of many ethnic groups that form a mosaic of different peoples.
- Canada has a developed economy that depends on valuable natural resources and includes service industries, manufacturing, and agriculture.
- Canada's British heritage includes its government, which is a parliamentary democracy modeled on the British system, and many customs and forms of recreation.

REVIEWING VOCABULARY

Number a sheet of paper from 1 to 10. Beside each number write **C** if the underlined word in the sentence is used correctly. If it is not, write the word that would correctly complete the sentence.

1. A <u>Commonwealth of Nations</u> is land set aside for Indians to live on.
2. A system in which the provincial governments share power with the central government is called a <u>parliamentary democracy</u>.
3. After independence Canada joined the <u>United Kingdom</u>.
4. In a <u>developed economy</u> the workers serve people.
5. Canada grows so much wheat that it can <u>export</u> some of it to other countries.
6. The population of Canada grew mainly through <u>representatives</u>.
7. Some of Canada's electricity is <u>hydro-electric power</u>, generated by the force of falling water.
8. The trading of goods without tariffs is called <u>separatism</u>.
9. Taking care of foreign visitors is an example of a <u>service industry</u>.
10. An <u>import</u> is a fee that the government places on goods brought into the country.

REVIEWING FACTS

1. What are Canada's two largest ethnic groups?
2. How can the population of Canada be compared to a mosiac?
3. Which province of Canada shows the most French influence?
4. What is population density?
5. What are four of Canada's most important natural resources?
6. Why is the area around Lake Ontario known as the "Golden Horseshoe"?
7. What is the capital of Canada?
8. Describe Canada's present-day relationship to Great Britain.
9. What is Canada's most popular sport?
10. Give two examples of ways in which the influence of French culture appears throughout Quebec province.

WRITING ABOUT MAIN IDEAS

1. **Writing an Opinion Paragraph:** Review the types of recreation enjoyed by Canadians. Which would you most like to watch or do? Write a paragraph explaining why you chose that activity.
2. **Writing a Paragraph:** You have read that Canadians like to remember the ethnic traditions and special legacies of each ethnic group. Describe three things that families can do to pass their heritage on to their children.

In 1990 the governments of Canada and the United States agreed to remove all limits on trade. As a result of the free-trade agreement, a new spirit of cooperation has grown up along the border of the two countries. This cooperation is strongest in the states of Minnesota, Montana, South Dakota, North Dakota and Kansas and the provinces of Ontario, Manitoba, Saskatchewan and Alberta. For example, plans have been made to coordinate health services in the neighboring areas. Leaders have agreed to consider the environmental impact on their neighbors across the border when planning factories, dams, or roads. Experts have shared ideas about developing education programs for rural areas by way of satellite television.

Each of these and other projects have brought the two countries even closer than they have been in the past. Some Canadians and Americans believe that we may be moving toward one economy. The trade between the two countries is the largest in the world.

3. Writing About Perspectives: Write a paragraph in which you discuss whether or not one of the following people might like to live in Ontario:
   a. an auto assembly line worker
   b. a schoolteacher
   c. a singer
   d. a wheat farmer

BUILDING SKILLS: UNDERSTANDING CAUSE AND EFFECT

Read the paragraph above. Use it and what you already know to answer the questions.

1. What is the difference between a cause and an effect?

2. Which steps should you use to identify causes and effects?

3. Identify three causes and three effects in the statement above.

4. Is the phrase *as a result of* a clue for a cause or an effect? Explain.

5. Is the agreement by the governments of the United States and Canada to remove all limits on trade a cause or an effect of the new spirit of cooperation between them?

6. Why is it useful to be able to identify causes and effects?

UNIT 3 - REVIEW

REVIEWING VOCABULARY

colony
ethnic group
export
federal system
free trade

legacy
legislature
missionary
province
suffrage

Number a sheet of paper from 1 to 10. Beside each number write the word or term from the list above that best matches the statement.

1. A person who is sent by a church to spread its beliefs among nonbelievers
2. An item that is sent to another country for sale or trade
3. A division of Canada, similar to a state in the United States
4. The trading of all goods without the use of tariffs
5. The right to vote
6. People who share the same language, customs, history, and religion
7. Something handed down from earlier generations
8. A group of people with the power to make laws for a country or area
9. A place that is under the control of another country
10. A type of government in which power is shared between the national and state or provincial governments

WRITING ABOUT THE UNIT

1. **Writing a Comparison:** Consider the economy of Canada in the early 1800s. How is it the same as or different from Canada's economy in the late 1900s? Write a paragraph comparing and contrasting the economy of the two periods.

2. **Writing a Newspaper Article:** Choose one event in Canadian history. Write a newspaper article giving the main facts and some background about the event.

3. **Writing About Perspectives:** Imagine that you are an English speaker from Quebec. Write a paragraph that provides an argument against separatism. Then imagine you are a French speaker from Quebec. Write a paragraph that argues for separatism. Write a final paragraph that notes which position you support.

ACTIVITIES

1. **Planning a Trip:** Plan a trip to a city in Canada. Do research to find out the interesting places to see. Then plan an itinerary, or list of places you would visit. Make a map locating the places on your itinerary.

2. **Preparing a Picture Essay:** Locate pictures showing examples of Canadian Indian art. Organize the pictures to include in a picture essay. Write a caption for each one. If you can't use the actual pictures, write a short description of each piece of art.

3. **Working Together to Make a Canada Handbook:** Divide into pairs or small groups to learn about Canada's provinces and territories. Each pair or group should concentrate on one province or territory. Find out interesting facts about its history, geography, economy, and culture. Prepare a one-page report of your findings. Then bind all the pages together to make a Canada Handbook for the class.

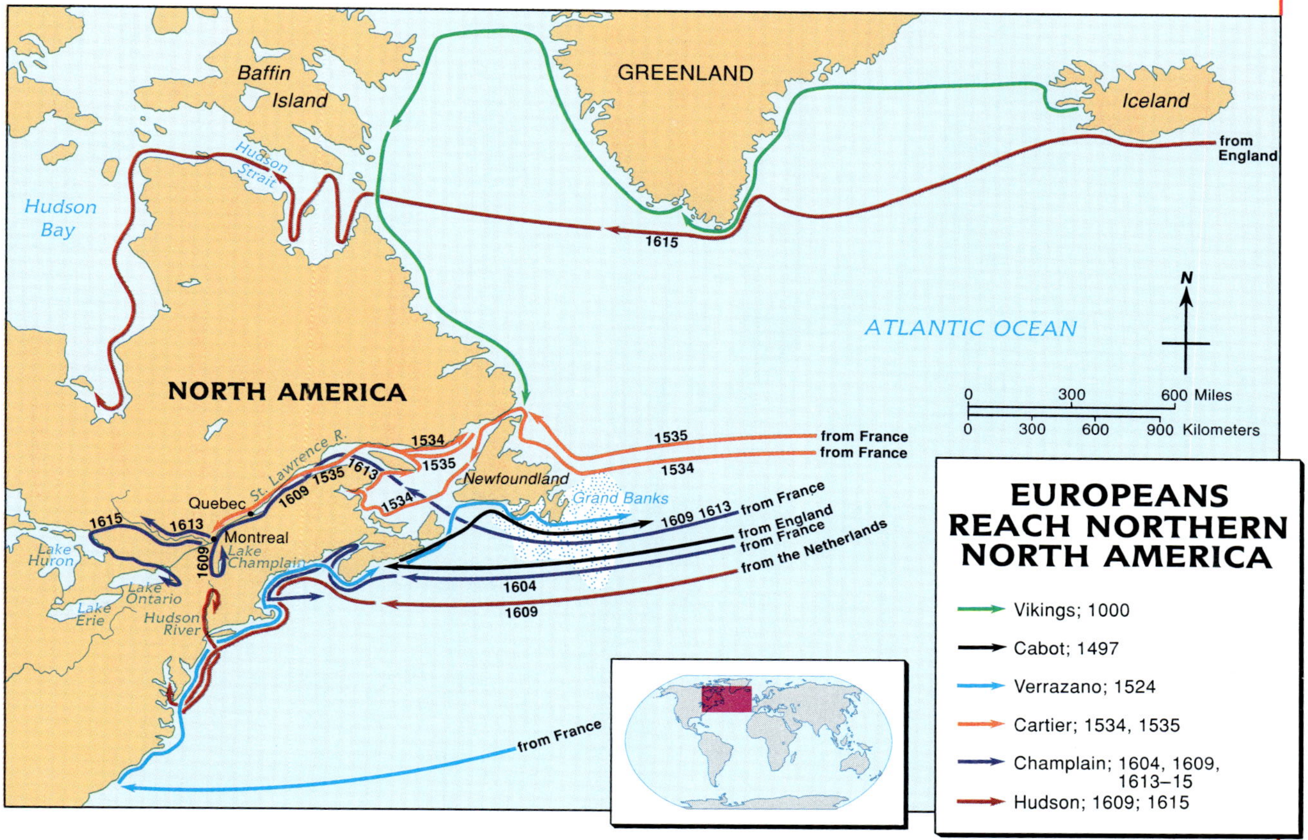
EUROPEANS REACH NORTHERN NORTH AMERICA
Vikings; 1000
Cabot; 1497
Verrazano; 1524
Cartier; 1534, 1535
Champlain; 1604, 1609, 1613–15
Hudson; 1609; 1615
Baffin Island
GREENLAND
Iceland
from England
Hudson Strait
Hudson Bay
1615
N
ATLANTIC OCEAN
0 300 600 Miles
0 300 600 900 Kilometers
NORTH AMERICA
St. Lawrence R.
1534
1535
1613
1609
Quebec
Montreal
Newfoundland
Grand Banks
from France
from France
from England
from France
from the Netherlands
1604
1609
Lake Huron
Lake Ontario
Lake Erie
Lake Champlain
Hudson River
from France

BUILDING SKILLS: READING HISTORICAL MAPS

Use the map above to answer the following questions.

1. What is a historical map?
2. How are the Vikings' routes of exploration shown?
3. Who was the first explorer to reach what became Canada?
4. When did Champlain go farther north, in 1604 or in 1609?
5. Name a main waterway of North America that some of the early explorers used.
6. Why are historical maps useful?

LINKING PAST, PRESENT, AND FUTURE

Canada and the United States share most of the continent of North America. What else do the two countries have in common? Name at least three things. Why might the future of Canada be important to you as a citizen of the United States?

NORTH AMERICA

60°N

45°N

30°N

Gulf of Mexico

MEXICO

Tropic of Cancer

CARIBBEAN ISLANDS

Caribbean Sea

CENTRAL AMERICA

15°N

ATLANTIC

OCEAN

0° Equator

PACIFIC OCEAN

SOUTH AMERICA

15°S

Tropic of Capricorn

105°W

90°W

75°W

45°W

30°W

135°W

120°W

30°S

60°W

45°S

60°S

ANTARCTICA

South Pole

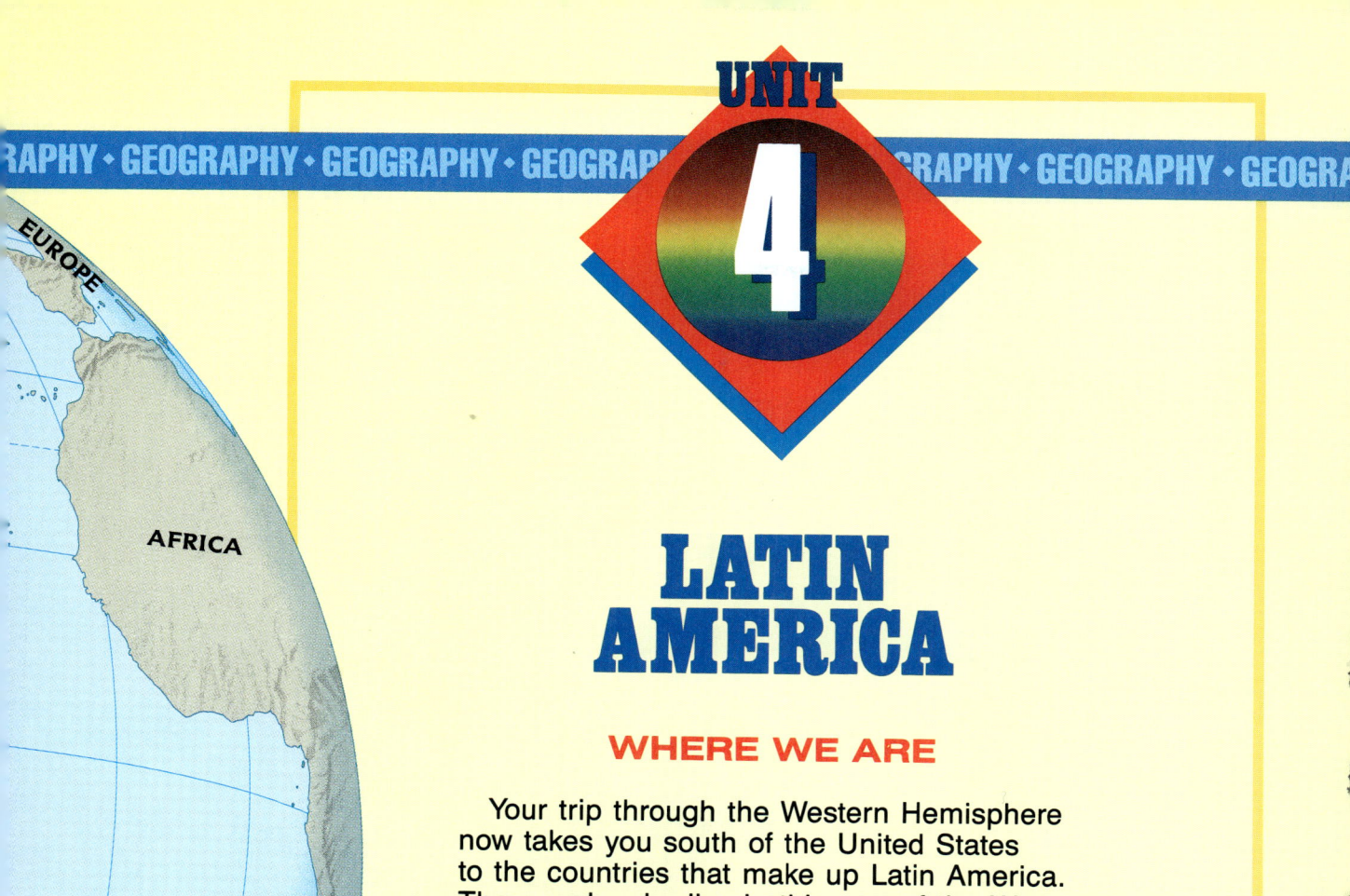

UNIT 4

LATIN AMERICA

WHERE WE ARE

Your trip through the Western Hemisphere now takes you south of the United States to the countries that make up Latin America. The people who live in this part of the Western Hemisphere today speak different languages and belong to many different cultures.

In this unit, you will learn about the geography of Latin America—from northern Mexico to the southern tip of South America. You will read about the early peoples who built great cities in Latin America and about how the arrival of Europeans influenced the history of this region. As your knowledge about Latin America grows, think about how the history of Latin America is similar to, and different from, the history of Canada.

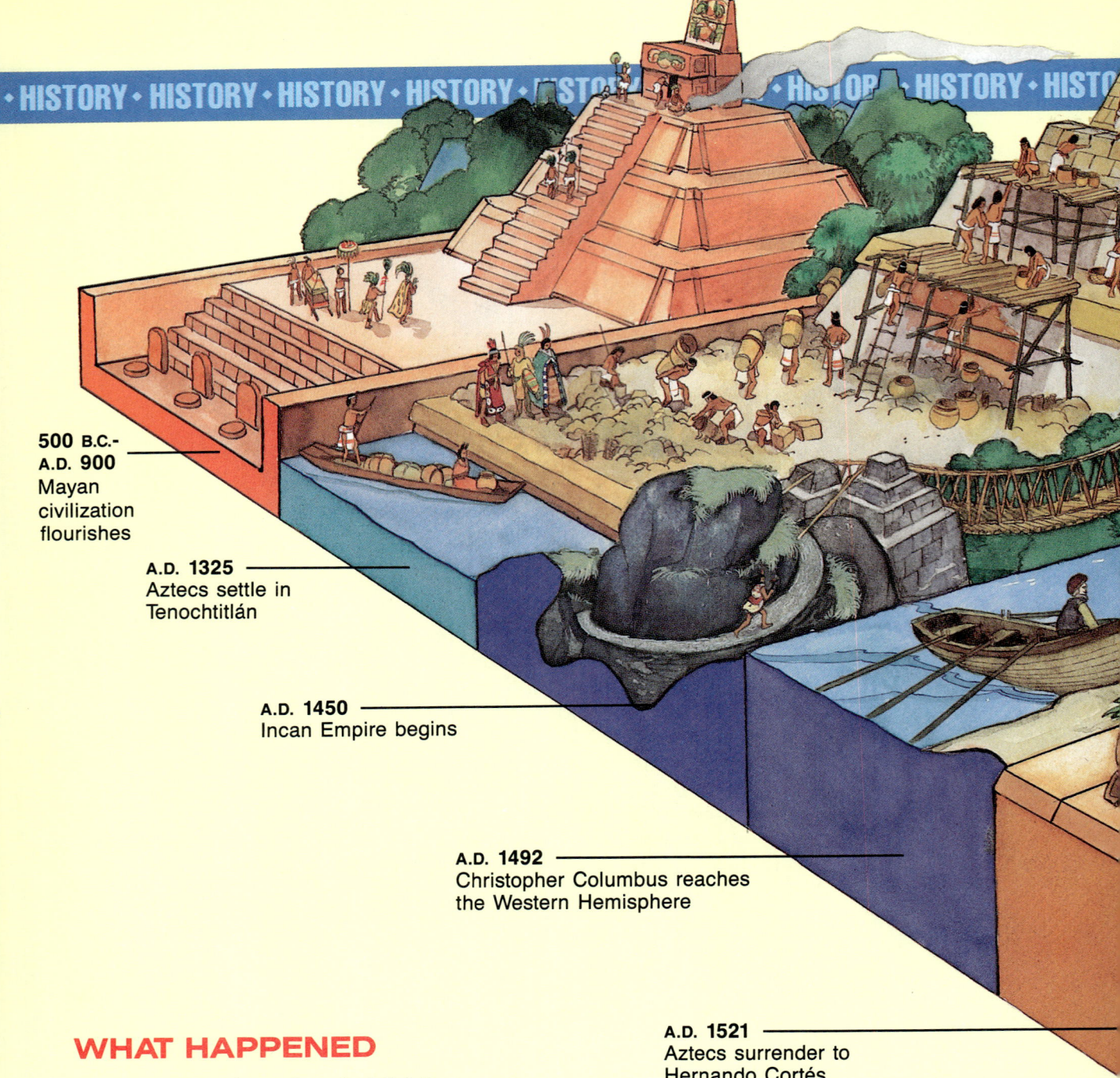

500 B.C.–
A.D. 900
Mayan
civilization
flourishes

A.D. 1325
Aztecs settle in
Tenochtitlán

A.D. 1450
Incan Empire begins

A.D. 1492
Christopher Columbus reaches
the Western Hemisphere

A.D. 1521
Aztecs surrender to
Hernando Cortés

A.D. 1533
Francisco Pizarro
captures the Incan
capital of Cuzco

WHAT HAPPENED

The peoples of early Middle
America and South America had
many different cultures. Some of these
peoples built large and splendid cities and
ruled over large areas. When the Spanish
and Portuguese reached the Americas, their
armies conquered the Indians and colonized
their lands. New Latin American cultures
began to develop.

182

LEARNING ABOUT LATIN AMERICA

FOCUS

I resolved . . . to make a journey that would span the Latin American experience, to see how history . . . had shaped the fortunes of some of the fastest-changing, most varied societies in the world. I also wanted to observe the human face of each society as shaped by extreme geography.

Like the journalist Robert Harvey, who is quoted above, you will make a journey through Latin America. In this chapter you will begin your journey by reading about the geography of this fascinating land and the people who shaped its history.

1 The Geography of Latin America

READL TO LEARN

 **Key Vocabulary**

navigable   tierra fría
tierra caliente   tropical rain
tierra templada   forest

Key Places

Rio Grande   Pampas
Andes Mountains   Orinoco River
Amazon River   Río de la Plata

 **Read Aloud**

My head hurt terribly and I felt like a stranger inside my own body, with my heart beating 90 times a minute (instead of the usual 60), as I got acclimatized [adapted] to 14,000 feet. At this altitude you have to do everything with painstaking care to avoid exhaustion and sickness.

This is how the writer Patrick Tierney described some of the problems of traveling in the high elevations. Since there is less oxygen in the air at higher elevations, it is harder to breathe. But the people of Latin America who live in the Andes Mountains have adapted to their environment. Many other regions of Latin America also present challenges. In this lesson you will read about the geography of Latin America. You will read also about the ways in which people have adapted to these different environments.

 **Read for Purpose**

1. **WHAT YOU KNOW:** Which mountains are found in Canada?
2. **WHAT YOU WILL LEARN:** How has Latin America's geography affected its people's ability to develop its resources?

SOUTH OF THE RIO GRANDE

As you know, Latin America, like Canada and the United States, is part of the Western Hemisphere. You read in Chapter 2 that "Latin America" is a cultural region that was influenced by Spain and Portugal. Within this one cultural region, there are two geographic regions—South America and Middle America. As you read in Chapter 1, Middle America includes Mexico, Central America, and the islands of the Caribbean.

You may know that the **Rio Grande**, which means "Great River" in English, forms much of the border between the United States and Mexico. It also forms the northern border of Latin America.

LATIN AMERICA: Elevation

Elevations

Feet	Meters
Above 14,000	Above 4,000
7,000	2,000
1,500	500
700	200
0	0

Below sea level

✳ National capital

▲ Mountain peak

MAP SKILL: High, rugged mountains cover much of Latin America. In which part of South America are the Andes Mountains located?

186

Look at the map on the opposite page. It shows that Cape Horn is at the southern boundary of Latin America.

LANDFORMS

The Andes Mountains, which Patrick Tierney explored, are the longest mountain chain in the world. Find the Andes Mountains on the map. How have the people who live in the Andes adapted to the high elevation? The writer Charles Frazier has offered an explanation.

> [They] maintain a somewhat elevated internal temperature to combat the mountain cold. Their hearts beat almost as slowly as a marathon runner's and are up to one fifth larger than the hearts of similarly sized sea-level dwellers.

As the map shows, there are other mountainous areas in Latin America besides the Andes. Parts of Mexico and Central America are mountainous. Most of the Caribbean islands are the tops of mountains that jut up from the bottom of the sea.

The elevation is just one challenge posed by Latin America's mountains. The mountains also form barriers. The Andes, for example, could be described as a huge wall that separates the people on each side. Because there are few passes through the Andes Mountains, transportation is often extremely difficult.

PLAINS AND PLATEAUS

Not all of Latin America is mountainous. East of the Andes Mountains, along the equator, lies a huge plain that is drained by the Amazon River. South of the Amazon's vast river valley are plains called the Pampas. The Pampas have rich soil that is good for farming and raising cattle. You will read more about the people who raise cattle on the Pampas in Chapter 25.

Among Latin America's plateaus are the Central Plateau in Mexico and the

Many of Peru's highest mountains remain covered by snow all year. Roads through these mountains (*above*) are often unpaved.

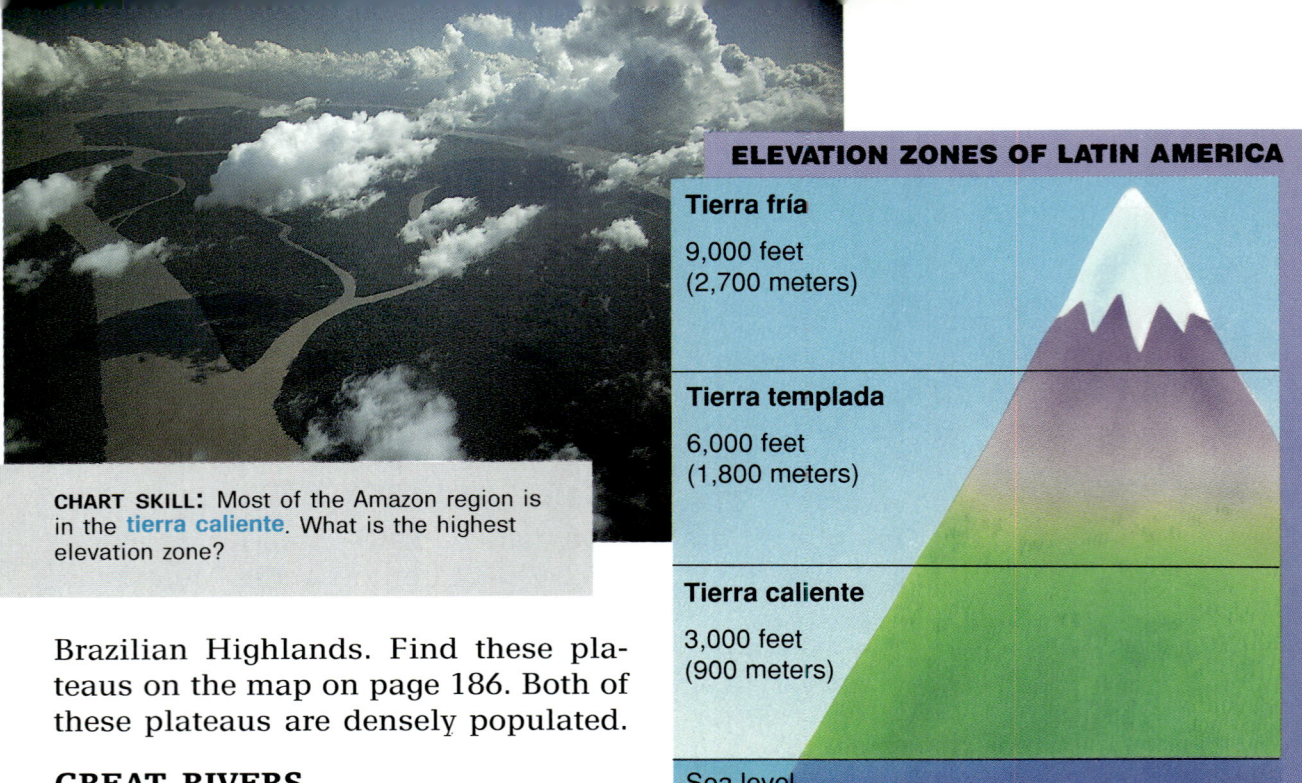

ELEVATION ZONES OF LATIN AMERICA

Tierra fría

9,000 feet
(2,700 meters)

Tierra templada

6,000 feet
(1,800 meters)

Tierra caliente

3,000 feet
(900 meters)

Sea level

CHART SKILL: Most of the Amazon region is in the tierra caliente. What is the highest elevation zone?

Brazilian Highlands. Find these plateaus on the map on page 186. Both of these plateaus are densely populated.

GREAT RIVERS

The Amazon is unrivaled [unmatched].
*From its mouth it pours out one
fifth of all the river water on earth.*

As you read in Chapter 1, the Amazon River in South America is the second-longest river in the world. But it carries more water than any other river in the world.

There are two other great river systems in South America. The **Orinoco River** begins in Colombia and flows across Venezuela to empty into the Atlantic Ocean. The **Río de la Plata** system is in the southeastern part of South America. It provides important transportation routes for that part of the continent.

In contrast to the river systems in South America, few rivers in the rest of Latin America are **navigable**. A navigable river is one on which boats can travel. The Rio Grande is the only navigable river in all of Middle America. This has always made transportation and communication in this part of Latin America very difficult.

ELEVATION ZONES

*The aircraft landed . . . I climbed out,
and was hit as though by something
resembling . . . hot wet towels. . . .
The heat and humidity were over-
powering.*

The journalist Robert Harvey wrote these words to describe the tropical climate he encountered in the Amazon region of South America. Much of Latin America lies in the tropics, or low latitudes. Because of these low latitudes, many parts of Latin America, including the Amazon region, have a warm, wet tropical climate.

Although many areas of Latin America are located in the tropics, not all of them have the same type of climate. How can this be? You read in Chapter 1 that many factors affect climate and cause temperatures to vary from place to place. For example, latitude and ocean currents have an effect on climate. Elevation, or height above sea level, also affects climate. As a result, there are some areas in the tropics that have colder climates than others.

You may recall from Chapter 1 that temperatures become lower at high elevations. For each 1,000-foot (300-m) increase in elevation, the temperature drops about 3.6°F. (2°C). For this reason temperatures remain cool in the high Andes, even in those parts near the equator.

Use the chart on page 188 to learn more about Latin America's climate. As you can see, three elevation zones are shown. The zone near sea level is called the **tierra caliente** (tyer′ ə kä lyen′ tā). In English *tierra caliente* means "hot land." This lowland zone is hot all year long.

Lands higher than 3,000 feet (900 m) but lower than 6,000 feet (1,800 m) are in the elevation zone called the **tierra templada** (tem plä′ də), or "temperate land." The Central Plateau of Mexico and many of Latin America's other highland plateaus are found in this mild zone.

As the chart shows, the zone with the highest elevation is called the **tierra fría** (frē′ ə), or "cold land." It includes all land higher than 6,000 feet (1,800 m). Chimborazo (chim bə roz′ ō), Ecuador's highest mountain peak, is in the tierra fría. This peak is near the equator, but it remains covered with snow all year long.

RESOURCES

Latin America has a great variety of valuable natural resources. But these resources are unevenly distributed. Central America, for example, has few minerals, while Brazil has an abundance of iron, gold, and diamonds. In South America only 5 percent of the land can be farmed. The soil is either too rocky or too dry. But on the islands of the Caribbean and in Central America, good soil is plentiful.

Besides being unevenly distributed, many of Latin America's natural resources are located in places that are hard to reach, such as the Andes Mountains. For example, in the Andes in Bolivia there are mines with large amounts of tin and zinc. However, some mines are located more than 16,000 feet (4,800 m) above sea level. This makes it difficult both to mine and to transport these minerals.

As you read in Chapter 1, rain forests are important resources. Latin America has many **tropical rain forests**, including the largest one in the world. It is located in the Amazon River Valley in Brazil. A tropical rain forest is a warm area where many trees and plants grow

Scientists use special equipment to study the treetops of the Amazon **tropical rain forest**

The Amazon rain forest is home to many kinds of snakes, monkeys, and birds.

closely together because of the high annual rainfall. Among the many kinds of trees that grow in the Amazon rain forest are hardwood trees such as rosewood and mahogany. The rain forest also yields valuable products such as nuts, fibers, and rubber.

During the past 15 years, large areas of the Amazon rain forest have been destroyed. Thousands of trees have been cut down by loggers. Thousands of acres of the forest have been burned to clear the land for farming. Many people are afraid that this unique environment will be completely destroyed. Large numbers of plants and animals already have died because of the shrinking of the rain forest.

Why are people all over the world so concerned? The Amazon rain forest is sometimes called the "lungs of the world." Scientists estimate that one fifth of the world's oxygen is given off by the trees in this forest. Destruction of the rain forest will decrease the amount of oxygen in the air throughout the world. Since oxygen is needed to form moisture, a decrease in oxygen will cause the world's climate to become drier. Many people also want to

preserve the way of life of the Indians who have lived in the rain forest for hundreds of years. People throughout the world are looking for ways to save the rain forest.

A LAND OF CONTRASTS

As you have read, Latin America is a land of mountains and great plains and plateaus. There are huge river systems, the largest of which is the Amazon. But most parts of Latin America have few navigable rivers. The region has many natural resources, but these resources are distributed unevenly and are often difficult to reach. One of Latin America's most important resources is the Amazon rain forest.

 Check Your Reading

1. What is a navigable river?
2. Identify three elevation zones in Latin America.
3. Why is the Amazon rain forest so important?
4. **GEOGRAPHY SKILL:** Look at the map on page 186. What is the highest mountain peak in Latin America?
5. **THINKING SKILL:** What has been the effect of geography on Latin America's ability to develop its resources?

PRESERVING THE AMAZON

As you know, many people throughout the world are concerned about preserving the rain forests of Latin America. Latin Americans are especially concerned about the people, plant life, and animals living in the Amazon Basin.

In 1978 a Brazilian graduate student named Mary Helena Allegretti (äl i gret′ ē) went to the Amazon rain forest in the northwestern part of her country. She wanted to study the culture of a group of people called the *seringueiros* (ser in gā′ rōs), or rubber tappers. The *seringueiros* walked for miles on winding trails through the rain forest, collecting sap from wild rubber trees. They also gathered fruits and nuts from the jungle. Mary was impressed by the way of life of the rubber tappers and their families. She called them "natural conservationists" because they used the forest without destroying it.

At that time, the Brazilian government was encouraging miners, loggers, ranchers, and farmers to develop the Amazon Basin. Mary and Chico Mendes, the leader of the *seringueiros*, organized the 70,000 rubber tappers scattered across the Amazon region. They helped the *seringueiros* to work together to protect their way of life.

Mary and Chico decided to show the people of Brazil that the area planned for development was already inhabited. They brought 130 rubber tappers to Brasília,

the capital of Brazil, to speak with government officials. People were surprised to see that rubber tappers still existed, and were not just romantic figures of the past.

Mary continued working to save the rain forest and its people. She helped bring schools and health-care facilities to the isolated communities of the *seringueiros*.

Mary asked the government to set aside preserves in the Amazon. A preserve is an area set aside for the protection of plant and animal life. Here rubber tappers could continue to harvest, or gather in, rubber, fruits, nuts, and herbs from the rain forest without being disturbed. Other more destructive forms of development would not be allowed in the rain forest.

The Brazilian government adopted the preserve plan in 1987. It set aside more than 5 million acres (2 million ha) of Amazon rain forest. Mary is now helping to establish preserves in other parts of Brazil. She is continuing to help protect the rain forest and the people who have lived in harmony with it.

191

Reading Climographs

Key Vocabulary

climograph

In this textbook, you are reading about many different countries in the Western Hemisphere. You are learning that each of these countries has special features. Each country has unique landforms and different natural resources. You also are reading about the varied climates of these countries. You may remember from Chapter 1 that the two most important parts of a place's climate are temperature and precipitation.

This textbook includes a number of climate maps, such as the one on page 73. Climate maps use colors to show the different types of climate in various regions.

Another way to learn about the climate of a place is to look at a **climograph**. A climograph is a graph that shows information about the temperature and precipitation of a place over a period of time.

Parts of a Climograph

Climographs are different from climate maps because they give information about climate for each month of the year. Look at **Climograph A** on this page. Notice that it is really two graphs—a line graph in blue, and a bar graph in red. The line graph shows the average monthly temperature in Mexico City. The bar graph shows the average monthly precipitation in Mexico City.

You read a climograph the same way that you read other graphs. Begin by looking at the title. It names the place described by the climograph. What place

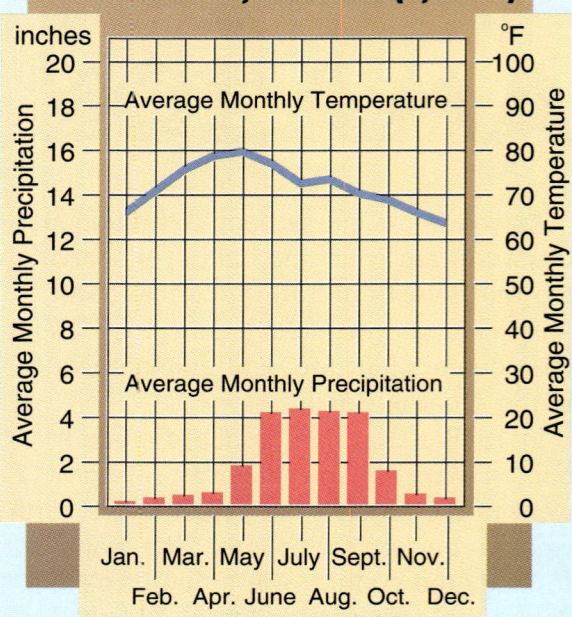

CLIMOGRAPH A:
MEXICO CITY, MEXICO
ELEVATION: 7,340 FEET (2,229M)

is described by **Climograph B** on page 193? Then read the labels along the sides of the climograph. On each climograph in this lesson, the labels on the left side tell you the average monthly precipitation. The labels on the right side measure monthly temperature. Now look at the labels along the bottom of the climograph. What do they tell you?

Look again at **Climograph A**. You will notice that the bar graph is made up of 12 vertical bars. They show the average precipitation during each month of the year. In which month does Mexico City get the most precipitation? Now look at the line graph. In which month is the average temperature the highest?

Interpreting Climographs

A climograph helps you to determine in which months the temperature and precipitation of a place are the highest

CLIMOGRAPH B: CARACAS, VENEZUELA ELEVATION: 3,418 FEET (1,042M)

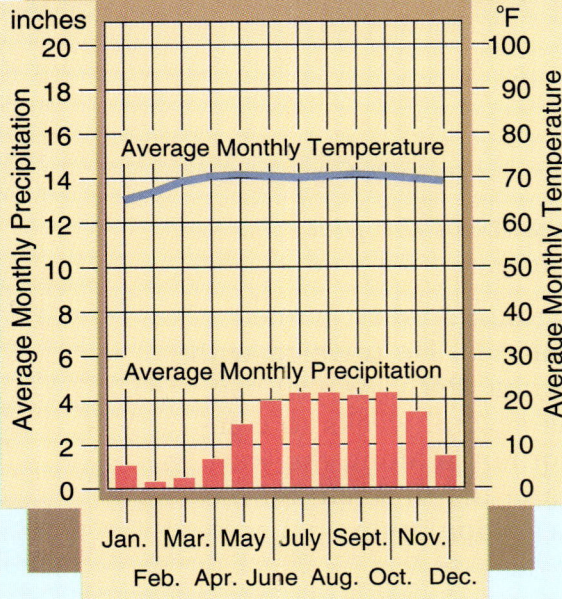

CLIMOGRAPH C: BUENOS AIRES, ARGENTINA ELEVATION: 89 FEET (27M)

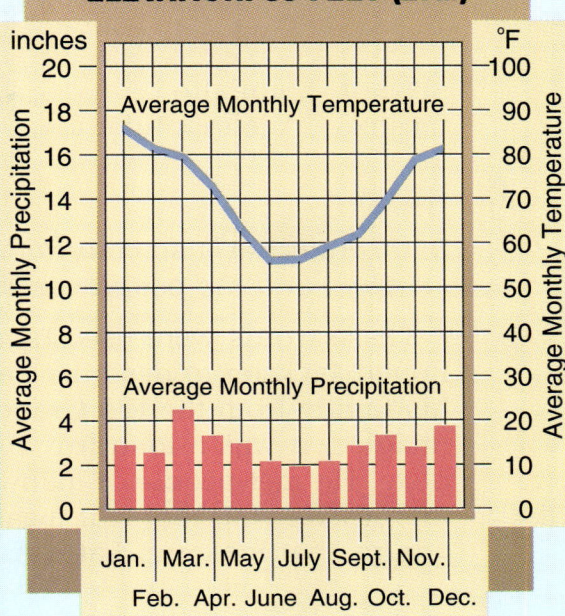

and the lowest. Look at **Climograph C**. In which month does Buenos Aires have the most precipitation?

You can use climographs to compare the climates of different places. Study **Climograph B** and **Climograph C** above. In which month does Caracas have the lowest temperature? In which month does Buenos Aires have the lowest temperature? Which city has more precipitation during the year?

Now find Mexico City and Buenos Aires on the map on page 195. Notice that Buenos Aires is south of the equator and that Mexico City is north of the equator. The climate is very different because the seasons of places south of the equator is the opposite of the seasons of places north of the equator. Which months are the winter months in Buenos Aires? During those same months, what season is it in Mexico City?

By reading a climograph, you can get a detailed picture of the climate of a place. You can learn if it is wet or dry, hot or cold. You can learn during which times of the year it might be most pleasant to live or visit there.

Reviewing the Skill

1. What is a climograph?
2. In Mexico City, what is the average temperature in May?
3. In Caracas, in which months is the precipitation greater than 2 inches?
4. Do you think it rains or that it snows in Mexico City in December? How can you tell?
5. In which month do you think it would be most pleasant to visit Buenos Aires? Explain your answer.
6. Why is it helpful to know how to read a climograph?

2 People of Many Cultures

READ TO LEARN

■ Key Vocabulary

slavery   mulatto
mestizo   metropolitan area

■ Read Aloud

Latin America is so colorful. The beauty of the place is startling and the people are so friendly.

These words were used by a Canadian student named Robert Jackson to describe Latin America. He traveled with his family from the Rio Grande to Lima, Peru. As you can imagine, it was a long trip and took several weeks to complete. He met people of many backgrounds along the way. In this lesson you, too, will meet some of the different ethnic groups that make up Latin America's population.

■ Read for Purpose

1. **WHAT YOU KNOW:** What is an ethnic group?
2. **WHAT YOU WILL LEARN:** Which ethnic groups are found in Latin America?

ETHNIC DIVERSITY

In order to study the geography and history of Latin America, you must understand its people. Throughout the world people make history. People and their activities are also a part of the study of geography.

You can see the countries that today make up Latin America on the map on page 195. Latin America is home to people of many backgrounds. For example, there are Indians, people of European descent, people of African descent, and people of mixed descent.

As you know, scientists believe that the ancestors of the Indians were the first people to live in the Americas. You read in Chapter 2 that these earliest Americans may have entered North America from Asia by way of a land bridge during the Ice Age. The land bridge vanished thousands of years ago. But the people who had come to the Western Hemisphere had spread out and had established many different cultures. In the next chapter you will read about some of the magnificent cities of these people.

EUROPEANS AND AFRICANS

For thousands of years, the Indians were the only inhabitants of the Western Hemisphere. In the late 1400s, however, Europeans began to arrive.

LATIN AMERICA:
Political

⊛ National capital   • Other city

MAP SKILL: Which country in Latin America has two capital cities?

195

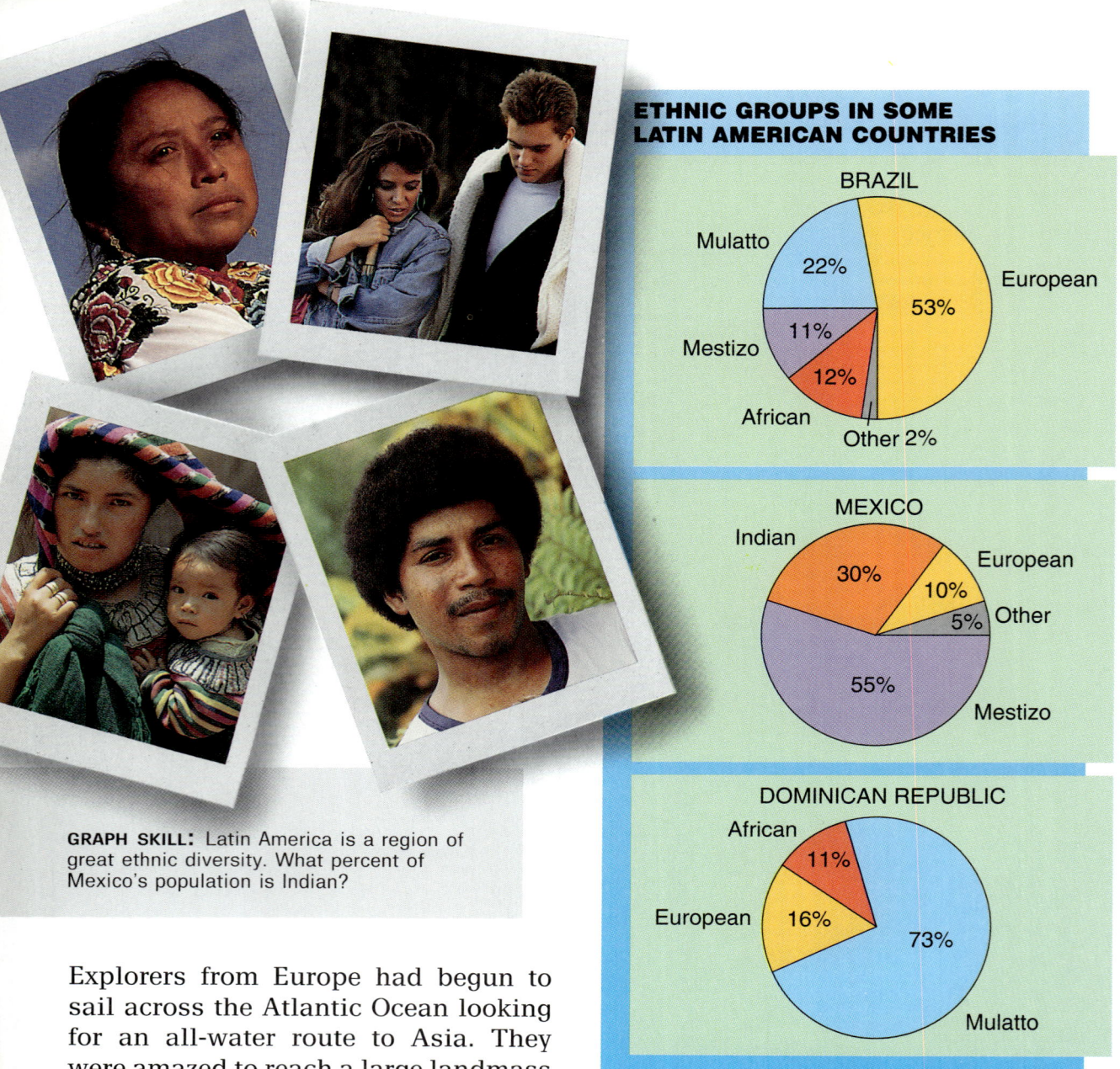

ETHNIC GROUPS IN SOME LATIN AMERICAN COUNTRIES

BRAZIL

- Mulatto 22%
- European 53%
- Mestizo 11%
- African 12%
- Other 2%

MEXICO

- Indian 30%
- European 10%
- Other 5%
- Mestizo 55%

DOMINICAN REPUBLIC

- African 11%
- European 16%
- Mulatto 73%

GRAPH SKILL: Latin America is a region of great ethnic diversity. What percent of Mexico's population is Indian?

Explorers from Europe had begun to sail across the Atlantic Ocean looking for an all-water route to Asia. They were amazed to reach a large landmass blocking their route. As you will read in Chapter 10, Spanish and Portuguese settlers soon conquered the Indians and set up large colonies in what would become known as Latin America. Today many of the people in Latin America are descended from these European settlers.

People of African descent make up another large ethnic group in Latin America. Upon their arrival, many Europeans set up large farms in Latin America. At first they forced the Indians into **slavery** to work on these farms. Slavery is the practice of making a person the property of another person. Many Indians died from disease and overwork. Then the Europeans began to take people from Africa and force them into slavery.

Historians believe that more than 5 million Africans were forced into slavery by the Europeans in Latin America.

Today many people of African descent live on the Caribbean islands, in Brazil, and in parts of Central America.

A MIXTURE OF PEOPLE

You read in Chapter 7 that the word *mosaic* is often used to describe Canada's people. Canada's ethnic groups have kept their separate identities. In Latin America, however, *melting pot* is a good term to describe the people because most Latin Americans are of mixed ancestry. Many are mestizos (mes tē′ zōz), people of mixed Indian and European ancestry. Others are people of mixed African and European descent, called mulattoes (mə lat′ ōz). Still others are of mixed African and Indian descent.

The graphs on page 196 show the ethnic groups that make up the population of three countries in Latin America. What percent of Brazilians are mulattoes? What is the largest ethnic group in the Dominican Republic? What is the largest ethnic group found in Mexico?

A RICH CULTURE

Latin America's ethnic groups have helped this region to develop a rich culture. Indians, Africans, and Europeans have all contributed to this culture.

Religion is a good example of the way in which cultures have blended in Latin America. Europeans introduced Roman Catholicism to Latin America in the 1500s. As a result, most Latin Americans today are Catholic. However, in Brazil and Haiti, some people of African descent practice a mixture of African religions and Catholicism. In other parts of Latin America, Indians have mixed elements of their traditional religions with Catholicism.

WHERE DO PEOPLE LIVE?

Where do the people of Latin America live? The most populated areas of Latin America are the mountain valleys and highlands that were settled by the Indians thousands of years ago. Other areas with large populations are found along the coasts. It is there that the Europeans built cities to be used as trading centers. São Paulo, Brazil, and Lima, Peru, are among these cities.

Look at the population density map on the next page. As you may recall, a place with a high population density

As Catholics, these Mayan Indians are celebrating Palm Sunday. Many Mayas also worship Mayan gods.

197

has many people living in a given place. As you can see from the map, Latin America has many large cities. Which country in Latin America has the most cities with more than 1 million people?

VAST CITIES

Today some of the world's largest urban areas are found in Latin America. For example, the urban area of Mexico City, Mexico, has a population of about 18 million people. This number is more than one half the population of the entire country of Canada. Mexico City is the largest **metropolitan** area in the world. A metropolitan area includes a large city and its surrounding suburbs and towns.

The metropolitan areas of Latin America are growing very rapidly because they are centers for industry. Many people from rural areas of Latin America go to the cities hoping to find jobs. Often they find only poverty. Without jobs or good housing, these urban newcomers are usually forced to live in the slums that surround many Latin American cities. You will read more about these growing cities of Latin America in later chapters.

RURAL AREAS

Located between Latin America's metropolitan areas are rural areas that

MAP SKILL: Is Jamaica or Puerto Rico more densely populated? Which cities in Mexico have more than 1 million people?

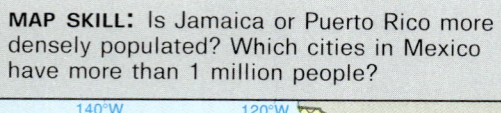

LATIN AMERICA: Population Density

People per square mile	People per square kilometer
0–2	0–1
2–25	1–10
25–125	10–50
125–250	50–100
250–500	100–200
over 500	over 200

• Cities with more than 1 million people

Crowded Mexico City, Mexico, contrasts sharply with Colombia's quiet rural areas.

stretch for thousands of miles. According to Canadian Robert Jackson:

After we left Bogotá [in Colombia], the land seemed deserted. All of a sudden, there was so much open land. We had been crushed in the city but were suddenly free to roam in the lush Colombian countryside. . . . Villages were separated by miles and miles of unused land.

Much of Latin America is still rural. Many people still earn a living by farming. However, more and more people are leaving the countryside hoping to find a better life in the cities.

A LAND OF MANY PEOPLES

In this lesson you have read about the many ethnic groups of Latin America. They include Indians, people of European descent, mestizos, people of African descent, and mulattoes. These people make up one of the world's greatest melting pots. Increasingly Latin Americans are leaving the countryside to look for jobs and new opportunities in the cities. As a result, Latin America has some of the largest and fastest-growing metropolitan areas in the world.

✔ Check Your Reading

1. Why is Latin America often called a melting pot?
2. Name the ethnic groups found in Latin America.
3. Why are Latin America's urban areas growing very rapidly?
4. **THINKING SKILL:** Compare and contrast Canada's mix of people with that of Latin America. What is the major difference between the two?

199

CHAPTER 8 · SUMMARY AND REVIEW

IDEAS TO REMEMBER

- Latin America has some of the world's highest mountains, as well as the world's second-longest river. Among its many resources is the Amazon rain forest, the "lungs of the world."
- The population of Latin America is a mixture of Indian, European, and African peoples, most of whom live in the region's rapidly growing urban areas.

REVIEWING VOCABULARY

Number a sheet of paper from 1 to 5. Beside each number write the letter of the best definition for the word or term.

1. *mestizo*
   a. enslaved person
   b. person of European ancestry
   c. person of mixed Indian and European ancestry
   d. person who lives in Mexico
2. *tropical rain forest*
   a. area that has been stripped of any growth
   b. warm, humid region in which many trees and plants grow
   c. area of river basins
   d. rainy area
3. *mulatto*
   a. person of African ancestry
   b. person who lives in Mexico
   c. person of mixed African and European ancestry
   d. person who lives in a city
4. *navigable*
   a. able to be traveled on by boat
   b. able to be eaten safely
   c. able to be breathed at high altitudes
   d. able to stay frozen even in summer
5. *slavery*
   a. people working for low wages
   b. people living in poor conditions in a city
   c. farming poor land
   d. forcing a person to become the property of another person

REVIEWING FACTS

1. Give one example of mountains, of a plain, and of a plateau in Latin America.
2. What are three important river systems in South America?
3. Why have transportation and communication been difficult in Middle America?
4. What is the tierra caliente? Where is it located?
5. In which elevation zone is Mexico's Central Plateau located?
6. Why is Chimborazo, near the equator, snow-covered all year round?
7. What is a tropical rain forest?
8. What are the main groups in Latin America's population?
9. Why is Latin America's population thought of as a melting pot?
10. What mixture of religions is sometimes practiced? What religion do most Latin Americans practice?

✎ WRITING ABOUT MAIN IDEAS

1. **Writing a Story:** Think about what might happen if large sections of the Amazon rain forest were cut down. Write a story that dramatizes some of the possible effects.

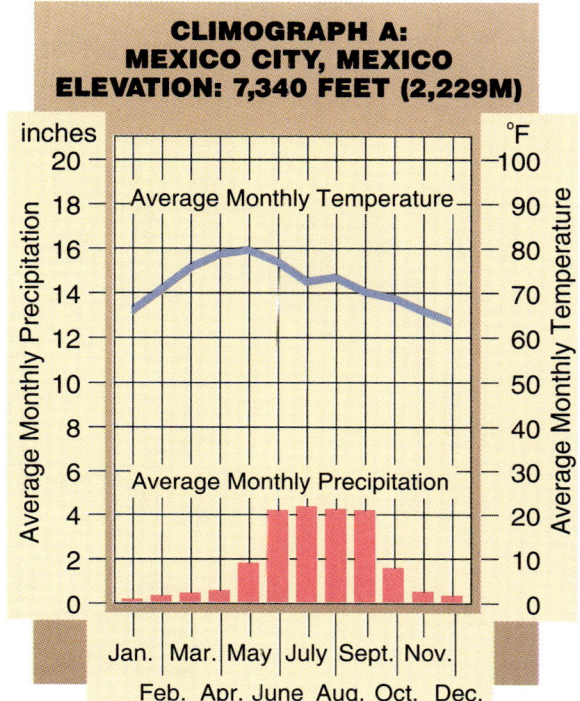

CLIMOGRAPH A:
MEXICO CITY, MEXICO
ELEVATION: 7,340 FEET (2,229M)

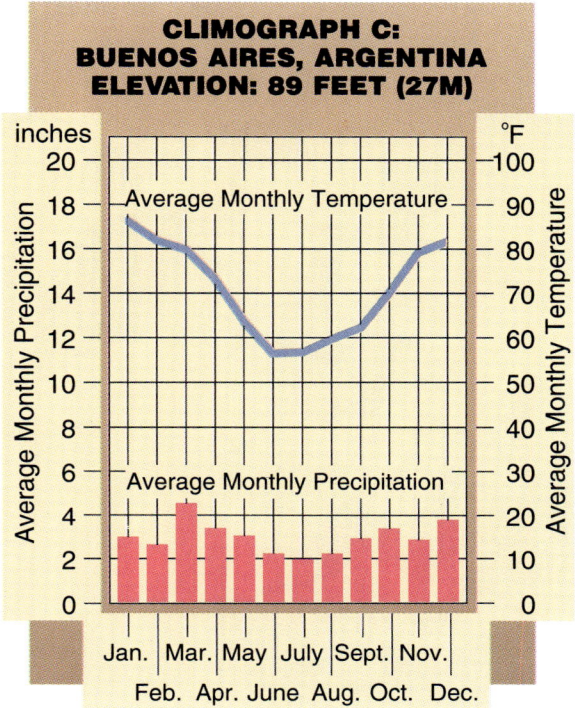

CLIMOGRAPH C:
BUENOS AIRES, ARGENTINA
ELEVATION: 89 FEET (27M)

2. **Writing an Opinion Paragraph:** The Andes Mountains are both helpful and challenging to the people of Latin America. Do you think they are more helpful or more challenging? Write a paragraph presenting your opinion.

3. **Describing a Plan:** Suppose that you are planning to make a poster entitled "Latin America: the Melting Pot." You can use words and pictures on the poster. What would your poster look like? Write one or more paragraphs describing your poster.

4. **Writing About Perspectives:** Imagine a family living in rural Latin America. It is hard to make a good life there. The family is discussing whether to move to the city. What arguments might be made for and against the move? Write a skit about the family's dilemma.

BUILDING SKILLS: READING CLIMOGRAPHS

Use the climographs above to answer the following questions.

1. What does a climograph show?
2. About how much precipitation does Mexico City get in May?
3. What is the average temperature in Buenos Aires in March?
4. Judging from these climographs, are Mexico City and Buenos Aires on the same side of the equator? Explain.
5. When is a climograph more helpful than a climate map?

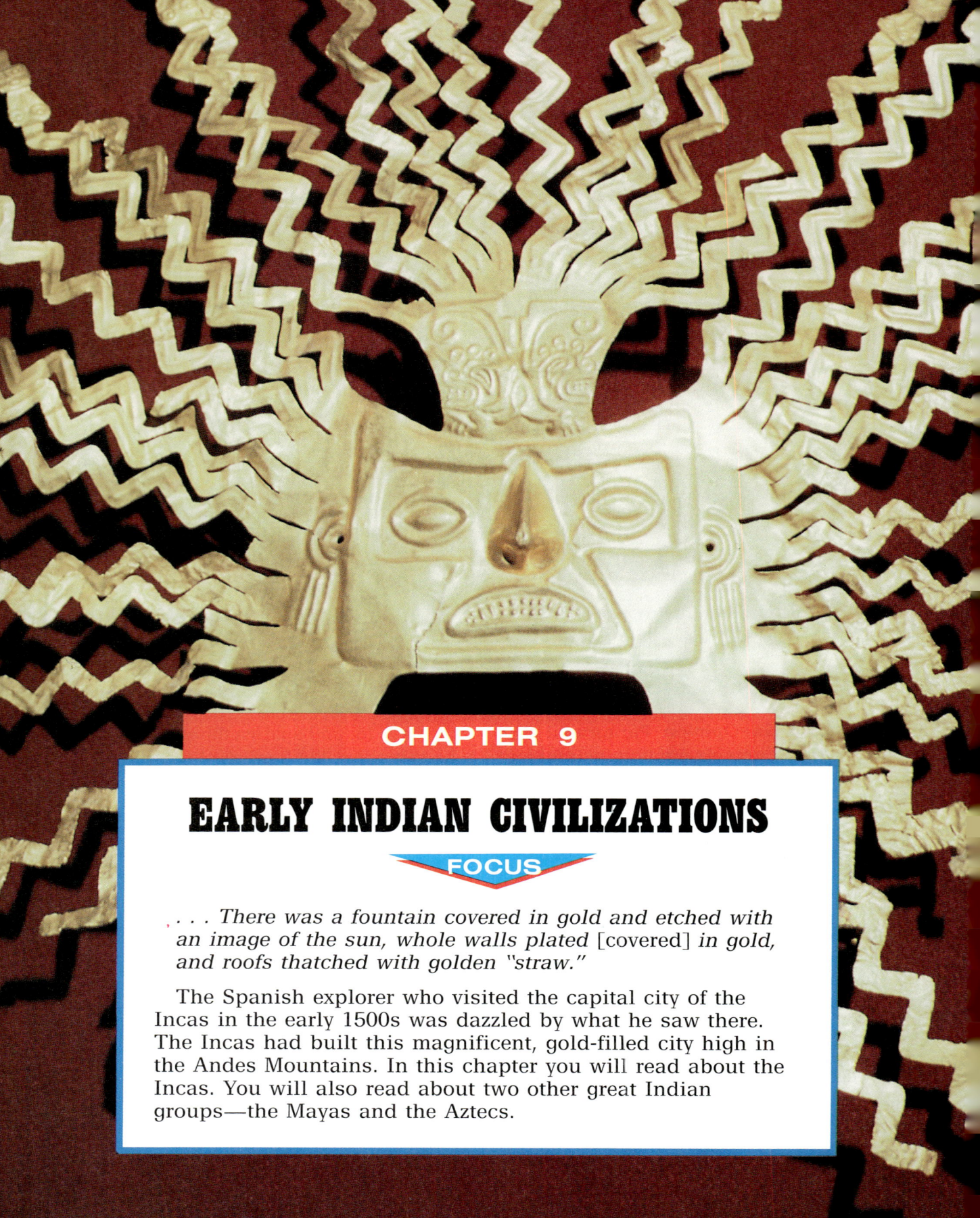

CHAPTER 9

EARLY INDIAN CIVILIZATIONS

FOCUS

. . . There was a fountain covered in gold and etched with an image of the sun, whole walls plated [covered] in gold, and roofs thatched with golden "straw."

The Spanish explorer who visited the capital city of the Incas in the early 1500s was dazzled by what he saw there. The Incas had built this magnificent, gold-filled city high in the Andes Mountains. In this chapter you will read about the Incas. You will also read about two other great Indian groups—the Mayas and the Aztecs.

READ TO LEARN

Key Vocabulary

civilization
pyramid
hieroglyphics

Key Places

Copán
Tikal

Read Aloud

The clump of dark forest . . . shrouds [hides] *the most extraordinary feature of the whole valley—a royal city . . . whose ornate buildings and sculptures, even in ruin, make it one of the greatest treasuries of art and architecture in all the Americas.*

George F. Stuart, an archaeologist, wrote these words after exploring the ruins of a city called Copán (kō pän′). Located in what is today Honduras in Central America, Copán was one of the centers of early American culture. In this lesson you will read about the builders of this magnificent city.

Read for Purpose

1. **WHAT YOU KNOW:** What is a culture?
2. **WHAT YOU WILL LEARN:** What were the most important characteristics of Mayan civilization?

EARLY AMERICAN CIVILIZATION

Throughout Latin America there are ruins of lost cities such as Copán. You may wonder what happened to these cities and their people. No one knows for sure, but scientists and archaeologists continue to seek clues. They have already found enough artifacts to provide many answers about the way of life of the people who built these cities.

As you read in Chapters 2 and 4, many different Indian cultures developed in the Western Hemisphere. Almost 10,000 years ago, Indians in Peru and Mexico learned how to farm. They also began to settle in communities. Before long some of these groups developed into complex societies. One of these groups was the Mayas, the builders of Copán.

THE CIVILIZATION OF THE MAYAS

From about the year 500 B.C. to about A.D. 900, the Mayan civilization dominated a large part of what is today Mexico and Central America. A civilization is a culture that has developed systems

203

of government, religion, and learning. Many early civilizations also had developed methods of writing.

Why were the Mayas able to develop a great civilization in the Western Hemisphere? Maize, or corn, is a big part of the answer. The Mayas were able to grow enough corn to feed their people. This allowed some people to spend their time doing things other than growing food. They could make pottery, weave cloth, or study the stars. People also had time to build cities.

You can find Copán and some of the other cities the Mayas built on the map below. The map shows where the Mayan civilization flourished. Cities were built by the Mayas throughout the Yucatán (ū kə tan′) Peninsula from the Gulf of Mexico to the Pacific Ocean. Ruins of Mayan cities also have been found in northern Central America.

MASTER BUILDERS

If you were to visit the Yucatán Peninsula today, you could see for yourself the remains of the buildings and cities of the Mayas.

The diagram on the opposite page shows one of the Mayas' great cities. Called Tikal (ti käl′), this city is located on the Yucatán Peninsula in what is today Guatemala. There are many pyramids in Tikal. A pyramid is a building with a square base and four triangular sides. Pyramids were used as tombs and as temples for religious ceremonies. As the diagram shows, there was also a ball court in Tikal where the Mayas played a game that was something like a blend of basketball, volleyball, and soccer. You will read more about this game in the Traditions lesson on pages 214–217.

A SYSTEM OF WRITING

In Tikal there is a special pyramid. Its back wall is completely covered with carvings of human figures, masks, animals, and symbols. These symbols are part of a system of writing called hieroglyphics (hī ər ə glif′ iks). Hieroglyphs are the symbols, signs, or pictures used in ancient writing. The Mayas were probably the first civilization in the Western Hemisphere to develop a system of writing.

What did the Mayas write about? For a long time the meaning of their writings was lost. However, scholars have solved some of the mystery. For example, they have learned that the Mayas wrote about their leaders and the key events in their cities. It also has been learned that the Mayas had developed a calendar. According to one scholar, their "method of keeping track of time was more accurate than any calendar

MAP SKILL: Which Mayan city is closest to the Pacific Ocean? How far is Tikal from Copán?

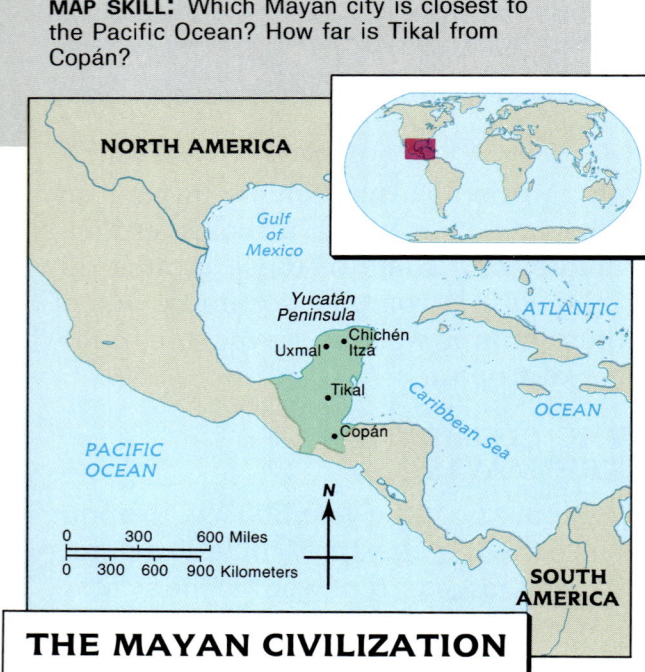

NORTH AMERICA

Gulf of Mexico

Yucatán Peninsula

Uxmal • • Chichén Itzá

• Tikal

• Copán

ATLANTIC OCEAN

Caribbean Sea

PACIFIC OCEAN

N

0   300   600 Miles
0 300 600 900 Kilometers

SOUTH AMERICA

THE MAYAN CIVILIZATION

TIKAL

Ball Court

Pyramid

Temple

Market

DIAGRAM SKILL: People who lived near Tikal would travel to the city to attend important religious ceremonies. What other activities are taking place?

Carved hieroglyphs (*above*) cover the wall over a door of a Mayan temple. These hieroglyphs (*above right*) represent the names of three days in one of the Mayan calendars.

Michael Holford/The British Museum

ever used in the ancient world." The illustrated hieroglyphs above represent three days on a Mayan calendar.

MAYAN LIFE

What was life like for the Mayas during the great period of Mayan civilization? The answer to this question depends on what a person's particular role was within Mayan society. Mayan society was organized like a pyramid. At the top were a small number of priests and nobles. Below them were craftsworkers and traders. At the largest section of the pyramid—the base—were farmers, other workers, and enslaved people. Most enslaved people were captured from other Indian groups.

The priests and nobles held the most power. Nobles were responsible for governing and for making nearly all important decisions. Nobles were regarded with awe by the people they ruled. They were considered so important that attendants held cloths in front of the nobles' faces so that no one could talk to them directly.

Nobles appointed people to help them run the government. These officials collected taxes and enforced laws. They also acted as judges who decided on the punishment to be given for breaking the law. For example, thieves became the captives of their victims. People who committed crimes less serious than stealing were punished by having their hair cut short. Short hair was a sign of disgrace.

MAYAN FARMERS

Farmers formed the essential base of the Mayan social pyramid. What was life like for a Mayan farmer? Imagine that you are visiting a farming village near the city of Tikal. It is just before dawn. Families are beginning to wake up in the thatch-roofed houses of the village. After a breakfast of corn porridge, the men of the village leave to work in the cornfields. They spend much of the day ridding the fields of fast-growing weeds. Some weeds can be pulled out. Others must be cut with a stone ax.

While the men of the village work in the fields, you watch the women grind corn to make flour. They use the flour to make tortillas (tôr tē´ yəz), or thin, flat cakes. The tortillas, along with vegetables and sometimes dried fish, are eaten for lunch and dinner.

The older children of the village help their parents. Boys help their fathers in the fields, and girls help their mothers prepare the meals. Some of the older girls watch the very young children.

Mayan farmers were so successful that they grew more corn than their families needed. Extra corn was given to the nobles and priests. When the corn-growing season ended, the farmers, along with enslaved people, worked on large public-building projects. The farmers and slaves provided the tremendous amounts of labor needed to build Mayan cities.

MAYAN RELIGION

Because religion was very important, priests as well as nobles were at the top of the Mayan social pyramid. The Mayas believed in many gods and goddesses. For example, they believed in a rain god, a moon goddess, and a god of the sun. Mayan life revolved around religion. It was the priests who decided where and when cities should be built. They decided when crops should be planted. They also decided when animal or human sacrifices should be made. The Mayas carried out human sacrifices because they believed that the sacrifices pleased their gods.

AN UNSOLVED MYSTERY

By A.D. 900 Mayan civilization was showing signs of weakening. People began to leave the cities. Gradually, once thriving and powerful urban centers were swallowed up by thick forests. The giant buildings of the Mayas crumbled and turned into ruins. Archaeologists and historians do not know why this happened. It remains an unsolved mystery.

Many parts of Mayan culture have been preserved, however. More than 2 million Indians of Mayan descent live in Mexico and Guatemala today. Most of them live near the ruins of their ancestors' great centers of civilization.

The Mayas probably abandoned Tikal around A.D. 900. Today the ruins of Tikal's many **pyramids** can still be visited.

MAYAN CIVILIZATION

The Mayas developed a great civilization in the Western Hemisphere. They built large cities and created complex systems of government and religion. They also developed a system of writing that used hieroglyphs. Although Mayan civilization declined, many Indians of Mayan descent still live in parts of Middle America today.

 Check Your Reading

1. Explain what a civilization is.
2. Describe Mayan civilization.
3. GEOGRAPHY SKILL: Look at the map on page 204. Which Mayan city was located the farthest south?
4. THINKING SKILL: List three questions you could ask to learn more about Mayan religion.

Distinguishing Fact from Opinion

Key Vocabulary

fact
opinion
value judgment
reasoned opinion

Have you ever heard a story about a friend that you are not sure you should believe? How can you tell if something is true about a person or not? Distinguishing **facts** from **opinions** can help you decide what to believe.

A fact is a statement that can be proven true. An opinion is a personal view or belief. It cannot be proven true. One type of opinion is a **value judgment**. It tells how someone feels about something. A second type of opinion is a **reasoned opinion**. This is a personal belief supported by reasons or evidence.

The story that you heard about a friend might be a fact. If it cannot be proven true and is based solely on someone's feelings, it is a value judgment. If reasons or evidence are given, however, the story is a reasoned opinion.

Trying the Skill

Which of the following statements about the Mayas are facts? Which are opinions? Which opinions are supported by evidence?

The Mayas achieved a higher level of culture than other Indian societies that developed in Middle America. Even by modern-day standards, the Mayan civilization was very advanced. The Mayas built impressive cities, large ball courts, and awesome temples. They developed a calendar and a system of numbers and writing. Their writing, however, was very simple. It took the form of hieroglyphs, or pictures.

1. Which facts and opinions did you find?
2. Which opinions were supported by reasons?
3. How were you able to separate facts from opinions?

The steps on the left outline one way to distinguish facts from opinions. The example on the right shows how these steps can be used to distinguish facts from opinions in the paragraph about the Mayas.

One Way to Distinguish Facts from Opinions	Example
1. Recall the meaning of *fact*, *value judgment*, and *reasoned opinion*.	A fact is a statement that can be proven true. A value judgment is a personal belief or judgment. A reasoned opinion is an opinion that is supported by evidence or reasons.
2. Look for clues that signal statements of fact. Look for statements that can be proven true.	The statement that the Mayas built cities, ball courts, and temples can be proven true.
3. Look for clues that signal value judgments. Look for adjectives such as *best*, adverbs such as *probably*, and words such as *I think* that signal statements of opinion.	Words such as *higher level* and *very advanced* signal value judgments. The writer makes value judgments about facts by using words such as *awesome* and *impressive*.
4. Look for clues to reasoned opinions. Look for words such as *because* and value judgements supported by evidence.	The writer supports his opinion about the advanced level of Mayan civilization with specific examples.
5. Read each statement carefully to find clues to facts, value judgments, and reasoned opinions.	The statement that the Mayas developed a calendar and a system of numbers and writing can be checked. The statement that the writing was simple is a value judgment. Because the writer supports the opinion with the fact that Mayan writing took the form of hieroglyphs, he or she is giving a reasoned opinion.

Applying the Skill

Read each statement below. Decide which are facts and which are opinions. Explain your answers.

1. In Middle America there are the remains of cities built by the Mayas.
2. The temples built by the Mayas were awesome.
3. A writing system of hieroglyphs was an important factor in helping the Mayas to achieve a high level of culture.

Reviewing the Skill

1. What is a fact? What is a reasoned opinion?
2. What are some steps you can take to separate facts from opinions?
3. What are two things you could look for to distinguish facts from opinions?
4. Why is it important to distinguish facts from opinions?

READ TO LEARN

Key Vocabulary
specialize
empire
tribute

Key Places
Tenochtitlán

Read Aloud

Our walls are keening [crying],
Our tears fall down like rain.
Weep, weep, our people,
For we have lost Mexico.

The Aztec poet who wrote these words in 1523 was mourning the loss of one of the world's great civilizations. It had lasted for only a few hundred years. In this lesson you will read about how the Aztecs grew from a small group of people into a great power in Mexico.

Read for Purpose

1. WHAT YOU KNOW: What is a civilization?
2. WHAT YOU WILL LEARN: What were the achievements of Aztec civilization?

THE VALLEY OF MEXICO

The Aztec civilization developed in the Valley of Mexico. This valley is wedged between high mountains in what is today central Mexico. Water flowing off the mountain ranges fed a series of shallow, marshy lakes that covered a large part of the valley floor.

According to the Aztecs' legends, the Aztec people came from a northern land called Aztlan (äz' tlän). After migrating to the Valley of Mexico, the Aztecs wandered until one of their gods told them where to build a city. "Look for an eagle perched on a cactus and holding a snake," said the god.

After generations of Aztec people had wandered for about 200 years, Aztec priests stood on the shore of Lake Texcoco (tā skō' kō). Legend says that suddenly they saw an eagle with a snake wriggling in its beak. The cactus on which the bird was perched grew on one of Lake Texcoco's islands. The Aztecs would build their city here. They named the island Tenochtitlán (te nôch tē tlän'), "the Place of the Prickly Pear Cactus."

(*left*) Today farmers in Mexico still use chinampas like those that were used by the Aztecs. (*above*) This vase was made by an Aztec artist in Tenochtitlán.

USING THE ENVIRONMENT

It was about 1325 when the Aztecs settled on Tenochtitlán. The Valley of Mexico was an ideal environment for a settlement. The surrounding lakes provided not only water, but also fish and waterfowl for food, and reeds for thatching and weaving.

The Aztecs also found a way to increase the amount of land available for growing food. They did this by making chinampas (chi nam′ pəs), or floating gardens. Along the shores of the lakes that surrounded the city, Aztec farmers floated mats made of reeds woven together. They then covered the mats with soil and planted seeds in the soil.

The chinampas yielded abundant crops. Vegetables such as chili peppers, squash, corn, tomatoes, and beans were grown. Today farmers in Mexico continue to use chinampas in the south-central part of the country.

AZTEC SCHOOLS

Like the Mayas, Tenochtitlán's people had a stable food supply that gave them more time to do other things. They were able to **specialize**. In other words, these people were able to concentrate on doing particular kinds of work. For example, some people began to specialize as builders, engineers, weavers, or painters. In fact, teaching specialized skills became very important to the Aztecs. As the historian Albert Marrin explains:

The Aztecs were the only people in the world at that time to have free schools that every child had to attend. . . . Girls went to schools attached to temples to learn religion and women's crafts of weaving and embroidery. There were two types of boys' schools: those for ordinary citizens, including slaves, and those for the sons of nobles and the wealthiest merchants.

The boys' schools trained specialists such as traders, engineers, doctors, builders, and astronomers. These specially trained builders and engineers created cities such as Tenochtitlán.

211

TENOCHTITLÁN

Great Pyramid

Central Plaza

Temple

Chinampas

Bridge

Causeway

Weaving

Pottery

Farming

DIAGRAM SKILL: Causeways linked together the islands that made up the city of Tenochtitlán. How do you think Tenochtitlán's geography helped the Aztecs?

TENOCHTITLÁN FLOURISHES

Tenochtitlán became a great city with tall temples, broad open plazas, and large marketplaces. By the mid-1400s, Tenochtitlán had a population of about 300,000. It was the largest city in the world at that time.

As the diagram on the opposite page shows, broad causeways linked the island city of Tenochtitlán with the mainland. A causeway is a raised road made of earth.

BUILDING AN EMPIRE

Aztec civilization soon spread from Tenochtitlán. The Aztecs often waged war to expand their **empire**. An empire is a group of lands and people under the control of one government. You can see the range of the Aztec Empire on the map on this page.

War was also important to the Aztecs because they demanded **tribute** from those they conquered. Tribute was a tax that was paid in goods or services. Tribute often included food, clothing, precious stones, or feathers. People were also taken as tribute. Many were forced into slavery and used as laborers on large building projects.

Many enslaved people were also sacrificed. In fact, many Aztec wars were waged in order to capture people to be sacrificed. Like the Mayas, the Aztecs believed that human sacrifices pleased their gods. Often thousands of enslaved people were sacrificed at one time.

As you can imagine, the Aztecs were hated and feared by the people they had conquered. It was with the help of these conquered Indian groups that the European invaders eventually were able to conquer the Aztecs. In the next chapter you will read more about the conquest of the Aztecs.

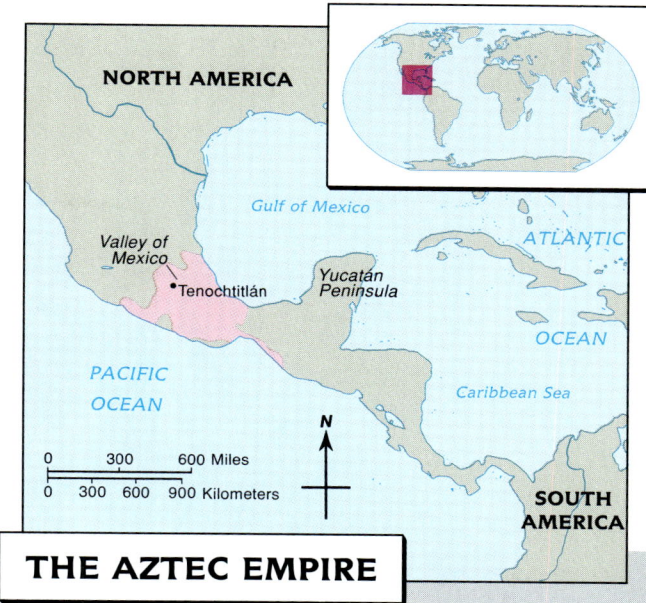

THE AZTEC EMPIRE

MAP SKILL: This statue (*below*) came from a temple in Tenochtitlán. Where is Tenochtitlán located in relation to the Yucatán Peninsula?

AZTEC CIVILIZATION

As you have read in this lesson, the Aztecs created a great civilization. By the mid-1400s they had built the largest city in the world—Tenochtitlán. However, their wars and demands for tribute gained the Aztecs many enemies and helped lead to their eventual downfall.

Check Your Reading

1. Why were chinampas important to the Aztecs?
2. Why were some of the Aztecs able to specialize?
3. How were the Aztecs able to enlarge their empire?
4. **THINKING SKILL:** Imagine that your area has just been conquered by the Aztecs. What do you predict the Aztecs will demand from your people?

A Serious Sport

 **by Eric Kimmel**

In Lesson 1 you read that the Mayas played a game resembling a blend of basketball, volleyball, and soccer. The Aztecs played a similar game. Like the Mayas, they took their sports very seriously. In fact, they sometimes settled disputes by playing ballgames instead of fighting wars! As you read, think about how the traditional sport of tlachtli (tläch' tlē) is similar to sports you may enjoy today.

AN AFTERNOON AT AN AZTEC BALLGAME

Imagine for a moment that you are living among the Aztecs. Along with the rest of the members of your village, you are gathered at a large court to watch a ballgame. With less than one minute left to play, your team is trailing. A player on your team checks the ball with his hip and tries to pass it on. Three members of the opposing team cut off your team's player. Can he pass? None of his teammates is in the clear. He tries for one last shot. The ball bounces off the wall. It teeters on the edge of the ring. It's in. Your team has won the game!

TLACHTLI

Wait a minute! What game is this? It isn't football. It isn't basketball or soccer, either. But its rules resemble those of all three. The Aztecs called it tlachtli (tläch' tlē), though it had many names during its long history. Many hundreds of years before the Aztecs, the Mayas played a version of this game on larger ball courts. They called it "pok-a-tok."

Tlachtli was played with a solid rubber ball that had a diameter of about 6 inches (15.2 cm), approximately the size of a bowling ball. The game took place in a special sunken court called the tlachco. Spectators looking down from above had a clear view of the action. The court itself was shaped like the capital letter *I*. A narrow gallery that might be as long as 200 feet (61 m) connected two square end zones, or the areas at the end of the field. A black or green line marked the boundary of each team's territory. High walls surrounded the court itself. Two stone rings hung down from the gallery walls at either side of this line.

THE RULES OF THE GAME

The object of the game was to drive a ball over a center dividing line into your opponent's territory. The ball could be bounced off the walls as in racquetball, but it could not touch the ground. It had to be kept in the air at all times. In order to score a point, players had to pass the ball across the goal line. If the ball touched the ground at any point, the goal did not count. The ball could not be kicked or thrown. A player could only touch the ball with his knees or hips. While scoring points was difficult, getting penalties was easy. A team lost points if a player touched the ball with any part of his body other than his knees or hips. Fouls were called if the ball touched the ground or went into the end zones.

215

THE WINNING POINT

No matter how far behind a team might find itself, or how little time remained, the losing team always had a chance to win the game. That's because the real object of tlachtli was to pass the ball through the hole in one of the stone rings that hung down on either side of the gallery walls in the center of the court. As soon as that happened, the game ended. It did not matter how many points ahead the other team was. The team that was the first to pass the ball through the stone ring automatically won.

Getting the ball through the ring, however, was not that easy. The rings were hung about 8 to 10 feet (2 to 3 m) above the ground. And the hole was less than 1 foot (0.3 m) wide. The rings of one elaborate tlachtli court were actually 35 feet (10 m) off the ground. No one knows if anyone ever scored a goal on that court, but it certainly would have been one for the record books.

A DANGEROUS GAME

Not only was tlachtli difficult, it was also dangerous. Imagine a solid 5-pound (2.2-kg) rubber ball about the size of a bowling ball bouncing around a narrow court! It was

not unusual for players to be seriously hurt or even killed while playing tlachtli. To protect themselves from the ball, the players wore thick, wide leather belts and heavy collars that covered most of their upper bodies. Knee pads, elbow pads, and special gloves allowed the players to drop to the ground to recover low-flying balls.

Both teams played with an intensity that cannot be matched even in today's most exciting sports contests. That's because the results of tlachtli could be more serious than the outcome of any game played today.

Sometimes two rival cities would have their best teams play each other as a way to solve disputes without going to war. At other times tlachtli games played a part in religious ceremonies. The losers did not just go home empty-handed. Sometimes they never went home at all. Members of the losing team were sometimes sacrificed to the gods. The players lost their lives, but war was avoided.

SUPERSTAR ATHLETES

The Aztecs treated tlachtli players in much the same way that superstar athletes are treated today. A player who scored the winning goal was regarded as a hero. The Aztecs honored him as they would a famous chief. The athlete was entitled to wear a special uniform. People surrounded him wherever he went, dancing around him and singing songs of praise. He also gained considerable wealth. According to an ancient custom, a tlachtli player who sent a ball through the ring was automatically entitled to the clothes and jewelry of everyone watching the game.

PAST AND PRESENT

The ancient ball courts of the Aztecs stand silent today. This ancient game is played in only a few small villages. Other sports games have become more popular. Although the results of these newer games are not as serious as the outcome of a game of tlachtli was in ancient times, excitement over sports in Latin America lives on.

How do modern-day sports resemble the traditional sport of tlachtli? How do they differ?

3 The Incas

Key Vocabulary

emperor
irrigation
terrace

Key Places

Cuzco
Machu Picchu

Read Aloud

When, at long last, the harvest was gathered in, there was a great festival of thanksgiving. The first grains of corn were offered to the gods on family shrines which were set up in fields.

According to the writer of these words, Brenda Ralph Lewis, the Incas held harvest festivals of thanksgiving. The Incas had much to celebrate. They were very successful farmers. They were also very successful builders. In this lesson you will read about the Incan civilization that developed in the Andes Mountains of South America.

Read for Purpose

1. **WHAT YOU KNOW:** Where are the Andes Mountains located?
2. **WHAT YOU WILL LEARN:** How was the empire of the Incas united?

THE LAST INDIAN EMPIRE

The civilization of the Incas was not the first to develop in the Andes Mountains. People have been living and farming in the western part of South America for thousands of years. Early societies lived along the Pacific Coast and fought with each other for control of important food resources.

Several of these societies developed flourishing civilizations. By about 1450, however, the Incas became the dominant society. They created the last great Indian empire in the Western Hemisphere.

As the map on the opposite page shows, the Incan Empire stretched for about 2,500 miles (4,000 km) along the western part of South America. The Incas ruled an area that included what is today the countries of Ecuador, Peru, Bolivia, Chile, and Argentina. The Incas ruled more than 12 million people. They lived in environments that varied from desert coastal lowlands to the rugged Andes Mountains.

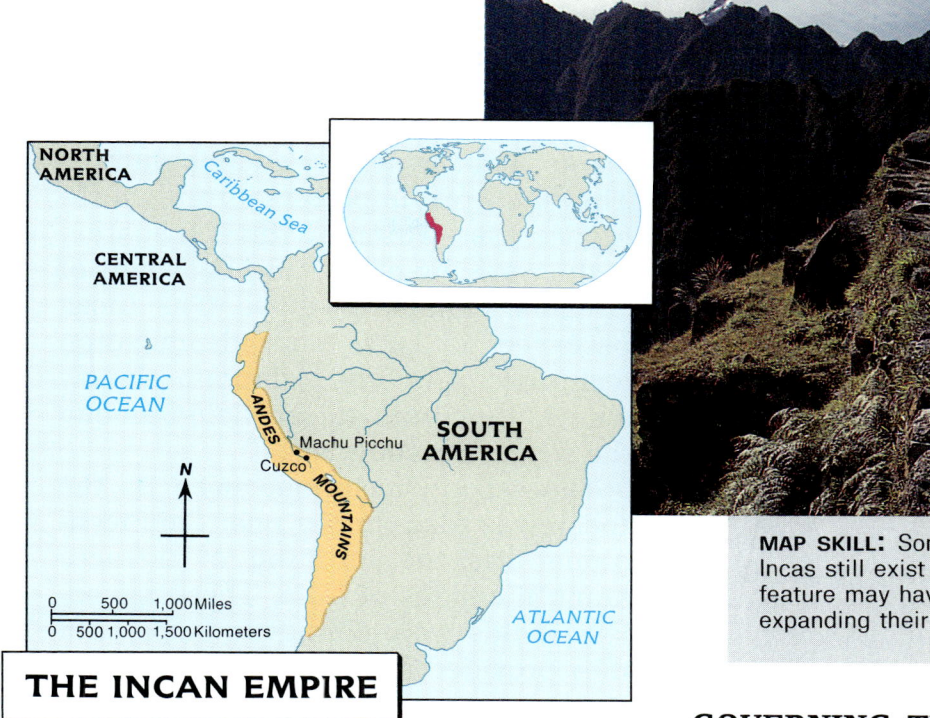

THE INCAN EMPIRE

MAP SKILL: Some of the roads built by the Incas still exist today. What geographic feature may have prevented the Incas from expanding their empire inland?

CHILDREN OF THE SUN

How did the Incas come to power? Like the Aztecs, they did so by conquering neighboring Indian groups. As each group was conquered, a road was built connecting the newly conquered area with the rest of the Incan Empire. In fact, the Incas built thousands of miles of roads. Specially trained runners were stationed along these roads. They would relay messages throughout the empire. This efficient communication system was the fastest in the world at that time.

Cuzco (küs' kō) was the capital of the Incan Empire. It was from Cuzco that the Incan leader ruled his empire. The Incan leader was an emperor, or an absolute ruler. According to Incan legend, the emperor was descended from the sun. His ancestor was Inti, the sun god. The Incas worshiped many gods, but the sun god was the most important. In fact, all Incas called themselves "Children of the Sun."

GOVERNING THE EMPIRE

How did the Incan emperor rule his people? His government held a tight grip on society. Almost all the activities of the emperor's subjects were watched closely. Every person had to report to a local official. These officials controlled almost every aspect of Incan life. They decided what each farmer should plant and when. Food, clothing, and even cooking utensils were distributed by government officials.

These officials also decided how much a person should pay the government in taxes. The Incas did not use money. Instead, the officials collected part of each farmer's harvest. Taxpayers also had to work for the government for part of the year. They built bridges and roads, and performed other kinds of labor.

Although the people of the Incan Empire had little freedom, they were secure. The government made sure that each person received enough food and clothing. The Incas never went hungry and were never homeless.

FARMING TECHNOLOGY

As you have read, the Incas were successful farmers. In fact, farming is perhaps the area of this civilization's greatest achievement. One historian has estimated that more than half of the kinds of foods the world eats today were developed by the Incas. Among the many crops they grew were beans, potatoes, corn, squash, tomatoes, and peppers. The Incas raised animals called llamas (lä′ məz) for their meat and their wool. They also had domesticated the llamas so that they could be used to carry goods.

The Incas managed to be successful farmers in some very harsh environments, such as deserts and mountains. They used two important farming techniques. One was irrigation. Irrigation is the watering of dry land by means of streams, canals, or pipes. The Incas perfected a 3,000-year-old irrigation technique. As the diagram below shows, they built raised fields among the irrigation channels.

The second technique used by the Incas was also an old one. This technique was the building of terraces along the sides of hills. These raised, level fields were similar to steps, and they provided more flat land for farming in a rugged area. Terraces also helped to catch and hold rainfall. The

DIAGRAM SKILL: With the use of irrigation and terraces, the Incas became very successful farmers. Why were irrigation channels necessary?

Terraces

Terraces

Raised field

Reservoir

Irrigation channel

Raised field

INCAN AGRICULTURE

Incas' terraces and irrigation systems helped them to produce a surplus of food. This means they had more food than their people needed.

THE INCAN SPECIALISTS

As you know, a surplus of food allowed the Mayas and Aztecs to specialize. A surplus of food also enabled the Incas to specialize. During the height of Incan civilization in the 1500s, people worked as potters, goldsmiths, jewelers, architects, engineers, carpenters, and builders. Today visitors to Incan cities, such as Cuzco, still marvel at the skill of Incan builders.

Incan architects and builders also created some of the most impressive buildings in the world. Many Incan buildings were made from huge stones. Incan engineers were able to cut the stones to fit together perfectly without the use of mortar or cement. Sheets of gold often covered the walls of important buildings.

High in the Andes the Incas built Machu Picchu (mäch ü pēk′ chü), one of the most spectacular works of engineering in the world. This city was made up of stone buildings that sprawled across a high ridge.

A DRAMATIC CHANGE

In the early 1500s the Incan Empire reached its greatest size. But the days of the empire were drawing to a close. In the year 1526, only months after the death of an emperor, a conflict between his sons grew into a terrible war. Finally one brother defeated the other and gained power. But the war left the empire greatly weakened. As you will read in the next lesson, soldiers from the faraway country of Spain were about to arrive.

Machu Picchu was eventually abandoned by the Incas. Its ruins were not found until 1911.

INCAN ACHIEVEMENTS

The Incas developed the last great Indian empire in the Western Hemisphere. Successful agricultural techniques, such as irrigation and terraces, allowed the Incas to grow a surplus of crops. They built roads and buildings that still exist today.

Check Your Reading

1. Over the lands of which present-day countries did the Incas rule?
2. Describe the two techniques that helped the Incas to become successful farmers.
3. How did the Incas control their empire?
4. THINKING SKILL: What effects do you think the spread of Incan power had on the other peoples of the Andes?

221

IMPORTANT EVENTS

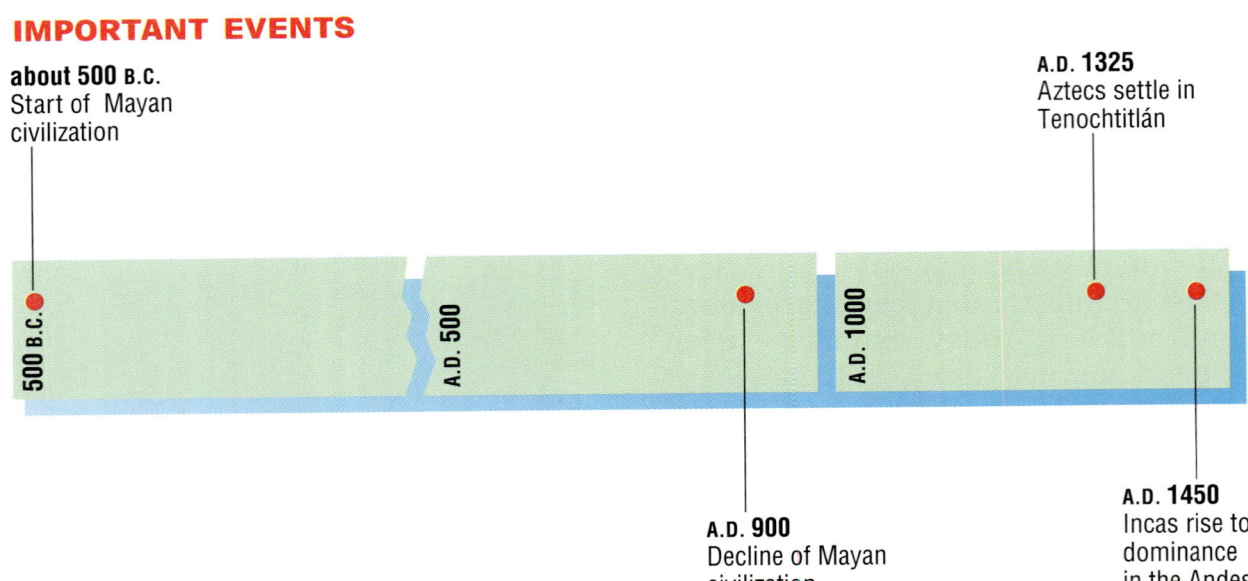

about 500 B.C.
Start of Mayan
civilization

A.D. 1325
Aztecs settle in
Tenochtitlán

500 B.C.

A.D. 500

A.D. 1000

A.D. 900
Decline of Mayan
civilization

A.D. 1450
Incas rise to
dominance
in the Andes

IDEAS TO REMEMBER

■ The Mayas developed a complex society in which religion played a key role. They also built large cities and created a system of writing.

■ The Aztecs, builders of the magnificent city of Tenochtitlán, fought many wars to expand their empire and, as a result, made many enemies.

■ The Incas started the last great Indian empire in the Americas. They used advanced farming techniques, such as irrigation, and built a vast network of roads and a number of cities.

REVIEWING VOCABULARY

civilization   pyramid
emperor   specialize
empire   terrace
hieroglyphics   tribute
irrigation

Number a sheet of paper from 1 to 10. Beside each number write the word or term from the list above that best completes the sentence. One of the words is used more than once.

1. The farmer used ____ to bring water to his fields.
2. The Mayas developed a ____ in what is today Mexico and Central America.
3. The Aztecs fought their neighbors in order to increase the size of their ____.
4. The Aztecs made the peoples they conquered pay ____ in the form of food, clothing, or enslaved people.

5. The Incas were ruled by an ____, who was an absolute ruler.
6. The Mayas developed a system of writing called ____.
7. When people ____, they each learn to concentrate on a certain job and to do that job well.
8. A ____ is a culture that has developed systems of government, religion, and learning.
9. The farmer will make a ____ on the land so that crops can be planted on the steep hills.
10. The ____ was a huge structure with a square base and four triangular sides.

REVIEWING FACTS

Number a sheet of paper from 1 to 10. Beside each number, write whether the item is associated with the Mayas, the Aztecs, or the Incas. Some items might be associated with more than one of the civilizations.

1. built pyramids
2. built chinampas, or floating gardens
3. used irrigation
4. developed a system of writing
5. specialization
6. regularly went to war
7. built many roads
8. developed a calendar
9. schools for boys and girls
10. known as "Children of the Sun"

WRITING ABOUT MAIN IDEAS

1. **Writing a Comparing Paragraph:** Write a paragraph in which you discuss the similarities of and differences between the Mayas and the Incas. Consider such topics as their achievements, their type of government, and how long their civilization lasted.
2. **Writing a Table of Contents:** Imagine that you are writing a book about ancient cities of the Mayas, Aztecs, and Incas. Write a table of contents that lists at least four chapters in the book. Write a sentence summarizing the content of each chapter.
3. **Writing a Paragraph:** Choose one of the civilizations discussed in this chapter. What do you think was its main achievement? Write a paragraph describing the achievement and telling why you think it was most important.
4. **Writing About Perspectives:** Pretend that you are a farmer under the rule of the Incas. Write an imaginary journal in which you describe your everyday life.

BUILDING SKILLS: IDENTIFYING FACT AND OPINION

Number a sheet of paper from 1 to 5. Beside each number write whether the statement is a fact or an opinion. Then explain how you can tell.

1. Indians in Peru probably learned how to farm 5,000 years ago.
2. The Mayas built cities throughout the Yucatán Peninsula from the Gulf of Mexico to the Caribbean Sea.
3. By the mid-1400s, Tenochtitlán was the largest city in the world.
4. Incan architects and builders created some of the most impressive architecture in the world.
5. Why is it important to be able to tell the difference between a fact and an opinion?

CHAPTER 10

EUROPEANS COME TO AMERICA

FOCUS

That night of destiny was clear and beautiful. . . . The men were tense and expectant. . . . At 2:00 A.M., 12 October, Rodrigo de Triana, lookout on Pinta, sees something like a white cliff shining in the moonlight and sings out, Tierra! Tierra! Land! Land!

The historian Samuel Eliot Morison used these words to describe the night in 1492 when one of Christopher Columbus's sailors sighted American land. That "night of destiny" would change the history of the Western Hemisphere.

1 European Explorers

READ TO LEARN

Key Vocabulary

astrolabe
compass
caravel

Key People

Christopher Columbus
Amerigo Vespucci
Pedro Álvares Cabral
Juan Ponce de León
Vasco Núñez de Balboa
Ferdinand Magellan

Key Places

Strait of
Magellan

Read Aloud

Gentlemen, we are now steering into waters where no ship has sailed before.

Ferdinand Magellan, a Portuguese explorer, said these words as he sailed into the Pacific Ocean in the early 1500s. Magellan was wrong, of course. Only ships from Europe had never sailed into the Pacific Ocean. In this lesson you will read about some of the Europeans who began to explore the waters and lands of the Western Hemisphere.

Read for Purpose

1. **WHAT YOU KNOW:** What dangers might explorers face when they travel into areas unknown to them?
2. **WHAT YOU WILL LEARN:** Which European voyages started a race for land and riches in the Western Hemisphere?

EUROPEAN TRADING

By the early 1400s, at the height of the Aztec Empire, Europeans were busy traders. For many years they had used land routes across Asia to reach India, China, and "the Indies." The Indies are the islands of Southeast Asia. Why did these faraway lands fascinate Europeans? Because there they knew that they could buy products such as spices, silks, cottons, and dyes, which were unavailable in Europe. In the mid-1400s, Europeans began to look for faster and easier routes to their rich trading partners in Asia.

IMPROVEMENTS IN NAVIGATION

Many people felt that an all-water route was the answer. Advances in mapmaking helped to make voyages of exploration possible. For example, European mapmakers began to include lines of latitude on charts and maps of

225

Explorers like Columbus used new instruments such as this Arabian **astrolabe** (*above*) and the **caravel** (*right*) for long journeys at sea.

the oceans. As you know, lines of latitude show distance north and south of the equator. Mapmakers also showed the directions of the ocean currents on these maps and charts.

European navigators also improved sea travel. They developed better ways to chart courses at sea. Sailors could determine their ship's latitude by using the **astrolabe** (as′ trə lāb), an instrument that measured the positions of stars and planets. Europeans also improved the magnetic **compass**, which the Chinese had invented. A compass shows the direction of the magnetic north. With it, sailors could determine their location even on days when clouds blocked the sun or stars.

Another improvement was the development of the **caravel** (kar′ ə vel). The caravel was a sailing vessel designed for rough seas and long voyages. It was large enough to hold supplies for a long trip of several months. The caravel's smooth hull and large sails helped sailors to make their way safely through ocean currents and storms.

THE VOYAGES OF COLUMBUS

As you read in the Chapter Focus on page 224, **Christopher Columbus** and his sailors first saw land in the Western Hemisphere in 1492. Columbus was born in Genoa, Italy, but he was sailing for the king and queen of Spain. Columbus believed that one could sail west to reach India and China in the East. Most people in Europe at that time were trying to reach Asia by sailing south and then east around Africa. Columbus, however, believed that his route would be faster.

Columbus's fleet of three ships—the *Niña*, the *Pinta*, and the *Santa María*—set sail from Spain on August 3, 1492. As his ships sailed farther west into the Atlantic Ocean, his sailors became more and more frightened. When they still had not seen land by October 10, they were terrified. They demanded that the ships be turned around and that they return to Spain. But Columbus was determined. He promised to return if they did not sight land in two days. As you read in the Chapter Focus, land was finally sighted by a sailor on October 12.

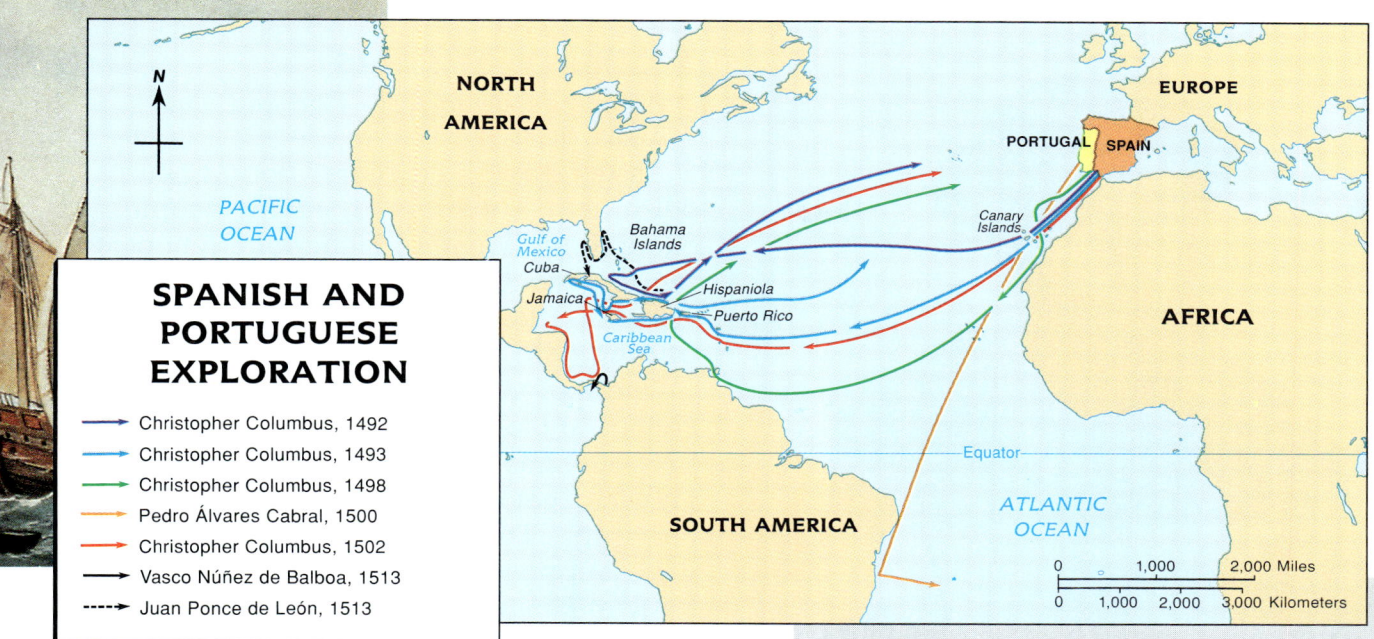

SPANISH AND PORTUGUESE EXPLORATION

→ Christopher Columbus, 1492
→ Christopher Columbus, 1493
→ Christopher Columbus, 1498
→ Pedro Álvares Cabral, 1500
→ Christopher Columbus, 1502
→ Vasco Núñez de Balboa, 1513
⇢ Juan Ponce de León, 1513

MAP SKILL: In what year did Christopher Columbus make his last voyage to the Western Hemisphere?

Columbus and his men had reached one of the small islands of the group now known as the Bahamas. Look at the Bahamas on the map on page 566 of the Atlas. You will find these islands off the coast of what is today the state of Florida. Columbus mistakenly called these islands the Indies because he thought he had reached the islands of Southeast Asia.

Columbus made three more voyages to the Western Hemisphere. You can trace his routes on the map above. Even after his fourth voyage Columbus still remained convinced that he had reached Asia.

NAMING THE AMERICAS

Of course, Columbus did not realize he had reached a continent previously unknown to Europeans. A merchant from Florence, Italy, named **Amerigo Vespucci** (äm ə rē′ gō ves pü′ chē) was the first European to realize the importance of this land. Vespucci crossed the Atlantic Ocean in 1499 and 1501. In his letters he described the coastline of the land that we know as Brazil. This was not Asia, he wrote, but a continent unknown to Europeans.

Vespucci's letters were read by Martin Waldseemüller (vält′ zā mül ər), a German mapmaker. In 1507 he published a new map of the world showing a great mass of land west of the Atlantic Ocean. He labeled this land *America,* in honor of Amerigo Vespucci.

THE RACE BEGINS

Columbus may have been wrong about reaching Asia, but his voyages started a race for land and riches among all of the powerful European nations of the time. Spain was the first country to begin carving out an empire in the Western Hemisphere. As you read in Chapter 5, English, French, and Dutch explorers also claimed vast amounts of land in North America.

In 1500 Portugal claimed the land that is now Brazil. A Portuguese ship

227

Balboa's sighting of the Pacific Ocean (*bottom*) led Magellan (*top*) to try to reach Asia by sailing around South America.

A VARIETY OF GOALS

We came here to serve God and also to get rich.

As the Spanish explorer Bernal Díaz del Castillo explained, many people came to the Western Hemisphere hoping to serve God. They wanted to convert the Indians to Christianity. But finding gold was also important.

One explorer, however, set out to find something else. His name was **Juan Ponce de León** (wän pons də lā on'). He was seeking a legendary "fountain of youth." The waters of this fountain were supposed to keep people young forever. He never found the fountain of youth, but he did become the first European to reach the large peninsula known today as Florida.

Other Spanish explorers fanned out across the Caribbean Sea. In 1513 **Vasco Núñez de Balboa** (väs' kō nün' yäs dā bal bō' ə) pushed through the thick rain forest of Central America. From a hilltop on the Isthmus of Panama, he saw a vast body of water. Balboa named it the South Sea, thinking it lay south of Asia. In fact, he was the first person from Europe to see the Pacific Ocean.

A VOYAGE AROUND THE WORLD

In 1519, only six years after Balboa's sighting of the Pacific Ocean, five ships left Spain and began a long voyage. The sailing expedition was led by **Ferdinand Magellan**, an explorer from Portugal. Magellan hoped to be able to reach Asia by sailing around South America and then west across the ocean sighted by Balboa. You can follow the route of Magellan and his crew on the map on page 229.

A year after he had left Spain, Magellan reached a stormy waterway at the

reached Brazil because of a sailing accident. **Pedro Álvares Cabral** (pā' drō äl' vär is kə bräl') and his crew were blown off course on a journey along the coast of western Africa. Their ship was blown far west and eventually reached the eastern coast of South America. Cabral was the first of many Portuguese explorers to reach the Western Hemisphere in the 1500s.

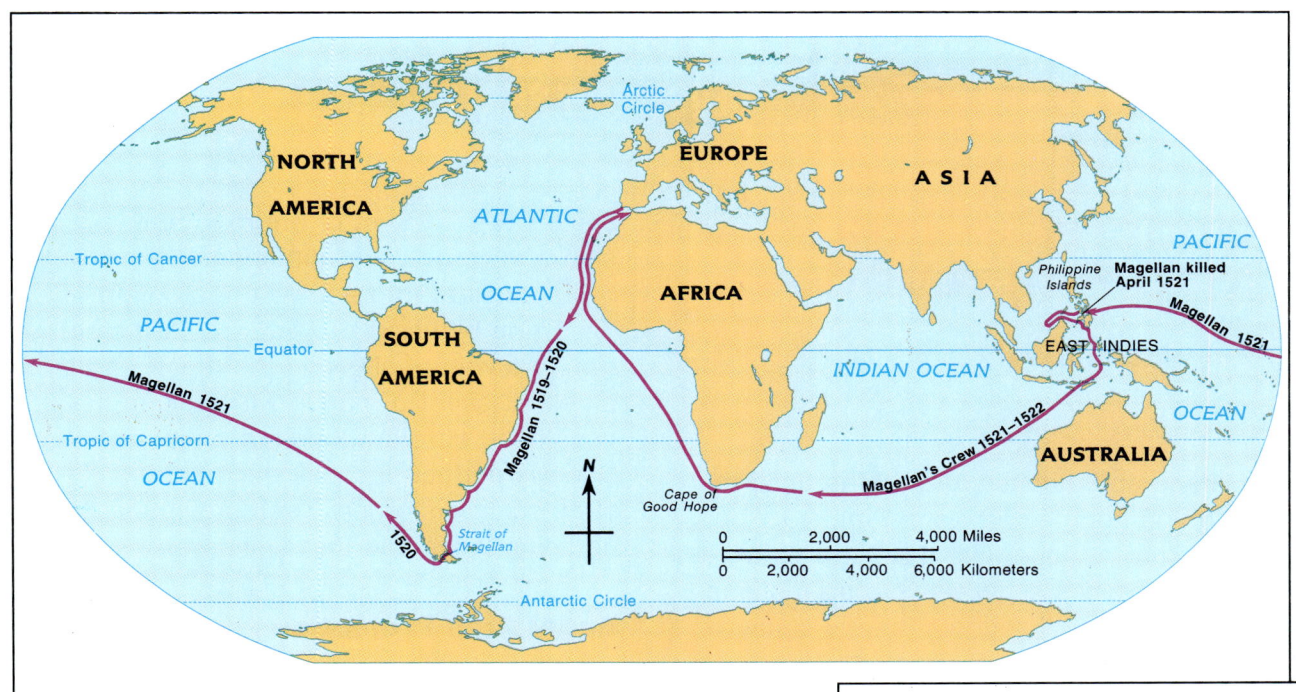

MAP SKILL: How many times did Magellan's ships cross the equator?

southern tip of South America. This narrow waterway is now called the **Strait of Magellan**. By this time one of Magellan's ships had been wrecked and another had returned to Spain. From the stormy strait, Magellan's small fleet sailed into the ocean that Balboa had seen. Magellan gratefully named it *El Pacífico*, or "the peaceful" ocean. Two years later, in 1522, one of Magellan's ships finally struggled back to Spain. The other ships had begun to leak and had been abandoned. Of the 237 people who had set out on the expedition, only 17 returned. Magellan was not among them. He had been killed during a small battle on an island in Southeast Asia. Magellan had been correct, however. Asia could be reached by sailing around South America and continuing west.

A CHANGING WORLD

After the success of Columbus's first voyage in 1492, other explorers began crossing the Atlantic Ocean. The voyages of these explorers enabled some European countries to claim vast areas of the Western Hemisphere. In the next lessons, you will read about what happened when the Europeans and Indians encountered each other.

Check Your Reading

1. Which advances in navigation helped sailors to make long ocean voyages?
2. Why were the voyages of Columbus important?
3. How did the voyage of Balboa help Magellan?
4. **THINKING SKILL:** List in chronological order the dates and leaders of the voyages of exploration that were discussed in this lesson.

Understanding Map Projections

Key Vocabulary
distortion
projection

Maps and globes can both be used to help you learn about Latin America. You know that a globe, like the earth, is a sphere. Globes show relative size, shape, distance, and direction correctly because a globe is a model of the earth.

Maps, on the other hand, show the earth less accurately. They are drawn on a flat surface, such as paper. In order to transfer what is on a round globe onto a flat map, parts of the globe must be cut or stretched. This cutting or stretching causes distortions, or errors in size, shape, distance, and direction.

Mapmakers try to solve the problem of distortion by using projections. A projection is a way of showing the round earth on a flat sheet of paper. Mapmakers have developed different kinds of projections. None is perfect because each one contains some distortion. Each projection has its advantages and disadvantages.

Equal-Area Projection

Map A below is an example of an equal-area projection. This type of projection is often used to give a view of the whole earth. Equal-area projections show the relative size of land and water areas fairly accurately. They are also used to compare the sizes of different places.

MAP A: Equal-Area Projection

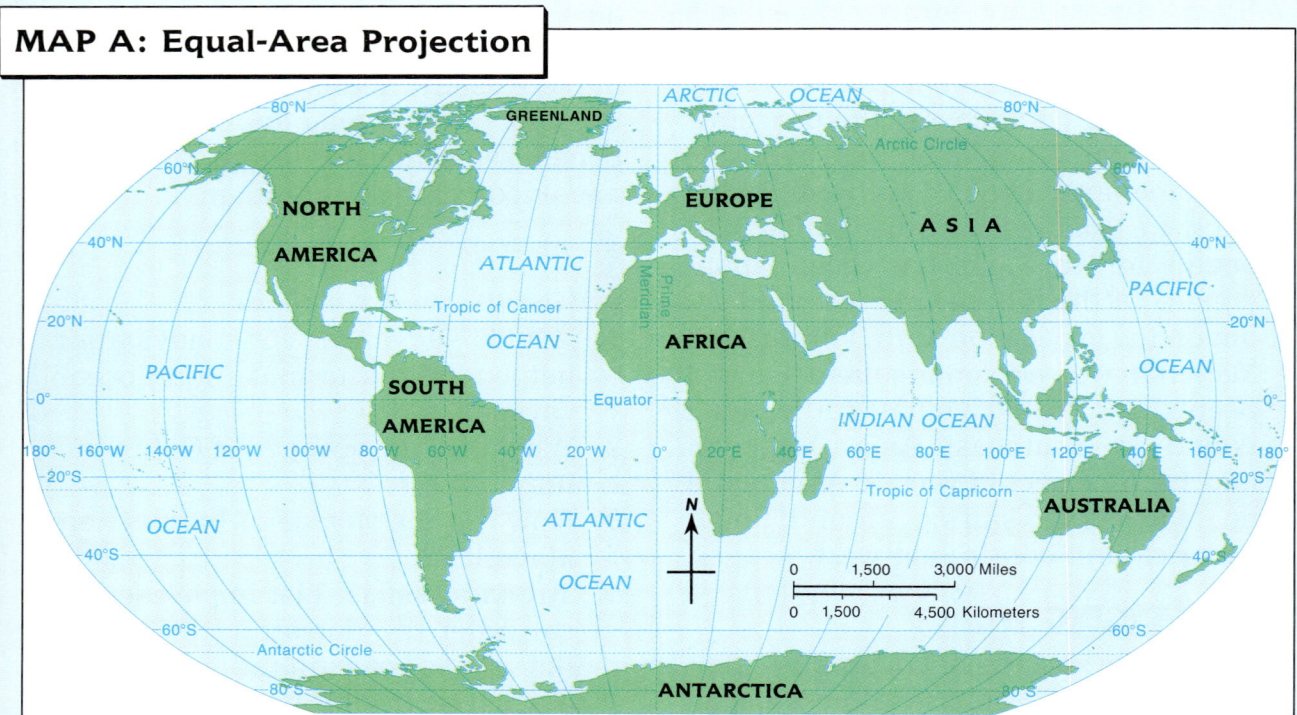

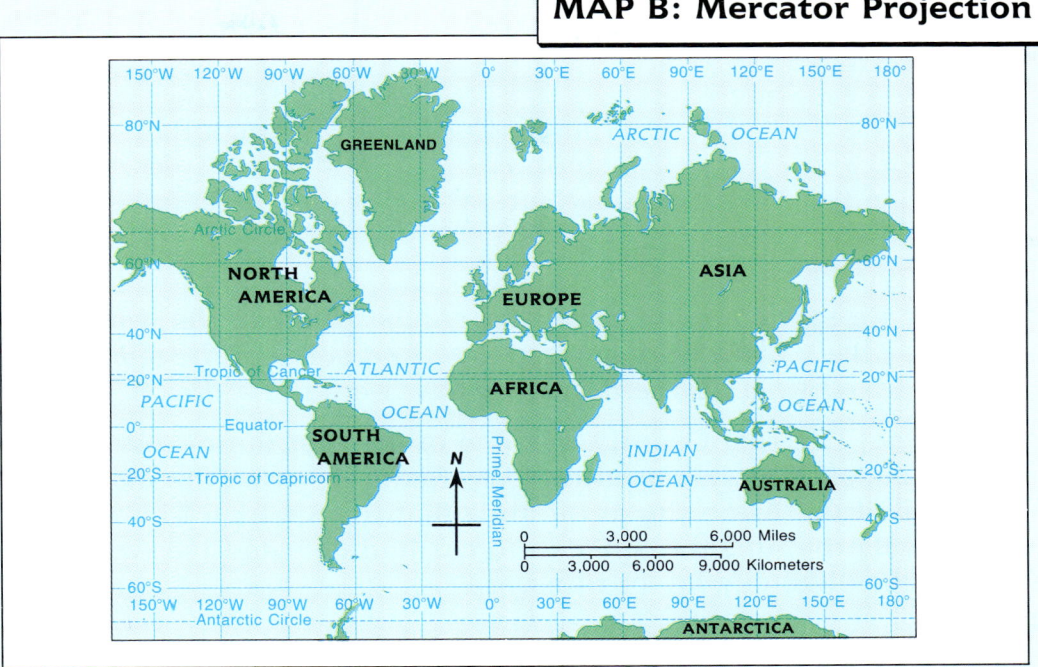

MAP B: Mercator Projection

However, there are some problems with equal-area projections. Shapes and distances are fairly accurate near the center of the map. At the edges they are badly distorted. Also, latitude lines are shown correctly on an equal-area map. But longitude lines are not shown as straight lines, except at the prime meridian. Find 20°E on **Map A**. Notice its curved shape. Now look at 140°E. As you can see, directions become more and more distorted as you move away from the center of the map.

The Mercator Projection

Another commonly used projection is the Mercator projection. On **Map B**, which uses this kind of projection, all lines of latitude and all lines of longitude are shown as straight lines. These lines and all lines accurately drawn on the map show compass directions. As a result,

north is always toward the top of the map, and east is to the right. Ship navigators use Mercator projections because they are able to draw their courses in straight lines.

Mercator projections show shapes accurately. However, they do not show size correctly. Places near the equator are shown more or less to scale. But the farther a place is from the equator, the more its size is distorted. You can test this by comparing a landmass on the map above to the same place on a globe.

Reviewing the Skill

1. What is distortion on maps? What is a projection?
2. Which projection shows sizes more accurately?
3. Why is it helpful to understand map projections?

231

2 The Conquest of Mexico

READ TO LEARN

Key Vocabulary

conquistador

Key People

Hernando Cortés
Moctezuma
Doña Marina

Key Places

Tenochtitlán

Read Aloud

When we saw so many cities and villages built in the waters of the lake . . . we were amazed. . . . And some of the soldiers even asked whether the things we saw were not a dream.

Bernal Díaz del Castillo was one of the first Europeans to see Tenochtitlán. He used these words to describe the magnificence of the Aztec city at the time that the Spanish first arrived. By the time the Spanish forces had defeated the Aztecs, the dreamlike city lay in ruins.

Read for Purpose

1. **WHAT YOU KNOW:** What was life like in Tenochtitlán?
2. **WHAT YOU WILL LEARN:** How did the Spanish conquer the Aztec Empire?

CONQUISTADORS

As you read in Chapter 9, by the early 1500s the Aztec and the Incan peoples had built two huge empires in the Western Hemisphere. However, Columbus never knew about these empires. The first Spanish explorers in the Western Hemisphere stayed mainly on the islands of the Caribbean Sea. Soon, however, their desire for riches and adventure led them to explore the mainland. During their expeditions, the Spaniards conquered the Indian groups they met. Thus, they were called conquistadors (kon kēs' tə dôrz). This name comes from the Spanish word meaning "to conquer."

HERNANDO CORTÉS

Like many conquistadors, **Hernando Cortés** (er nän' dō kôr tez') was said to be courageous, charming, and ruthless. Cortés had come from Spain to Cuba, an island in the Caribbean, when he was 19. He was given some land by the Cuban governor for farming. But Cortés had other ideas.

Land? I don't want land. I didn't come here to till [plow] the soil like a peasant. I came for gold!

Cortés soon had his chance to look for gold. The governor of Cuba had heard tales of Aztec wealth in Mexico. He decided to send an expedition to Mexico in search of the Aztecs. Cortés eagerly accepted the governor's invitation to lead the expedition. He sailed from Cuba to Mexico on November 18, 1518. His fleet of 11 vessels carried 508 soldiers, 2 priests, 16 horses, and a few small cannons. Cortés's group quickly set up a small settlement along the Gulf of Mexico.

As you read in Chapter 9, religion was very important to the Aztecs. They worshiped many gods, including one called Quetzalcoatl (ket säl kō ä′ təl). According to Aztec legend, Quetzalcoatl had vanished over the ocean, but promised to return one day. The Aztecs even predicted the year in which he would return. It was the same year in which Cortés and his soldiers arrived in Mexico.

Word of the arrival of Cortés reached Moctezuma (mäk tə zü′ mə), the Aztec ruler. Moctezuma is sometimes also known as Montezuma. It was Moctezuma's belief that Cortés and his men were gods, or at least messengers from Quetzalcoatl.

Moctezuma's soldiers outnumbered the Spaniards and could have killed them easily. But Moctezuma was not sure of the Spaniards' intentions. He sent ambassadors to Cortés's settlement with gifts of gold and colorful feathers. He hoped that the Spaniards would accept the gifts and leave. But the golden gifts only made the Spaniards want to find their source.

THE MARCH TO TENOCHTITLÁN

Cortés was anxious to reach the Aztec capital of Tenochtitlán. But his soldiers were frightened because they were outnumbered by the Aztec soldiers. Most of the Spaniards wanted to return to Cuba. To prevent them from leaving, Cortés burned his ships.

Cortés received help from a woman who was called Doña Marina (dōn′ yä mä rē′ nä) by the Spanish, and *La Malinche* (lä mä lēn′ chä) by the Indians. Doña Marina had been an Aztec princess until she was enslaved. As a captive, she had lived with several different Indian groups and had learned their languages. She was able to help Cortés communicate with the different Indian groups that he met on his way to the Aztec capital.

The Granger Collection

With Doña Marina's help, Cortés (*right*) was able to communicate with many of the enemies of the Aztecs.

A RETURNING GOD?

As you read in Chapter 9, the Aztecs were disliked by many other Indian groups. With the help of Doña Marina, Cortés was able to persuade many of these groups to join him on his march toward Tenochtitlán. On August 16, 1519, he set out for Tenochtitlán with his small army.

This Aztec drawing shows Cortés and Doña Marina arriving in Tenochtitlán.

Moctezuma waited as the conquistadors marched toward Tenochtitlán. He could not decide what to do. Who was Cortés, Moctezuma wondered. Was he the returning god? Or was he an enemy that had to be crushed?

THE DEFEAT OF MOCTEZUMA

Nevermore will there be a Mexico; it is already gone forever.

An adviser used these words to warn Moctezuma as Cortés approached Tenochtitlán. Cortés and Moctezuma met on a causeway leading to the city. Tens of thousands of Aztecs watched from rooftops and canoes as the conquistadors marched into the city.

Cortés took Moctezuma prisoner. At first he tried to rule the Aztec Empire by issuing orders through Moctezuma. But the Aztecs soon realized that Cortés was not a god and that he was interested only in gold and power. The furious Aztec soldiers attacked the conquistadors. Cortés lost so many soldiers that his only hope was to escape from Tenochtitlán. As Cortés and his men were fleeing from the city, Moctezuma was killed.

A year later Cortés returned with an army of Spanish soldiers and Indian allies, or supporters. He and his army surrounded the city. No food or fresh water could be brought into Tenochtitlán. The city fell to the Spanish army after several months. Almost every building in the city had been destroyed. "The city looked as if it had been plowed up," one witness wrote.

The Spaniards won partly because of their horses and superior weapons—iron muskets and cannons. Another great help to the Spaniards were the Aztecs' enemies.

The Spaniards also won because of the diseases they unknowingly brought with them. These diseases swept through Aztec villages and cities.

THE END OF AN EMPIRE

It is hard to believe that a small but determined group of gold-hungry adventurers could bring about so much destruction. Cortés and his Spanish forces not only defeated the Aztecs, they also destroyed their civilization.

Check Your Reading

1. Why did Cortés go to Mexico?
2. How did Doña Marina help Cortés?
3. List four things that helped Cortés to defeat the Aztecs.
4. **THINKING SKILL:** List two things Moctezuma could have done when Cortés arrived in Tenochtitlán.

3 The Conquest of South America

READ TO LEARN

Key People

Francisco Pizarro
Atahualpa

Key Places

Tumbes
Cuzco

Read Aloud

With shots ringing, swords clashing, and horses rushing out from hiding places, the square was suddenly a scene of terror. . . . It was all over in a few minutes.

These words describe the fall of the Incan Empire in 1532. The Spanish used surprise and trickery to quickly topple this great civilization. In this lesson you will read about the defeat of the Incas.

Read for Purpose

1. WHAT YOU KNOW: Where was the Incan Empire located?
2. WHAT YOU WILL LEARN: How did the Spanish conquer the Incan Empire?

A LAND OF GOLD

When the Spanish explorer Balboa crossed the Isthmus of Panama in 1513 and saw the Pacific Ocean, a man named Francisco Pizarro (pi zär′ ō) was with him. While he was on the isthmus, Pizarro heard legends from the local Indians about an amazingly rich land of gold far to the south. As you know, the great Incan Empire lay south of the Aztec lands. The Incan Empire was isolated and protected by the Andes Mountains. Pizarro, however, was determined to find it.

Pizarro made two failed attempts to find the Incas' capital city. He failed both times because he did not have enough supplies. On his second trip, however, he had his first glimpse of Incan riches when he visited the Incan city of Tumbes (tüm′ bās). Visiting Tumbes made Pizarro more anxious than ever to find the rest of the vast Incan Empire.

When Pizarro returned to Spain in 1528, he visited the king of Spain. One historian wrote:

Pizarro showed the king golden drinking vessels acquired at Tumbes as well as a live llama and two young Indians whom he was training as interpreters.

According to the same historian, the king was pleased and gave Pizarro permission to attack the Incan lands and "gain possession of them."

MAP SKILL: Pizarro (*above*) made several attempts to reach Cuzco, the Incan capital. How far is Cuzco from the Isthmus of Panama?

PIZARRO'S ROUTES

→ With Balboa, 1513 → 1526–1527
→ 1524 → 1531–1532

FIGHTING THE INCAS

In 1531 Pizarro and 180 Spanish soldiers were ready to begin their attack on the Incas. You can follow Pizarro's route on the map on this page.

Pizarro and his army began to attack the many small Incan villages that lined the Pacific Coast. Pizarro soon learned that the Incas were in the middle of a war. Taking advantage of the conflict among the Incas, Pizarro headed east to Cuzco, the capital of the empire.

Atahualpa (ä tə wäl′ pə), the Incan ruler, had heard about the arrival of Pizarro. When the Spaniards entered Atahualpa's court, the Incan ruler greeted the intruders. He said:

Tell your commander that I am keeping a fast that will end tomorrow. Then I will visit him.

When Atahualpa visited Pizarro the next day, the Spaniards were waiting. They attacked the surprised and unarmed Incas. Although the massacre lasted for less than half an hour, more than 1,500 Incas were killed. Many of them were government officials who had come to witness the meeting. As you may recall from Chapter 9, Incan government officials had always maintained strict control over the Incan people. Pizarro and his soldiers shattered this control by killing many of these government officials. With most of their leaders dead, the Incas were unable to defend their land.

A ROOM FILLED WITH GOLD

Atahualpa was not killed in the massacre, but he was captured. For nine months, Pizarro and Atahualpa lived closely together in a remote city. Pizarro was waiting for more help from

A room filled with Incan gold objects similar to these was not enough to gain Atahualpa his freedom.

Spain. Atahualpa was waiting to regain his freedom. During this time Atahualpa had noticed something strange. The Spanish soldiers loved gold.

One day Atahualpa and Pizarro were sitting in the same room. Atahualpa turned to the conquistador and offered to fill the room with gold in exchange for his freedom. The conquistador was amazed but accepted the offer.

Astonishing amounts of gold were brought to Atahualpa. The gold began to pile up on the floor of the room. Long sheets of gold, pieces of finely crafted jewelry, golden chairs, and golden ears of corn lay on the floor. The Spaniards watched eagerly. When the room was filled with gold, Atahualpa demanded his freedom.

THE END OF AN EMPIRE

Atahualpa, however, was not given his freedom. On the same day that Atahualpa had finished filling the room with gold, Pizarro ordered that he be put to death.

After Atahualpa's death, Spain conquered much of South America. Just as they had succeeded in Mexico, the Spaniards succeeded in this region because they had horses and superior weapons. The diseases that they had brought with them also killed many of the Indians. By 1535 Spain had built one of the world's largest empires. It stretched from Mexico to the southern tip of South America. But throughout the empire, the Incas and other Indians never stopped fighting against Spanish rule.

THE CONQUEST OF THE INCAS

The conquest of the Incas by a small group of Spanish soldiers was led by Francisco Pizarro. In order to gain the wealth of the Incas, Pizarro used both trickery and military means to defeat the Indians of the Andes.

 Check Your Reading

1. How did Pizarro conquer the Incas?
2. Who was Atahualpa?
3. GEOGRAPHY SKILL: Look at the map on page 236. Is Tumbes north or south of Cuzco?
4. THINKING SKILL: Compare and contrast the Spanish conquests of the Incas and of the Aztecs.

IMPORTANT EVENTS

1492
Columbus's first
voyage to America

1513
Ponce de León
explores Florida;
Balboa sights the
Pacific Ocean

1521
Cortés conquers
the Aztecs

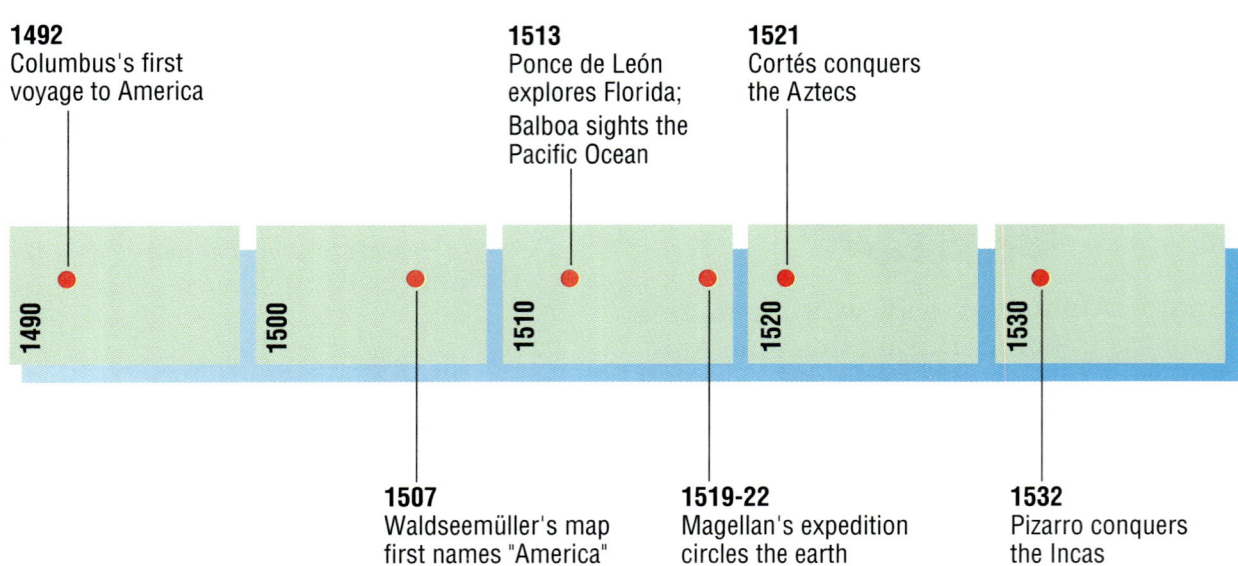

1490

1500

1510

1520

1530

1507
Waldseemüller's map
first names "America"

1519-22
Magellan's expedition
circles the earth

1532
Pizarro conquers
the Incas

PEOPLE TO KNOW

Christopher Columbus 1451?–1506

Amerigo Vespucci 1454–1512

Hernando Cortés 1485–1547

Vasco Núñez de Balboa 1475?–1517

Doña Marina 1501–1550

Ferdinand Magellan 1480?–1521

Moctezuma 1480?–1520

IDEAS TO REMEMBER

■ Following Columbus's landing in the Americas, other Europeans sailed to the Western Hemisphere and beyond, exploring lands, seeking routes westward to Asia, and claiming territories for their home countries.

■ Spanish conquistador Hernando Cortés and his soldiers destroyed the Aztec civilization with weapons, with the help of other Indian groups opposed to Aztec rule, and by the spread of contagious diseases.

■ Francisco Pizarro defeated the Incas in order to gain their wealth and claim their territory.

REVIEWING VOCABULARY

Each of the following statements contains an underlined vocabulary word or term. Number a sheet of paper from 1 to 5. Beside each number write whether each of the statements is true or false. If the statement is true, write **T**. If it is false, rewrite the sentence, using the vocabulary term correctly.

1. The <u>astrolabe</u> is a device that helps you to find which direction is north.
2. The <u>compass</u> is a kind of swift boat.
3. The <u>caravel</u> was an animal that Pizarro took to show to the king of Spain.
4. Cortés was a famous <u>conquistador</u>.
5. The <u>astrolabe</u> is an instrument that was used to measure the position of stars and planets.

REVIEWING FACTS

1. How did the caravel help sailors make long voyages?
2. Why did Columbus call the islands he reached the "Indies"?
3. Why was Portugal able to claim parts of South America?
4. Who was Amerigo Vespucci?
5. List one important fact about Balboa's exploration and Magellan's voyage.
6. Why did the Aztecs not fight Cortés and his men at first?
7. How did other Indians help the Spanish to defeat the Aztecs?
8. What was Pizarro's goal in fighting the Incas?
9. What bargain did Atahualpa make with Pizarro?
10. What were two reasons that the Spanish were able to defeat the Incas?

WRITING ABOUT MAIN IDEAS

1. **Writing a Character Sketch:** Make a list of character traits of Francisco Pizarro based on the information in this chapter. Then use the words on the list to write a character sketch of Pizarro.
2. **Writing a Paragraph:** In this chapter you read about the explorations of Columbus, Vespucci, Balboa, and Magellan. How did each man's expedition help make possible the later expeditions? Write a paragraph or series of sentences showing the connections among the expeditions.
3. **Writing About Perspectives:** Write a story in which you retell the conquest of the Aztecs as Moctezuma might have told it. Think about how Moctezuma might have viewed those events.

BUILDING SKILLS: UNDERSTANDING MAP PROJECTIONS

Use what you already know and the maps on pages 230–231 to answer the following questions.

1. Why do mapmakers use projections?
2. What is distortion?
3. What is the advantage of a Mercator projection?
4. Compare the size of South America and Greenland on **Map A**. On **Map B**. Which map shows their relative sizes more accurately? Why?
5. Why is Antarctica so much larger on **Map A**? Explain.
6. Why is it important to understand map projections?

239

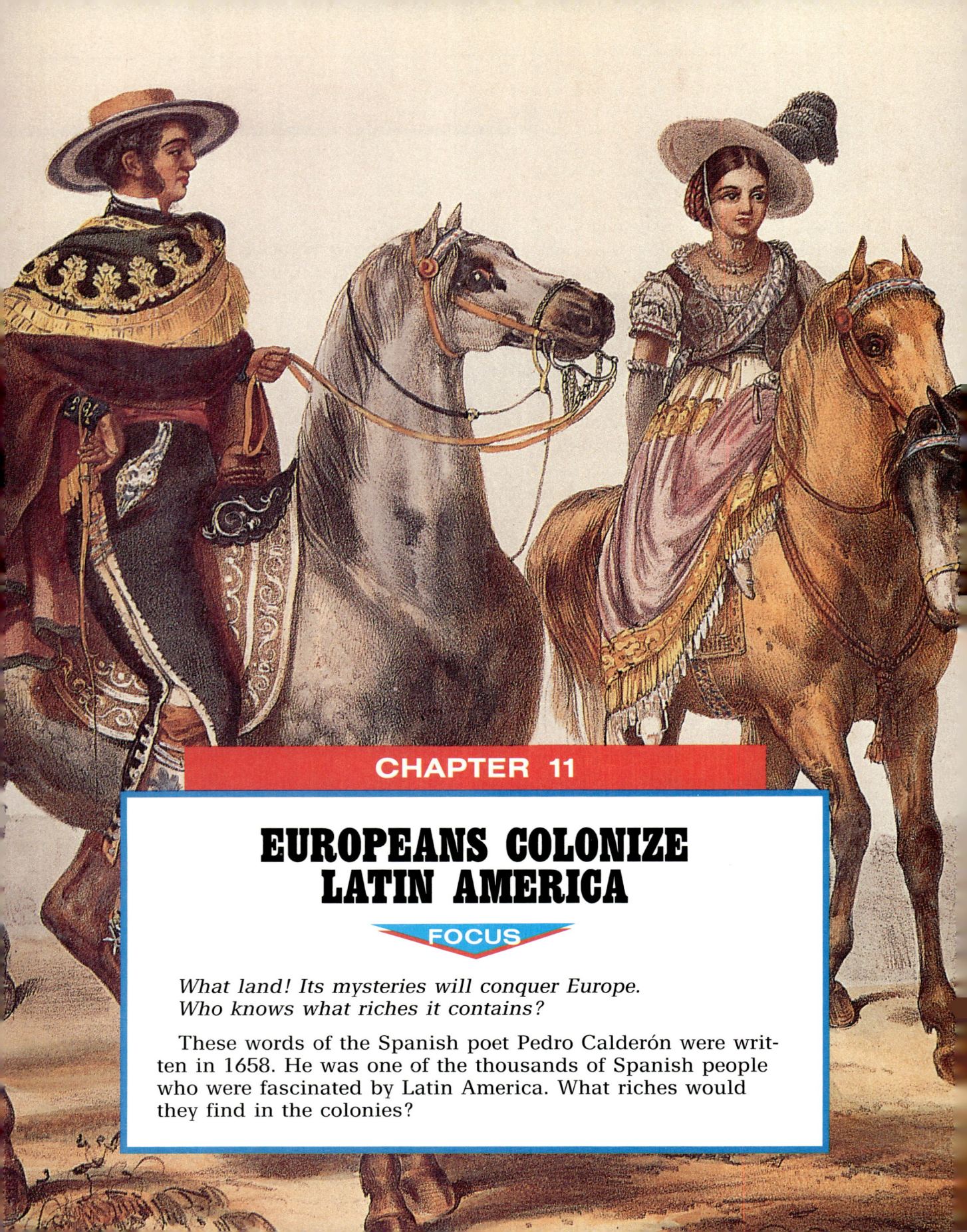

CHAPTER 11

EUROPEANS COLONIZE LATIN AMERICA

FOCUS

What land! Its mysteries will conquer Europe.
Who knows what riches it contains?

These words of the Spanish poet Pedro Calderón were written in 1658. He was one of the thousands of Spanish people who were fascinated by Latin America. What riches would they find in the colonies?

1 Spanish and Portuguese Colonies

READ TO LEARN

■ Key Vocabulary

viceroyalty   captaincy
encomienda
mission

Key Places

Viceroyalty of
  New Spain
Viceroyalty of Peru

Key People

Bartolomé de
  Las Casas

■ Read Aloud

It was not until a decade [ten years] *after the conquest that the whole of Mexico, or New Spain, was under secure Spanish control. Some Indians were easily subdued* [conquered]; *others resisted to the death.*

These words were written by a Spanish soldier who took part in the Spanish conquest of Mexico. The Spanish took ten years to gain control of the Aztec Empire. Then they began to establish colonies in the newly conquered lands. In this lesson you will read how the colonies developed.

■ Read for Purpose

1. **WHAT YOU KNOW:** Why did the Spanish want to conquer the Aztec Empire?
2. **WHAT YOU WILL LEARN:** How did Spain and Portugal establish colonies in Latin America?

THE SPANISH EMPIRE

You have read about the conquests by Cortés and Pizarro of the Aztec and Incan empires during the early 1500s. After these victories, huge areas of Latin America were claimed by Spain. The king of Spain encouraged his people to settle the colonies in Latin America before other European groups tried to claim them. Thousands of Spanish made the long journey to Latin America. They hoped to make their fortunes by acquiring land or finding precious metals such as gold or silver.

When they arrived, the Spanish destroyed much of the civilization that had taken generations for the Indians to build. One Spanish official wrote:

The Spanish did more harm in 4 years than the Incas had done in 400.

GOVERNING THE EMPIRE

To help him govern the Latin American colonies, the Spanish king divided them into political divisions called **viceroyalties** (vīs′ roi əl tēz). During the early 1500s there were two viceroyalties established in Latin America.

MAP SKILL: Which **viceroyalty** was located in North America?

One was the **Viceroyalty of New Spain** in North America, and the other was the **Viceroyalty of Peru** in South America. Later, during the mid-1500s, the Portuguese established the Viceroyalty of Brazil. Find the Spanish and Portuguese viceroyalties on the map on this page.

THE INDIANS AND THE SPANISH

The Spanish king had two goals in Latin America. The first was to gain wealth from the colonies. The second was to bring Christianity to the Indians. The king tried to accomplish these goals with the **encomienda** (en kō mē en' də) system. An encomienda was a group of Indians granted to a colonist. A typical grant read:

Unto you are given in trust [a certain number] of Indians for you to make use of in your farm and mines.

Often an encomienda included more than 5,000 Indians. The Spanish rulers also granted control of land to friends and loyal subjects. In return for the grants, the colonists sent a part of their income from the land to the rulers in Spain. They also took responsibility for converting the Indians to the Christian religion.

Most Spanish colonists did not live on the land that was worked by the Indians. They preferred to live near one another in cities. They visited their fields or mines occasionally to make sure that the land was being managed well. The colonists wanted to make as large a profit from their land grants and encomiendas as possible. Most colonists overworked the Indians and treated them as slaves.

Imagine how the Indians felt about the encomienda system. Most of them had lost control of their land and their freedom. One Spanish observer, Hernando de Santillan, wrote this description in 1563.

They live the most wretched and miserable lives of any people on earth. As long as they are healthy they are fully occupied in working. . . . Even when they are sick, they have no respite [rest], and few survive their first illness, however slight, because of the appalling [shocking] existence they lead.

SILENT ENEMIES

Many Indians died from forced labor and harsh punishments, but their worst enemy was disease. The Spanish unknowingly brought with them diseases from Europe that were new to the colonies. Because they had no natural resistance to these diseases, hundreds of thousands of Indians died from measles and the common cold. In some areas of New Spain, the Indian population dropped to one third of what it had been before the Europeans arrived. One Aztec wrote about the illness all around him.

. . . People could not walk. They only lay in their resting places and beds. They could not move. They could not stir.

MISSIONARIES

The Spanish rulers believed it was their duty to convert the Indians to Christianity. To accomplish this, they sent missionaries to teach their religion to the Indians. As you know, missionaries were people who taught their religion to others who had different beliefs. The missionaries established **missions** on land granted to the Catholic Church. The missions were settlements that contained a working farm, living quarters, churches, schools, and workshops.

The Indians were forced to live and work at the mission. There the missionaries taught the Indians the Catholic religion, the Spanish language, and European farming methods. Spanish soon became the major language of the colonies. But many Indians refused to convert to a new religion. One missionary was told by an Aztec:

Our ancestors taught us that we live by and through the gods. We ask them for rain so that the plants may take root and grow. We know to whom we owe life and how to pray. Do not make us do what will cause our destruction.

The Indians shared many of their skills with the Spanish. They taught them farming methods, mining techniques, and information about their environment. They also introduced

This mural by Mexican artist Diego Rivera shows Indians mining and working precious metals for the Spanish rulers.

crops such as corn, squash, potatoes, tomatoes, and pumpkins to the Spanish colonists. Over time both Indian and Spanish ways became part of a new Latin American way of life.

PROTECTOR OF THE INDIANS

Many missionaries became concerned about the way in which the Spanish colonists treated the Indians. In their churches the priests protested against the colonists' cruel behavior, but the wealthy landowners ignored them. However, one priest, **Bartolomé de Las Casas** (bär tō lō mä′ də läs käs′ əs), insisted on being heard.

Like other colonists, Bartolomé de Las Casas had come to New Spain seeking his fortune. But he soon became sickened by the terrible cruelty he saw around him. Las Casas gave up his land and decided to become a priest. He was the first person to become a priest in New Spain.

243

Las Casas wrote many letters to the Spanish rulers protesting the colonists' cruelties toward the Indians. In one of his reports he wrote:

All the Indians to be found here are to be held as free: for in truth so they are, by the same right as I am free. . . . These people are the most humble, patient, and peaceable, holding no grudges [anger].

His pleas persuaded the rulers, who in 1516 appointed Las Casas "Protector of the Indians." For the next 50 years he worked to protect the Indians' rights and tried to limit their suffering.

PORTUGUESE SETTLEMENT

The Spanish colonies developed earlier than the Portuguese colonies did. You read in Chapter 10, about the Portuguese explorers who claimed parts of Brazil. Unlike the Spanish, the Portuguese did not rush to settle their claims in Latin America.

The first Portuguese explorers of Brazil did not find gold and silver or any great Indian empires to conquer. Instead they saw Indian settlements scattered throughout the dense rain forests. These Indians, unlike the Aztecs and the Mayas, lived simply and had gathered little material wealth.

The colonies that were started in Brazil at this time served as collection stations. These were centers where goods were gathered before shipment to Europe. The Portuguese discovered that the brazilwood trees in the forests could be used to make red dyes. The colonists collected the brazilwood and prepared it for shipment to Portugal.

Brazil was governed much like the Spanish colonies, except that the colonies were not called viceroyalties but **captaincies** (kap′ tən sēz). The Portuguese colonists who were granted captaincies agreed to bring in Portuguese settlers and to develop their land.

A NEW CULTURE

In this lesson you have read how European settlers established colonies in Latin America. You also have read about the terrible hardships suffered by the Indians. In the next lesson you will read about the way of life that grew out of the fact that the Spanish and the Indians lived side by side.

Check Your Reading

1. What did the Spanish and Portuguese settlers hope to find in Latin America?
2. Why did the king of Spain want to settle the colonies quickly?
3. Describe the encomienda system.
4. Explain why disease had such terrible effects on the Indians.
5. **THINKING SKILL:** Identify the following statement as fact or opinion: "The Spanish colonists improved living conditions for the Indians." Explain your answer.

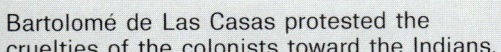
Bartolomé de Las Casas protested the cruelties of the colonists toward the Indians.

2 Life in the Colonies

READ TO LEARN

Key Vocabulary

social class   creole   peon
peninsular   hacienda

Key People

Juana Inés de la Cruz

Read Aloud

I remember that in those days, although I had the healthy appetite of most children . . . I would not eat cheese because I heard that it made one dull-witted, and the desire to learn was stronger in me than the desire to eat. . . .

These words were spoken by Juana Inés de la Cruz (wän' ä ē nās' dā lä krüs), who lived in the Spanish colonies in the 1600s. When she was three years of age she already wanted to learn to read. In this lesson you will read more about the life of this unusual young girl. You will also read about life in the colonies for other groups of people.

Read for Purpose

1. **WHAT YOU KNOW:** What is one characteristic of your culture?
2. **WHAT YOU WILL LEARN:** What was life like in the Latin American colonies?

AFRICANS FORCED INTO SLAVERY

As you have read, the Spanish and Portuguese colonists started a new way of life in Latin America. The colonists acquired land through grants from Spain and Portugal. They also acquired Indians through the encomienda system. The Indians were forced into slavery, and thousands of them lost their lives.

So many Indians died that the colonists began to look for workers to replace them. Portuguese traders began kidnapping people who lived in Portuguese colonies in West Africa.

Soon thousands of men, women, and children were being kidnapped in Africa to be sold to colonists in Latin America. These enslaved Africans were then brought against their will to the Latin American colonies.

The Africans suffered terribly. They were forced to work so hard and were treated so badly that thousands of them became sick and died. Africans were brought as captives to many parts of Latin America, including Brazil, the

Spanish colonies, and the islands of the Caribbean region. You will read more about slavery in the Caribbean region in Chapter 19.

SOCIAL CLASSES

The arrival of enslaved Africans added a new social class to Latin American society. A social class is a division of society in which the people share similar economic, educational, and social characteristics. Each social class played an important role in the history of Latin America. Look at the diagram of Latin America's social pyramid on this page.

The most powerful social class was the peninsulares (pe nēn sü lä′ rās). They were called peninsulares because they were born in Spain or Portugal.

Find Spain and Portugal, which are part of a huge peninsula in Europe, on the map on pages 562–563 of the Atlas. The peninsulares held all of the most important positions in the colonial governments.

The next Latin American social class was the creoles, who were descendants of the Spanish or Portuguese settlers. Many creoles were owners of huge farms or mines. However, because they were not born in Spain or Portugal, they were not given powerful roles in government.

You read in Chapter 8 that the mestizos were part Indian and part Spanish. The mestizos were regarded as less important than either the peninsulares or the creoles. Although they sometimes gained wealth, the mestizos rarely held important jobs.

You also read that the mulattoes were part African and part European. The mestizos and the mulattoes were

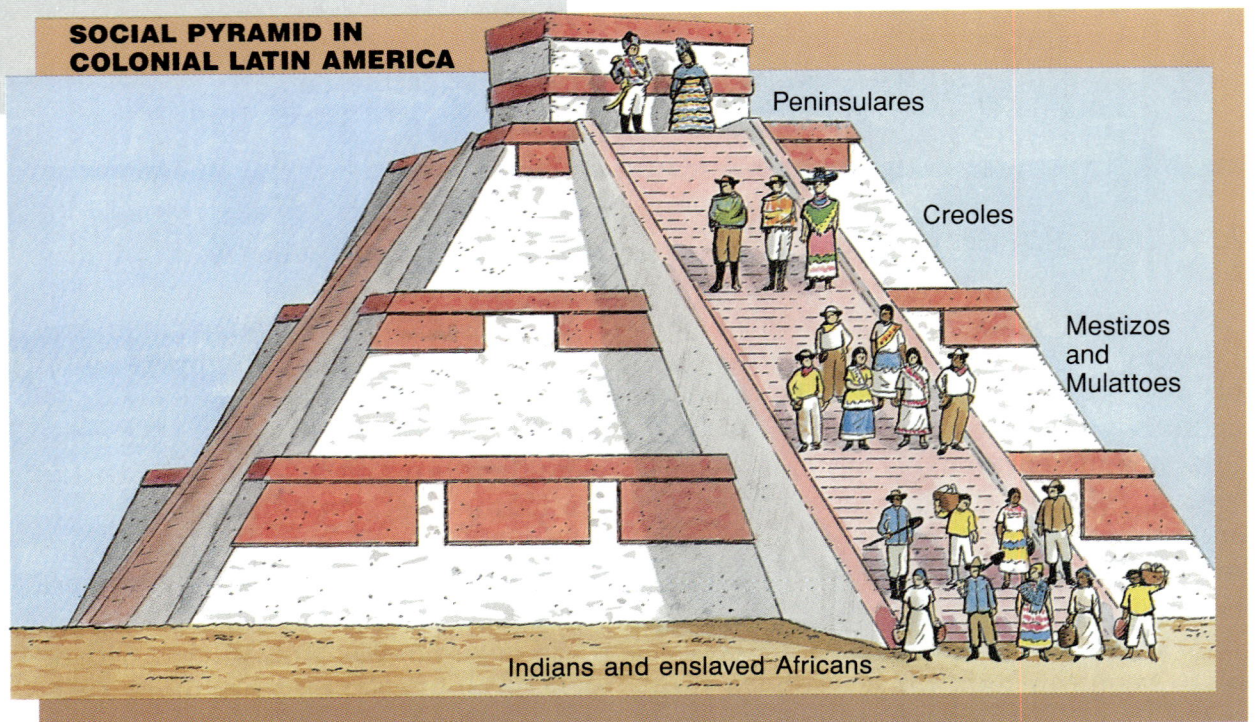

DIAGRAM SKILL: Which social class was at the top of Latin American society? Which social class was at the bottom?

SOCIAL PYRAMID IN COLONIAL LATIN AMERICA

Peninsulares

Creoles

Mestizos and Mulattoes

Indians and enslaved Africans

one step above the bottom of the social classes. The Indians and enslaved Africans had the fewest rights and privileges in Latin American society. You can see from the diagram on page 246 that the Indians and the enslaved Africans were the largest social class.

JUANA INÉS DE LA CRUZ

Women in all of the social classes in Latin American society were expected to care for their homes and their families. They could also choose to become nuns and devote their lives to the Catholic Church. One woman called Juana Inés de la Cruz tried to overcome the social rules. You read about her in the beginning of this lesson.

Juana Inés de la Cruz was born in Mexico in 1651. You may recall that she enjoyed learning. At that time women were not educated. When she was 14 years old, she tried to attend Mexico University, but she was refused entry because the university was open to men only. At the age of 18, Juana Inés de la Cruz decided to become a nun so that she could continue to study and write. As a nun, Juana was called Sor Juana. *Sor*, which means "sister" in Spanish, is the title used by nuns.

For 25 years Sor Juana wrote poetry, plays, and essays about religion and social issues. She often wrote about the unequal treatment of women. Today Sor Juana is remembered and honored as one of Mexico's greatest scholars and most talented poets.

LIVING ON A HACIENDA

In Lesson 1 you have read about the encomienda system. During the 1700s the encomienda system finally ended. The European rulers hoped that their ending the system would stop the cruel

What clues in this painting of Juana Inés de la Cruz tell you that she fulfilled her desire to become a nun and to study?

treatment of the Indians and the Africans. Most of the huge land grants were divided and gradually replaced by haciendas (hä sē en' dəs). Haciendas were large ranches or plantations. The haciendas were owned by the peninsulares or the creoles.

The haciendas were self-sufficient villages. The most important buildings surrounded a central plaza, or open square. Several buildings, including the owner's large house, a church, some workshops, and stables, faced the central plaza.

A difference between the haciendas and the land grants was that the owners lived on the haciendas instead of in the city. Also, on the haciendas the Indians were given some land on

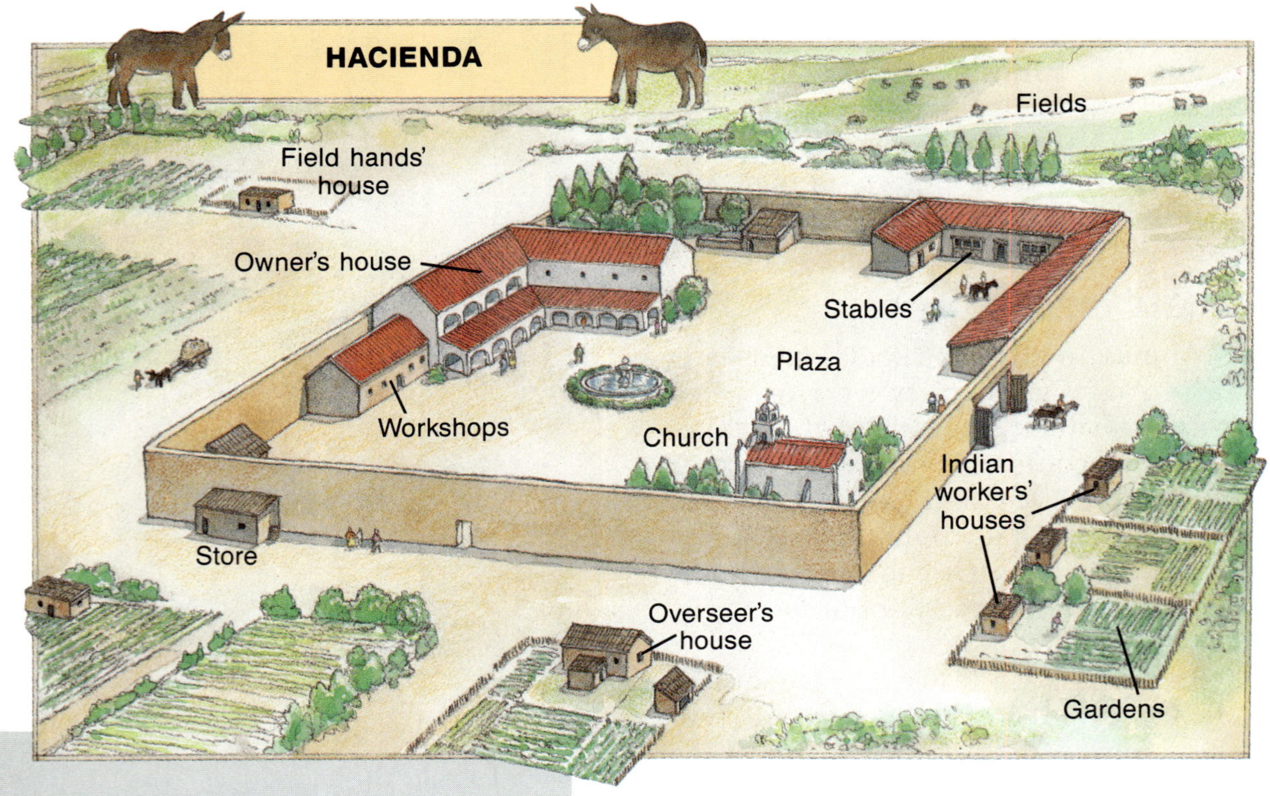

HACIENDA

Fields

Field hands' house

Owner's house

Stables

Plaza

Workshops

Church

Store

Indian workers' houses

Overseer's house

Gardens

DIAGRAM SKILL: Where was the plaza located in relation to the other buildings on the hacienda?

which they could live and raise crops. However, most of their time was spent working for the owner. As you can see in the diagram above, the Indian workers had only a small piece of land.

These Indians were called peons, or people who were forced to work to pay off their debts. The Indians went into debt because they earned very low wages. Because they did not have enough money for their needs, they borrowed from the landowner. Week after week the debt increased as the Indians borrowed more money, until they were paying all of their earnings to the owner. This system was one more way in which the Indians were kept at the bottom of the social pyramid in Latin America.

SOCIAL UNREST

As you have read, the people in the colonies formed distinct social classes. The less powerful and poorer groups resented those with greater wealth and power. During the years following the colonial settlement, these resentments continued to grow. In the next lesson you will read how these feelings of unrest developed into revolts.

Check Your Reading

1. Why were Africans forced to come as slaves to Latin America?
2. Name the main social classes in Latin America.
3. Why did the creoles resent the peninsulares?
4. THINKING SKILL: State three facts from the section, "Africans Forced into Slavery." Tell how you determined that each one is a fact.

3 Revolt Comes to Latin America

Key Vocabulary

monopoly

Key People

Tupac Amarú II

Read Aloud

For once and all, know that you have been born to be silent and to obey, and neither to discuss nor to hold opinions on the affairs of government.

These words were once spoken by a Spanish official to his creole subjects. Imagine how the creoles felt when they heard this speech. It is no wonder that many creoles argued that the time had come to break away from Spain and Portugal.

Read for Purpose

1. **WHAT YOU KNOW:** What were some of the reasons for dissatisfaction in the Latin American colonies?
2. **WHAT YOU WILL LEARN:** How did the movement toward independence begin in the Latin American colonies?

RESISTING SPANISH RULE

In Lesson 2 you read about the social classes in the Latin American colonies. Struggles among these social groups caused an increase in unrest during the 1700s. For example, the creoles resented the peninsulares because they held the most powerful positions.

Dissatisfaction was also growing among the Indians and the enslaved Africans. Uprisings against the landowners and the government officials were occurring more and more often.

In Peru a mestizo landowner who lived in comfort saw the poor conditions of the Indians. His name was José Condorcanqui (kon dôr kän′ kē). When he complained to Spanish officials about the terrible conditions, Condorcanqui was ignored.

Hundreds of years before, Condorcanqui's ancestors had been members of the Incan ruling family. One Incan emperor had continued to fight the Spanish even after the conquest of the Incas. The emperor, Tupac Amarú I (tü päk′ äm är ü′), was killed by the Spanish in 1571. In memory of that emperor, Condorcanqui decided to call himself **Tupac Amarú II**. The people respected Tupac Amarú II and accepted his leadership.

In November 1780 Tupac Amarú II asked mestizos, Africans, mulattoes, and creoles to join him in an uprising.

The anger shown by the revolutionaries terrified the Spanish, who fled the area or hid behind barricades. Nearly one half the population of Peru was involved in the fighting. Finally, however, more than 60,000 Spanish soldiers equipped with horses and guns stopped the revolt. In 1781 Tupac Amarú II was captured and killed.

REVOLUTIONS IN OTHER PLACES

During the late 1700s events in other parts of the world began to have an effect on Latin Americans. For example, in 1776 Britain's 13 colonies in North America declared their independence and formed the United States. Britain was forced to recognize the independence of the United States at the end of the American Revolution. A revolution is the complete overthrow of a government. Then, in 1789, the French Revolution began, leading to the overthrow of the French king.

During the late 1770s, many wealthy young creoles attended school in Europe. They returned home with new ideas they had learned there about liberty and equality. More and more Latin Americans began to think about gaining freedom from Spain and Portugal.

Imagine how you would have felt as a colonist who was being treated unfairly by your rulers who lived in Europe. Then suppose you learned that in other countries, ordinary citizens had overthrown their European rulers in revolutions. With these examples in mind, groups of colonists throughout Latin America began to make plans for their own revolutions.

CONTROLLING TRADE

While discontent grew among the colonists, the rulers in Spain and Portugal found new ways to control the colonies. As you have read, the rulers of Spain and Portugal had gained enormous wealth from their colonies.

Since the 1500s the Spanish and Portuguese rulers had ordered their

Spanish ships loaded with goods sailed to and from the colonies in Latin America.

The Granger Collection

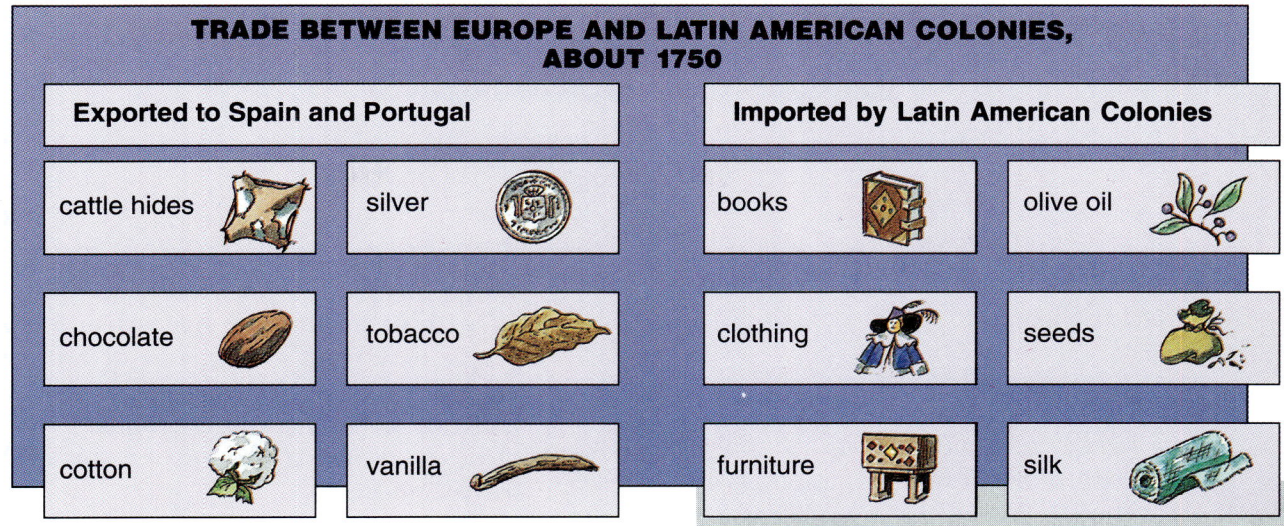

TRADE BETWEEN EUROPE AND LATIN AMERICAN COLONIES, ABOUT 1750

Exported to Spain and Portugal

cattle hides	silver
chocolate	tobacco
cotton	vanilla

Imported by Latin American Colonies

books	olive oil
clothing	seeds
furniture	silk

CHART SKILL: Which goods did the Latin American colonies receive from Europe?

colonists to use only ships that sailed under official orders when they traded. Furthermore, the colonies were not allowed to trade with any other country. The king of Spain had said that anyone trading with foreigners "shall be punished with death. . . ."

Now laws also limited the goods that the colonists could trade and those that they could manufacture. These new laws gave Spain and Portugal a **monopoly**, or complete control, over the trade and business of their colonies. The chart above shows some of the goods that were controlled by the Spanish and Portuguese monopoly. The chart shows exports to Spain and Portugal and imports by the colonies.

The great distance between Europe and Latin America created problems for colonial trade. Colonists smuggled goods and committed acts of piracy more frequently as their anger over the monopoly increased. Some colonists also began to believe that they should keep their profits instead of giving them to the rulers in Europe. More and more colonists began to talk about independence for the colonies.

A TIME OF CHANGE

As you have read, the resentments among the social classes within Latin America continued to grow. The colonists also were angry because the Spanish and Portuguese rulers used a monopoly to restrict their trade. You will read more about these and other problems that developed in Latin America in Chapter 13.

 Check Your Reading

1. List two reasons for unhappiness in Latin American colonial society.
2. Which social classes took part in the Latin American uprisings of the late 1700s?
3. How did the Spanish and Portuguese establish a monopoly over colonial trade?
4. THINKING SKILL: Imagine that you are a visitor to the Latin American colonies in the late 1700s. Predict what would happen to the colonies during the next 50 years. Explain.

Using Primary and Secondary Sources

Key Vocabulary

primary source
secondary source

You have been reading about unrest in the Spanish and Portuguese colonies of Latin America. As you read, you learned how the people there lived and worked. How did the authors of your textbook find out about the everyday lives of the Spanish, the Portuguese, and the Indians? After all, these people lived hundreds of years ago.

Primary Sources

One way your authors uncovered the information was by looking at **primary sources**. A primary source is a firsthand account. It is written by someone who actually witnessed an event or saw a place. Primary sources include diaries, newspapers, letters, and official documents. Primary sources can also be nonwritten items, such as artifacts, clothing, or pictures. These sources help a historian to study how people worked, dressed, or even styled their hair.

Primary sources always tell something true about the past. But they do not always tell the whole truth. For example, a letter written by Bartolomé de Las Casas would have painted a very dreary picture of Indians' lives. A diary entry by the Spanish viceroy might have told how successful the colonial mining business was. Each account might have included some truth. But each one also would have reflected the writer's opinion.

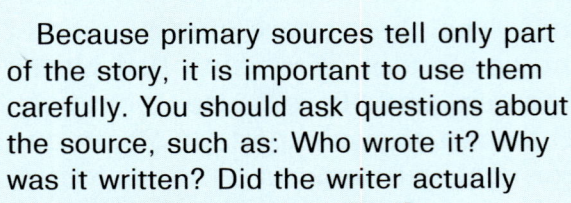

The chief place in the city is the marketplace. It is fair and wide, built all with arches on one side where the people may walk dry in time of rain. There are shops of merchants furnished with all sorts of stuffs and silks. Before them sit women selling all manner of fruits and herbs.

Over against these shops and arches is the palace of the viceroy. The viceroy's palace runs almost the whole length of the marketplace. At the end of the palace is the chief prison, which is strong of stonework. Next to this is a beautiful street called Goldsmith Street. Here a man's eye may behold in less

Because primary sources tell only part of the story, it is important to use them carefully. You should ask questions about the source, such as: Who wrote it? Why was it written? Did the writer actually witness the events described?

Secondary Sources

Not everything written about the past is a primary source. This textbook, for example, is not an eyewitness account of past events. Instead, it is a **secondary source**. Secondary sources are accounts that bring together the information from many primary sources. They are written not by someone who witnessed events but by

than an hour millions of dollars worth of gold, silver, pearls, and jewels.

The gallants [nobles] of this city show themselves daily, some on horseback and most in coaches. They gather about 4:00 in the afternoon in a pleasant shady field, called *La Alameda*. *La Alameda* is full of trees and walks. Here about 2,000 coaches full of gallants, ladies, and citizens come to see and to be seen. Each coach is accompanied by a train of slaves, some a dozen and some a half dozen, waiting upon them. The slaves wear beautiful uniforms which are heavy with gold and silver lace.

The cities were laid out around a central plaza, or open square. Facing the plaza were a town hall and other buildings for the government officials. The principal church, or cathedral, was the most important church in the city. The plaza served as a marketplace and as a meeting place for the people of the city.

From the plaza a broad main street led away from the center of the city. Sometimes this street was paved with stone blocks. Old records tell us that the buildings were beautiful, but the streets were not kept too clean. Often people threw garbage and other waste materials into the streets. There were no street cleaners. Instead, birds, dogs, and pigs ate the garbage in the streets.

someone who later describes the events. Other secondary sources include encyclopedias and atlases.

Secondary sources can be very useful. They can give an overview of past events. They summarize facts and opinions presented by many other sources.

Comparing Sources

The first excerpt above is an example of a primary source. It was written by a person who lived in Mexico City in 1625. The second is from a textbook. After reading the excerpts, compare their descriptions of city life in Mexico.

Reviewing the Skill

1. What is the difference between a primary source and a secondary source?
2. Based on the primary source, give two or three adjectives that could describe Mexico City in 1625. Based on the secondary source, give two or three adjectives that could describe the city at that time.
3. Which account do you find the most interesting? Why?
4. Why might a primary source be more reliable than a secondary source?
5. When might a primary source be less reliable than a secondary source?

IMPORTANT EVENTS

1500s
Encomienda system set up

Mid-1500s
Captaincies flourish

1600s
Social pyramid develops

1720
Encomienda system ends

1790s
Ideas of revolution spread throughout Latin America

1500

1600

1700

1516
Las Casas named Protector of the Indians

1651
Sor Juana born

1780
Tupac Amarú II leads revolt in Peru

PEOPLE TO KNOW

Bartolomé de Las Casas
1474–1566

Juana Inés de la Cruz
1651–1695

Tupac Amarú II
1742?–1781

IDEAS TO REMEMBER

■ While many European colonists came to Latin America and became rich, Indians suffered from overwork and disease.

■ Latin American colonies had a clear division of social classes—the highest class being the Spanish and Portuguese nobles, followed by the creoles. The middle class consisted mainly of mulattoes and mestizos. The lowest class was made up of Indians and enslaved Africans.

■ Dissatisfaction with Spain and Portugal grew among the colonists. During the late 1700s this dissatisfaction led to revolts.

REVIEWING VOCABULARY

creole   mission   peon
encomienda   monopoly   social class
hacienda   peninsular   viceroyalty

Number a sheet of paper from 1 to 10. Beside each number write the word or term from the list above that best matches the definition. One of the words is used more than once.

1. A poor farm worker living in the Spanish colonies
2. A descendant of a Spanish or Portuguese settler
3. A settlement set up by priests where Indians learned about Christianity
4. A member of the social group with the most power in Latin America
5. A group of Indian laborers given to a Spanish colonist
6. A political division in the Spanish colonies in America
7. A division of society in which the people share similar economic, educational, and social characteristics
8. A self-sufficient farming village owned by a peninsular or creole
9. The complete control over trade and business in the colonies
10. A person in the highest Latin American social class who was born in Spain or Portugal

REVIEWING FACTS

Number a sheet of paper from 1 to 10. Beside each number write **T** if the statement is true. If it is false, rewrite it to make it true.

1. Latin America was divided into three viceroyalties—New Spain, Peru, and Brazil.
2. The rulers of Spain had two goals in Latin America—to find a new passage to Asia and to gain wealth.
3. On an encomienda, the Indians owned the land they lived on and could earn money from farming that land.
4. Bartolomé de Las Casas wrote to the king that more people from Spain should come and live in New Spain.
5. Latin American uprisings were led mainly by peninsulares.

WRITING ABOUT MAIN IDEAS

1. **Writing a Comparing Paragraph:** How were missions and haciendas the same? How were they different? Write a paragraph comparing these two types of communities.
2. **Writing About Perspectives:** Do you agree or disagree with this statement: "The people of Latin America would have been better off if Europeans had never come there"? Write a paragraph in which you express your opinion.

BUILDING SKILLS: USING PRIMARY AND SECONDARY SOURCES

1. What is a primary source?
2. What is a secondary source?
3. Is each of the following a primary or secondary source?
   a. a diary   **c.** a photograph
   b. this textbook   **d.** an encyclopedia

REVIEWING VOCABULARY

captaincy
civilization
conquistador
irrigation
mestizo
metropolitan area

mission
slavery
social class

Number a sheet of paper from 1 to 10. Beside each number write the word or term from the list above that best completes each sentence. One of the words is used more then once.

1. The practice of making a person the property of another person is _____.
2. The Aztecs developed a _____ in the Valley of Mexico.
3. In the 1600s the lowest _____ in Latin America was made up of Indians and enslaved Africans.
4. In many places, the Spanish priests set up a _____, where they hoped to convert the Indians to Christianity.
5. The Incas used _____, a system of bringing water to their fields using ditches and channels.
6. Pizarro was a _____ who eventually conquered the Incas.
7. The Portuguese colonist who was granted a _____ agreed to bring in Portuguese settlers and to develop their land.
8. The peninsulares made up the most powerful _____ in Latin America during the 1600s.
9. A _____ is a city and its surrounding communities.
10. A _____ is a person of mixed Indian and European ancestry.

WRITING ABOUT THE UNIT

1. **Writing to Answer Questions:** How did the environment affect the great civilizations of Latin America? Write a paragraph describing at least three ways. How did the Indian civilizations change their environments? Write a paragraph describing at least three ways.
2. **Writing About Perspectives:** Imagine you are either an Indian or an enslaved African in Latin America in the year 1700. Write a journal entry that tells how you feel about the European colonists.

ACTIVITIES

1. **Conducting Research:** Find out more about one of the European explorers discussed in Chapter 10. Research such topics as the explorer's background and results of his voyage. Write a report presenting what you find out.
2. **Drawing a Diagram:** Find out more about one of the the Indian cities, such as Cuzco or Tenochtitlán. Draw a diagram of the city. Be sure to label the main features of the city.
3. **Working Together to Present a TV News Report:** Imagine that you lived in the times discussed in this unit. Choose one important event. With a small group of classmates, plan a TV report about the event. One person could be the reporter on the scene, others could be people being interviewed, and another could be the anchor reporter. Present your report to the class.

"The Indies were discovered in the year 1492.... There were numberless...islands, and very large ones...that were all—and we have seen it—as inhabited and full of their native Indian peoples as any country in the world....

Among these gentle sheep [the Indians]...the Spaniards entered...like wolves, tigers, and lions which had been starving for many days, and since forty years they have done nothing else; nor do they otherwise at the present day, than outrage, slay, afflict, torment, and destroy them.... To such extremes has this gone that, whereas there were more than 3 million souls, whom we saw in Hispaniola, there are today, not 200 of the native population left....

The reason why the Christian [the Spanish] have killed and destroyed such infinite numbers of souls is solely because they have made gold their ultimate aim, seeking to load themselves with riches in the shortest time..."

BUILDING SKILLS: IDENTIFYING PRIMARY AND SECONDARY SOURCES

The account shown above was written by Bartolomé de Las Casas between 1540 and 1542. It was published in a book called *Very Brief Account of the Destruction of the Indies*. Read the account. Then answer the questions that follow.

1. Is the account a primary or secondary source? How do you know?

2. Approximately how many years passed between the events that Las Casas is describing and his account of them?

3. According to Las Casas, what happened to the people of the Indies?

4. Why did the Spanish in the Indies act as they did, according to Las Casas?

5. Do you think this account is accurate and reliable as a source of information about the Indies in the 1500s? Why or why not?

LINKING PAST, PRESENT, AND FUTURE

You might have noticed there are few women mentioned in this unit. This is not because the authors of your textbook ignored the important contributions of women. It is because, in the past, women were not usually allowed to actively participate in public life. As your textbook points out, Sor Juana was an exception for her time. What do you think most women were doing while some men were exploring, conquering, and ruling? What is your reaction to this reality of the past? What do you think the role of women will be in the future?

ARCTIC OCEAN

75°N

Baffin
Bay

60°N

Gulf of Alaska

Hudson
Bay

NORTH

AMERICA

75°W

60°W

Tropic of Cancer

Gulf of Mexico

PACIFIC

MEXICO

Gulf of California

OCEAN

Caribbean   Sea

SOUTH

165°W

150°W

135°W

120°W

105°W

90°W

AMERICA

Tropic of Capricorn

PACIFIC   OCEAN

60°S

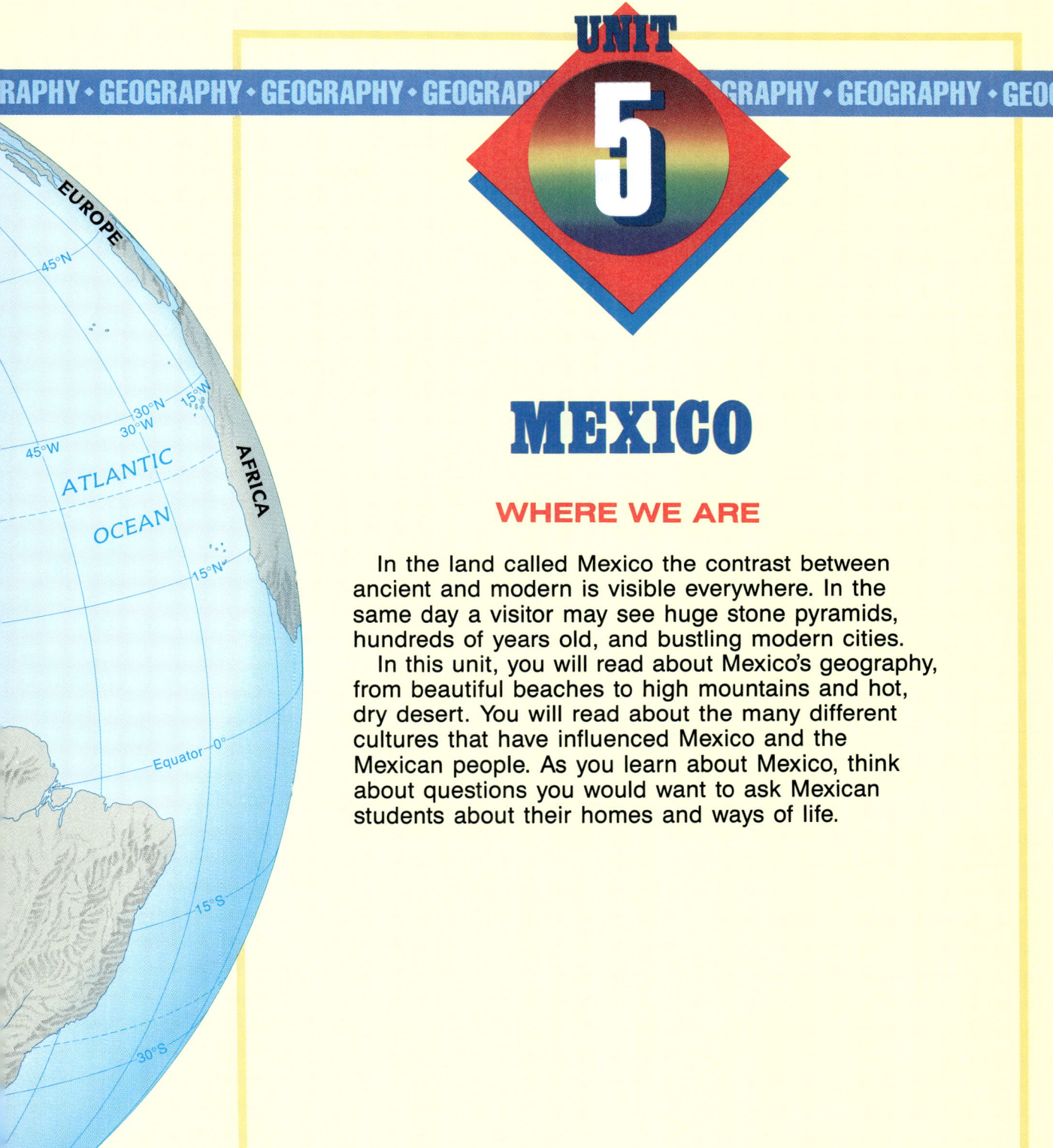

5

MEXICO

WHERE WE ARE

In the land called Mexico the contrast between ancient and modern is visible everywhere. In the same day a visitor may see huge stone pyramids, hundreds of years old, and bustling modern cities.

In this unit, you will read about Mexico's geography, from beautiful beaches to high mountains and hot, dry desert. You will read about the many different cultures that have influenced Mexico and the Mexican people. As you learn about Mexico, think about questions you would want to ask Mexican students about their homes and ways of life.

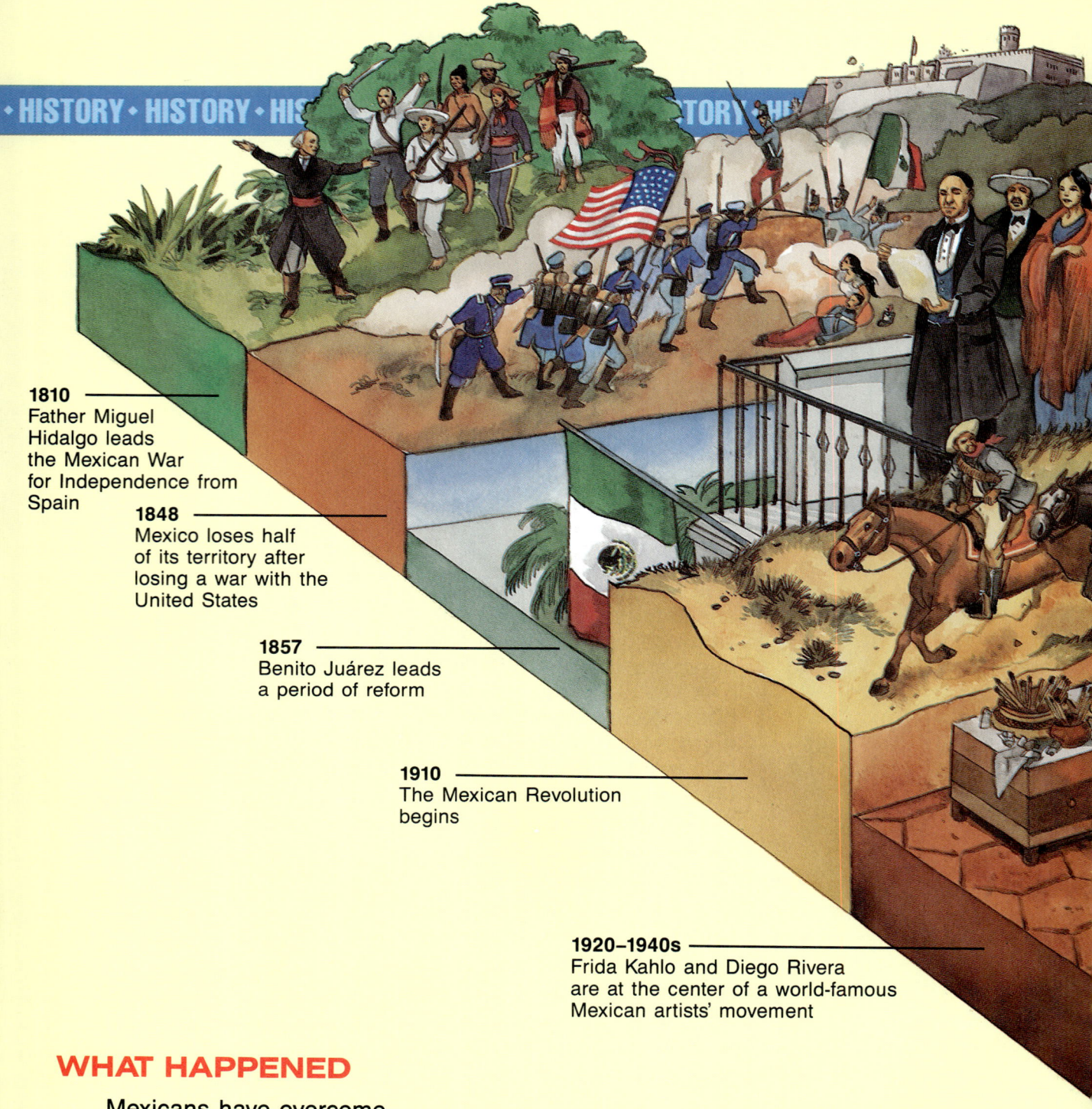

1810
Father Miguel Hidalgo leads the Mexican War for Independence from Spain

1848
Mexico loses half of its territory after losing a war with the United States

1857
Benito Juárez leads a period of reform

1910
The Mexican Revolution begins

1920–1940s
Frida Kahlo and Diego Rivera are at the center of a world-famous Mexican artists' movement

1988
New oil fields are discovered in the Gulf of Mexico

WHAT HAPPENED

Mexicans have overcome many obstacles in their struggle for freedom and prosperity. After a long rebellion, Mexico became independent from Spain. In the next 100 years, Mexico lost half its territory, endured dictatorships, and fought another revolution. Today, Mexicans are working hard to make their economy strong.

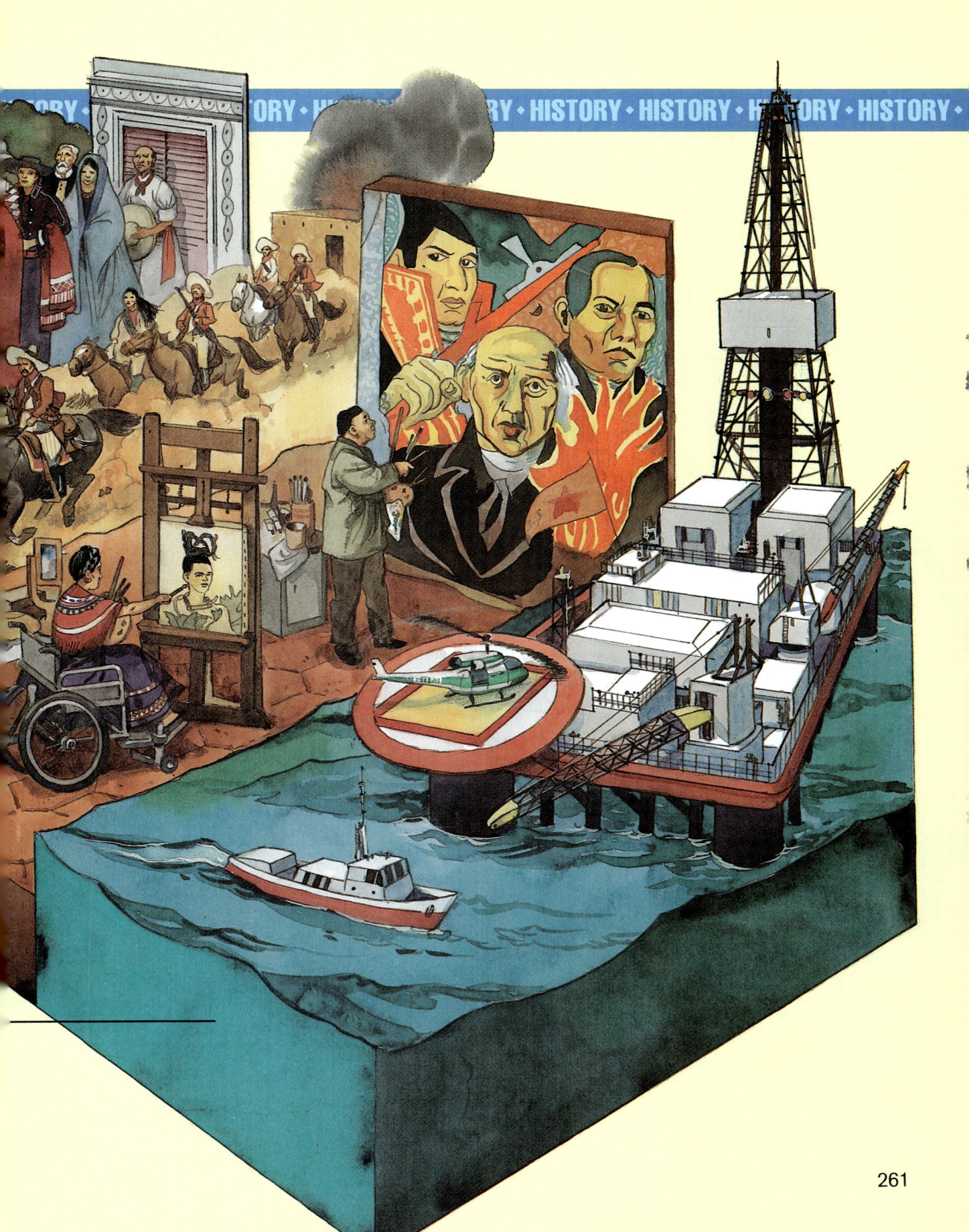

MEXICO

Werner Forman Archive/
British Museum London

MEXICO

Capital ✪
Mexico City

Major language: Spanish
Population: 85.7 million
Area: 761,604 sq mi; 1,972,550 sq km
Leading exports: oil and cotton

262

263

CHAPTER 12

THE GEOGRAPHY OF MEXICO

FOCUS

Thunder and avalanches in the mountains, huge floods and storms on the plains. Volcanoes exploding. The earth shaking and splitting.

This is how the writer Christopher Isherwood described the geography of Mexico, a land of contrasts in which nature was always changing. In this chapter you will visit Mexico, a land of contrasts.

1 The Land of Mexico

READ TO LEARN

Key Places

Gulf of Mexico	Yucatán Peninsula	Gulf Coastal Plain
Baja California	Western Sierra Madre	Central Plateau
Gulf of California	Eastern Sierra Madre	

Read Aloud

When Hernando Cortés returned to Spain and appeared before King Charles, the king ordered, "Tell me about our new land across the sea." Cortés crumpled a piece of paper before the king. "This is your map of Mexico, Your Majesty," he said. In this lesson you will read that Cortés was only partly right. The country is mostly mountainous, but it is also flat in certain areas.

Read for Purpose

1. WHAT YOU KNOW: What are some of the major landforms in your state?
2. WHAT YOU WILL LEARN: What are some of the major landforms of Mexico?

THE SHAPE OF MEXICO

Look at the map of Mexico on page 266. As you can see, the country is shaped like a great, curving horn. To the north, it shares a 1,900-mile (3,040-km) border with the United States. About half of that border follows the Rio Grande. To the south, Mexico is bordered by Guatemala and Belize. The Pacific Ocean lies to its west, and the Gulf of Mexico lies to its east.

Mexico has two large peninsulas, one on each coast. On the west coast is a narrow peninsula called Baja (bä′ hə) California, or Lower California. The Gulf of California separates Baja California from the rest of Mexico.

On the east coast is the Yucatán (ū kə tan′) Peninsula, which juts into the Gulf of Mexico like a fat thumb. The Yucatán Peninsula separates the Gulf of Mexico from the Caribbean Sea. You read in Chapter 9 that the Mayas built some of their magnificent cities on this peninsula.

A MOUNTAINOUS LAND

As Cortés demonstrated with the crumpled paper, mountains cover much of Mexico. Beginning in southern Mexico and stretching north in the form of a huge *V* are two mountain ranges, the Sierra Madre (sē er′ ə mä′ drā) or the "mother mountains."

MEXICO: Elevation

Elevations

Feet	Meters
Above 14,000	Above 4,000
7,000	2,000
1,500	500
700	200
0	0

⊛ National capital

• Other city

▲ Mountain peak

Iztaccíhuatl 17,343 ft. (5,236 m)
Popocatépetl 17,887 ft. (5,452 m)
Citlaltépetl 18,700 ft. (5,700 m)
El Chichón 3,478 ft. (1,060 m)

MAP SKILL: Mexico has few lowlands for farming. In which region shown on the map would flat land be located?

The **Western Sierra Madre** stretch along the Pacific Ocean on the west coast of Mexico. The **Eastern Sierra Madre** border the Gulf of Mexico on the east coast. In northwestern Mexico another mountain chain forms the backbone of Baja California.

HIGHLANDS AND LOWLANDS

As you know, Mexico is a mountainous country with few lowland regions. One very flat area, a coastal plain, runs along the Pacific Coast. This area, the **Gulf Coastal Plain**, is the largest lowland in Mexico. This plain borders the Gulf of Mexico and covers the Yucatán Peninsula. Find the Gulf Coastal Plain on the map on this page.

Mexico's largest land area is called the **Central Plateau**. This plateau is a broad, high area that lies between the V formed by the two Sierra Madre mountain ranges. Find the Central Plateau on the map above. It was in the Central Plateau that the Aztecs built their beautiful cities. Today most of Mexico's population and all of its largest cities are found in the Central Plateau.

EARTHQUAKE COUNTRY

The Mexicans of the Central Plateau live with the knowledge that an earthquake could happen at any time. You read about the causes of earthquakes in Chapter 1. You may recall that the movement of tectonic plates that are in contact with each other can cause an earthquake. There was a major earthquake in 1985. It toppled hundreds of buildings in Mexico City, causing more than 20,000 people to lose their lives.

Carlos Granillo, his wife, and six children survived the 1985 earthquake, but their lives were changed because of it. The Granillo family was 1 of more than 100,000 families left homeless by that earthquake. Almost one year later, Carlos and his family still lived in a yellow plastic tent. Nearby, on the spot where their house once stood, nothing remained but some dirt. The Granillos ate their meals in a larger tent, which they shared with other families. It took many years for the homes destroyed by the earthquake to be rebuilt.

Most earthquakes, though, are small. Only rarely does an earthquake cause as much damage as the one in Mexico City in 1985.

MEXICO'S VOLCANOES

The movement of the plates in the earth's crust can also cause volcanoes to form. Some of Mexico's highest mountains are volcanoes. Hundreds of volcanoes cover the landscape in the southern part of the Central Plateau.

There are so many volcanoes in Mexico that no one has counted them.

Imagine living near a volcano that might erupt at any time. Today most of Mexico's volcanoes are inactive, but from time to time a sleeping volcano erupts in a cloud of ash and dust.

As strange as it may seem, most of Mexico's people live in the valleys between the volcanoes. Because the soil that surrounds the volcanoes is rich and fertile, many farmers live in the valleys despite the danger from volcanoes. The ash from volcanoes adds nutrients to the soil. A nutrient is a substance that is needed by animals and plants for life.

El Chichón erupted violently in 1982. One survivor reported:

Fire started coming out of the sky.
Ash and sand were falling, and rocks came through the roof like bullets.

A LAND OF BEAUTY

As you have read, Mexico is a mountainous land with very few lowland areas. Nearly one half of Mexico is covered by the Central Plateau, which is also the center of earthquake country. It is no wonder that Mexico is called a "land of contrasts."

 Check Your Reading

1. Name two important mountain ranges in Mexico.
2. Why do many of Mexico's people live in the valleys that are located between volcanoes?
3. **GEOGRAPHY SKILL:** Which peninsula is located in the northwestern part of Mexico?
4. **THINKING SKILL:** What are three questions you could ask to find out more about volcanoes?

Understanding Great-Circle Routes

Key Vocabulary

great circle   great-circle route

As you know, Mexico, Canada, and all the countries and regions you have been studying this year lie west of the prime meridian and east of the 180° line of longitude. The line that circles the earth at 0° line of longitude and 180° line of longitude is called a **great circle**. A great circle is any line that divides the earth into equal halves. It is the largest imaginary circle that can be drawn on the earth.

The equator is another example of a great circle. Look at **Map A** on this page. As you can see, the equator divides the earth into its northern and southern halves—the Northern Hemisphere and the Southern Hemisphere. Every line of longitude and the line of longitude opposite it make up a great circle. The equator is the only line of latitude that makes up a great circle.

With a globe, a piece of string, and a pen, you can see for yourself how great circles work. Wrap the string around the globe at the equator. Mark the distance on the string. Now measure with the string any other circle around the globe. If the circle measures the same distance as the equator, it is a great circle.

Great-Circle Routes

What is the importance of great circles? The answer is that the shortest distance between any two places on the earth is along a great circle. So airplane pilots, for

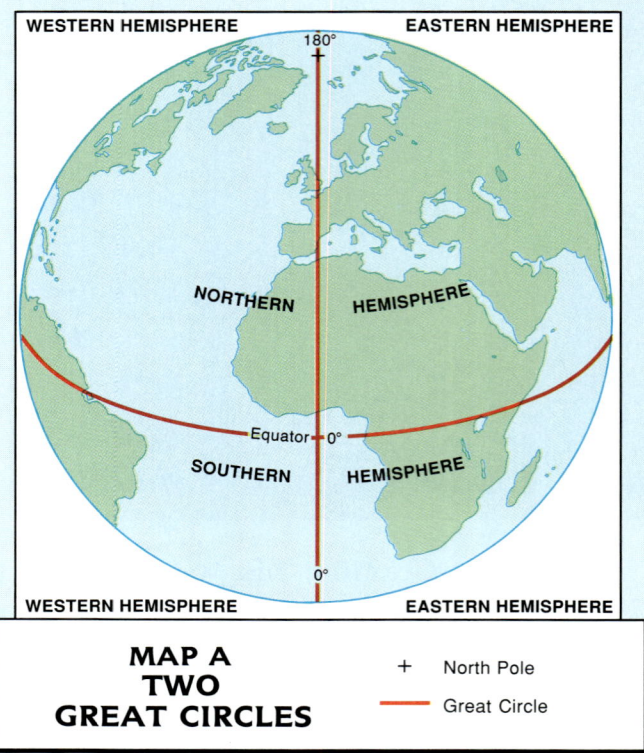

MAP A
TWO
GREAT CIRCLES

+ North Pole
— Great Circle

example, fly along great circles in order to save time, fuel, and money. Routes that follow great circles are called **great-circle routes**.

You can use the string and globe again to learn something about great-circle routes. Choose two places on the globe; for example Tokyo, Japan, and Los Angeles, California. Place your string so that it stretches between the two cities. You have now measured the shortest distance between them. The string shows a portion of the great-circle route that passes through Tokyo and Los Angeles.

Using Great-Circle Routes

It is easy to understand great-circle routes when you look at a globe. However, it is more difficult to imagine them when you look at a map. That is because a map is a flat surface, while the earth it represents is round. So, a great-circle route that follows the round shape of the earth might become distorted when shown on a flat piece of paper.

For instance, **Map B** shows three great-circle routes. Because this is a Mercator projection, all lines of latitude and longitude are shown as straight lines. Notice that the great-circle route between Libreville and Singapore looks like a straight line. It follows the line of the equator which, as you know, is a great circle. The great-circle route between Washington, D.C., and Lima, Peru, also

looks like a straight line. It follows the line of longitude on which both cities are located. Remember, each line of longitude and the line of longitude opposite it forms a great circle.

Now look at the great-circle route between Los Angeles and Tokyo. It appears as a longer, curved line. It does not seem possible that this could be the shortest route between the two cities. But actually, the curved line on the map is the way a flat map shows a rounded great-circle route on the earth.

You have read that understanding great-circle routes is especially important for airplane pilots. One common airline route passes between opposite sides of the world by flying over the North Pole. To use these routes, pilots have special maps that show great-circle routes as straight lines. **Map C** is an example of this type of map. Suppose that you were flying from Anchorage to St. Petersburg. You would first fly directly north to the North Pole along 150°W longitude. Then you would proceed directly south along 30°E longitude to Leningrad.

Reviewing the Skill

1. What is a great circle? What is a great-circle route?
2. Why are all lines of longitude part of a great circle?
3. On **Map B**, would the great-circle route between Santiago and Cape Town appear as a straight line or as a curved line? Why?
4. Why is it helpful to understand about great-circle routes?

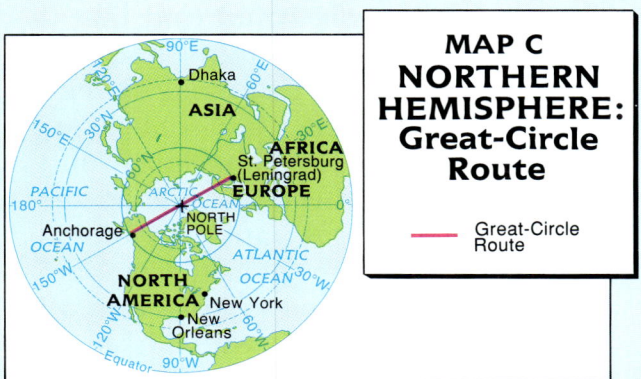

MAP B
THE WORLD:
Great-Circle Routes

—— Great-Circle Route

MAP C
NORTHERN
HEMISPHERE:
Great-Circle
Route

—— Great-Circle Route

2 Climate and Resources

READ TO LEARN

Key Vocabulary

humid
arable
fossil fuel

Key Places

Sonora Desert
Veracruz

Read Aloud

For 1,400 years a statue of the Aztec rain god, Tlaloc (tlä′ lŏk), stood near the village of Coatlinchan (kwä tlin chän′), Mexico. Then, in 1964, the huge stone statue was moved to Mexico City. As the statue was rolled through the streets, dark thunderclouds gathered overhead. Rain poured down on Mexico City, and many people believed that the rain god was grateful to them for moving his statue. Today Tlaloc's statue stands in Mexico City and continues to remind Mexicans of the value of rain to their country.

Read for Purpose

1. **WHAT YOU KNOW:** How is rain important to your community?
2. **WHAT YOU WILL LEARN:** What are the major climate zones and the most important resources of Mexico?

AN ARID REGION

If you were to travel to the northern half of Mexico, you would find that the climate is very dry, or arid. Sometimes as little as 5 inches (12 cm) of rain fall in this area in one year. Land with so little rain is called a desert. The huge Sonora Desert covers much of northern Mexico. Find the Sonora Desert on the Atlas map on page 573.

In the Read Aloud on this page you read about Tlaloc, the Aztec rain god. Hundreds of years ago, when the Spanish first arrived, most of Mexico did not receive enough rain to meet the needs of its people. Today many Mexicans say that lack of water is still their biggest worry.

If you were to travel to the southern half of Mexico, you would find that it has two seasons, one rainy and one dry. The dry season begins in November and lasts until May. The rainy season begins in June and lasts until October. During the rainy season the area may receive as much as 60–80 inches (150–200 cm) of rain. Compare that with the average annual rainfall for the earth as a whole, which is about 36 inches (91 cm).

In contrast with the Sonora Desert, the Gulf Coastal Plain is a lowland region that is hot and **humid**, or damp. You may know already that humid areas attract mosquitoes. The coastal city of **Veracruz** was once surrounded by mosquito-infested swamps. In the past so many people died of diseases carried by mosquitoes that Veracruz was called the "City of Death." Find the coastal city of Veracruz on the climate map below.

MEXICO'S CLIMATE

In Chapter 8 you read about the three elevation zones found in Latin America. In Mexico the lowlands along both the east coast and the west coast lie in the tierra caliente, or hot zone. Here daytime temperatures often rise to over 90°F. (32°C). Temperatures at night are usually cooler.

The higher Central Plateau lies in the tierra templada, or temperate zone, where days are warm and nights are cool. As you know, elevation has an effect on temperature. It is no wonder that most people in Mexico live in the gentle climate of the Central Plateau.

Mexico's mountains rise into the coldest elevation zone, the tierra fría. Here the tallest volcanic peaks glisten with snow year-round. Look at the climate map on this page. If you lived in Mexico, in which climate would you choose to live?

NEED FOR WATER

Imagine trying to grow crops in Mexico, where little rain falls and the land is often mountainous. Only a very

MAP SKILL: Which part of Mexico has a warm and wet climate all year?

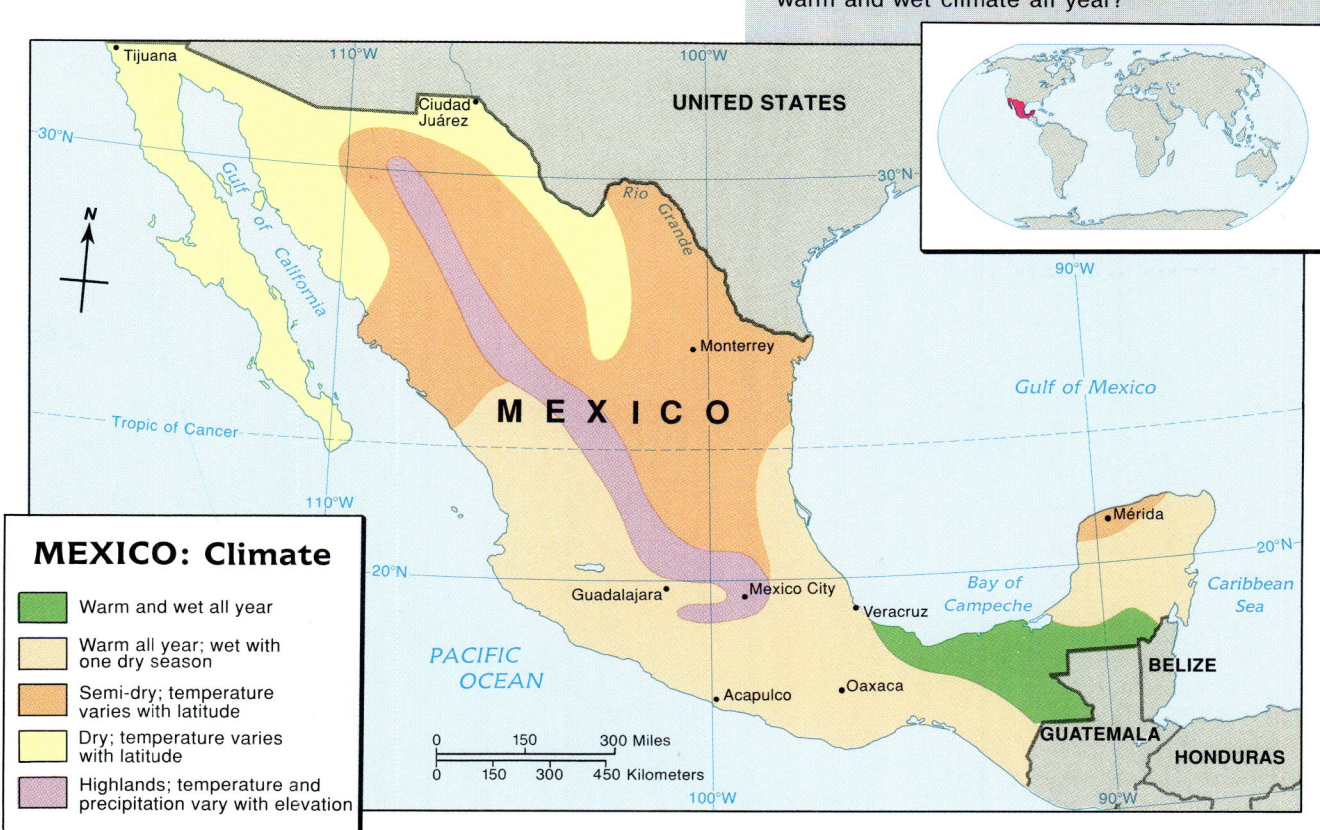

MEXICO: Climate

- Warm and wet all year
- Warm all year; wet with one dry season
- Semi-dry; temperature varies with latitude
- Dry; temperature varies with latitude
- Highlands; temperature and precipitation vary with elevation

small part of Mexico's land is **arable**, or suitable for growing crops.

Mexicans have tried to increase their arable land through irrigation. You may recall that irrigation is a method of supplying water to fields by means of canals, streams, or pipes. The fact that Mexico does not have many large rivers or lakes contributes to the difficulty of developing irrigation systems.

In addition, Mexico's mountains form natural barriers to transporting water. Despite these hardships, Mexicans have developed systems of irrigation in many parts of the country. Today, because of irrigation, one of Mexico's major farming regions is in the arid northwest. Find the arid northwest on the rainfall map below.

MEXICO'S NATURAL RESOURCES

Although rain is scarce in much of Mexico, valuable minerals are not. These buried treasures take the form of minerals, gems, and **fossil fuels**. Fossil fuels are sources of energy such as coal, natural gas, or petroleum. Fossil fuels have developed from the remains of plants and animals.

Large coal deposits are mined in the northeast. In 1977 huge reserves of oil and natural gas were discovered beneath the Gulf Coastal Plain and the Gulf of Mexico. Natural gas and petroleum are found in such large amounts in Mexico that the country is able to export what it does not need. In the 1980s, Mexico became the world's fourth-largest producer of oil.

As you read in Chapter 11, hundreds of years ago the Spanish mined gold and silver in Mexico. Mexico is still one of the world leaders in silver production, as you can see from the graph on page 273. Gold is mined in the northern deserts and mountains. Gemstones such as opals, amethysts, and turquoise are found in Mexico.

MAP SKILL: The photograph shows crop irrigation in Mérida. How can you tell from the map that irrigation is important in Mérida?

MEXICO: Annual Rainfall

Inches	Centimeters
Less than 10	Less than 25
10-20	25-50
20-40	50-100
40-80	100-200
More than 80	More than 200

272

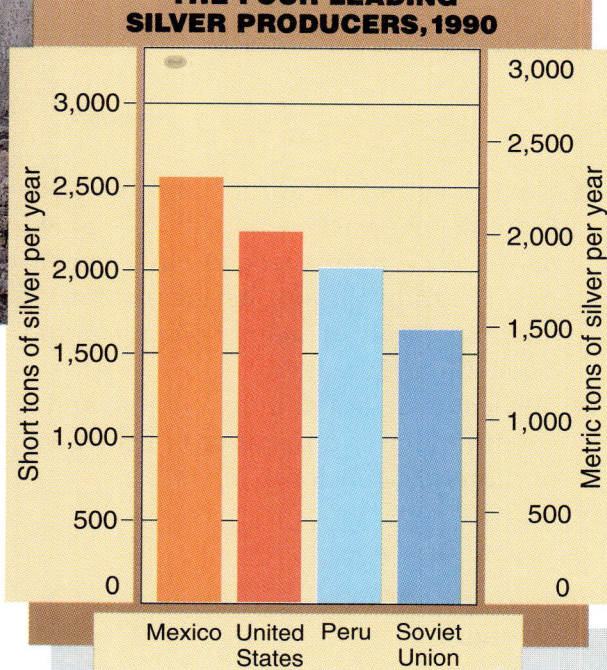

THE FOUR LEADING SILVER PRODUCERS, 1990

GRAPH SKILL: Silver is one of Mexico's leading natural resources. How many tons of silver does Mexico produce annually?

Mexico is also a leading producer of such minerals as lead, zinc, and mercury. Other important minerals include iron, copper, gypsum, sulfur, and manganese. These minerals are used in products that are sold in Mexico and around the world.

A HOT AND DRY COUNTRY

You read that Mexico is a mostly dry country with limited arable land. You also read that irrigation helps farmers to grow crops in arid areas. Beneath Mexico's surface are rich deposits of minerals and fossil fuels. In the next chapter you will read more about how Mexicans have used their land and their mineral wealth.

 Check Your Reading

1. Why is rain so important to the people of Mexico?
2. Which area of Mexico receives the most rain each year?
3. In which elevation zone is Mexico's Central Plateau located?
4. What is a fossil fuel? Name two examples of fossil fuels.
5. THINKING SKILL: What effect has irrigation had on farming in northwest Mexico?

IDEAS TO REMEMBER

■ Mexico is a beautiful land of geographic contrasts in which rugged mountain chains edged by coastal plains sandwich an interior plateau. It also is a land of many volcanoes and frequent earthquakes.

■ Mexico has a hot and dry climate and a wealth of natural resources in the form of minerals and fossil fuels.

REVIEWING VOCABULARY

arable
fossil fuel
humid

Number a sheet of paper from 1 to 5. Beside each number write the word or term from the list above that matches the statement or definition. Some of the words are used more than once.

1. Coal is an example of this source of energy, which developed from remains of plants and animals.
2. This type of land is suitable for growing crops.
3. Enough rain falls to make it damp in this climate.
4. Large deposits of this energy source are located in the northeast corner of Mexico.
5. The Gulf Coastal Plain has this type of climate.

REVIEWING FACTS

1. Name one contrast in landforms and one contrast in climate in the geography of Mexico.
2. Which bodies of water border Mexico on the east and on the west?
3. List the three countries that border Mexico, and tell in which direction from it each one lies.
4. Which mountain ranges form the gigantic *V* that stretches from the south to the north of Mexico?
5. Which major landform is located within the *V*?
6. What are Mexico's two major peninsulas, and where is each located?
7. In which part of the country are Mexico's gold mines located?
8. Why has irrigation become so important in Mexico?
9. Which area of Mexico is the most heavily populated? Why?
10. Why do many people in Mexico risk living near volcanoes?

WRITING ABOUT MAIN IDEAS

1. **Writing a Brochure:** Mexico is truly a land of beauty and contrasts. Write a travel brochure in which you describe examples of these places. Describe which geographic sights you think people would like to see in Mexico.
2. **Writing a Journal Entry:** Imagine that you have witnessed a volcano erupting in Mexico. What did you see, hear, smell, and feel? Use your imagination to create the whole experience for yourself. Then write a journal entry describing it.
3. **Writing a News Story:** Imagine that you are a reporter who is on the scene as an earthquake occurs in Mexico. Write a news story in which you describe what happens while it is going on and what effects it has on the surroundings. Also tell how it affects the people of the area.

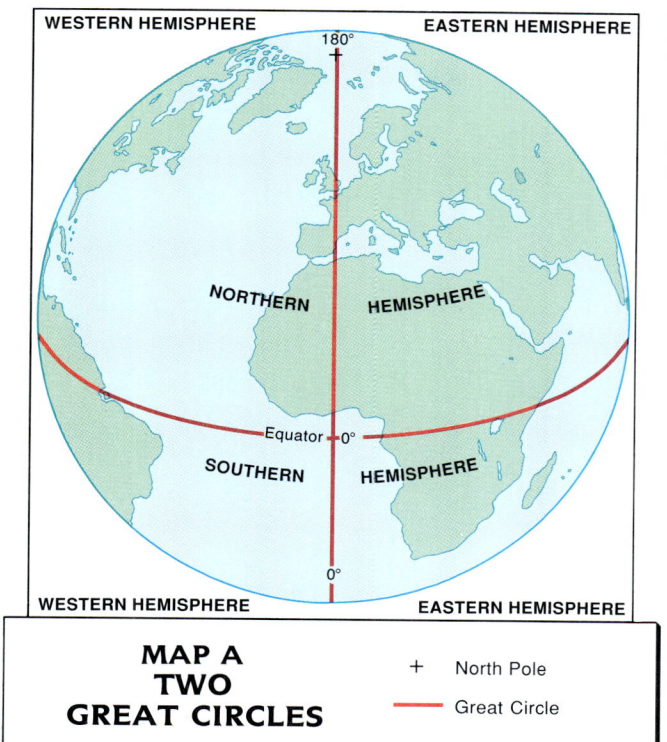

WESTERN HEMISPHERE · EASTERN HEMISPHERE

NORTHERN HEMISPHERE

Equator 0°

SOUTHERN HEMISPHERE

WESTERN HEMISPHERE · EASTERN HEMISPHERE

**MAP A
TWO
GREAT CIRCLES**

+   North Pole

——   Great Circle

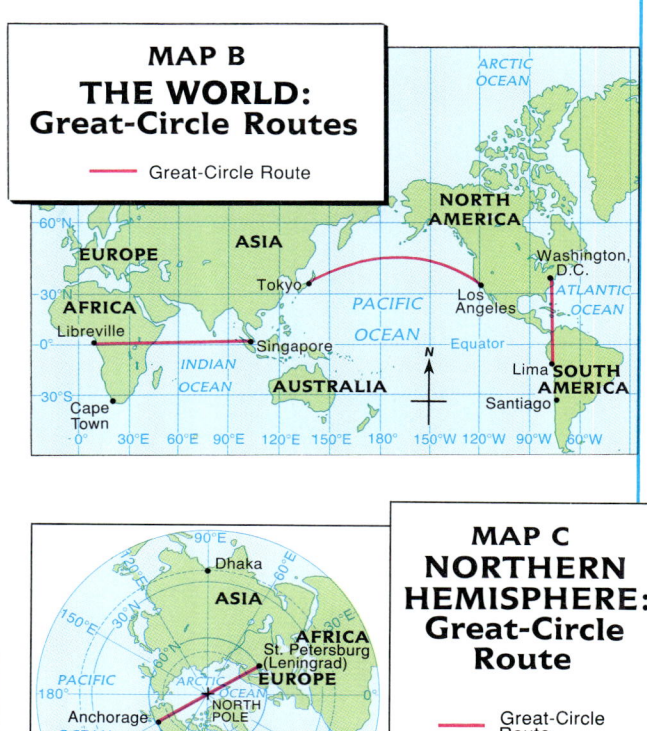

**MAP B
THE WORLD:
Great-Circle Routes**

——   Great-Circle Route

**MAP C
NORTHERN
HEMISPHERE:
Great-Circle
Route**

——   Great-Circle Route

4. **Writing About Perspectives:** Write one or more paragraphs in which you contrast how a person living in the Sonora Desert and a person living in the Central Plateau would describe their land and their climate.

BUILDING SKILLS: UNDERSTANDING GREAT-CIRCLE ROUTES

Use what you already know and the maps above to answer the questions.

1. What is a great circle? Why is the distance around any great circle always the same?

2. What is the connection between a great circle and a great-circle route?

3. Can great-circle routes be traced between any two points on earth? Explain.

4. On **Map A**, what is the name of the only line of latitude that makes up a great circle? Why is it that no other line of latitude is a great circle?

5. On **Map B**, why does the route from Los Angeles to Tokyo appear to be a curved line?

6. On **Map C**, describe the great-circle route from New Orleans to Dacca.

7. For whom are great-circle routes useful and why?

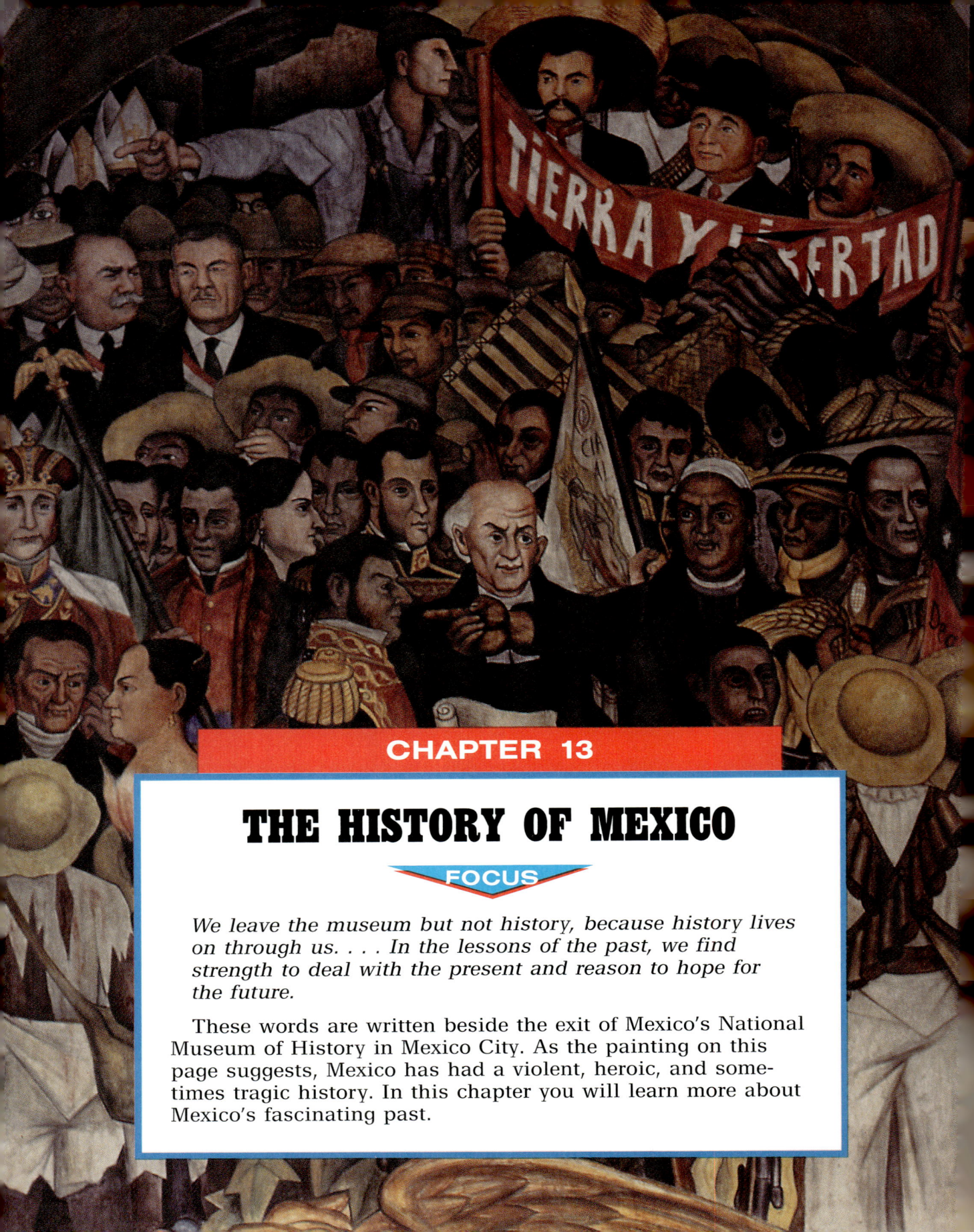

CHAPTER 13

THE HISTORY OF MEXICO

FOCUS

We leave the museum but not history, because history lives on through us. . . . In the lessons of the past, we find strength to deal with the present and reason to hope for the future.

These words are written beside the exit of Mexico's National Museum of History in Mexico City. As the painting on this page suggests, Mexico has had a violent, heroic, and sometimes tragic history. In this chapter you will learn more about Mexico's fascinating past.

1 The Struggle for Independence

READ TO LEARN

 **Key People**

Miguel Hidalgo
José Morelos
Agustín de Iturbide

 **Read Aloud**

Friends and countrymen, you are the sons of this land, yet have been for three centuries in bondage. The Europeans have everything. We propose to end their rule. Come march with us for country and religion. . . . Death to the bad government!

With these words Miguel Hidalgo (mē gel' ē däl' gō) called on the people of Mexico to fight for their freedom from Spain. In this lesson you will read about Hidalgo and how the movement for independence that he led grew from a small number of people into an army of thousands.

 **Read for Purpose**

1. **WHAT YOU KNOW:** What were some of the reasons for unrest in the Spanish colonies?
2. **WHAT YOU WILL LEARN:** How did the Mexicans win their independence from Spain?

MIGUEL HIDALGO

In Chapter 11 you read about the early uprisings in Mexico. You have also read that Mexico's Indians and mestizos were trapped in conditions of intense poverty and despair. These terrible conditions had existed under Spanish rule for nearly 300 years.

In 1803 a priest called **Miguel Hidalgo** was assigned to a church in Dolores, a village in central Mexico. Hidalgo was shocked by the poverty that he found in Dolores. He tried to help poor Indian and mestizo farmers by teaching them to grow olives and grapes. However, it was illegal to raise these crops in Mexico because they could be imported, or brought, into Mexico from Spain. The Spanish wanted the Mexicans to buy only olives and grapes grown in Spain. Officials chopped down the new olive trees and the grape vines. Hidalgo realized that the lives of the poor would never improve under Spanish rule. He felt that the only way to help his people was to end Spanish control over Mexico.

277

Many students come to see a mural showing Miguel Hidalgo calling on Mexicans to fight for their freedom. The church in Dolores, where he made his speech, is at the left.

THE CRY OF DOLORES

On September 16, 1810, church bells rang in the village of Dolores. Hidalgo climbed to the top of the church steps and addressed the Indians and mestizos who had gathered below. Hidalgo told them that the time had come to free Mexico from Spanish rule. You read some of his words in the Read Aloud that begins this lesson. Hidalgo's famous speech is known as the "Cry of Dolores."

That day in 1810 was the beginning of the War for Independence. Eight hundred men, women, and children followed Hidalgo out of the village on the way to Mexico City. In the days that followed, Hidalgo gathered everyone that he could to increase his army. He said the following words to a young man who could not decide whether to join the rebels.

It is not right that we Mexicans, having a rich and beautiful country, should remain under the rule of the [Spanish]. They treat us as slaves; we cannot speak freely or enjoy the fruits of our soil, for they own everything. . . . We must all unite and run out the [Spanish]. What do you say? Will you take arms and join me? Will you give your life, if necessary, to free your country?

The young man finally agreed to join Hidalgo. One by one the poor people of Mexico joined the ragged army. Shouting and singing, they marched along the dusty roads toward Mexico City. With farm tools and homemade weapons, they attacked any Spanish soldiers along the way. Behind them they left a path of destruction.

As they marched toward Mexico City, their rebel army numbered 90,000. But the rebels were poorly armed and lacked training. A force of 6,000 Spanish soldiers attacked and scattered Hidalgo's army. In 1811 Hidalgo was captured and later killed. The priest's head was displayed in an iron cage as a warning to other rebels.

THE STRUGGLE CONTINUES

The struggle for independence did not end with Hidalgo's death. José Morelos (hō sā′ mō rā′ lōs), a mestizo priest, continued to lead the poor in the rebellion against the Spanish. Morelos became a skillful leader who won many victories in battle. But the Spanish, with their well-armed troops, finally exhausted the rebels. Morelos was captured and killed in 1815. It seemed to many Mexicans that their hopes for independence were over.

INDEPENDENCE AT LAST

Although most of the rebels were deeply discouraged, the dream of independence was kept alive by small bands of people who hid in the hills. They continued to make scattered raids on the Spanish troops.

A creole officer, Agustín de Iturbide (ä gùs tēn′ dā ē tùr bē′ dā), was appointed to defeat the rebellion. Earlier in the struggle Iturbide had helped to defeat Hidalgo and Morelos. However, he had secretly switched sides and now supported the rebels. Although Iturbide did not really believe in the cause of the poor people, he switched sides because he saw an opportunity to gain power for himself. Iturbide had a plan to seize that power.

Agustín de Iturbide (on horseback) defeated Miguel Hidalgo and José Morelos (*left*) before switching sides to support the rebels.

Mexicans celebrate Independence Day each year on September 16—the day that Miguel Hidalgo made his famous speech, the "Cry of Dolores." Here Mexicans enjoy a parade.

THE PLAN OF IGUALA

In 1821 Iturbide wrote an independence plan for Mexico called the Plan of Iguala (i gwäl' ə). This plan contained three promises to Mexicans. It called for Iturbide to become emperor of Mexico. It declared that the Roman Catholic Church would remain the official church of Mexico. And most important, the plan promised equal rights to all Mexicans.

The Plan of Iguala won the support of almost everyone in Mexico, from wealthy creoles to poor mestizos and Indians. But the plan did not win the support of the Spanish government. The Spanish did not want to lose control of an enormously rich colony. It is no wonder that the Spanish viceroy would not agree to the plan. As a result, Iturbide's troops surrounded the viceroy and forced him to sign the plan. On August 24, 1821, 11 years after Hidalgo's "Cry of Dolores," the long struggle for Mexico's independence was over.

FREE AND INDEPENDENT

You read that Mexico's struggle for its independence began in 1810 and lasted 11 years. During those difficult years the people of Mexico attempted to free themselves from Spanish rule. In the next lesson you will read about the problems that arose despite this new independence.

Check Your Reading

1. What was Miguel Hidalgo's role in Mexico's long and difficult struggle for independence?
2. Describe how Hidalgo's forces grew from 800 to over 90,000 Mexicans.
3. What were the three promises of the Plan of Iguala?
4. **THINKING SKILL:** Compare and contrast the leaders Miguel Hidalgo and Agustín de Iturbide to explain which man had a greater effect on Mexico.

2 Independent Mexico

 Key Vocabulary

republic
North American Intervention

Key People

Antonio López de Santa Anna

 Read Aloud

Independence brought happiness to very few Mexicans. After years of war, the country was in ruins. Behind fire-blackened hacienda walls, fields lay unplowed. Mines had become flooded. Bandits roamed the roads.

The people of Mexico needed a time of peace and strong leadership in order to rebuild their country. But as you will read, they had neither peace nor leadership.

Read for Purpose

1. **WHAT YOU KNOW:** How did Spanish rule come to an end in Mexico?
2. **WHAT YOU WILL LEARN:** Why did independence fail to bring peace to Mexico?

PROBLEMS OF INDEPENDENCE

Early in 1822 soldiers ran through the streets of Mexico City shouting, "Long live Agustín I!" Bells rang and cannons boomed. A congress chosen by Agustín de Iturbide had declared him emperor of Mexico. Remember that Iturbide had written the Plan of Iguala, which called for Mexico to have an emperor. But Emperor Agustín I lived in luxury and did very little to help the Mexican people. He ruled so badly that he was soon driven out of power.

The Mexican people decided that Mexico should become a republic. In a republic, power rests with the citizens and their chosen representatives. Then in 1824 the Mexicans finally elected their first president.

The new republic faced huge problems. Poverty was common. The nation was in debt. But instead of working together to solve these problems, the leaders fought among themselves. Rebellions were widespread. Presidents gained and lost power rapidly.

These difficulties were described by Fanny Calderón in a book called *Life in Mexico*. Her husband was Spain's representative in Mexico during the 1840s. In her book she wrote, "All is decaying . . . one revolution follows another, yet the remedy is not found."

Agustín de Iturbide (on balcony) was declared emperor of Mexico in 1822, but was quickly driven out of power. Santa Anna (*right*) was elected president of Mexico in 1833.

THE TEXAS REBELLION

One of Mexico's first presidents was called Antonio López de Santa Anna (an tō′ nyō lō pās dā san′ tə an′ ə). Following his election, Santa Anna became a powerful ruler who often ignored the people's rights. Many Mexicans opposed Santa Anna's actions and protested his presidency.

At that time Mexico was much larger than it is today. The land that today forms the states of Texas, California, New Mexico, and Arizona was all part of Mexico. People from the United States had moved to Texas, and many of them wanted Texas to join the United States. In 1836 the Texans rebelled against Santa Anna, declaring Texas an independent republic.

Santa Anna called the Texas rebels "worthless land thieves." He led an army north to Texas and captured the Alamo, a fort in San Antonio. Santa Anna's army then marched across Texas to destroy the rebels. At the same time, however, an army of Texans took up the battle cry, "Remember the Alamo!" Led by Sam Houston, the Texans killed most of the Mexican troops and captured the others. To save his life, Santa Anna gave up Texas.

Mexicans were very unhappy about the loss of Texas. They dreamed that this land would someday return to Mexico. Meanwhile, people from the United States went to Mexico with offers to buy land that later formed California and New Mexico. The Mexicans replied firmly that the land was not for sale.

THE NORTH AMERICAN INTERVENTION

In 1845 Texas became the twenty-eighth state of the United States. Mexicans were furious about the loss of so much land. In response, Mexico broke all ties with its northern neighbor. Mexican troops entered a part of Texas claimed by both countries.

In 1846 those troops clashed with a United States force that was in the same area. The United States declared war on Mexico. In the United States this conflict is called the Mexican-American War. In Mexico it is called the **North American Intervention**. *Intervention* means "interference in the affairs of another country."

Across Mexico, local leaders raised their own armies. However, instead of uniting against the United States, they fought against each other. Meanwhile, United States troops were invading Mexico by land and by sea.

A BITTER DEFEAT

Mexicans turned to Santa Anna to save their country. The general formed an army of 18,000 troops. With this army he slowed the advance of the United States troops into northern Mexico, but his efforts were not good enough to stop them.

In 1847 United States troops landed on Mexico's coast near Veracruz. From there they fought their way across the mountains to Mexico City. Thousands of Mexicans died trying to stop this invasion. However, by the end of the year, the United States troops controlled the capital. The war was over.

In 1848 a peace treaty was signed in the town of Guadalupe Hidalgo. Under its terms, Mexico agreed to sell a huge piece of land to the United States. That land today forms the states of California, Nevada, Utah, and parts of Colorado, Arizona, and New Mexico. The United States paid Mexico $15 million for this vast territory.

In 1853 the United States bought more land, called the Gadsden Purchase. The map on page 284 shows the total amount of land that Mexico lost during these years. For Mexicans, this

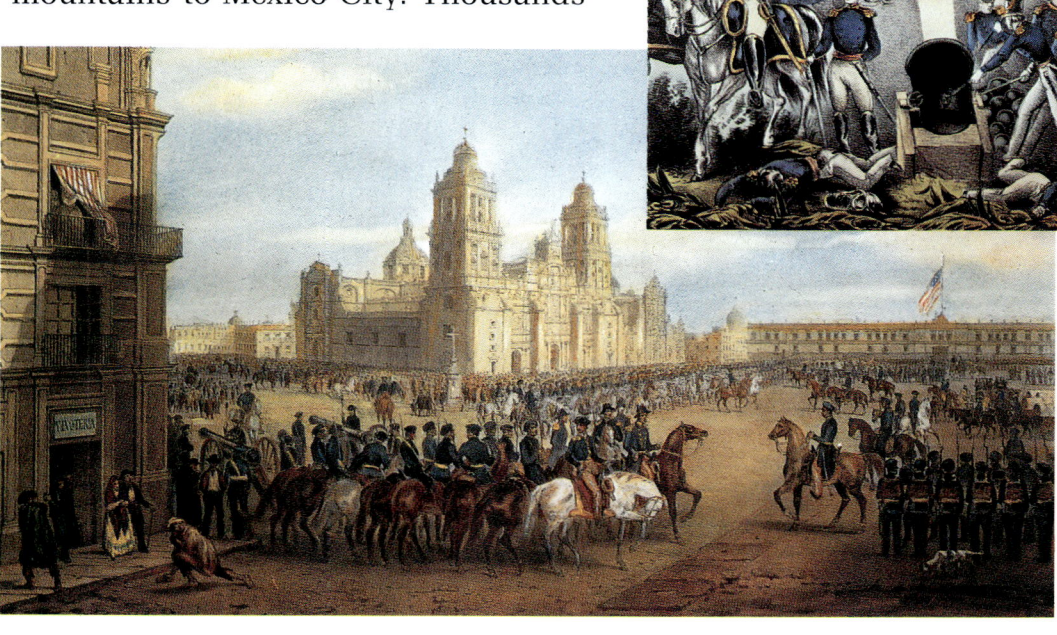

(*top*) General Scott at the siege of Veracruz. (*bottom*) Scott's army entering Mexico City.

MEXICO'S CHANGING BORDERS

———	Mexico's borders in 1823
▨	Land lost in 1836 (Republic of Texas)
▨	Land lost 1836 to 1845
▨	Land sold to United States in 1848
▨	Land sold to United States in 1853 (Gadsden Purchase)

Present-day boundaries and state names are shown.

MAP SKILL: Mexico lost half of its territory between 1821 and 1853. In which year did it lose the largest single piece of land? Which states were at one time entirely part of Mexico?

or to defend their country in battle. The result for Mexicans was tragic. By 1848 Mexico had lost half of its territory to the United States.

loss was a bitter defeat. Not only had they lost a war, but they had also lost half of their country. Santa Anna declared sadly, "Mexicans! We have brought this tragic misfortune on ourselves by our endless disputes."

A DEEPLY DIVIDED NATION

In this lesson you have read that independence left Mexico a deeply divided nation. The people of Mexico could not unite to solve their problems

Check Your Reading

1. How did Agustín de Iturbide become emperor of Mexico?
2. What kind of a leader was Santa Anna?
3. How did Mexico lose the land that today is the state of Texas?
4. **THINKING SKILL:** List the following events in sequence: Texas becomes a state; the North American Intervention; Mexico declared a republic; Santa Anna captures the Alamo.

3 Reform And Revolution

READ TO LEARN

Key Vocabulary

reform   investor
civil war
dictator

Key People

Benito Juárez   Francisco Madero
Maximilian   Pancho Villa
Porfirio Díaz   Emiliano Zapata

Read Aloud

I decided before very long that only by going to the city could I learn anything more. I often asked my uncle to take me there and he always replied, "We'll go there someday," but he never made a move to begin the journey.

These are the words of Benito Juárez (be nē′ tō hwä′ rez). At the age of 12, he decided to leave his Zapotec Indian village to attend school in the city. Many years later Juárez was elected president of Mexico. In this lesson you will read more about this national hero known as *El Indio*, or the Indian.

Read for Purpose

1. **WHAT YOU KNOW:** How did Mexico lose half of its territory?
2. **WHAT YOU WILL LEARN:** How did Mexicans try to improve their country during the 1850s?

JUÁREZ AND THE REFORM

When Benito Juárez left his village, he went to Oaxaca (wə häk′ ə), where he attended school and became a lawyer. In 1834 he was elected state representative for Oaxaca. Juárez was a quiet man with strong ideas. He said:

Our ship of state is still drifting. Soon it is going to strike the rocks.

Juárez and his friends in the government called for reforms to make Mexico stronger. Reforms are changes for the better. He was eager to replace Mexico's leaders who, he believed, had almost destroyed the country.

In 1855 the reformers seized control of the government. Juárez became minister of justice and began to write laws that would reform the government. Mexicans call this period of their history la Reforma, or the Reform.

THE WAR OF THE REFORM

For hundreds of years, the Roman Catholic Church had been a powerful force in Mexico's government. The church owned nearly one half of Mexico's arable land. But the reformers claimed that the church did not use its wealth and power to help the poor.

This mural by José Orozco shows Benito Juárez during the War of the Reform.

They accused church leaders of stopping efforts to improve society.

Juárez recommended reform laws that would reduce the wealth and power of the church. In 1857 the reformers wrote these laws into a new constitution. The constitution also allowed Mexicans to practice religions other than the Catholic faith.

Church leaders were outraged by these reforms. They called on Catholics to take up arms to defend their religion. As a result, civil war broke out. A civil war is a war between groups of people in the same country. The civil war in Mexico was called the War of the Reform.

In 1861 the War of the Reform ended in victory for the reformers. Juárez became the first Indian to be elected president of Mexico. His motto was "Nothing by force. Everything through law and reason."

THE FRENCH INVASION

The Mexicans who had opposed Juárez decided to ask the French for help. The leaders of France had already been dreaming of building an empire in Mexico. Within months after Juárez took office, French troops landed in Veracruz. Fighting began in 1862 and continued for many months. In 1863 the French captured Mexico City and Juárez had to flee. Mexico was ruled again by a European power. This time an Austrian prince named Maximilian was chosen by the French to rule the Mexican empire.

Maximilian tried to rule Mexico fairly, but the Mexican people would not accept a ruler from another country. Meanwhile, Juárez was in northern Mexico where he was building a new army. His followers begged him to leave the country for his own safety, but Juárez refused, saying:

*Show me the highest, driest . . .
mountain, and I will climb to the top
and die there of hunger and thirst. But
leave Mexico? Never!*

In 1866 France brought its troops from Mexico. They were needed to fight in Europe. While the French troops marched away, Juárez's army swept across Mexico. Maximilian was taken prisoner and killed in 1867.

Juárez was a national hero when he returned to Mexico City. He continued to work to rebuild his country until his death in 1872.

ORDER AND PROGRESS

In 1876 a leader named Porfirio Díaz (pôr fē′ ryō dē′ äs) seized power in Mexico. Like Juárez, Díaz wanted to make Mexico strong and successful. His motto was "Order and Progress." But unlike Juárez, Díaz cared little about the rights of the people. For the next 35 years, Díaz ruled Mexico as a dictator, a ruler with complete power and authority over a country. Elections were held, but Díaz decided who would run for office, who would vote, and who would win.

However, Díaz did bring order to his country. During the years of his rule there were no civil wars in Mexico. His police force, the *rurales* (rù rä′ läs), cleared the roads of outlaws and made travel safe for the first time in years. The dictator brought some progress as well. During his rule railroads and ports were built. Mines were opened and oil wells drilled. Electrical systems lighted cities and ran factories.

Most of the money for these projects came from foreign investors. An investor is someone who puts money into a project in the hope of making a profit. By 1910 foreign investors owned half of Mexico's wealth and a third of its land. "Mexico is the mother of foreigners," it was said, "and the stepmother of Mexicans." During the 35 years of Díaz's dictatorship, progress was made, but many people continued to suffer.

"VIVA LA REVOLUCIÓN"

Among the people who suffered most from Díaz's long rule were the farmers. One million poor Mexican farmers lost their land to rich landowners during Díaz's rule. By 1900 only 3 rural families out of 100 owned land.

In 1910 a reformer named Francisco Madero called on Mexicans to overthrow Díaz. Madero wanted Mexico to be a democracy. The people were so unhappy with Díaz that they supported Madero and joined his uprising. Poor farmers and workers soon took up Madero's call. "Viva la Revolución!" (vē′ və lä re vō lü sē ōn′) they cried. "Long Live the Revolution!"

Porfirio Díaz (*left*) ruled Mexico as a dictator for more than 30 years. Díaz's *rurales* brought order to Mexico.

The Granger Collection

Mexican
NATIONAL ANTHEM

Translated by Miss B. Romero
Versified by J. E. Hales

Words by Francisco González Bocanegra (1824–1861)
Music by Jaime Nunó (1824–1908)

CHORUS

Me - xi - ca - nos al gri - to de gue - rra El a -
Mex - i - cans, when the trum - pet is call - ing, Grasp your

ce - ro ap - res - tad y el bri - dón. Y re -
sword and your har - ness as - sem - ble. Let the

tiem - ble en sus cen - tros la tie - rra, Al so -
guns with their thun - der ap - pal - ling Make the

no - ro ru - gir del ca - ñón, Y re -
Earth's deep foun - da - tions to trem - ble. Let the

tiem - ble en sus cen - tros la tie - rra al so -
guns with their thun - der ap - pal - ling Make the

no - ro ru - gir del ca - ñón.
Earth's deep foun - da - tions to trem - ble.

288

Emiliano Zapata led an army of poor landless farmers in the fight against Porfirio Díaz's long dictatorship.

Now bands of rebels sprang up across Mexico. In the north they were led by **Pancho Villa** (vē′ ə), who wanted to improve the lives of the poor people. In the south **Emiliano Zapata** (ā mēl yän′ ō sä pä′ tə) formed an army of landless farmers. Zapata's battle cry was "Land and Liberty." For the next few years the rebels fought the army, the rich landowners, and each other for power. Finally Díaz was overthrown by "the Madero Revolution."

The Mexican people elected Madero president, but the government was still very weak. Madero held office for only 15 months before he was assassinated. During the next ten years many other presidents were elected and then overthrown by the people of Mexico.

THE CONSTITUTION OF 1917

Finally, in 1917 the Mexican people agreed on a new constitution for their country. This plan of government included many changes that the reformers had been fighting for during the past 100 years.

The 1917 Constitution created a democratic government with power coming from the people. It gave the government the power to break up estates in order to give land to the poor. It also said that the people of Mexico, not foreigners, should control Mexico's natural resources. At last, the Mexican Revolution was over. Mexicans could celebrate by singing the Mexican anthem, which you can find on page 288.

A HISTORY OF CONFLICT

As you have read, Mexico has a long history of violent conflicts. These conflicts led to struggles for power among the poor, the landowners, the church, and foreign leaders. When the Mexican Revolution was over, Mexico had a new government.

Check Your Reading

1. Which two groups of Mexicans fought in the War of the Reform?
2. How did Benito Juárez overcome Maximilian?
3. What kind of a leader was Díaz?
4. **THINKING SKILL:** Which of the leaders described in this chapter would you follow? Explain your choice.

Determining Point of View

You read in this chapter that Mexican president Santa Anna called the Texas rebels "land thieves." Do you think the people who wanted Texas to break away from Mexico and join the United States thought of themselves as "land thieves"? They probably viewed themselves as rebels who no longer wanted to be part of Mexico. Santa Anna and the Texas settlers had differing points of view toward the Texas rebellion. Point of view is the way a person views or feels about a subject or topic.

It is important to recognize a person's point of view. How a person feels about a topic affects the accuracy of what he or she has to say or write about that topic.

Trying the Skill

The excerpt below is from an 1850s newspaper article on the war between the United States and Mexico. The article was written by Frederick Douglass, an African-American leader of the struggle to end slavery. As you read, think about how Douglass feels about the subject.

> Those who have all along been loudly in favor of the war, glorifying the terrible deeds of barbarous heroism, have no sincere love of peace. . . . They had robbed Mexico of her territory. Had they not succeeded in robbing Mexico of her most valuable territory, many of those now loudest in favor of peace would be loudest and wildest for war. We are not the people to rejoice. We ought to blush and hang our heads for shame. We ought to crave [beg] pardon for our crimes at the hands of God, whose mercy lasts forever.

1. What was Douglass's point of view?
2. How were you able to determine his point of view?

HELPING YOURSELF

The steps on the left can help you to determine the point of view of a writer or speaker. The example on the right shows how to apply these steps to Douglass's newspaper article.

One Way to Determine Point of View	Example
1. Identify the subject or topic.	The topic is the war between the United States and Mexico.
2. Identify statements of fact.	There are no statements of fact.
3. Identify statements of opinion.	The entire article is a statement of opinion. Douglass thinks that people in favor of the war "have no sincere love of peace," "robbed Mexico of her territory," and glorify the "terrible deeds of barbarous heroism."
4. Look for words or phrases that suggest how the writer feels about the topic.	The phrases "We ought to blush and hang our heads for shame" and "We ought to crave pardon for our crimes" show how the writer feels.
5. Identify aspects of the topic that the author does not include but probably could have.	The writer does not include reasons that the United States went to war against Mexico.
6. Describe the point of view expressed.	The writer's point of view is that the United States was wrong to go to war against Mexico to acquire territory.

Applying the Skill

Now apply what you have learned. Determine the point of view expressed in the passage below.

Benito Juárez is one of the most honored men in the history of Mexico. This plain and honest man, a Zapotec Indian, was the author of reform measures in the Constitution of 1857. As president he helped to create the modern country of Mexico by encouraging industry, transportation, and public education. This liberal thinker was truly a man of vision.

1. Identify one fact and one opinion stated in the passage.
2. What are some aspects of the subject that the writer did not include?
3. What is the writer's point of view?

Reviewing the Skill

1. What does the term *point of view* mean?
2. What are some steps you can follow to determine the point of view of a writer or a speaker?
3. When is it important to identify a person's point of view?

IMPORTANT EVENTS

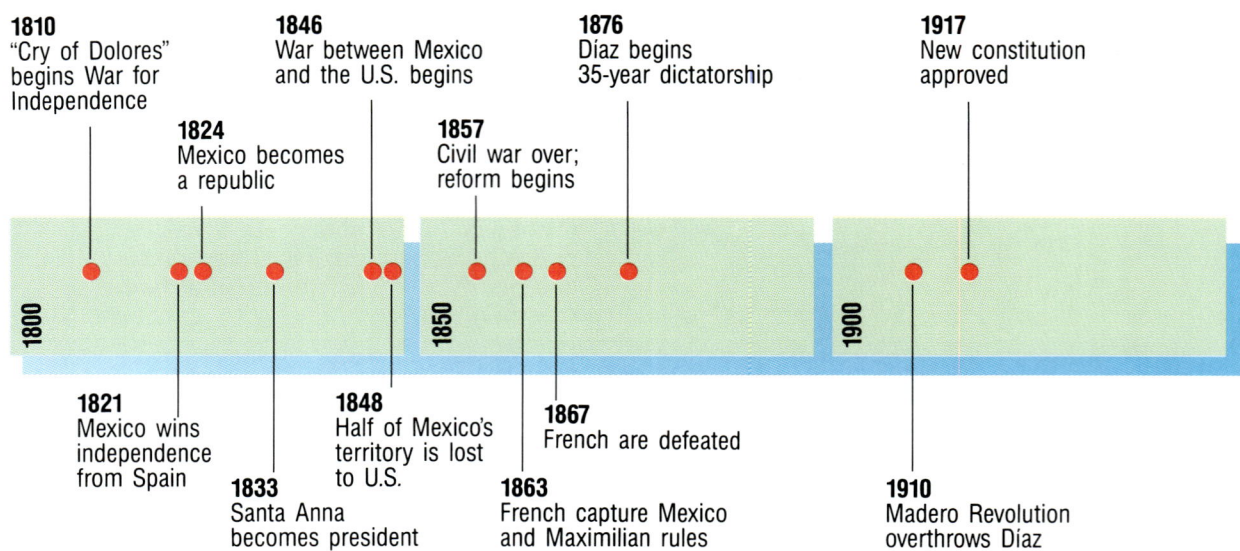

1810
"Cry of Dolores" begins War for Independence

1824
Mexico becomes a republic

1846
War between Mexico and the U.S. begins

1857
Civil war over; reform begins

1876
Díaz begins 35-year dictatorship

1917
New constitution approved

1800

1850

1900

1821
Mexico wins independence from Spain

1833
Santa Anna becomes president

1848
Half of Mexico's territory is lost to U.S.

1863
French capture Mexico and Maximilian rules

1867
French are defeated

1910
Madero Revolution overthrows Díaz

PEOPLE TO KNOW

Miguel Hidalgo 1753–1811

Porfirio Díaz 1830–1915

Antonio López de Santa Anna 1794–1876

José Morelos 1765–1815

Benito Juárez 1806–1872

Francisco Madero 1873–1913

Pancho Villa 1877?–1923

IDEAS TO REMEMBER

■ Mexicans fought to free themselves from Spanish rule so that they could develop their country in their own way and for their own benefit.

■ Mexican independence tragically led to a deeply divided nation torn by internal struggle and a loss of territory.

■ Nearly 70 years that saw attempted reform, civil war, foreign invasion, dictatorship, and another revolution finally led to the Constitution of 1917.

REVIEWING VOCABULARY

civil war   reform
dictator   republic
investor

Number a sheet of paper from 1 to 5. Beside each number write the word or term from the list above that best completes the sentence.

1. A _____ is a change for the better.
2. Santa Anna and Díaz could each be called a _____ because each ruled with absolute power over his nation.
3. When groups of people in the same country go into armed conflict with each other, they are fighting a _____.
4. A nation in which governing power rests with the citizens and their chosen representatives is a _____.
5. An _____ is someone who puts money into a project in the hope of making more money.

REVIEWING FACTS

1. What was the "Cry of Dolores"?
2. Why did Mexico's first attempt to win independence fail?
3. List what the Plan of Iguala promised
   a. to Agustín de Iturbide.
   b. to the Roman Catholic Church.
   c. to all the people of Mexico.
4. Give two reasons for the continued unrest in Mexico after independence.
5. How did the Treaty of Guadalupe Hidalgo change Mexico's boundaries?
6. List two reforms that Juárez called for to make Mexico a stronger nation.
7. What part did France play in Mexican history?
8. Name two positive and two negative effects that Díaz had on Mexico.
9. What is one way foreign investors can help a country? What is one way they can hurt a country?
10. List three reforms that the 1917 Constitution brought about in Mexico.

WRITING ABOUT MAIN IDEAS

1. **Writing a Feature Article:** Imagine that you are a journalist and your magazine has assigned you to write a feature article on Father Miguel Hidalgo. You are supposed to both interview him and discuss what he is trying to do. Write a brief feature article in which you report on your interview and discussion.
2. **Writing a Character Sketch:** Review what you have read about Santa Anna and make a list of the character traits he seemed to have had. Use this list to write a brief sketch of what kind of man you think he was.
3. **Writing About Perspectives:** Agustín de Iturbide and Benito Juárez had very different ideas on how Mexico should be governed. Write a paragraph in which you contrast their ideas.

BUILDING SKILLS: DETERMINING POINT OF VIEW

1. What is a point of view?
2. List three steps in finding point of view.
3. Where, outside of school, would it be useful to try to determine the point of view of a writer or a speaker?
4. Why is it important to identify the point of view behind any given information?

CHAPTER 14

MEXICO TODAY

FOCUS

The solution is all of us.

José López Portillo spoke these words to the people of Mexico before he was elected president in 1976. Portillo wanted all Mexicans to realize that they have an important role to play in their country. The children in this photograph live in Mexico today. They will help to shape the future of modern Mexico. In this chapter you will read about the problems and the promises of Mexico—a growing country.

1 People

■ Key Vocabulary

Nahuatl   extended family

■ Read Aloud

To me the men in Mexico are like trees, forests that the white men felled in their coming. But the roots of the trees are deep and alive and forever sending up new shoots.

The English writer D. H. Lawrence, like many others who have studied Mexico, knew that the Indian culture would survive. Like trees with deep roots, ancient customs and values remain strong in modern-day Mexico.

■ Read for Purpose

1. **WHAT YOU KNOW:** What are some ways that customs and traditions of the past affect the lives of people in the United States today?
2. **WHAT YOU WILL LEARN:** How have Mexicans combined Indian and Spanish traditions to form a uniquely Mexican way of life?

A LIVING HERITAGE

Today Mexico is the world's largest Spanish-speaking country. However, Mexico's 88 million people are very different from the people of Spain and other countries where Spanish is spoken. The people of Mexico trace their roots to three cultures—Spanish, Indian, and mestizo. As you read in Chapter 11, *mestizo* means neither Spanish nor Indian, but a mixture of both peoples.

LANGUAGE IN MEXICO

For 300 years Mexico's Spanish rulers tried to get rid of the Indian languages, religions, and customs. They wanted all of the Indians to learn Spanish and to change nearly everything about the way they lived.

For many years after Mexico gained its independence the only language taught in Mexican schools was Spanish. In some areas Indian children who spoke only their Indian languages could not understand their teachers. The Indians protested this practice. Finally schools began to teach Indian children to read and write their own languages as well as Spanish.

Nahuatl (nä′ wa təl), the language of the Aztecs, is the most widely spoken Indian language. Today about 3.5 million Mexicans speak Nahuatl.

UNITED STATES

BAJA CALIFORNIA NORTE
SONORA
CHIHUAHUA
COAHUILA
BAJA CALIFORNIA SUR
SINALOA
DURANGO
NUEVO LEÓN
TAMAULIPAS
ZACATECAS
SAN LUIS POTOSÍ
NAYARIT
AGUASCALIENTES
GUANAJUATO
QUERÉTARO
HIDALGO
JALISCO
MÉXICO
Mexico City
FEDERAL DISTRICT
TLAXCALA
VERACRUZ
YUCATÁN
QUINTANA ROO
CAMPECHE
COLIMA
MICHOACÁN
PUEBLA
MORELOS
TABASCO
GUERRERO
OAXACA
CHIAPAS
BELIZE
GUATEMALA
HONDURAS

Gulf of California
Pacific Ocean
Gulf of Mexico
Rio Grande
Tropic of Cancer

30°N 20°N 110°W 100°W 90°W

N

MEXICO: Political
⊛ National capital
— State boundary

0   150   300 Miles
0   150   300   450 Kilometers

MAP SKILL: Mexico shares a border nearly 2,000 miles (3,200 km) long with the United States. Which two countries share Mexico's southern border?

RELIGION IN MEXICO

As you have read, Spanish colonial rulers also tried to get rid of the Indian religions and replace them with Christianity. While it is true that most Mexicans today are Catholics, the Indian religions have not completely disappeared. For example, one of Mexico's most important holidays has its roots in both the Roman Catholic and Aztec religions.

On November 1 and November 2, All Saints' Day and All Souls' Day are observed by Catholics throughout the world. Mexicans also celebrate these holy days honoring the memory of saints and the dead. They go to church and say prayers with their families. But

at the same time they also observe an important Aztec holiday, the Day of the Dead, on which dead relatives are remembered. In observance of the Day of the Dead, Mexicans carry food, flowers,

and lighted candles to the graves of their relatives. Later they eat the food that has been prepared for the holiday. There is bread shaped like animals, sugar candy shaped like skulls, and chocolate shaped like bones.

For many years the Catholic Church tried to forbid these Aztec customs. Today, however, the Mexican people continue to observe both the Day of the Dead and the Catholic holy days. Two cultures have come together to form a unique Mexican holiday.

LARGE FAMILIES

Holidays are times for Mexican families to gather together. Large families and strong family ties are common among most Mexicans. Jaime (hī' mā) Gómez is a 12-year-old boy who lives in Mexico City. Mexico City is the capital of Mexico. Find Mexico City on the map on page 296.

Jaime lives with his parents, his four sisters, and his two brothers. Soon the family will be even larger because Jaime's sister, Lucía, will be getting married. Lucía and her new husband will move into the Gómez house until they can afford their own home.

The Gómez house is always a busy place. Visitors often include members of Jaime's large extended family. An

The Day of the Dead is one holiday that brings together Spanish and Aztec traditions. On that day extended families visit the graves of their relatives.

Many schools in Mexico City are overcrowded because of the city's fast-growing population.

extended family includes aunts, uncles, cousins, and grandparents. Jaime also visits often with María and Carlos Ruiz, who live nearby. María and Carlos are Jaime's *padrinos*, or "godparents." When Jaime was born, his parents asked their good friends María and Carlos to be his padrinos, and they agreed.

Jaime's sister, Ana, will soon celebrate her fifteenth birthday. On that day, according to Mexican custom, her childhood will end, and she will become a young woman. Ana's fifteenth birthday party, one of the most important events in her life, will be given by her padrinos.

A GROWING CITY

Mexico City has one of the fastest-growing populations in the world. The huge population is stretching government services. For example, officials at Jaime's school realized that there were not enough teachers and classrooms. To solve the problem, they divided the school day. Now Jaime attends the morning session at school while another group of students attends classes in the afternoon. You will read more about Mexico City's population growth in the next lesson.

A RICH CULTURE

As you have read, Mexico's population has roots that are Indian and Spanish. Most Mexicans are Spanish-speaking. However, many of the Indian groups in Mexico still speak Indian languages. Indian and European customs have mixed to form a unique Mexican culture.

 ## Check Your Reading

1. Which three cultures form the roots of the Mexican people?
2. Who speaks Nahuatl today?
3. Which Mexican holiday today unites both Aztec and Catholic traditions?
4. What is an extended family?.
5. **THINKING SKILL:** Was the point of view of the writer D. H. Lawrence sympathetic or unsympathetic to the Mexican people? Explain.

HOUSES FOR THE POOR

In Lesson 1 you read about Mexico City having one of the fastest-growing populations in the world. On September 19, 1985, a tremendous earthquake brought disaster to many of the people of Mexico City. As you read in Chapter 12, this earthquake caused terrible suffering to the people around Mexico's capital. When their small houses collapsed during the earthquake, millions of the poor found themselves suddenly without a place to live.

In the days that followed, families set up tents on the streets near the ruins of their homes. Many had lost the few possessions they had struggled so hard to acquire. They worried about ever having the time or money to build again.

Antonio Paz Martinez did not just worry. He was sure that if all the families in his neighborhood worked as a team they could build decent houses for each other faster and cheaper than if each family tried to build its own home. He explained his idea to people in the area of the city where he lived. Six hundred families formed *Campamentos Unidos*, or "Tent-dwellers United," and began to rebuild their homes.

Antonio found a local architect who showed the members of *Campamentos Unidos* how to build pleasant homes with shared courtyards for half the cost of ordinary construction. Once they were in the habit of working together, the men and women of *Campamentos Unidos* began to look around for other business opportunities. Some started small businesses building windows, doors, and furniture from the rubble of the quake. Others began making tortillas, raising chickens, and selling basic foods at low prices. Women who had once made crafts or candies at home alone formed groups so they could work together as they watched their children in the courtyards.

Under Antonio's leadership, the members of *Campamentos Unidos* have used teamwork to improve their lives. People from poor neighborhoods in countries all around the world visit them in hopes of copying their success.

How were 600 homeless families able to change themselves into 600 families with decent homes and brighter futures? Antonio points to the three founding principles of *Campamentos Unidos*: people try to fill their needs within the group, they use teamwork to get the job done, and they rebuild not only homes but also lives and families.

299

READ TO LEARN

 **Key Vocabulary**

land reform
ejido
subsistence farmer
commercial farm

Read Aloud

Every day, just after sunrise, several soldiers march to the center of the Plaza of the Constitution in Mexico City. While a band plays, one of the soldiers slowly raises the green, white, and red flag of Mexico. A new day has officially begun in Mexico City.

Read for Purpose

1. **WHAT YOU KNOW:** Which different cultural traditions influence the people of Mexico?
2. **WHAT YOU WILL LEARN:** How is Mexico City trying to provide for its rapidly growing population?

A GROWING POPULATION

Mexico City is the fastest-growing city in the world. You read in Lesson 1 that there are not enough schools for all the students in Mexico City. Neither are there enough homes or jobs or services for the city's 9 million people.

Why has the population of Mexico City increased so rapidly? One reason, as you read in the last lesson, is that families in Mexico are often very large.

But the main reason for Mexico City's growth is the arrival of millions of people from all over the country. These Mexicans have come to the city in search of work. There is not enough work for them in rural areas.

A CROWDED CITY

Each year about 400,000 people move to Mexico City from rural areas. Most of these people arrive with no place to live. These newcomers are called *paracaidistas* (par ə kä dis′ təs), which means "parachutists." The paracaidistas seem to drop from the sky as new towns spring up almost overnight.

Miguel Méndez, his wife, and their six children are paracaidistas. They moved to Mexico City from their home in Oaxaca (wə häk′ ə). They live in one of the city's huge slums called *ciudades perdidas* (sē ū däd′ āz pâr dēd′ əz), or lost cities. There are 1,500 other para-

caidistas living in the same ciudad perdida. When asked why his family moved to Mexico City, Miguel said, "It was plain ignorance. We came because we thought it would be heaven here. But it's not, is it?"

Despite all the difficulties, the Méndez family will not go back to Oaxaca. Miguel explained why.

In Oaxaca I went to school, but I didn't really learn to read or write. But here, if my children go to school, well, maybe it will be better for them.

FARMING A DIFFICULT LAND

Those Mexicans who remain in rural areas are mostly farmers who are trying to raise enough food for the country's growing population. However, farming is a difficult business in Mexico. As you have read, most of Mexico's land is not suitable for farming.

Another problem is that much of the fertile farmland is taken up by the large estates of rich landowners. To help the farmers who are not wealthy, Mexico's government began a program of **land reform**. Land reform is a

Mexico City attracts thousands of rural people in search of work. Many of them live in *ciudades perdidas*, or lost cities.

change in the pattern of ownership of land. As part of the land reform program, the government purchased the old haciendas and divided them into **ejidos** (ā hē′ dōz). An ejido is government-owned farmland on which a group of farmers work together. Farmers on ejidos can sell their crops but they cannot sell the land since it belongs to the government.

Most of the ejidos are small. The farmers working on ejidos usually are subsistence farmers. Subsistence farmers grow just enough food to feed themselves and their families. They usually have nothing left over to sell. The ejidos cannot support all of the members of a large family. Often some of the younger members must leave the ejido to try to find work in the cities.

COMMERCIAL FARMING

Life is very different for the owners of large farms and ranches. Jorge Roiz manages a huge cattle ranch for his father 115 miles (184 km) northwest of Mexico City. The ranch is one of the 10 largest milk producers in Mexico. The ranch also raises bulls for the popular Mexican sport of bullfighting. About 300 people work on the ranch.

Some of the largest farms in Mexico are in the arid Pacific northwest. In Chapter 12 you read about the success of irrigation projects in this area. Irrigation has turned the northwest into a region of commercial farms. Commercial farms raise crops and livestock for sale, not for the farmer's own use.

Despite the success of commercial farms, Mexico is not producing enough food for its population. Therefore the country has to import food. How does Mexico get the money to buy food for its growing population?

JOBS IN NEW INDUSTRIES

One way to meet the food shortage and to create more jobs is through new industries. Today one in five Mexicans works in manufacturing industries. As Mexico's economy grows, more Mexicans are finding jobs in industries such as petroleum, steel, and automobile production. In 1988 new oil fields were discovered in Mexico, creating thousands of new jobs.

Subsistence farmers who work on ejidos continue to use simple farm tools. The commercial farmer at right uses more modern machinery.

Automobile factories provide new jobs for workers in Mexico. This worker helps to assemble parts of an automobile.

Other Mexicans work in factories called *maquiladoras* (ma kil ə dôr′ əs). Workers in maquiladoras assemble parts into finished products. For example, Mexican workers assemble cars, toys, and computers for export to the United States. A number of large companies from Japan and the United States have built maquiladoras in Mexico because wages there are lower. Thousands of new jobs have been created because of the maquiladoras.

THE BORDER

You have read that Mexico shares a long border with the United States. About 3 to 4 million Mexicans cross that border each year in search of work. In the United States, Mexicans can earn as much money in one week as they can earn in three weeks at home. Many Mexicans entering the United States are illegal immigrants, or people who do not have legal permission to cross the border.

These Mexicans often must leave their families behind them. However, Mexican workers continue to cross the border looking for work because there are higher-paying jobs for them in the United States.

PROGRESS AND PROBLEMS

Mexico's fast-growing population has created many problems for the government. You have read that as more people move to the cities, new jobs are needed for them. The government has developed new industries that have created thousands of jobs. Today Mexico continues to try to meet the needs of a growing population.

Check Your Reading

1. Why is Mexico City's population increasing so rapidly?
2. How did land reform help poor farmers?
3. Describe the difference between subsistence farms and commercial farms.
4. Why do some large companies build maquiladoras in Mexico?
5. **THINKING SKILL:** What choices did Miguel Méndez probably consider when he decided to leave Oaxaca? Explain your answer.

Reading Line, Bar, and Circle Graphs

Key Vocabulary

graph
line graph
horizontal axis
vertical axis

bar graph
circle graph

Earlier in this chapter you read about the different types of people who live and work in modern Mexico. One way you can show information about this is in a **graph**. A graph is a diagram that shows amounts in a visual way. Graphs make it easier to understand statistics, or numerical facts. How many children attend each of the schools in your community? In your after-school hours, what part of your time do you spend doing homework? The answers to each of these questions could be shown on some type of graph.

Line Graphs

One useful kind of graph is a **line graph**. Line graphs are used to show changes over time. **Graph A** is a line graph that shows changes in Mexico's population. A line graph is set up as a grid, with horizontal and vertical lines. The **horizontal axis** is the bottom line of the graph. It shows the intervals of time into which the graph is divided. The horizontal axis in **Graph A** shows 30-year periods. What is the earliest year on the graph?

The **vertical axis** on a line graph is the outside left line. It usually shows amounts. In **Graph A** the vertical axis is marked with numbers that stand for millions of people.

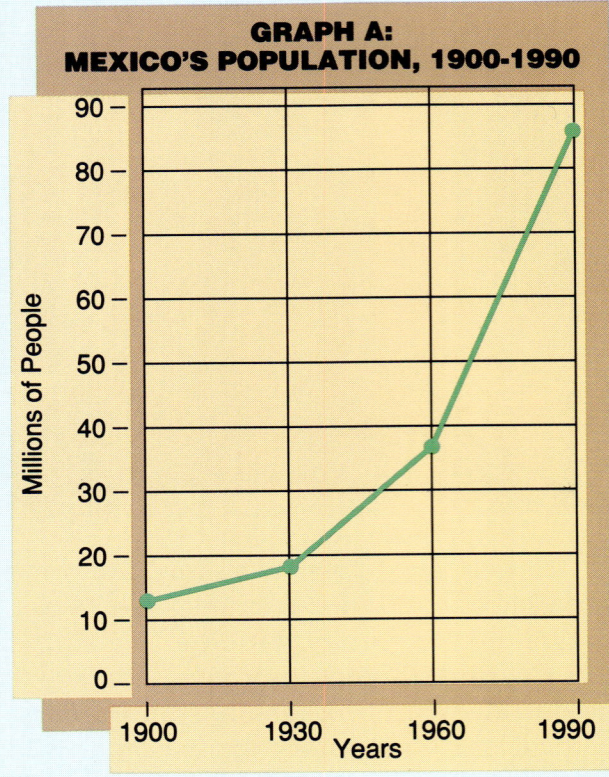

GRAPH A: MEXICO'S POPULATION, 1900-1990

To read this line graph you must find the point where a year and an amount cross each other. For example, suppose you want to know Mexico's population in 1960. You begin by finding the year 1960 on the horizontal axis. Then move your finger up to the dot on the line above that year. Now move your finger left until you come to the vertical axis. The number on the axis tells you how many millions of people lived in Mexico in 1960. **Graph A** can help you to see that Mexico's population has grown dramatically since 1900.

Bar Graphs

A **bar graph** can also help you understand statistics. It is used to compare amounts. It might compare amounts of the same thing at different times. Or it might compare different things. **Graph B**

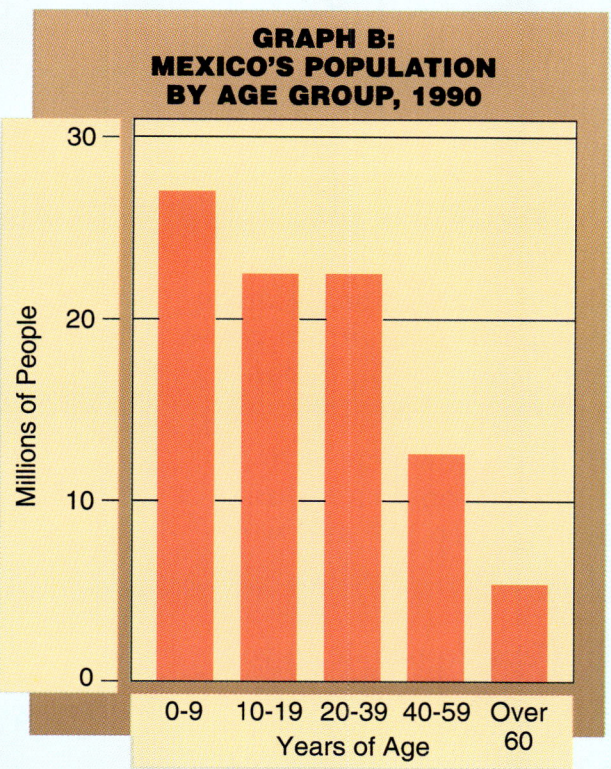

GRAPH B: MEXICO'S POPULATION BY AGE GROUP, 1990

Millions of People

30
20
10
0

0-9   10-19   20-39   40-59   Over 60

Years of Age

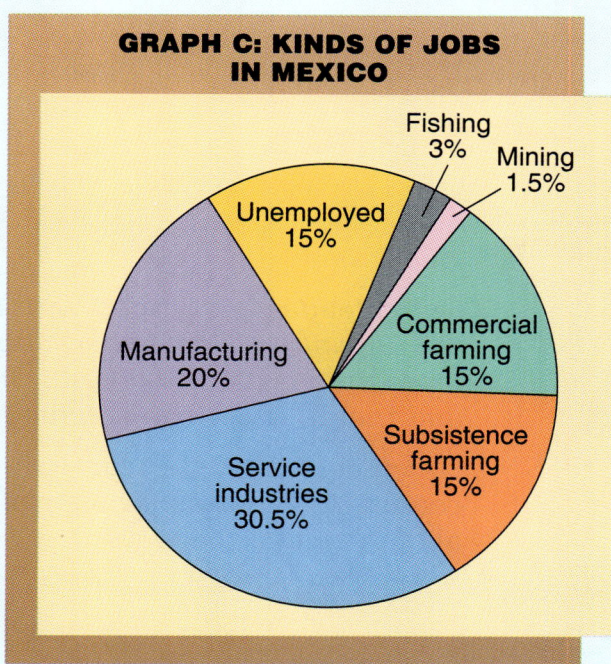

GRAPH C: KINDS OF JOBS IN MEXICO

Fishing 3%
Mining 1.5%
Unemployed 15%
Commercial farming 15%
Manufacturing 20%
Subsistence farming 15%
Service industries 30.5%

is a bar graph that compares different age groups within the Mexican population.

You read a bar graph in the same way as a line graph, by using the horizontal and vertical axes. A horizontal bar graph is one in which you read the bars from left to right. **Graph B** is a vertical bar graph, because you read the bars from bottom to top. The graph shows that the largest population group in Mexico is people under the age of 10. Which age group is the smallest?

Circle Graphs

A third kind of graph is a circle graph. A circle graph shows how a whole is divided into parts. It is sometimes called a pie graph, because it looks like a pie cut into slices. **Graph C** is a circle graph. It shows the different types of work the

Mexican people do. The whole circle graph stands for 100 percent of something—each slice shows a part, or percentage, of the whole.

Graph C shows that there are six main ways of earning a living in Mexico today. Miners make up the smallest group. What percentage of the population is employed in farming?

Reviewing the Skill

1. What is the purpose of a graph?
2. Could the information on **Graph B** be plotted on a line graph instead? Why or why not?
3. According to **Graph C**, one in five Mexicans is employed in which type of work?
4. A circle graph can be called a pie graph. Are all the slices of **Graph C** the same size? Explain.
5. Why is it important to be able to read different types of graphs?

READ TO LEARN

■ Key People

Octavio Paz   Diego Rivera

■ Read Aloud

Our calendar is crowded with fiestas [festivals]. Each year on the fifteenth of September, at eleven o'clock at night, we celebrate the Fiesta of the Grito in all the plazas of the Republic, and the excited crowds actually shout for a whole hour.

Octavio Paz, a Mexican writer, describes how people in his country love fiestas, or festivals. In this lesson you will read about some of the ways that people in Mexico live and work.

■ Read for Purpose

1. **WHAT YOU KNOW:** In what special ways do people in your community celebrate holidays?
2. **WHAT YOU WILL LEARN:** How have the Mexican people preserved their traditions through the arts?

FIESTAS

The Fiesta of the Grito, which is described above, is celebrated to remember an event that took place in 1810. Do you remember the "Cry of Dolores," which you read about in Chapter 13? Mexicans still gather to shout the cry of Miguel Hidalgo, which started their country on the road to independence. This celebration, like many others in Mexico, brings together the old and the new. Across Mexico, throughout the year, Mexicans celebrate many different fiestas.

Imagine that you have arrived in Mexico just in time for a fiesta. You see people dressed in brightly colored costumes. You smell the spices used in

Mexican food. You watch dancers performing traditional and modern folk dances. They are dancing to music played by small bands.

The bands play many different kinds of music, but *mariachi* (mär ē äch′ ē) is a favorite of most people. Mariachi music began in the highlands and later spread to the rest of Mexico. *Mariachi* music is played on stringed instruments and trumpets. Sometimes the band is accompanied by the rattle of gourds, or hard-shelled fruits. The bands may still be playing as the sun sets. Then, as darkness falls, the sky overhead explodes with a colorful fireworks display.

SPORTS

Many fiestas also include sporting contests or exhibitions. Some Mexican sports are based on ancient traditions. You read about the Aztec game of tlachtli in Chapter 9. Another sport, bullfighting, came from Spain and is very popular in Mexico.

Jai alai (hī′ lī) is a game that also comes from Spain. Jai alai is a fast-paced game played by two to four people with a small rubber ball. The game is played on a long, three-walled court. The players toss and catch the ball with a *cesta* (ses′ tə), a curved straw basket strapped to one arm. Jai alai is a game which is also played in some parts of the United States.

These girls are playing musical instruments at a fiesta. Traditional dances and sporting events, such as *jai alai* games, may also be part of a celebration.

Cowhands display their skills at a *charreada* in Mexico.

Another popular sporting event in Mexico is the *charreada* (chär rē a' də), or "rodeo." The charreada is held to display the skills of cowhands. Rodeos in the United States had their beginnings in the charreadas of Mexico.

OCTAVIO PAZ

Poetry has been an important form of expression in Mexico since before the Spanish conquest. In modern times Octavio Paz, whose words you read in the Read Aloud, has written many stories and poems about Mexico. In 1989 Paz was honored for his writing when he received the Nobel Prize in literature. The Nobel Prize honors writers,

scientists, and humanitarians from all over the world. One of Octavio Paz's poems is about poetry itself.

> Between what I see and what I say
> Between what I say and what I
>   keep silent
> Between what I keep silent and
>   what I dream
> Between what I dream and what I
>   forget:
> Poetry

Through his writing Paz is carrying on an ancient tradition. Mexicans have been writing poetry for hundreds of years. In 1583 a poetry contest in Mexico City brought entries from more than 300 poets.

AN ARTISTIC TRADITION

When the Spanish arrived in Mexico, they were amazed by the beauty of the art and architecture they found. As you read in Chapter 9, Mayan and Aztec builders had created splendid architecture. Magnificent buildings were painted with brightly colored designs.

During the 1930s Diego Rivera, a talented Mexican painter, became world famous for his murals. Murals are huge pictures that are painted directly on a wall or a ceiling. Rivera wanted all Mexicans, rich and poor, to

Diego Rivera's colorful murals (*left*) were often painted on the walls of buildings. Zapotec weavers (*above*) create beautiful designs based on ancient traditions.

see his work. You will read more about Rivera in the Traditions lesson on pages 310–313 in this chapter.

For hundreds of years the Zapotec have been known for their weaving. In a small, quiet village near Oaxaca, two cousins, Isaac García and Alberto Jiménez, carry on a family tradition. They continue to create beautiful weavings. Many of the designs used in their weavings have been passed from one generation to the next for hundreds of years. These designs are exact copies of images created by their ancestors. Isaac García explains.

When I was eight or nine years old, I would stand for hours by my father's side staring with amazement as he glided from foot pedal to foot pedal, and as his fingers seemingly flew across the yarn. . . .

By producing tapestries of these designs, which are as fine as I possibly can create, perhaps new generations of my countrymen will find a new reverence and respect for their cultural heritage.

CULTURAL RICHES

Mexico's rich tradition of literature and art is expressed in the daily life of its people. The heritage of its people continues in traditions that have been preserved for hundreds of years.

 Check Your Reading

1. What is a fiesta? What kind of music might you hear at a fiesta?
2. Name two sports that Mexicans enjoy.
3. Who is Octavio Paz?
4. How do Isaac García and Alberto Jiménez help to preserve tradition in Mexico?
5. **THINKING SKILL:** State one fact that is mentioned in the section called "Fiestas." Then state one opinion from the quotation by Isaac García. Tell how you can distinguish fact from opinion.

309

FRIDA KAHLO

ARTIST AND TEACHER

by Eric Kimmel

Self Portrait, 1937 by Frida Kahlo

You have just read that Mexico is a land with strong artistic traditions. Since the time of the Mayas and the Aztecs, many gifted artists have made their homes there. In our century, one of the most interesting and talented Mexican artists was Frida Kahlo (frē' dä kä' lō). Kahlo was a great teacher as well as a great painter. Although she was handicapped with a painful spine disease, she spent ten years teaching children to paint at a special school in Mexico City called La Esmeralda (lä ez mə räl' dä). As you read this story, think about how Frida Kahlo helped her students to appreciate Mexico's artistic traditions.

LA ESMERALDA

I will never forget the day I met Frida Kahlo. None of us had been at La Esmeralda for very long. Few of us thought of ourselves as artists. We were all girls and boys from poor families, hungry for an education. If being artists would allow us to go to school, then we would be artists. Our school was officially called The School of Painting and Sculpture of the Mexican Ministry of Public Education, but that was too long a title for us to use. We called it La Esmeralda because it was located on Esmeralda Street, even though that name makes the school sound grander than it really was.

The school consisted of one classroom where we had formal lessons and a patio where we could paint outdoors. Because the patio flooded whenever it rained, we had to walk over it on planks. We didn't mind. All our books and materials were free, our teachers were famous artists, and we had all of Mexico for our studio.

One day we were told that our new teacher was going to be Frida Kahlo, Diego Rivera's wife. We all knew about the great Rivera and the wonderful murals he had painted all over Mexico. Rivera was like a god to us! But who was Frida

Kahlo? Some of the boys maintained that any woman who was married to Diego Rivera had to be a great artist herself. We girls weren't so sure. Just because her husband was a famous painter didn't mean that she knew anything about art. One of our instructors had met her in the office a few days before. "What is this about teaching? I don't know anything about teaching!" Frida Kahlo had said. This made me angry. If she didn't know anything about teaching, what was she doing in our school?

Frida swept into our lives like a whirlwind. She was the most striking woman I had ever seen. Her thick eyebrows met at the bridge of her nose, making it look as if she had one huge eyebrow going straight across her forehead. She was certainly not beautiful in the way that movie stars were. Frida's beauty came from within. She was a walking flower, bursting with life and laughter, enthusiastic about everything life had to offer.

LEARNING TO PAINT

"Well, kids," she said, "let's get to work. I am your so-called teacher, but really I am no such thing. I am always learning." She went on to say, "To paint is the most terrific thing there is, but doing it well is difficult. You need skill and practice and self-discipline. Above all, you need love. I will make a few comments about your work from time to time, and I hope that when I show you my paintings, you will do the same about them." Then she asked us what we wanted to paint. No one knew what to say. Nobody knew what to make of this astonishing person who had just walked into our lives. "**Doña** (don′ yä) Frida," I stammered, "would you pose for us?" She nodded yes with a smile. Someone brought her a chair. She sat down and was immediately surrounded by easels.

Doña a Spanish term of respect for women

Frida meant what she said. She never corrected our work. Instead she would say, "I would make the color a little stronger. But that's only my opinion. If it's useful, take it. If not, leave it alone."

Frida opened our eyes to the world around us. She taught us to see the pageant that was Mexico. "**Muchachos**, we can't learn anything locked up in school. Let's go out into the street and paint the life out there." We would follow her to the markets, the many different neighborhoods, the old colonial quarters. Once we traveled to the pyramids at Teotihuacán (tä ō tē wə kän′). Along the way Frida taught

muchachos a Spanish word for young people

us **corridos** and songs of the Mexican Revolution. We sang at the top of our voices as the miles flew by. We would follow our Frida anywhere. We called ourselves *Los Fridos*, in her honor.

The day that we completed our studies at La Esmeralda was the saddest day of my life. Frida invited us to her home to say good-bye. She told us, "I'm going to be very unhappy because you're not going to be here anymore." She spoke from her heart, as she always did. Her husband Diego Rivera comforted her by saying, "It is the moment in which they are going to walk alone. Although they go their own ways, they will come and visit us always, because they are our comrades."

Years have passed since then. My friends from La Esmeralda have gone their separate ways. Frida Kahlo and Diego Rivera are gone. But we have not forgotten them. They are still our comrades.

corridos a Spanish word meaning folk songs

Why did Frida Kahlo want her students to appreciate Mexico City's neighborhoods and historic monuments?

313

IDEAS TO REMEMBER

- The Mexican people, most of them mestizos, have a rich and proud heritage that springs from Indian, Spanish, and mestizo roots.
- Mexico has a fast-growing population, almost one third of which makes its living from subsistence farming and commercial farming. However, manufacturing is increasing.
- Mexico's rich culture embraces joyous fiestas, a variety of musical forms, many sports, and very strong artistic traditions.

PEOPLE TO KNOW

Diego Rivera
1886–1957

Frida Kahlo
1907–1954

Octavio Paz
1914–

REVIEWING VOCABULARY

ejido   Nahuatl
extended family subsistence farmer
land reform

Number a sheet of paper from 1 to 5. Beside each number write the word or term from the list above that matches the statement or definition.

1. One's relatives, such as aunts, uncles, cousins, and grandparents, are all part of this group.
2. The name given to a government policy of changing the pattern of land ownership by dividing large holdings into smaller sections.
3. Small sections of farmland owned by the government but worked by a group of farmers.
4. This is the language of the ancient Aztecs and the most widely spoken Indian language in Mexico today.
5. People who work the land and grow just enough food to feed themselves and their families are called this.

REVIEWING FACTS

1. Why is Spanish not the only language spoken in Mexico today?
2. Give an example of how some Mexicans combine the customs of the Catholic and Aztec religions.
3. Why does the Mexican government have difficulty meeting its population's need for public services?
4. Why do millions of Mexicans from rural areas move into the cities?
5. Give two examples of the problems these people find when they do move.
6. Why does the Mexican government

want to encourage the rapid growth of manufacturing?

7. Why are foreign companies eager to build manufacturing facilities in Mexico?

8. Name three sights you might see at a fiesta in Mexico.

9. Describe three sports that are particularly popular in Mexico.

10. Which highly respected international prize was Octavio Paz awarded?

WRITING ABOUT MAIN IDEAS

1. **Writing a Letter:** Pretend that you are taking a trip through Mexico. Write a letter to a friend or relative back home in which you describe three experiences you have had during your visit.

2. **Writing a Paragraph of Contrast:** Review what you have learned about subsistence farming and commercial farming. Write a paragraph in which you contrast the aims of the two methods, the kinds of crops grown, and the working conditions of each method.

3. **Writing a Journal Entry:** Imagine that you have just found a job at a maquiladora. Write a journal entry in which you tell what the job is, why you wanted it, and what you hope to gain for your family by having the job.

4. **Writing About Perspectives:** Imagine that you work for the Mexican government and your job is to attract foreign companies to invest in businesses in Mexico. Write an advertisement in which you give reasons why this would be a good investment for them.

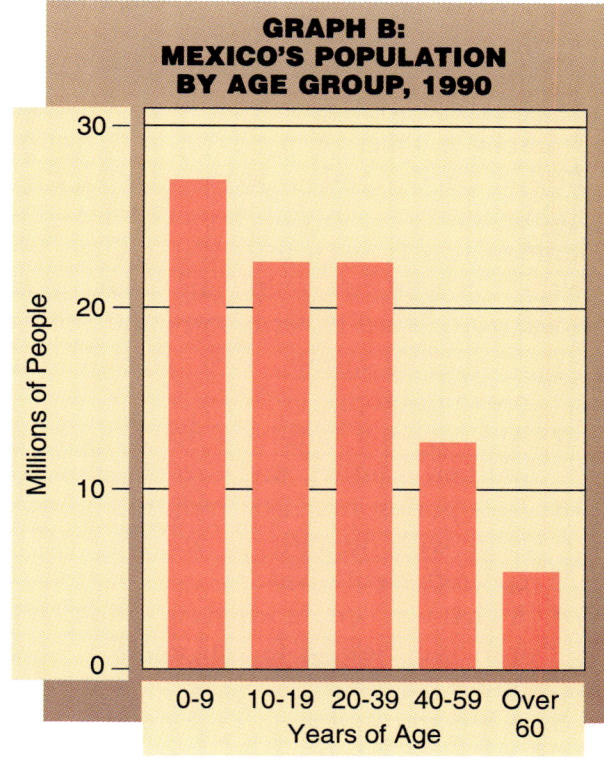

GRAPH B:
MEXICO'S POPULATION BY AGE GROUP, 1990

BUILDING SKILLS: READING LINE, BAR, AND CIRCLE GRAPHS

Use the graph above and what you already know about graphs to answer the following questions.

1. What kind of graph is shown above?

2. Could this same information be shown in a circle graph? Why or why not?

3. What advantage is there in presenting information in graph form?

4. Suppose that you wanted to compare the population of Mexico and the population of Canada. What kind of graph would you use?

5. Why is it helpful to be able to read and construct graphs?

REVIEWING VOCABULARY

Number a sheet of paper from 1 to 10. Beside each number write whether the following statements are true or false. If a statement is true, write **T**. If it is false, re-write the sentence using the underlined vocabulary word or term correctly.

1. If land is <u>arable</u>, it is suitable for growing crops.
2. An <u>extended family</u> is made up of a mother, a father, and two children.
3. In a nation that is a <u>republic</u>, power rests with the citizens and their chosen representatives.
4. A <u>civil war</u> occurs when two neighboring countries go to war against each other.
5. A <u>dictator</u> is a ruler of a country who shares political power with other government departments and officials.
6. Sources of energy that are taken from under the ground such as coal, natural gas, or petroleum are called <u>fossil fuels</u>.
7. Someone who puts money into a project in the hope of making more money is an <u>investor</u>.
8. Dividing large land holdings into smaller sections for groups of farmers to work together is an example of <u>land reform</u>.
9. When the United States army declared war on Mexico in 1846, Mexicans called the war the <u>North American Intervention</u>.
10. When a government tries to make <u>reforms</u>, it is trying to keep conditions just as they are.

WRITING ABOUT THE UNIT

1. **Writing a List:** List the advantages and disadvantages that Mexico as a nation faces today.
2. **Writing a Letter:** Imagine that you have moved from your rural home in Mexico to find work in the city. Write a letter to a friend back home describing your new life. Include advice on whether or not your friend should do as you did.
3. **Writing About Perspectives:** Explain what you think this inscription, written on the National Museum of History in Mexico City, might mean to Mexicans today: "In the lessons of the past, we find strength to deal with the present and reason to hope for the future."

ACTIVITIES

1. **Presenting a Television Report:** Imagine that you can go back in time to witness one of the events described in this unit. Write an "on the scene" report of it to present on the evening news.
2. **Working Together to Make a Bulletin Board Display:** With a group of classmates, make a bulletin board display about what you now know about Mexico. Include a map, as well as pictures and captions for your display. You could show traditional costumes, or dances, or excerpts from stories and poems. Photographs of cities or drawings of volcanoes could be included. Make your bulletin board as varied and interesting as possible. You might want to put it on display for your class in school.

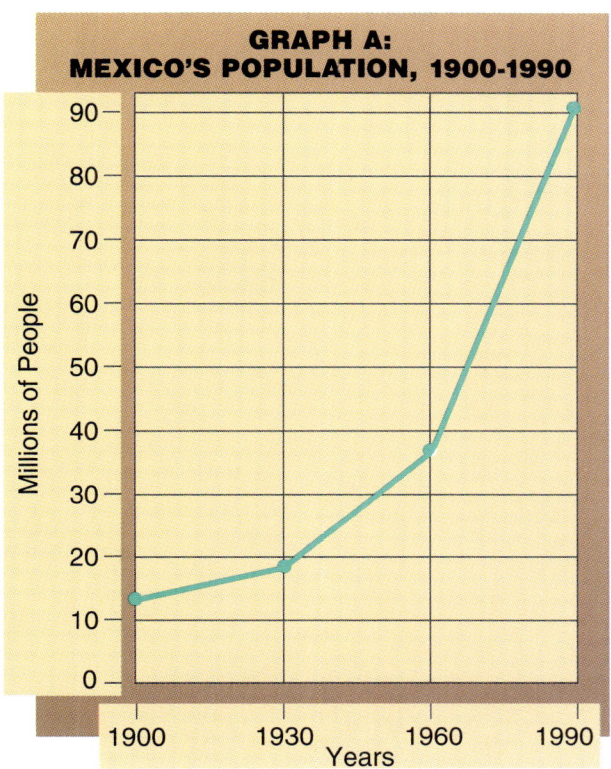

**GRAPH A:
MEXICO'S POPULATION, 1900-1990**

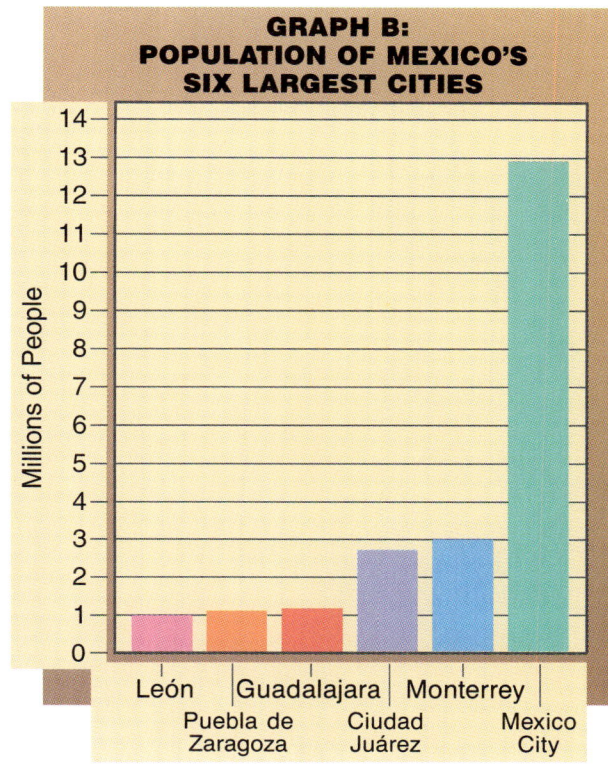

**GRAPH B:
POPULATION OF MEXICO'S
SIX LARGEST CITIES**

BUILDING SKILLS: READING LINE, BAR, AND CIRCLE GRAPHS

Use what you have already learned about graphs to answer the following questions.

1. How does **Graph A** above differ from **Graph B**? What is one thing they have in common?

2. According to **Graph B**, which cities have populations under 2 million?

3. Could the information in these graphs be shown in a circle graph? Why or why not?

4. Why is it important to know how to read and construct graphs?

LINKING PAST, PRESENT, AND FUTURE

In this unit you have read that highly valuable oil and natural gas reserves have been discovered in Mexico. Imagine that you are running for president of Mexico. How do you think the Mexican government should spend its share of oil and gas profits? What would you tell voters that you would want to spend these funds on in the future? Explain.

317

ARCTIC OCEAN

75°N

Baffin
Bay

Gulf of Alaska

Hudson
Bay

60°N

NORTH
AMERICA

75°W

60°W

PACIFIC

Tropic of Cancer

Gulf of Mexico

Gulf of California

CARIBBEAN
ISLANDS

OCEAN

Gulf of Honduras

Caribbean   Sea

CENTRAL
AMERICA

165°W

150°W

135°W

120°W

105°W

90°W

SOUTH

AMERICA

Tropic of Capricorn

PACIFIC   OCEAN

60°S

UNIT 6

CENTRAL AMERICA

WHERE WE ARE

Between Mexico and South America lie the countries of Central America. These seven countries are located on the narrow strip of land between the vast Pacific Ocean and the beautiful turquoise waters of the Caribbean Sea.

In this unit, you will learn about the geography, history, and people of Central America. You will investigate some of the problems facing modern Central America and the efforts to solve them. As you read, think about how the history of Central America has been influenced by the large countries to the north and south.

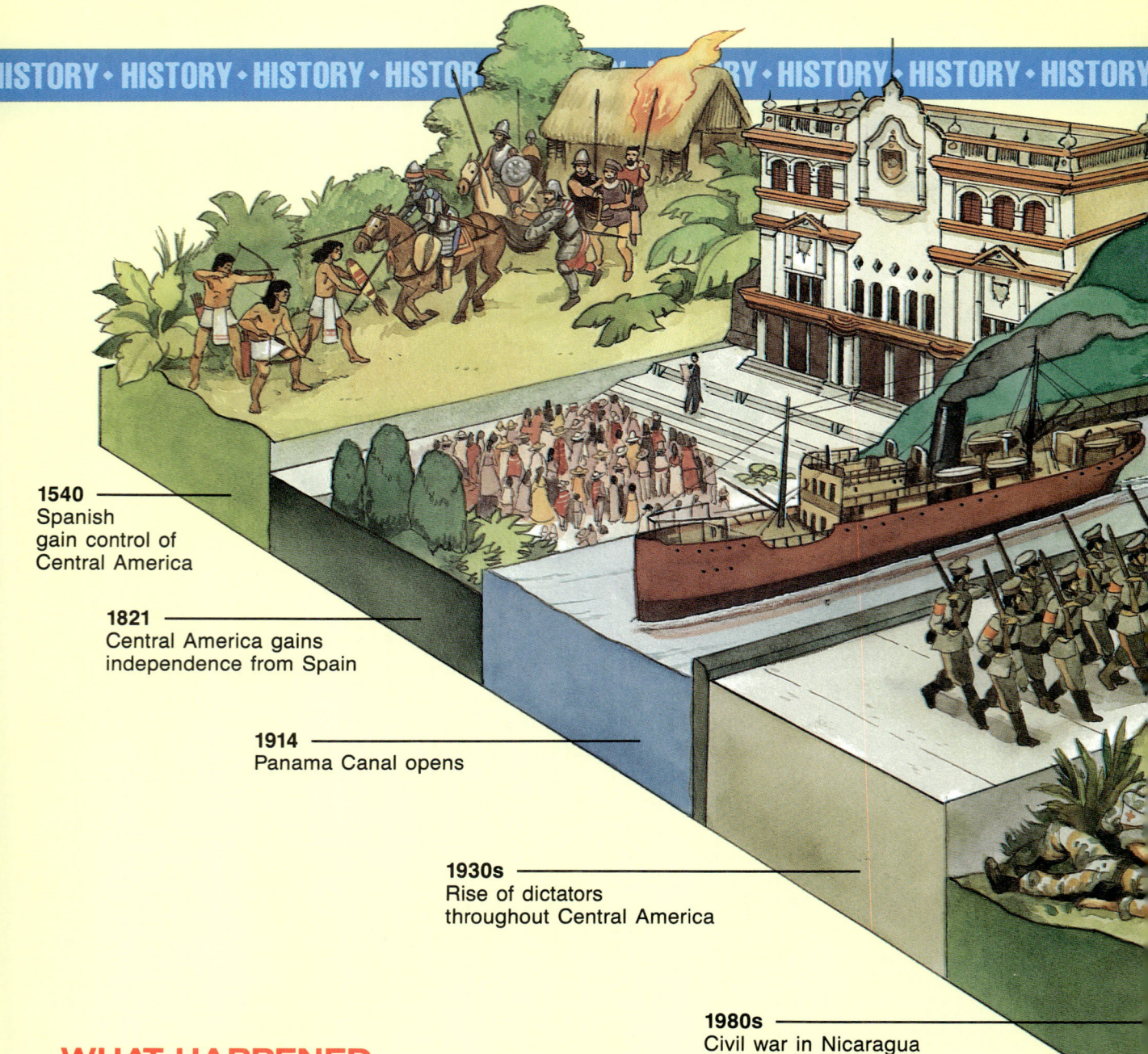

1540
Spanish
gain control of
Central America

1821
Central America gains
independence from Spain

1914
Panama Canal opens

1930s
Rise of dictators
throughout Central America

1980s
Civil war in Nicaragua

1990
Violeta Chamorro is
elected president
of Nicaragua

WHAT HAPPENED

When the people of Central America announced their independence from Spain in 1821, they ended nearly 300 years of colonial rule. Central Americans then faced the task of bringing peace, democracy, and economic growth to their countries. In this unit you will read about some of the challenges that the Central Americans faced as they worked to achieve these goals.

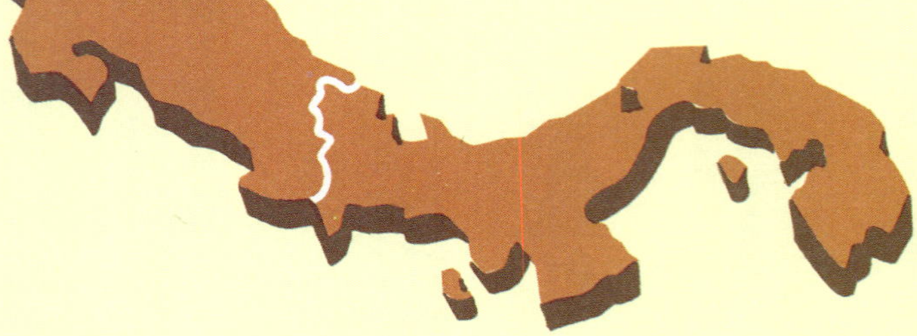

CENTRAL AMERICA

BELIZE

Capital ✪
Belmopan

Major languages: English and Spanish
Population: 0.2 million
Area: 8,865 sq mi; 22,960 sq km
Leading export: sugar

COSTA RICA

Capital ✪
San José

Major language: Spanish
Population: 3.1 million
Area: 19,652 sq mi; 50,900 sq km
Leading export: coffee

EL SALVADOR

Capital ✪
San Salvador

Major language: Spanish
Population: 5.4 million
Area: 8,124 sq mi; 21,040 sq km
Leading export: coffee

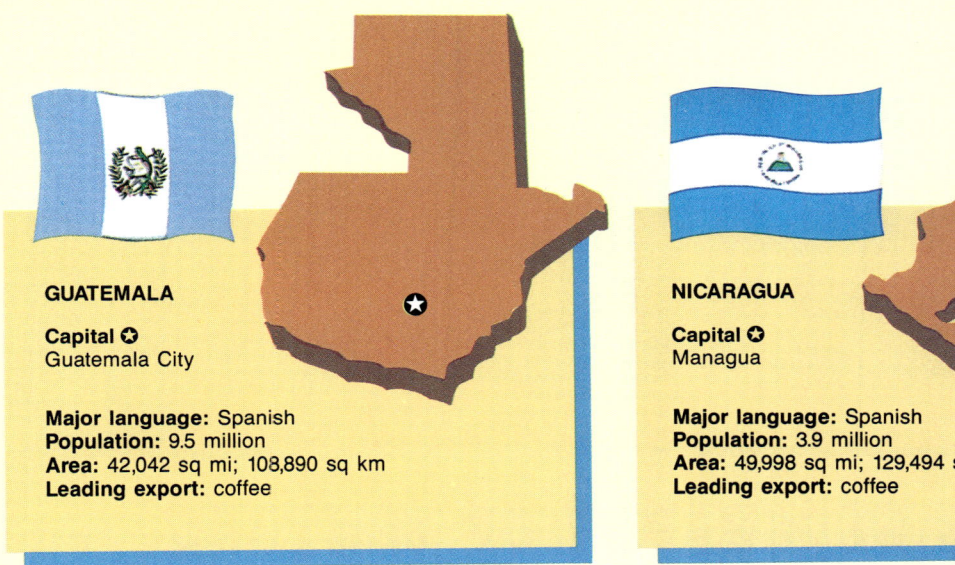

GUATEMALA

Capital ✪
Guatemala City

Major language: Spanish
Population: 9.5 million
Area: 42,042 sq mi; 108,890 sq km
Leading export: coffee

NICARAGUA

Capital ✪
Managua

Major language: Spanish
Population: 3.9 million
Area: 49,998 sq mi; 129,494 sq km
Leading export: coffee

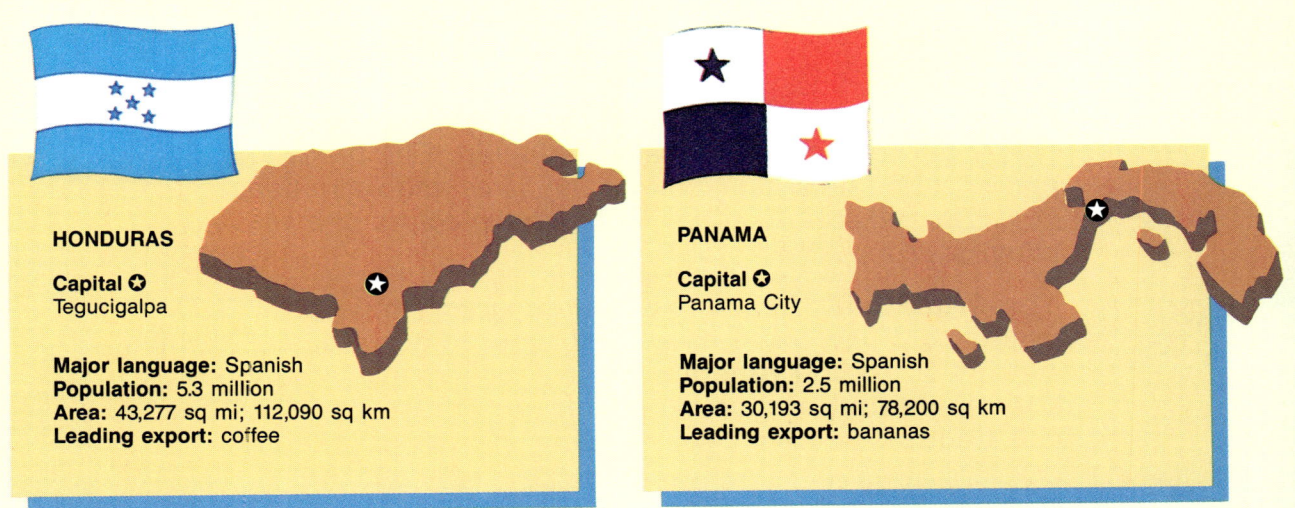

HONDURAS

Capital ✪
Tegucigalpa

Major language: Spanish
Population: 5.3 million
Area: 43,277 sq mi; 112,090 sq km
Leading export: coffee

PANAMA

Capital ✪
Panama City

Major language: Spanish
Population: 2.5 million
Area: 30,193 sq mi; 78,200 sq km
Leading export: bananas

CHAPTER 15

THE GEOGRAPHY OF CENTRAL AMERICA

FOCUS

El Salvador is made up of land and people as varied as the colors and designs in a Mayan weaving. The blues and greens in the weaving could be the lakes and mountains . . . . The reds and oranges look like the colors of a volcano when it erupts.

The writer Faith Adams used these words to describe El Salvador, but she could have used them to describe any of the countries of Central America. Central America is a region of lakes, mountains, and volcanoes. In this chapter you will read about Central America's sometimes explosive geography.

1 The Land Of Central America

Key Vocabulary

fault

Key Places

Lake Nicaragua

Read Aloud

In 1835 a great explosion rocked Central America. Mount Cosigüina (kō sə gwē′ nə), a lofty snowcapped volcano in the Central American country of Nicaragua, had erupted in violent fury. The volcano's roar was heard hundreds of miles away. Nearby villages were buried under rock and ash. Days later, when the dust and smoke had cleared, Nicaraguans saw that the fiery volcano had blown its top. The height of Mount Cosigüina had been reduced from about 10,000 feet (3,048 m) to about 3,500 feet (1,067 m)!

Millions of years ago, volcanoes helped to form Central America. Today they are one of the forces that influence where and how the people of this region live.

Read for Purpose

1. WHAT YOU KNOW: On which continent is Central America located?
2. WHAT YOU WILL LEARN: How do the landforms in Central America influence life in this region?

A LAND BRIDGE

Twenty-five million years ago, North America and South America were separated by seas. As you read in Chapter 1, the earth's tectonic plates are constantly pushing against and pulling each other. As the plates under North America and South America began approaching each other, faults appeared in the ocean floor between the two large landmasses. Faults are great cracks in the earth's crust.

Over time, volcanoes formed along these faults. Lava pouring out of the volcanoes created underwater mountains. Eventually these mountains rose above the sea, creating a land bridge.

Today this land bridge is known as Central America. This region begins at the southern border of Mexico. You can see from the map on page 326 that it curves like a stretched-out, backward S toward South America. The warm waters of the Caribbean Sea wash against its eastern shore. The rolling waves of the Pacific Ocean pound against its western shore.

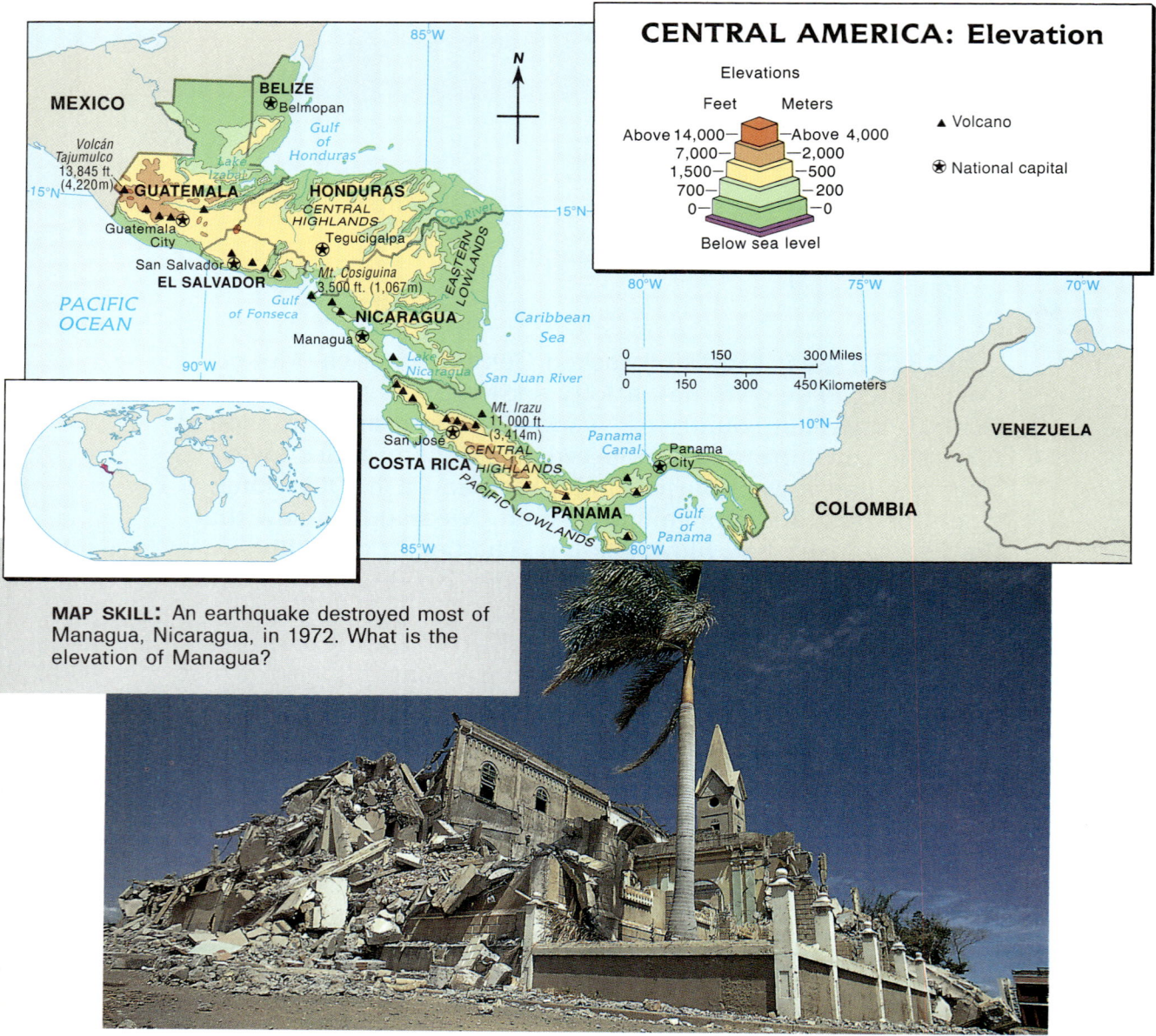

CENTRAL AMERICA: Elevation

Elevations

Feet	Meters
Above 14,000	Above 4,000
7,000	2,000
1,500	500
700	200
0	0
Below sea level	

▲ Volcano

✪ National capital

MAP SKILL: An earthquake destroyed most of Managua, Nicaragua, in 1972. What is the elevation of Managua?

VOLCANOES AND EARTHQUAKES

The forces that have shaped Central America are still at work today. Volcanoes continue to boil and bubble. From time to time, a volcano erupts and spits out huge clouds of dust and ash into the air. Sometimes it pours out lava from the depths of the earth. Volcanic eruptions sometimes bury entire villages under the flow of lava. Volcanic ash damages crops and forests.

Earthquakes are an even greater danger in this region than volcanoes. An earthquake is a sudden movement or shaking of the ground. Such movements occur along faults in the earth's surface. The fault that runs below Central America is often in motion. Over the past 30 years this region has experienced about 150 major earthquakes.

Few towns in Central America have never experienced an earthquake. San

326

Salvador, the capital of the country of El Salvador, has been destroyed and rebuilt nine times since it was founded in 1528. Earthquakes have forced Guatemala to move its capital, Guatemala City, twice. In 1972 a huge earthquake destroyed much of Managua, the capital of Nicaragua. After that earthquake the writer Robert Harvey visited Managua and described the destruction.

> There were broad streets, but no buildings overlooking them. . . . When one came upon buildings, these were huge shipwrecked hulks. . . . The center of Managua was no more.

THE CENTRAL HIGHLANDS

Although volcanoes cause much destruction, they also have some positive effects. Over the years ash from volcanic eruptions has covered much of the mountainous region of Central America. As you read in Chapter 12, volcanic ash adds nutrients to the soil. These nutrients have made the soil of the mountainous region of Central America, called the Central Highlands, very fertile.

Indians began farming these fertile highlands more than 3,000 years ago. When the Spanish arrived in Central America, they also set up farms in the Central Highlands. Today most Central Americans still live in this fertile mountainous area.

THE COASTAL LOWLANDS

Not all of Central America is mountainous. Flat lowland plains line both coasts of the region. You can see from the map on page 326 that the widest lowland plains are found along the Caribbean coast. These plains, called the Eastern Lowlands, are hot, wet, and swarming with mosquitoes. Storms here cause frequent floods. As a result, the Eastern Lowlands area always has been sparsely settled.

A tropical rain forest covers much of the Eastern Lowlands. When the Spanish came to this area, they cleared patches of the rain forest for farms. However, they soon found that heavy rains washed most of the nutrients out of the soil. Only those nutrients that were buried deep beneath the earth's

Most of Central America's farms are in the fertile Central Highlands region.

This cattle ranch is located in the Pacific Lowlands of Costa Rica.

surface were not washed away by the rains. For this reason, only deep-rooted crops, such as bananas, are able to grow in this area.

The plains along the Pacific coast are dry grasslands called the Pacific Lowlands. Here a lack of water is as much a problem as flooding is in the Eastern Lowlands. The Spanish introduced cattle ranching in this area. Today irrigation has opened up the Pacific Lowlands to farming. Farmers in this area grow crops such as cotton, sugarcane, and cacao. Cacao is used to make chocolate.

RIVERS AND LAKES

Many rivers flow out of the Central Highlands. As you read in Chapter 8, none of the rivers of Central America is navigable. They are too small and fast to be used for transportation. Farmers living in the Pacific Lowlands, however, depend on these rivers as a source of water for irrigation.

Central America is also dotted with blue lakes. **Lake Nicaragua**, the largest lake in Central America, is of great interest to scientists. They are interested in Lake Nicaragua because it is the only freshwater lake in the world that contains swordfish and sharks—fish that normally live in salt water.

Why are sharks and swordfish able to live in the lake? Scientists believe that Lake Nicaragua was once part of a large ocean bay. Long ago, rising volcanoes cut this bay off from the Pacific Ocean, forming a lake. Many ocean fish were trapped in the newly formed lake. As the lake water became less salty, some of the fish adapted to the change and were able to survive.

A DANGEROUS PARADISE

With its beautiful volcanic peaks, lush tropical rain forest, and sky-blue lakes, Central America has been called a paradise. But as you have read, it is a dangerous paradise. Earthquakes and volcanic eruptions often shake this region, causing death and destruction.

 ### Check Your Reading

1. How was Central America formed?
2. Why is the soil of the Central Highlands very fertile?
3. **GEOGRAPHY SKILL:** Why do most Central Americans live in the Central Highlands?
4. **THINKING SKILL:** List three questions you could ask to learn about Central America's volcanoes. Tell what you hope to learn by asking these questions.

2 Climate and Resources

READ TO LEARN

Key Vocabulary

rain shadow

Read Aloud

Then there was the rain—always the rain, sometimes three cloudbursts in a single day.

This is how George Meegan described Central America in his book called *The Longest Walk.* The book tells the story of the author's walk from the southern tip of South America to the northern tip of North America. As George Meegan discovered, parts of Central America are very rainy.

Read for Purpose

1. **WHAT YOU KNOW:** How often does it rain where you live?
2. **WHAT YOU WILL LEARN:** How does the climate of Central America influence where the people of the region live?

A TROPICAL LAND

Central America lies in the climate zone nearest the equator. You read in Chapter 1 that places near the equator have tropical climates. Most places in the tropics are warm year-round. In fact, the difference between day and night temperatures is usually far greater than that between summer and winter temperatures. Central Americans have a saying that "night is the winter of the tropics."

As you read in Chapter 8, tropical areas often have different climates because of elevation differences. Because Central America has both lowlands and highlands, it has areas in the tierra caliente, the tierra templada, and the tierra fría.

The highest parts of Central America are in the tierra fría. Days are pleasant in this elevation zone, but nights can be cold and even frosty.

Most of the Central Highlands are in the tierra templada. Days in this zone are warm and nights are cool. Most Central Americans prefer to live in this comfortable climate. The climate in this area is perfect for growing coffee.

Both the Eastern Lowlands and the Pacific Lowlands lie in the tierra caliente. Tropical crops such as cacao, bananas, and sugarcane thrive in this hot climate. Look at the song on the next page. It tells about growing sugarcane in Costa Rica. What do the words of the song tell you about the climate of the tierra caliente?

Sweet Sugar Cane
(Cañas Dulces)

Costa Rican Folk Melody

Ya yo me voy _____ pa - ra ca - ñas dul - ces
Sweet su - gar cane, _____ I will there be get - ting

don - de se pro - du - ce muy bien el fri - jol.
Yon - der where our beans are grown so fat and fine.

Her - mo - sa tie - rra que sus ce - rros
A bla - zing sun _____ 'gainst clear skies sil -

lu - ce en los cla - ros dí - as de ar - do - ro - so sol.
houett - ing ver - dant hills in that fair land of gold sun - shine.

Vi - va, vi - va ca - ñas dul - ces, Tie - rra de mi co - ra -
Grow, sweet su - gar cane for - ev - er, In the land of my de -

zón. Vi - va, vi - va ca - ñas dul - ces,
sire. Grow, sweet su - gar cane for - ev - er,

y go - yi - to de la O! Que a fa - ma - ron Mo - li -
Fes - tive land of gay at - tire. Which our lit - tle mill made

ni - ta. y go - yi - to de la O!
fa - mous. Fes - tive land of gay at - tire.

RAINY AND DRY

Because the Pacific Lowlands and the Eastern Lowlands both lie in the tierra caliente, you might think the two areas have the same climate. However, as the map on this page shows, the climates of the two areas are, in fact, quite different. This is because they receive different amounts of rainfall.

Warm winds from the Caribbean Sea make the Eastern Lowlands a very rainy area. How does this occur? As the warm winds blow across the Caribbean Sea, they absorb large amounts of seawater. When this moist air reaches Central America, it rises and cools, forming rain clouds. The result, as George Meegan experienced, is rain.

As clouds move across the Central Highlands, they lose most of their moisture. The western slopes of the highlands and the Pacific Lowlands lie in a **rain shadow**. Look at the diagram on this page. An area in a rain shadow is protected from rain-bearing winds and gets little rain most of the year.

THE RAIN SHADOW

1. Air moving over ocean picks up water vapor which forms into clouds
2. Warm winds push clouds up mountain
3. Cooler temperatures cause rain or snow
4. Clouds have less moisture

Ocean

MAP/DIAGRAM SKILL: Which city lies in the **rain shadow**—Belmopan or Managua? Which city receives more rain?

CENTRAL AMERICA: Climate

- Warm and wet all year
- Warm all year; wet with one dry season
- Highlands; temperature and precipitation vary with elevation

The jaguar (*left*) and the quetzal (*right*) live in Central America's shrinking rain forest.

TREES AND ANIMALS

Once most of Central America was covered with trees. Swamps with tangled mangroves edged the Caribbean shore. The mangrove is a tropical evergreen tree. You can see from the photograph on this page that its branches sprout huge roots.

The rest of the Eastern Lowlands was covered with a vast rain forest. Oak and pine forests carpeted the Central Highlands.

Over the last 500 years, however, much of the rain forest has been cut down. The trees have been cut for lumber and firewood or to create farmland. Like the Amazon rain forest, Central America's rain forest is in danger of being destroyed.

The forest that has survived is home to a great variety of wildlife. Crocodiles and snakes lurk in the mangrove swamps. Jaguars and pumas prowl the rain forest in search of anteaters, monkeys, and deer. Parrots, macaws, and other birds bring color to the highland forests.

Perhaps the most beautiful bird that lives in Central America is the quetzal (ket säl'). The quetzal is a rare highland bird with brilliant green, red, and white feathers. The Mayas used the green feathers of the quetzal for their royal robes. Today the quetzal is the national bird of Guatemala.

NATURAL RESOURCES

Central America's most important natural resource is its fertile volcanic soil. About two thirds of the people in Central America are farmers.

Forests are another resource. The rain forest of Central America yields valuable hardwood trees such as mahogany and teak. These woods are

332

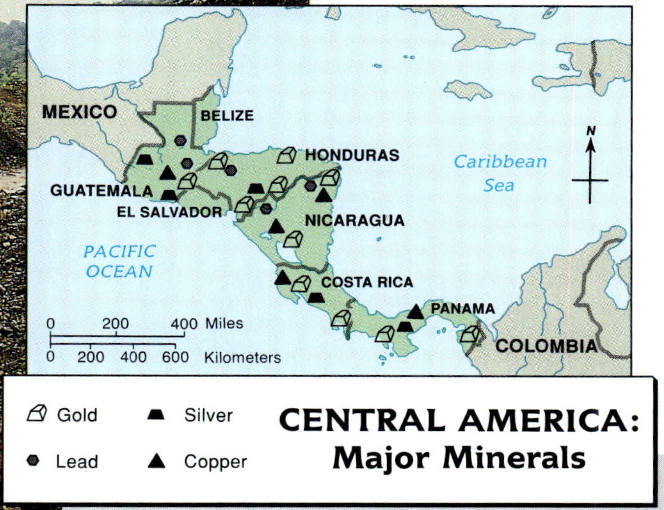

CENTRAL AMERICA:
Major Minerals

Gold Silver
Lead Copper

MAP SKILL: These Costa Rican miners are searching for gold. What other minerals are mined in Costa Rica?

prized by furniture makers and boat builders. The sapodilla tree is the source of chicle, the main ingredient of chewing gum. Other trees are sources of oils, drugs, and dyes.

Central America does not have many mineral resources. Look at the map above. It shows where small amounts of gold, silver, lead, and copper have been found in Central America. Zinc and nickel also have been discovered in the highlands. The Central American nation of Panama has large deposits of copper and iron.

Central America is poor in energy resources. No coal deposits have been discovered in this region, and only Guatemala has found oil. To meet their energy needs, Central American nations are building dams and power plants on rivers. The power plants produce electricity for this region.

A WARM AND FERTILE REGION

You have read that the Eastern Lowlands of Central America are hot and rainy all year long. The Pacific Lowlands are also warm all year but drier because they lie in a rain shadow. Most of the Central Highlands are in the tierra templada and have a pleasant climate. Central America's most important resources are its rich soil and dense forests. In the next two chapters you will read more about how people live in Central America.

Check Your Reading

1. Why do the Eastern Lowlands receive a lot of rain each year?
2. Name the areas of Central America that lie in the tierra caliente.
3. How has the landscape of Central America changed in the last 500 years?
4. GEOGRAPHY SKILL: Look at the map on page 331. What kind of climate does Panama City have? What kind does San Salvador have?
5. THINKING SKILL: What effect has climate had on where the people of Central America live?

Reading Contour Maps

Key Vocabulary

contour map
contour line
relief
contour interval

You have been reading that the geography of Central America varies greatly. It includes landforms ranging from flat plains to rugged mountains. Cartographers, or people who make maps, have several ways to show this varied landscape. For example the climate map on page 331 uses colors to show the climate of the land. Elevation maps such as the one on page 326 use colors to show areas at different heights above sea level.

Contour Maps

Another type of map that helps you picture the shape of the land is a **contour map**. *Contour* means "shape." Contour maps give detailed information about the earth's surface. They show the actual elevation and features of a place.

Contour maps use lines, colors, or both to show different elevations. A **contour line** on a map connects areas of the same elevation or height. If you were to walk along an area following a contour line, you would not go up or down. You would remain at the same elevation.

Using the Diagrams

Diagram A on this page will help you understand contour lines. It shows a

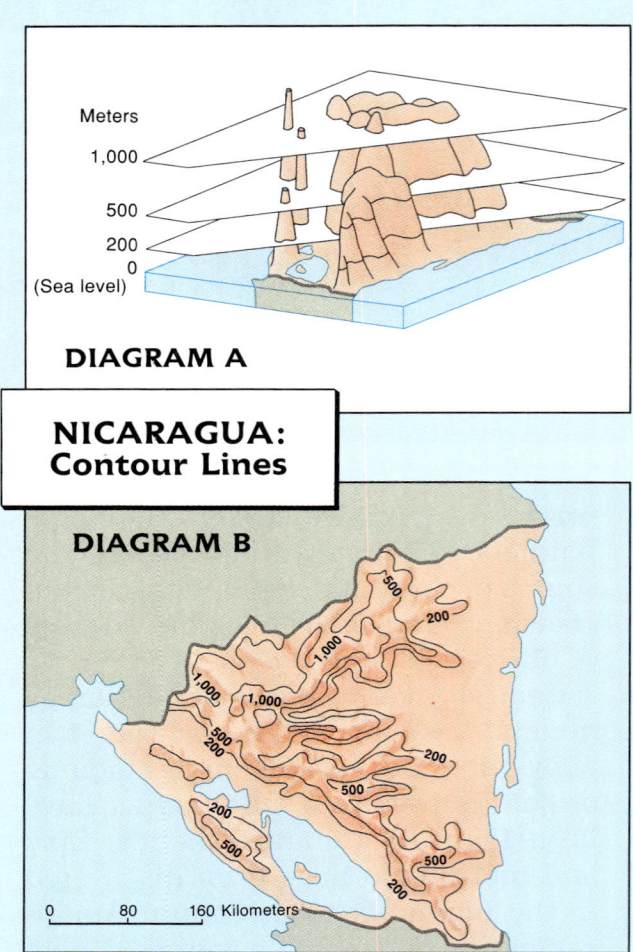

DIAGRAM A

NICARAGUA: Contour Lines

DIAGRAM B

model of Nicaragua. This diagram shows how the land can be cut into layers by using horizontal sheets that seem to intersect the land. Note the elevation on each sheet is in meters. Imagine you could push the sheets down onto the model. They would line up directly above one another. Then imagine tracing the outline of each "cut" onto the sheet below it. If you then took each outline you had made in turn and positioned it correctly over the previous outline on a piece of paper, you would have a contour map of Nicaragua, as shown in **Diagram B**. The closed, somewhat circular lines on **Diagram B** show Nicaragua's various elevations.

Contour Maps Show Relief

As you have read, when you look at a contour map you can see the variety of elevations. In addition, a contour map shows the **relief** of an area. Relief is variation in elevation. It describes the roughness of the land. For example, an area of steep, rugged mountains with great variation in elevation is an area of high relief. On the other hand, plateaus and plains, which have little variation in elevation, are areas of low relief.

Cartographers show relief on a map by the way they space the contour lines. Widely spaced contour lines indicate that the land is flat or gently sloping. In contrast, closely spaced contour lines show a steep slope. The contour map of Guatemala on this page shows low relief around Lake Izabal and high relief around Tajumulco. Try to imagine the shape of the land.

When you read a contour map, the best way to begin is to check the **contour interval** of the map. This is the difference in elevation between any two contour lines. The contour interval, which may vary from one map to another, is usually shown in the legend. Look at the map of Guatemala. What is the contour interval on the map?

CONTOUR MAP OF GUATEMALA

- • City or town
- ▲ Mountain peak

——— International boundary
Contour interval is 500 meters

Reviewing the Skill

1. What is a contour map?
2. According to the map of Guatemala above, how many meters below Tajumulco is Lake Izabal located?
3. Is the part of Guatemala with high relief located in the north or south of the country?
4. Are Chimaltenango and Escuintla located at the same elevation? How can you tell?
5. How do contour maps help you to picture the elevation of the land?

335

IDEAS TO REMEMBER

- Central America is a colorful land of coastal lowlands, interior highlands, lush rain forests, tumbling rivers, and sky-blue lakes—as well as frequent earthquakes and erupting volcanoes.
- Central America has tropical climates, both wet and dry, which give it rich and varied animal and plant life; volcanoes give it fertile soil.

REVIEWING VOCABULARY

fault
rain shadow

Number a sheet of paper from 1 to 5. Beside each number write the word or term from the list above that best completes the sentence. Both of the words are used more than once.

1. Sometimes the side of a mountain receives little precipitation and is said to lie in a _____.
2. Because the earth's tectonic plates are constantly pushing against and pulling each other, a _____ may appear in the earth's surface.
3. The western slopes of the highlands and the Pacific Lowlands lie in a _____.
4. The movement of the plates under North and South America create a _____ on the ocean floor.
5. A _____ is an area that is protected from rain-bearing winds.

REVIEWING FACTS

1. Central America has been described as a land bridge. List the landmasses that this bridge connects and the bodies of water that surround it, telling the direction in which each is located from Central America.
2. Name a positive role that volcanoes have played in the development of Central America.
3. Why are earthquakes so frequent in Central America?
4. In which area of their region do most Central Americans live? Why?
5. Tell why the Eastern Lowlands get so much rain, and name two effects that heavy rains have on this area.
6. Why is the climate drier in Central America's Pacific Lowlands?
7. Where are the coolest climates in Central America? The warmest?
8. How do Central America's rain forests encourage a rich and varied animal life?
9. What effect can cutting down rain forests have on the soil?
10. Name Central America's two most important natural resources.
11. The Pacific Lowlands receive very little rain. Where do the farmers get water for their crops?
12. What is the temperature range in the tierra caliente in the daytime?
13. Name some uses for trees other than as sources for wood.
14. How was the land bridge that connects North and South America formed?
15. What is the name we have given to this land bridge?

WRITING ABOUT MAIN IDEAS

1. **Writing a Letter:** Imagine that you work for a zoo and your employer has sent you to visit Central America. Your job is to identify Central American animal life that your zoo might like to import. Write a letter to your employer in which you name and describe the animals that you think would be good additions to the zoo.

2. **Giving Directions:** Suppose that you know someone who is planning a trip from Belize to easternmost Honduras to Costa Rica. In which directions will your friend travel and through which countries? Use the map on page 331 to find out and write down these directions for your friend.

3. **Writing an Adventure Story:** Central America has been called a "dangerous paradise." Imagine an adventure that you might have in a Central American rain forest, with the title "Lost in a Dangerous Paradise."

4. **Writing About Perspectives:** Write a paragraph that shows how a person from the highlands would describe Central America's land and climate. Then write a paragraph that shows how a person from the lowlands would describe these features.

BUILDING SKILLS: READING CONTOUR MAPS

Use the two diagrams above to answer the following questions.

1. What is a contour line? What is a contour interval?

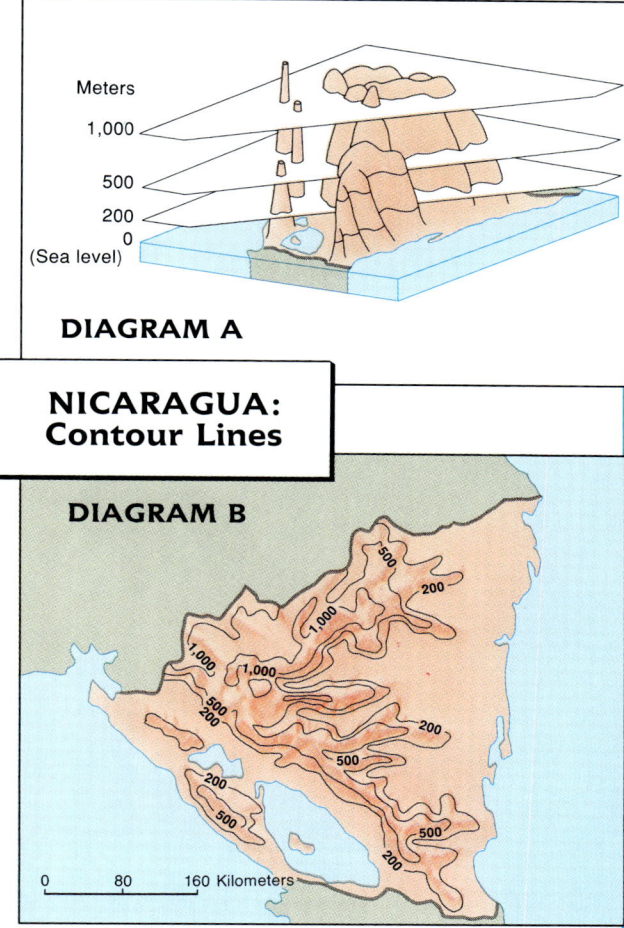

DIAGRAM A

NICARAGUA: Contour Lines

DIAGRAM B

2. When using contour maps, why is it a good idea to first check the contour intervals?

3. What does **Diagram A** show? What does **Diagram B** show?

4. What is the highest elevation shown in the two diagrams? The lowest?

5. On the basis of these diagrams and the map on page 335, how would you compare the major landforms of the countries of Nicaragua and Guatemala?

6. How do contour lines show the shape of an area's land?

337

CHAPTER 16

THE HISTORY OF CENTRAL AMERICA

FOCUS

Either to live in violence for another century, or reach a peace . . . this is the challenge facing [us]. Only peace can write a new history.

Costa Rican President Oscar Arias Sánchez used these words in a peace plan that he proposed for Central America in 1987. As Arias knew, the history of Central America is a story of conflict. Arias and other leaders in Central America hope that the plan will bring peace to their region.

1 Gaining Independence

READ TO LEARN

Key Vocabulary

Monroe Doctrine   coup
caudillo

Key People

James Monroe

Read Aloud

As rumors spread across Guatemala City, a huge crowd gathered at the government palace. The captain-general, who governed Central America for Spain, was meeting with a few wealthy landowners in the government palace. Mexico had already declared its independence from Spain. Was independence for Central America being discussed in the palace?

The people cheered while church bells rang out. Perhaps the noisy roar helped the men in the palace to make their decision. A paper was hastily written, signed, and read to the crowd. On September 15, 1821, Central America declared its "absolute independence" from Spanish rule.

Read for Purpose

1. **WHAT YOU KNOW:** In which year did the United States declare its independence?
2. **WHAT YOU WILL LEARN:** What kinds of governments developed in Central America in the 1800s?

CENTRAL AMERICA'S INDIANS

Central America declared its independence almost 300 years after a small army of Spanish soldiers had marched south from Mexico. The soldiers had found many different groups of people living in Central America. In the north the descendants of the Mayas still farmed fields of corn and beans. The southern part of the region was home to many other groups of Indians who got their food by farming, fishing, and hunting.

The Central American Indians had tried to defend their lands. However, their spears had been no match for the conquistadors' swords and guns. One group after another had been defeated by the well-armed Spanish invaders. By 1540 most of Central America was controlled by Spain.

COLONIAL SOCIETY

After the conquest Spain divided Central America into five provinces. A new society took shape slowly in the provinces of Central America. This society was like the other colonial societies that you read about in Chapter 11.

Indians made up the bottom social class. Above the Indians was a social class made up of thousands of mestizos and mulattoes. Creoles and peninsulares formed the top social class. They controlled most of the land and wealth in the provinces. They also controlled the government.

THE UNITED PROVINCES

When Central America became independent in 1821, the creoles agreed to make it part of Mexico. But in 1823 Central America broke away from Mexico to form a new republic. This new republic was called the United Provinces of Central America. The map on this page shows the provinces. What was the capital of the United Provinces of Central America?

MONROE DOCTRINE

At the same time that the United Provinces of Central America was being formed, the United States feared that European countries like France and Great Britain might try to establish colonies in Latin America. In 1823 James Monroe, the President of the United States, issued a warning to these European countries. He made it clear that the United States would oppose any attempt by a European country to gain control over any part of the Western Hemisphere. This policy became known as the Monroe Doctrine.

With the Monroe Doctrine, the United States was protecting more than the nations of Latin America. It was also trying to protect its own interests. The United States wanted to make it clear to European countries that it intended to be the major power in the Western Hemisphere. As you will read in later chapters, the Monroe Doctrine marked the beginning of a series of attempts by the United States to influence events in Latin America.

LIBERALS VERSUS CONSERVATIVES

From the beginning the United Provinces of Central America were far from united. High mountains separated some of the provinces from each other. People in one area knew little about the problems of people in other areas. Lack of agreement among Central America's creoles about the way in which their new republic should be governed also divided the United Prov-

MAP SKILL: What are the names of the five provinces that made up the United Provinces of Central America?

UNITED PROVINCES OF CENTRAL AMERICA, 1823

☐ United Provinces   ✷ Capital of United Provinces

inces. On one side of the issue were the Conservatives, who were opposed to change. They favored a strong government run by wealthy landowners.

On the other side were the Liberals, who were eager to bring reforms to Central America. For example, they wanted to educate the poor. The Liberals also wanted to bring new business and industry to Central America.

Conflict between the Conservatives and the Liberals led to war. In 1830 the Liberals gained control of Central America. Foreigners were invited to Central America to start new businesses. As you might expect, these changes upset the Conservatives.

CENTRAL AMERICA BREAKS APART

In 1837 a deadly epidemic struck Central America. An epidemic occurs when a sickness spreads very rapidly. Many Conservatives blamed the epidemic on the Liberals. They said that the government had caused the spread of the disease by poisoning the water supply.

This was the moment that the Conservatives had been waiting for. They quickly formed an army. With shouts of "Death to Foreigners," the rebels overthrew the Liberal government. The United Provinces would never again be ruled by one government.

The five new nations of Guatemala, Honduras, El Salvador, Nicaragua, and Costa Rica were created out of the ruins of the United Provinces. Later they would be joined by two more nations, Panama and Belize. Until 1903, Panama was part of Colombia, a South American country. Belize, a colony of Great Britain, did not become independent until 1981.

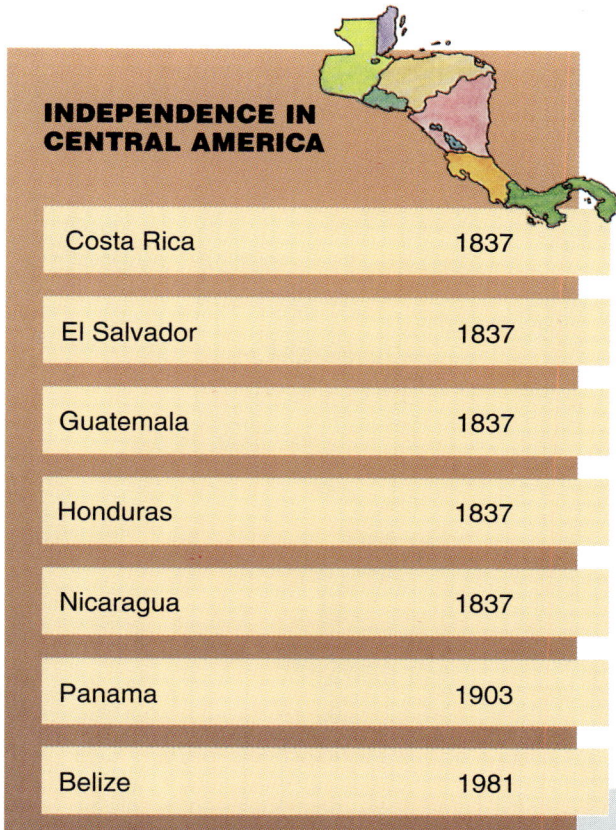

INDEPENDENCE IN CENTRAL AMERICA

Costa Rica	1837
El Salvador	1837
Guatemala	1837
Honduras	1837
Nicaragua	1837
Panama	1903
Belize	1981

CHART SKILL: Belize was the last Central American country to become independent. In what year did that happen?

RULE BY CAUDILLOS

Some people hoped to establish democratic governments in their new nations. However, most of the creoles saw no reason to share their power with the Indians and mestizos. For the next 100 years, the countries of Guatemala, Honduras, El Salvador, and Nicaragua were all ruled by **caudillos** (kou dē′ yōs), or military dictators.

A caudillo's power depended on his control of the army. Most caudillos used their power to make themselves and their creole friends rich. They did little to improve the lives of the poor.

Caudillos seldom gave up their power without a struggle. Sometimes a caudillo's opponents would form a

A system of free public schools in Costa Rica has helped the people of this country to become some of the best-educated people in Latin America.

did not have a society made up of rich creoles on one side and poor Indians and mestizos on the other. Because few Indians had lived in Costa Rica before the Spanish arrived, the Spanish settlers had to work the land themselves. As a result, most Costa Ricans owned small farms and were neither very rich nor very poor.

After independence, Costa Rica was ruled by caudillos. However, unlike the caudillos of that time in most other parts of Central America, these leaders were eager to improve their country. One of them, for example, set up a system of free public schools to educate all the children of Costa Rica.

In 1889 Costa Rica held its first free elections. Since then most of Costa Rica's leaders have been democratically elected.

DICTATORS AND DEMOCRACY

By 1838 there were five independent Central American nations. Panama and Belize became independent much later. Independence brought rule by dictator to most of Central America. Power changed hands as a result of civil wars and coups. In Costa Rica, however, it was different. There democracy took hold, and leaders were freely elected.

 Check Your Reading

1. What is a caudillo?
2. Why have there been many civil wars in Central America?
3. Why did the United Provinces of Central America break apart?
4. THINKING SKILL: Compare and contrast Costa Rica's history with that of the other four former Central American provinces.

rebel army to drive the dictator from power. The usual result was civil war. As you read in Chapter 13, a civil war is fought within a country.

More often, an unpopular dictator was removed from power in a military coup (kü). A coup is a sudden overthrow of a government. Officers of the armed forces lead military coups. Once the officers seized power, they replaced the dictator with their own caudillo. Coups took place very frequently in Central America. Honduras alone had 134 coups in its first 134 years as an independent country.

COSTA RICA

Costa Rica was the only Central American country to develop a tradition of democratic government. Unlike the rest of Central America, Costa Rica

Using the Library

Key Vocabulary

reference
atlas
dictionary
call number
encyclopedia
almanac

In your study this year of Latin America and Canada, you are learning about many different lands and peoples. Along the way, you may want to learn more about a certain subject. For instance, you may wonder how deep Lake Nicaragua is. Or you may want to know why the United Provinces of Central America did not succeed. To find the answers to such questions, you could look for the information in the library.

Using Reference Books

A library has information about many different subjects. You can find a quick answer to a question in the **reference** section. In this part of the library, you will find many different sources of information. Called reference books, these include **dictionaries**, **encyclopedias**, **almanacs**, and **atlases**. Each of these sources is useful for finding particular kinds of information.

A dictionary provides the meanings of words and shows how to pronounce them. An encyclopedia is made up of articles about thousands of different subjects. Almanacs are published every year and give the latest facts on many subjects. Atlases give information about the geography of places and include maps, charts, and tables.

Finding Books

Reference books can be very useful in helping you to find the answer to a question. However, usually you cannot borrow reference books from the library. You must use them in the library and then return them to the shelves. But there are many other books in a library that can be borrowed and that contain useful information. How would you go about finding a book that might help you?

Most libraries have a card catalog that lists all the books in the library, including the reference books. Some libraries have the same information in a computer list. No matter how information is shown, each book is listed three different ways—by author, by title, and by subject. Authors' names are shown with their last names listed first, followed by their first names. One of the most important pieces of information on the card or computer listing is the book's **call number**. The call number tells you where to find the book on the library shelves.

Reviewing the Skill

1. Name four kinds of reference books.
2. Which reference book would you use to find out how to pronounce *literacy*?
3. In which reference book would you look to find the name of the current president of Honduras?
4. Which reference book would show you the present-day borders of Costa Rica?
5. Why is it important for you to know how to use the library?

READ TO LEARN

Key People

Theodore Roosevelt
William Gorgas
George W. Goethals
Ronald Reagan

Manuel Noriega
George Bush
Oscar Arias Sánchez

Key Places

Canal Zone

Read Aloud

The strange-looking yellow fruit caused a sensation at Philadelphia's Centennial Exposition. Three million people had come to this fair in 1876 to celebrate 100 years of United States independence. There, many of them saw and tasted their first banana. Each piece of the rare tropical fruit was carefully wrapped and being sold at an incredibly high price.

Clearly there was money to be made in growing bananas. Soon people from the United States were buying huge amounts of land in Central America for growing bananas.

Read for Purpose

1. WHAT YOU KNOW: In which elevation zone do bananas grow?
2. WHAT YOU WILL LEARN: What role has the United States played in Central America?

GROWING INTEREST

The demand for bananas brought businesspeople from the United States to Central America. The hot swamps of the Eastern Lowlands are ideal for growing bananas. So much land was devoted to growing bananas that they became the most important product of Central America.

In 1899 the two largest banana growers joined together to form the United Fruit Company, or UFCO. Central Americans had mixed feelings about this giant company. UFCO created thousands of jobs. The company built houses, schools, and hospitals for its workers. However, the company also paid its workers very low wages. It forced small independent growers out of business. Many people in Central America were upset because the largest business in their region was owned and operated by foreigners.

THE PANAMA CANAL

Some people in the United States were interested in more than growing bananas in Central America. In 1898 the United States naval ship *Oregon* was sent from San Francisco, California, to the Caribbean Sea. It took so long for the ship to travel around South America that by the time it had reached the Caribbean Sea, it was no longer needed there.

As a result, the leaders of the United States decided that a canal was needed across the Isthmus of Panama. It would shorten the trip by ship from New York City to San Francisco by 8,000 miles (12,875 km).

At that time Panama was part of Colombia. In 1902 United States President Theodore Roosevelt offered $10 million to Colombia for a 10-mile-wide (16-km-wide) strip of land across Panama. This land is called the Canal Zone. Colombia said no to Roosevelt's offer. In 1903 the United States helped a group of people in Panama rebel against Colombia. After Panama won its independence, it accepted President Roosevelt's offer.

BUILDING THE CANAL

The United States was not the only country interested in building a canal across Panama. France had attempted to build a canal in Panama in 1881.

After nine years, millions of dollars, and the loss of thousands of workers' lives, the French gave up. Diseases such as yellow fever and malaria took the lives of many workers.

Could the United States succeed in building a canal when the French had failed? Doctor William Gorgas thought that he had the solution to the spread of yellow fever and malaria. Gorgas knew that mosquitoes carried the germs that caused these diseases. As soon as the mosquitoes were controlled, fewer people became sick.

When the problem of disease was at last under control, work on the canal began. George W. Goethals (gō' thəlz) was the engineer in charge of the project. Dynamite and steam shovels were used to blast and dig through the mountains. Under Goethals's direction, thousands of workers completed the canal in August 1914, five months ahead of schedule.

THE CANAL TODAY

The Panama Canal has been a tremendous success. It has saved a great deal of time for ships traveling from

More than 43,000 people worked during the 10 years it took to cut through the mountains of Panama to build the Panama Canal.

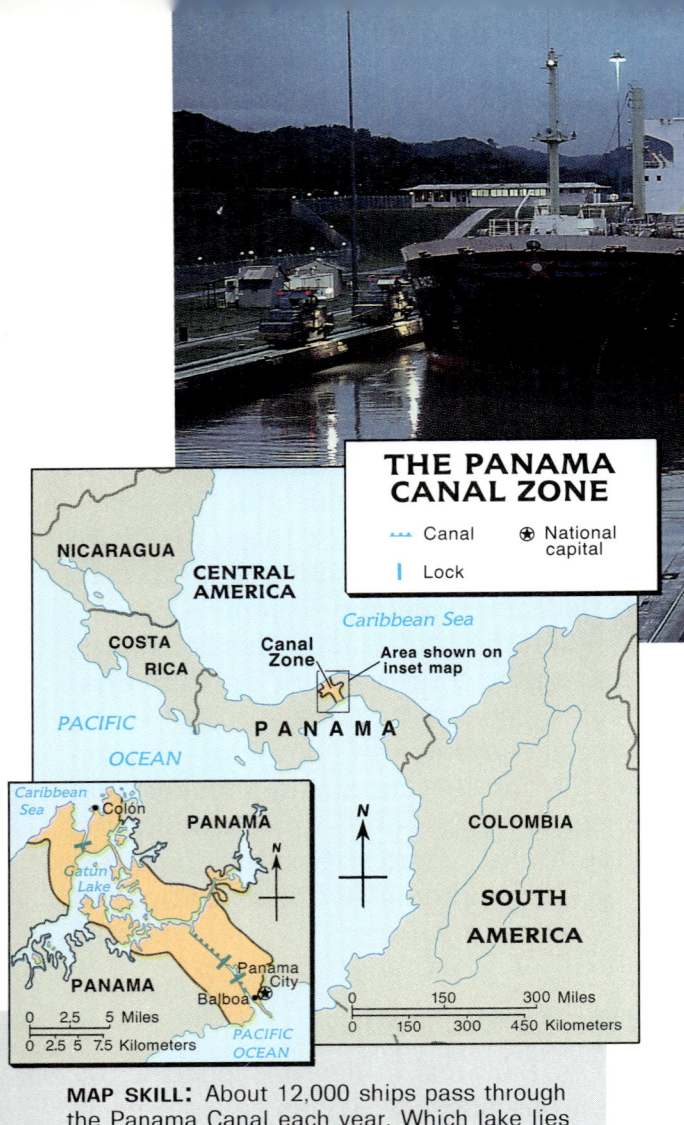

THE PANAMA CANAL ZONE

- ···· Canal
- ⊛ National capital
- | Lock

NICARAGUA

CENTRAL AMERICA

Caribbean Sea

COSTA RICA

Canal Zone

Area shown on inset map

PACIFIC OCEAN

PANAMA

COLOMBIA

SOUTH AMERICA

N

0   150   300 Miles
0   150   300   450 Kilometers

Caribbean Sea

Colón

PANAMA

Gatún Lake

N

Panama City

PANAMA

Balboa

PACIFIC OCEAN

0 2.5 5 Miles
0 2.5 5 7.5 Kilometers

MAP SKILL: About 12,000 ships pass through the Panama Canal each year. Which lake lies within the Canal Zone?

the Atlantic Ocean to the Pacific Ocean. You can trace the canal's route through Panama on the map above.

However, many people in Panama resented having the United States control a large part of their small country. Since the opening of the canal, the leaders of Panama have tried to gain control of it. An agreement between Panama and the United States was finally reached in 1977. Under its terms the United States agreed to turn over control of the canal and the Canal Zone to Panama by the year 2000.

UNITED STATES INTERESTS

The presence of the Panama Canal and businesses like the United Fruit Company made Central America very important to the United States. For many years the United States wanted one thing above all from the governments of Central America—stability.

The United States sometimes used force to bring stability to Central America. For example, the United States Marines were sent into Nicaragua several times between 1909 and 1933 to put down rebellions and to supervise elections.

In the 1930s powerful caudillos seized power in every country of Central America except Costa Rica. These dictators crushed all opposition to their rule. The leaders of the United States sometimes supported the dictators because these leaders believed that the dictators brought stability to Central America.

DEMANDS FOR REFORM

The dictators did keep order. However, they did little to help the majority of their people. Most Central Ameri-

346

cans remained desperately poor. By 1950 demands for reform to improve the lives of the people were heard all across Central America.

The reformers often clashed with those who opposed any change. By the 1980s these clashes became conflicts in which thousands of people died.

Two of the worst conflicts took place in Nicaragua and El Salvador. You will read more about the war in Nicaragua in the next chapter.

The United States took sides in many of these conflicts. However, government leaders in the United States often disagreed about which side to support. During the 1980s United States President Ronald Reagan supported a rebel force in Nicaragua. But other United States leaders in Congress favored a more neutral approach.

In Panama, the United States at first gave its support to a dictator named Manuel Noriega. Later, after Noriega was accused of trading illegal drugs, the United States turned against him. In 1989 United States President George Bush sent troops to Panama to help drive Noriega from power.

A PEACE PLAN

Costa Rican President Oscar Arias Sánchez believed that Central Americans should solve their own problems. In 1987 he brought together the leaders of Central America to talk about an end to the fighting in Nicaragua. At that meeting they agreed on a peace plan. You can find part of the peace plan in the box on this page.

By 1990 elections had been held in every Central American country. For the first time in the history of the region, its seven countries were all ruled by democratically elected leaders.

CENTRAL AMERICAN PEACE PLAN

The following is an excerpt from the Central American Peace Plan.

"*W*e, the Presidents of the five states of Central America, with political will to respond to the longings for peace of our people, sign [this document] in the city of Guatemala, on August 7, 1987."

The Central American Peace Plan was signed by the leaders of Costa Rica, Honduras, Guatemala, El Salvador, and Nicaragua.

A MOVE TOWARD DEMOCRACY

The United States first became interested in the business of growing bananas in Central America and later in the building of a canal. The United States often supported dictators to protect the canal and United States business interests. By the early 1990s democratically elected governments had come to power in all of the Central American countries.

Check Your Reading

1. Why did some Central Americans dislike the United Fruit Company?
2. How did Oscar Arias Sánchez help to bring peace to Central America?
3. THINKING SKILL: What was the United States' point of view regarding dictators in Central America?

IMPORTANT EVENTS

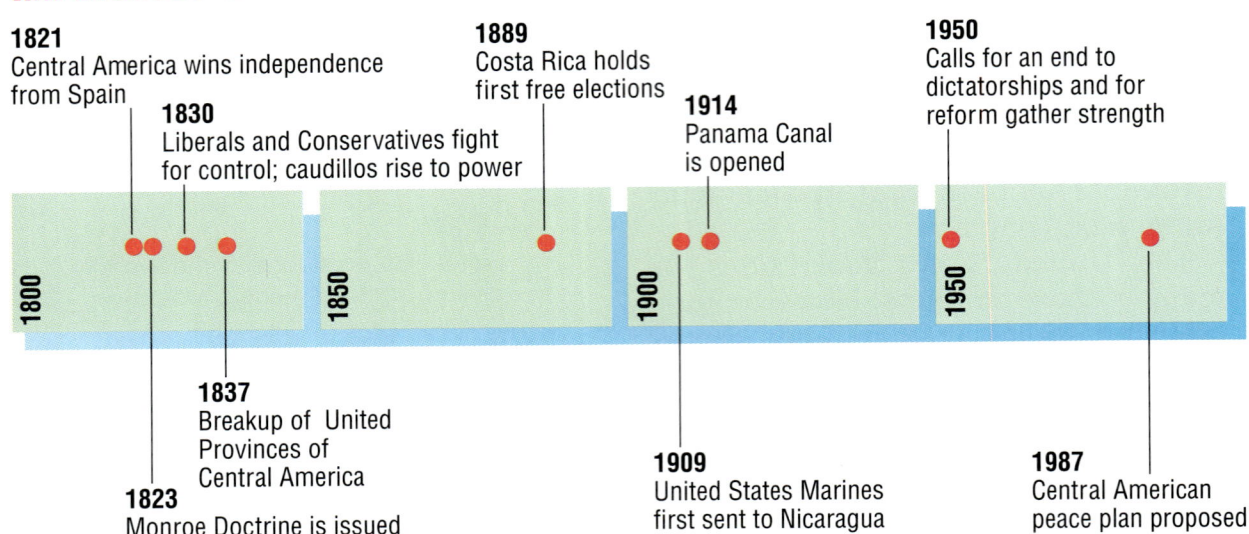

1821
Central America wins independence from Spain

1830
Liberals and Conservatives fight for control; caudillos rise to power

1889
Costa Rica holds first free elections

1914
Panama Canal is opened

1950
Calls for an end to dictatorships and for reform gather strength

1800

1850

1900

1950

1837
Breakup of United Provinces of Central America

1823
Monroe Doctrine is issued

1909
United States Marines first sent to Nicaragua

1987
Central American peace plan proposed

PEOPLE TO KNOW

George W. Goethals 1858–1928

Theodore Roosevelt 1858–1919

Manuel Noriega 1938–

William Gorgas 1854–1920

George Bush 1924–

Ronald Reagan 1911–

Oscar Arias Sánchez 1943–

IDEAS TO REMEMBER

■ Since the people of Central America won their independence from Spain in 1821, they have waged a constant struggle for democratic government and political stability.

■ Foreign investment and foreign intervention have had a strong effect on Central American life, and the movement to lessen foreign influence and to make internal reforms continues to grow.

REVIEWING VOCABULARY

caudillo   Monroe Doctrine
coup

Number a sheet of paper from 1 to 5. Beside each number write the word or term from the list above that matches the statement or definition. Some of the words are used more than once.

1. It marked the beginning of attempts by the United States to influence events in Latin America.
2. Guatemala, Honduras, El Salvador, and Nicaragua were all ruled by this kind of dictator after independence.
3. This warned European countries that the United States would oppose any attempt by them to gain control of parts of the Western Hemisphere.
4. This is an act by which rebel officers seize power.
5. This is an event that has occurred in Central America numerous times as one dictator or military group suddenly takes over the government.

REVIEWING FACTS

1. List three effects that the Spanish had on the Indians of Central America.
2. List three social classes in colonial Central America.
3. Name the seven nations that eventually emerged in Central America.
4. Why have dictatorships flourished in Central America?
5. Why have civil wars occurred in Central America so frequently?
6. Which Central American nation has had the only consistently democratic government?
7. Why did the United States want to build the Panama Canal?
8. Name two kinds of problems that building the Panama Canal posed.
9. What did Oscar Arias Sánchez believe that the Central Americans should do when he brought their leaders together in 1987?
10. Whom did reformers struggle against?

WRITING ABOUT MAIN IDEAS

1. **Writing Sentences:** Develop your own peace plan for Central America. Write at least three sentences, each of which describes a way to work for greater democracy and stability.
2. **Writing About Perspectives: Paragraph of Contrast:** Liberals and conservatives have historically clashed over how Central America should be ruled. Write a paragraph contrasting their ideas about proper government.

BUILDING SKILLS: USING THE LIBRARY

Imagine that you are a teacher and you want to create an activity to test your students' library skills. Make a list of four questions about Central America that students must go to the library to answer, for example: "Who was president of Costa Rica in 1935? How far is Managua, Nicaragua, from San Salvador, El Salvador?" Then exchange your list with a partner. Go to the library to find the answers to the questions your partner gives you. Write each answer and the kind of source in which you found it. Then meet with your partner to discuss both your findings.

CHAPTER 17

CENTRAL AMERICA TODAY

FOCUS

The democratic instrument of peace is participation, working together to resolve problems.

José Napoleon Duarte (dwär′ tā), a president of El Salvador, wrote these words about his country in his 1986 book *My Story*. He could have been writing them about any of the countries of Central America. In this chapter you will read about how the people of Central America are working together to resolve their problems.

READ TO LEARN

Key Vocabulary   **Key Places**

ladino   Udirbi Park

Read Aloud

A story is told in Guatemala about a Maya who left his farm to live in a city. He found a job as the caretaker of a sky-scraper. Within a few months people noticed something green on the building's roof. A closer look revealed that the patch of green was corn growing. The Mayas have always believed that corn is the source of life. So no matter where Mayas go, they plant corn.

For almost 500 years descendants of the Indians and the Spanish colonists have lived side by side in Guatemala. Guatemala is not the only country in Central America with a mixed population. As you will read, Central America is a region of many peoples and cultures.

Read for Purpose

1. **WHAT YOU KNOW:** Where did the Mayas build their cities?
2. **WHAT YOU WILL LEARN:** Which ethnic groups are shaping life in Central America today?

SEVEN SMALL COUNTRIES

You can find the seven small coun-tries that make up Central America on the map on page 352. The smallest country is El Salvador and the largest is Nicaragua. Taken together, the land area of all the countries of Central America would fit easily inside the state of Texas. This small region is home to many different ethnic groups.

MANY ETHNIC GROUPS

As you read in the Read Aloud above, Indians and the descendants of Spanish colonists live in Central America. The Indians were Central America's first people. In most coun-tries of Central America today, Indians form the smallest ethnic group. How-ever, in Guatemala more than half the people are Mayas.

The descendants of Spanish colo-nists are also a minority. Only in Costa Rica do people of Spanish descent make up the largest ethnic group.

Most people in Central America are mestizos, or of mixed Indian and Span-ish descent. Mestizos are a majority in Honduras, El Salvador, Nicaragua, and Panama.

Other Central Americans trace their roots to Africa. The first Africans were forcefully brought to the Eastern Lowlands as slaves by British planters and woodcutters. Many Africans escaped and lived with Indians. Today their descendants are known as Black Caribs or Afro-Indians.

Most of the people of African descent came to Central America as workers in the early 1900s. They came from the Caribbean islands to plant bananas, build railroads, and dig the Panama Canal. Most of their descendants now live along the Caribbean coast of Central America. A majority of the people of Belize are of African descent.

THE LADINOS

Ladino (la dē′ nō) is a word used in Central America for a Central American who follows Latin American customs. Most people in Central America consider themselves to be ladinos. Ladinos speak Spanish and usually belong to the Catholic Church.

Only two groups in Central America are not considered ladinos. One group is the people of Belize, who speak English. The other group is made up of those Indians who follow a traditional way of life and speak their own languages rather than Spanish.

Ladino families are both large and close-knit. Whether rich or poor, families have tended to live in the same place for hundreds of years. When a son marries, he brings his wife home to his family. Then the family helps the couple to build a home nearby.

In recent years the ladino tradition of family closeness has begun to break down. Civil war and violence have disrupted family life in many places.

TRADITIONAL LIVES

A few of the Indian groups of Central America have been able to preserve

MAP SKILL: What is the capital of Costa Rica? Of Honduras? Which countries share a border with Mexico?

The Cuna of Panama live in Udirbi Park, a protected area. Many of their colorful blankets show some of the animals found in the park.

their traditional ways of life. For example, in the mountains of Guatemala, about 3 million Indians still speak Mayan languages and mix Christianity with their Mayan religious beliefs.

However, in the Eastern Lowlands traditional Indian cultures are being threatened by land-hungry people. The Cuna (ku′ nə) Indians of Panama have found a way to protect their land and culture. In the early 1980s the Cuna decided to turn their rain-forest home into a protected area called Udirbi (ū dir′ bē) Park. The Panamanian government asked the Cuna, "Why do you Cuna need so much land?" The leader of the Cuna explained:

The forest is my pharmacy [drugstore]. If I have sores on my legs, I go to the forest and get the medicine I need to cure them. The forest is also a great refrigerator. It keeps the food I need fresh. So we Cuna need the forest, and we use it and take much from it. But we can take what we need without having to destroy everything.

This answer persuaded the government to help create the park. Today the Cuna live in Udirbi Park, which is protected from further development.

COLORFUL CONTRASTS

You have read that Central America contains a mix of people. There are Indians, people of Spanish descent, people of African descent, mestizos, and Afro-Indians. Most people in Central America are ladinos, but not all. As a result, Central America is a land of colorful contrasts.

Check Your Reading

1. What is a ladino?
2. Which ethnic groups live in Central America?
3. Why was Udirbi Park created?
4. **THINKING SKILL:** List three questions that you might ask to learn more about Central America's Indians. Why are these good questions to ask?

Poets

of
CENTRAL
AMERICA

by
Eric Kimmel

In Lesson 1 you learned that the people of Central America have inherited the traditions of three rich cultures. Over centuries, the ways of the Indians, the Africans, and the Spanish have collided and combined with one another. One important expression of Central American culture is poetry. Throughout the region's history, its poets have spoken out for freedom. Sometimes poets have held political office or influenced events through the force of their ideas. In this lesson you will meet two Central American poets, Rubén Darío (rü ben′ dä rē′ ō) and Claribel Alegría (äl ə grē′ ə). As you read, think about how the tradition of poetry helps Central Americans to express their feelings and beliefs.

RUBÉN DARÍO

Rubén Darío (1867–1916) is considered one of the greatest Latin American poets. He was born in Nicaragua, but spent a great part of his life living in Europe and South America. Darío learned to read at a young age and began writing poems when he was about 12. He read the works of many writers, especially poets, in both South and North America. Extensive travel and reading shaped his poetry.

While living in Europe as a representative of the government of Nicaragua, Darío realized that Latin America needed its own poets. He turned his efforts toward developing a powerful Latin-American voice. Although Darío spent most of his life in Europe, in poems such as "Allá Lejos" (ä yä′ lä′ hōs) he remembered the bright colors of his faraway homeland, Nicaragua.

354

ALLÁ LEJOS

Buey que vi en mi niñez echando
   vaho un día
bajo el nicaragüense sol de
   encendidos oros,
en la hacienda fecunda plena de la
   armonía
del trópico; paloma de los bosques
   sonoros
del viento, de las hachas, de pájaros
   y toros
salvajes, yo os saludo, pues sois la
   vida mía.

Pesado buey, tú evocas la dulce
   madrugada
que llamaba a la ordeña de la vaca
   lechera,
cuando era mi existencia toda
   blanca y rosada;
y tú, paloma arrulladora, y
   montañera,
significas en mi primavera pasada
todo lo que hay en la divina
   Primavera.

FAR AWAY

Ox of my childhood, hot under
the burning gold Nicaraguan sun,
on the fertile farm filled with
   tropical harmony;
Dove of forests filled with the
sounds of wind, axes, birds, and
   wild bulls,
I greet you, for you are my life.

Heavy ox, you bring back the
sweet dawn that called the cows to
   be milked,
when my life was still white and
   pink;
and you, cooing, mountain dove,
I see in you the springs of my past
as well as the Eternal Spring.

CLARIBEL ALEGRÍA

Claribel Alegría (1924–) grew up in Santa Ana, El Salvador. Like Rubén Darío she has traveled a great deal and lived in many countries. In 1943 she visited the United States and since then has lived in Mexico, Chile, Uruguay, Nicaragua, and Spain. Alegría has published ten books of poetry, five novels, and a book of children's stories.

Alegría has written many poems of political protest about Latin America. She is considered a brave and powerful force in Latin American poetry today. Her poems have been praised for their rich language and passion.

In her poem "Flowers from the Volcano," an excerpt of which you will read on these pages, Alegría writes about the violent physical and political history of El Salvador.

FLORES DEL VOLCAN

Catorce volcanes se levantan
en mi país memoria
en mi país de mito
que día a día invento
catorce volcanes de follaje y piedra
donde nubes extrañas se detienen
y a veces el chillido
de un pájaro extraviado.
¿Quién dijo que era verde mi país?
es más rojo
es más gris
es más violento:
el Izalco que ruge
exigiendo más vidas
los eternos chacmol
que recogen la sangre
y los que beben sangre
del chacmol
y los huérfanos grises
y el volcán babeando
toda esa lava incandescente
y el guerrillero muerto
y los mil rostros traicionados
y los niños que miran
para contar la historia.
No nos quedó ni un reine
uno a uno cayeron
a lo largo de América

FLOWERS FROM THE VOLCANO

Fourteen volcanos rise
in my remembered country
in my mythical country.
Fourteen volcanos of **foliage** and stone
where strange clouds hold back
the screech of a homeless bird.
Who said that my country was green?
It is more red, more gray, more violent:
Izalco roars,
taking more lives.
Eternal **Chacmol** collects blood,
the gray orphans
the volcano spitting bright lava
and the dead **guerrillero**
and the thousand betrayed faces,
the children who are watching
so they can tell of it.
Not one kingdom was left us.
One by one they fell
through all the Americas.

foliage leaves

Izalco an active volcano of western El Salvador
Chacmol a stone figure named after a Mayan god
guerrillero the Spanish word for rebel soldier

What important Central American beliefs are expressed in the poems of Rubén Darío and Claribel Alegría?

2 Living and Working

■ Key Vocabulary

campesino   diversify

■ Read Aloud

Elena Guzmán lives with her parents and brother on a farm in Costa Rica where they grow coffee. When the coffee is harvested, everyone in the Guzmán family helps to pick the coffee beans from the trees. Coffee is very important to the Guzmán family and to many other families in Central America.

Many people in Central America earn their living from growing crops such as coffee. But this is beginning to change. In this lesson you will read about how the people of Central America live and work.

■ Read for Purpose

1. **WHAT YOU KNOW:** Which natural resources are found in Central America?
2. **WHAT YOU WILL LEARN:** How have Central Americans developed their resources and economies?

FERTILE LAND

Central America's most valuable resource is its land. As you read in Chapter 15, volcanic ash has made the soil of the Central Highlands very fertile.

For many years coffee and bananas were the most important crops grown in Central America. But Central American governments have been encouraging farmers to grow other crops. This is because depending on one or two crops is dangerous. Bad weather or plant diseases sometimes destroy whole crops. For example, in 1974 Honduras lost 70 percent of its banana crop during a hurricane.

COFFEE AND BANANAS

In most countries of Central America, coffee is not grown on small farms. Coffee trees do not produce beans for at least three years after planting. People who owned small farms often could not afford to wait that long to harvest their first crop. Therefore, most of the coffee was raised by landowners on large coffee estates.

Like coffee, bananas are not grown on small farms. Bananas are grown in the tropical rain forest of the Eastern Lowlands. Growing bananas is difficult. Trees must be cut down before bananas can be planted. Roads must be built to move the fruit to the coast for shipment to other countries. This is why people in Belize say, "Bananas are not a small man's crop."

RICH AND POOR

Coffee growers on large estates have become very rich. In fact, over the years, coffee has always sold so well that growers have used their profits to buy more land and plant more coffee. Often this meant pushing people with small farms off land they had farmed for generations. As a result, more and more land was owned by fewer and fewer people. For example, until recently 60 percent of the land in El Salvador was owned by a few thousand people. Many people want to change this pattern of land ownership. You will read more about this in the Point/Counterpoint on pages 362–363.

The vast majority of Central Americans see none of the wealth that comes from crops such as bananas and coffee. Most are **campesinos** (käm pə sē′ nōz), or poor farmers. They scratch out a living by growing corn and beans on tiny plots of poor land. Campesinos often raise barely enough food to feed their families. Life is even harder for those without any land at all. They must try to find jobs on large coffee or banana estates.

NEW INDUSTRIES

Many campesinos in Central America are moving from the countryside to the cities. They go to the cities hoping to find work in the new industries that have been started there. Since the 1950s, the countries of Central America have been trying to **diversify**, or add variety, to their economies. Encouraging the growth of new industries

Many workers are needed on coffee estates because coffee beans are picked by hand.

is one way in which Central American governments have tried to diversify their economies.

For example, food processing has become a major industry in many Central American countries. Food processors produce packaged foods and bottled drinks. Other new industries produce clothing, shoes, furniture, paper, and building materials. The growth of these industries has helped to create many new jobs.

359

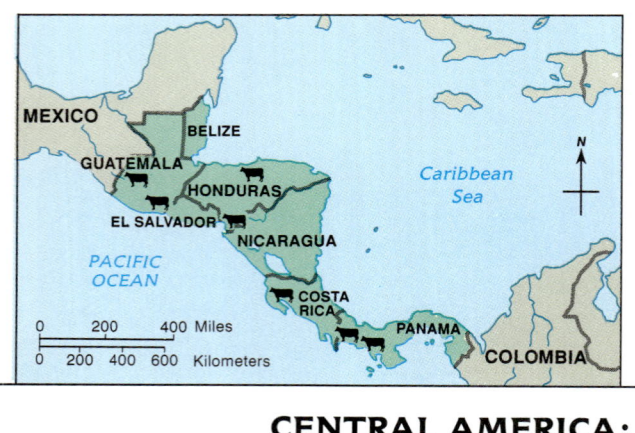

CENTRAL AMERICA: Cattle

🐄 Cattle raising

🍌 Bananas   ⊘ Coffee
🟤 Cacao   ♀ Cotton

CENTRAL AMERICA: Major Crops

MAP SKILL: In which countries are cattle raised? Which crops does Panama grow?

NEW CROPS

Central American governments have also encouraged farmers to diversify by growing different crops. For example, many farmers now raise cacao and cotton. The map above shows where these crops are grown in Central America. It also shows where coffee and bananas are grown.

Farmers also raise cattle for meat and milk. The map at the top of this page shows where most cattle is raised in Central America.

HAVING FUN

Although Central America has many economic problems, its people have many ways of having fun. For example, most Central Americans enjoy sports. Soccer is the most popular sport in Central America. In Honduras and El Salvador, outstanding soccer players are regarded as national heroes.

United States fruit companies introduced baseball to Central America. The popularity of the game spread and it is especially popular in Nicaragua. Many young Nicaraguans dream of playing in *Las Ligas Grandes*, or "The Big Leagues," in the United States.

CELEBRATIONS

Central Americans celebrate many holidays throughout the year. Most holidays are religious. Catholics often celebrate Christmas, Easter, and special saints' days with parades. Guatemalan Indians celebrate ancient Mayan religious holidays with songs and dances.

There are also festivals to celebrate the culture and history of Central

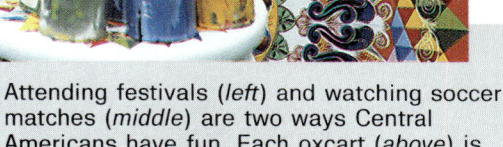

Attending festivals (*left*) and watching soccer matches (*middle*) are two ways Central Americans have fun. Each oxcart (*above*) is painted in a unique pattern.

America. For example, the people of Guatemala have a festival called the Dance of the Conquest. As you can see in the photograph on page 360, some Mayas at the festival remember their history by dressing as the Spanish conquistadors. Costa Ricans celebrate Columbus Day with four days of parades and fireworks.

ART AND MUSIC

As you have read in the Traditions lesson on pages 354–357, Central America's poetry reflects the cultures of the many peoples of this region. Central America's art and music also reflect this cultural mix. Artists bring together European painting and Indian designs. Composers create music for a mixture of Indian, African, and European instruments.

Central American art is often useful as well as beautiful. In Costa Rica farmers use gaily painted oxcarts to go to the market. The designs on the carts have been passed down in families for generations.

A POOR REGION

Many Central Americans earn a living from farming. Growing crops such as coffee and bananas has made some people rich. But most campesinos remain poor. New industries have drawn many people from the countryside to jobs in the cities.

Check Your Reading

1. How do the people of Central America use resources to earn a living?
2. Why are coffee and bananas usually grown on large farms?
3. What are three ways in which people in Central America have fun?
4. **THINKING SKILL:** What effect has the growing of coffee had on the people of Central America?

Is Land Reform Good for El Salvador?

As you read in this chapter, most of the farmland in El Salvador is owned by a few powerful families. Seventy percent of El Salvador's campesinos either work on large plantations or rent land from one of these families.

Although these landowners earn good profits from their plantations, the campesinos do not share in the profits. Wages are low. In addition, thousands of campesinos are hired to work only during harvesttime. This means that they cannot find work for eight months out of each year. Because they have no land of their own on which to plant food crops, many campesinos and their families often face starvation.

Since the 1970s, El Salvador's campesinos have called for land reform, or improvements in the way land is owned. They state that it is unfair for most of the land to be owned by a few landowners. If large plantations were broken up and redistributed among the people, campesinos argue, there would be less hunger and poverty throughout the country.

The landowners argue that the land legally belongs to them. If their land were to be taken from them without their consent, their constitutional right to own property would be violated.

POINT

Land Reform Is a Positive Step

On March 6, 1980, El Salvador's leaders announced a sweeping land-reform program. The government proposed to transfer ownership of some farmland from landowners to campesinos. Colonel Adolfo Majano (mä hä′ nō), a government leader, went on national radio to present the case for land reform to El Salvador's people.

This new land-reform program will take the land out of the hands of a few and will distribute it among the many. It will allow people who have known only landlessness and despair to create their own destiny [future].

Such redistribution will help people who have been living in poverty for years. Once these farm workers and renters get the land, they must organize and work it efficiently, to produce as much as possible. And they should produce food to feed the people of their own communities, rather than produce only for export, as is now the case.

This redistribution of land is not taking us down the road toward centralized government control. Instead, we are trying to find the way to a true democracy.

● Why is Adolfo Majano in favor of land reform?

COUNTERPOINT

Land Reform Is a Threat

Landowners have strongly opposed the land-reform movement in El Salvador. They state that land reform opposes the spirit of free enterprise upon which business is based. One group of landowners, called the National Association of Private Enterprise (NAPE), published the following statement.

As the representative of Salvadoran free enterprise, we object to an economic policy that uses the methods and principles of centralized government planning. This reflects a tendency toward total government control, covered with an apparent clothing of democracy.

It is not possible to destroy the spirit of free enterprise without creating more misery. Redistribution of land will punish efficient production. It also threatens to destroy the spirit of enterprise. . . . When our Constitution guarantees private property, these principles cannot be thrown aside for purely political motives.

The grave economic and social problems of our country will not be solved by attacking private property and other constitutional rights and freedoms.

● Why is the NAPE opposed to land reform?

UNDERSTANDING THE POINT/COUNTERPOINT

1. Which side do you think presents the stronger argument? Give reasons for your answer.
2. What other opinions might people in El Salvador have about this issue?
3. Do you think the two sides can reach a compromise? Explain your answer.

363

3 Nicaragua: Building a Democracy

READ TO LEARN

Key Vocabulary

Sandinista
communism
Contra

Key People

Augusto César Sandino
Anastasio Somoza
Anastasio "Tachito" Somoza

Daniel Ortega
Violeta
Chamorro

Read Aloud

We don't want the gains of the revolution lost, just the opposite. Rescue them and rescue the economy and the culture, not for the State, but for men and women. Our responsibility is the Nicaraguan people.

Pablo Antonio Cuadra, a poet and journalist in Nicaragua, wrote these words in 1987 while Nicaragua was involved in its second civil war in 20 years. Why were these wars fought? In this lesson you will learn the answer to this question.

1. **WHAT YOU KNOW:** What is a civil war?
2. **WHAT YOU WILL LEARN:** Why have the people of Nicaragua fought civil wars?

THE UNITED STATES IN NICARAGUA

In order to understand the civil wars in Nicaragua, you must know something about Nicaragua's earlier history. The roots of Nicaragua's conflicts go back to the early 1900s. As you have read in Chapter 16, the United States Marines were sent to Nicaragua several times between 1909 and 1933 to supervise elections and put down rebellions. Many Nicaraguans wanted the marines to leave. They did not think the United States should be involved in their country's affairs.

In the early 1930s one Nicaraguan became an important leader in the struggle to remove the marines from Nicaragua. His name was **Augusto César Sandino**. The people who fought alongside Sandino called themselves **Sandinistas**.

There were many clashes between the Sandinistas and the United States Marines. Although the Sandinistas were never able to defeat the marines, they refused to give up. As Sandino explained:

I will die with the few that follow me because it is preferable to die as rebels . . . than to live as slaves.

In 1933 the marines finally left Nicaragua. In their place they left a new Nicaraguan army led by **Anastasio Somoza**. Somoza and members of his family would control Nicaragua for the next 45 years.

Augusto César Sandino (*left, in checked jacket*) was murdered after Anastasio Somoza came to power. "Tachito" Somoza (*above*) was the last Somoza dictator.

THE SOMOZA DICTATORSHIP

Somoza was anxious to control Nicaragua without any opposition. Because he was afraid that Sandino would continue to lead rebellions, Somoza had his own soldiers murder Sandino in 1934. In 1936 Somoza became president of Nicaragua. He ruled the country as a dictator.

During the Somoza dictatorship, the Somoza family became very rich. The dictator used his power as president of Nicaragua to force farmers to sell him their land at very low prices. He forced owners of profitable businesses to turn their businesses over to him. Although Somoza tried to appear as if he cared about the welfare of the people of Nicaragua, he did very little to improve life in his country.

Somoza was disliked by many Nicaraguans. In 1956 an angry student murdered him. But after his death, power passed first to his oldest son and then to his youngest son, Anastasio "Tachito" Somoza. Tachito continued to rule as his father had. Soon the Somoza family owned one fifth of all the wealth in Nicaragua.

While the Somozas became richer, the people of Nicaragua became poorer. Many Nicaraguans were unemployed, poorly fed, and unable to read and write. Many children died from hunger and disease.

A REVOLUTION

Elections offered little hope of change in Nicaragua. It was dangerous to openly oppose the Somoza government. People who did could be jailed or killed. Many Nicaraguans believed that revolution was the only way to bring about change.

Small groups of rebels began to form in towns and villages across Nicaragua. These rebels called themselves Sandinistas, after Augusto César Sandino and his followers. The Sandinistas began to demonstrate against the Somoza government. By 1978 their rebellion had become a civil war.

After battling Somoza's army for 18 months, the Sandinistas succeeded.

Tachito, the last Somoza dictator, was driven out of Nicaragua in 1979. The war had taken more than 50,000 lives. Thousands of people had been injured and left homeless.

SANDINISTA RULE

The Sandinistas wanted to build a new Nicaragua. They began land reform measures in order to distribute Somoza's land among the poor. Programs were started to teach people to read and write. Under the Somozas only 50 percent of the people in Nicaragua could read and write. Under the Sandinistas this number grew to almost 90 percent.

Despite these changes, many people were unhappy with Sandinista rule. It seemed to many that the Sandinistas were trying to establish a system of government based on communism. Under a communist system, the entire economy of a country is controlled by the central government. People in a communist system have little personal freedom.

The Sandinistas began to take control of parts of Nicaragua's economy. They also limited freedom of the press. Newspapers were not allowed to criticize the government. When Nicaragua's most important newspaper continued to write critically about life in Nicaragua, the Sandinistas closed down the paper.

THE CONTRA WAR

By 1980 rebels who were called Contras began to oppose rule by the Sandinistas. *Contra* is the Spanish word for "against." Years of civil war and violence followed. More than 30,000 people died in the civil war between the Sandinistas and the Contras.

The United States, led by President Ronald Reagan, supported the Contras by sending them money and weapons. But other United States leaders did not want the United States to take sides.

These children are carrying chairs to one of the new schools that have been opened throughout Nicaragua.

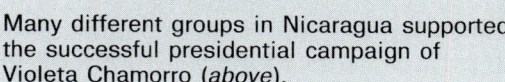
Many different groups in Nicaragua supported the successful presidential campaign of Violeta Chamorro (*above*).

As you have read in Chapter 16, President Oscar Arias Sánchez of Costa Rica proposed a peace plan for Central America in 1987. His plan called for free elections to be held in Nicaragua. In 1990 Sandinista leader Daniel Ortega (ôr tä′ gə) agreed to hold the elections to end the civil war. To Ortega's surprise the Sandinistas were voted out of office. In April 1990 Violeta Chamorro (vē ō lät′ ə chä môr′ ō) became Nicaragua's president.

BUILDING A NEW NICARAGUA

The civil wars in Nicaragua had devastated the country. The loss of life was staggering. The Sandinista government had used most of its money to support the army against the Contras. This left Nicaragua's economy weak. Poverty remains a major problem for Nicaraguans.

But the people of Nicaragua are rebuilding their country. Education and health programs started by the Sandinistas have been continued by the Chamorro government. Freedom of the press also has been restored.

A TROUBLED HISTORY

In the 1970s the Sandinistas led a successful rebellion against the Somoza dictatorship. Some Nicaraguans, called Contras, opposed rule by the Sandinistas, who were beginning to set up a communist government. This led to another civil war. In 1990 free and honest elections were held in Nicaragua. Today the people of Nicaragua are hoping they can work together to rebuild their country.

Check Your Reading

1. Who was Augusto César Sandino?
2. Why did many Nicaraguans dislike the Somoza government?
3. Why did the Sandinistas and the Contras fight a civil war?
4. **THINKING SKILL:** What is the correct order of the major events that were discussed in this lesson?

Determining the Accuracy of Information

One day a friend tells you that tickets are selling fast for next month's rock concert. She says that Saturday's performance is sold out, and there are only a few good seats available for Friday night's show. She suggests that after school you both go to the stadium to buy tickets.

Before you run off to the box office, wouldn't you want to know if your friend is giving you accurate information? Information that is accurate is free of errors. You need accurate information to make good decisions.

Trying the Skill

Suppose that you have to give a report to your class about the economy of Central America. One day you hear a reporter on a news program say the following:

According to several international organizations, most Central American nations will continue to need financial aid to deal with widespread poverty and severe inflation. For example, in Honduras the average amount a working person makes in a year is slightly less than $600. In recent years, the inflation rate in Nicaragua has reached as high as 200 percent. That means that a loaf of bread that once cost $.50 now sells for $2.00.

1. Do you think the information in the news report is accurate? Explain.
2. How could you determine the accuracy of what you just read?

HELPING YOURSELF

The steps on the left can help you to determine the accuracy of information that you hear or read. The examples on the right show how these steps can be used to evaluate the information about the economic problems of Central America.

One Way to Determine the Accuracy of Information	Example
1. Identify the source of the information.	The sources are several international organizations.
2. Determine whether the source is credible, or believable, by asking the following questions. • Is the author or speaker an expert or well informed about the topic? • Does the author or speaker have anything to gain by giving inaccurate information?	These groups are probably well informed about the topic. The author appears to have nothing to gain by giving inaccurate information.
3. Determine if the information is current.	The report was broadcast recently, so the figures given are probably for the current year.
4. Compare the information with similar information in other sources.	Checking the same information in other sources helps you to determine its accuracy. In this case, you might look up the same information in current world almanacs, World Bank reports, or government publications.

Applying the Skill

Now apply what you have learned. Determine the accuracy of the following information from a book written in 1988. The author is a college professor who has lived and taught in different Central American countries for over 20 years.

Costa Rica is unique among the Central American countries. It has the most democratic and politically stable government in the region as well as the highest standard of living. Costa Rica's literacy rate, the percentage of people in the country who can read and write, is over 90 percent. Primary and secondary education are free and compulsory. More than 20,000 students attend the two public universities.

1. Is the information that is presented accurate? How can you tell?
2. Is the source of the information credible? How do you know?
3. What are two sources you might check to determine the accuracy of this information?

Reviewing the Skill

1. What does the word *accuracy* mean?
2. When should you try to check the accuracy of statements?
3. What are three ways to check the accuracy of information in a speech or book?
4. Why is it important to determine whether or not information is accurate?

IMPORTANT EVENTS

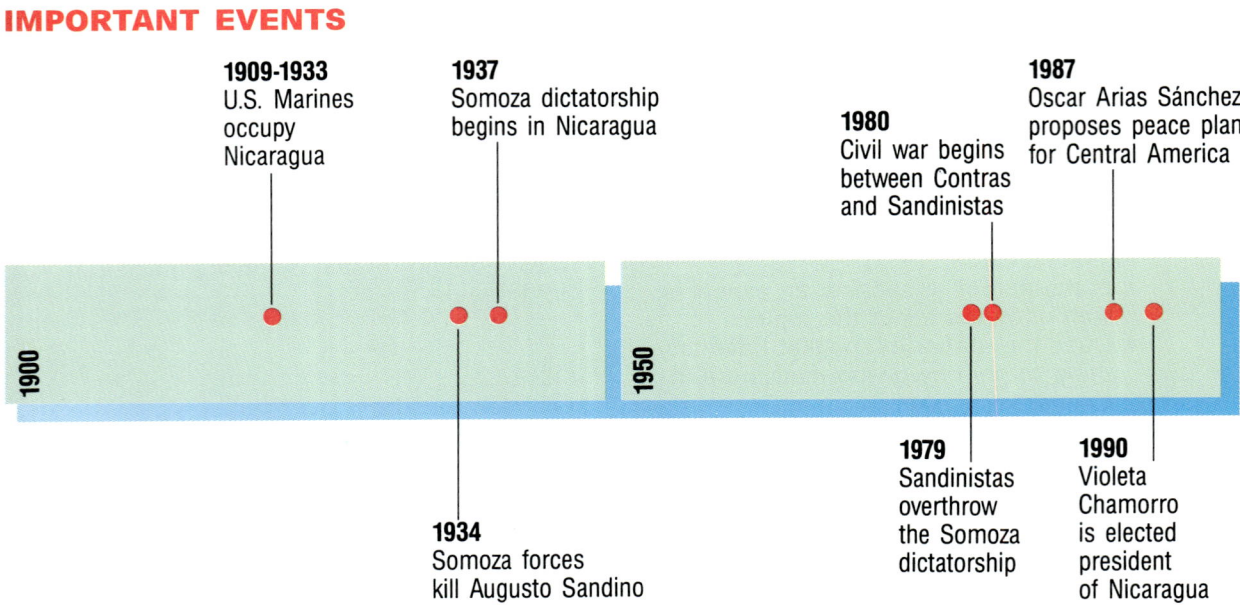

1909-1933
U.S. Marines occupy Nicaragua

1937
Somoza dictatorship begins in Nicaragua

1980
Civil war begins between Contras and Sandinistas

1987
Oscar Arias Sánchez proposes peace plan for Central America

1900

1950

1934
Somoza forces kill Augusto Sandino

1979
Sandinistas overthrow the Somoza dictatorship

1990
Violeta Chamorro is elected president of Nicaragua

PEOPLE TO KNOW

Augusto César Sandino 1895–1934

Anastasio Somoza 1896–1956

Violeta Chamorro 1929–

Anastasio "Tachito" Somoza 1925–1980

Daniel Ortega 1945–

IDEAS TO REMEMBER

■ Central America has a rich and colorful mix of people—Indians, people of European descent, people of African descent, mestizos, and Afro-Indians—most of whom live as ladinos.

■ Central Americans earn their livings as large landowners raising cash crops, campesinos raising subsistence crops or working on large farms, and city dwellers working in developing industries like food processing.

■ The people of Nicaragua hope that they are finally emerging from a troubled history of foreign intervention, dictatorship, and civil war.

REVIEWING VOCABULARY

campesinos   ladino
communism   Sandinistas
diversify

Number a sheet of paper from 1 to 5. Beside each number write the word from the list above that best completes the sentence.

1. _____ is the name that revolutionary fighters took for themselves in honor of an important Nicaraguan rebel of the 1930s.
2. Poor farmers in Central America are referred to by the name _____.
3. Under the system of government called _____, the entire economy of a country is controlled by the central government.
4. When Central Americans try to add variety to the industries that make up their economies, they are attempting to _____ them.
5. A Central American who adopts Latin American customs and values is known as a _____.

REVIEWING FACTS

1. In which Central American country are more than half the people Mayas? In which is the majority of Spanish descent? In which is the majority of African descent? In which four are mestizos in the majority?
2. Who make up the only two groups in Central America that are not considered ladinos? Why are they not considered ladinos?
3. Why is the traditional Indian lifestyle changing?

4. Which important cash crops are difficult for campesinos to raise?
5. Name three problems that campesinos face today.
6. Describe two ways that Central American governments have tried to improve their economies.
7. Name two favorite sports in Central America.
8. Why were many Nicaraguans dissatisfied with Somoza rule?
9. Why were many Nicaraguans dissatisfied with Sandinista rule?
10. What has given Nicaragua new hope for a democratic government?

WRITING ABOUT MAIN IDEAS

1. **Writing a News Story:** Imagine that you are a television newscaster who has the assignment of reporting the Ortega-Chamorro election. Write a script for your television appearance and be sure to rehearse reading it. Then present the television news story to your class.
2. **Writing About Perspectives:** Pretend that you are trying to end the long Somoza dictatorship. Write a flier convincing others to join your cause.

BUILDING SKILLS: DETERMINING THE ACCURACY OF INFORMATION

1. What is the difference between accurate and inaccurate information?
2. What is another word for credibility?
3. List three ways to check the accuracy of information.
4. Why is it so important to determine whether information is accurate or not?

371

REVIEWING VOCABULARY

campesino	fault
caudillo	ladino
communism	Monroe Doctrine
coup	rain shadow
diversify	Sandinistas

Number a sheet of paper from 1 to 10. Beside each number, write the word or term from the list above that matches the statement or definition.

1. The name of the people who fought on the side of Augusto Sandino
2. A crack that can appear in the earth's crust when plates within the earth push and pull against each other
3. A name most Central Americans call themselves because they wear western clothes and follow Latin American customs and values
4. The United States policy that carried the message "European nations, do not try to gain control over any part of the Western Hemisphere"
5. A poor Central American farmer
6. An area that is protected from rain-bearing winds
7. Central American countries have often been ruled by this kind of military dictator, whose main interest is power rather than the people
8. What many Central American nations have wanted to do to their economies since the 1950s by encouraging the development of new industries
9. A sudden overthrow of government often staged by army officers
10. A system of government under which a nation's entire economy is controlled by the central government

WRITING ABOUT THE UNIT

1. **Writing a Menu:** Write a menu for a meal featuring mainly food products from Central America. Your menu should include a soup, a main course, a dessert, and a beverage.
2. **Writing a Paragraph:** Which place in Central America would you most like to visit? Write a paragraph describing this place and telling why you chose it.
3. **Writing About Perspectives:** Imagine you are one of the Cuna shown in the photographs on page 353. Write a short story based on the photographs that shows what your everyday life might be like.

ACTIVITIES

1. **Constructing a Time Line:** Review this unit to identify major events that took place in the various Central American countries. Then draw a time line that shows the major events that occurred in Nicaragua.
2. **Using an Almanac:** Farming is a very important activity throughout Central America. Look up the seven countries of Central America in an almanac and find the percentage of land in each that is used for agriculture. Make a chart of your findings.
3. **Working Together to Make a Country Booklet:** List the seven countries of Central America on the chalkboard. Form seven groups and have each group choose a country from the list. Work together to research your country, using encyclopedias and almanacs. Prepare a booklet on your country for the classroom library.

REFORM IN CENTRAL AMERICA

The following account was written by Central America scholar Robert Leiken:

"Rising protests and demands for reform reflected deeply rooted . . . changes in Central America. Economic expansion there had altered Central America's class structure, producing a middle class and an urban working class. The shock of earthquake and massive relief efforts heightened social awareness. In Guatemala, Indians in remote villages learned that their welfare was now not only of national but international concern."

BUILDING SKILLS: USING THE LIBRARY

Use what you have already learned and the account above to answer the following questions.

1. Name four examples of reference books found in the library.
2. What purpose does a card catalog serve?
3. If you wanted to find the meanings of *structure* and *awareness* from the account above, in which kind of reference book would you look?
4. Which kind of reference book would help you learn which countries make up Central America?
5. Where would you look to find out which country is larger or smaller?
6. Which kind of reference book might give you the most current information on what percentage of the Guatemalan population is Indian?
7. Which library tool might you use to look for information about the life of the middle class in one of the countries of Central America?

 ### LINKING PAST, PRESENT, AND FUTURE

You have read about Central America's troubled and often violent past. And you have learned how this past has caused problems that continue there today. Recall that in 1987 Costa Rican president Oscar Arias Sánchez brought the leaders of Central America together to solve their own problems. Write two or three paragraphs describing ways that peace in the future might change life in Central America for the better.

ARCTIC OCEAN

75°N

Baffin
Bay

60°N

Gulf of Alaska

Hudson
Bay

NORTH

AMERICA

75°W

60°W

Tropic of Cancer

Gulf of Mexico

THE
BAHAMAS

CARIBBEAN
ISLANDS

PACIFIC

Gulf of California

OCEAN

GREATER ANTILLES

Caribbean   Sea

LESSER
ANTILLES

165°W

150°W

135°W

120°W

105°W

90°W

SOUTH

AMERICA

Tropic of Capricorn

PACIFIC   OCEAN

60°S

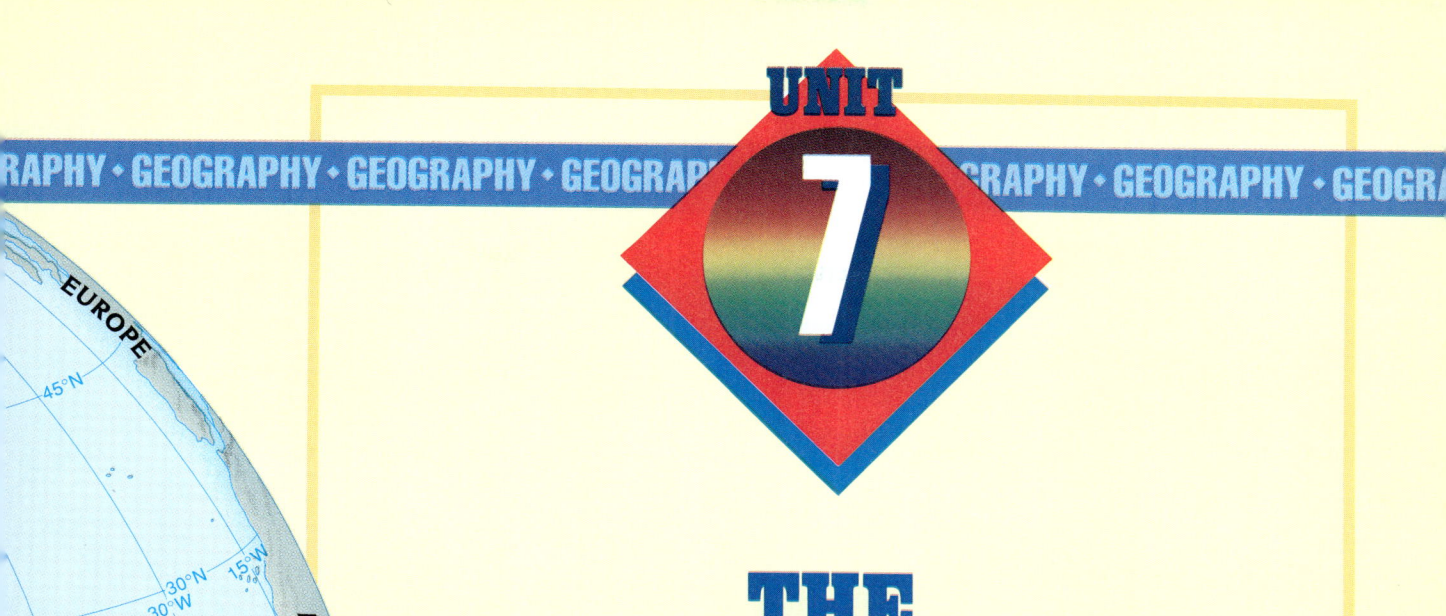

UNIT 7

EUROPE
45°N
30°N   15°W
45°W   30°W
ATLANTIC
OCEAN
AFRICA
15°N
Equator 0°
15°S
30°S

THE CARIBBEAN

WHERE WE ARE

You are about to travel through a region of beautiful beaches, colorful coral reefs, and steep volcanic mountains. Several chains of islands make up the land of the Caribbean. Some of the islands are just tiny specks on a map, but others are big enough to have large populations and growing cities.

In this unit, you will read about the many different groups of people that have contributed to the present cultures of the Caribbean islands. You will read about a group of Indians named the Arawak, who were the first inhabitants of the Caribbean region. You will also read about the explorers and settlers from Europe and the Africans who were forcibly brought to the region as slaves. As you learn about the Caribbean today, try to recognize how these diverse groups have contributed to the modern cultures of the region.

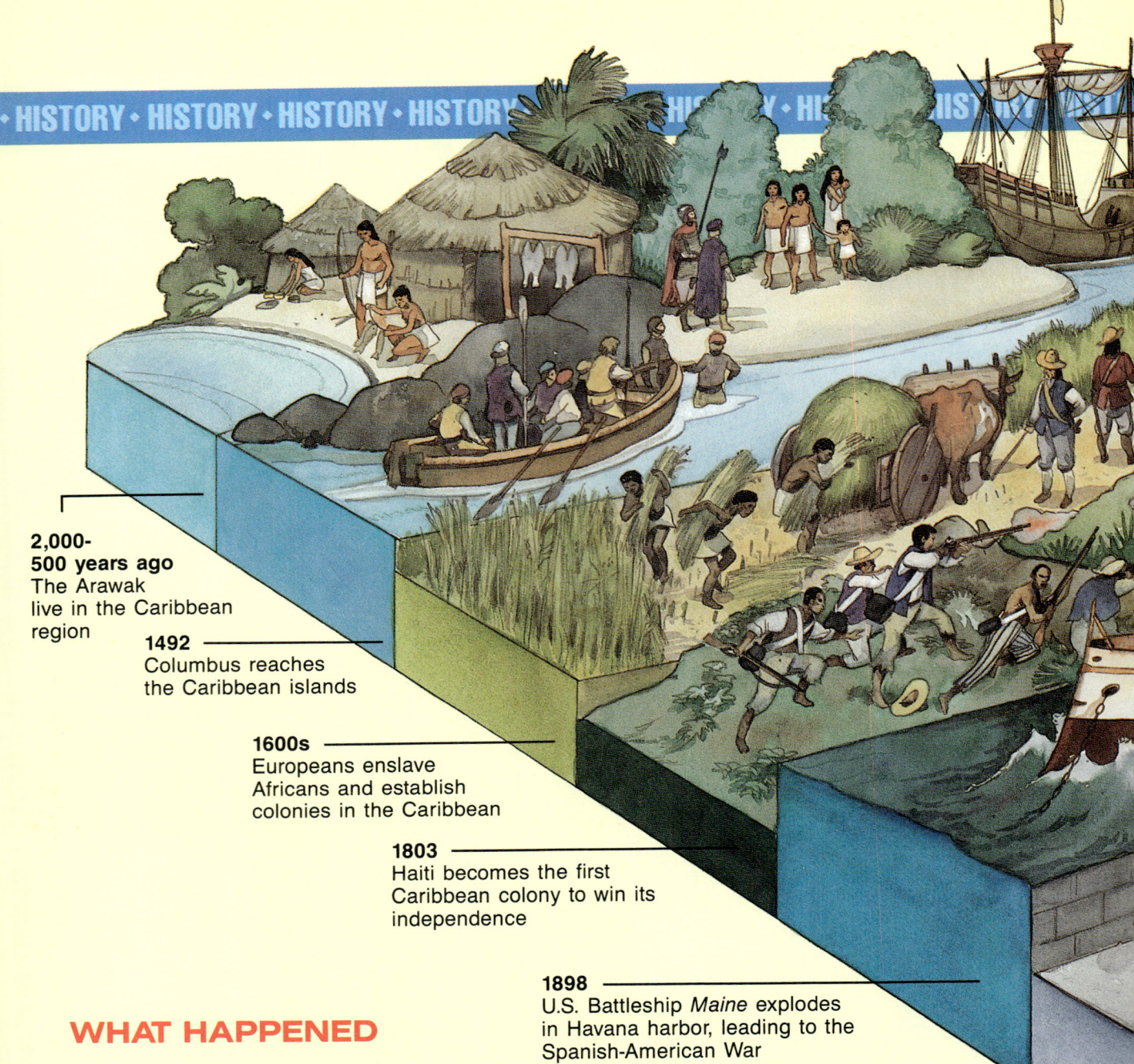

**2,000-
500 years ago**
The Arawak
live in the Caribbean
region

1492
Columbus reaches
the Caribbean islands

1600s
Europeans enslave
Africans and establish
colonies in the Caribbean

1803
Haiti becomes the first
Caribbean colony to win its
independence

1898
U.S. Battleship *Maine* explodes
in Havana harbor, leading to the
Spanish-American War

1959
Fidel Castro leads the
Cuban Revolution

1990s
Puerto Ricans
debate independence,
statehood, and
commonwealth status

WHAT HAPPENED

　　Thousands of years ago,
the Arawak Indians settled on the
islands of the Caribbean. The arrival
of Christopher Columbus in 1492 was the
first step toward European colonization of
the Caribbean region. The European rulers
set up plantations where sugarcane and other
products were harvested, first by Indians and later
by enslaved Africans. Haiti became the first colony to win
its independence. Today most Caribbean islands
are independent and have growing economies.

376

377

THE CARIBBEAN

ANTIGUA AND BARBUDA
Capital ✪
St. John's

Major language: English
Population: 0.1 million
Area: 170 sq mi; 440 sq km
Leading export: clothing

CUBA
Capital ✪
Havana

Major language: Spanish
Population: 10.7 million
Area: 42,803 sq mi; 110,860 sq km
Leading export: sugar

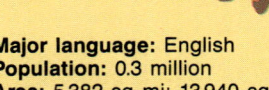

BAHAMAS
Capital ✪
Nassau

Major language: English
Population: 0.3 million
Area: 5,382 sq mi; 13,940 sq km
Leading export: lobster

DOMINICA
Capital ✪
Roseau

Major language: English
Population: 0.1 million
Area: 290 sq mi; 750 sq km
Leading export: bananas

BARBADOS
Capital ✪
Bridgetown

Major language: English
Population: 0.3 million
Area: 166 sq mi; 430 sq km
Leading export: sugar

DOMINICAN REPUBLIC
Capital ✪
Santo Domingo

Major language: Spanish
Population: 7.3 million
Area: 18,816 sq mi; 48,730 sq km
Leading export: sugar

GRENADA

Capital ✪
St. George's

Major language: English
Population: 0.1 million
Area: 131 sq mi; 340 sq km
Leading export: nutmeg

**ST. KITTS
AND NEVIS**
Capital ✪
Basseterre

Major language: English
Population: 40,000
Area: 139 sq mi; 360 sq km
Leading export: sugar

HAITI

Capital ✪
Port-au-Prince

Major languages: French and
Haitian Creole
Population: 6.3 million
Area: 10,714 sq mi; 27,750 sq km
Leading export: coffee

ST. LUCIA

Capital ✪
Castries

Major language: English
Population: 0.2 million
Area: 239 sq mi; 620 sq km
Leading export: bananas

JAMAICA

Capital ✪
Kingston

Major language: English
Population: 2.5 million
Area: 4,243 sq mi; 10,990 sq km
Leading export: aluminum

**ST. VINCENT AND
THE GRENADINES**
Capital ✪
Kingstown

Major language: English
Population: 0.1 million
Area: 131 sq mi; 340 sq km
Leading export: bananas

PUERTO RICO

Capital ✪
San Juan

Major languages: Spanish
and English
Population: 3.5 million
Area: 3,515 sq mi; 9,104 sq km
Leading exports: chemicals

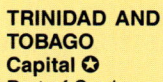

**TRINIDAD AND
TOBAGO**
Capital ✪
Port-of-Spain

Major language: English
Population: 1.3 million
Area: 1,980 sq mi; 5,130 sq km
Leading export: oil

CHAPTER 18

THE GEOGRAPHY OF THE CARIBBEAN

FOCUS

There are enormous quantities of fish here. . . . I took a boat and entered a small river at the end of a harbor. . . . I took a net with me to fish; before I reached land a fish jumped into the boat.

This is how Christopher Columbus described what it was like to go fishing in the Caribbean Sea in 1492. Today fishing is still an important part of life for the people of the Caribbean islands. In this chapter you will read about how the sea and the land shape life in this region.

READ TO LEARN

Key Vocabulary

coral

Key Places

Bahamas
Greater Antilles
Lesser Antilles

Read Aloud

. . . like nothing else on earth . . . a ribbon of turquoise lost in the midnight blue of the world's oceans . . .

This is how an astronaut soaring high above the earth described the islands known as the Bahamas. From space, the Bahamas look like tiny green jewels set in a sea of "midnight blue" water. In this lesson you will read about these and other "jewels" that make up the islands of the Caribbean Sea.

Read for Purpose

1. **WHAT YOU KNOW:** Which part of the Western Hemisphere did Christopher Columbus first see in 1492?
2. **WHAT YOU WILL LEARN:** Which three island groups are part of the Caribbean region?

THE CARIBBEAN SEA

Find the Caribbean Sea on the map on page 382. As you can see, it is set off from the Atlantic Ocean by a long, curving arc of islands. These islands are known as the Caribbean islands. They are also called the West Indies. In Chapter 10 you read that Christopher Columbus named the Caribbean islands the "Indies" because he thought that he had sailed all the way to Asia.

The Caribbean islands occupy a special location in relation to the rest of the Americas. Ships traveling through the Gulf of Mexico and the Caribbean Sea always pass near these islands. This fact has played an impor-

tant part in the history of the Caribbean islands, as you will see in the next chapter.

The Caribbean region includes three groups of islands. Each group has its own special characteristics.

THE BAHAMAS

As you read in Chapter 10, the first land Christopher Columbus saw in the Americas was an island in the Bahamas. The Bahamas are a group of islands that stretch to the south and east for 500 miles (805 km). As you can see from the map on page 382, the Bahamas mark the northern entrance to the Caribbean Sea.

The Bahamas are coral islands. They were formed slowly as skeletons of tiny sea animals built up layer by layer. These tiny sea animals are called coral. Most coral islands are small, flat, and covered with trees.

THE GREATER ANTILLES

South and west of the Bahamas is a group of large islands. When Columbus reached these islands, he thought he had arrived at the entrance to India. As a result, he named the islands the Antilles (an til′ ēz), which means "to come before."

The four islands in this group are known as the Greater Antilles. In this case, *greater* means "larger." The Greater Antilles include Cuba, Jamaica, Puerto Rico, and Hispaniola—the island that is divided into the countries of Haiti and the Dominican Republic. The largest island, Cuba, is about the size of Pennsylvania.

Millions of years ago, the modern-day Caribbean Sea was probably a dry valley. At some point the land in the valley began to sink. Waters from the Atlantic Ocean flooded the valley, forming a sea.

The islands of the Greater Antilles are made up of the mountain peaks that remained above water when the Caribbean Sea was formed. Unlike the flat coral islands of the Bahamas, the land on the Greater Antilles is rugged and mountainous.

The four islands of the Greater Antilles have towering mountains, lush

MAP SKILL: What is the tallest mountain in the Caribbean region? How tall is it, and where is it located?

CARIBBEAN: Elevation

Elevations

Feet	Meters
Above 14,000	Above 4,000
7,000	2,000
1,500	500
700	200
0	0

⊛ National capital
• Other city
▲ Mountain peak
△ Volcano

The Caribbean islands include both volcanic islands like Montserrat (*left*) and coral islands like the Bahamas (*above*).

forests, and deep harbors. The islands also have plains and valleys with rich soil for growing crops.

THE LESSER ANTILLES

South and east of the Greater Antilles are the Lesser Antilles. As their name suggests, these islands are smaller than the Greater Antilles. The Lesser Antilles stretch southward for 500 miles (805 km) from Puerto Rico toward the coast of South America.

Some of the islands in the Lesser Antilles are coral islands like the Bahamas. Many others, including Martinique (mär tə nēk′) and Montserrat, are volcanic islands.

Like the land bridge between North and South America, which you read about in Chapter 15, these volcanic islands were formed when the plates under North and South America collided against each other millions of years ago. Volcanoes pushed upward from the faults in the ocean floor and finally rose above the sea. Today most of the volcanoes on these islands are dormant, or inactive.

In 1902, however, a volcano on the island of Martinique erupted. A cloud of fiery lava and gas swiftly rolled down the side of Mount Pelée (pə lā′)

and covered the town of St. Pierre (sän pyâr). One observer later wrote:

In three minutes St. Pierre was completely devastated. . . . No one could have survived for longer than a few minutes. But for them they must have been terrible minutes.

AN ISLAND REGION

On a map, the Caribbean islands look like stepping stones linking North and South America. The islands are divided into three groups: the Bahamas, the Greater Antilles, and the Lesser Antilles. In the next lesson you will read about the climate and natural resources of these island groups.

Check Your Reading

1. What are coral islands? Name one example of a group of coral islands.
2. How are the Greater Antilles different from other islands?
3. **GEOGRAPHY SKILL:** Explain how Columbus's mistaken sense of location led to the naming of the Antilles islands.
4. **THINKING SKILL:** Compare and contrast the geography of the Bahamas with that of the Lesser Antilles.

Using Maps at Different Scales

Key Vocabulary

small-scale map
large-scale map

In this textbook you have looked at many maps. On page 227, you studied a map that showed Columbus's voyages across the Atlantic Ocean from Europe to the Americas. On page 242, you looked at another map that showed Spanish and Portuguese Viceroyalties. A map on page 296 presented a close-up look at the states of Mexico. A map of the islands of the Caribbean and their elevation is on page 382. One major difference among these maps was their scale.

As you know, most maps include a scale of distance. The scale shows how actual distances on the earth have been translated into distances on the map. Mapmakers use many different scales, depending on how much detail they want to show on a map.

Small-Scale Maps

Maps that show a large area of the earth in a small space are called small-scale maps. They use a small measure, such as an inch, to stand for a large distance, such as 1,000 miles. The map of Puerto Rico on this page (**Map A**) is a small-scale map.

As you can see, if you use your ruler, 1 inch stands for 25 miles. Two centimeters stand for 25 kilometers.

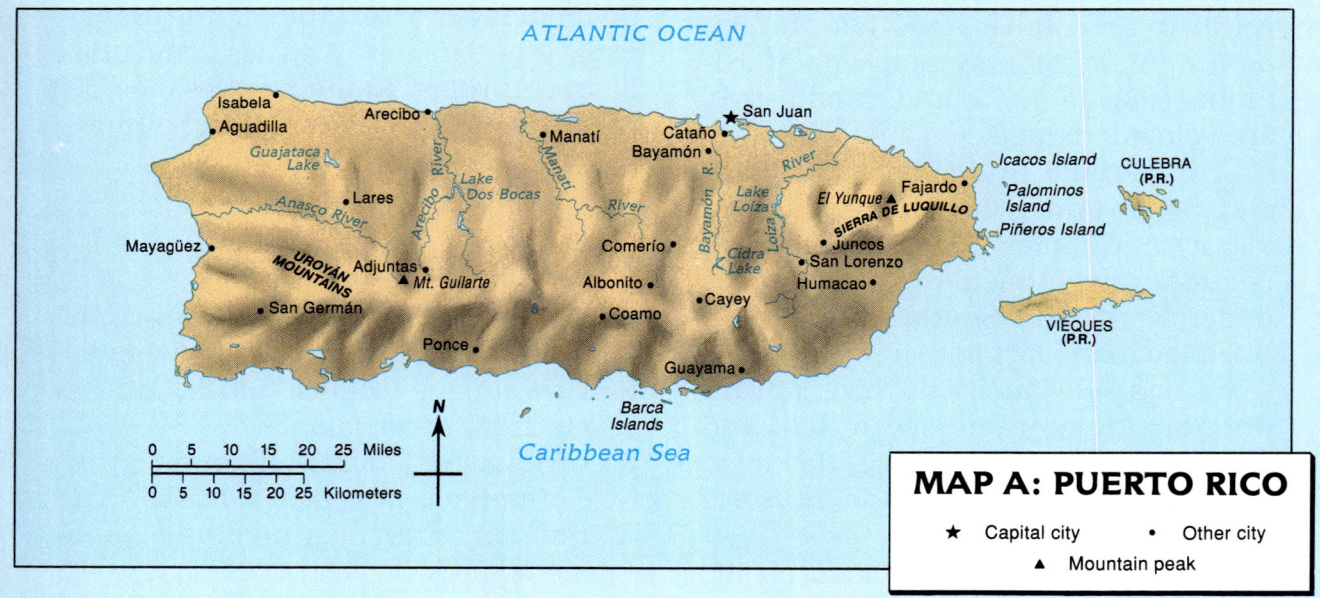

MAP A: PUERTO RICO
★ Capital city • Other city ▲ Mountain peak

Using a small-scale map can be helpful when you want to get a general idea about a place. For example, notice how **Map A** shows the major cities in Puerto Rico, as well as its important rivers and other physical features.

Large-Scale Maps

Suppose that you want a more detailed view of a place—for example, you want a closer look at San Juan, the capital of Puerto Rico. Then you could use a **large-scale map**. Large-scale maps generally show small parts of the earth in a fairly large space. On a large-scale map, 1 inch would stand for a smaller distance than it would on a small-scale map. **Map B** is an example of a large-scale map. What does 1 inch stand for on **Map B**? What do 2 centimeters stand for?

Because it is a large-scale map, **Map B** is able to show more detail than **Map A** does. Compare the two maps. Notice that **Map B** shows a number of streets in San Juan. It also shows some sights of interest, such as the Castillo El Morro.

The city of San Juan appears larger on **Map B** than it does on **Map A**. Notice on **Map B** that the entire distance across San Juan is only a little more than 10 miles (18.8 km). The distance covered by the whole island of Puerto Rico on **Map A** is more than 100 miles (135 km). Remember that even though maps can be drawn to different scales, actual distances on the earth do not change.

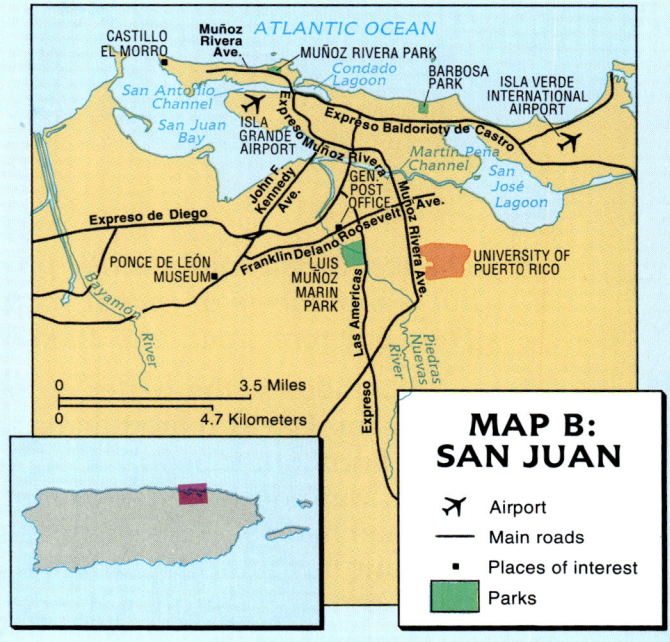

MAP B: SAN JUAN

- ✈ Airport
- — Main roads
- ▪ Places of interest
- ▮ Parks

Reviewing the Skill

1. What is a small-scale map? What is a large-scale map?
2. From which map, **Map A** or **Map B**, could you learn the names of major cities in Puerto Rico?
3. Which map, **Map A** or **Map B**, shows more details of San Juan?
4. Describe the location of San Juan in Puerto Rico. Which map did you use to find the answer?
5. Name two airports in Puerto Rico. Which map did you use to find the answer? Explain.
6. How can it be helpful to use maps drawn at different scales?

2 Climate and Resources

READ TO LEARN

Key Vocabulary

trade winds   leeward
windward

Key Places

Grenada

Read Aloud

The air turned into a milky green swirl of mud, water, coco-nuts, and sheets of [metal roofing] like flying razor blades. Then our roof went, and I knew we were dead.

Miraculously, the writer of these words did not die when Hurricane David roared across the island of Dominica in 1979. Forty other people died, however, and thousands of homes were destroyed. Coconut palms were snapped in two like matchsticks. For most of the year, Caribbean weather is pleasant day after day. In late summer and fall, though, hurri-canes can bring sudden danger and destruction.

Read for Purpose

1. **WHAT YOU KNOW:** What types of weather do you experience in your community during the course of the year?
2. **WHAT YOU WILL LEARN:** How do the trade winds affect life in the Caribbean region?

THE TRADE WINDS

The temperature of the Caribbean islands changes little throughout the year because of their tropical latitude. In Jamaica, for example, the average temperature in July is 81°F. (27°C). In February it is 76°F. (24°C). Imagine what it would be like to live in a place where it is warm enough to wear shorts all year long!

The tropical heat in the Caribbean region is eased by steady breezes that blow across the Caribbean Sea day and night. These breezes are known as the trade winds. The trade winds begin over the Atlantic Ocean and blow to-ward the west most of the year.

As well as cooling the islands, the trade winds have had other effects on geography. Over many years, the trade winds helped the seeds of plants from distant lands to drift across the Atlan-tic Ocean. Some washed up on Carib-bean beaches and took root. One of the plants brought by the trade winds from Africa was the coconut palm. You can see a picture of this tree on page 389.

Today palms provide welcome shade on Caribbean beaches. Some islanders use palm branches to make roofs for their houses. They weave the leaves into baskets. They eat the coconut fruit or press it to get cooking oil. They also burn the coconut shell for fuel. You can see why islanders call the coconut palm "the tree of life."

THE RAINY SEASON

The trade winds not only bring cooling breezes and useful plants to the Caribbean. They also provide islanders with the rain they need to live.

Look at the diagram on this page. It shows how the trade winds bring rain to the Caribbean. As the trade winds blow across the Atlantic Ocean, they pick up moisture and form rain clouds. When these clouds come into contact with the higher elevation of island land, they rise, cool, and drop their moisture as rain.

The trade winds blow against the north and east coasts of the Caribbean islands. These coasts are known as windward coasts. They are usually fertile and green because they receive so much rain.

Coasts sheltered from trade winds are called leeward coasts. They receive much less rain than windward coasts. The windward coast of Haiti, for example, receives about 100 inches (254 cm) of rainfall each year. On Haiti's leeward coast, only about 20 inches (51 cm) of rain fall each year.

HOWLING GIANTS

In the late summertime, the trade winds bring hurricanes to the Caribbean region. The Taino (tä ē′ nō) Indians of Puerto Rico believed these storms were caused by an evil god named Juracan (hür′ ä kän). It was Juracan, they said, who darkened the

DIAGRAM SKILL: Leeward coasts are drier than windward coasts. According to the diagram, why is there more rainfall on windward coasts?

TRADE WINDS IN THE CARIBBEAN

Rain

Trade Winds

Windward Side (wet)

Leeward Side (dry)

sky and brought the terrifying winds. The English word *hurricane* comes from the name Juracan.

Most hurricanes begin as tropical storms near the west coast of Africa. As the trade winds push these storms westward across the Atlantic Ocean, some storms blow themselves out. But other storms grow into howling giants. The largest hurricanes measure 500 miles (805 km) across. Their fierce, swirling winds whip up the sea into mountainous waves.

Almost every year, at least one island in the Caribbean region is struck by a hurricane. The wind hits the land like a giant fist, flattening homes and trees. Blinding rains flush crops and villages down hillsides. Huge waves smash against the shores. Towering walls of seawater flood coastal towns. Recovering from such a storm can take years.

The roofs of these houses in the Caribbean region were blown off by a hurricane.

Some islands are rarely hit by hurricanes. As the people of **Grenada** learned in 1955, however, no island is completely safe. That summer Hurricane Janet struck this island in the Lesser Antilles, killing 137 people. "Grenada looked like a plucked chicken," reported one survivor. Another recalled that:

> *Many roofs from the houses on the slope below ended in our yard. People kept coming by asking if I had "seen a red roof," or "a green roof," and I'd say to go look, we had plenty to choose from!*

NATURAL RESOURCES

When Columbus first landed in the Bahamas, he saw gold jewelry on the people living there. "Without a doubt," he wrote, "there is in these lands a vast quantity of gold." These words set off a

Sugarcane and the coconut palm are both products of the Caribbean's fertile soil. People make sugar from sugarcane and baskets from palm leaves.

gold rush to the Caribbean region. Spanish treasure hunters searched the islands for precious metals. To their sorrow, they found almost nothing worth mining.

Most of the Caribbean islands are poor in minerals. The exception is Jamaica, which has large bauxite (bôk′ sīt) deposits. Bauxite is the ore from which aluminum is made.

The most valuable resource in the Caribbean is the fertile soil found on many islands. Farmers grow corn, beans, peanuts, potatoes, peppers, and tobacco in this soil. Sugarcane, coffee, and spices such as nutmeg and vanilla also grow well in this region.

The sea is another important resource. Both the Atlantic Ocean and the Caribbean Sea are good sources of fish and shellfish.

SUNSHINE AND RAIN

You have read that the Caribbean region is blessed with a warm climate and trade winds that bring much rainfall to the region. Aside from its climate, its rich soil, and the sea, however, most Caribbean islands are poor in natural resources. In the next chapter, you will see how these facts have shaped the history of the Caribbean region.

Check Your Reading

1. Why are the trade winds important to the Caribbean islands?
2. Where does the word *hurricane* come from, and what is the story behind that word?
3. GEOGRAPHY SKILL: How does the leeward coast of an island differ from the windward coast?
4. THINKING SKILL: Name three ways in which the coconut palm affects life in the Caribbean region.

IDEAS TO REMEMBER

■ Three island chains make up the West Indies in the Caribbean Sea—the Bahamas, the Greater Antilles, and the Lesser Antilles.

■ The West Indies are blessed with a warm climate, rainfall borne by trade winds, sunshine, fertile soil, and the sea, although they are poor in mineral resources.

REVIEWING VOCABULARY

coral   trade winds
leeward   windward

Number a sheet of paper from 1 to 5. Beside each number write the word or term from the list above that best matches the statement or definition. One of the words is used more than once.

1. Tiny sea animals that, layer by layer, can build up into islands
2. Steady breezes that blow off the Atlantic Ocean westward across the Caribbean Sea
3. Coasts that are fully open to the effects of the steady westward-blowing breezes over the Caribbean
4. Coasts that are sheltered from the westward-blowing breezes
5. These helped the seeds of plants drift across the Atlantic Ocean

REVIEWING FACTS

1. Where is the Caribbean Sea in relation to North and South America?
2. The Caribbean island groups form a long, curving arc. Describe the order in which the island groups form this arc, from north to east to south.
3. How do the Greater Antilles differ from the Bahamas and the Lesser Antilles in the way in which they were formed?
4. Name the four islands of the Greater Antilles.
5. What part did plate movements in the earth play in the origin of the volcanic Caribbean islands?
6. Why do temperatures on the Caribbean islands change little over the course of a year?
7. Name four uses that islanders make of the coconut palm.
8. Why are the windward coasts in the Caribbean likely to be greener than the leeward coasts?
9. How do hurricane winds affect the sea? How do they affect the land?
10. How rich in mineral resources are the islands of the Caribbean? Which island is an exception?

WRITING ABOUT MAIN IDEAS

1. **Writing Directions:** Imagine that you are going to sail from Florida to Jamaica. Write a letter to a friend describing the directions you are going to follow on your sail.
2. **Writing a Postcard:** Make a postcard that shows a Caribbean landscape on one side, either drawn by you or cut from a newspaper or magazine. On the other side, write a message describing what you saw on your visit there and address it to a friend or relative.

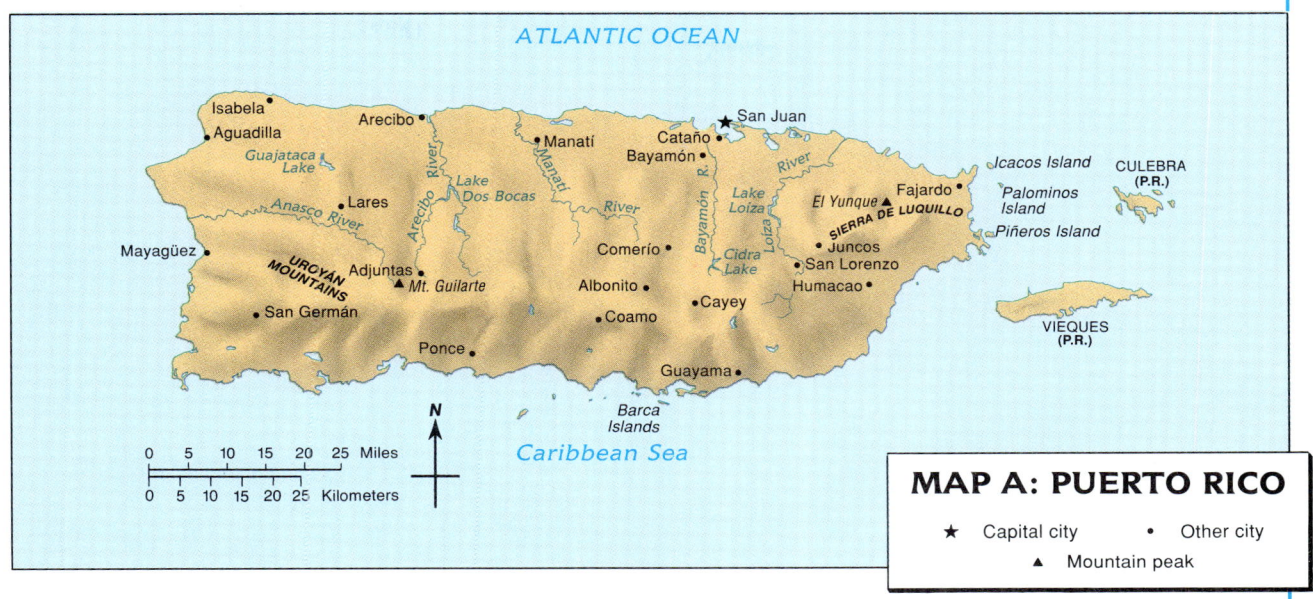

MAP A: PUERTO RICO

★ Capital city   • Other city
▲ Mountain peak

3. **Writing a Travel Brochure:** Pretend that you work for the Caribbean Tourist Board. Write a travel brochure in which you describe geographic features that would attract tourists.

4. **Writing About Perspectives:** Pretend that you lived in Martinique and were one of the two people who survived when the Mount Pelée volcano erupted in 1902. Everyone is asking you to describe what your experience was like, so you decide to write it down.

BUILDING SKILLS: USING MAPS AT DIFFERENT SCALES

Use the maps above and on the right to answer the following questions.

1. What does a map scale tell you?
2. Would you use **Map A** or **Map B** to locate the University of Puerto Rico?
3. How do small-scale and large-scale maps differ in what they can show?

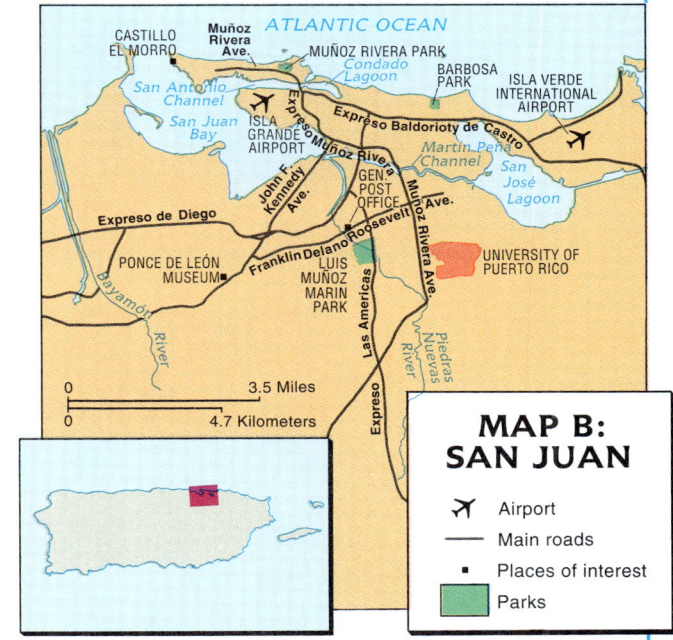

MAP B: SAN JUAN

✈ Airport
— Main roads
▪ Places of interest
▇ Parks

4. How do mapmakers decide what scale to use on a map?
5. Why is it important to be able to use maps of different scales?

CHAPTER 19

THE HISTORY OF THE CARIBBEAN

FOCUS

The Citadel symbolized [the ruler of Haiti's] determination to keep Haiti free.

The Citadel (sit' ə del) in Haiti is the largest fortress in the Western Hemisphere. It was built in the early 1800s to protect the newly independent country from invaders. In this chapter you will read why, as writer Charles Cobb put it, the ruler of Haiti was so determined "to keep Haiti free."

1 From Slavery to Freedom

READ TO LEARN

Key Vocabulary

emancipate

Key People

Toussaint L'Ouverture
Jean-Jacques Dessalines

Key Places

Haiti

Read Aloud

I want Liberty and Equality to reign. I work to bring them into existence. Unite yourselves to us brothers and fight for the same cause.

With these words a Haitian called on the people of Haiti in 1791 to fight for their freedom. In this lesson you will read about this leader and other people of the Caribbean region who fought to regain their freedom.

Read for Purpose

1. **WHAT YOU KNOW:** What did the Spanish hope to find when they colonized the Caribbean?
2. **WHAT YOU WILL LEARN:** How did sugarcane change life in the Caribbean region?

THE FIRST SETTLERS

People had been living and working in the Caribbean region for hundreds of years before Christopher Columbus and his sailors arrived in 1492. One group of people was called the Arawak (ar' ə wak). These people had migrated to the Caribbean islands from South America around 400 B.C.

The Arawak lived by farming and fishing. They planted crops in the rich soil of the Greater Antilles, and caught fish and shellfish in the clear waters of the Caribbean Sea. They slept in *hamacas*, or hammocks.

In time, another group of people moved into the Caribbean region.

These people were hunters known as the Carib (kar' ib). The Caribbean Sea is named after them.

THE EUROPEANS ARRIVE

When Columbus arrived in the Caribbean region in October 1492, he was greeted by Arawak people bearing gifts of parrots, spears, and cotton cloth. The Arawak were even more generous when Columbus's ship the *Santa María* ran aground off the shore of present-day Haiti on Christmas Eve. They helped Columbus and his sailors to bring the ship's goods ashore and let the crew rest in the Arawak village.

393

Arawak women used stone dishes and clay bowls like these to prepare food. Wooden rattles (*left*) were favorite Arawak musical instruments.

Columbus left 39 men there to build a fort and look for gold on the islands, and he sailed back to Europe. What happened next is unknown. Columbus returned the next year to find the burned ruins of a fort and all of his men dead. This was the beginning of tense relations between Europe and the Americas—the clash of two cultures.

A PEOPLE DESTROYED

Despite these tense relations, treasure seekers from Spain were soon flocking to the Americas. You have already read about Hernando Cortés and conquistadors who traveled to Mexico looking for gold. After they had defeated the Aztecs, the Spaniards began shipping the fabulous riches of Mexico east to Spain. Pirates began to rob these ships as they sailed through the Caribbean islands. To protect its important shipping lanes, Spain built fortresses on the Greater Antilles.

During this time the Spanish enslaved the Arawak and forced them to build settlements for the Spanish. Those who fought back were killed. In just a few years the Arawak were destroyed by the Europeans whom they had once welcomed to their lands.

Other European countries moved in to build colonies in the Caribbean. By the 1600s France, England, and the Netherlands had established colonies in the Carib people's territory as well. The map on page 395 shows the location of each country's colonies.

Some countries used their Caribbean colonies as bases for raids against Spanish ships. Others looked for a crop that would turn the Caribbean sun and soil into profit. The crop that fulfilled this wish was sugarcane.

SUGARCANE AND SLAVERY

On his second journey to the Americas, Columbus brought the first stalk of sugarcane from Spain to the Caribbean region. This reedlike plant, originally from India, would forever change life on the Caribbean islands.

Sugarcane grew well on most of the islands. The warm climate and the rich soil of the Caribbean islands were perfect for growing it. Europeans loved the sweet taste of sugar and were willing to pay almost any price for it. Caribbean planters saw this as their golden opportunity to make a fortune.

Sugarcane was raised on large plantations, each with its own sugar mill. Sugarcane required a great deal of work to grow, harvest, and process into sugar. The European planters, not wanting to work so hard themselves, first used the Arawak as laborers. After the Arawak were killed by disease and overwork, the planters turned to Africa for new workers.

Millions of Africans were brought by force to the Caribbean by European colonists between the 1600s and 1800s. These enslaved Africans turned the Caribbean into thriving, wealthy colonies. So much wealth flowed from these colonies that they were called the "jewels of empire."

CARIBBEAN SOCIETY

Slavery and the plantation system created a troubled society in the Caribbean. At the top of this society were a few wealthy planters. Below the planters were small groups of "poor whites." Some were merchants or government officials. Others were managers who ran the plantations for the planters.

Still lower in Caribbean society were the mulattoes. Many had been freed by their owners. But although free, they were not considered equal with whites.

At the bottom of society were the enslaved Africans, who vastly outnumbered whites. They were overworked, underfed, and brutally treated. Half of all enslaved children died before reaching the age of ten. Adults were literally worked to death.

MAP SKILL: Which islands were colonies of Spain in the early 1800s?

COLONIES OF THE CARIBBEAN: Early 1800s

- Spanish
- Dutch
- French
- British

REBELLIONS AGAINST SLAVERY

Imagine that you have been taken by force from your family and sold to someone in a strange land. Your new life offers you little but hard work and sorrow. What would you do?

Some Caribbean captives responded to this question by running away into the mountains. Others joined together and rebelled against slavery.

The greatest rebellion broke out in the French colony of Haiti. One August night in 1791, enslaved Haitians attacked their owners shouting, "Better to die than be slaves." Two months later, 2,000 people were dead and 180 plantations had become mounds of ashes.

THE HAITIAN REVOLUTION

Toussaint L'Ouverture (tü sant' lü vər tür'), a Haitian soldier, shaped the rebels into a strong army. This army conquered all of Hispaniola and named Toussaint its ruler. His first act was to emancipate, or free, all enslaved islanders.

These actions angered the ruler of France, Napoleon Bonaparte. In 1802 Napoleon sent a large force of French troops to Hispaniola. Their leader, Charles Leclerc, had orders to recapture the island and return the Haitians to slavery.

Plantation life was brutal for enslaved people in the Caribbean. Chains were used to imprison them. Abandoned sugar plantations can still be seen in the Caribbean today.

The Granger Collection

The Granger Collection

Leclerc soon captured Toussaint and sent him to France. As he left Haiti, Toussaint warned:

In overthrowing me, you have cut down only the trunk of the tree of black liberty. It will spring up again by the roots, for they are many and deep.

Haiti's great emancipator died alone in a French prison in 1803.

The roots of black liberty were many and deep. Former slaves led by **Jean-Jacques Dessalines** (zhän zhäk de sä lēn') fought hard against the French. In 1804 Napoleon admitted defeat. Haiti became the first colony in Latin America to gain independence.

THE END OF SLAVERY

In the early 1800s, a movement to end slavery began to spread across Europe. Its leaders called slavery a crime against humanity and worked hard to destroy it. The revolution in Haiti added great weight to their words.

The first support for ending slavery came from Great Britain. In 1833 the British government banned slavery in its colonies. France emancipated its enslaved people in 1848 as did the Netherlands in 1863. Spain was the last to act. Slavery ended in Spanish Cuba in 1886.

The emancipated captives fled the sugarcane plantations. Most struggled to get their own piece of land to farm. Others worked in towns. Life was hard, but at least they were free at last.

CARIBBEAN COLONIES

Columbus's arrival in the Bahamas in 1492 brought many important changes to life in the Caribbean. You

The Granger Collection

Toussaint L'Ouverture (*above*) **emancipated** the slaves of Hispaniola. Jean-Jacques Dessalines (*right*) led Haiti's people to victory over the French.

read how it brought about the destruction of the Arawak people. It paved the way for the enslavement of millions of Africans. Haiti's independence in 1804 brought a ray of hope to a troubled region. As you will read, however, the end of slavery did not necessarily mean the end of colonial rule.

Check Your Reading

1. Who were the Arawak?
2. Why were Africans brought by force to the Caribbean?
3. How was society in the Caribbean organized?
4. Name two ways in which sugarcane affected life in the Caribbean.
5. **THINKING SKILL:** Express in your own words Toussaint L'Ouverture's point of view regarding his capture and Haiti's fight for freedom.

CRAFTS
OF · THE · PAST
TODAY

Ada Balcácer lives in Santo Domingo, the capital of the Dominican Republic. As you read in Lesson 1, many groups played a role in the history of the Caribbean and in the creation of Caribbean culture. Ada is an artist who is proud of her country's heritage of Indian, European, and African cultures. But she worried that the younger people were losing touch with the traditions and crafts of the past. As a volunteer in a poor section of the city, she was also concerned about the lack of jobs for women.

Ada's two concerns came together in 1976 when she was asked to give a speech to a group of poor women. She said, "These women are tired of speeches. Why don't we teach them something so they can earn a living?"

That was the beginning of *Women in Industry*, Ada's program to teach women how to make traditional crafts for modern markets. Her plan was to teach skills to a small group of women, who would train other women, who would in turn train still more women. First she designed jewelry, dolls, masks, and pottery, all of which could be made from local materials. Using themes about the Dominican Republic, she created beautiful fabrics to be made into clothing. She taught her first class of nine women how to make these things to sell. Then they each brought five more women into the program.

Ada ran the program for its first ten years. Determined to see her project succeed, she worked many hours each week. By 1983 *Women in Industry* had grown to 545 members. As small groups of trained women left the original centers to open their own businesses, new students took their places. By 1990 Ada could look with pride at thriving businesses run by women who had once had neither skills nor hope. Ada is counting on these women to pass on not only their skills but a new awareness and appreciation of their cultural heritage to the younger women.

Because one of her former students now runs *Women in Industry*, Ada can finally devote more time to her own art. She'll continue helping others, of course. Ada says:

I will never be satisfied just working for myself. Never. I have to work for myself and others. I feel it is the only way to be happy.

2 The Road to Independence

Key Vocabulary

exile
autonomy

Key People

Ramon Betances
Antonio Maceo
José Martí
François Duvalier
Jean-Claude Duvalier
Mary Eugenia Charles

Key Places

Dominican Republic
Puerto Rico
Cuba

Read Aloud

By agreement with [Cuban] generals . . . José Martí gives the order to rise [revolt]. The order travels from . . . Florida and reaches Cuba concealed within a Havana cigar.

Author Eduardo Galeano describes this moment in 1895. Cubans wait impatiently for their hero, José Martí, to return from Florida and lead them to freedom from Spain. Then his secret message arrives. Finally, the time to revolt has come! In this lesson you will read more about Martí and Cuba's struggle for independence.

Read for Purpose

1. WHAT YOU KNOW: What was the first Caribbean colony to become independent?
2. WHAT YOU WILL LEARN: How did other colonies in the Caribbean win their independence?

REVOLUTION!

In Lesson 1 you read about Haiti's successful fight for independence in the early 1800s. Calls for independence soon rang out throughout the Caribbean region.

The second colony to take up the call of revolution was Santo Domingo. In 1821 people in Santo Domingo declared their independence from Spain. The following year, however, they were conquered by their Haitian neighbors. For the next 22 years Santo Domingo was ruled by Haiti. In 1844 Santo Domingo revolted against Haitian rule and became an independent country called the **Dominican Republic**.

In nearby **Puerto Rico** the fight for independence was unsuccessful. It was led by a doctor named **Ramon Betances** (rä món′ be tän′ ses). On a warm September night in 1868, he led

Antonio Maceo (*top*) and José Martí (*below*) led the Cuban struggle for freedom from Spain during the late 1800s.

to be independent of Spain. They called on other enslaved people and free Cubans to join their army.

Within a month their army numbered 12,000 troops. Spain responded by sending thousands of troops to the capital city of Havana. The ten-year war that followed was one of the bloodiest in Latin America's history.

Cuba's army was led by a Cuban soldier named **Antonio Maceo** (mä sä′ ō). He wore down the Spanish with quick hit-and-run attacks. Between raids, Maceo and his troops hid in the mountains of eastern Cuba.

Finally, in 1878, Spain promised to improve the government of Cuba and gradually end slavery. Many war-weary colonists agreed to stop fighting. Others, however, held onto their dream of an independent Cuba. Antonio Maceo was one of them. He chose to move to Jamaica rather than continue to live under Spanish rule.

"FREE CUBA"

The dream of *Cuba libre* (lē′ brā), or "free Cuba," was kept alive by a famous poet and patriot named **José Martí** (hō sā′ mär tē′).

In 1879 Martí was **exiled** from Cuba. *Exile* means "to send away by law." He went to the United States and quickly plunged into the task of organizing a new revolution.

Martí returned from exile with Antonio Maceo in 1895. The word spread like wildfire. "Martí is here. Long live Cuba libre!" Thousands of Cubans left their homes to join the revolution.

Once again, fighting broke out in Cuba. This time Spain sent 200,000 troops to Cuba. Their instructions were to crush the rebellion at any cost. Both Maceo and Martí were killed early in

hundreds of Puerto Ricans in a rebellion against Spanish rule. Their flag had the words, "Liberty or Death. Long Live Free Puerto Rico."

The Spanish governor of Puerto Rico viewed the rebellion as "tomfoolery." His troops crushed the uprising.

THE TEN YEARS' WAR

One month after Puerto Rico's struggle, planters in **Cuba** revolted. They were angry because taxes were soaring, Spain's government was corrupt, and they, as colonists, had no voice in the government that ruled them.

On October 10, 1868, a group of planters led by Carlos Manuel de Céspedes (dā ses pe′ des) freed their enslaved workers and declared Cuba

the fighting. Thousands of other Cubans were put into prison camps. There they died of hunger and disease. Around the world, people were outraged by Spain's cruelty.

THE SPANISH-AMERICAN WAR

Leaders in the United States watched closely as the war in Cuba continued. They were worried about United States property in Cuba that was worth millions of dollars.

On February 15, 1898, a United States battleship, the *Maine*, mysteriously exploded in Havana Harbor and 260 crew members were killed. Many people in the United States blamed Spain and cried out for revenge. Amid shouts of "Remember the *Maine*," the United States declared war on Spain.

The Spanish-American War lasted only four months. A defeated Spain signed a treaty with the United States giving it control over Cuba and Puerto Rico. You will read about the United States' relationship with Cuba and Puerto Rico in the next chapter.

UNITED STATES TROOPS IN THE CARIBBEAN

At the time of the Spanish-American War, the governments of Haiti, the Dominican Republic, and Cuba were not meeting the needs of their people. Centuries of slavery and colonial rule had left these islands unprepared for democratic self-government.

The United States was concerned about the unstable political conditions on these islands. It was also concerned about its business interests in the Caribbean. Between 1906 and 1934, United States troops were sent to occupy Cuba, the Dominican Republic, and Haiti. Most of the people in these countries resented the presence of these "Yankee" troops.

THE DICTATORS

After the United States soldiers left, dictators took control of Cuba, the Dominican Republic, and Haiti. These rulers denied people the right to have a say in government and stole money from their countries' treasuries.

One of the most feared dictators in the Caribbean was François Duvalier (frän swä′ dü väl yā′), who took over Haiti in 1957. Duvalier ruled through terror. His special police, the *Tonton Macoutes* (ton ton mä küt′), murdered all those who opposed him.

United States newspapers questioned Spain's role in the explosion of the *Maine* in Havana Harbor.

The Granger Collection

CHART SKILL: These women of Antigua and Barbuda are celebrating Independence Day. When did their country become independent?

INDEPENDENCE IN THE CARIBBEAN

Country	Year of Independence
Haiti	1804
Dominican Republic	1844
Cuba	1902
Jamaica	1962
Trinidad and Tobago	1962
Barbados	1966
Bahamas	1973
Grenada	1974
Dominica	1978
St. Lucia	1979
St. Vincent and the Grenadines	1979
Antigua and Barbuda	1981
St. Kitts and Nevis	1983

When Duvalier died in 1971, power was passed to his son **Jean-Claude** (zhän klod) **Duvalier**. Jean-Claude was driven out of power in 1986. He left Haiti the poorest country in the Western Hemisphere. In late 1990, Jean-Bertrand Aristide (ä ris teed′) was elected president in the country's first free elections. On September 30, 1991, a military coup ousted Aristide. The struggle for stability continues in Haiti.

THE END OF COLONIAL RULE

While countries in the Greater Antilles struggled with rule by dictators, other islands were finding ways to end colonial rule. In 1946 the people of Guadeloupe and Martinique voted to become part of France. Dominica gained **autonomy**, or the right of self-government, from Britain in 1978. **Mary Eugenia Charles** has led this island nation since 1980. In 1990 she was elected for her third term of office.

The chart on this page shows you which Caribbean islands voted to become independent nations.

A SEA OF MANY NATIONS

You have read that a wave of independence movements swept through the Caribbean in the early 1800s. Some colonies were able to achieve independence at that time. For others, independence would be achieved only after painful struggles. Today, the Caribbean region has become a sea of many independent nations.

 Check Your Reading

1. What caused the Ten Years' War?
2. Why is José Martí a hero in Cuba?
3. In what ways did the Duvaliers cause harm to Haiti?
4. **THINKING SKILL:** Identify three sources to check the accuracy of the statement, "Many people in the United States blamed Spain for the *Maine* explosion." Tell why these sources would be useful.

Writing a Summary

Key Vocabulary

summary
topic sentence

You have just read about many people and events in the history of the Caribbean. How can you remember such a variety of interesting information?

Identifying What Is Important

One way to keep track of information is to write a short summary. A summary is a few sentences telling the main ideas in a piece of writing.

There are several steps to follow to write a good summary. You start by reading through the material about which you will write the summary. Then, as you reread each paragraph, look for the topic sentence. The topic sentence states the main idea. The other sentences give details that support the main idea. When you have found the topic sentence, write down the main idea that it expresses.

Often a topic sentence is found at the beginning of a paragraph. In other paragraphs, though, it might appear in the middle or even at the end, summing up the supporting information. Wherever it appears, however, it states the main idea of the paragraph.

Summarizing the Lesson

Suppose you wanted to write a summary of Lesson 2 in this chapter. You can tell from its title that it is about the road to independence in the Caribbean. Notice the main headings that are printed in bold

type. These headings give you an idea about main topics covered in the lesson.

First, read through the lesson. Then go back to the beginning and reread each paragraph. Identify the topic sentence of each paragraph and write it down.

Look at the first paragraph under the bold heading **Revolution!** on page 399. The paragraph is about Caribbean independence. In this example the topic sentence can be found at the end of the paragraph. It says, "Calls for independence soon rang out throughout the Caribbean region." Now try the next paragraph yourself. What is the topic sentence? Write it down. It is the main idea of the paragraph.

When you have identified the main idea of each paragraph, you will be ready to write a summary of the material you have read.

Reviewing the Skill

Read the paragraph below and then write a summary in two or three sentences.

After Hurricane Gilbert finished howling and hammering Jamaica last Monday, the lovely green-and-gold island had been transformed [changed] into a strew of twisted, tilted, ripped and battered debris [rubbish]. Kingston and outlying areas alike were an immense litter of downed trees, broken utility poles, tangles of electrical wires, a vista of demolished houses and blown tin roofs....Of the 2½ million inhabitants, 500,000 were suddenly homeless; four-fifths of the nations' homes had been damaged or destroyed. Obstructions blocked and sealed off streets and roads. Said Prime Minister Edward P.G. Seaga: "It's the worst natural disaster in our modern history. The storm has left a trail of wreckage the length of the island."

IMPORTANT EVENTS

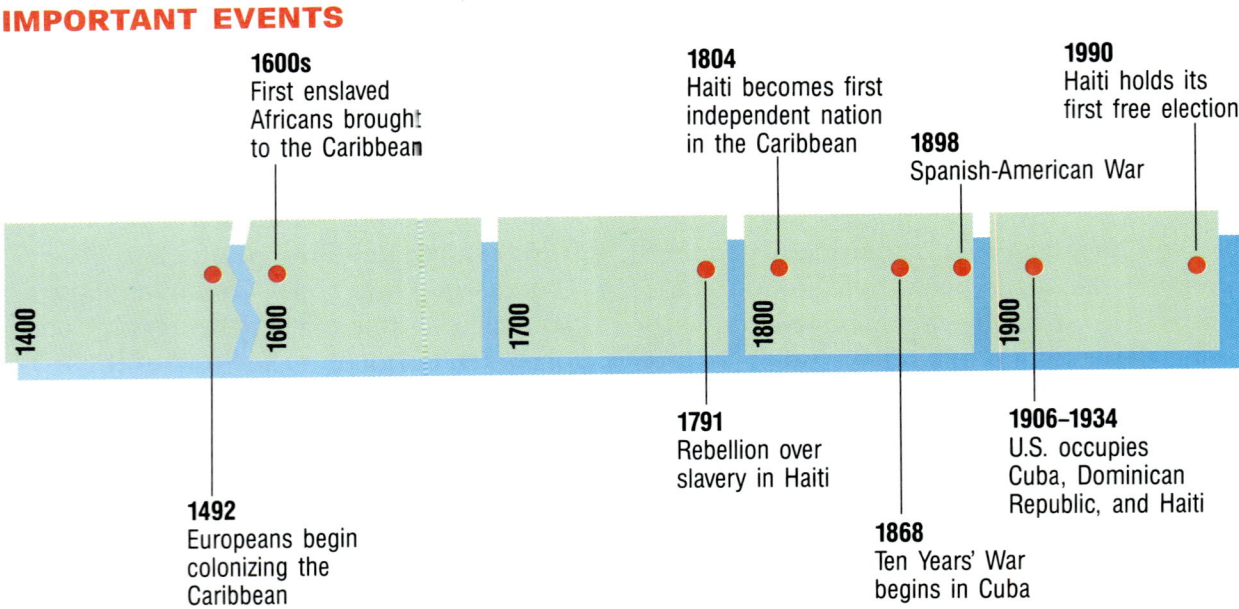

1600s
First enslaved
Africans brought
to the Caribbean

1804
Haiti becomes first
independent nation
in the Caribbean

1898
Spanish-American War

1990
Haiti holds its
first free election

1400

1600

1700

1800

1900

1492
Europeans begin
colonizing the
Caribbean

1791
Rebellion over
slavery in Haiti

1868
Ten Years' War
begins in Cuba

1906–1934
U.S. occupies
Cuba, Dominican
Republic, and Haiti

PEOPLE TO KNOW

Toussaint L'Ouverture about 1743–1803

Jean-Jacques Dessalines 1758?–1806

José Martí 1853–1895

Ramon Betances 1827–1898

François Duvalier 1907–1901

Jean-Claude Duvalier 1951–

Mary Eugenia Charles 1919–

IDEAS TO REMEMBER

■ Columbus's arrival in the Caribbean
began an era of European colonization,
the destruction of the Indians, and the
enslavement of Africans.

■ The people of the Caribbean underwent
almost 200 years of struggle to achieve
freedom and political independence.

REVIEWING VOCABULARY

autonomy   exile
emancipate

Number a sheet of paper from 1 to 5. Beside each number write the word from the list above that best completes the sentence. Some of the words are used more than once.

1. When Caribbean peoples won the right to self-government, they had achieved ____.

2. Haitians, led by Jean-Jacques Dessalines, fought for ____ from the French in 1803.

3. José Martí went to the United States in 1879 because of his ____ from Cuba.

4. To send people forcibly from their native land and forbid them to return is to ____ them.

5. To free enslaved people is to ____ them.

REVIEWING FACTS

1. Describe two major effects that sugarcane had on life in the Caribbean islands.

2. Identify the four social classes in early Caribbean society and rank them from the highest to the lowest.

3. Give three examples of revolutions that have taken place in the countries of the Caribbean region.

4. Name three trials that Cuba has had to undergo in its troubled history.

5. Contrast the type of government chosen by Guadeloupe and Martinique with the type of government chosen by the island of Dominica.

WRITING ABOUT MAIN IDEAS

1. **Writing a News Story:** Imagine that you are a war correspondent sent to cover the Ten Years' War in Cuba. Write a news story in which you answer the journalist's five *W* questions: Who? What? When? Where? Why?

2. **Writing About Perspectives:** Imagine you are José Martí. Tell how you would feel about the presence of United States troops in Cuba between 1906 and 1934.

BUILDING SKILLS: WRITING A SUMMARY

Write a summary of the following paragraph. Your summary should be only one sentence.

Columbus was thoroughly enraptured by Hispaniola after landing there. He wrote a long letter to a friend describing its attractions. It was rich in spices and in gold, he said. Its people were kind and gentle. And of its mountains, he wrote: "All are most beautiful, of a thousand shapes...and filled with trees of a thousand kinds and tall, and they seem to touch the sky...."

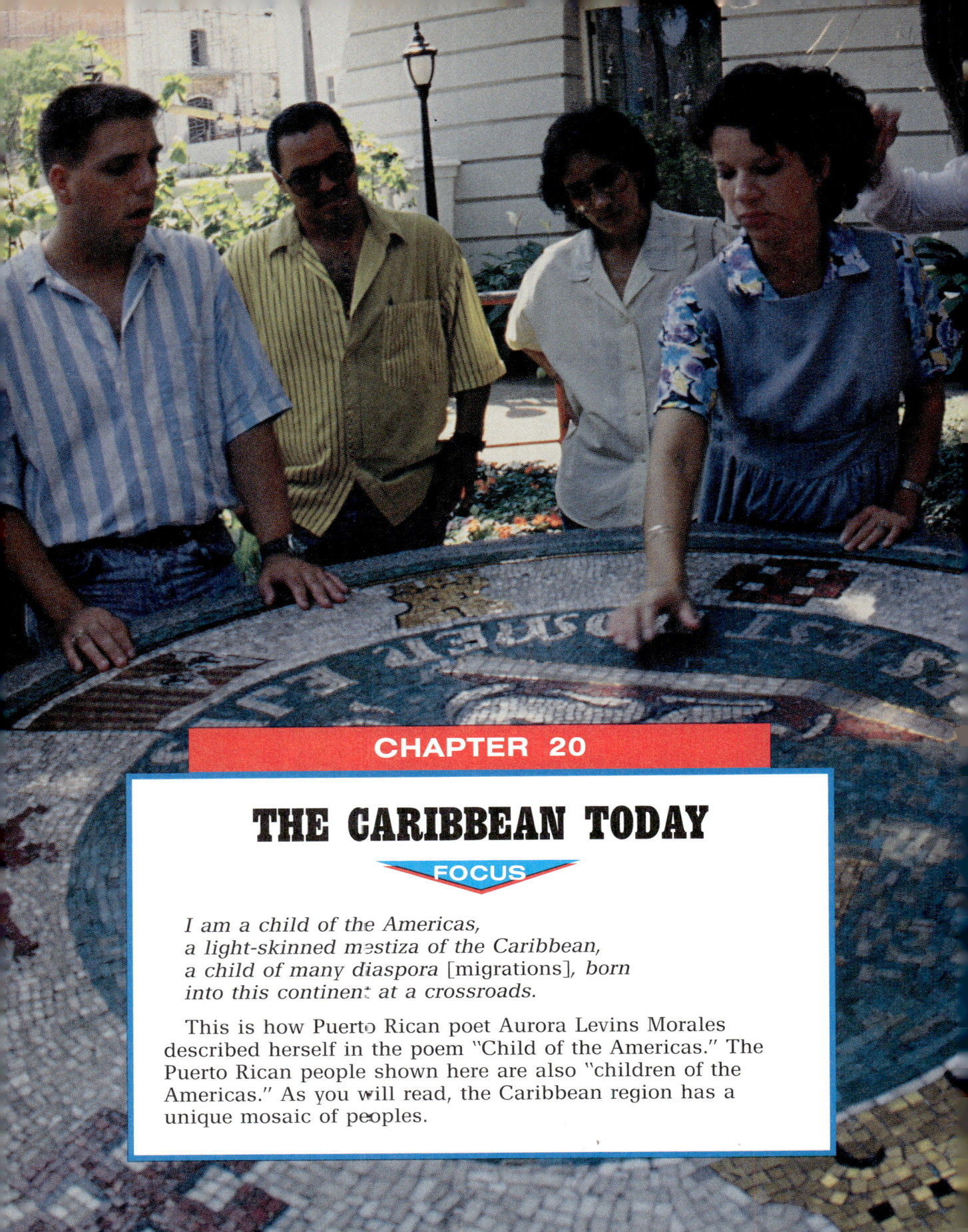

CHAPTER 20

THE CARIBBEAN TODAY

FOCUS

I am a child of the Americas,
a light-skinned mestiza of the Caribbean,
a child of many diaspora [migrations], *born*
into this continent at a crossroads.

This is how Puerto Rican poet Aurora Levins Morales described herself in the poem "Child of the Americas." The Puerto Rican people shown here are also "children of the Americas." As you will read, the Caribbean region has a unique mosaic of peoples.

1 People

READ TO LEARN

Key Vocabulary

racism

Key People

Norman Manley

Key Places

Trinidad and Tobago
Jamaica

Read Aloud

In the days before refrigerators, many Caribbean cooks kept a "pepper pot" of meats, vegetables, and peppers simmering on the back of their stoves. Once begun, a pepper pot was never emptied. New ingredients were simply added to replace what was eaten. With the passage of time, the flavor of the pepper pot grew richer and more interesting.

In many ways the Caribbean is like a giant pepper pot. For over 500 years, people from many lands have come together here. Each group of people has added richness and flavor to life in this region.

Read for Purpose

1. **WHAT YOU KNOW:** Why were Africans brought to the Caribbean against their will?
2. **WHAT YOU WILL LEARN:** Which ethnic groups shape life in the Caribbean today?

AN ETHNIC MOSAIC

Today there are 13 independent countries in the Caribbean region. Other islands are still controlled by European nations. If you were to visit each of these places in the Caribbean, you would find an amazing mixture of ethnic groups. People who live here trace their roots to Africa, Europe, Asia, the Middle East, and North America. Most are of African descent.

In the last chapter, you read about how Africans were enslaved and forced to come to the Caribbean to work on sugarcane plantations. When slavery was banned throughout the islands in the 1800s, sugarcane planters searched the world for new workers. Between 1838 and 1917, the planters brought thousands of people from India, China, and Indonesia to work as laborers on their plantations.

Few of these workers chose to stay on the plantations because the work was so hard and the wages were so low. As soon as they could, workers left the plantations and started their own farms or businesses. These immigrants became yet another part of the Caribbean's ethnic "pepper pot."

407

A WEALTH OF LANGUAGES

Each ethnic group brought its own language to the Caribbean. Spanish, English, French, and Dutch can all be heard throughout the Caribbean today. In some countries, such as Trinidad and Tobago, you can also hear Arabic and Chinese being spoken. Locate Trinidad and Tobago on the map shown below.

In Haiti most people speak a language that dates back to slavery. The enslaved people who came to Haiti spoke many different African languages. In the sugarcane fields, they had to find some way to communicate with each other and with their French owners. In time, a language developed that was a mixture of French and African languages.

Today this language is called Haitian Creole. Creole is a language based on the mixture of two or more other languages. As you know, it is also the name for a descendent of Spanish or Portuguese settlers. In the Netherlands Antilles people speak Papiamento, a Creole language that combines Dutch, English, and Spanish.

CARIBBEAN SOCIETY

In the last chapter, you read that a plantation society developed in the Caribbean. This society was based on racism, or the belief that one race is superior to another. The lighter a person's skin was, the higher his or her place was in plantation society.

MAP SKILL: What are the names of two French territories that are located in the Lesser Antilles?

These students go to school in Havana, Cuba. Like most people throughout the Caribbean, their roots can be traced to Africa, Europe, and Asia.

The end of slavery did little to end racism in Caribbean society. A minority of people of European descent still controlled the wealth and power in the Caribbean. The majority of people, who were of African descent, remained poor, uneducated, and powerless.

BUILDING NEW SOCIETIES

By the 1950s this old society began to break down. "Massa day done," people said, meaning that time had run out for the old masters and rulers. As Caribbean colonies moved toward independence, new leaders gained power. Many were of African descent. They began the task of ending racism and building new societies based on equal opportunity for all people.

Norman Manley was one of these new leaders. Manley was born in 1892 and grew up poor on a farm in Jamaica. Despite his poverty he went on to graduate with a degree in law from Oxford University in England. Manley returned to Jamaica and used his law background to help poor farmers.

In the 1930s Manley became involved in politics, and in 1953 he was elected prime minister of the British colony of Jamaica. Throughout his nine-year term in office, Manley worked to help the people of Jamaica. His greatest achievement was Jamaican independence, which became official in 1962.

"OUT OF MANY, ONE PEOPLE"

You have read that many ethnic groups make their home in the Caribbean. In the past, racism often divided one group from another. Today, the people of the Caribbean are working to build new societies that will bring their people together. This goal is stated well in the national motto of Jamaica: "Out of many, one people."

 Check Your Reading

1. Why are there so many ethnic groups in the Caribbean?
2. How does the Caribbean's wealth of languages reflect the region's ethnic diversity?
3. What is racism?
4. THINKING SKILL: List three questions that you could ask to learn more about how different ethnic groups interact in the Caribbean. What would you hope to learn by asking each question?

READ TO LEARN

◼ Key Vocabulary

cash crop
reggae

Key People

Bob Marley

◼ Read Aloud

*You're going to lively up yourself
'cause reggae is another bag.
You lively up yourself and don't say no,
You're gonna lively up yourself
'cause I say so.*

So sang the Jamaican musician Bob Marley in his 1974 song "Lively Up Yourself." In this lesson, you will read about some of the things that Caribbean islanders do to "lively up" themselves and to earn a living.

◼ Read for Purpose

1. **WHAT YOU KNOW:** When you listen to your favorite kind of music, how does it make you feel?
2. **WHAT YOU WILL LEARN:** What are some of the ways in which people live and work in the Caribbean?

LIFE ON THE LAND

In Chapter 18 you read that the Caribbean's most valuable resource is its land. Many people in this region work as laborers on plantations or as farmers on small plots of land.

Today large plantation companies own much of the Caribbean's fertile land. They use it to grow **cash crops**, or plants raised to be sold, such as sugarcane, bananas, and coffee. The map on page 411 shows where different cash crops are grown throughout the Caribbean. Which cash crops are grown in Puerto Rico?

Caribbean farm families work hard to grow food crops such as potatoes and squash on less fertile land. While men work in the fields each day, women act as their family's business agents, selling crops at local markets.

Besides being salespeople, women must also prepare their family's meals and wash their family's clothes. This does not mean putting clothes into a washing machine. In rural Haiti, for example, it means scrubbing each piece of laundry in a stream, then laying it out to dry on stones or on nearby bushes.

PROBLEMS WITH AGRICULTURE

Agriculture is central to the lives of many Caribbean islanders. But the way in which land is used has created many problems in this region.

First of all, as you read earlier, most of the fertile land in the Caribbean is planted with cash crops. In fact, so much land is used for cash crops that some islands must import 50 percent of their food.

Secondly, many Caribbean countries depend almost entirely on one cash crop for income. For example, Cuba and St. Kitts and Nevis depend heavily on sugarcane for their national incomes. Such dependence is dangerous for a country. If crop prices fall, or a natural disaster such as a hurricane damages crops, the country and its people will suffer hard times.

Finally, the land cannot support the Caribbean's growing population. In the last 30 years the region's population has almost doubled. People in rural areas have flocked to cities hoping to find work. Each year thousands of others "go foreign," or move to Europe or to North America. Today there are twice as many Puerto Ricans living in New York City as there are in Puerto Rico's capital city of San Juan.

OTHER INDUSTRIES

Caribbean leaders have been working to diversify their economies and to provide jobs for the people of their countries. However, doing this has been anything but simple.

MAP SKILL: Which islands grow only one of the agricultural products shown in the key?

CARIBBEAN: Agricultural Products

- 🍌 Bananas
- Cacao
- 🌴 Coconuts
- Coffee
- Cotton
- Nutmeg
- Oranges
- Sugarcane
- Tobacco

One reason for the Caribbean islands' dependence on agriculture is that they are poor in mineral resources, as you have read in Chapter 18. Jamaica is one of the few Caribbean countries that has a large mining industry. Bauxite, a mineral used in making aluminum, is mined there. Another island that has a valuable resource is Trinidad, which has reserves of oil.

Although most Caribbean islands do not contain such valuable resources, all are rich in three things: sun, sand, and sea. As a result, tourism has been

Tourists love to visit the beautiful beaches of the Caribbean islands.

developed as a major industry in the Caribbean. Thousands of people now work in hotels, shops, restaurants, and entertainment spots that have been built especially for tourists.

Unlike most of the other Caribbean islands, Puerto Rico's most important industry is manufacturing. Its factories produce many products, ranging from clothing to computers. In the next lesson you will read more about the reasons for the development of Puerto Rico's manufacturing industry.

CARIBBEAN CULTURE

Although many islanders leave the Caribbean to find work elsewhere, most migrants would rather live on the islands. This is partly because their families and friends are there. But it is also because the Caribbean is home to a rich and vibrant culture that is like none other in the world.

For 400 years Caribbean islanders of African descent were not taught to value their African cultural heritage. In school children studied only the works of European artists, musicians, and writers. One author, Lloyd Best, has written:

> We denied our music while we loved it. We suppressed [held back] our art. We became Afro-Saxons [African-Europeans], black skins, white masks.

In recent years Caribbean islanders have reclaimed their African heritage. This is heard most clearly in the musical sounds of the region.

MUSIC AND STORYTELLING

Enslaved Africans brought the rhythms of their homeland to the Caribbean. In African religions, drummers create powerful rhythms to prepare dancers for a visit by the spirits. Drumming and dancing are still important parts of religious ceremonies in the Caribbean today.

In recent years Caribbean islanders have blended European or North American musical styles with African rhythms. The result is a distinctive Caribbean sound. Musicians added strong rhythms to folk songs to create calypso (kə lip' sō) music.

Jamaican musicians combined North American "pop" music with Caribbean rhythms. The result was fast-paced dance music known as ska. Jamaican

People throughout the Caribbean enjoy listening to the reggae music of Bob Marley (*left*) and playing baseball.

singers like **Bob Marley** made popular a slower version of this music, called **reggae** (reg' ā). You have read Marley's words in the Read Aloud on page 410. Reggae music has become popular throughout North America and the entire world.

Africans also brought the art of telling stories to the Caribbean. Some stories told today are old African folktales. Others are based on recent events. You will read a Haitian folktale called "Owl" in the Traditions lesson on pages 414–417.

CARIBBEAN SPORTS

Baseball and basketball are both popular games in Puerto Rico, Cuba, and the Dominican Republic. Baseball is considered a national sport in the Dominican Republic. Many Dominican players, such as José Rijo (rē' hō) and Tony Fernandez, have gone on to become stars on major-league teams in the United States.

A "LIVELY-UP" REGION

The Caribbean is a region filled with contrasts. For some, life is filled with the struggle just to survive from day to day. For others, it is a land where profits can be made. For still others, the Caribbean is the beloved homeland that they left behind in order to find work elsewhere in the world.

The Caribbean's cultural heritage helps to tie all of these diverse experiences together. The region's music, storytelling tradition, and sports help to make it a "lively-up" place to live for all Caribbean islanders.

Check Your Reading

1. What is daily life like for Caribbean women in rural areas?
2. How has the development of the tourist industry helped people in the Caribbean?
3. What role has the Caribbean's African heritage played in the development of Caribbean music?
4. **THINKING SKILL:** Reread the quote by Lloyd Best on page 412. What is his point of view regarding his heritage?

A Haitian Folktale As Retold
by Diane Wolkstein

*In the last lesson you read that storytelling is an
important tradition in the culture of the Caribbean. On
Saturday nights in Haiti, entire communities throughout the
mountains and countryside gather to exchange stories.
These stories are filled with singing and dancing. All the
listeners, young and old, join in. In this lesson you will
read "Owl," a Haitian story that appeared in a book called
The Magic Orange Tree. Like many Haitian stories, "Owl"
has both animals and people as characters. After you have
read "Owl," perhaps you will carry on the tradition of
storytelling by telling it to somebody you know!*

*In Haiti a person with a story to tell traditionally begins
by saying "Cric?" If the audience wants to hear the story,
they will answer "Crac!" Until the audience answers "Crac!"
the story cannot begin.*

Cric?
Crac!
And so our story begins.

Owl thought he was very ugly. But one evening he met a
girl and talked with her and she liked him. "If it had been
day," Owl thought, "and she had seen my face, she never
would have liked me." But still she had liked him.

So Owl went to her house the next night. And the next.
And the night after that. Every evening he would arrive at

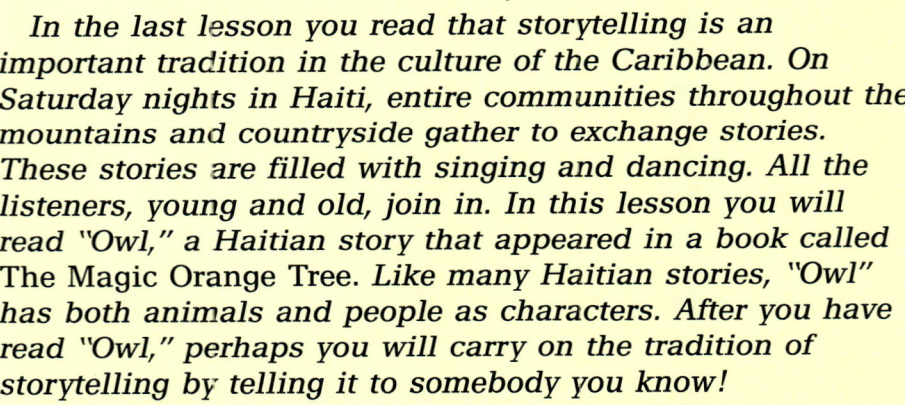

the girl's house at seven, and they would sit outside on the porch steps, talking together politely.

Then one evening after Owl had left, the girl's mother said to her, "Why doesn't your fiancé come and visit you during the day?"

"But Mama, he's explained that to me. He works during the day. Then he must go home and change and he cannot get here before seven."

"Still, I would like to see his face before the marriage," the mother said. "Let's invite him to our house for a dance this Sunday afternoon. Surely he doesn't work on Sunday."

Owl was very pleased with the invitation: a dance in his honor. But he was also very frightened. He told his cousin, Rooster, about the girl and asked him to accompany him to the dance. But that Sunday afternoon, as Owl and Rooster were riding on their horses to the dance, Owl glanced over at Rooster. Rooster held himself with such assurance, he was so elegantly and fashionably dressed, that Owl imagined the girl seeing the two of them and was filled with shame.

was so elegantly and fashionably dressed, that Owl imagined the girl seeing the two of them and was filled with shame.

"I can't go on," he choked. "You go and tell them I've had an accident and will be there later."

Rooster rode to the dance. "Tsk tsk, poor Owl," he explained. "He has had an accident, and he has asked me to let you know that he will be here later."

When it was quite dark, Owl tied his horse a good distance from the dance and stumbled up to the porch steps.

"Pssst," he whispered to a young man sitting on the steps. "Is Rooster here?"

"Well now, I don't know."

"Go and look. Tell him a friend is waiting for him by the mapou tree."

Rooster came out. "OWL!"

"Shhhhhh—"

"Owl!"

"Shhh—"

"Owl, what are you wearing over your head—I mean your face?"

"It's a hat. Haven't you ever seen a hat before? Look, tell them anything. Tell them I scratched my eyes on a branch as I was riding here and the light—even the light from a lamp—hurts them. And you must be certain to watch for the day for me, and to crow as soon as you see the light, so we can leave."

"Yes, yes," Rooster said, "Come in and I shall introduce you to the girl's relatives."

Rooster introduced Owl to everyone, explaining Owl's predicament. Owl went around shaking hands, his hat hung down almost completely covering his face. Owl then tried to retreat into a corner, but the girl came over.

"Come into the yard and let's dance," she said.

Dong ga da, Dong ga da, Dong ga da, Dong.
Dong ga da, Dong. Eh-ee-oh.

Owl danced. And Owl could dance well. The girl was proud of Owl. Even if he wore his hat strangely and had sensitive eyes, he could dance.

Dong ga da, Dong ga da, Dong ga da, Dong.
Dong ga da, Dong. Eh-ee-oh.

Rooster was dancing too. When Owl noticed that Rooster was dancing, instead of watching for the day, Owl was afraid that Rooster would forget to warn him, and he excused himself to the girl. He ran out of the yard, past the houses to a clearing where he could see the horizon. No, it was still night. Owl came back.

> Dong ga da, Dong ga da, Dong ga da, Dong.
> Dong ga da, Dong. Eh-ee-oh.

Owl motioned to Rooster, but Rooster was lost in the dance. Owl excused himself again to the girl, ran to the clearing; no, it was still night. Owl returned.

> Dong ga da, Dong ga da, Dong ga da, Dong.
> Dong ga da, Dong. Eh-ee-oh.

Owl tried to excuse himself again, but the girl held on to him. "Yes, stay with me," she said. And so they danced and danced and danced.

> Dong ga da, Dong ga da, Dong ga da, Dong.
> Dong ga da, Dong. Eh-ee-oh.

The sun moved up in the sky, higher and higher, until it filled the house and the yard with light.

"Now—let us see your fiancé's face!" the mother said.

"*Kokioko!*" Rooster crowed.

And before Owl could hide, she reached out and pulled the hat from his face.

"MY EYES!" Owl cried, and covering his face with his hands, he ran for his horse.

"Wait, Owl!" the girl called.

"*Kokioko!*" Rooster crowed.

"Wait, Owl, wait."

And as Owl put his hands down to untie his horse, the girl saw his face. It was striking and fierce, and the girl thought it was the most handsome face she had ever seen.

"Owl—"

But Owl was already on his horse, riding away, farther and farther away.

Owl never came back.

The girl waited. Then she married Rooster. She was happy, except sometimes in the morning when Rooster would crow "*kokioko-o-o.*" Then she would think about Owl and wonder where he was.

Why do people enjoy the tradition of telling—and listening to—stories?

Drawing Conclusions

When you draw a conclusion, you pull together facts or pieces of evidence so that they mean something to you. Suppose you come home from school one afternoon after a thunderstorm, and you notice that the electric clocks are two hours behind. The lights on the VCR and clock radio are flashing. You probably would conclude that your house had been without power for about two hours during the storm. By putting all these pieces of information together, you were able to understand what had probably happened, even though you had not been at home when the power went out.

Trying the Skill

Read the facts below. Think about how the facts relate to each other. Then state a conclusion based on those facts.

- Between 1950 and 1980, the number of Caribbean cities with populations of over 100,000 more than doubled. People from rural areas flocked to the cities in search of work.
- Too often there were more people than jobs. Unemployment became a problem in the cities.
- Cities could not keep up with the increased demand for housing, so many people crowded together in makeshift shelters.

1. What conclusion did you draw?
2. What steps did you take to arrive at your conclusion?
3. When is it important to be able to draw conclusions?

One Way to Draw Conclusions	Example
1. Identify the topic or subject of all the information given.	The subject is population growth in Caribbean cities.
2. Skim, or quickly read through, the information.	In this step you read the information quickly to get a general sense of the facts. Each piece of information describes the effect of population growth on people living in Caribbean cities.
3. Look for ideas that are common to all the pieces of information.	You might find that all three statements involve large numbers of people.
4. Write a sentence stating how the subjects or ideas common to all the pieces of information relate to one another. This sentence is your conclusion.	One conclusion you might draw is that population growth led to economic and social problems in Caribbean cities.

Applying the Skill

Now apply what you have learned by drawing a conclusion from the following pieces of information.

- The calypso, which originated with blacks in Trinidad, combines African traditions of singing and dancing.
- African dances were brought to the Caribbean by the Ashanti from what is now Ghana and by the Yoruba from Nigeria.
- European as well as West African influences are reflected in such Caribbean dances as the guaracha, the mambo, and the cha-cha.

1. What is the topic of the given facts?
   a. The Caribbean
   b. Caribbean dances
   c. West Africans

2. What common feature do all of the statements share?
   a. The African influence on Caribbean dances
   b. The popularity of Caribbean dances
   c. The European influence on Caribbean dances

3. Write a sentence that states a conclusion you can draw from the facts given.

Reviewing the Skill

1. Describe in your own words what it means to draw a conclusion.
2. Name some instances when it is necessary or useful to draw conclusions in school.
3. Why is it important to draw conclusions about information?

3 Cuba and Puerto Rico

READ TO LEARN

Key Vocabulary

Platt Amendment
nationalize
commonwealth

Key People

Fulgencio Batista
Fidel Castro
Luis Muñoz Marín
Felisa Rincón de Gautier

Key Places

Bay of Pigs

Read Aloud

Cuba and Puerto Rico are two wings of one bird.

This is how the poet Lola Rodríguez de Tió described Cuba and Puerto Rico in the 1800s, when both were Spanish colonies struggling for independence from Spain. In this lesson, you will read about the struggles of Cuba and Puerto Rico for economic growth in the 1900s.

Read for Purpose

1. **WHAT YOU KNOW:** What does independence mean to you?
2. **WHAT YOU WILL LEARN:** How have Cuba and Puerto Rico tried to achieve economic diversity in the 1900s?

UNITED STATES INVOLVEMENT

In Chapter 19 you read that the United States gained control over Cuba and Puerto Rico after the Spanish-American War. This was the beginning of United States ties to these islands.

After the war the United States set up a military government in Cuba. Troops remained in Cuba for three years. During that time they helped Cubans to build roads, hospitals, and schools. They also protected United States interests on the island.

In 1902 the military government yielded its power to the leaders of the newly formed Republic of Cuba. The republic's constitution included the Platt Amendment, which was written by United States leaders. The Platt Amendment stated that the United States could send troops into Cuba if needed "for the preservation of Cuban independence." The amendment also allowed the United States to establish military bases in Cuba.

Puerto Rico, too, was occupied by troops from the United States after the Spanish-American War. Unlike Cuba, however, this island was made a colony of the United States. In 1900 the United States established a government for Puerto Rico. Its governor and other top officials were appointed by the President of the United States.

Living conditions were harsh for many Puerto Ricans in the early 1900s.

GROWTH OF BIG BUSINESS

United States businesses quickly became important to the economies of Cuba and Puerto Rico. They bought up the best land and planted it with sugarcane. By the 1950s United States companies had gained control of more than 75 percent of Cuba's farmland.

Big business profited at the expense of Cuban and Puerto Rican farmers, as it had during the time of Spain's colonial rule. Many people lived in shacks. There were no schools for farmers' children to attend. Few farm families had enough to eat, and some even faced starvation.

People on both islands became angry and frustrated. To many Cubans and Puerto Ricans, it seemed that Spain's powerful landowners had simply been replaced by landowners from the United States.

CUBA'S ROAD TO REVOLUTION

In 1934 a leader named Fulgencio Batista (fùl hān′ syō bə tēs′ tə) took control of Cuba. Batista was a harsh military dictator, but the United States supported him because he did not interfere with United States business in-terests. Batista was in and out of power for the next 24 years. Throughout this period Batista and other dictators crushed workers' protests against the poor living conditions in Cuba.

In the 1950s a young lawyer named Fidel Castro organized a group that wanted to overthrow Batista. Castro gained the support of poor people with his promise of a just society. Many Cubans joined his army. Once again the call for revolution rang through the air, just as it had in the 1800s. Another Cuban revolution had begun.

Batista ordered a harsh crackdown on those who opposed him, but his brutal methods turned most Cubans

After Fulgencio Batista (*top*) fled the country at the end of 1958, Fidel Castro (*bottom*) became Cuba's new ruler.

is nationalized it belongs to the government. The United States owners were not paid for their property.

Many people in the United States were angered by Castro's efforts to nationalize companies in Cuba. They were also concerned about his ties to communist countries, especially the Soviet Union. As a result, the United States government banned all trade with Cuba in 1960.

A year later President John F. Kennedy launched an invasion of Cuba at the **Bay of Pigs**, in western Cuba. The invaders were Cubans who opposed Castro's rule. They hoped to spark a popular uprising against him. But when they landed in Cuba, they were captured by Castro's army.

GOVERNMENT PLANNING

By 1963 the Castro government controlled all of the land and businesses in Cuba. Government planners, not farmers or businesspeople, decided what Cubans should plant or produce.

Castro's planners tried to break Cuba's dependence on sugar by ordering farmers to plant other crops. They told businesspeople to produce goods for export. However, nothing that Cubans grew or produced under this system sold as well as sugar.

In later years Castro wrote the following words:

At the time of the revolution, we thought it was sugar that kept our people poor. We have tried many crops and looked into even more. But we always have to return to sugar, because of the money it can bring.

There are also other problems in Cuba today. One of the greatest is that free speech is not permitted by the Castro government. People who speak

against him. In the end he even lost the support of his own army. On December 31, 1958, Batista fled to the Dominican Republic, and Fidel Castro became Cuba's new ruler. Under Castro great changes were made in Cuba.

COMMUNIST CUBA

Castro was determined to drive foreign businesses out of Cuba. Only in this way, he said, could Cuba develop its economy for the good of Cubans, not foreigners. Castro began to turn Cuba into a communist country. As you read in Chapter 17, communism is an economic system in which land and businesses are controlled by the government.

In 1960 Castro ended free elections and began to **nationalize** United States companies in Cuba. When a company

out against Castro are jailed. Many Cubans have fled their homeland as a result. They have had to leave their families and possessions behind. Cuba also has become isolated since the collapse of communism in the Soviet Union in the summer of 1991.

Fidel Castro, however, has been successful at raising the standard of living of poor Cubans. More than 1 million homes have been built for the poor. Before the revolution, fewer than 40 percent of all Cubans could read. Today, almost all Cubans can read.

PUERTO RICO'S ROAD TO ECONOMIC DIVERSITY

Like Cuba, Puerto Rico was heavily dependent on the sugar industry in the early 1900s. But Puerto Ricans took a different road to reach the goal of breaking sugar's hold on their island.

In 1948 Puerto Ricans were allowed by the United States government to elect their own governor for the first time. The winner of that election, Luis Muñoz Marín (lù ēs′ mùn yōs′ ma rēn′), was determined to improve living conditions in Puerto Rico.

OPERATION BOOTSTRAP

Muñoz Marín set up an economic plan called "Operation Bootstrap." The name comes from a saying that describes people who work their way out of poverty as "pulling themselves up by their own bootstraps."

Operation Bootstrap had two parts. The first was to use Puerto Rico's sun, sand, and sea to attract tourists. The second part of the plan offered tax savings to United States companies that set up factories in Puerto Rico.

Muñoz Marín traveled throughout the Americas, seeking support for Op-

eration Bootstrap. Helping him in this effort was the mayor of San Juan, Felisa Rincón de Gautier (rin kōn′ dā gō tē yär′). Gautier had been involved in politics since 1932, when Puerto Rican women first were allowed to vote. She quickly rose to power in local politics and became one of Muñoz Marín's strongest supporters.

ECONOMIC SUCCESS

As the graph below shows, Muñoz Marín's plan was a success. Manufacturing boomed because of Operation

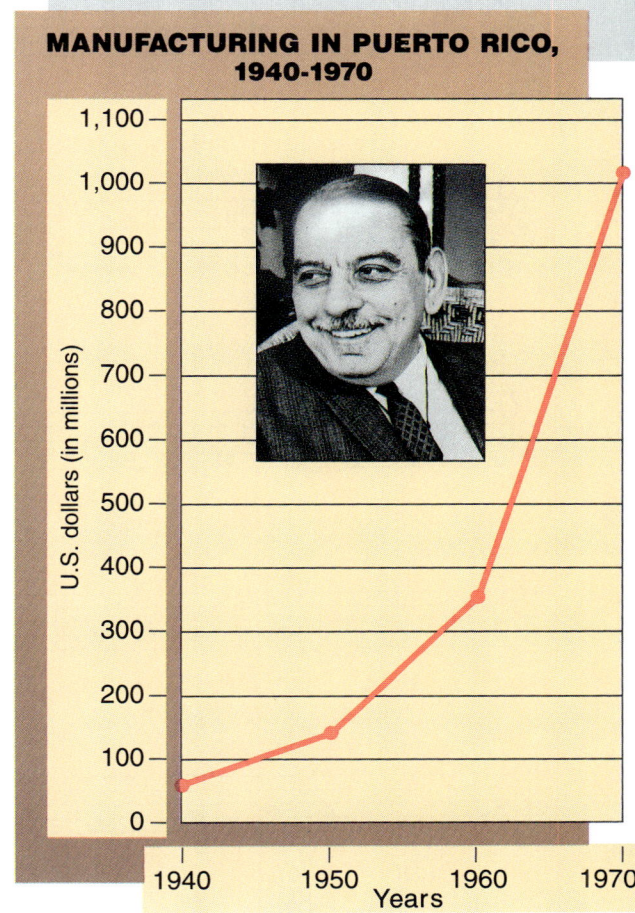

GRAPH SKILL: Luis Muñoz Marín helped Puerto Rico to grow economically. Between which years did Puerto Rico's manufacturing output more than double?

MANUFACTURING IN PUERTO RICO, 1940-1970

U.S. dollars (in millions)

Years

423

La Borinqueña

Poem by Manuel Fernandez Juncos
Music by Don Felix Astol

La _____ tie-rra de Bo - rin - quén _ don - de he na ci - do yo, _____
Is - land of rar-est splen-dor,_ My Puer-to Ri-can land, _____

es _____ un jar-dín flo - ri - do _____ de már - gi-co pri - mor.
Beau - ti - ful flow - er gar - den,_ Your ma-gic I un - der - stand.

Un cie-lo siem-pre ní - ti - do le sir-ve de do - sel Y dan a - rru-llos
Bright is your sky that seems to be Round-er than an - y dome, Sweet is the lap-ping

(cue notes 2nd time)

plá - ci - dos las o - las a sus pies. Cuan-do a sus Pla-yas vi - no Co -
of the sea, Lull-ing my na - tive home. When first Co - lum-bus be-held your

lón, ex - cla - mó lle - no de ad-mi - ra - cíon: O _____
strand, He shout-ed, "This is a love-ly land!" Oh, _____

És - ta es la lin-da tie - rra _ que bus-co yo! _____
We _____ found the land we looked for, _ This is the one, _____

Es _____ Bo-rin-quén la hi - ja, _ la hi - ja del mar y el sol.
You _____ are the love-ly, beau-ti - ful daugh-ter of sea and sun!

del mar _ y el sol, del mar _ y el sol.
Of sea _ and sun! Of sea _ and sun!

424

Bootstrap. In 1947 there were only 13 United States factories in Puerto Rico. Today there are more than 2,000.

Puerto Rico's tourism industry also boomed. In 1950 only 65,000 tourists visited Puerto Rico. Today more than 1 million tourists visit Puerto Rico each year.

Operation Bootstrap ended Puerto Rico's dependence on sugar. Puerto Rico still faces other challenges, however. The number of new jobs in Puerto Rico has not kept up with the island's growing population. Despite the success of Operation Bootstrap, unemployment and poverty remain difficult problems in Puerto Rico.

A COMMONWEALTH

Today Puerto Rico is a United States commonwealth. As members of a commonwealth, Puerto Ricans are United States citizens. They elect their own government officials and have their own anthem, which appears on page 424. They must obey the laws of the United States, but they do not have to pay United States taxes. Although Puerto Rico sends a representative to the United States Congress, he or she has no voting power. Puerto Rican residents also cannot vote in Presidential elections.

Some Puerto Ricans want Puerto Rico to remain a commonwealth of the United States. Others would like it to become a state of the United States. Still others would like Puerto Rico to become an independent country. You can read more about this issue in the Point/Counterpoint on pages 426–427.

A CENTURY OF CHANGE

Both Cuba and Puerto Rico struggled for independence and economic devel-

These workers make medical equipment in a factory in San Juan, Puerto Rico.

opment in the 1900s. Today Cuba is an independent country that is still struggling to lessen its dependence on the sugar industry. Puerto Rico is a part of the United States today, and it has successfully diversified its economy.

Check Your Reading

1. What was the result of the Spanish-American War for Cuba and Puerto Rico?

2. Why were some Cubans and Puerto Ricans angry with the United States in the early 1900s?

3. As residents of a United States commonwealth, what rights do Puerto Ricans have? Name one right they do not have.

4. THINKING SKILL: Compare and contrast the approaches that Fidel Castro and Luis Muñoz Marín took to lessen their islands' dependence on the sugar industry.

Should Puerto Rico Become a State?

The question of Puerto Rico's political future is a continuing topic of discussion among Puerto Ricans. Should Puerto Rico remain a self-governing commonwealth of the United States, should it become a state of the United States, or should it seek independence?

Many Puerto Ricans believe that being a commonwealth is valuable because it encourages United States companies to build factories—and create jobs—in Puerto Rico. However, if Puerto Rico were to become a state, it would no longer be able to provide tax benefits to companies. Without those tax savings, the companies might leave Puerto Rico, adding to the island's problems of unemployment and poverty.

Other Puerto Ricans believe that being a commonwealth is damaging because it denies them full political rights. As you read in the previous lesson, the Puerto Rican representative in Congress does not have voting rights, and Puerto Ricans cannot vote in presidential elections. Statehood would grant Puerto Ricans full political equality with other United States citizens.

POINT ☆\☞

Puerto Rico Should Become a State

The movement to make Puerto Rico the fifty-first state of the United States has grown in recent years. Supporters believe that statehood would give full equality to the people of Puerto Rico. In April 1990 a Puerto Rican named Gilberto Pagán wrote the following letter to the *San Juan Star*.

> I want statehood for Puerto Rico because I am tired of being considered a second-class citizen and having our contributions to this nation go unrecognized. Many people think we are taking a free ride in this country and I want them to know that . . . we did not simply fill out an application to join the country. We have paid many, many dues. I want my father's contributions as a soldier in World War II and the Korean War, for example, to be recognized.
>
> The opportunity for voting for statehood is an opportunity to protect our dignity and our pride. We should not tolerate inequality, even if it means having to make financial sacrifices. . . . Our dignity as a people should not be assigned a dollar value.

● Why does Gilberto Pagán believe Puerto Rico should become a state?

COUNTERPOINT ☜\☆

Puerto Rico Should Remain a Commonwealth

Many Puerto Ricans believe that the economic benefits of being a commonwealth outweigh its political negatives. The governor of Puerto Rico, Rafael Hernandez Colón, explained this viewpoint in an essay that appeared in *The New York Times* in February 1990.

> Under statehood our economic development could not continue. Why? Because . . . no Federal taxes are [collected] on the island. This has enabled Puerto Rico to undertake a highly successful economic development program. . . . It has raised its income [per person] from $342 in 1950 to $5,574 in 1989.
>
> Our industrial development program could not exist under statehood. Federal taxes throughout the nation must be uniform, thus making our Federal-tax incentive [for companies] impossible.
>
> Statehood would destroy our economic achievements and the possibilities of commonwealth—a noble experiment in flexible political relationships for people with different cultures.

● Why does Hernandez Colón think Puerto Rico should remain a commonwealth?

UNDERSTANDING THE POINT/COUNTERPOINT

1. Who makes the stronger argument? Give three reasons for your answer.
2. What other opinions might Puerto Ricans have about this issue?
3. How might a compromise be reached?

IMPORTANT EVENTS

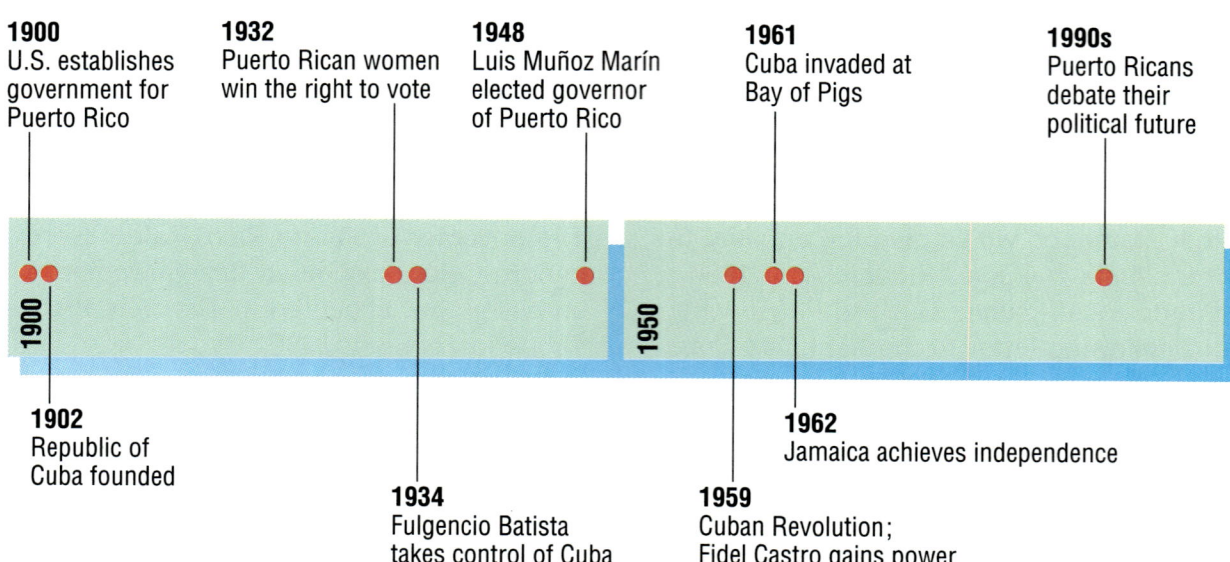

1900
U.S. establishes government for Puerto Rico

1932
Puerto Rican women win the right to vote

1948
Luis Muñoz Marín elected governor of Puerto Rico

1961
Cuba invaded at Bay of Pigs

1990s
Puerto Ricans debate their political future

1900

1950

1902
Republic of Cuba founded

1934
Fulgencio Batista takes control of Cuba

1959
Cuban Revolution; Fidel Castro gains power

1962
Jamaica achieves independence

PEOPLE TO KNOW

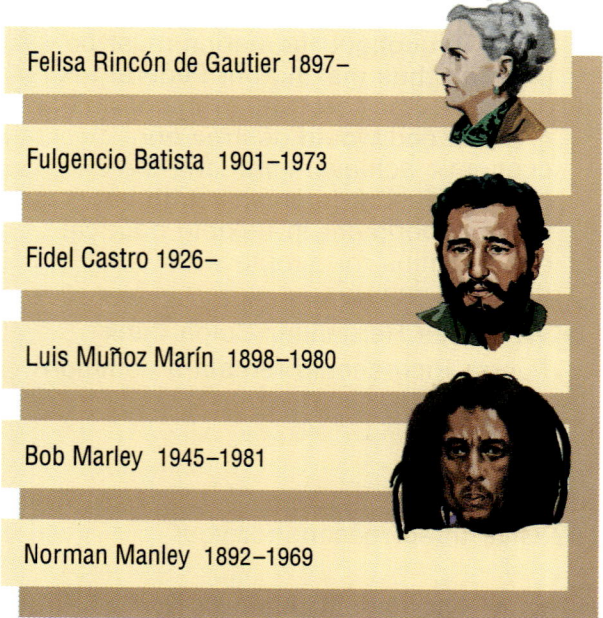

Felisa Rincón de Gautier 1897–

Fulgencio Batista 1901–1973

Fidel Castro 1926–

Luis Muñoz Marín 1898–1980

Bob Marley 1945–1981

Norman Manley 1892–1969

IDEAS TO REMEMBER

■ The people of the Caribbean islands are a rich mixture of ethnic groups.

■ Making a living in the Caribbean region can be difficult, but the cultural heritage of music, storytelling, and sports enriches life there.

■ For Cuba and Puerto Rico, the 1900s have been a time of great struggle for economic and political strength.

REVIEWING VOCABULARY

cash crop   racism
nationalize   reggae
Platt Amendment

Number a sheet of paper from 1 to 5. Beside each number write the word or term from the list above that matches the statement or definition.

1. The idea that one race is superior to another
2. A plant or plant product that is grown strictly to be sold in order to earn money
3. A style of slow-paced music, developed by Jamaican musicians, that combines pop music from the United States with Caribbean rhythms
4. According to this document, the United States could send troops to Cuba if needed "for the preservation of Cuban independence" and could set up military bases there
5. The Cuban government did this to various industries when it took over ownership of them

REVIEWING FACTS

1. Why is it possible to call the Caribbean "an ethnic pepper pot"?
2. Name two languages that have developed from combining other languages in the Caribbean.
3. How has political independence changed social structure in the Caribbean region?
4. Describe three problems that agriculture faces in the Caribbean region.

5. Name three resources that make the islands of the Caribbean so attractive to tourists.
6. How has African influence affected Caribbean music?
7. What part did United States businesses play in the economies of Cuba and Puerto Rico after the Spanish-American War?
8. Name two of the ways in which communist government changed Cuba.
9. Describe the two major parts of Puerto Rico's Operation Bootstrap.
10. In which way is Puerto Rico currently linked to the United States?

WRITING ABOUT MAIN IDEAS

1. **Writing a Paragraph of Contrast:** Write a paragraph in which you contrast the current governments of Cuba and Puerto Rico.
2. **Writing About Perspectives:** What wishes might the people of the Caribbean have for their future? List three wishes and explain why they would be held by Caribbeans.

BUILDING SKILLS: DRAWING CONCLUSIONS

1. Explain what it means to draw a conclusion.
2. State in a single sentence the steps you could take to draw a conclusion.
3. Why is it important to draw conclusions about information that you read?
4. What do you suppose might cause you to change a conclusion once you have drawn it?

429

REVIEWING VOCABULARY

Number a sheet of paper from 1 to 10. Beside each number write **T** if the statement is true. If it is false, rewrite the sentence using the underlined vocabulary word or term correctly.

1. Autonomy refers to the right of people to be free of taxation.
2. To emancipate people is to free them from slavery.
3. Trade winds are warming breezes that begin over the Pacific Ocean and blow east most of the year.
4. A person who believes that one race is superior to another is guilty of racism.
5. Tiny sea animals whose shells build up layer by layer to create islands are called coral.
6. To exile someone is to welcome him or her to become a citizen of a country.
7. A coast that receives a good deal of rain from ocean breezes is called a windward coast.
8. A coast that receives little rain from ocean breezes is called a leeward coast.
9. A cash crop is one that is grown to feed a farmer's family.
10. If a government decides to nationalize an industry, it takes over ownership of that industry.

WRITING ABOUT THE UNIT

1. **Writing a Biography:** The Caribbean has produced several leaders who have tried to bring greater freedom to their people—Toussaint L'Ouverture, Jean-Jacques Dessalines, José Martí, Norman Manley, and Luis Muñoz Marín. Choose one of these leaders and do some library research on him. Use your research to write a brief biography of the leader of your choice.
2. **Writing a Story:** Reread the beginning of Chapter 19 and then write a story about the Arawak people. You might write about their voyage from the mainland to the islands, or the ways they farmed and fished when they got there so very long ago.
3. **Writing About Perspectives:** Choose a Caribbean country and imagine that you are a young citizen of it. What would you want to contribute to your country? Write a pledge in which you state what you will do to make life better there.

ACTIVITIES

1. **Writing a Paragraph:** Think about the status of people of African descent in the Caribbean over time. Write a paragraph in which you compare their status when they first arrived with their status today.
2. **Working Together to Plan a Tour:** With your classmates, plan a tour that you think would give a traveler a good picture of life in the Caribbean. This tour should be both recreational and educational. Consider such matters as scenery, ways of making a living, political conditions, and the local culture as you choose your tour stops. You might want to make a map showing your stops along the way. Then you could hang the map on your classroom bulletin board.

JOSÉ MARTÍ SPEAKS

The following words are those of José Martí, Cuban poet and patriot:

Let us rise up so that freedom will not be endangered by confusion or apathy or impatience in preparing it. Let us rise up for the true republic, those of us who, with our passion for right and our habit of hard work will know how to preserve it. Let us rise up to give graves to the heroes whose spirits roam the world, alone and ashamed. . . .And let us place around the star of our new flag this formula of love triumphant: "With all, and for the good of all."

BUILDING SKILLS: DRAWING CONCLUSIONS

Read the quotation above and use it and your personal knowledge to answer the following questions.

1. What is meant by drawing conclusions about information?
2. Name four steps you could take in order to draw conclusions.
3. What is the subject of the information in the box above?
4. What can you conclude about who Martí thinks must serve Cuba?
5. What can you conclude about what Martí believes the overwhelming aim is for Cuba?
6. Why is it important to draw conclusions about this information?

 ### LINKING PAST, PRESENT, AND FUTURE

It has now been 500 years since Christopher Columbus first sailed into the Caribbean. Try to imagine the peoples and the condition of the land when he first saw them. Suppose that he were able to return to the Caribbean today. What changes would he see? What additional changes might he see if he returned 50 years from now?

NORTH
AMERICA

60°N

45°N

30°N

Gulf of Mexico

Tropic of Cancer

15°N

ATLANTIC

OCEAN

0° Equator

SOUTH AMERICA

PACIFIC   OCEAN

15°S

Tropic of Capricorn

75°W

45°W

30°W

105°W

90°W

135°W   120°W
30°S

60°W

45°S

60°S

ANTARCTICA

South Pole

UNIT 8

SOUTH AMERICA

WHERE WE ARE

Jagged mountain peaks, dense rain forests, vast plains, and tumbling waterfalls are some of the major physical features of South America. This large continent will be the last stop on your trip through the Western Hemisphere.

In this unit, you will become acquainted with the many peoples who have played a role in the history of this continent. You will visit the dramatic mountain cities of the Andes and the small villages of the Amazon rain forest. As you read, think about how the ways of life of people in different parts of South America are influenced by the physical features and climate of the places in which they live.

EUROPE

AFRICA

15°W

0°

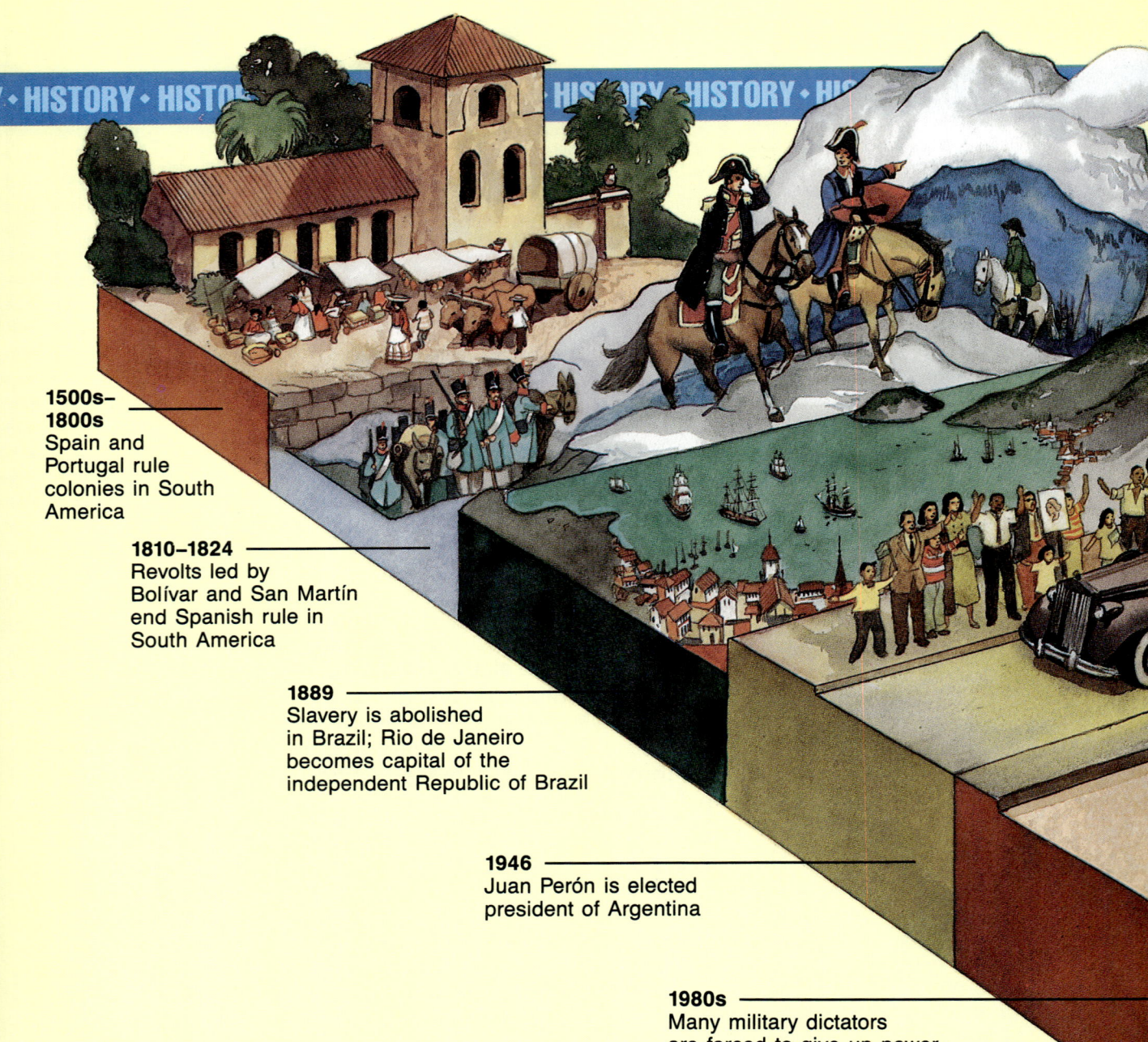

1500s–1800s
Spain and Portugal rule colonies in South America

1810–1824
Revolts led by Bolívar and San Martín end Spanish rule in South America

1889
Slavery is abolished in Brazil; Rio de Janeiro becomes capital of the independent Republic of Brazil

1946
Juan Perón is elected president of Argentina

1980s
Many military dictators are forced to give up power to elected officials

1990s
Preservation of the Amazon rain forest becomes a major issue in Brazil

WHAT HAPPENED

South America was ruled by Spain and Portugal for almost 300 years. During the 1800s, most of the continent became a region of independent countries. In the twentieth century many South Americans have struggled for freedom against dictators. Today, many South American countries have replaced dictators with freely elected governments. Now South Americans are striving to preserve their new freedoms and improve their economies.

4

SOUTH AMERICA

BRAZIL

Capital ✪
Brasília

Major language: Portuguese
Population: 153.3 million
Area: 3,286,480 sq mi; 8,511,970 sq km
Leading exports: iron ore and coffee

ARGENTINA

Capital ✪
Buenos Aires

Major language: Spanish
Population: 32.7 million
Area: 1,068,299 sq mi;
         2,766,890 sq km
Leading exports: meat and corn

CHILE

Capital ✪
Santiago

Major language: Spanish
Population: 13.4 million
Area: 292,259 sq mi;
         756,950 sq km
Leading export: copper

BOLIVIA
Capital ✪
Sucre (judicial)
and La Paz
(administrative)

Major languages: Spanish, Quechua
         and Aymará
Population: 7.5 million
Area: 424,163 sq mi; 1,098,580 sq km
Leading exports: tin and copper

COLOMBIA

Capital ✪
Bogotá

Major language: Spanish
Population: 33.6 million
Area: 439,734 sq mi; 1,138,910 sq km
Leading export: coffee

ECUADOR

Capital ✪
Quito

Major languages: Spanish and Quechua
Population: 10.8 million
Area: 109,483 sq mi; 283,560 sq km
Leading export: oil

PERU

Capital ✪
Lima

Major languages: Spanish, Quechua, and Aymará
Population: 22.0 million
Area: 496,225 sq mi; 1,285,220 sq km
Leading export: copper

FRENCH GUIANA
Capital ✪
Cayenne

Major languages: French and Creole
Population: 0.1 million
Area: 35,135 sq mi; 91,000 sq km
Leading export: shrimp

SURINAME

Capital ✪
Paramaribo

Major languages: Dutch, English, and Hindi
Population: 0.4 million
Area: 63,039 sq mi; 163,270 sq km
Leading exports: bauxite and aluminum

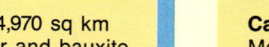

GUYANA

Capital ✪
Georgetown

Major languages: English, Hindi, and Urdu
Population: 0.8 million
Area: 83,000 sq mi; 214,970 sq km
Leading exports: sugar and bauxite

URUGUAY

Capital ✪
Montevideo

Major language: Spanish
Population: 3.1 million
Area: 68,039 sq mi; 175,220 sq km
Leading export: meat

PARAGUAY

Capital ✪
Asunción

Major languages: Spanish and Guaraní
Population: 4.4 million
Area: 157,047 sq mi; 406,750 sq km
Leading export: copper

VENEZUELA

Capital ✪
Caracas

Major language: Spanish
Population: 20.1 million
Area: 352,143 sq mi; 912,050 sq km
Leading export: oil

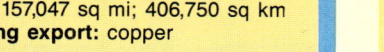

437

CHAPTER 21

THE GEOGRAPHY OF SOUTH AMERICA

FOCUS

Almost at the end of a 20-mile [32-km] valley is Angel Falls—the king of waterfalls, its . . . path a creamy, frothy milk shake of a river that bubbles down to the center of the valley.

In this passage writer John Wilcock is describing the highest waterfall in the world. Located in Venezuela, Angel Falls drops more than 3,000 feet (900 m). This makes it about 19 times higher than Niagara Falls, which is on the border between the United States and Canada. In this lesson you will read about many of the dazzling wonders of South America.

1 The Land

READ TO LEARN

Key Vocabulary

altiplano
mesa

Key Places

Tierra del Fuego   Angel Falls   Pampas
Lake Titicaca   Amazon Basin   Patagonia
Guiana Highlands   Chaco

Read Aloud

No bridge crosses the Amazon for 3,900 miles [6,275 km], and ocean-going vessels can journey . . . for much of its length. Its [streams] contain ten times as many fish species as all the European rivers combined, and about 20 percent of the world's river water. For all that, the Amazon is not well known.

English writer Anthony Smith tells us above that even today parts of the Amazon River are not well known. In this lesson you will read about why the Amazon River is one of the major features of South America. Some parts of it are so wide that a person standing on one bank can't see the other side. Some parts are so deep that a ten-story building could be sunk in them.

Read for Purpose

1. **WHAT YOU KNOW:** What kinds of physical features can make travel difficult?
2. **WHAT YOU WILL LEARN:** What are the major landforms and bodies of water in South America?

THE SHAPE OF THE LAND

As you read in Chapters 1 and 8, the Andes Mountains and the Amazon River are the major physical features of South America. Learning about these features will tell you much about the continent and its people.

First, let's look at the continent. The world's fourth-largest continent, South America is about twice the size of the United States. Shaped like a long kite that narrows to a thin tail, South Amer-ica bulges far eastward into the Atlantic Ocean. The Amazon River flows across most of that bulge, just south of the equator.

On the continent's western side, the Andes Mountains form the continent's spine. As you can see on the elevation map on page 440, the Andes run down the whole 4,750-mile (7,650-km) length of South America. At the kite's tail is a cold, stormy place where the Atlantic and Pacific oceans meet. In the passage

SOUTH AMERICA: Elevation

Elevations

Feet	Meters
Above 14,000	Above 4,000
7,000	2,000
1,500	500
700	200
0	0

Below sea level

⊛ National capital
• Other city
▲ Mountain peak
⟋ Dam
⫽ Waterfall

MAP SKILL: The Andes Mountains are high and rugged. In which countries of South America are the Andes Mountains located?

440

that follows, Chilean reporter Hernán Muñoz Villegas points out that the continent breaks up into storm-pounded islands at its southern tip.

> *The southernmost tip is actually a vast archipelago where the waves have gradually [destroyed] everything except the rock, [rubbing away at] what underbrush has been able to survive, and where the blizzards continue to beat their age-old [way] to the ocean.*

The weather is cold at the tip of South America because the tip is near the South Pole. Nevertheless, in 1520 explorer Ferdinand Magellan named the large island at the tip Tierra del Fuego (tyer′ ə del fwā′ gō), which is Spanish for "Land of Fire." Magellan had noticed that the Indians who lived there kept fires burning all the time.

THE LONGEST MOUNTAIN CHAIN

Find the Andes again on the elevation map on page 440. The map does not show that the Andes begin under the Caribbean Sea off the coast of Venezuela. From there, the Andes continue south along South America's Pacific coast all the way to Cape Horn at the southern tip of the continent. You may recall from Chapter 1 that the Andes are part of the great chain of mountains that stretches from Alaska all the way to the tip of South America.

If you were to take a trip through the Andes, you would find that the mountains get higher as you go farther south. The highest point is Mount Aconcagua, which is on the border between Chile and Argentina. It is 22,834 feet (6,960 m) above sea level.

In Peru and Bolivia the mountain ranges are far apart. In between some of the ranges are lovely lakes such as

The gentle mountain slopes and the high altiplano (*inset*) are among the important farming areas of the Andes.

Lake Titicaca. Actually, Lake Titicaca is on the altiplano (al ti plän′ ō), which is a high plateau. The altiplano is about 12,000 feet (3,657 m) above sea level. Yet it is one of the most crowded parts of the Andes because it is flat.

Fewer people live farther south in the mountains. There the Andes are rugged. Winds of hurricane force often blow through the peaks, which are close to one another.

LIVING IN THE ANDES

Many people of the Andes live in fear of natural disasters, such as earthquakes and volcanic eruptions. You read in Chapter 1 that the earth's tectonic plates grind against each other. The plates along South America's west coast meet with such power that one of them slides under the other. This meeting often causes the earth to split and quake. One effect was noted by the writer Robert Harvey, who visited Chile in the 1980s. He wrote that a recent earthquake had "made the glass in the windows bend and ripple."

The force of the moving tectonic plates also causes hot liquid rock within the earth to escape to the surface, at which point it is called lava. As you have read, a cone-shaped opening through which lava and ash escape is called a volcano. Lava and volcanic ash are rich in minerals.

HIGHLANDS

No other mountains in South America are as high as the Andes. For example, the Guiana (gē an′ ə) Highlands in eastern Venezuela have been worn down by the wind and rain. Their highest peak, Mount Roraima, only reaches 9,094 feet (2,772 m).

Within the Guiana Highlands are many mesas. A mesa is a flat-topped hill that rises steeply above the land around it. In addition to the mesas, there are also a few very high cliffs. Tumbling over one of them is Angel Falls, which you read about in the chapter Focus on page 438.

THE AMAZON RIVER

The main stream of the Amazon River begins with trickles of melting snow high in the Andes in Peru. Along its route it is joined by about 1,100 tributaries. At least six tributaries are more than 1,000 miles (1,600 km) long. The entire Amazon River is 3,900 miles (6,275 km) long. In comparison, the Mississippi River in North America is 3,710 miles (5,936 km) long and has far fewer tributaries.

As the land of South America drops sharply from west to east, the Amazon River and its tributaries gain speed and power. They roar through rapids and over waterfalls as mountains drop to plateaus and plateaus slope down to flat plains. The area drained by the Amazon River and its tributaries is called the Amazon Basin. You can find the Amazon Basin on the map on this page. The Amazon Basin, which is often called Amazonia, includes about 40 percent of South America's land. The size of the Amazon Basin is almost equal to that of the United States, not including Alaska.

MAP SKILL: The Amazon Basin is mainly in Brazil. Into which other countries does the Amazon Basin extend?

AMAZON BASIN

OTHER WATERWAYS

South America's other large rivers include the Orinoco River and the Río de la Plata. The Orinoco River, in northern South America, flows across eastern Colombia and Venezuela.

The Río de la Plata, in the southeast, is made up mainly of the Paraná and Uruguay (yùr′ ə gwī) rivers. A major transportation route, the Río de la Plata has three capital cities along its shores: Buenos Aires in Argentina, Montevideo (mon tə vi dā′ ō) in Uruguay, and Asunción in Paraguay.

SOUTHERN LOWLANDS

Many people live on the plains of the Río de la Plata. The plains are among the few places in South America on which people can live and travel easily. Unlike the United States with its broad Atlantic coastal plain, South America has narrow plains along its coasts.

South of Bolivia, between the Brazilian Highlands and the Andes Mountains, lie miles and miles of plains. The northern part of these plains is a dry, harsh land called the Chaco. South of the Chaco is a milder area, the Pampas. It is the major wheat-growing region of South America. The plains end at Patagonia, the high plateau in the south of the continent.

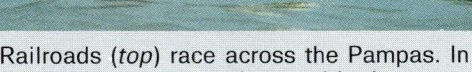

Railroads (*top*) race across the Pampas. In Amazonia, many people travel by boat.

A LAND OF EXTREMES

South America is a continent of great beauty. But rugged or unpleasant conditions make it difficult for people to live on much of its land. The continent is dominated by its two major physical features—the Andes Mountains and the Amazon River.

 ## Check Your Reading

1. Where is Tierra del Fuego located?
2. Why can more people live on the altiplano than in many other parts of the Andes?
3. List two distinctive features of the Amazon River.
4. **THINKING SKILL:** Review Lesson 1. What conclusions can you draw about transportation throughout South America? Give evidence to support your conclusions.

Reading Time Zone Maps

Key Vocabulary

time zone   International Date Line

In the last lesson you learned about many important features of the geography of South America. In addition to the deep valleys and high mountains, when people who live in these countries want to communicate with each other, they have another thing to consider—time.

Suppose Eva Cruz in Buenos Aires goes to work at 9:00 A.M. and calls a business partner in San Francisco. He, however, is still in bed. Is he lazy? Not at all. It is only 4:00 A.M. in San Francisco.

Time Zones

This situation could happen because the two cities are in different time zones. In 1884 the nations of the world divided the earth into 24 standard time zones. In all places within each zone, the time would be the same. To understand time zones we must first think about the division of the day into hours. In one day, or 24 hours, the earth rotates 360° of longitude. Because there are 24 hours in a day, the earth rotates 1/24th, or about 15°, in an hour. The time zone lines of longitude do not always follow exactly at 15° intervals. In some places the boundaries of time zones zigzag so that people living in the same region or country can have the same time.

The prime meridian was chosen to be the line of longitude that represented noon. The time zone to the east would be one hour later. The time zone to the west would be one hour earlier. The 180° line of longitude became the line for midnight. The map on the next page shows the world's standard time zones. The time is shown for each zone when it is 12 noon in the zone centered on the prime meridian. Use the map to find out what time it is in Anchorage when it is 12:00 noon in London.

The International Date Line

The line that determines the date, originally established at 180°, has been redrawn to avoid as many land areas as possible. This line, the International Date Line, marks the boundary between one day and the next. It is important to remember that there are always two days happening at the same time around the world.

How do you know what date it is in another part of the world?

1. If you cross the time zone where it is midnight going eastward, today becomes tomorrow. If you cross the time zone where it is midnight going westward, today becomes yesterday.
2. If you cross the International Date Line going eastward, today becomes yesterday. If you cross the International Date Line going westward, today becomes tomorrow.
3. If you cross both the midnight time zone and the International Date Line going either eastward or westward, today remains today. (When the midnight time zone coincides with the zone centered on the International Date Line, rule 2 applies.)

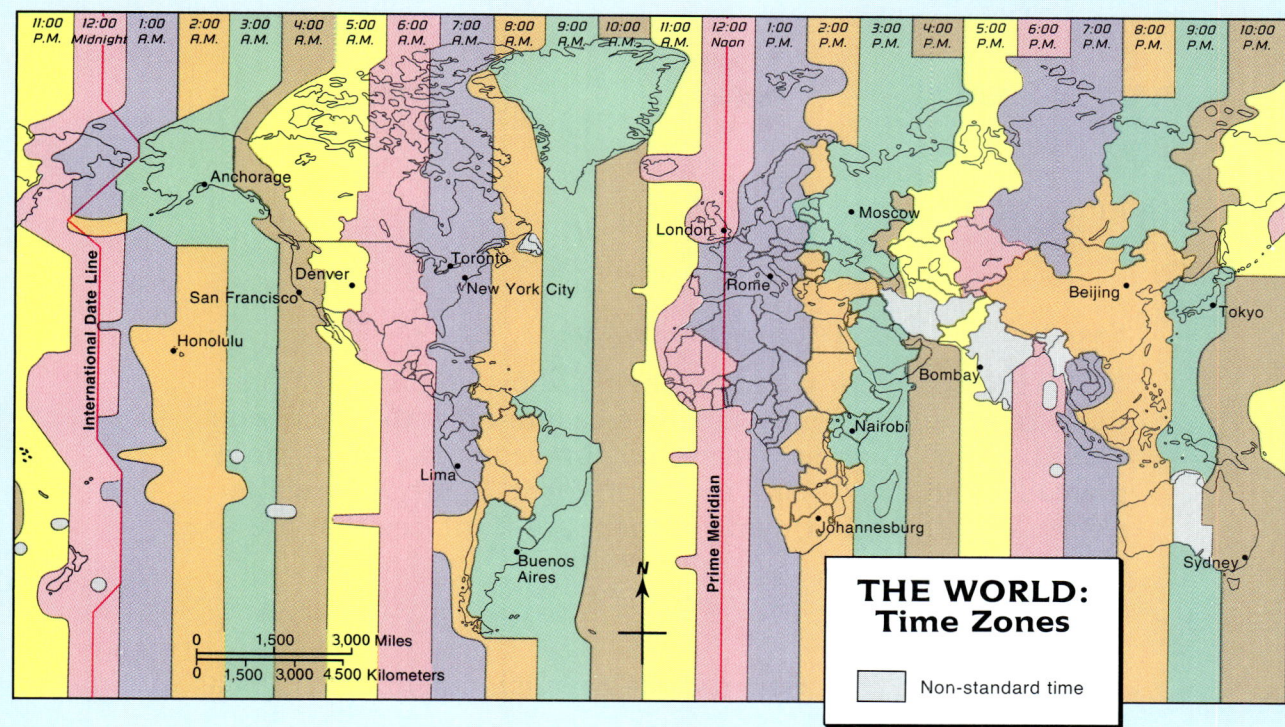

The time zone map showing clock times across the top from 11:00 P.M. through Midnight, A.M. hours, Noon, and P.M. hours. Cities labeled include Anchorage, San Francisco, Denver, Honolulu, Toronto, New York City, Lima, Buenos Aires, London, Rome, Moscow, Beijing, Tokyo, Bombay, Nairobi, Johannesburg, and Sydney. The International Date Line and Prime Meridian are marked.

THE WORLD: Time Zones

Non-standard time

Using the Time Zone Map

Use the time zone map to follow these examples of how time zones work.

A. When it is 7:00 A.M. in Lima, it is 2:00 P.M. in Johannesburg. (The map shows that Johannesburg is seven time zones to the east of Lima.)

B. When it is 6:00 A.M. on Monday in Honolulu, it is 2:00 A.M. on Tuesday in Sydney. (Sydney is four time zones west of Honolulu and is across the International Date Line.)

C. When it is 9:00 P.M. on Tuesday in Tokyo, it is 3:00 A.M. on Tuesday in Anchorage. (Anchorage is six time zones east of Tokyo and across the International Date Line and the midnight time zone.)

Reviewing the Skill

1. What is a time zone? What is the International Date Line?
2. Why are there 24 time zones?
3. If you cross the International Date Line traveling east, does it become a day later or a day earlier?
4. If you were traveling through time zones from west to east, would you turn your clock ahead or back?
5. If it is noon in London, what time is it in Beijing? In Sydney?
6. If it is 12:00 noon in Lima, what time is it in Denver?
7. If you leave San Francisco at 9:00 A.M. on Tuesday, what time and day will it be when you arrive in Beijing 12 hours later?
8. Why is it helpful to know how to read a time zone map?

445

READ TO LEARN

Key Places

Atacama Desert

Read Aloud

Sweat of the Sun; Tears of the Moon.

The Incas of Peru used the saying above to describe their treasure of gold and silver. This treasure drew the conquistadors to South America, where they braved wild rivers, windy plateaus, and dry deserts to search for it. South America is rich in resources, but many of them are in places that are hard to reach.

Read for Purpose

1. **WHAT YOU KNOW:** Why did the Spanish colonize vast areas of South America?
2. **WHAT YOU WILL LEARN:** What are the major climates and resources of South America?

FINDING MINERALS

Imagine working at an elevation of 20,262 feet (6,176 m). That is the elevation at which a large sulfur mine is located in the Bolivian Andes. Miners climb the snowy mountains on foot each day, carrying sleds to be used for their return trip from the mines. Farther west, in Chile's stony Atacama (ät ə käm′ ə) Desert, copper is mined from great open pits.

South Americans mine and search for valuable metals in many parts of their continent. For example, divers in the Amazon Basin use hoses run by motors to draw up soil from the bottom of the Madeira (mə dîr′ ə) River as they search for gold. Not far from the search for gold in the Madeira River, other people can be found standing knee-deep in swamp mud while they dig for tin ore.

REACHING RESOURCES

Clearly, South America is rich in natural resources. Besides the ones you have already read about, there are manganese, nitrates, lead, zinc, iron, and oil. However, some of these resources are located in places that are difficult to reach.

South America's land is so rugged that important railroad lines and highways run along the coasts. The continent's longest highway system is the Pan-American Highway. This is an

Miners in this gold mine climb uphill every day. The rugged land in South America makes many of its resources hard to reach.

international highway that runs from Mexico to the tip of South America. During the past 30 years engineers have found ways to link the east and west coasts by cutting through forests and building roads across mountains.

Even though new highways have been built, many places in South America today can be reached only by airplane. River transportation is limited because most rivers have rapids or waterfalls. The Amazon River is an important transportation route. But, as you read in Chapter 8, one of the world's largest rain forests grows in its basin. Near the river, thick vines, deep mud, poisonous snakes, and great numbers of biting, clinging insects make walking slow and dangerous.

HARNESSING RIVERS

In spite of these challenges, South Americans are harnessing their rivers to make them usable for travel and irrigation. Falling water is used to run machinery to make hydroelectricity, or electric energy from water power. For example, the Brazilians and the Paraguayans have built the world's largest hydroelectric plant on the Paraná River between Paraguay and Brazil. It is called the Itaipu (ē tī′ pü) project. Its plant provides most of Paraguay's electricity.

GIGANTIC FORESTS

South America has many rain forests. Therefore, wood is an important natural resource. Brazil has the world's largest forest reserves. However, as you read in Chapter 8, South Americans have been clearing the rain forests rapidly in order to open up land for development. Some people fear for the future of these giant forests. You will read more about their efforts to save the Amazon rain forest in the Point/Counterpoint on pages 450–451.

LAND FOR FARMING

As a result of South America's mountains, deserts, and rain forests, only about 5 percent of its land is arable, or fit for farming. Much of the arable land lies south of the Paraná River, in the Pampas of Argentina and Uruguay. The soil of the Pampas is rich.

The volcanic soil of the Andes also is fertile. However, the land is so steep that people have to carve terraces, or steplike platforms of earth, into the hillsides before they can plant their crops. Without these terraces, their crops would slide downhill when it rained. Yet it was on these same terraces that the Incas discovered how to grow many of the food crops that are popular today. They include potatoes, peppers, tomatoes, and beans.

In the 1980s scientists in the United States recreated the ways of farming used by the people who lived near Lake Titicaca 1,500 years ago. They rebuilt the narrow channels of water that the farmers of long ago had dug around

raised platforms on their terraces. The scientists found that the water in the channels held the heat of the sun during the night. This warmth protected the plants growing on the platforms from cold nighttime temperatures.

To the surprise of the scientists, this method produced seven times the amount of crops grown by modern methods. Scientist William Deneven said, "It's fantastic. Here's a whole system, abandoned before any Europeans came, now being restored."

A VARIETY OF CLIMATES

The lowland areas of South America have many kinds of climates. East of the Andes, northern South America has the largest area of wet tropical climates in the world. Look at the climate map below to name some of these climates.

South of the Tropic of Capricorn, South America has mostly temperate climates. Notice that the three most

MAP SKILL: Which countries are all or mostly south of the Tropic of Capricorn? How many climates are found in South America?

SOUTH AMERICA: Climate

- Very cold winter, cold summer, dry
- Warm and wet all year
- Mild or warm winter, hot summer, wet
- Warm all year, wet with one dry season
- Mild winter, cool summer, wet
- Mild, wet winter; hot, dry summer
- Semi-dry, temperature varies with latitude
- Dry, temperature varies with latitude
- Highlands, temperature and precipitation vary with elevation

heavily populated cities of the continent are in areas with temperate climates. These cities are São Paulo, Buenos Aires, and Rio de Janeiro.

RAINFALL

The Andes affect rainfall in much of South America. Towering above the clouds, the mountains trap moist air blowing from east to west across the Amazon Basin. When these moist winds hit the Andes, the moisture forms rain or snow.

Most of South America's heavy rain falls in the tropics, near the equator. North of the equator on Colombia's Pacific coast, rainfall can reach 280 inches (711 cm) a year. However, farther south little moisture gets past the high Andes. As you read in Chapter 15, the dry side of the mountains is called the rain shadow. Because of the rain shadow, parts of coastal Peru and Chile do not get any rain for many years at a time.

RAIN FORESTS AND CLIMATE

Forests in the tropics are rich in plant and animal life. In the Amazon rain forest, 2.5 acres (1 ha) of land have more kinds of plants than all of Europe does. About 2,000 different kinds of fish have been found in the Amazon River, compared with 250 in the Mississippi River.

Rain forests help to make their own climate. You know that trees create oxygen. Did you know that the thick vegetation of the Amazon rain forest produces about one half of the forest's rainfall? Scientists measured 12.1 feet (4 m) of rainfall in one year in a French Guiana rain forest. "The trees gave off so much moisture," they said, that it was "raining from the ground up."

Many orchids and brightly colored birds, such as the wire-tailed manakin, are found in the rain forests of South America.

THE CHALLENGES OF DEVELOPMENT

You have read that South America is rich in natural resources. Yet its land and climates make it difficult and costly for South Americans to develop many of these resources. People are meeting these challenges by harnessing the power of rivers and by building roads to improve transportation.

 ### Check Your Reading

1. List three of the important natural resources of South America.
2. Why are some of South America's rivers important natural resources?
3. Why does so much rain fall in the Amazon Basin?
4. THINKING SKILL: Reread the paragraph on this page mentioning the scientists in French Guiana. Write down one fact that appears in the paragraph. Is there an opinion?

What Is the Best Way to Use the Amazon Rain Forest?

As you have read, the Amazon region contains the largest rain forest in the world. The Amazon rain forest houses a spectacular variety of plants and animals found nowhere else in the world. It is often called the "lungs of the world" because it produces almost one fifth of the earth's supply of oxygen.

Today many people who live in the rain forest earn their living by harvesting rubber, fruits, nuts, and oils from the forest. Harvesting does not hurt the rain forest because in this process no trees are cut down and no land is burned. For this reason, many people believe that harvesting is the best way to use the Amazon rain forest.

Other people believe that more money could be made by using the Amazon rain forest in other ways. Ranchers and farmers have been burning down parts of the forest to clear the land for cattle raising and farming. They argue that clearing the land makes development in the Amazon region possible—and such development could help Brazil to solve its pressing economic problems.

POINT

The Rain Forest Should Be Used and Conserved

Scientist Charles M. Peters recently completed a three-year study of plant life in the Amazon rain forest. He concluded that the harvesting of Amazon plants is both profitable and good for the environment.

Tropical forest resources have traditionally been divided into two main groups: (1) timber resources, and (2) nonwood resources, which include fruits, oils, rubber, and medicines.

Given that fruit and rubber can be collected every year, we estimate the value of a hectare *[2.4 acres]* of fruit and rubber harvest at $6,330. Felling *[cutting down]* the timber of the same area would bring a revenue of $1,000.

The results from our study clearly show that nonwood resources . . . yield higher [profits] than timber. . . . Without question, harvesting nonwood resources represents the most immediate and profitable method for both using and conserving the Amazon forests.

● Why does Charles Peters believe that harvesting is the best way to use the Amazon rain forest?

COUNTERPOINT

The Rain Forest Should Be Developed

Assuero Veronez is a rancher in the Amazon region. He believes that ranching is helping to open up the Amazon region to economic development. This development, he states, is important to the economic health of Brazil.

Cattle raising is always the pioneering activity that opens regions. . . . It's the cheapest way to do an economic activity in a recently tamed area. In time, grain producers come and push the cattle raisers farther out on the frontier. Once the [tree] trunks have been removed, it's easy for mechanized agriculture to move in. . . .

Look at São Paulo. It was all forest, now it's all production. And this doesn't make it an ecological disaster. . . . What are we supposed to do? Leave all the Amazon as a sanctuary *[protected area]*? Brazil can't afford the luxury of leaving the Amazon untouched. We are not such a rich country.

● Why does Assuero Veronez believe that development of the Amazon rain forest is important to Brazil?

UNDERSTANDING THE POINT/COUNTERPOINT

1. Which side makes a stronger case? Give three reasons for your answer.
2. What other people might have opinions about how the rain forest should be used?
3. Do you think the two sides can reach a compromise? Explain your answer.

IDEAS TO REMEMBER

■ The two main geographic features of South America are the Andes Mountains and the Amazon River. Many areas of South America have physical features that make them difficult for people to live in. The abundant natural resources of South America have sometimes been difficult to reach and use.

■ Although the task has been difficult, new roads have been built and many rivers have been harnessed to create hydroelectric power.

REVIEWING VOCABULARY

List the numbers 1 and 2 on a sheet of paper. Beside each number write the letter of the phrase that best defines the vocabulary term.

1. *altiplano*
   a. Spanish word for airplane
   b. A great plain
   c. A high plateau in the Andes
   d. A plateau in the coastal region of Colombia
2. *mesa*
   a. A flat-topped hill that rises steeply above the surrounding land
   b. A bowl-shaped valley
   c. A coastal plain
   d. A gently sloping hill

REVIEWING FACTS

1. In which countries are the Andes Mountains located?
2. Name two results of the presence of tectonic plates along the west coast of South America.

3. What is Amazonia? How much of South America's land does it include?
4. Why do you think that three major capital cities are located along the Río de la Plata?
5. Name two mining areas in South America in which it is difficult to mine for minerals.
6. What is the Itaipu project?
7. Why is only 5 percent of South America's land arable?
8. What farming method have the people of the Andes used in order to farm the steep hillsides?
9. How does the rain shadow affect the climate in South America?
10. Where in South America is Tierra del Fuego located?

WRITING ABOUT MAIN IDEAS

1. **Writing a Paragraph:** Write a paragraph that explains how the Andes Mountains have both helped farmers and made farming difficult for them.
2. **Writing a Travel Description:** Imagine that you are a travel writer for a newspaper or a magazine. Write an article about a trip that you took from the source of the Amazon River to its mouth. Describe what you saw as you traveled.
3. **Writing a Paragraph:** Study the Amazon Basin map on page 442 and the elevation and climate maps on pages 440 and 448. Write a paragraph telling at least three conclusions that you can draw from the maps.

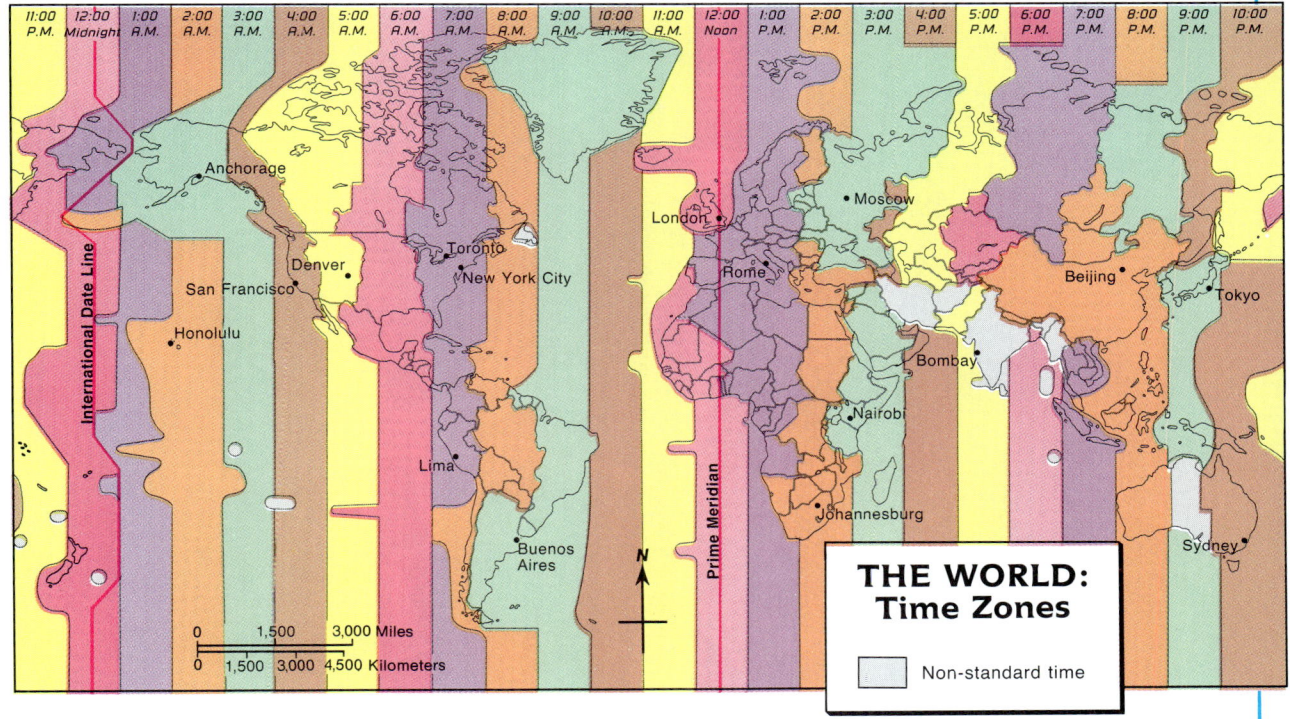

THE WORLD:
Time Zones

International Date Line

Prime Meridian

0   1,500   3,000 Miles
0 1,500 3,000 4,500 Kilometers

Non-standard time

Anchorage · Toronto · Denver · San Francisco · New York City · Honolulu · Lima · Buenos Aires · London · Rome · Moscow · Beijing · Tokyo · Bombay · Nairobi · Johannesburg · Sydney

4. **Writing Paragraphs:** Think about the ways in which people in South America interact with their environment. Then write a paragraph that lists at least two important ways in which the environment affects life in South America. Write a second paragraph that tells about two important ways in which South Americans have changed their environment to improve their lives.

5. **Writing About Perspectives:** Write a story about a young man's first day at work with his father in a sulfur mine in the Bolivian Andes. In the story try to describe how they got to work so high up in the mountains and how they got home.

BUILDING SKILLS:
READING TIME ZONE MAPS

Use what you already know and the map above to answer the following questions.

1. Why were time zones set up?
2. In how many time zones is South America located?
3. If it is 10:00 P.M. on Tuesday in Moscow, what day and time is it in Lima?
4. Why do you think some of the time zone lines are not one straight line?
5. Why is it important to know how to use a time zone map?

453

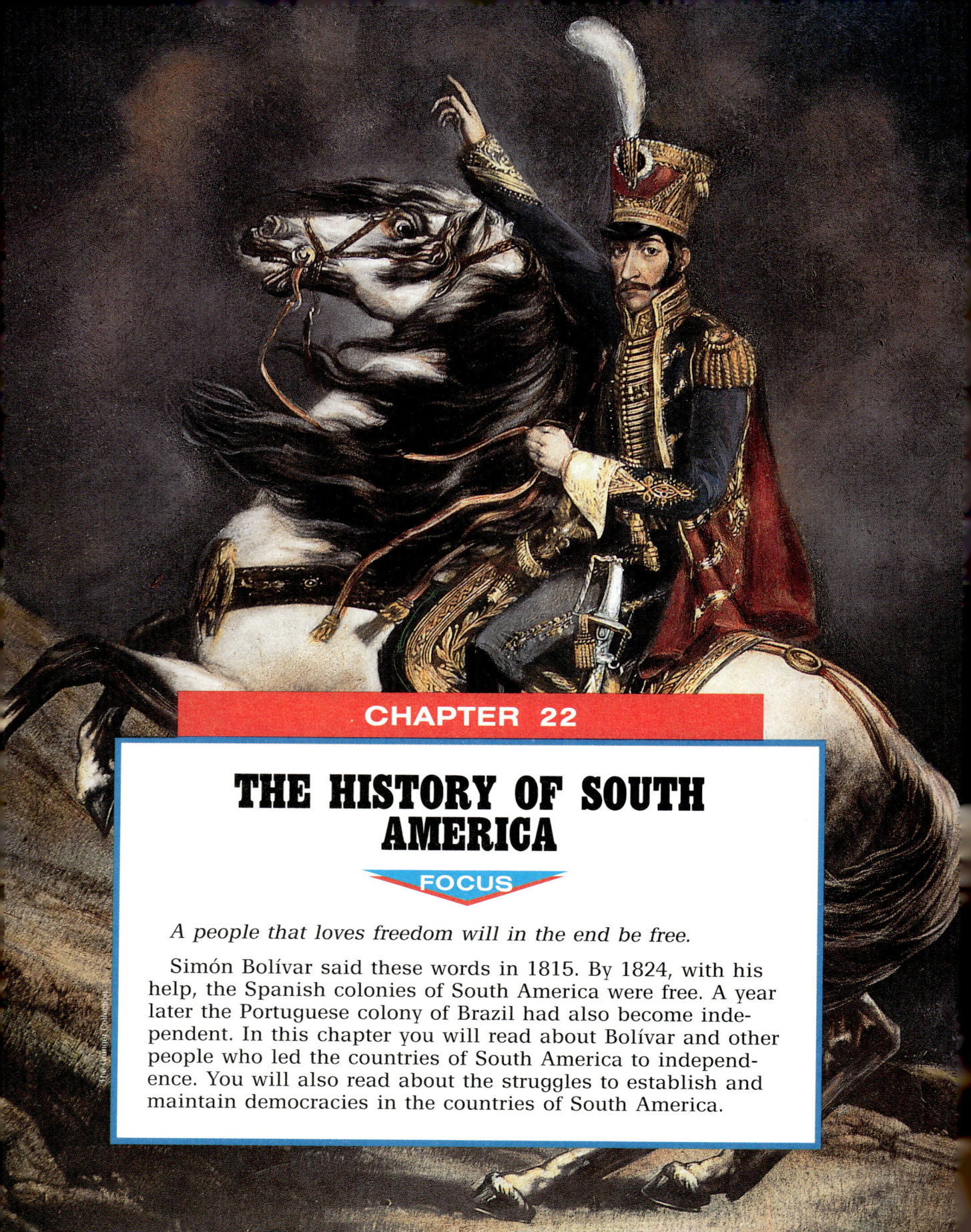

CHAPTER 22

THE HISTORY OF SOUTH AMERICA

FOCUS

A people that loves freedom will in the end be free.

Simón Bolívar said these words in 1815. By 1824, with his help, the Spanish colonies of South America were free. A year later the Portuguese colony of Brazil had also become independent. In this chapter you will read about Bolívar and other people who led the countries of South America to independence. You will also read about the struggles to establish and maintain democracies in the countries of South America.

1 Independence in the Spanish Colonies

READ TO LEARN

Key People

Napoleon Bonaparte   José de San Martín

Simón Bolívar   Bernardo O'Higgins

Key Places

Gran Colombia

Ayacucho

Read Aloud

The time has come for us to be a united and free people.

Simón Bolívar (sē mōn′ bō lē′ vär) wrote these words in 1810. After fighting for almost 15 years, he and others did help to bring freedom to most of South America, but not unity. In this lesson you will read about the struggles for independence.

Read for Purpose

1. **WHAT YOU KNOW:** How was South America governed during colonial times?
2. **WHAT YOU WILL LEARN:** How did the Spanish colonies in South America win their independence?

CAUSES OF DISCONTENT

By 1800, Spanish South America was divided into three viceroyalties—Peru, New Granada, and Río de la Plata. In all three regions discontent was widespread, especially among the creoles.

In 1808 an event outside the colonies helped to lead to their independence. At that time **Napoleon Bonaparte** was the power-hungry dictator of France. In 1808 Napoleon invited the king of Spain and his son to France. When they arrived, Napoleon put them both in jail. He then appointed his brother to be the king of Spain.

In South America colonists began to wonder if they should be loyal to Spanish officials who were taking orders from a French king. For many the answer was no. In 1810 creoles in New Granada and Río de la Plata rebelled and declared their independence. A revolution had begun.

LIBERATOR OF THE NORTH

The revolts of 1810 triggered a 14-year war for independence in Spanish South America. **Simón Bolívar** led the fight for freedom in the north. Bolívar was born in Caracas, Venezuela, to a rich, land-owning family. When he was a boy, a tutor had opened his mind to exciting new ideas about freedom. Bolívar later wrote to this teacher:

You have molded my heart for liberty, justice, greatness, and beauty. I have followed the path you traced for me.

In 1810 Bolívar joined the movement to free Venezuela from Spanish rule. By 1813 he was leading the Venezuelan rebels against forces loyal to Spain. The people of Venezuela began calling Bolívar "The Liberator" because he wanted to liberate, or free, them. But it would be many years before he would succeed in liberating any part of South America.

FROM DEFEAT TO VICTORY

In 1814 thousands of Spanish troops were sent to South America to regain control of the rebellious colonies. By 1815 the Spanish forces had crushed the rebels in Venezuela.

Bolívar was forced to flee from Venezuela. He escaped to Jamaica, where he became more determined than ever to free the colonies from Spain. He wrote about his ideas in his famous "Letter from Jamaica." You can read part of this letter below.

In 1816 Bolívar returned to Venezuela, where he found large numbers of Spanish troops waiting for him. Bolívar decided to attack the Spanish in Colombia instead of in Venezuela. In 1818 he marched his troops west to Colombia, where he hoped to surprise the Spanish.

Why would the Spanish be surprised? In order to reach Colombia, Bolívar had to cross the flooded plains of Venezuela, and then the steep, snow-covered Andes Mountains. Most people considered this to be impossible. One of Bolívar's officers, General Daniel Florencio O'Leary, described the troops' difficult journey.

The whole route was flooded. . . . [It was] more like a small sea than solid ground. The gigantic Andes loomed ahead. The ascent [climb] was made even more difficult by . . . rain and increasing cold. . . . Few horses survived, and the dead ones obstructed the path.

Bolívar wrote the words below after he had escaped to Jamaica from Venezuela.

LETTER FROM JAMAICA

The hatred that the Peninsula [Spain] has inspired in us is greater than the ocean between us. It would be easier to have the two continents meet than to reconcile [make agree] the spirits of the two countries. . . . For this reason [South] America fights desperately. . . .

As you read in Chapter 8, the air at high elevations has little oxygen in it. As the soldiers climbed over mountain passes of 15,000 feet (4,570 m), their lungs screamed for oxygen. Those soldiers who survived the march swore that they would rather die in battle than return the way they had come. But Bolívar's plan worked. His battered army surprised the Spanish forces, and Colombia was liberated. Venezuela fell to Bolívar's army two years later.

GRAN COLOMBIA

Bolívar had hoped to unite all of South America. In 1819 he was able to unite parts of what are today Brazil, Venezuela, Colombia, Panama, and Ecuador. As you can see on the map on this page, the new country was called Gran Colombia. Bolívar was asked to be president of this new country. But rather than serve as president, Bolívar decided to continue to help other Spanish colonies gain their freedom.

LIBERATOR OF THE SOUTH

While Bolívar was leading the fight for freedom in the north, a soldier from Argentina named José de San Martín (hō sä′ dä san mär tēn′) had been leading the fight in the south.

In 1816, after fighting for six years, San Martín had helped to liberate the people of the Río de la Plata Viceroyalty from Spanish control. But he knew that Spain still had an army across the Andes in Peru. "You can be sure that the war will not be finished," he wrote, "until we capture [Peru]."

San Martín devised a daring plan to do just that. He planned to march an army across the Andes into Chile. Between Chile and Peru lies the Atacama Desert. San Martín knew that it would

GRAN COLOMBIA, 1819

Gran Colombia, 1819

Present-day boundaries
(Present-day country names)

MAP SKILL: Which present-day country that was once a part of Gran Colombia is not in South America?

be impossible to cross this desert. Therefore, he decided that he would build a fleet of wooden ships in order to sail his army to Peru.

ACROSS THE ANDES

In January 1817, San Martín left Argentina for Chile with 5,000 troops. Almost one third of them were people of African descent who had been freed from slavery. They had joined the army in the hope of ending slavery.

Like Bolívar's journey, San Martín's journey across the Andes was difficult. There were no paths up the rugged, snow-covered slopes. The nights were so cold that some soldiers never awoke from their frozen sleep.

457

Despite all the hardships, most of San Martín's troops reached Chile. There they joined forces with Chilean rebels led by a creole soldier named Bernardo O'Higgins (ber när′ dō ō hig′ ənz). By 1818 this combined army had freed Chile from Spanish control. O'Higgins became independent Chile's first leader.

San Martín then left Chile for Peru. As his fleet left Chile in 1820, O'Higgins remarked, "On those few timbers depends the fate of [South] America."

TWO LIBERATORS MEET

In 1820 San Martín landed his small army on Peru's coast and by 1821 he had liberated its capital, Lima. But most of the colony was still being held by forces loyal to Spain.

In 1822 San Martín wrote to Bolívar suggesting that they combine their armies. The two leaders met in Guayaquil (gwī ə kēl′), Ecuador. What did they say at the meeting? No one is sure. However, after the meeting San Martín returned to Argentina. The fate of Peru was suddenly left in Bolívar's hands.

THE END OF SPANISH RULE

On the morning of December 9, 1824, two rival armies faced each other on a plateau near Ayacucho (ī ə kü′ chō), Peru. As the Spanish troops looked at Bolívar's ragged rebel forces, they felt confident of victory. They outnum-

MAP SKILL: Bolívar (*right*) and San Martín (*left*) met in Guayaquil. How far did San Martín travel from Santiago to Guayaquil?

ROUTES OF BOLÍVAR AND SAN MARTÍN

→ Bolívar   → San Martín
Present-day boundaries are shown.

bered the rebels by 3,000 men and had 10 times as many guns.

One hour later their confidence had vanished. By then 1,400 Spanish troops lay dead. Another 700 were hurt. The rebel army had won a great victory.

The Battle of Ayacucho was the final big battle in the war for independence. A few weeks later, the last Spanish troops left Peru.

INDEPENDENT COUNTRIES

The people of Spanish South America were now free to shape their own future. But Bolívar's plan for unity soon failed. By 1830 the government of Gran Colombia had collapsed. Geography was one of the reasons for the collapse. It was difficult to unite people who lived in places separated by rain forests and high mountains. As Gran Colombia struggled to establish a central government, it became clear that the people of Venezuela, Colombia, and Ecuador wanted to rule themselves as separate countries.

Look at the chart on this page. It shows the countries that had been formed from the Spanish colonies in South America by the year 1830.

Although Spanish South America was now independent, life there continued almost unchanged. A small group of creoles still controlled the land and wealth in the new countries. Millions of Indians, mestizos, and people of African descent still faced a lifetime of hard work and hunger, just as they had under Spanish rule.

STRUGGLING NATIONS

The fight for independence for the colonies of Spanish South America was led by Simón Bolívar and José de San Martín. After independence new

FROM SPANISH COLONIES TO INDEPENDENT COUNTRIES

Spanish Viceroyalty	Independent Country	Date of Independence
New Granada	Colombia	1830
	Ecuador	1830
	Venezuela	1830
Peru	Chile	1818
	Peru	1824
Río de la Plata	Argentina	1810
	Paraguay	1811
	Bolivia	1825
	Uruguay	1828

CHART SKILL: Which countries were part of the Viceroyalty of New Granada? When did Bolivia become independent?

governments were established, but for most people life remained unchanged. In the next lesson you will read about Brazil's move toward independence.

Check Your Reading

1. What events led the colonists to rebel against Spain in 1810?
2. How did Bolívar and San Martín help the Spanish colonies to gain their independence?
3. GEOGRAPHY SKILL: How did geography affect the struggles for independence in the Spanish colonies of South America?
4. THINKING SKILL: Predict what might have happened if Bolívar had remained in Jamaica in 1815.

Evaluating Information

"Are you sure that's right? How do you know?" How many times have you asked those questions and wondered how to decide if information is accurate and if the source of your information should be trusted?

You can apply many of the thinking skills you have learned in this book to evaluate information you hear and read. A first step is to separate facts from opinions, and reasoned opinions from value judgments. Remember that a reasoned opinion is a personal belief supported by reasons or evidence. Once you have made this separation, you will be able to identify the point of view of the writer or the speaker. The way a person views a topic can limit or distort the information presented. Another step in evaluating information is to determine if the source of the information is credible. Does the writer or speaker have anything to gain by presenting inaccurate information?

Trying the Skill

Following are two accounts of political conditions in South America after the countries of that region gained independence from Spain. **Account A** was written by a professor of history. **Account B** was written by Simón Bolívar. Read both accounts and then evaluate the information in **Account A**.

1. How would you evaluate the information in **Account A**?
2. How did you reach this conclusion?

Account A

Most Latin American countries were characterized by political instability and violence after they gained independence from Spain. Caudillos, many of them revolutionary war heroes, seized power with the help of the military. With their armed bands of followers, these ruthless tyrants killed any opponents who stood in their way. Of the northern countries, only Colombia was not controlled by a caudillo. In Argentina, Juan Manuel de Rosas, ruled as a dictator during the 1830s and 1840s.

Account B

There is no good faith among the nations in America. Treaties are scraps of paper; constitutions, printed matter; elections, battles; and life, a torment. Elections were characterized by riots and intrigue. . . . Virtually every government official has been replaced by a blood-stained victor. Rare are the elections that are free of terrible crimes. Rivadavia [an Argentinian leader] was unable to stay in office half the legal term.

One Way to Evaluate Information	Example
1. Identify the subject or topic.	The subject is politics in newly independent South American countries.
2. Separate the facts and opinions, the value judgments and reasoned opinions.	Most of the information in the account is factual. The writer's description of the caudillos as "ruthless tyrants" is a reasoned opinion.
3. Determine if the source is credible.	The writer is a credible source. Since the writer is a professor of history, it can be assumed that he or she is well informed on the topic and has nothing to gain by presenting inaccurate information.
4. Identify the writer's point of view.	The writer's point of view is that South American countries were unstable after independence.
5. State your evaluation of the information. Should you trust it?	The information appears to be factual, credible, and accurate.

Applying the Skill

Now reread **Account B** and evaluate its information.

1. Which statement in the account is a fact?
   a. There is no good faith among the nations in America.
   b. Elections were characterized by riots and intrigue.
   c. Rivadavia was unable to stay in office half the legal term.
2. How would you describe Bolívar's point of view?
   a. His point of view is similar to that expressed in **Account A**.
   b. His view is that South American countries do not deserve to be independent.
   c. He views treaties and constitutions as nothing more than pieces of paper.
3. What is your evaluation of the information presented in Bolívar's account?

Reviewing the Skill

1. What are some thinking skills you can use to evaluate information that you hear or read?
2. What are some steps you can take to help you evaluate information?
3. What are you doing when you evaluate information?
4. Why is it important to be able to evaluate information?

2 Brazil: From Colony to Republic

Key People

João
Pedro I
Pedro II

Key Places

Rio de Janeiro

Read Aloud

All Brazil is a fresh-blooming garden.

A Portuguese priest wrote the words above to describe Portugal's new colony of Brazil in the early 1500s. Over the next 300 years, this "fresh-blooming garden" attracted thousands of colonists from Portugal. The Portuguese planted crops, raised cattle, and mined diamonds and gold. Then, as revolution spread like wildfire across the rest of South America, they began to think and talk about independence for Brazil.

Read for Purpose

1. **WHAT YOU KNOW:** How did the Spanish colonies become independent?
2. **WHAT YOU WILL LEARN:** How did Brazil become a republic?

COLONIAL BRAZIL

By 1800 there were over 3 million people in Brazil. About two thirds were in slavery, the descendants of Africans brought by force to Brazil to work for the colonists.

Brazilian life centered around the *fazendas* (fä zen′ dəs), or plantations. Fazendas were like the haciendas of the Spanish colonies. Most fazendas were huge. One fazenda was larger than all of Portugal!

Brazil's few towns and cities served the fazendas. Townspeople packed and shipped the sugar, cotton, and tobacco that the fazendas produced. In 1800 Rio de Janeiro (rē′ ō dā zhə när′ ō), with 80,000 people, was the largest city in Brazil. It was a poor city with run-down housing, unpaved streets, open sewers, and unsafe water.

MOVING TOWARD INDEPENDENCE

Life in Rio de Janeiro would soon change, however. In 1808 Napoleon Bonaparte sent French troops into Portugal. The Portuguese royal family, along with 15,000 of their supporters, fled to Brazil.

Most of these newcomers hated Brazil and were disliked by the Brazilians. But Dom **João** (dom zhwaů′), or King

John, loved Brazil from the beginning. He settled in Rio de Janeiro and began to improve his new homeland.

Dom João had factories built and opened up trade with the rest of the world. He helped to create Brazil's first bank, art museum, medical school, newspaper, naval academy, and national library.

In 1820 Dom João returned to Portugal to regain his throne. But he left behind his son, Prince Pedro, with these words of advice:

> If Brazil demands independence, grant it, but put the crown upon your own head.

"INDEPENDENCE OR DEATH!"

By this time many Brazilians were talking about independence. For a time Prince Pedro was not sure what to do. Then on September 7, 1822, he received orders from Portugal's parliament to return home at once. The prince answered by raising his sword and shouting, "The hour is now! Independence or death!"

Late in 1822 the prince was crowned Dom Pedro I, Emperor of Brazil. Unlike Spain, Portugal did not resist. By 1825 it had recognized Brazil's independence.

Dom Pedro I had a constitution written for his empire. This plan of government created an elected legislature, called the General Assembly. However, Dom Pedro I did not rule wisely. He gave the best government jobs to people from Portugal, not to Brazilians. The king also started a war with Argentina that he could not win. By 1829 many Brazilians had turned against him. Fearing a rebellion, Dom Pedro I gave up his throne in favor of his son Dom Pedro II.

FROM EMPIRE TO REPUBLIC

Dom Pedro II proved to be a better ruler than his father. Under his rule Brazil began to modernize. Towns were linked together by telegraph lines. Railroads were built.

Dom Pedro I (*left*) became very unpopular during his rule. Dom Pedro II (*right*) and his daughter are shown leaving Brazil.

The most difficult problem that the emperor faced was slavery. Dom Pedro II hated slavery. Yet the fazenda owners depended on it. They opposed any effort to end slavery.

Dom Pedro II moved slowly against slavery. He approved laws that freed children born to people in slavery and all people held as slaves over the age of 60. Then, in 1888, the General Assembly passed a bill freeing all remaining people from slavery.

The fazenda owners were angry because they were not paid for the people who were freed from slavery. They blamed Dom Pedro II for the end of slavery. With the landowners' support, the army rebelled against the emperor and declared Brazil a republic. On a rainy night late in 1889, Dom Pedro II boarded a ship and left Brazil. He lived in Europe for the rest of his life.

THE REPUBLIC OF BRAZIL

You have read that Brazil became an independent empire in 1822. During the long reign of Dom Pedro II, the country began to modernize. The end of slavery in 1888 brought with it the end of the monarchy. In that year the Brazilian Empire became the new Republic of Brazil.

Check Your Reading

1. Why did Dom João go to Brazil to live?
2. In what year did Dom Pedro I become emperor of Brazil?
3. How did Pedro II help Brazil?
4. How did the end of slavery help to bring about the end of the Brazilian Empire?
5. THINKING SKILL: List one fact and one opinion that were presented in the section "Independence or Death!" on page 463.

3 Struggles for Democracy

READ TO LEARN

Key Vocabulary
socialism
terrorist
guerrilla

Key People
José Batlle
Salvador Allende
Augusto Pinochet

Read Aloud

Good Morning, Democracy!

These words appeared on a banner that hung outside a government building in Brazil in 1985. Brazil had just replaced its military government with a democratically elected government. Like Brazil, many countries in South America today have democratically elected governments. However, both establishing and keeping these democracies have been difficult. In this lesson you will read about the struggles for democracy in South America.

Read for Purpose

1. **WHAT YOU KNOW:** How did Portuguese rule come to an end in South America?
2. **WHAT YOU WILL LEARN:** How have the 12 South American republics changed and developed since independence?

SOUTH AMERICAN REPUBLICS

As you have read, Spain's vast empire in South America broke apart into nine independent republics by 1830. The Portuguese colony of Brazil became independent in 1822 and South America's tenth republic in 1889. By the mid-1900s Guyana and Suriname had also gained their independence, bringing the number of South American republics to 12. You can find these republics on the map on page 466.

You will also find French Guiana on the map. Today French Guiana is an overseas department of France. This means that it is governed as if it were a part of France. French Guiana is the only nonindependent area on the continent of South America.

Each of the nations of South America has its own history. However, they all have faced many similar problems since gaining their independence.

THE RISE OF CAUDILLOS

One of the problems faced by the new independent countries of South America was the rise of caudillos. As

SOUTH AMERICA: Political

⊛ National capital • Other city

MAP SKILL: Today there are 12 republics and 1 nonindependent area, French Guiana, in South America. What is the capital of Chile? What is the capital of Argentina?

466

you read in Chapter 16, a caudillo is a military dictator. Why did caudillos come to power in South America? Although creoles like Simón Bolívar and José de San Martín led the struggle for independence, their armies had attracted people from many other social classes. The army was a place in South American society where talented people could succeed whatever their background.

After independence, most creoles left the army to return to their large estates. Most mestizos did not have this choice. For them the only ways to get ahead were to stay in the army or work for the government.

Throughout South America some of the powerful army officers took control of the new governments and ruled as caudillos. A few caudillos brought stability to their new nations. Most did not. Bolivia's government, for example, changed leaders, on average, more than once a year.

ECONOMIC DEVELOPMENT

In the late 1800s events throughout the world brought other changes to South America. The growth of industry in Europe and the United States cre-

ated new demands for South America's natural resources. These demands encouraged economic development throughout South America. Most countries concentrated on one or two key products. In Chile that product was copper. In Bolivia it was tin. Argentina and Uruguay exported beef and wheat. Brazil and Colombia became two of the world's major coffee producers.

Economic development began to change South America. Old colonial seaports such as Rio de Janeiro, Brazil, and Buenos Aires, Argentina, grew into booming centers of trade. These bustling cities were home to a new and growing middle class.

As these changes were taking place, very powerful dictators gained control of many South American countries. The Mexican leader Porfirio Díaz, about whom you read in Chapter 13, was an example of this kind of dictator.

In the late 1800s many South American seaports were busy shipping goods such as coffee and oranges.

467

Like Díaz, the dictators of South America wanted to make their countries strong and prosperous. However, this prosperity would be achieved at great cost because these dictators cared little about the rights of the people. Brazil and Argentina are two countries in which strong dictators came to power. You will read more about these countries in later chapters.

A DEMOCRATIC TRADITION

Two countries in South America did not come under the control of dictators. In Chile and Uruguay (yür′ ə gwī), a tradition of democratic rule began after the caudillos lost power. By the early 1900s Chile began to elect its leaders democratically.

In Uruguay a newspaper editor named José Batlle (bät′ yā) became president in 1903. He would be an important leader in Uruguay for the next 26 years, until 1929. During this time he introduced many reforms, such as social security. Social security provides payments to people who are no longer able to work. Free high schools were also established. Batlle helped Uruguay to become the most democratic country in South America.

SOCIAL PROBLEMS

Whether ruled by democratically elected leaders or by dictators, most of the countries of South America had many social problems. The gap between rich and poor continued to grow. Economic growth had brought wealth to the people of the small upper and middle classes. But most South Americans remained poor and powerless.

People began to take steps to end this inequality. In Peru in the 1920s a group called the American Popular Revolutionary Alliance (APRA) was formed. APRA hoped to help the poor Indians and mestizos who were not sharing in the nation's wealth. For example, APRA hoped to bring about land reform. Although it was not successful, the government of Peru finally did seize many large farms in 1969. These farms were made into cooperatives. This means that they were now owned by their workers.

In the late 1960s the Roman Catholic Church also took steps to end inequality in South America. The church began to speak out more strongly for the rights of the poor.

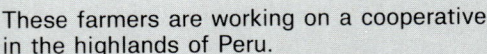
These farmers are working on a cooperative in the highlands of Peru.

SOCIALISM IN CHILE

By 1970 changes were also taking place in Chile. **Salvador Allende** was elected president of Chile in 1970. Allende believed that **socialism** would help solve many of Chile's problems. Socialism is an economic system. Under socialism all land, banks, factories, and other businesses are owned and controlled by the government, not by individuals, as in the United States. Allende was the first socialist to be democratically elected to lead a country in the Western Hemisphere.

After Allende was elected, he nationalized some of Chile's industries. As you read in Chapter 20, when an industry is nationalized, it then belongs to the government instead of to private companies. Allende also broke up many large farms and distributed the land to campesinos. Some people supported Allende's policies. But the people who lost land and businesses did not approve of the changes.

Leaders in the United States also disliked these changes. Many of the companies that were nationalized by Allende's government were owned by people in the United States. Because the United States was fearful of having a socialist government in the Western Hemisphere, it stopped sending economic aid to Chile. Chile's economy, which was already weakened, soon seemed about to collapse.

AN END TO DEMOCRACY

In 1973 General **Augusto Pinochet** (ou gü′ stō pē nō chā′) seized control of Chile in a military coup. Allende died during the coup. Pinochet was able to rebuild Chile's economy. But he also established a brutal dictatorship. People who disagreed with him were arrested, tortured, and often killed. Pinochet's dictatorship marked the end of Chile's long democratic tradition.

Salvador Allende (*left*) was killed during a coup led by Augusto Pinochet (*right*). These Chileans (*center*) are protesting against Pinochet's harsh rule.

TERRORISM AND TORTURE

Other South American countries besides Chile were having problems by the late 1960s and early 1970s. People in some countries began to call for a revolution. These revolutionaries were inspired by Fidel Castro's revolution in Cuba, which you read about in Chapter 20. Like Castro and his followers, they hoped to seize control of their nation's government. Once in power, they promised to strip the upper classes of their wealth and redistribute it more equally to all of the people.

In urban areas, bands of **terrorists** turned many cities into battlegrounds. A terrorist is a person who uses fear and violence to try to bring about change. Terrorists robbed banks, kidnapped officials, gunned down police, and set off bombs in public buildings.

In more rural areas, revolutionaries formed **guerrilla** (gə ril' ə) bands. A guerrilla is a soldier who makes hit-and-run raids on enemy positions. The guerillas attacked villages, police stations, power plants, and army bases. Their goal, like that of the urban terrorists, was to win the support of the poor and to bring down the government.

Few governments were prepared to deal with urban terrorism and guerrilla warfare. As the violence increased, the army often stepped in and took control. By 1980 most of South America was ruled by generals.

The military leaders declared war on the terrorists, the guerrillas, and anyone even suspected of supporting them. Thousands of people died. Many other people were thrown into jail and tortured.

This bus (*left*) was bombed by **terrorists** in Peru. A masked terrorist (*top, right*) paints graffiti on a building in Chile. These armed and masked **guerrillas** (*bottom, right*) were fighting in Peru.

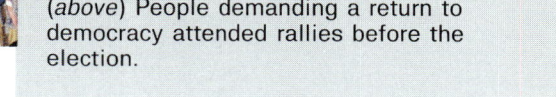

(*left*) These people were voting in Chile's first free election since Pinochet came to power. (*above*) People demanding a return to democracy attended rallies before the election.

A RETURN TO DEMOCRACY

By the 1980s the people of South America began to demand an end to military rule and a return to democracy. In one country after another, the generals were forced to give up power to elected leaders. In Chile, for example, elections were held in 1989, and General Pinochet was voted out of office. Today most South Americans live under democratic governments.

These new governments still face serious problems. Terrorists continue to disrupt life in some countries. Many countries have borrowed billions of dollars to keep their economies going. In spite of land reform, millions of campesinos remain landless and poor. Many of these campesinos have crowded into South America's cities. You will read more about these problems in later chapters.

None of these problems will be solved quickly or easily. But since the return to democracy, many South Americans have begun to look for new solutions to these old problems.

RICH AND POOR

As you have read, after independence caudillos rose to power in many South American countries. Economic development increased the gap between rich and poor. Socialism in Chile and revolutionary attempts in other countries have not succeeded in ending social problems. Today many South Americans are looking for new ways to create more just societies.

Check Your Reading

1. Why did caudillos rise to power in South America?
2. What is socialism?
3. Why did the gap between rich and poor increase as the economy of South America grew?
4. **THINKING SKILL:** What are three things that you could do to evaluate the accuracy of the information in this lesson?

471

IMPORTANT EVENTS

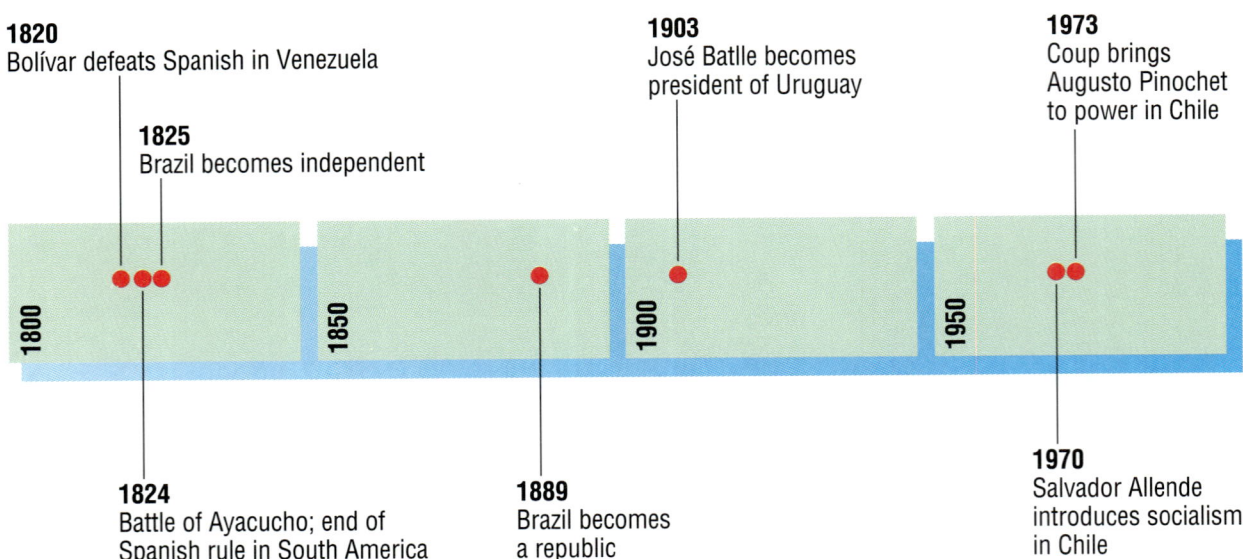

1820
Bolívar defeats Spanish in Venezuela

1825
Brazil becomes independent

1824
Battle of Ayacucho; end of Spanish rule in South America

1903
José Batlle becomes president of Uruguay

1889
Brazil becomes a republic

1973
Coup brings Augusto Pinochet to power in Chile

1970
Salvador Allende introduces socialism in Chile

1800   1850   1900   1950

PEOPLE TO KNOW

Simón Bolívar 1783–1830

Pedro I 1798–1834

Bernardo O'Higgins 1778–1842

Pedro II 1825–1891

José de San Martín 1778–1850

Salvador Allende 1908–1973

Augusto Pinochet 1915–

IDEAS TO REMEMBER

■ Under the leadership of Simón Bolívar and José de San Martín, Latin Americans gained independence from Spain. However, life did not change much for most people.

■ In 1822 Brazil became independent of Portugal, and in 1889 it became a republic. During the reign of Dom Pedro II, railroads and telegraph lines were built and slavery was gradually ended.

■ After independence most Latin American countries struggled to solve the problems of unstable and sometimes unjust governments and the wide gap between the rich and the poor.

REVIEWING VOCABULARY

guerrilla   terrorist
socialism

Number a sheet of paper from 1 to 5. Beside each number write the word or term from the list above that best completes the sentence. Some of the words are used more than once.

1. In the more rural areas there were _____ bands.
2. Under the system of _____, the government owns all land and businesses.
3. The _____ fighters turned some cities into battlegrounds.
4. A _____ is a soldier who makes hit and run raids on enemy positions.
5. Allende believed that _____ would help solve many of Chile's problems.

REVIEWING FACTS

1. Why was Simón Bolívar called "The Liberator"?
2. What was Gran Colombia?
3. Who led the forces against Spanish rule in the Río de la Plata and Peru?
4. Why was the Battle of Ayacucho important?
5. Name three ways in which Dom João helped Brazil.
6. What steps led to the end of slavery in Brazil?
7. What were two results in Latin America of the rise of industry in Europe and the United States?
8. How did José Batlle help Uruguay?
9. What changes did Salvador Allende bring to Chile? How did the United States react to these changes?

10. What are two problems that still face most Latin American countries?

WRITING ABOUT MAIN IDEAS

1. **Writing a Paragraph:** Choose one of the people discussed in this chapter. Write a paragraph explaining how that person helped or hurt his country.
2. **Writing a Paragraph of Contrast:** Review the careers of Dom João and Pedro II in Brazil. What similarities and differences do you see? Write a paragraph comparing their careers.
3. **Writing a Prediction:** You have read that Latin American countries began to develop one or two main products to sell to the industrializing countries in Europe and to the United States. Do you think that concentrating on one or two products would help or hurt the countries in Latin America? Why?
4. **Writing About Perspectives:** Imagine that you were with José de San Martín when he led his troops from Argentina to Peru. Write a letter home telling your family of your experiences.

BUILDING SKILLS: EVALUATING INFORMATION

Reread Bolívar's words on page 460. Then answer these questions.

1. What is the subject of the excerpt?
2. How could you determine if the writer should be believed?
3. Identify the facts and opinions in the excerpt.
4. What is Bolívar's point of view?
5. When is it important to know how to evaluate information?

CHAPTER 23

THE NORTH COAST COUNTRIES

FOCUS

Skyscrapers mix with colonial buildings, plazas, cathedrals, and slums.

In his description of the large cities of Colombia, writer Lionel Landry paints a picture that can be used to illustrate all of the large cities of South America's North Coast region. The fact that past and present meet here makes this an exciting and unique part of the world.

1 People

READ TO LEARN

Key Vocabulary

penal colony
patois

Key Places

Georgetown

Read Aloud

The greatest challenge facing the . . . people is that of drawing together the many . . . traditional ways of life.

This is how Charles Gritzner described the country of Guyana. As you will read, the "greatest challenge" he mentions faces people in all of the North Coast countries.

Read for Purpose

1. **WHAT YOU KNOW:** Into which social classes was society divided during Latin America's colonial period?
2. **WHAT YOU WILL LEARN:** Which groups of people live in the North Coast countries today?

THE TOP OF THE CONTINENT

You know that the equator runs through South America. North of the equator the continent grows narrower. There four countries sit atop the continent. They are Colombia, Venezuela, Guyana, and Suriname. East of Suriname is French Guiana, which, as you read in Chapter 22, is a department of France. A department is an area that is governed like a state. These areas are called the North Coast countries because they are all on the north coast of South America.

THE CROWDED COAST

Most of the people in the North Coast region live in cities. Look at the map on page 476. It shows that almost all of the region's cities are located along the Caribbean coast and on a few inland plains. This means that most of the population lives near the Caribbean coast. South of the coastal lowlands are the rugged Andes Mountains and the Guiana Highlands.

The North Coast cities have some of the world's most ethnically diverse populations. Imagine, for example, that you were to visit Georgetown, the capital of Guyana. On the streets you would see people of African, Portuguese, Chinese, South Asian, and American Indian descent. If you were to visit Maracaibo in Venezuela, on the other hand, you would see people who are mainly mestizos. What is today Venezuela was colonized by the Spanish, as was nearby Colombia.

THE GUIANAS

Guyana, Suriname, and French Guiana are together often called the three Guianas. When they were both colonies, Guyana was called British Guiana and Suriname was called Dutch Guiana. The name of French Guiana has remained the same.

The three Guianas are similar in culture. Their people come from similar ethnic groups and share many customs with the people of the Caribbean region. However, the Guianas have more people of African and southern Asian descent than of any other group. In Guyana, these two groups make up over 80 percent of the total population.

When Guyana was a British colony, thousands of Africans were forced to work there as slaves on the sugar plantations. After slavery was abolished in 1834, many people who had been enslaved moved to the cities.

The desire for farm workers caused Guyanese plantation owners to bring in thousands of people from India and Southeast Asia. Today many of their descendants work on Guyana's plantations and farms. They are called East Indians. Suriname also has many East Indians and people of African descent.

In the past, French Guiana was mainly a **penal colony**, or a colony for

MAP SKILL: Which North Coast countries are bordered on the north by the Atlantic Ocean? By the Caribbean Sea?

NORTH COAST COUNTRIES:
Political

⊛ National capital

★ Other capital

• Other city

people judged to be dangerous to society. France sent thousands of convicts and political prisoners to the prison camps in French Guiana. All of the camps were closed by 1940.

Their ethnic groups have affected the Guianas in many ways—in their governments, arts, customs, religions, and beliefs. A good example of the influence of their ethnic diversity is their languages. Each of the Guianas has a different official language. Guyana is the only English-speaking country in South America. Dutch is the official language of Suriname, and French is French Guiana's official language. However, most people speak in a **patois** (pat′ wä), which is a regional dialect of a language. In a patois words may be pronounced in a slightly different way, or they may have a different meaning. An example of Guyana patois is the phrase "Don tek your eyes fuh pas me," which means "Don't be rude" in standard English.

VENEZUELA AND COLOMBIA

Find Venezuela and Colombia on the political map on page 476. You can see from the map that Venezuela and Colombia are the two largest countries in land area in the North Coast region. They also have the largest populations. They are the only countries there in which Spanish is the major language.

Today most people in Colombia and Venezuela are mestizos. However, the opportunities for mestizos are different in the two countries. In Venezuela mestizos are powerful in all parts of society. In Colombia, on the other hand, mestizos have little power. The members of a small group of families of Spanish descent hold most of the important positions.

These East Indian students live in Georgetown, Guyana. East Indians are one of that country's largest ethnic groups.

Indians live mainly in the highlands. In both Venezuela and Colombia, people of African descent and mulattoes live along the Caribbean coast.

AN AMAZING VARIETY

As you have read, Venezuela, Colombia, Guyana, Suriname, and French Guiana are located on South America's North Coast. All of these countries have many ethnic groups. Colombia and Venezuela are the only two countries in the region that have Spanish as a main language.

Check Your Reading

1. Name at least three ethnic groups of the North Coast countries.
2. Which North Coast countries have many mestizos?
3. What is special about the language of Guyana?
4. **THINKING SKILL:** Classify the countries of the North Coast region into at least two groups. Explain your choice of groups.

2 Living and Working

READ TO LEARN

 **Key Vocabulary**   **Key Places**

barrio   Caracas   Bogotá   Llanos

Read Aloud

The real gold in Venezuela isn't gold or even oil; it is the country itself.

As Stephen Birnbaum notes above, the real value of a country includes more than its important natural resources. Its value includes the efforts of all its people. In this lesson you will read about the efforts of the people of the North Coast countries to develop their economies.

Read for Purpose

1. **WHAT YOU KNOW:** What is a diversified economy?
2. **WHAT YOU WILL LEARN:** Why have the North Coast countries found it difficult to develop their economies?

CHALLENGE TO DEVELOPMENT

The North Coast countries have many different kinds of natural resources. They have minerals such as oil and gold, large forests, and some areas of fertile soil. However, because of the rugged land and the climate, these resources have not always been easy to develop. For example, most of the fertile soil in the region is in a few lowland areas and highland valleys. Many minerals are located high in the Andes Mountains or deep in the rain forests. In addition, this rugged land makes it difficult to transport goods.

The North Coast countries also have the hard job of changing their economic systems, which were formed during their colonial days. At that time, Europeans forced their colonies to produce raw materials and crops for export. These were sent to Europe and were not used in Latin America. Colonies also could not manufacture goods but had to import them from Europe.

CROPS FOR EXPORT

Today the North Coast countries still grow crops for export because they are important ways to gain income. For example, Guyana and Suriname are among the world's largest exporters of sugar, rice, and bananas. Colombia and Venezuela are important coffee producers and are known for the excellent quality of the coffee they grow. Coffee makes up more than half of Colombia's export earnings.

478

To some Colombians, coffee growing is a way of life. Writer David Bowen describes a coffee farm in Colombia.

Coffee growing is a family business, and there are many small family farms in the coffee zones. Coffee growing requires a lot of hand labor, so the whole family helps, even small children. Sometimes a coffee farm grows with the family. More trees are set out when a son is born, and when he grows up, they will be his trees.

DANGER IN THE MOUNTAINS

It can be dangerous to depend on one crop such as coffee for income. If world prices for that crop fall, its farmers earn less money. When coffee prices fell in the 1980s, some of Colombia's campesinos, or poor farmers, grew other crops instead. For example, some campesinos secretly grow coca plants in the mountains. Andean people have long used the plant for medicine. However, growing the coca plant, which is used to make the drug cocaine, is illegal. Cocaine sells for high prices in overseas countries such as the United States, where it is illegal. Drug dealers pay Colombian farmers high prices for coca. This has led to an increase in the drug trade and has caused the Colombian government to do more to end this unlawful activity.

Unable to earn a living, some campesinos have joined small guerrilla bands in the mountains. As you have read in Chapter 22, guerrilla groups try to overthrow governments through violence. These guerrilla bands survive by charging farmers, ranchers, and coca growers a fee for their safety. Those who do not pay the fee may have their property destroyed. They may also be kidnapped or murdered.

The government of Colombia has held peace talks with some of these guerrilla groups. The government has also sent troops to destroy their mountain bases. However, in 1990 the army admitted that the bases were getting larger. One commander said that one of the bases the army had captured "had kitchens, dormitories, supply rooms, classrooms, [and] a theater."

Coffee is Colombia's main crop. Another important, but unlawful, crop is the coca plant, from which cocaine is made. These sacks of cocaine (*right*) were seized by the army.

A crowded city of more than 3 million people, Caracas has many traffic jams and **barrios**.

THE BARRIOS

Many North Coast farmers choose to migrate to large cities such as Caracas (kə rä′ kəs). Caracas is the capital and largest city of Venezuela. According to British traveler Geoff Crowther:

[Every day] thousands of people flock to Caracas in search of the . . . dream of wealth, or even just a job. They come mainly from the rural areas of Venezuela but also from other South American republics.

Unfortunately even a large city such as Caracas cannot take in all of the migrants. Some newcomers do not find jobs or even a decent place to live. Instead they end up living in **barrios**. Barrios are poorly built settlements on the edges of a city. These neighborhoods often lack running water and electricity. About 35 percent of the population of Caracas lives in barrios.

Why do so many people stay in the barrios? The farmer who migrates there may feel that life in the barrio is no worse than it was in the mountains.

In the city, according to writer Lionel Landry, the farmer may be lucky and find a job. The city offers:

education for the children, and the availability of doctors and hospitals. . . . His children, at least, will live longer and better than he. And, if he gets a job, the family may be able to move into a real house on a paved street, and begin to live like real city people.

BUSTLING CARACAS

In Venezuela, most of the migrants head for Caracas. Newcomers to this bustling city are amazed by the amount of activity they see on its streets. The traffic never seems to stop, and the city has some of the world's largest traffic jams. More than 3 million of the country's total population of 19 million people live in and around Caracas.

Like many cities in the United States, Caracas has highways that run in and out of the city. Shopping malls with expensive shops dot the wealthy suburbs. Caracas is called the "city of eternal spring" because of the many parks and gardens in its center.

BOGOTÁ, CENTER OF COLOMBIA

Colombia has 31 million people. This makes its population the second-largest in South America, after Brazil. Bogotá, the capital and largest city of Colombia, has more than 4 million people. Bogotá is a city of contrasts, with poor and wealthy neighborhoods. An old colonial city, Bogotá is known for its churches, museums, universities, and restaurants.

OIL AND OTHER MINERALS

As you have read, the North Coast countries have many mineral resources. These resources include gold, silver, iron, lead, emeralds, diamonds, tin, bauxite, and oil.

Until recently almost all of the minerals that were mined in the North Coast countries were exported. Before the discovery of oil in the early 1900s, gold and diamonds were Venezuela's most exported minerals. Today Venezuela is one of the world's leading producers of oil. You will read more about Venezuelan oil in Lesson 3. Suriname and Guyana are both rich in bauxite. Both countries export most of their bauxite and much of the aluminum that they make from the bauxite.

THE LLANOS

Venezuela is the only North Coast country to have a large cattle industry. It is centered in the inland plains called the Llanos (yä′ nōs). *Llanos* comes from the Spanish word meaning "plains." The Llanos is located between the Andes ranges of Colombia and the Guiana Highlands. Its coarse grass is ideal for cattle grazing. However, its weather changes often. According to writer John Wilcock, the weather can be described as follows:

A lovely day will turn violent. Either temperatures suddenly soar or skies burst open . . . burning or washing away every living thing.

Cattle raising, an important industry in Venezuela, is centered in the Llanos.

481

The weather is hot and dry for most of the year. Until dams were built there, heavy rains from May to October caused flooding in parts of the Llanos. The cowhands, called *llaneros*, usually managed to save their herds from drowning in the floods. When they could, the llaneros gathered around campfires to talk and sing. Venezuelan writer Rómulo Gallegos described the llaneros in the following way.

> [They] begin to talk and end by singing . . . for if there is anything which must be said, the Plainsman [llanero] always has a ballad [that can] say it better than speech.

These people are fishing off the coast of French Guiana. Fishing, especially for shrimp, is an important industry there.

In recent years the government of Venezuela has tried to develop the Llanos. It has built roads and has encouraged families to move there and to start more cattle ranches and wheat farms. The beef and wheat are used at home and are also exported.

OTHER INDUSTRIES

As you read in Lesson 1, most of the people in Guyana, Suriname, and French Guiana live along the narrow coastal plain. This plain is rarely more than 40 miles (65 km) wide. Rice is grown where the land is low. Also, many fishing villages hug the coast. In French Guiana, many people work in the shrimp industry. Shrimp are among French Guiana's chief exports.

ECONOMIC CHALLENGES

As you have read, the North Coast countries have many resources, but these resources are sometimes difficult to develop. Rugged land, uneven distribution of wealth, and economic systems inherited from the past are some of the challenges that the region faces.

 Check Your Reading

1. What is a barrio?
2. Give three reasons that many North Coast people migrate to the region's large cities.
3. **GEOGRAPHY SKILL:** Look at the Atlas maps on pages 578 and 579. Which national capital is near the Llanos?
4. **THINKING SKILL:** Imagine that you are a campesino in Colombia who wants to improve the life of your family. What alternatives would you consider? What would you decide to do and why?

HELPING THE HELPLESS

Ray Schambach walks through the poorest neighborhoods of Bogotá, Colombia, looking for the abandoned, the sick, and the dying. He brings them to clean, safe homes. There they are cared for by Ray and the other Brothers of the Divine Providence, a community of Catholic volunteers dedicated to helping the helpless.

The son of an American father and a Colombian mother, Ray grew up in very comfortable surroundings. He planned to be a doctor. But a spur-of-the-moment decision when he was in medical school started him down a very different path.

While at the university in Bogotá in 1973, Ray visited every day a home for abandoned street children where a friend worked. One day he arrived to discover that the children had been abandoned once again—the shelter had been closed by the government. Ray knew the children would starve unless someone helped them. Then and there, the 22-year-old student decided to care for them himself. He rented a house and set up a home for 17 children, all under the age of 10.

Ray's life changed overnight. He decided to put off his medical training and began working nights teaching English and days taking care of his new family. Life wasn't easy, but he found that his new role as a "parent" made him very happy. He began to encourage friends and members of a prayer group to which he belonged to work with him to help the abandoned children of Bogotá.

In 1976 Ray and his fellow caregivers formed a religious community called the Brothers of the Divine Providence. At first they ran homes for 300 street children. After a visit and training from Mother Teresa, they expanded their work with children to include helping the sick and the aged. Mother Teresa has devoted her own life to caring for the poor and sick throughout the world.

Under Ray's direction, the 70 women and men of the religious community now offer comfort and care to more than 1,000 needy people. They have 39 homes in Colombia, Bolivia, Peru, and Ecuador.

Ray Schambach is a quiet, gentle man who spends all day, every day, working with the poor. He says:

I'm very happy with what I'm doing. I'm getting even more back than I'm putting in.

Reading a Newspaper

Key Vocabulary

headline	classified ad
news article	dateline
feature article	byline
editorial	

END OF
LIMITS ON
COFFEE EXPORTS

In this chapter, you read about the many different kinds of people who live in the North Coast countries. And you also read about some of the difficulties faced when growing coffee as a cash crop for export in some of these countries.

When these events took place they were all reported in newspapers. The **headline** shown on this page might have introduced one of the newspaper stories. A headline is a sentence or phrase printed in large type at the beginning of a newspaper article. Its purpose is to grab the reader's attention.

The Parts of a Newspaper

The first part of a newspaper includes most of the **news articles**. News articles tell the latest facts about events going on in the local area, the nation, or around the world. News articles tell only facts about an event. They do not give opinions. The headline on this page introduces a news article. What is it about?

Other types of articles that appear in a newspaper are called **feature articles**. A feature article is a detailed report about a person, an issue, or an event. For example, a feature article might trace the history of Venezuela's search for oil and discuss the big discovery of oil in 1922.

Another part of a newspaper includes a special type of article called an **editorial**. An editorial gives the opinion of the people who run the newspaper about an important issue. For example, they might explain in an editorial why they support a certain candidate for governor of your state. Or they might tell why they support or oppose a new nuclear power plant.

The editorial section of the newspaper also includes letters to the editor. These are letters written by readers telling what they think about a particular issue.

Other parts of a newspaper include sports, comics, weather, and **classified ads**. Classified ads are short advertisements printed in small type. They might be "Help Wanted" ads, which describe job openings. Or they might list apartments for rent or homes for sale. People place classified ads in a newspaper to let other people know that they want to buy or sell something. What are some ads that might appear in your local newspaper?

COFFEE PRICES DROP TO 8-YEAR LOW

LONDON, JULY 4, 1989 – The International Coffee Organization today lifted all limits that had been placed on the amount of coffee each country could export. The announcement was made at the end of a one-day meeting of 74 coffee-producing and coffee-consuming countries. After the announcement, the price of coffee fell to an 8-year low. Delegates to the meeting said that the price of coffee would drop by at least 20 cents a pound as coffee-producing countries increase shipments.

Coffee is Colombia's main source of income. More than 3 million Colombians work in the coffee business. Any drop in world coffee prices will make it harder for the government to pay for roads, schools, and hospitals.

Parts of a News Article

The front page of a newspaper contains the most important news articles of the day. As you have read, each news article begins with a headline, which is meant to catch the reader's attention. Read the headline of the article above. What is it about? Just below the headline you will see a **dateline**. A dateline tells where and when the event took place. Sometimes you will also find a **byline**. A byline tells who wrote the article.

Within the article the most important information is presented in the first paragraph. Usually the reporter tries to answer several questions in the first paragraph. *Who* is the story about? *What* is it about? *When* did it take place? *Where* did it take place? The rest of the article fills in the other facts about the event.

Reviewing the Skill

1. Name at least four parts of a newspaper.
2. What is the purpose of a headline?
3. Read the first paragraph of the article above. Does it answer the questions *Who*? *What*? *When*? and *Where*? What is the answer to each question?
4. Is the article above a news article or a feature article? How can you tell?
5. How would the article be different if it were an editorial?
6. Why is it useful to know how to read a newspaper?

3 Changing Economies

READ TO LEARN

Key Vocabulary

foreign debt
recession

Key People

Rómulo Betancourt
Carlos Andrés Pérez

Read Aloud

On December 4, 1922, workers drilling for oil near Venezuela's Lake Maracaibo (mar ə kī′ bō) began to shout. After many drilling efforts, Los Barrios oil well number 2 had exploded, hurling oil and pieces of an oil derrick into the sky. As you will read, oil brought both great wealth and many challenges to the people of Venezuela.

Read for Purpose

1. **WHAT YOU KNOW:** What are some of Venezuela's important natural resources?
2. **WHAT YOU WILL LEARN:** How have oil resources affected Venezuela's economy?

VENEZUELA'S OIL INDUSTRY

Oil resources helped Venezuela to diversify its economy. After 1922 Venezuela began to change from a mainly farming economy to one of the world's top oil exporters. Look at the graph on page 171 to see which ten countries now produce the largest amounts of oil in a year.

Although it exported great amounts of oil, Venezuela did not earn large profits from oil until after 1973. The world's major oil-producing countries had formed the Organization of Petroleum Exporting Countries, or OPEC, in order to control oil prices in 1960. However, OPEC did not set high prices for oil until the early 1970s.

BENEFITS FROM OIL

As an OPEC member, Venezuela benefited greatly from the higher oil prices. What happened to this money? Some of it helped Caracas to grow larger and to modernize. Some wealthy Venezuelans used the money they earned to buy more foreign goods. As a result, more foreign ships could be seen in Venezuela's ports. They unloaded luxury goods to be sold in shopping malls and grocery stores. In the rich suburbs of Caracas, shops sold all kinds of foreign goods, from Swedish crystal and Japanese televisions to Italian suits.

Some Venezuelans believed that this spending was not the best way for their oil riches to be used. Juan Pablo Pérez Alfonzo, once in charge of Venezuela's oil industry, said the following:

Income from oil has discouraged us from trying to do with less and [from] arriving at solutions through hard work. That is why we have a line of ships at our harbors, loaded with goods; we think we can solve our problems by buying outside.

A MIXED BLESSING

Not everyone shared equally in Venezuela's oil boom. In the barrios of Caracas, more houses for the poor crowded the hillsides around the city. Venezuelans also found that their oil wealth was a mixed blessing. Oil brought undreamed-of riches to some. However, Venezuela did not diversify its economy, and it became dependent on world oil prices for its wealth.

As oil prices rose in the world and in Venezuela, the prices of everyday goods in Venezuela also rose. Increasingly high prices make it costly for people, especially the poor, to live in large cities like Caracas.

PETROLEUM PROFITS

In the 1960s Venezuelan president Rómulo Betancourt urged the country to start "sowing the petroleum." He was comparing the investment of oil profits to the sowing, or planting, of seeds. Investing profits from oil in new businesses, President Betancourt said, would cause other businesses to start. These new businesses were needed for Venezuela to industrialize—that is, build more factories and businesses.

In the 1970s another Venezuelan president, Carlos Andrés Pérez, introduced a policy to industrialize the country at a faster pace. For example, he created programs to build steel and aluminum plants.

BORROWING FOR GROWTH

During the late 1970s Venezuela began to borrow heavily from foreign banks to pay for the country's development. Many bankers were eager to lend money to oil-rich Venezuela. Few thought that the country would ever have trouble repaying its debts.

Many shopping malls, such as this one in Caracas, opened up after the Venezuelans discovered oil near Lake Maracaibo.

From 1973 to 1982, the **foreign debt** of Venezuela grew rapidly. The foreign debt is all of the money that a country owes to foreign banks and countries. Venezuela's debt rose to about one half of the amount shown on the graph below. Some of the money that Venezuela borrowed was spent to build housing projects, schools, and hydroelectric plants. But not all of the money was used wisely. For example, the government hired too many people.

After 1982 Venezuela's foreign debt rose even more. This happened because, as the graph on page 489 shows, the price of oil began to drop in 1982.

Many countries then faced a **recession**. A recession is a period of slower business activity. Even after the recession ended, oil prices remained low.

THE RISING DEBT

As a result of lower oil prices in the 1980s, Venezuela earned far less than it had expected from its sales of oil. Foreign bankers began to worry about the loans they had made to Venezuela and other oil producers during the boom years of the 1970s.

By 1988 Venezuela owed over $33 billion to foreign banks. This debt made Venezuela the fourth-largest debtor nation in South America. As you can see on the graph on this page, only Mexico, Argentina, and Brazil had larger foreign debts.

In order to make payments on its loans, the government of Venezuela had to reduce spending. Apartment buildings were left unfinished. Government workers lost their jobs. Venezuela's leaders had to make deep cuts in government spending programs. Such cuts hit the poor the hardest.

In February 1989, Venezuela's President Pérez raised the price of gasoline and of bus fares. This move and additional spending cuts shocked and angered Venezuelans. Riots broke out in cities throughout Venezuela.

ECONOMIC RECOVERY

Venezuelans have recently made great strides to improve their troubled economy. Venezuela still relies heavily on the export of oil. Venezuelans need to diversify the country's economy by developing new industries. Then they will be less affected by changes in oil prices.

However, Venezuela has begun to

GRAPH SKILL: What was the **foreign debt** of Venezuela in 1988? Of Brazil?

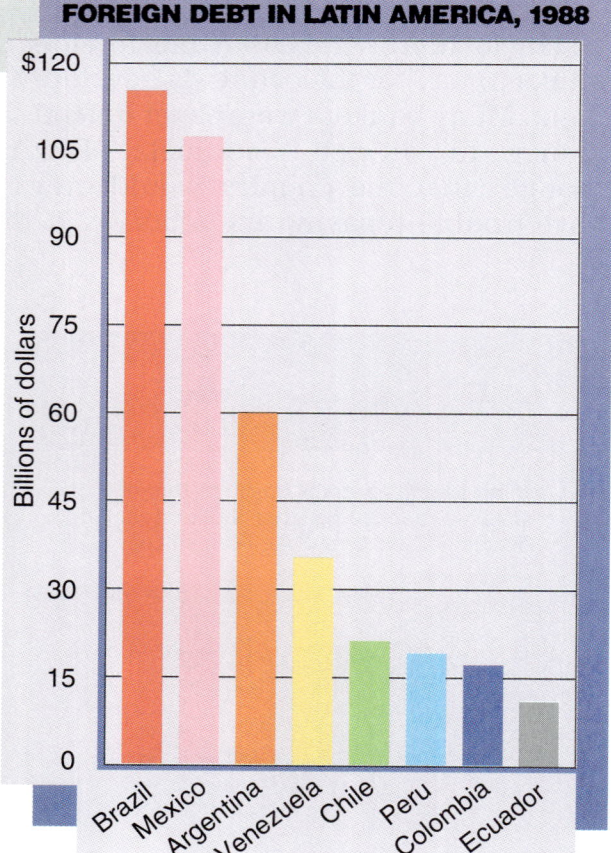

FOREIGN DEBT IN LATIN AMERICA, 1988

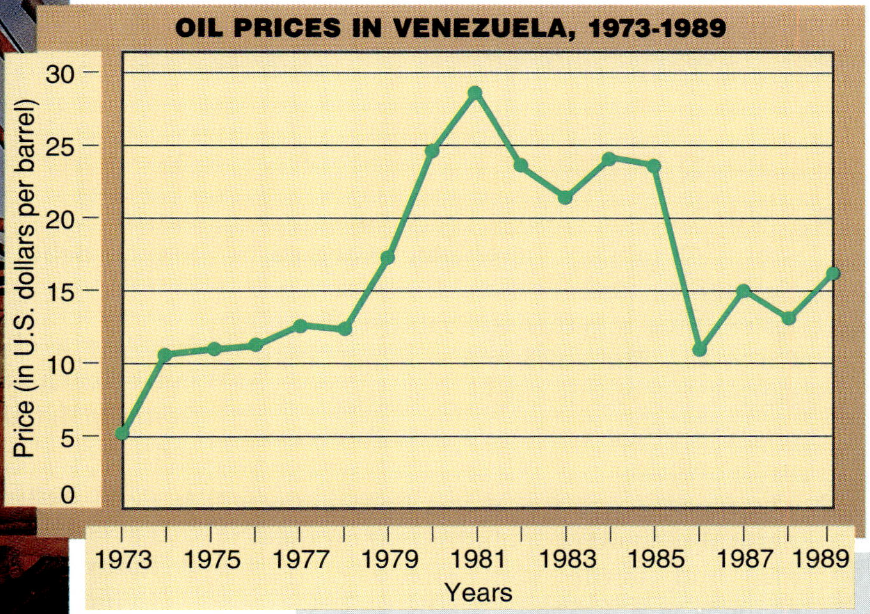

OIL PRICES IN VENEZUELA, 1973-1989

Price (in U.S. dollars per barrel) vs. *Years*

GRAPH SKILL: This graph shows oil prices in Venezuela over a 16-year period. When did the price of oil increase the most? When did it decrease the most?

explore ways of improving its economy by selling some of the companies it owns to private investors. For example, Venezuela recently reached an agreement with a company in Spain to sell part of its national airline.

Venezuela also is working hard to open up trade with other countries, including the United States. According to Andrés Sosa Pietri, president of a Venezuelan oil company,

> We are back to [being] the fastest-growing economy in the region. We lagged in the '80s, but now we are back on our feet.

The other North Coast countries do not have large reserves of oil. However, they, too, depend on one product or a few export products. They also need to diversify their economies.

A DIFFICULT TASK

You have read that Venezuela is rich in oil resources. The government has used oil profits to develop the economy. It also borrowed money from foreign banks to help industrialize the country and has had trouble repaying its debts. Since 1991 Venezuela has begun to experience economic growth.

Check Your Reading

1. Why was OPEC formed? How did its actions affect Venezuela?
2. Why did Venezuela borrow money from foreign banks in the 1970s?
3. What caused Venezuela's foreign debt to increase?
4. THINKING SKILL: Reread the quotation by Venezuelan oil company president Andrés Sosa Pietri on this page. Explain why he concluded that Venezuelans were "back on our feet."

CHAPTER 23 · SUMMARY AND REVIEW

IDEAS TO REMEMBER

■ South America's North Coast countries are Colombia, Venezuela, Guyana, Suriname, and French Guiana. The latter three together are known as the Guianas. The different groups that settled the North Coast countries created one of the most diverse populations in the world.

■ The North Coast countries have many natural resources, including oil, minerals, and fertile soil. However, the rugged, mountainous lands have presented a challenge to the people who try to use these resources.

■ The discovery of oil changed the economy of Venezuela. Venezuela entered the world economy, becoming one of the world's leading oil exporters. But economic dependence on oil brought problems as well as benefits to this South American country.

PEOPLE TO KNOW

Rómulo Betancourt
1908–1981

Carlos Andrés Pérez
1922–

REVIEWING VOCABULARY

barrio   penal colony
foreign debt   recession
patois

Number a sheet of paper from 1 to 5. Beside each number write the word or term from the list above that best completes the sentence.

1. After borrowing so much money, Venezuela had a huge _____.
2. Many convicts died due to the terrible living conditions in the _____.
3. People bought fewer goods during the worldwide _____, and many workers lost their jobs.
4. A _____ is a version of a language spoken in a region.
5. Many people live without running water or electricity in the _____.

REVIEWING FACTS

Number a sheet of paper from 1 to 10. Write whether the following statements are true or false. If the statement is false, rewrite it to make it true.

1. Suriname, Colombia, and Guyana are together known as the three Guianas.
2. French Guiana is not an independent country.
3. Today French Guiana is still mainly a penal colony.
4. Guyana is South America's only Russian-speaking country.
5. Some of the world's finest coffee is made from beans grown in Colombia and Venezuela.
6. Growing the coca plant is illegal in Colombia.

SURINAME INDEPENDENT AT LAST !

PARAMARIBO, November 25, 1975 – Today the government of the Netherlands granted complete independence to Suriname. After two years of talks, agreement was finally reached. Large-scale financial aid is also promised for the future. There is dancing in the streets, and the people are

INDEPENDENCE DAY CELEBRATION

7. Colombia has the second-largest population in all of South America.
8. After 1922 Venezuela's economy changed and became mainly a farming economy.
9. Everyone in Venezuela benefited equally from the discovery of oil.
10. Today in Venezuela less than half of the government's money comes from the export of oil.

WRITING ABOUT MAIN IDEAS

1. **Writing a Letter:** Imagine that you are on a tour of South America's North Coast countries. Write a letter home to your family describing some of the people you have met on your trip.
2. **Writing a Paragraph:** In which ways do you think the Venezuelan government could try to improve the nation's economy? How could financial planners make the country less dependent on oil? What do you recommend they do to help the citizens?
3. **Writing About Perspectives:** Imagine that you belong to a group of llaneros in Venezuela. Write the lyrics to a song about your day that you might sing around a campfire.

BUILDING SKILLS: READING A NEWSPAPER

Use what you already know and read the article at the top of the page to answer the following questions.

1. What is the most important information presented in the first paragraph above?
2. What kind of information would you find in an editorial?
3. If you wanted to find a part-time job after school, where in the newspaper would you look?
4. Why is it important to understand how to read newspapers?

CHAPTER 24

THE ANDEAN COUNTRIES

FOCUS

Bolivians like to talk about their future. They like to think that it will be a good one.

The writer William E. Carter wrote these words to describe the people of Bolivia. In this chapter you will read about life today in Bolivia and the other Andean countries—Peru, Ecuador, and Chile. As you will read, the people of these countries are working to make their future "a good one."

1 People

READ TO LEARN

Key Vocabulary
landlocked

Key Places
Cuzco

Read Aloud

It is late June, the start of winter in the Southern Hemisphere, the half of the earth that lies south of the equator. Indian women in colorful shawls and layers of full skirts and men in striped ponchos crowd the streets of Cuzco, Peru, once the capital of the Incan Empire. The Indian visitors are in Cuzco for the Incan sun festival. Long ago Incan worshipers of the sun god took part in this religious celebration. They believed that the celebration would ensure the sun's return to the Andes at winter's end. Today most Indians see the sun festival as a way of remembering their past.

Read for Purpose

1. **WHAT YOU KNOW:** What are some holidays that people in the United States celebrate to remind them of their past?
2. **WHAT YOU WILL LEARN:** How is life in the Andean countries a blend of the old and new?

THE ANDEAN REGION

You can find the four countries that make up the Andean region on the map on page 494. This region takes its name from the Andes Mountains, which cover parts of all four countries.

The smallest Andean country is Ecuador. Its name, which is the Spanish word for "equator," tells you a lot about its location. As you can see from the map on page 494, the equator runs through Ecuador. South of Ecuador is Peru. Almost three times the size of the state of California, Peru is the largest Andean country. Southeast of Peru is Bolivia, the region's only landlocked

country. As you can see on the map, Bolivia has no coast. It is surrounded by other countries. Chile, the southernmost Andean country, is sometimes called the "shoestring" country. This is because it stretches along the western coast of South America like a long, thin shoelace.

THE ANDEAN INDIANS

In two of the four Andean countries, Bolivia and Peru, Indians make up over half the population. About one fourth of all Ecuadorians are Indians. In Chile Indians are a minority. Most Andean Indians are Quechua (kech' wä)

ANDEAN COUNTRIES: Political

✪ National capital
• Other city

MAP SKILL: Which countries border the landlocked country of Bolivia? Which Andean country has the longest coastline? What is the capital of Ecuador?

Indians, the descendants of the Incas. The language they speak is also called Quechua. The Aymara (ī mä rä′) are another large Indian group. Their ancestors were conquered by the Incas in the 1400s.

The villages of the plateaus and valleys of the Andes are home to most of the region's Quechua. The Aymara live mostly along the shores and on the islands of Lake Titicaca, on the border between Peru and Bolivia.

EUROPEANS

People of Spanish descent are a small but powerful minority in the Andean countries. Although they do not make up more than one fourth of the population in any of these countries, they control most of the power and wealth. Most of them are descendants of the Spanish colonists who settled in South America when the continent was part of the Spanish Empire.

In the 1800s Chile began attracting small numbers of European immigrants from Great Britain and Germany. Chile's German settlers came mainly in the 1850s, after the Chilean government had set up immigration offices in Germany to attract settlers.

OTHER ETHNIC GROUPS

In Chile and Ecuador mestizos are the largest ethnic group. They also make up sizable percentages of the population of Peru and Bolivia. Most mestizos speak Spanish.

In Ecuador one person in ten people traces his or her roots to Africa. Most people of African descent live in Ecuador's coastal lowlands. Their ancestors were forced to come to Ecuador as slaves in the 1500s to work on plantations owned by Spanish colonists.

TRADITIONAL WAYS

"The Indians of the Andes," said one traveler to Peru, "have dual [double] citizenship in the worlds of the past and present." Their dances, clothing, music, and food date back to ancient times. Spanish missionaries had converted most of the Indians to the Catholic religion. However, many of their holidays combine elements of both Incan religion and Catholic customs.

Memories of the Incas' great civilization are still very much alive in the Andean highlands. Vicente Revilla (vi cen' tā rā vē' yə) was born in the city of Cuzco, Peru, and lived there until he was 20. He describes his early education this way:

Like other children growing up in the highlands, I learned about all the legends of the Incan Empire, the names of the . . . rulers and Incan heroes . . . who made . . . Peru what it was.

GROWING URBAN AREAS

In two of the four Andean countries—Bolivia and Ecuador—the population is almost evenly divided between rural and urban areas. Beginning in the 1950s, people from the rural areas of Chile and Peru began moving to the cities. Today over two thirds of all Chileans and Peruvians live in urban areas. You will read more about the growing urban areas of this region in Lesson 3.

A MIXED POPULATION

The countries of the Andean region are home to Indians, mestizos, and people of European and African descent. The populations of Ecuador and Bolivia are divided between rural and urban areas. The cities of Chile and Peru continue to grow.

 Check Your Reading

1. Which two large Indian groups live in the Andean countries?
2. Why can the Indians of the Andes be said to have "citizenship in the worlds of the past and present"?
3. GEOGRAPHY SKILL: Look at the map on page 494. Which countries share a border with Ecuador?
4. THINKING SKILL: Compare the ethnic groups that live in Chile with Ecuador's ethnic groups.

Using Graphs

While reading this book, you have often been referred to graphs or charts for specific information. For example, the line graph on this page shows how the population of Peru grew from 1986 to 1990. The circle graphs on page 497 show different kinds of information about the population of Bolivia.

Sometimes information is best described by showing two or more different graphs. Then you can compare the graphs and draw conclusions from the comparison. When you compare graphs, you can gain information that neither graph alone could have provided. In this lesson you can use graphs that show related information to find new information and to draw conclusions.

Using Line and Bar Graphs

Graph A shows the total population in Peru from 1986 to 1990. You recall that to read a line graph, you look first at the labels on the horizontal and vertical axes. To find the population of Peru in 1987, for example, you begin by finding the year 1987 on the horizontal axis. Move your finger up to the point on the line above that year. Then follow a straight line left to the vertical axis. It shows that the population of Peru was just under 20 million people in 1987. What was its population one year before, in 1986?

Now look at **Graph B**. It shows the percentage of Andean workers with jobs in agriculture in 1990. Which country has the lowest percentage? About what percentage of people in Peru's labor force work in agriculture?

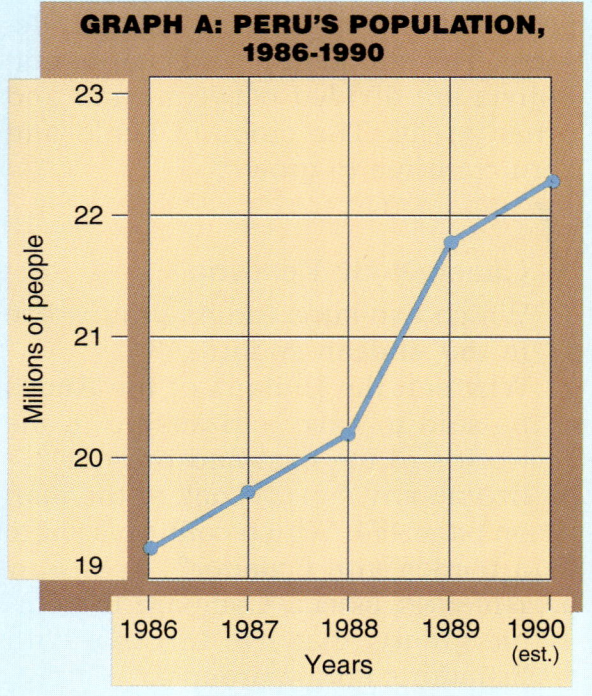

GRAPH A: PERU'S POPULATION, 1986-1990

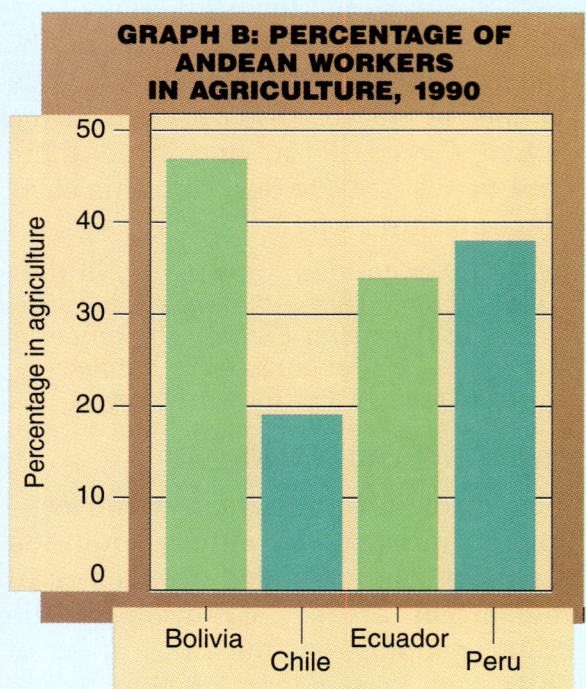

GRAPH B: PERCENTAGE OF ANDEAN WORKERS IN AGRICULTURE, 1990

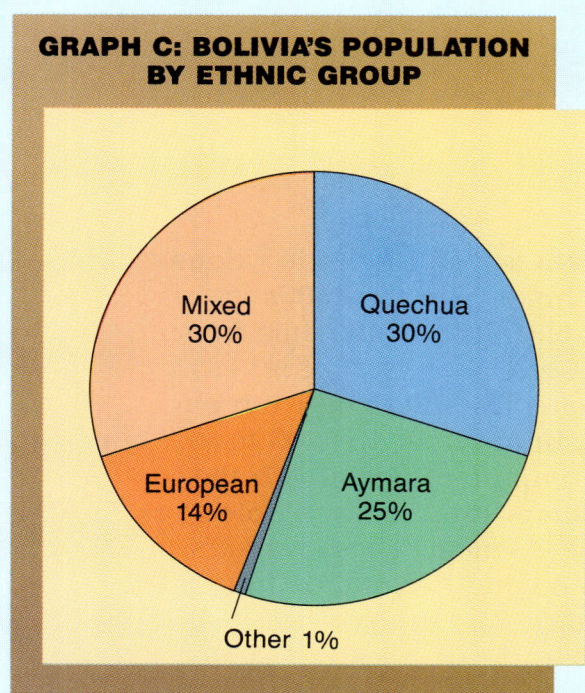

GRAPH C: BOLIVIA'S POPULATION BY ETHNIC GROUP

Quechua 30%
Mixed 30%
European 14%
Aymara 25%
Other 1%

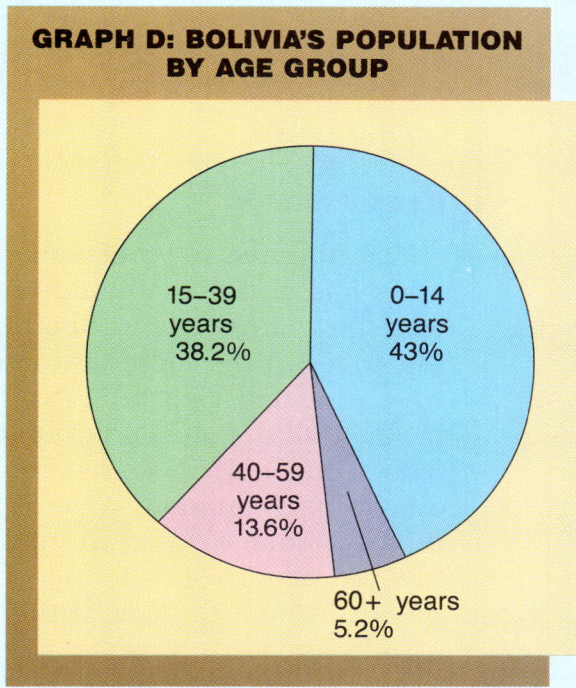

GRAPH D: BOLIVIA'S POPULATION BY AGE GROUP

15–39 years 38.2%
0–14 years 43%
40–59 years 13.6%
60+ years 5.2%

By using these graphs together, you can find out approximately how many people were in Peru in a particular year and the kind of work many of them did.

Using Circle Graphs

Graph C and **Graph D** are circle graphs. As you recall, circle graphs show how a whole is divided into parts. **Graph C** shows the ethnic groups into which Bolivia's population is divided.

Graph C also helps you see clearly that Bolivia's population is divided into four main ethnic groups. What percentage of the population is from the Quechua Indian group?

Now look at **Graph D**. It presents the breakdown of Bolivia's population according to age. The graph shows that the largest population group in Bolivia is people

under the age of 15 years. Which group is the smallest?

You could put together **Graph C** and **Graph D** to find out a great deal about the population of Bolivia. Do you think that most of the people in the Indian groups are young or old?

Reviewing the Skill

1. What is the purpose of using more than one graph?
2. Could the information on **Graph A** be plotted on a bar graph instead? Why or why not?
3. About what percentage of the labor force in Bolivia works in agriculture?
4. Which ethnic group in Bolivia is the smallest?
5. Why is it helpful to know how to use different kinds of graphs?

497

2 Living and Working

READ TO LEARN

Key Vocabulary
cash economy

Key Places
Otavalo

Read Aloud

The Bolivian town of Potosí (pōt ə sē′) in the Andes Mountains has had two chapters in its history. In the 1600s Potosí was the richest city in Spain's empire. Its wealth came from the silver in the mountain called Cerro Rico (ser′ ō rē′ kō), which means "rich hill" in Spanish. When the silver ran out in the 1800s, Potosí's population shrank from 150,000 to 8,000. But in 1905 Potosí became important again with the discovery of another mineral resource—tin. Today people work in government-owned tin mines near Potosí. These workers, like the people of the other Andean countries, are earning a living through the use of the region's resources.

Read for Purpose

1. **WHAT YOU KNOW:** Which ethnic groups live in the Andean countries?
2. **WHAT YOU WILL LEARN:** How do the people of the Andean countries earn a living?

A REGION OF FARMERS

In every Andean country except Chile, more people work in farming than in any other industry. In the Andean highlands, most farmers are subsistence farmers. The food they raise is enough to feed their families, with a little left over to exchange for goods at the local market.

The number of crops that these farmers grow is limited by geography. Most farms in this region are located on the altiplano. As you read in Chapter 21, the altiplano is a high plateau. Farmers must struggle to raise crops on the hard, barren soil.

The number of crops that can be grown is also limited by the lack of modern farm equipment. Throughout the Andes, farmers rely on wooden plows pulled by oxen to till their fields. On steep hillside slopes, farmers use digging sticks with iron tips, which are similar to the tools used by their Incan ancestors. These traditional methods help the Andean farmers grow food in steep places where modern farm machinery cannot be brought.

POTATOES AND LLAMAS

Throughout the Andes, farmers grow beans, barley, corn, wheat, and over 200 different varieties of potatoes. In the highlands, potatoes come in all shapes, sizes, and colors. The Indians have given interesting names to some. For example, the Quechua word for a knobby, hard-to-cook potato is *lumchipamundana* (lum chē pä mun dä′ nə), which means "potato that makes a young bride weep."

In grassy areas, Andean farmers also raise llamas, sheep, and alpacas. At dawn boys lead sheep and llamas up hillside trails to graze. The sure-footed llama serves as a pack animal, carrying heavy loads on mountain trails. Women and girls turn its wool into clothes and blankets. They weave on portable looms as they travel along mountain trails.

CASH ECONOMY

Indian families sometimes earn a little extra money by selling handicrafts, such as pottery, wood carvings, or woven goods, at the weekly market in the town plaza. Until recently Andean

(*left*) An Indian woman sells different kinds of potatoes at the market. (*center*) This Quechua Indian is spinning wool. (*right*) Handicrafts are being sold in Otavalo, Ecuador.

Indians had little contact with a **cash economy**. In a cash economy, goods are exchanged for money. The Andean Indians used to trade goods rather than buy and sell goods for money.

In recent years peddlers have brought plastic buckets, safety pins, aluminum pots, and other manufactured goods to all but the most remote areas. As more and more people buy cheap, factory-made goods, traditional crafts and skills like weaving have begun to die out.

However, in **Otavalo** (ōt ə väl′ ō), Ecuador, a group of Andean Indians have seen interest in their handicrafts grow. Otavalo women knit brightly colored sweaters, ponchos, blankets, and other woolen goods in distinctive patterns. Their beautiful creations are

499

sold many thousands of miles away in markets in other South American countries and Europe. The high quality of their work has made it possible for the people of Otavalo to earn more income than most Indians of the Andes.

OFFICIAL AND UNOFFICIAL EXPORTS

Since the time of the Incas, Andean Indians have chewed the coca leaf. Its numbing effects have helped them to endure long hours of work, bitter cold, and hunger. As you have read in Chapter 23, coca is used to make the illegal drug cocaine. In recent years the growth of the South American drug trade in cocaine has made coca an important but illegal crop in both Peru and Bolivia.

In lowland coastal areas farmers grow a variety of crops. Ecuador's com-mercial farmers grow cacao, bananas, and coffee. Bolivia's major lowland crops include rice, cotton, and sugarcane. On cooperative farms in Peru's highlands, farmers grow crops such as corn and potatoes. In Chile's fertile Central Valley farmers grow grapes and other fruits for export. Nearly three fourths of the grapes imported by the United States come from Chile. Wines made from Chilean grapes have become well known all over the world.

Harvesting the sea is another important industry in parts of the Andean region. Along the Pacific coast Peruvians catch anchovies, tuna, and other fish. In fact, Peru ranks first in Latin America in the size of its fishing industry. Chile ranks second. The catch of the Chilean fishing fleet includes anchovies and sardines. Cans of fish from both countries are sold in European and United States supermarkets. However, most of the fish is ground into fish meal and exported as fertilizer.

Farming and fishing are two of the most important economic activities in the Andean countries.

MINING DESERTS AND MOUNTAINS

As you read in the Read Aloud on page 498, long ago Potosí was an important center of mining. Today mining is big business in the Atacama Desert in northern Chile. Copper mining provides jobs for thousands of Chilean workers. The country contains one fifth of the world's copper reserves and is the world's largest copper producer. Towns in northern Chile celebrate the importance of mining with a festival honoring the patron saint of miners. Look at the map on this page. Which other minerals are mined in Chile?

A DIVERSIFIED ECONOMY

Although copper is still Chile's most important export, Chileans have successfully diversified their economy. In the past, sharp drops in the price of copper on world markets have left the Chilean economy badly shaken. Today, however, exports of fruit, fish meal, and wine and the growth of industries have made Chile less dependent on mining. The other Andean countries still face the difficult challenge of diversifying their economies.

RECREATION

The people of the Andean countries find many different ways to relax and have fun. In the cities people enjoy plays, movies, ballets, and operas. Ski resorts in the Chilean Andes are a popular vacation spot for the wealthy.

MAP SKILL: The copper-refining plant (*below*) is in the Atacama Desert in Chile. In which countries besides Chile is copper mined?

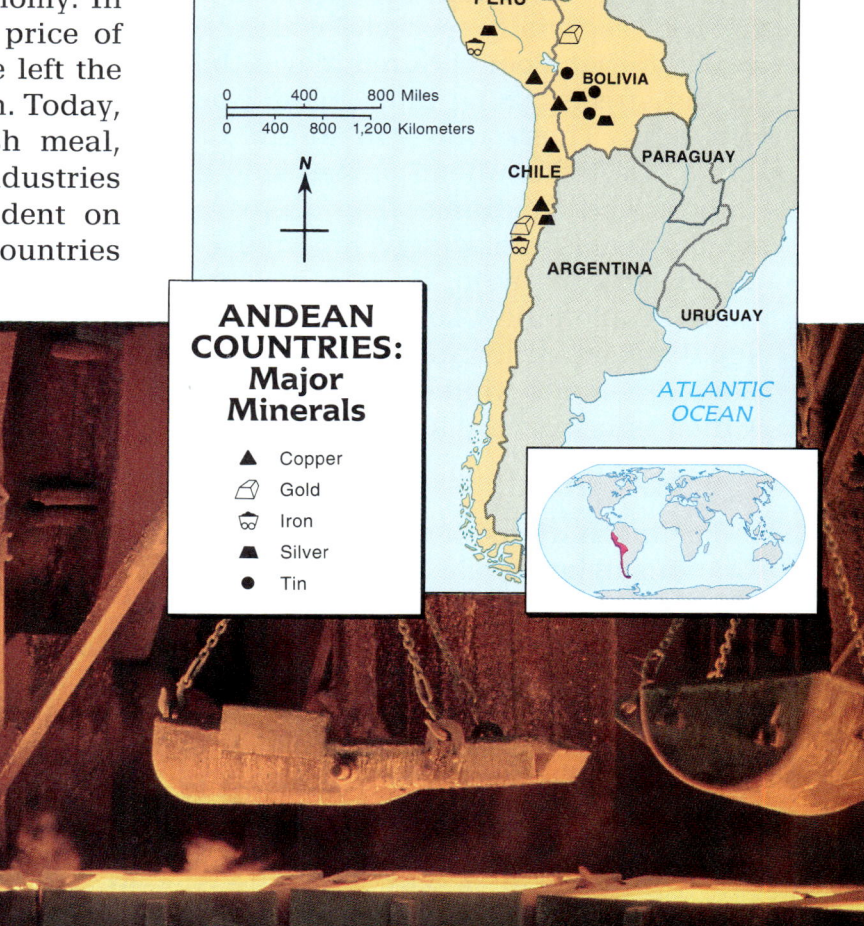

ANDEAN COUNTRIES: Major Minerals

▲ Copper
⬔ Gold
⬕ Iron
▲ Silver
● Tin

(*above*) These children have made a soccer ball from old rags. (*right*) Ski resorts in Chile attract many tourists.

Both the rich and the poor enjoy sports, especially soccer, which is called *fútbol*. Poor children play fútbol in the streets, using balls made from old rags. Those who can afford the price of a ticket attend games held at large soccer stadiums. The scores of soccer teams are widely reported on television, on radio, and in newspapers. People follow soccer closely during the competition for the World Cup, soccer's major international event, which is held every four years.

CELEBRATIONS

For the Indians of the Andes, celebrations in honor of a birth of a child, a saint's day, or the building of a house are a welcome break from daily chores. On festival days in the highlands, villagers march in parades, carrying statues of the saints to the village church. The air fills with the sad and lonely sounds of Andean songs played on the quena (kā' nə), a bamboo flute, and accompanied by the rhythms of drums. Families share a special meal of roast pig or chicken. These special meals are a welcome change from the daily diet of potatoes and vegetables.

A FARMING REGION

In this lesson you read that farming, fishing, and mining are all important in the Andean region. Farming employs the most people in all of these countries, except Chile. The people of this region have many ways of relaxing, such as watching or playing soccer and taking part in celebrations.

Check Your Reading

1. List four ways in which the people in the countries of the Andean region earn a living.
2. What is a cash economy?
3. Why was it important for Chile to diversify its economy?
4. **THINKING SKILL:** Based on your reading of this lesson, what can you conclude about manufacturing in the Andean countries?

502

HIGH HOPES IN THE ANDES

For years many of the young people who lived in Aquia (ä′ kē ä), a small village high in the Andes Mountains of Peru, had to leave their home to find work elsewhere. As you have read in Lesson 1, this situation is not uncommon in the Andean countries. Aquia, like other small mountain villages all over Chile and Peru, offered its young people little hope for the future. However, the situation in Aquia today is very different. Thanks to the efforts of the town council, Aquia has a thriving new industry and a brighter future.

After nearly 400 years, the Aquia town council decided in the early 1980s to bring alpacas back to their area. Alpacas are four-legged woolly animals, closely related to the llama. The council hoped that the alpacas would provide work for herders, as well as wool for spinners, weavers, and other craftspeople. As the new industry grew, the council hoped the young people of Aquia would not have to move to the cities in order to find work.

For hundreds of years, the alpaca was a main source of wool and meat for the people of the Andes Mountains. But the Spanish conquerors took over the lands on which the alpacas lived. This, in addition to the many diseases that Spanish livestock brought to South America, wiped out the native alpaca.

Finally, 400 years later, the Peruvian government returned the lands seized by the Spanish to the *campesinos*, or poor farmers, of Aquia. The town council voted to raise alpacas as a community project.

In 1986, men traveled from Aquia to southern Peru to buy a herd of alpacas. After a 7-day trip by foot, train, and truck, the campesinos put 1,000 alpacas in their new home in the meadows of Aquia.

There were problems at first. The herders had to get used to life in the cold, lonely fields, miles away from their families in the village. People had to learn how to care for the alpacas. They had to learn how to handle the alpaca's fleece, which is more delicate than the sheep's wool to which they were accustomed.

The alpaca herd is increasing rapidly now, and the campesinos of Aquia have great hopes for the future. Their efforts to improve their lives should be successful. As a village leader said, "We now have the seed. And the seed will bear fruit for the community."

3 Growing Cities

Key Vocabulary

squatter
pueblo joven

Key Places

Villa El Salvador
Lima

Read Aloud

Shortly after midnight on May 1, 1971, about 500 Peruvian families launched an invasion. These families took over an empty plot of state-owned land on the outskirts of Lima, the capital of Peru. Carrying cardboard, straw, and scrap metal, they quickly patched together homes to house their families. By the next morning, a small city had sprung up on Lima's south side. Although lacking in water, electricity, or plumbing, the new town had a name. Its new residents named it Villa El Salvador (vē′ yə el sal′ və dôr).

Read for Purpose

1. **WHAT YOU KNOW:** Would you rather live in a city or a rural area? Why?
2. **WHAT YOU WILL LEARN:** How has rapid population growth affected Lima?

A CHANGING LIFESTYLE

Nearly every day throughout Latin America, towns like Villa El Salvador spring to life around large cities such as Lima, Peru. The areas are settled by squatters. A squatter is someone who settles on land to which he or she has no legal right. As you read in People Who Make a Difference on page 503, more and more rural villagers are moving to the cities of Latin America. There housing shortages force these urban newcomers to become squatters.

In 1925 only one in three Latin Americans lived in cities. As you can see from the graph on page 505, more people now live in urban areas than in rural areas. The populations of cities such as Mexico City, Mexico; Caracas, Venezuela; São Paulo, Brazil; and Bogotá, Colombia, have skyrocketed. Chile is typical. Today about 86 percent of all Chileans live in urban areas. Santiago, the capital of Chile, is home to over one third of all Chileans.

FROM COUNTRY TO CITY

There are several reasons for the movement of people from rural areas to cities. In the Andean countries poverty and lack of opportunity lead the list. Newcomers from the highlands view the city as a place where they can find jobs, schools for their children, and better medical care.

Modesto Mamani is an Indian boy who lives in a small town in Peru near Lake Titicaca. He describes his vision of city life in this way:

I don't know what heaven is like. But I think heaven must be like a city. Because everybody is happy there. Nobody goes hungry. There are plenty of fruits. There is no water problem.

City dwellers who live in the slums would disagree with Modesto's rosy picture of city life. But his words suggest the wide gap that separates the urban from the rural, and the rich from the poor in parts of Latin America.

CITIES IN THE ANDEAN COUNTRIES

In recent years improved roads and railroads have helped to increase mountain villagers' awareness of city life. Andean villagers go to the cities to sell their crops or handicrafts. Some return to the highlands with tales of city life. Others decide to stay in the cities. Relatives who are assured of a place to stay until they can find work soon join family members in the cities.

When newcomers from the villages reach the cities, their first houses are often shacks. These shacks make up the slums surrounding many South American cities. Chileans call such slums *callampas* (kä yäm′ pəz), which

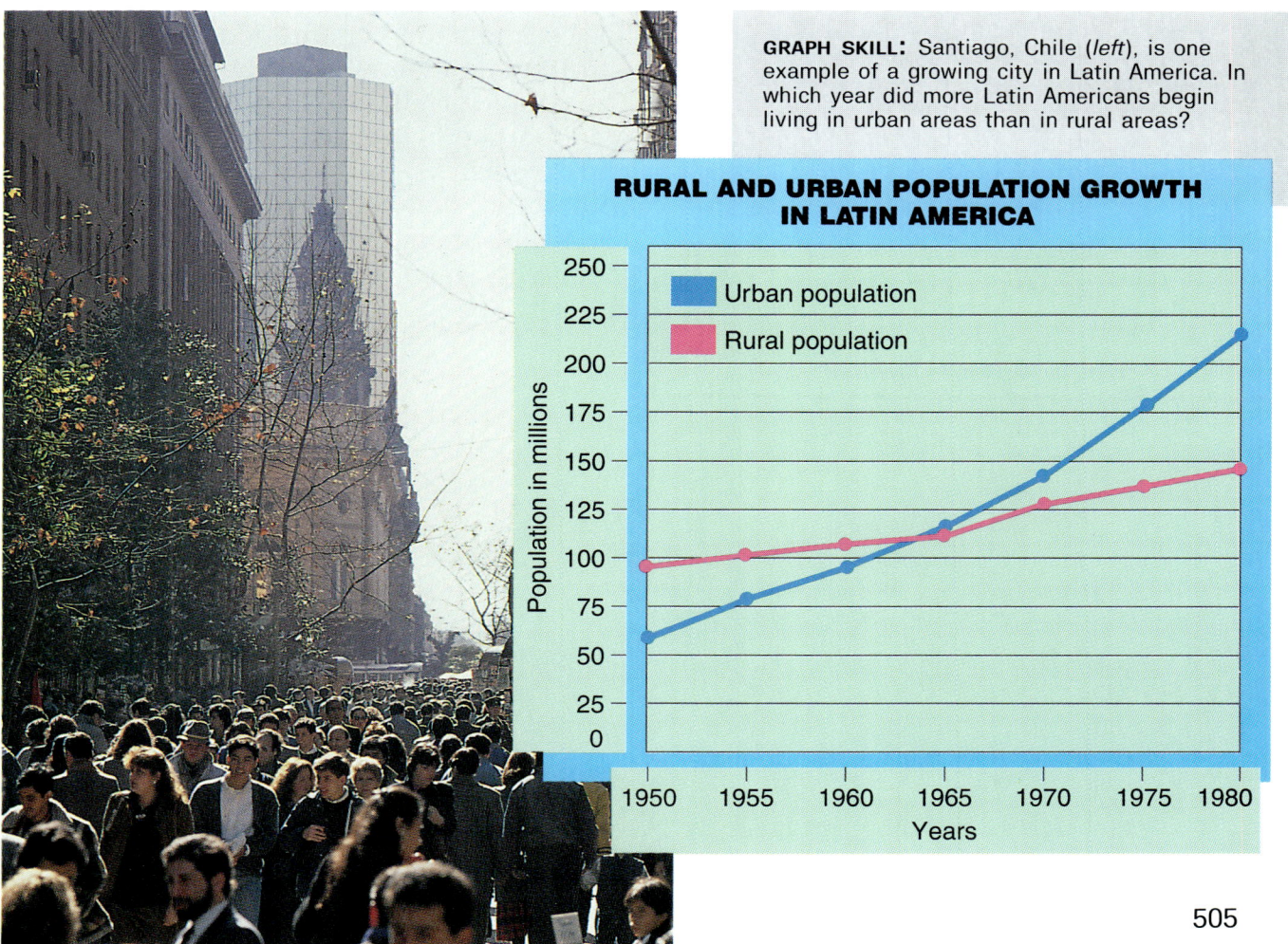

GRAPH SKILL: Santiago, Chile (*left*), is one example of a growing city in Latin America. In which year did more Latin Americans begin living in urban areas than in rural areas?

RURAL AND URBAN POPULATION GROWTH IN LATIN AMERICA

Urban population
Rural population

Population in millions

250
225
200
175
150
125
100
75
50
25
0

1950 1955 1960 1965 1970 1975 1980

Years

505

means "mushrooms," as they seem to spring up overnight like mushrooms after a heavy rain. Lacking paved roads, water, and electricity, these slums often offer little more than shelter.

For those who can find jobs, the stay in a slum is only a steppingstone to a better life. However, most newcomers find it hard, if not impossible, to get good jobs. In the crowded cities of this region, there are always many more job seekers than jobs. Most newcomers are unskilled and have little schooling. Many cannot read. Some get low-paying jobs in factories, or work as servants or messengers. However, many remain jobless.

YOUNG TOWNS

In Peru the government calls its new urban slums **pueblos jóvenes** (pwe' blōs hō' bā nes), or young towns.

MAP SKILL: (*left*) These Villa El Salvador residents are building a home. How far is Villa El Salvador from Lima's 1968 boundary?

Government leaders want to help the pueblos jóvenes. The government hopes that the settlements will grow into independent communities. Lima's Villa El Salvador, which you read about in the Read Aloud on page 504, is one such pueblo joven. You can find Villa El Salvador on the map below. From its start with 500 families over 20 years ago, it has grown to a community of more than 300,000 people. The Peruvian government has worked with the people of Villa El Salvador to improve life in this pueblo joven.

WORKING TOGETHER

The people of Villa El Salvador have helped build schools and houses of concrete or adobe, which is sun-dried brick. Community volunteers built over 200 schools and went door-to-door, enrolling students in these schools. The people of Villa El Salvador formed neighborhood groups, youth clubs, and women's groups. Working together, they were able to persuade the local government in Lima to provide them with water, electricity, and other city services.

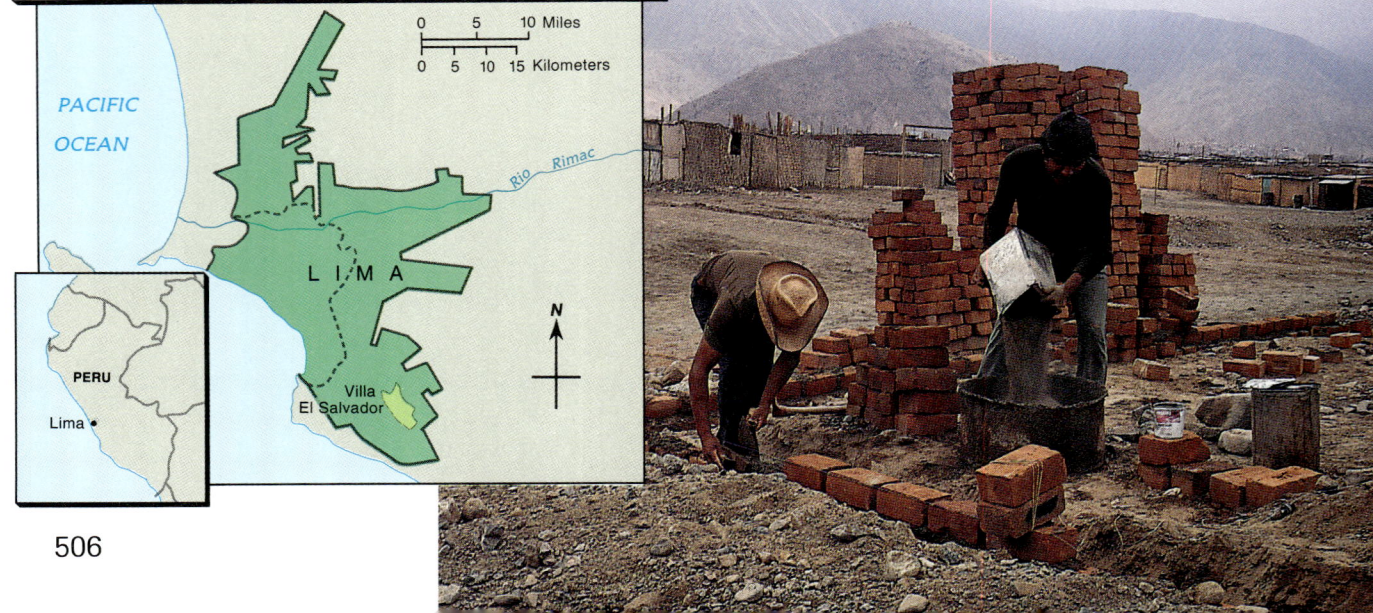

GROWTH OF LIMA

- - - - - - 1968 boundary of Lima
———— Present-day boundary of Lima

0   5   10 Miles

0   5   10   15 Kilometers

PACIFIC OCEAN

Rio Rimac

L I M A

N

PERU

Lima

Villa El Salvador

In 1983 Villa El Salvador became an independent city. Its voters elected a mayor who represents the community to the city government of Lima. The people of Villa El Salvador urged Lima city officials to pipe in water to irrigate nearly 100 acres (40 ha) of desert that lie close to Villa El Salvador. Today these city farmers grow oranges, sweet potatoes, papayas, and corn on the irrigated land.

EARNING A LIVING

Although few residents of Villa El Salvador have factory jobs or collect a regular salary, they work very hard. Toribia Chávez (tō rēb′ yə chäv′ əs), for example, has a one-room store next to her house. Here neighbors come to buy bread, cooking oil, pencils, and soda. Hernando García makes keys. He carries his workbench from street corner to street corner looking for new customers.

In Lima there is a huge marketplace on the banks of the Rímac River. Here people from the pueblos jóvenes buy and sell everything from radios and plumbing parts to carpets. Children shine shoes or sell newspapers and magazines. Their parents offer such services as auto repair or bargain with tourists over the price of a sweater, wall mirror, or fruits and vegetables.

AN URBAN CHALLENGE

Squatter cities are found throughout Latin America. Housing shortages force newcomers to live in quickly made shacks on the outskirts of these cities. Villa El Salvador in Peru is an example of a Latin American squatter city. By making places like Villa El Salvador more livable, Peru's leaders hope to include the poor in the economic and social life of the city.

Check Your Reading

1. How has Lima, Peru, changed since its population has increased?
2. What is a squatter?
3. How have the people of Villa El Salvador improved life in their city?
4. **THINKING SKILL:** State one opinion that is mentioned on page 505. Predict what facts would be needed to prove it to be true.

507

IDEAS TO REMEMBER

- The population of the Andean countries is made up of Indians, mestizos, and people whose ancestors came from Europe or Africa. People live in both rural and urban areas, but cities continue to grow as people move there looking for jobs.

- Important economic activities in the Andean countries are farming, fishing, and mining. Recreational activities include soccer and joining together in celebrations.

- On the outskirts of most Latin American cities, there are poor, crowded squatter cities, where many people must live when they come from the countryside in search of work. Government leaders are working to make squatter cities more livable.

REVIEWING VOCABULARY

cash economy
landlocked
pueblo joven
squatter

Number a sheet of paper from 1 to 5. Beside each number write the word or term from the list above that best completes the sentence. One of the words is used more than once.

1. A _____ is a person who settles on land to which he or she has no legal right.
2. _____, meaning "young town," is the Spanish name given to urban slums.
3. An arrangement in which goods are exchanged for money, not traded for other goods, is called a _____.
4. Many an urban newcomer in Latin America is forced to become a _____.
5. A country that has no coast is _____.

REVIEWING FACTS

Number a sheet of paper from 1 to 10. Beside each number write the name of the Andean country associated with the phrase. In some cases, the correct answer may be the names of more than one Andean country.

1. Population evenly divided between urban and rural
2. Largest fishing industry in Latin America
3. Only landlocked Andean country
4. Farming is the biggest industry
5. Smallest Andean country
6. "Shoestring" nation
7. Mestizos are the largest ethnic group
8. More than half the population is Indian
9. Capital: Santiago
10. Copper mining is big business

✏️ WRITING ABOUT MAIN IDEAS

1. **Writing an Outline:** Review on page 493 the subsection entitled "The Andean Indians." Make an outline of the information on population contained in the subsection. Include at least two main headings.

2. **Writing a Paragraph:** How do the Indians of the Andes combine traditional ways with modern ways? Write a paragraph describing at least two ways in

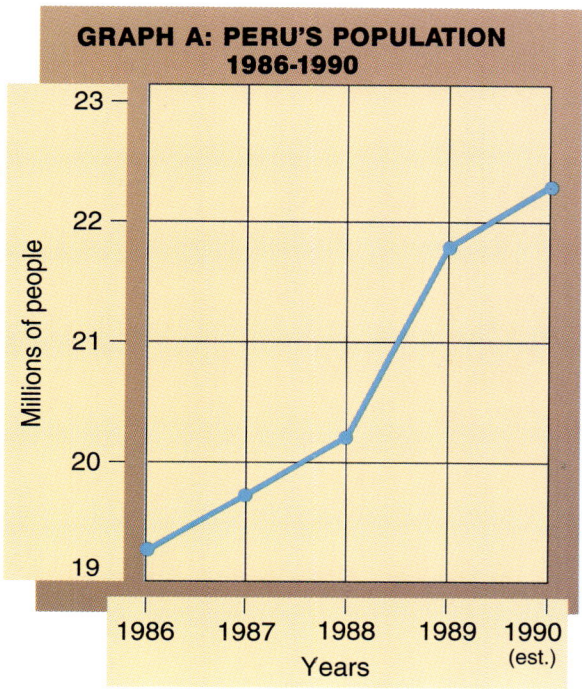

GRAPH A: PERU'S POPULATION 1986-1990

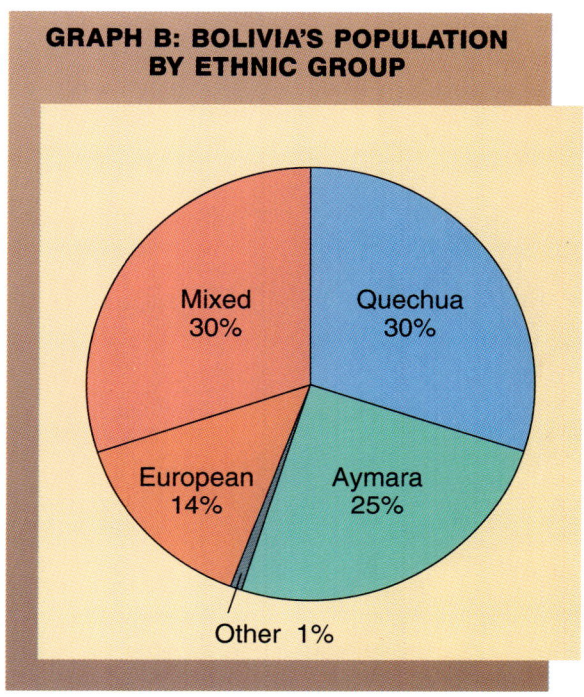

GRAPH B: BOLIVIA'S POPULATION BY ETHNIC GROUP

which they combine the traditional with the modern.

3. **Writing a Paragraph:** If you were in a position of power in the national government of an Andean country, what would be the first thing you would do to improve the situation of squatters? Write a paragraph that tells what you would do and why.

4. **Writing About Perspectives:** Write a story about an Andean family that moves from a country village to the city. In your story consider why they moved, what their life was like when they got to the city, and how they felt about what happened to them. Use the information in the chapter to make the story realistic, and use your imagination to make it interesting.

BUILDING SKILLS: USING GRAPHS

Use the graphs above to answer these questions.

1. Which type of graph is **Graph A**?
2. What is the subject of **Graph B**?
3. What was the population of Peru in 1988?
4. Which Indian group in Bolivia is larger—Quechua or Aymara?
5. About how many people in Bolivia are of European descent?
6. If you knew the population of Chile in 1970, 1980, and 1990, could you show those statistics on a circle graph? Why or why not?
7. Why is it helpful to know how to use graphs?

CHAPTER 25

THE COUNTRIES OF THE RÍO DE LA PLATA

FOCUS

The people want to know what it's all about.

Everyone in Argentina is familiar with this saying. People use it in conversation to mean, "Tell me more." In this chapter you will read more about Argentina, Paraguay, and Uruguay— the countries of the Río de la Plata.

1 People

Key Vocabulary

estuary
literacy rate

Key Places

Buenos Aires
Montevideo
Asunción

Read Aloud

The typical Argentine is an Italian who speaks Spanish but thinks he's British.

What do you think this old joke says about the people of Argentina? As you will read, Argentines come from a variety of backgrounds. In this lesson you will read about the different groups of people who live in Argentina, as well as those living in Uruguay and Paraguay.

Read for Purpose

1. **WHAT YOU KNOW:** How did the Río de la Plata countries win their independence from Spain?
2. **WHAT YOU WILL LEARN:** Which groups of people live in the Río de la Plata countries today?

COUNTRIES LINKED BY RIVERS

Río de la Plata means "silver river" in Spanish. But the Río de la Plata is actually neither silver nor a river. It is a murky, brown **estuary**. An estuary is the mouth of a river where the current meets the sea. Several rivers flow into the Río de la Plata estuary. This river system unites the three countries of this region: Paraguay, Uruguay, and Argentina. It also separates them, forming several of the borders between the three countries. In this lesson you will read about the people of the Río de la Plata region and about what unites and divides them.

ARGENTINA'S PEOPLE

Argentina, the second-largest country in South America, is more than four times the size of Texas. Its population is unlike that of most other Latin American countries.

Between 1850 and 1970 over 3 million European immigrants came to Argentina. As the immigrants arrived in the late 1800s, many of them moved west from the coast into the fertile Pampas. As they did so, Indian groups who had been living there for generations were often pushed off the land or killed. Fights started over farmland and cattle. Between 1878 and 1883

511

RÍO DE LA PLATA COUNTRIES:
Political

⊛ National capital   • Other city

MAP SKILL: The Río de la Plata is an **estuary** that opens into the Atlantic Ocean. Which three rivers feed into the Río de la Plata? How many countries do they reach?

almost all of Argentina's and Uruguay's Indians were killed.

Today very few Indians live in Argentina. Of the 33 million people living in the country today, 97 percent are of European ancestry.

In Argentina, as throughout the Río de la Plata region, cities have developed on the fertile land along the rivers. Over 80 percent of Argentina's population is urban, living in or near cities. Today almost one half of the entire population of Argentina lives in or near the capital city of **Buenos Aires** (bwā′ nəs ī rəs).

As the map on this page shows, Buenos Aires is located on the Río de la Plata. This location has enabled Buenos Aires to become a major port city. Ocean-going ships, as well as smaller ships bound for Uruguay, Paraguay, Brazil, and Bolivia, can be found docked in the harbor. The people of Buenos Aires are known as *porteños*, or "port dwellers."

Much of Argentina's culture has been affected by its European heritage. The famous Argentine dance, the tango, is a mixture of styles brought by immigrants from Spain and Italy.

URUGUAY—A SMALL NATION

Uruguay, the second-smallest country in South America, is slightly smaller than the state of Washington. Although Uruguay is much smaller than its giant neighbor, Argentina, the two countries have much in common. Like the people in Argentina, almost all of Uruguay's 3 million people are of European descent. Like Argentines, most Uruguayans are urban.

The two countries share another characteristic—they have the two highest **literacy rates** in Latin America.

The literacy rate is the percentage of people who can read and write. In Uruguay 95 percent of the population is literate. One reason for Uruguay's high literacy rate is its system of education. Education is required and is provided free of charge for all children. Many students go on to study at the university in Montevideo (mon tə vi dā′ ō), the capital of Uruguay.

PARAGUAY—POOR AND LANDLOCKED

Paraguay is one of the poorest countries in Latin America. Like Bolivia, Paraguay is landlocked, or surrounded on all sides by other countries. Willard L. Beaulac, a former United States Ambassador to Paraguay, explained in 1965:

Geography has seen to it that Paraguayans have changed little. Paraguay has probably changed more slowly than any other South American country.

About 95 percent of Paraguay's 4.4 million people are mestizos. They are descended from both Guaraní (gwär ə nē′) Indians and Spanish colonists.

Most Paraguayans are bilingual. Spanish is the official language of the schools, the church, and the government. However, when people in Paraguay want to express their emotions, they often do so in Guaraní. Magazines, plays, and poems are published in Guaraní.

Paraguayan society is divided into two groups, the rich and the poor. The rich control much of the best land and run the banks and businesses. They live in large houses in Asunción (ä sün syōn′), the capital of Paraguay. The poor, mostly Indians and mestizos, live as squatters in shacks scat-

Squatters like the family above live in shacks throughout Paraguay's countryside.

tered across the countryside. As one poor farmer says, "Land belongs to the one who works it."

THREE NATIONS AND PEOPLES

After Argentina and Uruguay were settled by European immigrants, the Indian populations of both countries were mostly destroyed. Paraguay, however, was closed to newcomers for much of its history. Its people are mostly mestizos who have both Spanish and Guaraní ancestors.

Check Your Reading

1. Why is Río de la Plata a misleading name?
2. What are the citizens of Buenos Aires called? Why?
3. What is one reason that Uruguay and Argentina have the highest literacy rates in Latin America?
4. **THINKING SKILL:** In which ways do you think being landlocked has caused Paraguay to remain a poor nation? Why?

2 Living and Working

READ TO LEARN

■ Key Vocabulary

estancia   industrialization   Itaipu Dam

■ Read Aloud

In 1984 the work was completed. An immense concrete dam spanned the mighty Paraná River in Paraguay. During 5 years of construction, enough concrete was poured to build a 350-story skyscraper. Entire towns were built just to house the workers who undertook this enormous task. In this lesson you will read about how this development changed life in Paraguay. You will also read about life and work throughout the Río de la Plata region.

■ Read for Purpose

1. **WHAT YOU KNOW:** Which groups of people settled the Río de la Plata countries?
2. **WHAT YOU WILL LEARN:** How do the people of these countries live and work today?

FARMING AND RANCHING

Land has always been the most valuable resource in the Río de la Plata countries. Argentina, Uruguay, and Paraguay were built by farmers, ranchers, and herders. Large numbers of people in each of these countries still earn their living from the land.

The cattle industry is a major part of Argentina's economy. One trucker who transports cattle notes:

Our own demand for meat is very high. We Argentines really like meat, and I've been told that we eat more meat than any other nation. But meat is an important part of our export business, too.

Argentina has some of the world's best farmland. On the fertile Pampas wheat grows without fertilizer, and cattle fatten without feedlots.

The rolling grasslands of Uruguay are ranching country. Sheep and cattle **estancias**, or ranches, cover most of this small nation. Beef and wool from the estancias have long been among Uruguay's most important exports.

Paraguay is a country of small farms. Most farmers use the same simple hand-held tools and ox-drawn plows that their ancestors used. Because the cost of shipping crops out of this land-locked country discouraged commercial farming, families used to grow just

Ranchers like those shown above raise sheep and cattle on the plains of Argentina's fertile Pampas region.

enough to live on and to sell locally. But the building of the Trans-Chaco Highway opened up transportation from the country to the sea. The highway changed farming in Paraguay. Now that they can move their crops across the Chaco, farmers are beginning to grow cash crops for export.

INDUSTRIALIZATION

Until the 1930s the economies of Argentina and Uruguay were based on farm exports. You may already know about the Great Depression in the United States. The rest of the world was also affected by this period of economic hardship. The prices of wheat, meat, and wool plunged. Prosperity gave way to poverty.

Argentina and Uruguay decided that the best solution was industrialization, or building new manufacturing industries. New businesses, it was hoped, would create jobs and produce goods that could replace costly imports.

The governments of Argentina and Uruguay helped new industries in many ways. They raised tariffs, or taxes on imports. This increase made imported goods more expensive and helped new local industries compete with foreign producers. If a business had trouble, the government often took it over.

Today both Argentina and Uruguay are industrial nations. Montevideo is ringed by meat-packing plants, textile mills, and food-processing plants. Factories in Argentina produce everything from textiles to tanks. In both countries one worker in four now works in manufacturing.

HYDROELECTRIC POWER FOR PARAGUAY

In the 1960s most of Paraguay did not have electricity. Other countries had developed hydroelectric power, or

515

electricity produced from the force of water. You have already read about the importance of hydroelectric power in Canada in Chapter 7. Paraguayans saw the power of their beautiful waterfalls and rivers, but they could not use it. Paraguay was too poor to build expensive dams and power plants.

In the early 1960s the United States government lent money to Paraguay to build its first hydroelectric power plant. Over the next 30 years many other countries, including Argentina, joined in lending Paraguay money.

Today the Itaipu Dam, which you read about on page 514, produces more electricity than any other hydroelectric power plant in the world. Now, hydroelectric power provides all of Paraguay with electricity. In fact, it produces enough electricity to make hydroelectricity Paraguay's leading export. The government makes more money from selling hydroelectric power than from all its other industries combined.

However, Paraguayans are still very poor compared to their neighbors in the Río de la Plata region. Much of the money the government earns is being spent to repay the loans it received from other countries. The building of dams created thousands of jobs for Paraguayan workers and boosted Paraguay's economy. However, when this project was completed in 1984, thousands of people were put out of work.

TRADITIONS REMAIN

Despite industrialization and growth, many old traditions remain in the countries of the Río de la Plata. One custom that unites all three countries is a simple beverage that people have been drinking for generations. *Yerba maté* (yer' bə mä' tā) is the national beverage of all three countries. Yerba is a kind of evergreen tree that grows naturally in the Río de la Plata region. The drink was first made by Indians. Branches from the yerba tree are harvested twice a year and taken to mills to be dried. The leaves and branches are dried and then ground into a powder.

The powerful river system of the Río de la Plata now produces hydroelectricity for the entire region. The Itaipu Dam, shown below, changed the economy of Paraguay.

Traditional gourds and metal straws are sometimes still used to drink yerba maté.

The powder is then brewed with boiling water, like tea. It tastes similar to tea but is slightly bitter. Some people sweeten it with sugar, while others come to love the unsweetened flavor. Traditionally, yerba maté was poured into a hollowed gourd and sipped through a silver straw. Today a metal bowl and straw replace the old utensils, but yerba is still drunk in a group, among friends. One Argentine yerba farmer explains the process today:

Traditionally yerba is drunk with a group of friends. You put the yerba in a maté [a metal bowl] *and then pour boiling water over it. You drink it through a bombilla* [a metal drinking straw].

It is considered an insult to refuse a sip of the yerba maté as it is passed around the circle.

CAFÉS IN MONTEVIDEO

In Montevideo friends and family gather in cafés to sip coffee and talk about their day. In Paraguay some workers take a break to sip yerba maté. The settings are different, but they show something that the Río de la Plata countries have in common.

The people in the Río de la Plata region value spending time with their friends and family. After work, family and friends often meet in a café for tea. Conversations begun in the afternoon often stretch long into the night.

A CHANGING REGION

You have read about how, over the past 50 years, the economies of Argentina, Uruguay, and Paraguay shifted from agriculture to industry. Today most people in these countries live and work in cities, not on farms. But wherever people live, traditions remain important in this changing region.

 ### Check Your Reading

1. What is one of the most valuable resources in the Río de la Plata region?
2. How did the economies of Argentina and Uruguay change after the Great Depression?
3. Name three ways in which life changed in Paraguay after hydroelectric power plants were built.
4. **THINKING SKILL:** If you decided to move to the Río de la Plata region, in which country would you choose to live? What were the reasons for your decision?

THE GAUCHO

by Eric Kimmel

You have just read that the fertile land of the Pampas helps Argentinians to raise beef cattle. Cattle ranching is a difficult job. The cattle must be rounded up, branded, and herded from one area to another. For almost 300 years, these tasks have been done by Argentinian cowhands called gauchos (gou' chōz). In this lesson you will learn about where the first gauchos came from and what their lives were like. As you read, think about why gaucho traditions have become an important part of the culture of Argentina.

"ORPHANS" OF THE PAMPAS

The first gauchos were Spanish outlaws who fled to the Pampas during the 1700s. They spent most of their time among the Indians. The word *gaucho* probably comes from the Indian word *hauchú* (ou chü'), which means "orphan." These first gauchos were thought of as orphans because they had left their families behind in Spain. Once in Argentina, many of them married the Indians they lived among and started families.

The gauchos were wanderers who captured and tamed the wild horses that roamed the Pampas. Gauchos had to become experts in using *boleadoras* (bō lā ä dō' räs), or *bolas*, for short. A bola consists of two or three rawhide thongs with a stone ball wrapped in rawhide on the end of each thong. The Indians taught the gauchos how to use the bola to capture horses, cattle, and especially rheas (rē′ əz), the ostrichlike birds native to the Pampas.

The gaucho would ride next to his prey, holding onto one of the stone balls of the bola and whirling the others around his head. At the right moment he would throw the bola, catching the legs of the animal and bringing it down to the ground.

A HARDY PEOPLE

Gauchos lived in the open. At night they slept on the ground with a sheepskin-covered saddle as a pillow and a poncho for a blanket. These tough, hardy people needed only a knife and a horse to survive.

The children of the gauchos learned to ride before they could walk. This is not surprising since gauchos seldom went anywhere on foot. A gaucho would sooner part with his last possession than sell his horse.

The first gauchos seldom went near a town. They lived off the land, trading hides and tallow for the few things they could not make themselves. Natural-ly, they dressed as sim-ply as they lived.

AN EARLY GAUCHO

A. bola
B. chiripá
C. facón
D. lace-trimmed leggings
E. poncho
F. open-toed riding boots

An early gaucho's costume was little more than a hand-woven shirt and poncho, a small felt hat, and a *chiripá* (chē rē pä'), a loose-fitting trouser made from a square of cloth that the gaucho wrapped around his waist and tucked between his legs.

The poorest gauchos went barefoot. Those with more money liked to dress up with lace-trimmed leggings and riding boots. They made their boots from animal skins. Most gauchos preferred to leave the front ends of their boots open because they rode by gripping the stirrups with their toes.

A COLORFUL COSTUME

The Pampas were becoming more settled by the middle of the 1800s. Gauchos began replacing their homemade clothes with manufactured goods. The well-dressed gaucho now wore factory-made boots, huge spurs, and brightly colored *bombachas* (bom bä' chäs). Bombachas are wide, baggy trousers that are gathered at the ankle.

Every gaucho also wore a long, double-edged knife thrust through the back of his belt. This knife is called a *facón* (fä cōn'). There is an old saying in Argentina that the gaucho cherishes three things: his horse, his sweetheart, and his facón. Gauchos used the facón for skinning cattle, for eating, for repairing their saddles and riding equipment, and, if necessary, for self-defense. No gaucho would think of riding out without his facón.

CHANGES FOR THE GAUCHO

The gaucho's way of life changed as Argentina became a modern nation. In order to force gauchos to settle down, the government of Argentina passed laws that made it possible for a gaucho to be arrested and put in jail if he could not prove he had a job. Since few gauchos could read or write, they were easily taken advantage of by dishonest officials. Some were driven to become outlaws.

EL GAUCHO MARTÍN FIERRO

In 1873 the Argentine poet José Hernández published a poem to protest what was happening to the gauchos. Titled *El Gaucho Martín Fierro* (mär tēn′ fyə′ rō), it has become Argentina's national poem. Martín Fierro is a typical gaucho who loves his old way of life as much as he hates the injustice that has driven him from his home and made him an outlaw.

> *Él anda siempre juyendo,*
> *siempre pobre y perseguido:*
> *no tiene cueva ni nido,*
> *como si juera maldito:*
> *porque el ser gaucho . . . ¡barajo!*
> *el ser gaucho es un delito.*

> *He's always on the run,*
> *always poor and hounded:*
> *he has neither a hole nor a nest,*
> *as if there were a curse on him:*
> *because being a gaucho . . . curse it!*
> *being a gaucho is a crime.*

It is certainly true that the gaucho's life was a hard one. The men often worked from sunup to sundown. Their legs became bowed from long days in the saddle. Their faces were lined and leathery, and their hands were calloused from holding rough ropes. And yet the gaucho's life was also appealing. In the words of Martín Fierro:

> *Mi gloria es vivir tan libre*
> *como el pájaro del cielo. . . .*

> *My joy is to live as free*
> *as the bird in the sky. . . .*

What makes the gaucho an appealing figure to the people of Argentina?

3 Argentina's Struggle for Democracy

READ TO LEARN

 Key People

Hipólito Yrigoyen   Eva Marie Perón

Juan Domingo Perón   Raul Alfonsín

 Read Aloud

The United States of the Southern Hemisphere.

This is how Argentina was often described in the 1920s. By 1920 both Argentina and the United States ranked among the world's ten richest nations. And both were ruled by democratically elected governments.

But in 1930 democracy collapsed in Argentina. Since that time, 25 governments have come to power, more than half of them by military coups. Making democracy work has not been easy in Argentina. In this lesson you will explore some of the reasons that account for this struggle.

 Read for Purpose

1. **WHAT YOU KNOW:** What problems did Latin American nations face after independence?
2. **WHAT YOU WILL LEARN:** Why has democracy often failed in Argentina?

ARGENTINA'S GAUCHO LEGACY

You have just read about the gauchos of Argentina. These "iron men of the Pampas" admired skill and courage. But they had little use for the rules and laws of government. The only leaders to win their loyalty were the caudillos who ruled with force.

Even now that the gauchos have become hired ranch hands, their legacy endures. Argentines still admire forceful leaders. Powerful dictators ruled Argentina for decades despite the country's repeated attempts at democracy.

THE BEGINNING OF DEMOCRACY

Democratic government came late to Argentina. Throughout the 1800s a series of caudillos ruled Argentina, ruthlessly seizing power from each other. These dictators often tortured and killed people who disagreed with them or threatened their power.

In 1916 the first democratic elections were held in Argentina. **Hipólito Yrigoyen** (ē rē goy′ ən) was elected president. When he took power, Argentines had not had time to develop democratic habits and values. Few leaders

522

understood the importance of listening to all points of view. Instead of teaching such values by his example, Yrigoyen ruled more like a caudillo than a democratic leader. He listened to no one and kept power to himself. One observer wrote:

> He decides, he orders, he makes and unmakes. He is president, treasurer, and secretary all at once. He surrounds himself with men who obey him and whom he can manage at will.

Yrigoyen often called on the army to help him maintain order in periods of unrest. In 1930 a group of military officers seized control of the government. However, they did more to destroy democracy than to save it. Over the next 16 years, no elected president ever completed his full term in office. The military ousted each one.

THE RISE OF JUAN PERÓN

In 1946 Argentina held its first democratic elections since the fall of Yrigoyen. The leading candidate for president was a new leader named Juan Domingo Perón. Campaigning with Perón was his wife, a popular radio actress named Eva Marie Perón. To her fans, she was known simply as "Evita."

The Peróns were beloved by Argentina's poor. Juan Perón reached out to these forgotten voters. He called them *descamisados* (des cä mē sä' dōs), or shirtless ones. Perón united the descamisados to form a powerful new political force, the Peronist Party.

Juan Perón inspired deep loyalty in his followers, who were called Peronists. He was the leader they had so long been waiting for. As one Peronist said, "Perón for many of us is an idol, a God."

Crowds gathered in 1946 to hail their popular new leaders, Juan and Evita Perón.

Juan Perón's speeches earned him more and more supporters. "I take off my shirt and join the *descamisados*," he once proclaimed, rolling up his shirt sleeves. When the election was held in 1946, Perón's victory was overwhelming. Many saw his election as a victory for democracy. At last Argentina had a government that represented the poor people and workers.

Perón also brought women into politics. Evita was very active in government programs to help the poor. By 1950 the Eva Perón Foundation had given away to poor families 200,000 cooking pots, 400,000 pairs of shoes, and 500,000 sewing machines.

Evita was also active in earning women the right to vote. She set up the Peronist Women's Party to encourage women to vote. In 1952 women helped elect Perón to a second term as president. A year later, when Evita died, the entire nation mourned.

By bringing workers and women into the political system, the Peróns expanded democracy in Argentina. But Juan Perón's new programs were very costly. Soon the country was in economic shambles. People became more and more dissatisfied.

Like Yrigoyen, Juan Perón cared more about power than about such basic democratic rights as freedom of speech and of the press. Perón labeled people who disagreed with him "traitors" and had them jailed. Newspapers that opposed Perón were ordered to close. Perón's opponents also cared more about power than about democracy. Rather than wait for the next election to run against Perón, they turned to the military for help. In 1955 army officers seized the government, and Perón was exiled, or ordered to leave his country.

GROWING UNREST

After 1955 democracy fell apart in Argentina. Elections were held regularly, but military leaders had little respect for the results. One president after another was removed from power and replaced by a military dictator.

The military justified each coup by pointing to the growing unrest in the

Mothers of the *desaparecidos* protested the disappearance of their sons and daughters during the 1970s.

country. In 1956 the government had outlawed the Perónist Party and jailed many of its leaders. Outraged Peronists reacted violently. Perón supported them from exile, writing that "the more violent we are, the better."

By 1973 unrest was so widespread that the military invited Perón back to Argentina to restore order. For the third time Perón was elected president by a huge majority. But in the following year, the aging leader died.

THE "DIRTY WAR"

After Perón died, angry young rebels and terrorists began a campaign of terror against the country's police, soldiers, and political leaders. By 1976 a bomb exploded somewhere in Argentina every three hours. Every five hours someone died in a terrorist attack.

That year the military again seized control of the country. The ruling generals declared war on all "enemies of the state." In the next few years, from 15,000 to 30,000 Argentines were kidnapped and tortured by military officials. Some of these people may have been terrorists. But most were innocent victims caught up in what Argentines called the "dirty war."

By the time the dirty war ended in 1980, 9,000 people, many of them teenagers, had disappeared. Only later were the *desaparecidos* (de sä pä rä sē' dōs), or "disappeared ones," found. Their bodies had been buried in graveyards, garbage dumps, and even under the lion's cage in the Buenos Aires Zoo.

THE FALKLANDS WAR

In 1982 Argentina was ruled by General Leopoldo Galtieri (gal tē âr' ē). The economy was suffering, and Galtieri was afraid that he would be overthrown by yet another military coup. He decided to attempt a risky military move of his own to try to demonstrate his strength.

On April 2, 1982, Argentine troops, led by General Galtieri, seized a small group of islands off the southern coast of Argentina. Argentina and Great Britain had both claimed that these islands were theirs. Argentina called them Malvinas and Great Britain called them the Falkland Islands.

Galtieri did not expect Great Britain to put up a fight, but he was wrong. Great Britain immediately sent its strong naval and air forces to the islands. The war lasted ten weeks, and Argentina was badly defeated. Galtieri's plan had backfired, and he was ousted from the government.

THE RETURN TO DEMOCRACY

In 1983 the military agreed to hold elections. Raúl Alfonsín became president based on his promise to return Argentina to democracy. "Our democratic order was disrupted," he said. "We must recover it."

President Alfonsín worked hard to make democracy a way of life in his country. He pushed schools to begin teaching students how democracy works. Unlike past presidents, Alfonsín did not rule like a caudillo. Instead, he worked with his political opponents to solve Argentina's problems. Alfonsín also tried to reduce the power of the military. He brought several military leaders to trial for their roles in the dirty war.

In 1989, for the first time in 60 years, power passed peacefully in a free election from one president to another. In his first speech as president, Carlos Menem said, "I don't bring simple

During the 1980s many of the leaders of the dirty war were brought to trial.

answers. I can offer only sacrifice, work, and hope."

"TIME TO CHANGE"

You have read that in the past Argentines have respected strong leaders more than democratic ideals. They have allowed presidents to rule like caudillos and generals to replace elected leaders. Today Argentines are trying to make democracy a way of life in their country. But as a Buenos Aries taxi driver says, after "years of bad governments, it's going to take time to change things."

 ## Check Your Reading

1. How was Yrigoyen's leadership like that of a caudillo?
2. Why were the Peróns popular among the *descamisados*?
3. How did Alfonsín try to make democracy work in Argentina?
4. **THINKING SKILL:** Predict what you think will happen to Argentina's government in the future. Give the reasons for your prediction.

Using Information

Imagine that your teacher has assigned as a group project an oral report on any topic related to the Río de la Plata countries. In order to prepare this report, you can use many of the thinking skills that you learned in this book. Start by choosing a topic and listing the questions that your report might answer about the topic. Next, identify the credible primary and secondary sources that will give you the information you want to know about the topic. Then evaluate and organize the information you collect into subtopics. Finally, use the information that you have collected to draw conclusions about the topic.

Trying the Skill

Use the information in Chapter 25 and in other sources to write a three-page report on Evita Perón. What questions might you ask to limit your topic and guide your research? What sources would you use? Look through the card catalog for books on the topic. Refer to the *Readers' Guide to Periodical Literature* for magazine articles. How might you organize the information you have collected? What conclusions might you draw about Evita Perón?

HELPING YOURSELF

The steps on the left will help you collect and use information to write a report. The example on the right shows one way to apply these steps to the report on Evita Perón.

One Way to Use Information	Example
1. Limit your topic to one that can be covered in a three-page report. List questions that focus on the topic.	"The Life of Evita Perón" is much too broad a topic for a short paper. A better topic would be "Evita Perón as First Lady." Ask questions such as: What did Evita do to help the poor? How did she encourage women to vote? Why is she such a popular figure in Argentina's modern history?
2. Look for answers to your questions in credible sources.	Look for answers in encyclopedia articles, biographies, and books on Argentina or Latin American politics.
3. Evaluate the information you collect.	Separate the facts from the opinions. Look for evidence supporting a writer's opinions. Verify the accuracy of information by comparing the same information in different sources.
4. Classify or group the information.	Group and label similar information. You may be able to organize your information into these subtopics: Economic Programs; Political Programs; Cultural Programs.
5. Look for common features or links in the data you collect. Draw a conclusion about the topic.	Read the information to get the general picture that the facts create. Draw a conclusion about Evita Perón and her role in Argentina's history.

Applying the Skill

Use the information in Chapter 25 and other sources, such as an almanac, to write a one-page paper describing the people of Uruguay.

1. Which of the following questions would help to guide your research?
  a. What is the per capita GNP in Uruguay?
  b. Which holidays are celebrated?
  c. Which immigrant groups have settled in Uruguay?
  d. What are Uruguay's most important exports?

Reviewing the Skill

1. What are some steps you can follow to find and use information about a topic?

2. Why is it important to evaluate and organize information before you use it?

3. Describe some occasions, outside of school, when you might need to collect, evaluate, and use information to draw a conclusion.

IMPORTANT EVENTS

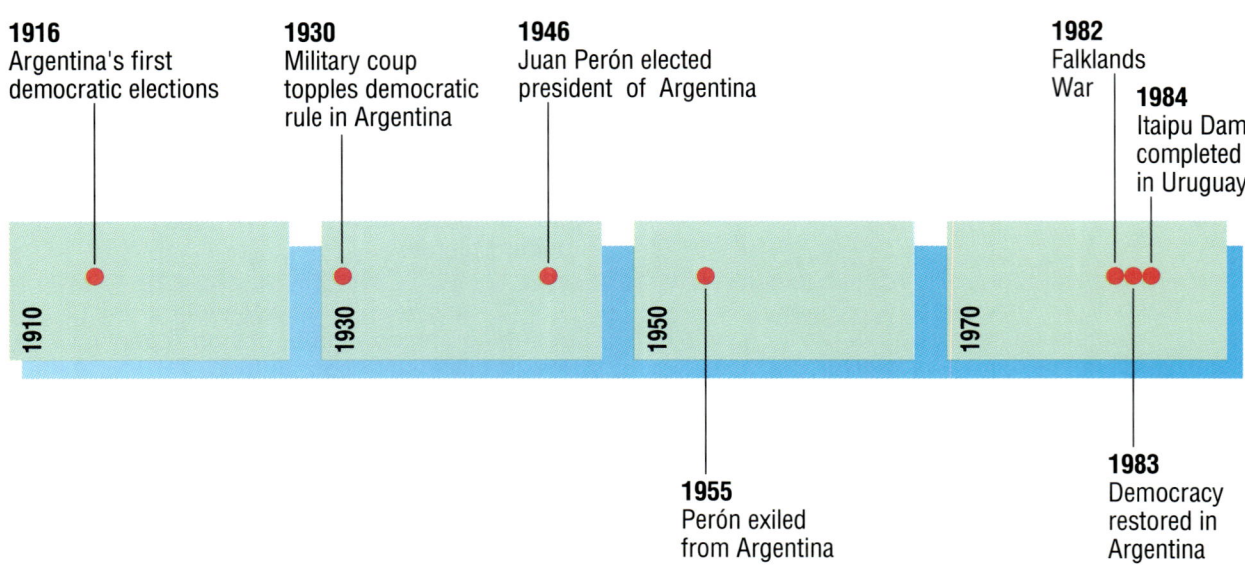

1916
Argentina's first democratic elections

1930
Military coup topples democratic rule in Argentina

1946
Juan Perón elected president of Argentina

1982
Falklands War

1984
Itaipu Dam completed in Uruguay

1910

1930

1950

1970

1955
Perón exiled from Argentina

1983
Democracy restored in Argentina

PEOPLE TO KNOW

Hipólito Yrigoyen 1852–1933

Juan Domingo Perón 1895–1974

Eva Marie Perón 1919–1952

IDEAS TO REMEMBER

■ After Argentina and Uruguay were settled by European immigrants, the Indian populations of these countries were mostly destroyed. Paraguay has changed little until recently because its geography has made the country difficult to reach.

■ While land has always been one of the most important resources in the countries of the Río de la Plata, recently these countries have turned to industry.

■ Argentina has recently returned to democracy, although in the past the country was led by a series of rulers who preferred to keep their own power rather than to promote democracy.

REVIEWING VOCABULARY

estancia   Itaipu Dam
estuary   literacy rate
industrialization

Number a sheet of paper from 1 to 5. Beside each number write the word or term from the list above that best completes the sentence.

1. An _____ is a ranch located in the rolling hills of Uruguay.
2. During the period of _____, the country built many factories and reduced its economy's dependence on farming.
3. The _____ is the percentage of people in a country who can read and write.
4. The _____ was built to increase hydroelectric power in Paraguay.
5. An _____ is the mouth of a river where the current meets the sea.

REVIEWING FACTS

1. Name two important facts about the size or population of Argentina.
2. Identify two ways in which Uruguay is similar to Argentina.
3. Of which ethnic group are most Paraguayans members?
4. What geographic fact has greatly affected the development of Paraguay?
5. From which two products do most Argentine farmers make a living?
6. What are Uruguay's most important exports?
7. How have the building of the Trans-Chaco Highway and the Itaipu Dam changed the economy of Paraguay?
8. How did the governments of Uruguay and Argentina help industrialization in their countries?
9. Name three Argentine rulers who were elected democratically.
10. What happened to the victims of Argentina's "dirty war"?

WRITING ABOUT MAIN IDEAS

1. **Writing a Paragraph:** How have the Río de la Plata countries used their natural resources to build their economies? Write a paragraph that gives at least one example for each country.
2. **Writing About Cause and Effect:** The literacy rate in Uruguay is very high. What effects do you think this fact has had on other areas of life in the country? List at least two effects of Uruguay's high literacy rate.
3. **Writing the Main Idea:** Reread in Lesson 1 the section called "Paraguay—Poor and Landlocked." Write a few sentences that tell the main idea of the section.
4. **Writing About Perspectives:** Pretend that you are writing a newspaper article about the history of Argentina under the rule of Perón. In your article focus on the gains made by women during this time.

BUILDING SKILLS: USING INFORMATION

Suppose that you were assigned to report on the architecture of Argentina today.

1. How would you go about finding information about the topic?
2. Which steps would you follow to evaluate the information you gathered?
3. Which thinking skills might you use in preparing the report?

CHAPTER 26

BRAZIL

FOCUS

In no other region is the sky more serene or the dawn which greets the day more beautiful. . . . Brazil, where the mighty rivers surge and flow, is an earthly paradise.

This is how the historian Sebastião José de Roca Pitta described Brazil in the early 1700s. The word *paradise* is used often in descriptions of Brazil. In this chapter you will read more about the people, problems, and promise of this "earthly paradise."

1 People

READ TO LEARN

Key Vocabulary

samba
discrimination

Key People

Jorge Amado
Pelé

Read Aloud

Mixture is the key word of Brazilian culture. . . . My grand-mother was Indian, my great-grandfather was black, and my name has definite Arab connections. Yet I am completely at ease as a Brazilian, with a feeling that I come from all over the world and am very much at home in Brazil.

This is how Brazil's most famous author, Jorge Amado (zhôr′ zhē ä mä′ dō), describes his family background. Like most Brazilians, Amado claims a heritage from all over the world. In this lesson you will find that *mixture* is indeed "the key word of Brazilian culture."

Read for Purpose

1. **WHAT YOU KNOW:** Which groups settled and built Brazil during colonial times?
2. **WHAT YOU WILL LEARN:** Which groups make up the population of Brazil today?

A UNIQUE PEOPLE

Brazil is a unique country in many ways. It is the only Portuguese-speaking nation in all of Latin America. More Indian groups live in Brazil than in any other country in Latin America. Communities of Brazilians of African descent thrive in cities such as Salvador. You can find Salvador on the map on page 532. Brazil is also home to people from the Middle East and Asia. Over 150 million people live in Brazil— about two thirds the population of the United States.

INDIANS OF BRAZIL

As you know, Indians were the first people to live in the land that is now called Brazil. In 1500 there were perhaps 4 million Indians in this land. They lived by hunting, fishing, and gathering wild plants from the rain forest. You read in Chapter 11 that the arrival of Europeans caused the deaths of millions of Indians throughout the Western Hemisphere. In 1900 only about 260 Indian groups were still living in Brazil. By the 1980s that number had been cut in half.

Today Brazil's government is trying to protect the country's remaining Indian groups. It has set aside parts of the Amazon rain forest as Indian reserves. As you read in Chapter 7, a reserve is land set aside by a government for special use. Brazil's largest Indian reserve is almost the same size as the state of West Virginia.

About 200,000 Indians live on Brazil's reserves. In recent years, though, highways have been built that run right through some reserves. These highways have made it possible for miners, loggers, and ranchers to invade the Indians' land. Find the Trans-Amazon Highway on the map below.

The newcomers often have little sympathy for the Indians and their way of life. "Why should Indians have a right to land," they ask, "when they don't produce anything on it?" In 1990 a Cayapo Indian responded with the following words.

We are owners of the land. Our grand-fathers and great-grandfathers were born here. We need the forest to go hunting.

Whether the Indians will survive these latest threats remains uncertain.

MAP SKILL: How many states and territories does Brazil have? Name two cities that are located along the Amazon River.

BRAZIL: Political

⊛ National capital
★ State capital
— Trans-Amazon Highway

Thousands of Indians live on reserves in the Amazon rain forest. Brazil's African heritage can be seen in the markets of Salvador.

BRAZIL'S AFRICAN HERITAGE

You have read that the Portuguese settled Brazil in the 1500s. Portuguese colonists brought over millions of people from Africa by force to work as slaves. Brazil was built by these men and women from Africa and the settlers from Portugal.

African slaves and their descendents gave more than their work to Brazil. They also gave many parts of their culture to the new land. Jorge Amado, the Brazilian author whose words you read in the Read Aloud on page 531, once said:

The source of Brazil's vitality [spirit] is Africa. Africans brought a rhythm and a vital energy to the new culture which are immediately recognizable. If you hear Brazilian music or watch a Brazilian dance, you will see it right away.

African beats and drums are at the heart of samba, Brazil's lively dance form. Samba is the soul of Brazil's most famous holiday, Carnaval. You will read more about the excitement of Carnaval and samba in the Traditions lesson on pages 536–539.

Brazil's African heritage also shapes daily life in Salvador, a city in northeastern Brazil. Most of the people here are of African descent. Women wear African headdresses to market. Restaurants serve spicy seafood stews just like those made in West Africa.

People here and elsewhere in Brazil mix African religious beliefs with those of Catholicism. The result is a new form of worship called Macumba.

THE IMMIGRANTS

Until the late 1800s Brazilian society was made up of three groups: Indians, Portuguese, and Africans. In Chapter 22 you read that slavery was outlawed in Brazil in 1888. After that the planters turned to Europe for workers. Between 1888 and 1929, over 100,000 immigrants moved to Brazil each year. Most were poor Italians and Portuguese who came to work on coffee and sugarcane plantations.

Brazilian
NATIONAL ANTHEM

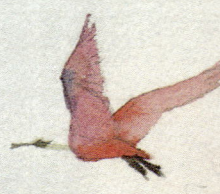

Translated by Gastão Nothman
Versified by Sebastian Shaw

Words by Joaquim Osório Duque Estrada (1870–1927)
Music by Francisco Manuel da Silva (1795–1865)

CHORUS
Ter - ra a - do - ra - da, en - tre ou - tras
A - mongst a thou - sand, you ev - er
mil, és tu, Bra - sil, Oh! Pá-tria a - ma - da! Dos fi - lhos
will be, oh Bra - zil, The one dear home - land! Oh bount-eous
des - te so - lo és mãe gen - til, Pá - tria a - ma - da, Bra - sil!
mo-ther, with such love you fill your proud chil-dren, Bra - zil!

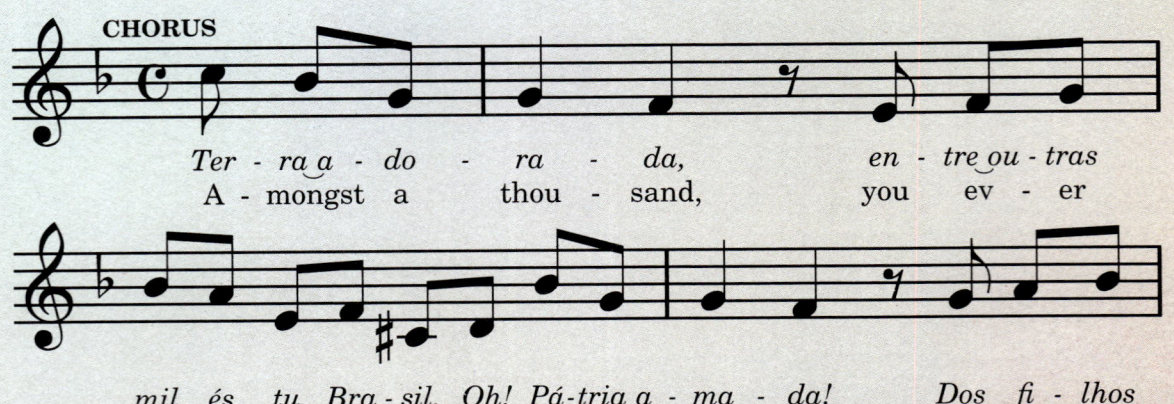

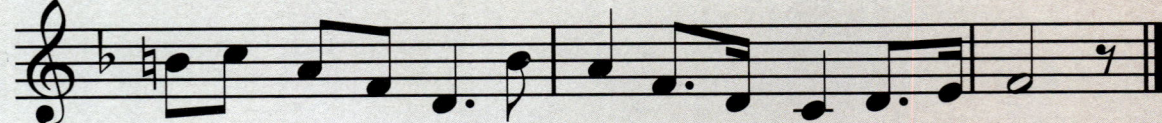

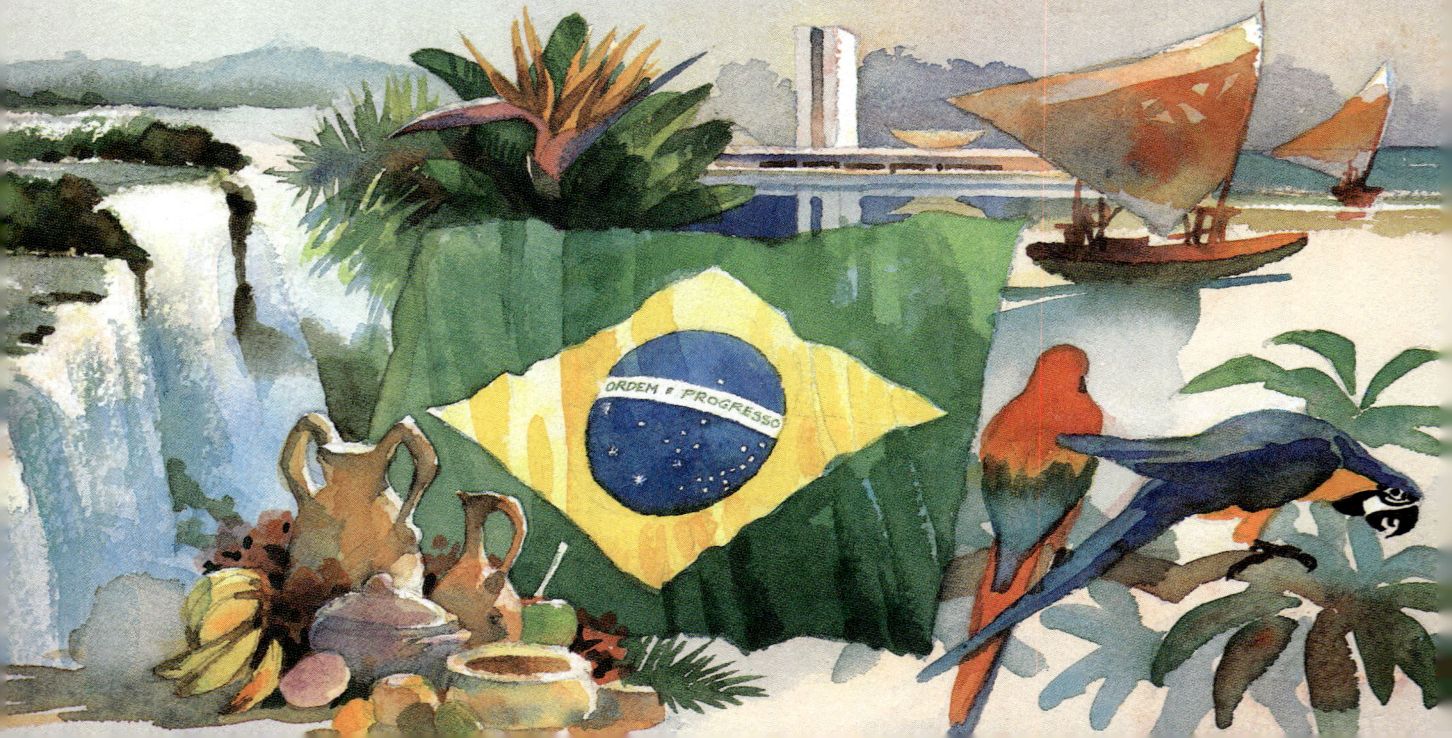
ORDEM E PROGRESSO

People have come from all over the world to live in Brazil. These merchants reflect Brazil's ethnic diversity.

Other immigrants came as well. Many Germans settled in southern Brazil, where they built farms and ranches. Brazil's cities attracted newcomers from Eastern Europe and the Middle East. More than 300,000 Japanese also moved to Brazil between 1900 and 1950 to work as farmers.

DISCRIMINATION

Brazilians like to describe their country as being a "racial democracy." By this they mean that Brazilians of every color and background are supposed to have the same rights and opportunities.

On the surface, Brazil is free of racial problems. The constitution of Brazil forbids discrimination, or an unfair difference in treatment based on color. A few Brazilians of African descent, such as the famous soccer player Pelé, have become heroes in Brazil.

A closer look shows that the poorest people in Brazil are also those whose skin is the darkest. Racism plays a clear role in Brazilian society. Author Antonio Callado once stated, "If you have black skin [in Brazil], you'd better be Pelé; otherwise you'll suffer for it."

Job discrimination is a problem for blacks and mulattoes, despite the words of the Brazilian constitution.

Help-wanted ads in Brazil sometimes state that a *boa aparencia*, or "good appearance," is required. Brazilians know that this means only white or pale-skinned people should apply.

A RICH MIXTURE OF PEOPLES

Brazil, as described in its national anthem on the opposite page, is a "dear homeland" to many people. These people are descended from Indians, Africans, Europeans, Middle Easterners, and Asians.

Check Your Reading

1. Why are reserves important to Brazil's Indians?
2. Is Brazil a true "racial democracy"? Explain your answer.
3. **GEOGRAPHY SKILL:** How has the geographical theme of movement played a role in Brazil's history?
4. **THINKING SKILL:** Suppose you were going to write a report about the people of Brazil. What steps would you follow to find and use information about your topic?

Carnaval!

by Eric Kimmel

You have just read that Brazilian society is a mixture of many different groups. Over the years, each group has contributed to a culture that is today no longer simply Potugese, or African, or Indian, but distinctly Brazilian. This blending of cultures is unmistakable in many of Brazil's traditions. One such tradition is the religious festival called Carnaval (kär nä väl').

Carnaval takes place just before Lent, the six-week period before Easter. During Lent, many Catholics give up some of their usual pleasures. Eating meat is one of them. In fact, that's how Carnaval got its name: "Carne, vale!" is Latin for "Good-bye, meat!"

Carnaval is a time for having fun before the serious observation of Lent begins. A street parade in Rio de Janiero is the high point of the holiday. In this parade Brazilians dance to the samba, a dance that came from Africa. All year long, people practice their steps in samba "schools." These are not actually schools but large neighborhood clubs devoted to the celebration of Carnaval.

Catholics in many other countries also celebrate some form of Carnaval. But no other country celebrates it quite the way Brazilians do, to the African beat of the samba. As you read, think about what the tradition of Carnaval means to the people of Brazil.

MUCH PREPARATION

Carnaval is a lot of fun. But it is also a lot of hard work and preparation. Members of each samba school prepare all year long for Carnaval. As one samba-school director said,

"Carnaval begins the day after Carnaval ends." Each school chooses a theme taken from Brazilian history or folklore. The theme might be anything from "Great Nations of Africa" to "Kingdoms of the Sea." Elaborate, glittering floats and costumes are designed around the theme. To raise money for their costumes and floats, samba schools sell items, such as key chains and headbands, that bear their school's emblem. They also hold raffles and Saturday night samba parties throughout the year.

In huge halls samba schools hold "harvests," or large gatherings. At a harvest each school chooses a samba theme song from the works of its own songwriters. The theme songs are then recorded and sold months before Carnaval. In that time, spectators can learn the words, so that they can accompany the paraders. The Carnaval participants spend endless hours in their halls practicing dance steps. In the following story you will read about what Carnaval means to a 12-year-old girl named Celinda.

IT'S HERE

Carnaval is here at last. Celinda is part of the moving blur of color and joy that is Rio de Janeiro. But she is in a panic because she can't find the area in which her samba

IT'S HERE

Carnaval is here at last. Celinda is part of the moving blur of color and joy that is Rio de Janeiro. But she is in a panic because she can't find the area in which her samba school is gathering for the parade. She makes her way through floats peopled with giants. Celinda hurries by tall giraffes and then ducks under a canopy hung with shiny silver tinsel. She finds herself face to face with "Indians," "kings and queens," "gangsters," and "rock stars." School directors, who are shouting orders through microphones, deafen her.

Just as Celinda makes her way around workers carrying a papier-mâché fountain, she sees people from her samba school. Some are practicing their steps. Others are putting on makeup. Celinda's schoolmates welcome her into the group by giving her a handful of green glitter gel. She spreads it on her face and arms and then rearranges her turban.

"We're on," someone yells. In a flash of pink and green, Celinda's samba school dances its way along the parade route, led by its floats. She gives herself to the dance. First she hears the drums. The big bass drums are the heartbeat of samba. Their sound rolls over Celinda like the waves of the ocean. She also moves to other instruments that whistle, rattle, jangle, and scratch. She remembers the words of her dance instructor:

Cross with your left foot as you hop on your right. Then hop on your right foot as you cross with your left. That's it! Let your hips slide side to side. Remember to keep your head and shoulders steady. Smile! The samba is joy, not work.

Celinda's heart quickens even more as she finishes the parade route and heads for the Sambadrome, a huge stadium built to hold samba competitions. The lights of the Sambadrome, reflecting from millions of sparkling sequins, dazzle her eyes. A roar goes up from the packed stadium crowd as the floats from Celinda's samba school roll in. Celinda is nervous, but somehow her feet and body seem to be moving by themselves.

It's over too soon. Now a spectator herself, Celinda watches the next groups compete in the Sambadrome. After the competition is over, she dances and sings at a party until well past her usual bedtime. She sleeps for a few hours and joins the Carnaval festivities again the next day.

CARNAVAL IS A PASSION

The parade in Rio de Janeiro, as well as the competition in the Sambadrome, is televised throughout Brazil. The announcement of the winners, which is also televised, lasts for several weeks after the end of Carnaval. Prizes are awarded for the best samba song, best theme, best dance, and best costume. Carnaval is viewed on television in Brazil with the same enthusiasm as the World Series is viewed in the United States.

Celinda's samba school won the prize for the best dance. Celinda was glad that she had practiced so much and that she had remembered the words of her dance instructor. Her samba school is already thinking about a song and steps for next year's dance! For Celinda and hundreds of thousands of other Brazilians, Carnaval has become an object of national pride and a year-round passion. Each year thousands of tourists from many different countries come to Rio de Janeiro to celebrate Carnaval.

How does the tradition of Carnaval reflect the mixture of Brazilian culture?

2 Living and Working

READ TO LEARN

◼ Key Places

sertão	Rio de Janeiro	Trans-Amazon
São Paulo	Brasília	Highway

◼ Read Aloud

We passed a row of pickup trucks parked in front of a bar. Within, a rowdy crew wearing finely tooled cowboy boots, Stetson hats, and revolvers on their hips was crowded around a pool table. . . . [The town] resembled a town in the Nevada desert.

Writer Alex Shoumatoff went to Brazil in the late 1970s to study the Amazon rain forest. To his surprise, he found that some places there looked more like frontier towns in the United States than the thick forest he expected to see.

◼ Read for Purpose

1. **WHAT YOU KNOW:** What words would you use to describe the Amazon rain forest?
2. **WHAT YOU WILL LEARN:** How do people live and work in the four regions of Brazil?

A VAST COUNTRY

Brazil is a huge country. It covers half of South America and is the fifth-largest nation on earth. To study this vast country, geographers divide Brazil into four regions: the Northeast, South, Center West, and the Amazon. The map on page 541 shows these four regions. Life in Brazil varies greatly from region to region.

THE NORTHEAST

The Northeast was the first region of Brazil to be colonized. In the 1500s Portuguese colonists and enslaved Af-

ricans built Brazil's first sugarcane plantations on the fertile soil of the northeastern coast. Salvador, which you read about in Lesson 1, was Portugal's first settlement in Brazil.

European colonists became rich thanks to the enslaved workers who grew their sugarcane, coffee, and cacao. For 150 years, the Northeast was Brazil's most prosperous and most populated region.

Today the northeastern coast is still an important agricultural area in Brazil. For example, sugarcane from this area is used to make ethanol, a kind of

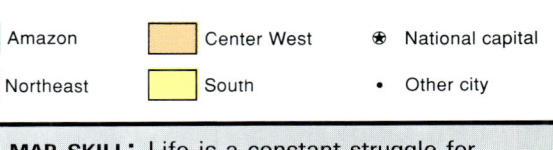

BRAZIL: Regions

🟩 Amazon	🟧 Center West	✹ National capital
🟥 Northeast	🟨 South	• Other city

MAP SKILL: Life is a constant struggle for residents of the sertão, such as the people at left. In which region is the sertão located?

fuel. More than half of Brazil's cars are powered by ethanol.

The effects of slavery are still present in the Northeast, however. Most people in the Northeast are blacks or mulattoes. For them, life is desperately hard. Many try to earn their livings by farming the dry lands of the region's inland area, known as the **sertão** (ser toun').

In times of drought, the sertão becomes so dry that nothing will grow. Millions of northeasterners leave the sertão and migrate to other places in Brazil. Yet they remain fiercely loyal to their homeland. Most return to the sertão when the rains fall again. The words of this song express the feelings of many northeasterners.

Today, many miles away,
In the saddest loneliness,
I wait for the rain to fall again
To return to my beloved sertão.

THE SOUTH

If the Northeast is a region of agriculture, the South of Brazil is a region of industry. This region was first settled by Europeans in the 1600s. Miners flocked to the South because of the gold and diamonds that lay buried in its hills. Today the South is Brazil's richest, most industrialized region. Yet it is also a region of great poverty, as you will read in Lesson 3.

Mining is still an important industry in the South. The southern hills are rich in iron, nickel, and other mineral resources. Farming also adds to the wealth of the region. Descendants of immigrants from Italy, Germany, and the Middle East grow crops and raise cattle on small farms here.

More than anything else, though, the South is known for its cities. There are more cities with over 1 million people in the south of Brazil than in all of the

541

United States. One out of five Brazilians lives in one of its two largest cities, **São Paulo** and **Rio de Janeiro**.

São Paulo is Brazil's largest city and its business center. More than 15 million people live here, making it the world's third-largest urban area. São Paulo's 30,000 factories produce everything from computers to canned foods.

Most of Brazil's factories are located in the cities of the South. This worker is wiring a radio in a factory in São Paulo.

Tucked among lush green hills by the Atlantic Ocean, Rio de Janeiro is considered Brazil's most beautiful city. It is also the banking and cultural center of the nation.

However, there is another side to life in Brazil's cities. Each year millions of poor northeasterners migrate to cities in the South, hoping to find work. Instead of jobs, though, the migrants find conditions of poverty that are almost impossible to imagine. You will read more about wealth and poverty in Brazil in the next lesson.

THE CENTER WEST

Unlike the urban South, the Center West is a region of dry land that is covered with small trees and shrubs. This region is also the home of the world's largest swamp, the Pantanal. The Pantanal is larger than the entire state of Indiana.

Until recently, few people lived in the Center West. Today, however, it is the fastest-growing region in Brazil. Much of the growth in this region was caused by the building of **Brasília** (brə zēl′ yə), Brazil's capital city.

In the 1950s the capital of Brazil was switched from Rio de Janeiro to a lonely plain 600 miles (960 km) inland. Brazil's leaders hoped that this would bring about growth in the country's huge inland regions. One leader predicted that Brasília would be "the magic trampoline for the integration of the Amazon into national life."

People nicknamed Brasília the "City of Hope." After five years of frantic building, the government was moved to Brasília in 1960. Today more than 1 million people live in this busy inland capital.

THE AMAZON

The Amazon is the largest region in Brazil. It contains the Amazon River Basin, which covers half of Brazil. For

thousands of years, Indian groups were the only people who lived and hunted in the Amazon rain forest. In the 1800s, however, other Brazilians began to settle along rivers in the rain forest. Most made a living by harvesting products from the forest such as nuts, lumber, and rubber.

The Amazon is an amazing source of natural resources. The rain forest contains the world's richest deposits of iron. Gold, copper, and other minerals can be found here as well. Untold numbers of stately trees grow in the Amazon forests—trees that can be turned into high-quality timber.

AMAZON DEVELOPMENT

In the 1950s Brazil's leaders set out to develop the Amazon. They saw its development as the solution to the nation's problems of poverty and unemployment. Poor Brazilians could make new lives for themselves in the Amazon frontier. The country could become rich by developing the many resources of the Amazon.

In the 1970s government leaders began offering land in the rain forest to anyone who was willing to settle it.

"Land Without People for People Without Land," their advertising read.

Government building was started on the **Trans-Amazon Highway**, a 3,350-mile (5,400-km) highway that cuts right through the rain forest. Before long buses streamed along the highway, carrying people who hoped to carve out land for themselves from the rain forest.

LIFE IN THE AMAZON

Life in the Amazon has many similarities with frontier life in the western parts of the United States during the 1800s. The promise of new lives and riches drew thousands of European Americans westward in the 1800s. The same promise lures settlers to the Amazon today.

Unfortunately for the Amazon settlers, however, the soil in the rain forest is very fragile. Once the land has been cleared, it becomes almost useless. Settlers must move on, hoping to find better soil elsewhere.

In the 1800s United States soldiers fought with Indians who were deter-

The sprawling city of Brasília was built in just five years. One of its most beautiful buildings is the Palace of the Arches, shown at left.

Thousands of miles of land were cleared to build the Trans-Amazon Highway. The highway has opened up the Amazon rain forest to new settlement and development.

mined to protect their lands. Amazon Indians, too, are fighting for their lands. But the Indians are losing their fight with disease, as did millions of other Indians of the Western Hemisphere.

United States pioneers had to clear the land of trees before they could do any farming or ranching. Ranchers and settlers in the Amazon, too, clear the land by burning down the trees on it. Alex Shoumatoff described what he saw as he traveled along an Amazon highway.

All the land in sight . . . had been reduced to a burnt-out wasteland, broken only by the occasional blackened pole of a dead tree. Flames swept the horizon . . . and licked the apron of the highway.

In 1987 alone, the area of rain forest that was burned equaled the size of the state of Minnesota.

In the Point/Counterpoint on pages 450–451, you read about how harmful the destruction of the rain forest is to Brazil's people and the environment.

The question remains: Will Brazil be able to save its rain forest before it is too late for Brazil and the world?

THE GIANT OF LATIN AMERICA

Brazil is a vast country, the giant of Latin America. Recently, efforts have been made to open up the Amazon rain forest to settlement and development. These efforts are gravely affecting Brazil's land and its people.

Check Your Reading

1. How is life in the South of Brazil different from life in the Northeast? How is it similar?

2. Why was Brazil's capital moved from Rio de Janeiro to Brasília?

3. GEOGRAPHY SKILL: How has the harsh climate of the sertão affected life in the Northeast?

4. THINKING SKILL: Suppose a tourist said, "Brazil has nothing in common with the United States." Evaluate the accuracy of this statement based on what you read.

Decision Making: Review

Decision making is selecting from a number of options, or alternatives, one that will help you to achieve a goal. You read in this chapter that the goal of Brazil's leaders was to encourage Brazil to develop its inland resources. After considering many different options, they selected the option of building a new capital city, Brasília, in the Center West region of Brazil. How did they arrive at this decision?

HELPING YOURSELF

The steps below outline one way to make a decision.

One Way to Make a Decision

1. Identify and define clearly the goal to be achieved.

2. Identify all possible alternatives, or options, for achieving the goal.

3. Predict the immediate and long-range outcomes of each option.

4. Evaluate each outcome by determining how it might be beneficial or harmful to you and others.

5. Choose the best alternative.

Applying the Skill

Many people in the United States have become involved in environmental movements to save the Amazon rain forest. Some Brazilian leaders have responded to United States interest in what they consider to be a local problem by pointing out environmental problems in the United States that need attention.

Imagine that you are head of the Environmental Protection Agency. Decide what United States government officials can do to convince Brazil's leaders that the United States is trying to solve its own environmental problems.

1. What is your goal as a government official?
2. What are some options you might consider?
3. Who would benefit and who would be harmed by each option?
4. Which alternative would you choose? Explain.

Reviewing the Skill

1. What are some steps to follow when making a decision?
2. Why should you consider all possible options, or alternatives, before making a decision?
3. Why is it important to consider the possible outcomes of each option?

3 Wealth and Poverty in Brazil

READ TO LEARN

 Key Vocabulary

favela
community development

Key People

Fernando Collor de Mello
Mary Helena Allegretti

 Read Aloud

Brazil suffers a famished [starved] *prosperity. Among countries selling food to the world, it stands in fourth place; among countries suffering hunger in the world, sixth place.*

Brazil is one of the world's leading industrial nations. As writer Eduardo Galeano pointed out, Brazil sells large amounts of food to the world. But for all of Brazil's economic power, millions of Brazilians remain trapped in poverty. In this lesson, you will read more about the "famished prosperity" of Brazil.

 Read for Purpose

1. WHAT YOU KNOW: How have some countries in Latin America and the Caribbean tried to solve the problem of poverty?
2. WHAT YOU WILL LEARN: Why has economic development failed to help many poor Brazilians?

TWO WORLDS

In many ways, there are two worlds in the country called Brazil. One world is made up of wealthy businesspeople, government officials, lawyers, doctors, and plantation owners. Most of these people are of European descent.

This is a small but very powerful world. About 10 percent of Brazil's population earns almost half of the country's income. A few of the people in this world are extremely wealthy, but most are not. All, however, have enough money to live comfortably.

Many have servants to help them with cooking, housework, and child care.

The remaining 90 percent of Brazil's population lives in another world—a world of desperate poverty. Most of the people in this world are of African or Indian descent.

POVERTY IN THE SERTÃO

The worst examples of Brazil's poverty are found in the dry and dusty sertão of the Northeast, which you read about in Lesson 2. In good years, a sertão resident earns only about half of what a person earns in the South. In bad years, sertão residents face starvation and even death.

Some northeasterners and their families survive by picking through city garbage dumps. Visitor Priit Visilind witnessed children searching for food in this way and was moved to write:

Hell [I believe] is when you are eight years old and you compete side by side with vultures for food. Hell is when you face bulldozers pushing ten-foot-high mounds of . . . garbage, and you must wade into it, knee-deep, clawing for tin cans or pieces of tomato. Hell is when you do this every day. And when it seems normal— when you are eight.

In the last 30 years millions of northeasterners have migrated to coastal cities and to the Amazon region in search of a better way of life.

POVERTY IN THE CITIES

As you read in Chapter 24, the cities of Latin America are growing rapidly. Brazil's cities have skyrocketed in size due to the mass migration of people from the Northeast. For example, the population of São Paulo has more than doubled in the last 20 years.

Because there is no housing for them, these poor Brazilians become squatters. They build little homes for themselves out of cardboard and tin. These homes form enormous slum neighborhoods, called favelas (fä vel' äz), that stretch out for miles around Brazil's cities.

Life in the favelas is hard. They have no water or sewage systems, garbage collection, lighting, or paved streets. Most have no schools, even though hundreds of thousands of people live in each favela.

Most of Brazil's cities are ringed by huge favelas (*above*). Many people who live in them come from rural areas, determined to make better lives for themselves.

THE "BRAZILIAN MIRACLE"

Beginning in the 1950s, the goal of Brazil's leaders was to make Brazil an industrial power. Development of the Amazon was at the heart of this plan.

In 1964 military leaders took control of Brazil. They were set on developing Brazil at any cost. Foreign companies and banks agreed to lend the leaders billions of dollars. This money was used to build highways, start new industries, and build the city of Brasília. By the 1970s, people were calling Brazil's amazing economic growth the "Brazilian miracle."

A few Brazilians made fortunes during this time of growth. Most people, however, were left out of the "Brazilian miracle." One reason was that Brazil's military leaders kept wages and taxes low to encourage foreign investment. With low wages, workers earned barely enough to live. The low taxes meant that the government had little money to spend on schools, health care, and other programs.

THE END OF THE MIRACLE

In the 1980s the "Brazilian miracle" collapsed. Heavy borrowing from foreign banks left Brazil more than $100 billion in debt, as the graph below shows. No other country in the world owed as much as Brazil. Worried that they might never be repaid, banks refused to lend more money to Brazil.

Growth and development in Brazil came to a halt. The entire economy was shifted toward paying back the nation's loans. Food crops were sold abroad, even though people at home

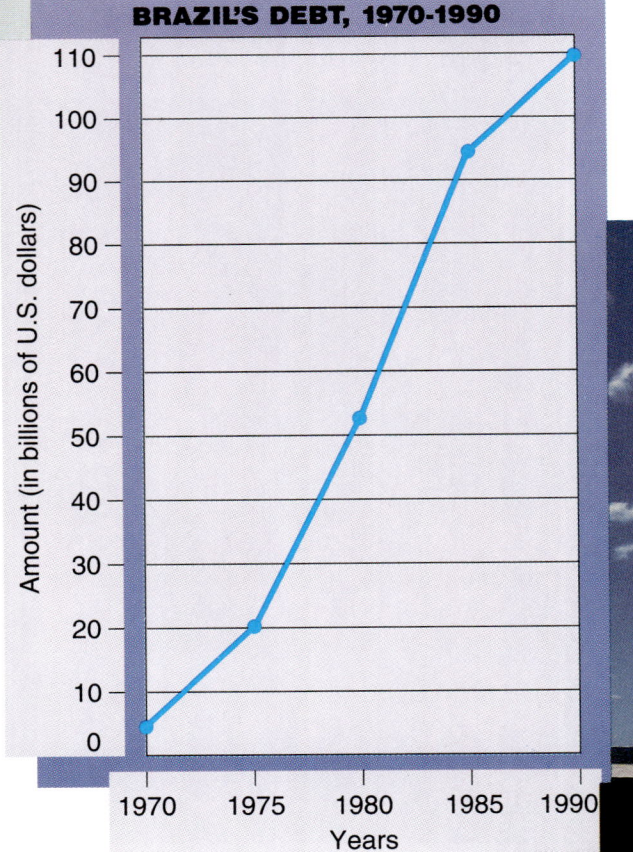

GRAPH SKILL: Brazil borrowed billions of dollars to build the city of Brasília. By how much did Brazil's debt grow between 1970 and 1975? Between 1980 and 1985?

BRAZIL'S DEBT, 1970-1990

Amount (in billions of U.S. dollars) vs. Years (1970, 1975, 1980, 1985, 1990)

were starving, because the government badly needed money.

Unrest spread throughout the country. People rioted as food prices skyrocketed and wages remained the same. With discontent growing, the military agreed to demands for a return to democracy.

In 1989 a young leader named Fernando Collor de Mello was elected president of Brazil. Upon taking office, he called for reforms in Brazil's "dramatically cruel and unjust" social system. One of his first acts in 1990 was to start a national reading program. His goal was to teach 32 million poor people to read and write by 1995.

COMMUNITY DEVELOPMENT

These new government programs are not the only way in which Brazil is addressing the needs of its poor. Community leaders are hard at work trying to improve life in Brazil's favelas and poor villages. Their work is called community development

You read about Mary Helena Allegretti in the Building Citizenship feature on page 191. She is helping Amazon rubber tappers to improve schools in their communities. Allegretti named her school program *poronga*, after the little lanterns the tappers carry to light their way in the forest.

LOOKING TO THE FUTURE

In the last 40 years, Brazil went through rapid economic growth known as the "Brazilian miracle." Economic growth, however, has done little to improve life for the poor of Brazil. Community development has given some poor Brazilians the tools they need to help themselves. One commu-

Medical care is an important part of community development. This team of doctors works among Amazon villagers.

nity worker, a Catholic nun named Sister Cecilia, explained how community development helps the poor.

Once they see children do not have to die, that health and disease do not just happen, and that their own actions are effective, then they understand themselves in a new way. Then they understand that they have the power to change things.

Check Your Reading

1. Why do people say that there are "two worlds" in Brazil?
2. What has caused rapid growth in the population of Brazil's cities?
3. Why is Brazil struggling with an enormous debt problem today?
4. THINKING SKILL: What is one of the most pressing problems facing Brazil's government leaders? State some options they might have to correct the problem.

IMPORTANT EVENTS

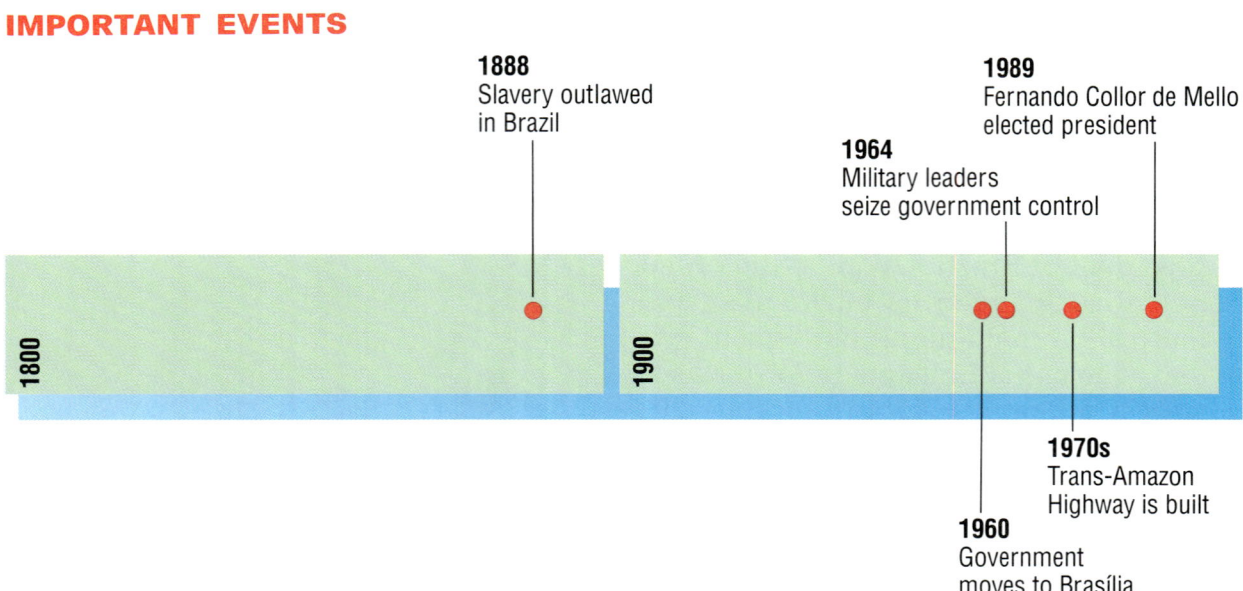

1888
Slavery outlawed
in Brazil

1964
Military leaders
seize government control

1989
Fernando Collor de Mello
elected president

1800

1900

1970s
Trans-Amazon
Highway is built

1960
Government
moves to Brasília

PEOPLE TO KNOW

Mary Helena Allegretti
1948–

Fernando Collor de Mello
1949–

Pelé
1940–

IDEAS TO REMEMBER

■ Brazil's population can be described as a mixture—made up of descendants of Indians, Africans, Europeans, Middle Easterners, and Asians.

■ Brazil is a giant land—the largest in Latin America. With the construction of Brasília, the inland areas have been opened to development.

■ Brazil is deeply divided between rich and poor, but today community development programs are trying to improve life for the poor. Unfortunately the country must repay huge debts created during the years of economic growth called the "Brazilian miracle."

REVIEWING VOCABULARY

community development   favela

discrimination   samba

Number a sheet of paper from 1 to 5. Beside each number write the word from the list above that best matches the definition. One of the words is used more than once.

1. The work done to try to improve life for poor people of Brazil
2. An example of Brazil's African heritage
3. An urban slum in Brazil
4. A type of dance that began in Brazil
5. Unfair difference in treatment

REVIEWING FACTS

Number a sheet of paper from 1 to 10. Beside each number write **T**, if the statement is true. If the statement is false, rewrite it to make it true.

1. Brazilian culture is called a mixture because immigrants from many Latin American countries have come to live there.
2. The Brazilian government has set aside areas in the cities, called reserves, for Indian groups.
3. Jorge Amado is the president of Brazil.
4. Brazil's African heritage can be seen in its dances and in the clothing and foods of people in the Northeast.
5. Brazil's constitution allows discrimination based on race.
6. European colonists first settled in the Northeast region.
7. The southern part of Brazil is an agricultural region.
8. Brazil's largest cities are São Paulo and Rio de Janeiro.
9. The Amazon is a vast area of many resources.
10. Most Brazilians have enough money to live decently.

◖◗ WRITING ABOUT MAIN IDEAS

1. **Writing a Paragraph:** Write a paragraph that answers these questions— why was Brasília called the "City of Hope"? Has the hope been realized?
2. **Writing a Comparison:** Write a paragraph that compares and contrasts Brazil and the United States. Consider their geography, history, people, and economy. Give at least four similarities or four differences.
3. **Writing About Perspectives:** Pretend that you are an Indian who lives in the Amazon. Describe how you might feel about the rapid growth of farming and ranching that is taking place in the Amazon today.

BUILDING SKILLS: DECISION MAKING

Suppose the government leaders of Brazil want to decide how to improve the lives of their country's poor people.

1. Which steps should they take to decide what to do?
2. List two alternatives that the leaders might try.
3. Name a possible outcome of each of the alternatives.
4. Why is it always a good idea to evaluate the possible consequences of each alternative before you actually make a decision?

REVIEWING VOCABULARY

cash economy	mesa
discrimination	recession
estuary	socialism
favela	squatter
literacy rate	terrorist

Number a sheet of paper from 1 to 10. Beside each number write the word or term from the list above that best matches the statement.

1. The name for one of many flat-topped hills that rise steeply above the surrounding land in South America.
2. In countries which have this kind of economy, individuals do not own or control businesses.
3. This person uses fear and violence to try to achieve change.
4. A country is in this condition when its economy worsens.
5. In this system, goods are exchanged for money, not for other goods.
6. A person who settles on land without purchasing it is known as this.
7. This is the mouth of a river where its current meets the sea.
8. This is the percentage of people in an area who can read and write.
9. The unfair difference in the treatment of people is known as this.
10. These are enormous slum neighborhoods that spread out for miles in Brazil.

WRITING ABOUT THE UNIT

1. **Writing Brochures:** Choose three of the countries you have read about in this unit. Write travel brochures for each one, including places and activities that a tourist would enjoy. Describe the land, the people, and the activities that make each country special.
2. **Writing a Survey:** Think of the questions you would ask people from the South American countries about how they feel about their country. Write a survey that has ten questions. You might ask about their jobs, their government, their entertainment, or anything else that is part of their culture.
3. **Writing About Perspectives:** Write a scene from a play based on the following situation: A gaucho from Argentina, a llanero from Venezuela, and a cowhand from the United States meet in the countryside of South America.

ACTIVITIES

1. **Reading Newspapers:** Collect newspapers for one week. Go through them and clip out all the articles that relate to South America. Make a presentation of the articles for your classmates.
2. **Making a Report:** Choose one country in South America to make a report on. Describe the features of the land, the exports of the country, or what kinds of people live and work there. You might attach a map to your report and point out the biggest cities and the rivers or mountains in that country.
3. **Working Together on a Debate:** With your classmates, divide into two groups. One side wants to harvest the resources of the rain forest. The other side wants to clear sections for farming. Refer to the Point/Counterpoint on pages 450–451 and conduct a debate. Give each side equal time.

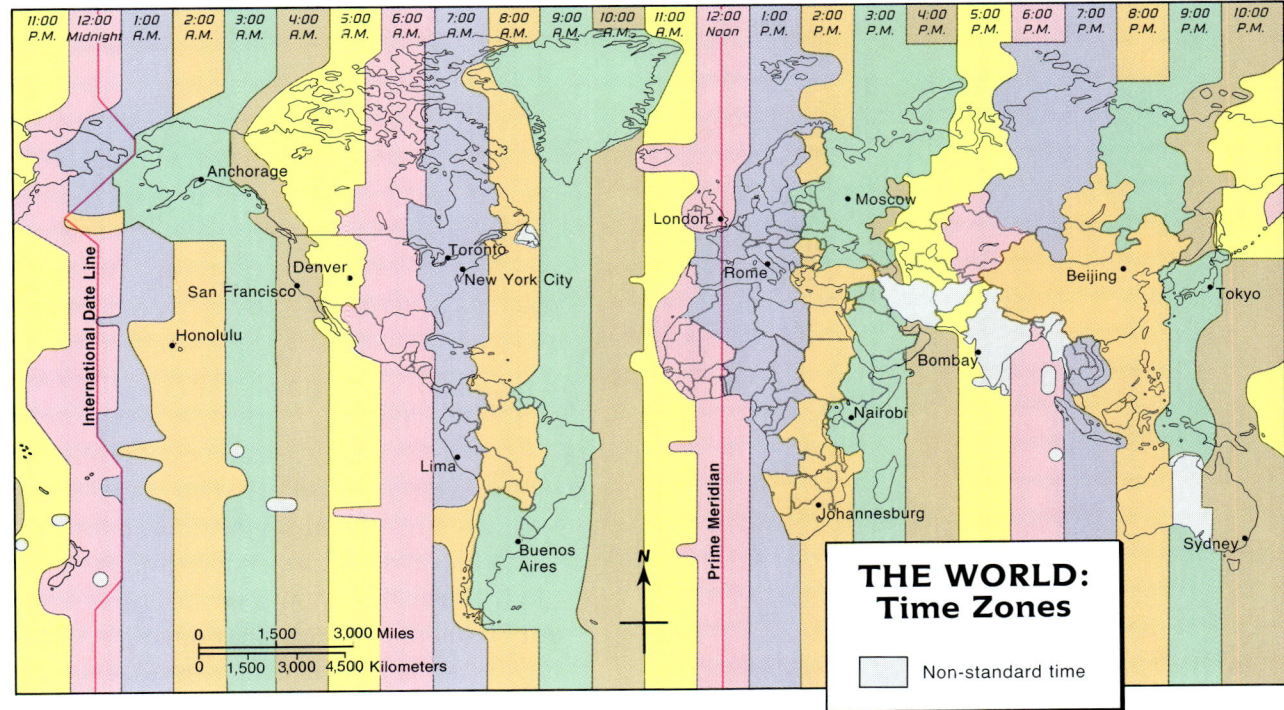

THE WORLD: Time Zones

Non-standard time

BUILDING SKILLS: READING TIME ZONE MAPS

Use the information shown on the map above to answer the following questions.

1. What is the International Date Line?
2. If it is 10:00 A.M. in Buenos Aires, what time is it in Denver?
3. If it is 7:00 A.M. Saturday in Beijing, give the day and time in Lima, San Francisco, Moscow, and Sydney.
4. If you were in a plane flying west across the Atlantic Ocean, would you set your clock back or forward?
5. Why is it important to understand how to read time zone maps?

 **LINKING PAST, PRESENT, AND FUTURE**

You have read in this unit about how the discovery of oil changed the economy and way of life in Venezuela. You have also read about how hydroelectric power changed life in Paraguay. Why do you think the discovery of different sources of energy is so important? How do you think energy developments in the future might affect life in South America?

CONCLUSION

Cooperation in the Western Hemisphere

Key Vocabulary

interdependent
Organization of American States
Pacific Rim

Interdependent Countries

In this book you have read about the many different ethnic groups that make their home in the Western Hemisphere. You also have studied the different countries that are located in this region.

Despite their differences, however, the countries of the Western Hemisphere are **interdependent**. This means that they

The Organization of American States works to promote peace in the Western Hemisphere.

depend upon one another in many ways. For example, the countries of the Western Hemisphere are politically interdependent. They must cooperate with one another in order to maintain peace in this region. In 1948 the **Organization of American States**, or OAS, was established to promote cooperation among the nations of the Western Hemisphere. Twenty-eight of the hemisphere's nations now belong to this organization, as the chart on this page shows.

The OAS has been important in helping to settle political problems in the Western Hemisphere. In 1969, for example, OAS troops helped to end a war between Honduras and El Salvador. The OAS also has provided economic aid to many countries in Latin America. It has raised money to build schools and hospitals.

Economic Ties

Economic interests also link the countries of the Western Hemisphere together. Each country needs products and goods that are grown or made in other countries. The United States imports natural gas and oil from Canada, Mexico, and Venezuela. Mexico imports wheat from the United States and Canada.

Government leaders are working to strengthen economic cooperation in the hemisphere. As you read in Chapter 7, Canada and the United States signed a free-trade agreement in 1988. In 1990 United States President George Bush announced a plan to increase trade among the countries of the Western Hemisphere.

President Bush's plan is called the "Enterprise for the Americas Initiative." An enterprise is a project, and an initiative is a first step or beginning. One part of the plan calls for making the entire hemisphere a free-trade zone, or an area in

ORGANIZATION OF AMERICAN STATES

Argentina	Honduras
Barbados	Jamaica
Bolivia	Mexico
Brazil	Nicaragua
Chile	Panama
Colombia	Paraguay
Costa Rica	Peru
Dominica	St. Kitts and Nevis
Dominican Republic	St. Lucia
Ecuador	Suriname
El Salvador	Trinidad and Tobago
Grenada	United States
Guatemala	Uruguay
Haiti	Venezuela

CHART SKILL: All but 8 of the Western Hemisphere's 36 countries belong to the OAS. Can you name a nonmember country?

which no taxes are collected for goods that are moved between countries.

Trade agreements are another way in which the countries of this hemisphere cooperate. But the people of these countries cooperate in still other ways.

Sister Schools

Two schools in the United States and Nicaragua have found a special way to work together. The Manhattan Country School in New York City and the Brenda Cano School in Tipitapa (tē pē tä′ pə), Nicaragua, have become sister schools. Students from each school send letters and cards to one another. In their letters they tell about their lives.

The students in the United States have learned about some of the problems in Nicaragua. One problem is that there are not enough school supplies for Nicaraguan students. Many schools do not have enough chairs and desks. Paper and pencils are too expensive for many schools and students to buy.

The students in one class at the Manhattan Country School decided to start a "pencil drive." Their goal was to supply each child at the Brenda Cano School with a pencil. The Manhattan Country School students made posters to let everyone in the school know about the pencil drive. They had special pencils designed, which they then sold to students in other classes. For each pencil sold, several were sent to the school in Tipitapa.

The pencil drive was a big success. In just one month the students were able to send 1,500 pencils to Nicaragua. Each student at the Brenda Cano School now has his or her own pencil.

The students at each school benefited from their contact with each other. They learned about life in each other's country. They also learned that they could take action to make a difference in other people's lives.

These United States students (*bottom*) have exchanged letters with students in Tipitapa, Nicaragua (*top*).

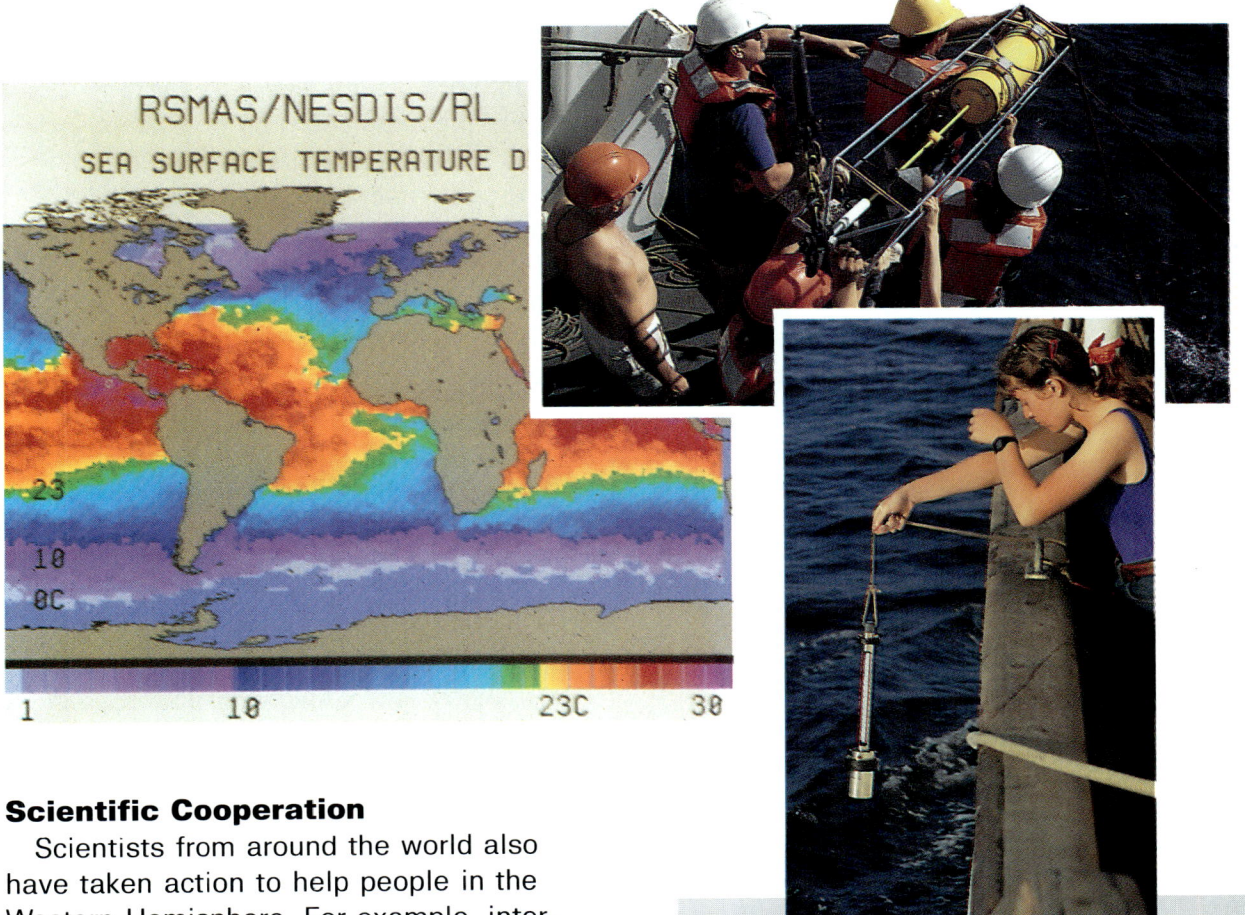

RSMAS/NESDIS/RL
SEA SURFACE TEMPERATURE D

This map shows how El Niño affected Peru and other countries in 1972. Scientists have worked together to understand El Niño.

Scientific Cooperation

Scientists from around the world also have taken action to help people in the Western Hemisphere. For example, international scientific cooperation helped to solve a problem that affects the fishing industry in Peru. As you read in Chapter 24, fishing is important to the economy of Peru.

In 1972 disaster struck Peru's fishing industry. The many fish that usually swim in the Pacific Ocean off the coast of Peru suddenly disappeared. What caused this sudden disappearance?

Scientists in Peru began working with scientists from the United Nations to find out the reason for this disappearance. They discovered that a shift in the currents of the Pacific Ocean causes the ocean's temperature near Peru to change every four or five years. When this happens, the ocean becomes much warmer, killing large numbers of fish. This event is called El Niño (el nēn' yō), because it happens around the time of year when

Christians celebrate the birth of Jesus. El Niño is Spanish for "the little boy."

The international team of scientists concluded that overfishing combined with El Niño had caused Peru's fishing disaster in 1972. Peruvian fishers had caught so many fish that there were few remaining when El Niño struck. Even fewer fish survived the effects of El Niño.

Today Peruvian scientists and scientists from the United Nations continue to watch for signs of El Niño. When it strikes, the number of people allowed to fish in Peru's coastal waters is limited. This helps to protect the country's fishing industry.

Illegal Drugs

An international effort also is being made to stop the illegal drug trade. As you read in Chapter 24, coca, from which cocaine is made, is grown in the Andes Mountains. Other drugs, such as marijuana (mar ə wä' nə), are also produced in Latin America. Many of these illegal drugs are bought by drug abusers in the United States and other countries.

Drug abuse has ruined millions of lives. Illegal drugs have also become a major cause of crime. In order to end the illegal drug trade, officials believe that both the supply of drugs and the demand for drugs must be stopped.

There is no easy way to stop the supply of drugs. In some ways the supply of drugs is linked to poverty in South America. Some poor campesinos in Peru, Bolivia, and Ecuador grow coca plants to earn a living. Drug producers then turn the coca leaves into cocaine.

United States police officers work with students in the DARE program.

The campesinos see very little of the profits made by the drug producers. However, the campesinos make more money from coca than from other crops. With help from the United States, government officials in these Andean countries are looking for ways to solve this problem.

How can the demand for drugs be stopped? In communities throughout the United States, police officers and teachers are working together to build self-respect in students. This program is called Drug Abuse Resistance Education, or DARE. DARE has taught more than 3 million students in the United States that they do not have to use drugs, even though people may pressure them to do so. This program and others are beginning to lessen the demand for drugs.

The Environment

You read in Chapter 8 that the destruction of the Amazon rain forest is harmful to the entire earth. Trees in the rain forest give off much of the earth's oxygen. As you know, many people are working to save the rain forest. You read about Mary Helena Allegretti's work with the rubber tappers on page 191. In the Point/Counterpoint on pages 450–451 you read about the disagreements among some people about how to use the rain forest.

Did you know that you, too, can help to protect this important natural resource? Learning about the rain forest is the first step. Many schools throughout Canada and the United States take part in Rain Forest Week during the month of October. During this week they try to find ways of working together to save the rain forest. For example, they learn about recycling paper to make new paper. To recycle means to use something again. Recycling paper helps to save trees from being cut down.

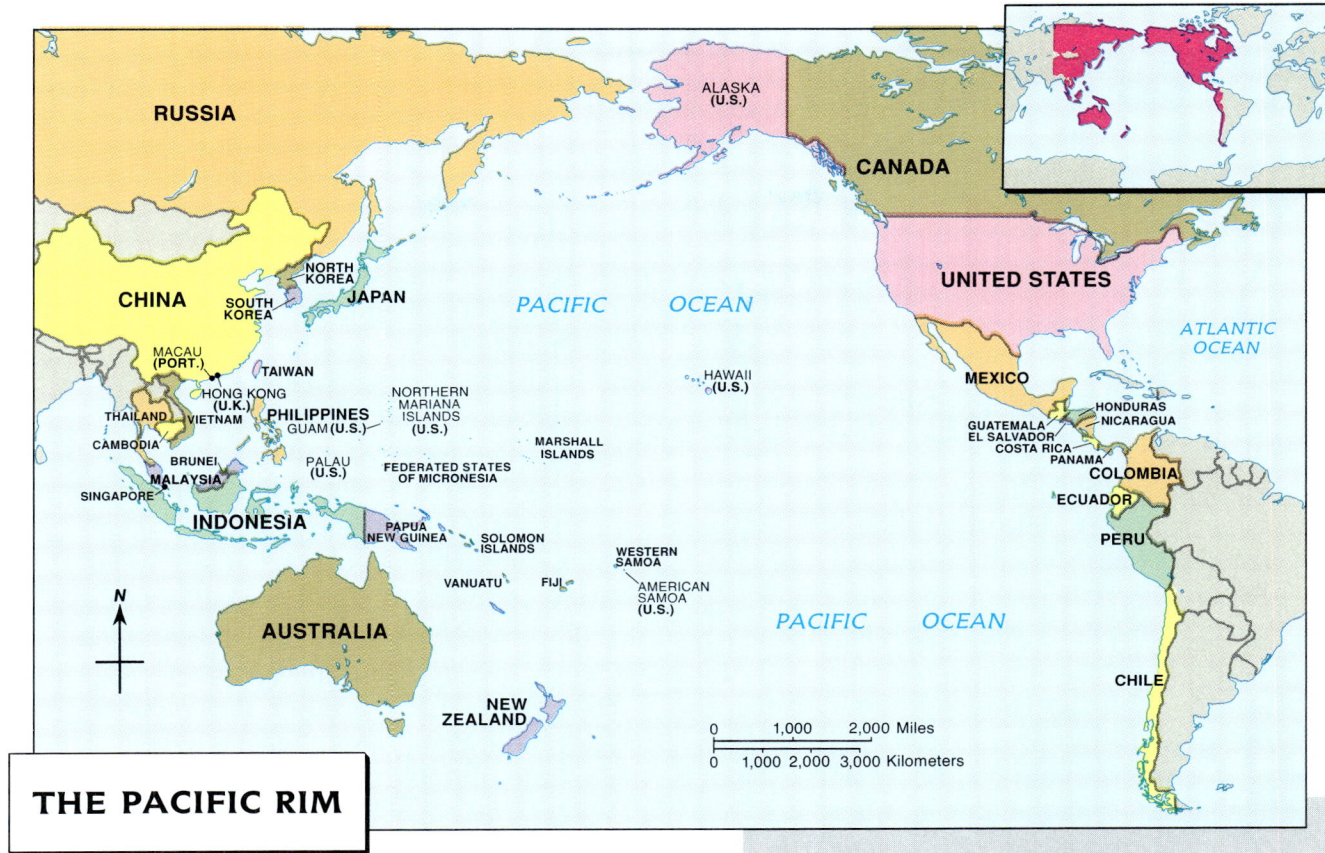

THE PACIFIC RIM

The Pacific Rim

The need for countries to cooperate reaches beyond the Western Hemisphere. The **Pacific Rim** is a term that refers to all the countries that border the Pacific Ocean. There are more than 30 countries in the Pacific Rim. In the Western Hemisphere, Pacific Rim countries are the United States, Canada, Mexico, all the countries of Central America except Belize, and four of the countries of South America. Locate all the Pacific Rim countries on the map on this page.

Like the countries of the Western Hemisphere, the countries of the Pacific Rim are interdependent. They depend upon one another for trade. Trade among these countries is growing so fast that the twenty-first century is sometimes called the "Pacific Century."

The Future

Geography has linked our Americas together for this flight of the future. An understanding of our differences [disagreements] is the true beginning of every great cooperative endeavor [effort].

The writer John A. Crow wrote these words about the countries of the Western Hemisphere. As he states, we are linked together by the land on which we live. We also share common goals for the region: political stability, economic growth, and environmental safety. In order to cooperate, Crow concludes, we must understand our differences. You have already begun to cooperate by learning about the similarities and differences between the peoples of the Western Hemisphere.

559

YOU CAN MAKE A DIFFERENCE

In your textbook this year you read about some very important men and women. Some of them developed new civilizations. Others traveled around the world. In this book you also read about many men and women who worked hard to make a difference in their own communities.

For example, you read about Jeff Gibbs. This young Canadian helped start an environmental club at his high school. You also read about Nancy Pocock. Over the years, Nancy has helped refugees from around the world begin new lives in Toronto, Canada.

You also read about Mary Helena Allegretti. With the help of Brazilian rubber tappers, she works hard to help save the Amazon rain forest.

Antonio Paz Martinez has made a difference in his community, too. After a devastating earthquake in Mexico, Antonio organized his neighbors to help them rebuild their homes and their schools.

Ada Balcácer is another person who saw a problem and tried to solve it. Ada, who is an artist, established a program that teaches women in the Dominican Republic how to make traditional crafts for modern markets. While Ada Balcácer was concerned about the lack of jobs for women, Ray Schambach was upset by the growing number of homeless children in Bogotá, Colombia. Today Ray tries to help the poor, the sick, and the aged.

Finally, you met the Aquia town council. This group helped bring alpacas back to the village of Aquia in Peru. Now the people there have new hope and new opportunities.

These are only a few of the many people who make a difference. Maybe you know someone in your own neighborhood who saw a problem and tried to solve it.

Is there a park or playground where you live that needs to be cleaned up? Or are there ways you can help your neighbors with recycling their trash? There are many ways to help others. The important thing to remember is that *you* can make a difference if you try.

REFERENCE SECTION

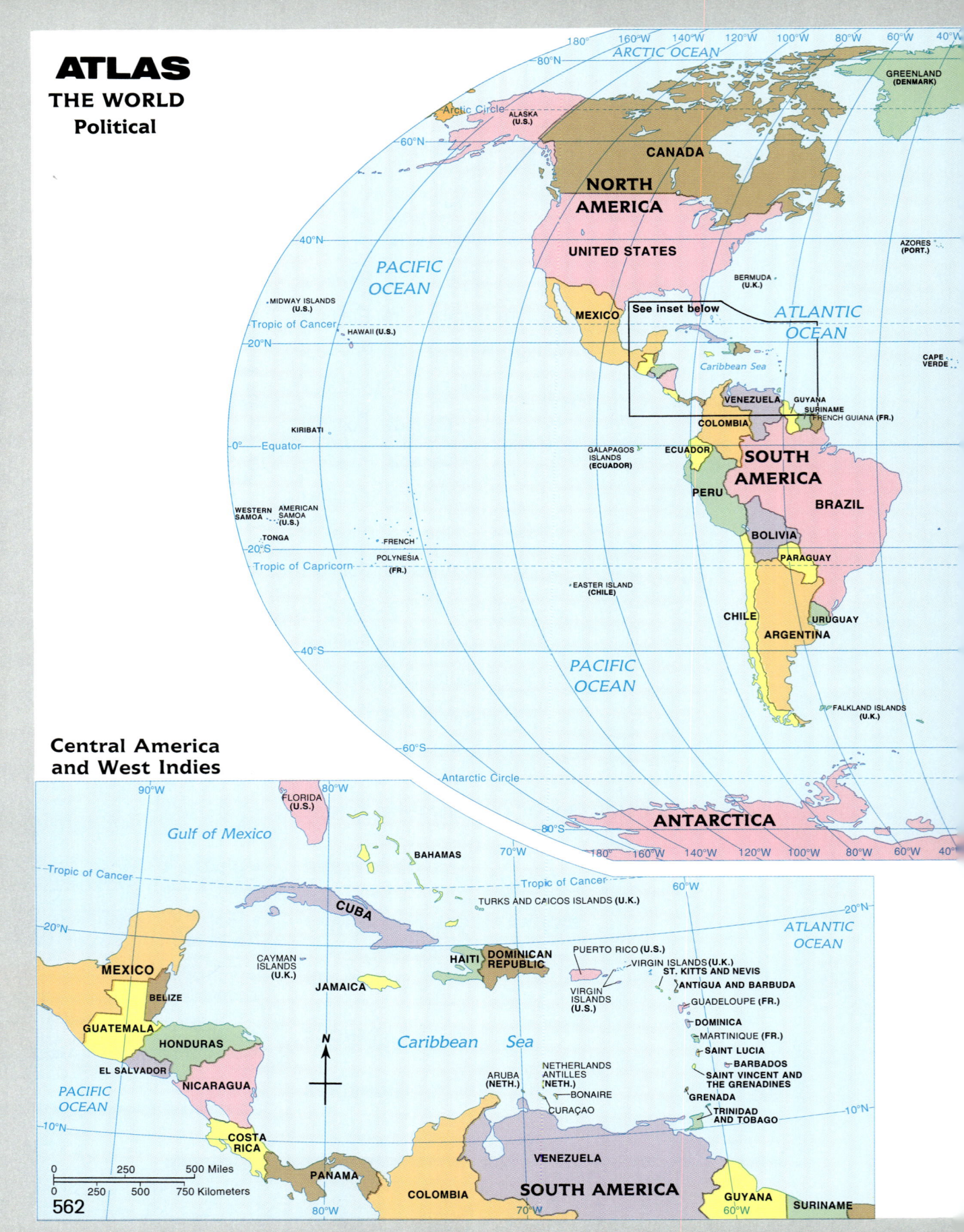

ATLAS
THE WORLD
Political

ARCTIC OCEAN

GREENLAND (DENMARK)

80°N

Arctic Circle   ALASKA (U.S.)

60°N

CANADA

NORTH
AMERICA

40°N

UNITED STATES

AZORES (PORT.)

PACIFIC
OCEAN

BERMUDA (U.S.)

ATLANTIC
OCEAN

MEXICO

See inset below

CAPE VERDE

Tropic of Cancer

20°N   HAWAII (U.S.)

Caribbean Sea

VENEZUELA   GUYANA
SURINAME
FRENCH GUIANA (FR.)

COLOMBIA

KIRIBATI

GALAPAGOS
ISLANDS
(ECUADOR)   ECUADOR

SOUTH
AMERICA

0°   Equator

PERU

BRAZIL

WESTERN
SAMOA   AMERICAN
SAMOA
(U.S.)

BOLIVIA

TONGA   FRENCH

20°S   POLYNESIA
(FR.)

PARAGUAY

Tropic of Capricorn

EASTER ISLAND
(CHILE)

CHILE   URUGUAY

ARGENTINA

40°S

PACIFIC
OCEAN

FALKLAND ISLANDS
(U.K.)

60°S

Antarctic Circle

80°S   ANTARCTICA

180°   160°W   140°W   120°W   100°W   80°W   60°W   40°W

Central America
and West Indies

90°W   80°W
FLORIDA
(U.S.)

Gulf of Mexico

70°W
BAHAMAS

60°W

20°N

Tropic of Cancer

Tropic of Cancer   TURKS AND CAICOS ISLANDS (U.K.)

ATLANTIC
OCEAN

20°N

CUBA

CAYMAN
ISLANDS
(U.K.)

MEXICO

BELIZE   JAMAICA

HAITI   DOMINICAN
REPUBLIC

PUERTO RICO (U.S.)

VIRGIN ISLANDS (U.K.)
ST. KITTS AND NEVIS
ANTIGUA AND BARBUDA

GUATEMALA

VIRGIN
ISLANDS
(U.S.)

GUADELOUPE (FR.)

HONDURAS

N

Caribbean   Sea

DOMINICA
MARTINIQUE (FR.)
SAINT LUCIA

EL SALVADOR

BARBADOS
SAINT VINCENT AND
THE GRENADINES

NICARAGUA

ARUBA
(NETH.)

NETHERLANDS
ANTILLES
(NETH.)

GRENADA

PACIFIC
OCEAN

BONAIRE

TRINIDAD
AND TOBAGO

CURAÇAO

10°N

COSTA
RICA

10°N

80°W

PANAMA

VENEZUELA

SOUTH AMERICA

COLOMBIA

70°W

GUYANA   SURINAME

60°W

0   250   500 Miles
0   250   500   750 Kilometers

562

ARCTIC OCEAN

80°N

SPITSBERGEN (NOR.)   SVALBARD (NOR.)

See inset below   Arctic Circle

ICELAND

RUSSIA   60°N

North Sea

EUROPE

ASIA   MONGOLIA

KAZAKHSTAN

GEORGIA   UZBEKISTAN   KYRGYZSTAN   NORTH KOREA   JAPAN   40°N

ARMENIA   TURKMENISTAN   TAJIKISTAN

TURKEY   AZERBAIJAN   SOUTH KOREA

TUNISIA   LEBANON   SYRIA   IRAQ   IRAN   AFGHANISTAN   CHINA

MOROCCO   ISRAEL   JORDAN

ALGERIA   LIBYA   KUWAIT   BAHRAIN   QATAR   PAKISTAN   NEPAL   BHUTAN   PACIFIC OCEAN

CANARY ISLANDS (SP.)

WESTERN SAHARA (MOROCCO)   EGYPT   SAUDI ARABIA   UNITED ARAB EMIRATES   BANGLADESH   MACAU (PORT.)   HONG KONG (U.K.)   TAIWAN   Tropic of Cancer   20°N

MAURITANIA   OMAN   INDIA   MYANMAR (BURMA)   LAOS   NORTHERN MARIANA ISLANDS (U.S.)   WAKE ISLAND (U.S.)

MALI   NIGER   CHAD   YEMEN   THAILAND   VIETNAM   GUAM (U.S.)   MARSHALL ISLANDS

SENEGAL   GAMBIA   AFRICA   SUDAN   DJIBOUTI   CAMBODIA   PHILIPPINES   PALAU (U.S.)   FEDERATED STATES OF MICRONESIA

GUINEA-BISSAU   BURKINA FASO   NIGERIA   ETHIOPIA   SRI LANKA   BRUNEI

GUINEA   CENTRAL AFRICAN REPUBLIC   MALDIVES   MALAYSIA   KIRIBATI   Equator   0°

SIERRA LEONE   COTE D'IVOIRE   BENIN   CAMEROON   SINGAPORE   NAURU

LIBERIA   GHANA   TOGO   EQUATORIAL GUINEA   ZAIRE   UGANDA   SOMALIA

SÃO TOMÉ AND PRINCIPE   GABON   CONGO   RWANDA   KENYA   INDONESIA   SOLOMON ISLANDS

CABINDA (ANGOLA)   BURUNDI   SEYCHELLES   PAPUA NEW GUINEA   TUVALU

TANZANIA   INDIAN OCEAN   VANUATU   FIJI   20°S

ANGOLA   COMOROS   NEW CALEDONIA (FR.)

ZAMBIA   MALAWI   MADAGASCAR

NAMIBIA   MOZAMBIQUE   MAURITIUS

WALVIS BAY (S.A.)   ZIMBABWE   AUSTRALIA

BOTSWANA   40°S

SWAZILAND   NEW ZEALAND

SOUTH AFRICA   LESOTHO

N

0   1,000   2,000 Miles
0   1,000   2,000   3,000 Kilometers
Scale accurate at Equator   60°S

Antarctic Circle   80°S

ANTARCTICA

20°W   0°   20°E   40°E   60°E   80°E   100°E   120°E   140°E   160°E   180°

ABBREVIATION KEY

Abbreviation:	Country:
(FR.)	FRANCE
(GR.)	GERMANY
(IT.)	ITALY
(NETH.)	NETHERLANDS
(NOR.)	NORWAY
(PORT.)	PORTUGAL
(S.A.)	SOUTH AFRICA
(SP.)	SPAIN
(U.K.)	UNITED KINGDOM
(U.S.)	UNITED STATES

Europe

FINLAND

NORWAY   SWEDEN   RUSSIA

IRELAND   North Sea   ESTONIA   Baltic Sea   LATVIA

UNITED KINGDOM   DENMARK   LITHUANIA (Russia)

NETHERLANDS   BYELARUS

ATLANTIC OCEAN   BELGIUM   GERMANY   POLAND

LUXEMBOURG   CZECHOSLOVAKIA   UKRAINE

FRANCE   LIECHTENSTEIN   AUSTRIA   HUNGARY   MOLDOVA

SWITZERLAND   SLOVENIA   ROMANIA

PORTUGAL   CROATIA   BOSNIA AND HERCEGOVINA   N

ANDORRA   MONACO   SERBIA   YUGOSLAVIA   BULGARIA

CORSICA (FR.)   ITALY   MONTENEGRO   Black Sea

SPAIN   ALBANIA   MACEDONIA   TURKEY

GIBRALTAR (U.K.)   BALEARIC IS. (SP.)   SARDINIA (IT.)   GREECE   SYRIA

0   250   500 Miles   SICILY (IT.)   CYPRUS   LEBANON

0   250   500   750 Kilometers   MALTA   CRETE (GR.)   Mediterranean Sea

THE WORLD
Physical

ARCTIC OCEAN

180°   160°W   140°W   120°W   100°W   80°W   60°W   40°W

80°N

60°N

ALASKA RANGE

Mt. McKinley
20,320 ft.
(6,194 m)

ROCKY MOUNTAINS

CANADIAN SHIELD

NORTH
AMERICA

40°N

Mississippi R.

APPALACHIAN MTS.

NORTH PACIFIC OCEAN

NORTH
ATLANTIC
OCEAN

Tropic of Cancer

Rio Grande

20°N

0°   Equator

Amazon R.

SOUTH
AMERICA

ANDES MTS.

20°S

Tropic of Capricorn

SOUTH PACIFIC OCEAN

Mt. Aconcagua
22,834 ft. (6,960 m)

40°S

Cape Horn

60°S

Antarctic Circle

Vinson Massif
16,864 ft. (5,140 m)

80°S

180°

ANTARCTICA

20°W 0° 20°E 40°E 60°E 80°E 100°E 120°E 140°E 160°E 180°

ARCTIC OCEAN

80°N

Arctic Circle

60°N

URAL MTS.

Ob River

Volga R.

EUROPE
ALPS
Mont Blanc
15,771 ft. (4,807 m)

Mt. Elbrus
18,481 ft.
(5,633 m)

ASIA

GOBI

40°N

HINDU KUSH

HIMALAYAS

Chang R.

SYRIAN
DESERT

SAHARA

Nile R.

Indus R.

Ganges R.

Mt. Everest
29,028 ft.
(8,848 m)

Tropic of Cancer

20°N

AFRICA

DECCAN
PLATEAU

PACIFIC OCEAN

Mt. Kilimanjaro
19,340 ft. (5,395 m)

Equator 0°

INDIAN OCEAN

20°S

NAMIB DESERT

KALAHARI
DESERT

GREAT
SANDY
DESERT

Tropic of Capricorn

AUSTRALIA

*SOUTH
ATLANTIC
OCEAN*

Cape of
Good Hope

Mt. Kosciusko
7,310 ft. (2,228 m)

0   1,000   2,000 Miles
0 1,000 2,000 3,000 Kilometers
Scale accurate at Equator

60°S

N

Antarctic Circle

ANTARCTICA

80°S

180°

ARCTIC OCEAN

Beaufort Sea

GREENLAND
(DEN.)

Baffin Bay

Yukon River

• Fairbanks

ALASKA
(U.S.)

Mackenzie River

• Yellowknife

• Iqaluit

Arctic Circle

Davis Strait

Nuuk •

• Anchorage

60°N

Hudson Bay

60°N

Labrador Sea

C A N A D A

NORTH AMERICA

• Edmonton

• Winnipeg

• Vancouver

• Quebec

Gulf of St. Lawrence

• Seattle

Missouri River

Great Lakes

Ottawa

• Portland

UNITED

• Minneapolis

• Toronto

• Boston

Great Salt Lake

• Salt Lake City

• Denver

• Detroit

• Chicago

• New York City

STATES

• St. Louis

Washington, D.C.

ATLANTIC OCEAN

• San Francisco

Colorado River

• Phoenix

Mississippi River

• Atlanta

BERMUDA
(U.K.)

30°N

• Los Angeles

• Houston

• New Orleans

30°N

Tropic of Cancer

HAWAII
(U.S.)

Gulf of California

Rio Grande

Gulf of Mexico

• Miami

PACIFIC OCEAN

• Monterey

MEXICO

• Havana

BAHAMAS

CUBA   HAITI

DOMINICAN REPUBLIC

• Guadalajara

Mexico City

Port-au-Prince

Santo Domingo

• San Juan

ST. KITTS AND NEVIS

Belmopan

JAMAICA

PUERTO RICO
(U.S.)

ANTIGUA AND BARBUDA

GUATEMALA

BELIZE

Kingston

DOMINICA

HONDURAS

ST. LUCIA

Guatemala City

Tegucigalpa

BARBADOS

San Salvador

NICARAGUA

Caribbean Sea

GRENADA

EL SALVADOR

Managua

ST. VINCENT AND THE GRENADINES

CENTRAL

COSTA RICA

San José

• Maracaibo

TRINIDAD AND TOBAGO

Panama

AMERICA

PANAMA

Panama City

Caracas

SURINAME

Bogotá

VENEZUELA

Georgetown

Paramaribo

Cayenne

COLOMBIA

GUYANA

FRENCH GUIANA (FR.)

0°   Equator

GALÁPAGOS ISLANDS
(ECUADOR)

ECUADOR

Quito

0°

Guayaquil

• Manaus

• Belém

Amazon River

• Recife

PERU

BRAZIL

• Callao

SOUTH AMERICA

• Bahia

• Lima

• La Paz

BOLIVIA

Brasília

• Santa Cruz

Sucre

• Río de Janeiro

N

PARAGUAY

São Paulo

Tropic of Capricorn

• Antofagasta

Asunción

Pôrto Alegre

30°S

30°S

• Tucimán

CHILE

• Rosario

URUGUAY

• Valparaíso

Santiago

Buenos Aires

Montevideo

• Concepción

La Plata

ARGENTINA

Mar del Plata

• Comodoro Rivadavia

Strait of Magellan

FALKLAND ISLANDS
(U.K.)

SOUTH GEORGIA
(U.K.)

• Punta Arenas

WESTERN
HEMISPHERE
Political

⊛ National capital   • Other city

| 0 | 500 | 1,000 | 1,500 Miles |

| 0 | 500 | 1,000 | 1,500 | 2,000 | Kilometers |

150°W   120°W   90°W   60°N

90°W   60°W

ARCTIC OCEAN

Point Barrow

Beaufort Sea

Queen Elizabeth Islands

Banks Island

Victoria Island

Baffin Island

Baffin Bay

Greenland

Davis Strait

Arctic Circle

Cape Farewell

60°N

Brooks Range

Yukon River

Mt. McKinley 20,320 ft. (6,194 m)

Alaska Range

Gulf of Alaska

Alaska Peninsula

Coast Mountains

Vancouver Island

ROCKY MOUNTAINS

Mackenzie River

Great Bear Lake

Great Slave Lake

Hudson Bay

Labrador Sea

Saskatchewan River

Lake Winnipeg

CANADIAN

SHIELD

LABRADOR

Great Lakes

St. Lawrence River

Newfoundland

Nova Scotia

Gulf of St. Lawrence

GREAT PLAINS

Missouri River

Platte River

NORTH AMERICA

Ohio River

APPALACHIAN MOUNTAINS

Cape Cod

Long Island

ATLANTIC OCEAN

Cascade Range

Snake River

Great Salt Lake

GREAT BASIN

Sierra Nevada

Coast Ranges

Cape Mendocino

Colorado River

Mississippi River

COASTAL PLAINS

Bermuda Islands

30°N

Rio Grande

Baja California

Gulf of California

SIERRA MADRE OCCIDENTAL

SIERRA MADRE ORIENTAL

Florida Peninsula

Tropic of Cancer

Hawaiian Islands

Gulf of Mexico

Straits of Florida

Cuba

WEST INDIES

Yucatán Peninsula

Gulf of Honduras

Greater Antilles

Hispaniola

Caribbean Sea

Lesser Antilles

PACIFIC OCEAN

CENTRAL AMERICA

Lake Nicaragua

Isthmus of Panama

Gulf of Panama

Lake Maracaibo

Orinoco River

LLANOS

GUIANA HIGHLANDS

Galápagos Islands

Magdalena River

Río Negro

AMAZON

Amazon River

Cape São Roque

0° Equator

ANDES

BASIN

Madeira River

São Francisco River

Tocantins River

SOUTH AMERICA

MATO GRASSO PLATEAU

BRAZILIAN HIGHLANDS

N

Lake Titicaca

GRAN CHACO

Paraguay River

Paraná River

Tropic of Capricorn

Mt. Aconcagua 22,834 ft. (6,960 m)

MOUNTAINS

Uruguay River

30°S

PAMPAS

PATAGONIA

Falkland Islands

WESTERN HEMISPHERE
Physical

0   500   1,000   1,500 Miles

0   500 1,000 1,500 2,000 Kilometers

Strait of Magellan

Tierra del Fuego

Cape Horn

567

South Georgia

RUSSIA

ARCTIC OCEAN

160°W

160°E

Bering Sea

AK

180°

Gulf of Alaska

40°N

PACIFIC OCEAN

WA

OR

N

CA

THE 50 UNITED STATES

✹ National capital

0	500	1,000 Miles
0	500	1,000	1,500 Kilometers

N

HI

20°N

568

140°W

120°W

Greenland
(DENMARK)

Arctic Circle

Hudson Bay

CANADA

Great Lakes

MT   ND   MN   MI   ME
                                WI   VT
ID   SD   MI   NY   NH
        WY   IA   PA   MA
                    NE   IL   IN   OH   CT RI
                                                              NJ   40°N
UT   KS   MO   KY   WV   Washington, D.C.
    CO   VA   MD DE
                    OK   AR   TN   NC
AZ   NM   SC   ATLANTIC
                                  MS   AL   GA   OCEAN

                    TX   LA   FL

MEXICO   Gulf of Mexico

                                            CUBA
Tropic of Cancer

569

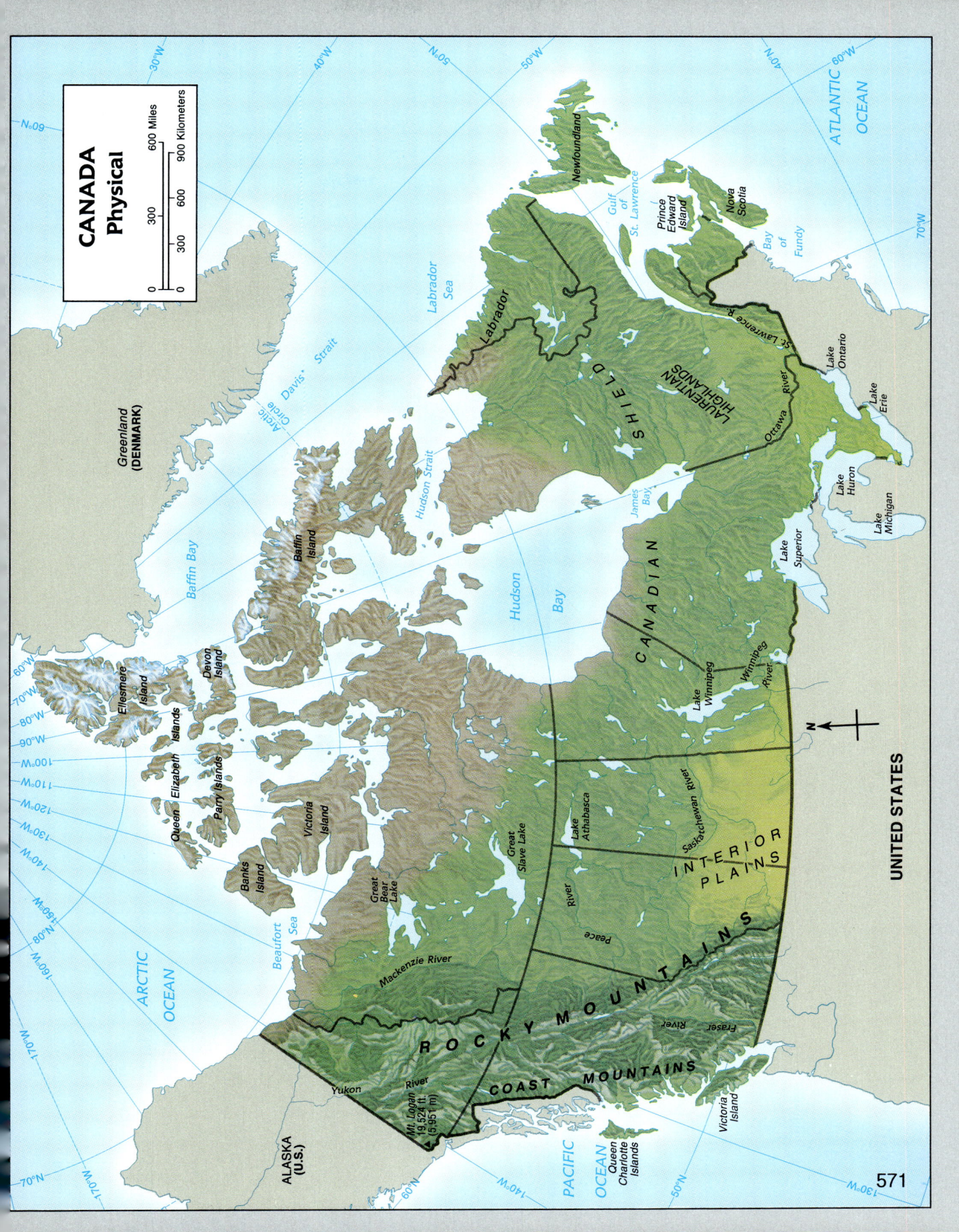

600 Miles

900 Kilometers

300

600

300

600

0

0

ATLANTIC
OCEAN

Newfoundland

Gulf
of
St. Lawrence

Prince
Edward
Island

Nova
Scotia

Bay
of
Fundy

Labrador
Sea

Labrador

St. Lawrence R.

Lake
Ontario

Lake
Erie

Davis Strait

Arctic Circle

Greenland
(DENMARK)

LAURENTIAN
HIGHLANDS

Ottawa
River

Lake
Huron

Baffin Bay

Baffin
Island

Hudson Strait

S
H
I
E
L
D

James
Bay

Lake
Michigan

Ellesmere
Island

Devon
Island

Queen Elizabeth Islands

Parry Islands

Hudson
Bay

Bay

C
A
N
A
D
I
A
N

Lake
Superior

Victoria
Island

Lake
Winnipeg

Winnipeg
River

Banks
Island

Great
Bear
Lake

Great
Slave Lake

Lake
Athabasca

Saskatchewan River

INTERIOR

PLAINS

Beaufort
Sea

Mackenzie River

River

Peace

R O C K Y   M O U N T A I N S

UNITED STATES

N

ARCTIC
OCEAN

Yukon

River

Mt. Logan
19,524 ft.
(5,951 m)

C O A S T   M O U N T A I N S

Fraser

River

Victoria
Island

ALASKA
(U.S.)

PACIFIC
OCEAN

Queen
Charlotte
Islands

60°N

50°N

40°N

30°W

40°W

50°W

60°W

70°W

60°W

70°W

80°W

90°W

100°W

110°W

120°W

130°W

140°W

150°W

160°W

170°W

160°W

150°W

140°W

130°W

60°N

70°N

80°N

MEXICO
Political

◉ National capital   ★ State capital

```
0        100        200 Miles
0   100   200   300 Kilometers
```

UNITED STATES

BAJA CALIFORNIA NORTE
★ Mexicali

SONORA
★ Hermosillo

BAJA CALIFORNIA SUR
★ La Paz

CHIHUAHUA
★ Chihuahua

SINALOA
★ Culiacán

DURANGO
★ Durango

COAHUILA
★ Saltillo

NUEVO LEÓN
★ Monterrey

ZACATECAS
★ Zacatecas

NAYARIT
★ Tepic

AGUASCALIENTES
★ Aguascalientes

SAN LUIS POTOSÍ
★ San Luis Potosí

TAMAULIPAS
★ Ciudad Victoria

JALISCO
★ Guadalajara

GUANAJUATO
★ Guanajuato

QUERÉTARO
★ Querétaro

HIDALGO
★ Pachuca

COLIMA
★ Colima

MICHOACÁN
★ Morelia

MEXICO
★ Toluca

MÉXICO CITY
FEDERAL DISTRICT

TLAXCALA
★ Tlaxcala

MORELOS
★ Cuernavaca

PUEBLA
★ Puebla

VERACRUZ
★ Jalapa

GUERRERO
★ Chilpancingo

OAXACA
★ Oaxaca

TABASCO
★ Villahermosa

CHIAPAS
★ Tuxtla Gutiérrez

CAMPECHE
★ Campeche

YUCATÁN
★ Mérida

QUINTANA ROO
★ Ciudad Chetumal

Gulf of Mexico

Bay of Campeche

PACIFIC OCEAN

Gulf of California

Rio Grande

Rio Grande de Santiago

Balsas River

Tropic of Cancer

GUATEMALA

BELIZE

HONDURAS

EL SALVADOR

N

572

UNITED STATES

Gulf of Mexico

Tropic of Cancer

Bay of Campeche

YUCATÁN PENINSULA

Terminos Lagoon

BELIZE

GUATEMALA

HONDURAS

EL SALVADOR

Gulf of Tehuantepec

GULF COASTAL PLAIN

Pánuco River

Citlaltépetl 18,700 ft. (5,700 m) ▲

Iztaccihuatl 17,343 ft. (5,286 m) ▲

Popocatépetl 17,887 ft. (5,452 m) ▲

Balsas River

Sierra Madre del Sur

EASTERN SIERRA MADRE

Salado River

Rio Grande

Lerma River

Rio Grande de Santiago

Lake Chapala

CENTRAL PLATEAU

Rio Grande

Bolson de Mapimi

Caballos Mesteños Plains

Conchos River

WESTERN SIERRA MADRE

Rio del Fuerte

Yaqui River

Sonora River

Concepción River

Marias Islands

San Benedicto Island

Socorro Island

Clarion Island

Gulf of California

BAJA CALIFORNIA

Magdalena Bay

PACIFIC OCEAN

Sebastian Vizcaino Bay

Cedros Island

Cerro del Pinacate 3,957 ft. (1,206 m) ▲

SONORA DESERT

N

MEXICO
Physical

▲ Mountain peak

200 Miles
300 Kilometers
100   200
100   200
0   0

30°N   25°N   20°N   15°N

115°W   110°W   105°W   100°W   95°W   90°W

573

JAMAICA

COLOMBIA

Caribbean Sea

Panama City
Colón
Gulf of Panama

Panama Canal

PANAMA

Santiago

David

Limón

Puerto Cabezas

Bluefields

San Juan del Norte

San José

COSTA RICA

Puntarenas

NICARAGUA

Matagalpa

Río Grande

Lake Managua

Lake Nicaragua

León

Managua

Granada

HONDURAS

La Ceiba

Tegucigalpa

San Pedro Sula

San Miguel

Belize City

Belmopan

BELIZE

Gulf of Honduras

Puerto Barrios

Lake Izabal

Motagua River

Usumacinta River

GUATEMALA

Cobán

Guatemala City

Santa Ana
San Salvador

EL SALVADOR

Antigua

Quetzaltenango

MEXICO

N

PACIFIC OCEAN

CENTRAL AMERICA
Political

⊛ National capital   • Other city

200 Miles
300 Kilometers
100
100   200
0   0

574

JAMAICA

Caribbean Sea

MEXICO

Turneffe Islands

Gulf of Honduras

Islas de la Bahía

MOSQUITO COAST

Lake Izabal

Belize River

Lake Petén Itzá

Usumacinta River

Motagua River

Sierra de las Minas

Sierra de la Merendon

Ulúa River

Lake Yojoa

Patuca River

Coco River

Isabella Range

Grande de Matagalpa

San Juan River

Darién Range

COLOMBIA

Gulf of Panama

Lake Gatún

Isthmus of Panama

Panama Canal

Azuero Peninsula

Coiba Island

Barú Volcano
11,410 ft.
(3,478 m) ▲

Talamanca Range

Cerro Chirripó
12,530 ft.
(3,819 m) ▲

Irazú Volcano
11,260 ft.
(3,432 m) ▲

Guanaca Mountains

Gulf of Nicoya

Nicoya Peninsula

Lake Nicaragua

Lake Managua

Río Grande

Lake Atitlán

Fuego Volcano
12,986 ft.
(3,958 m) ▲

Santa María
Volcano
12,363 ft.
(3,768 m) ▲

Tajumulco
Volcano
13,816 ft.
(4,211 m) ▲

San Miguel
Volcano
6,994 ft.
(2,132 m) ▲

Lempa River

Choluteca River

Santa Clara
Volcano
4,512 ft.
(1,375 m) ▲

Gulf of Fonseca

El Viejo
Volcano
5,839 ft.
(1,780 m)

PACIFIC OCEAN

N

CENTRAL AMERICA
Physical

200 Miles

300 Kilometers

0   100   200

0   100   200   300

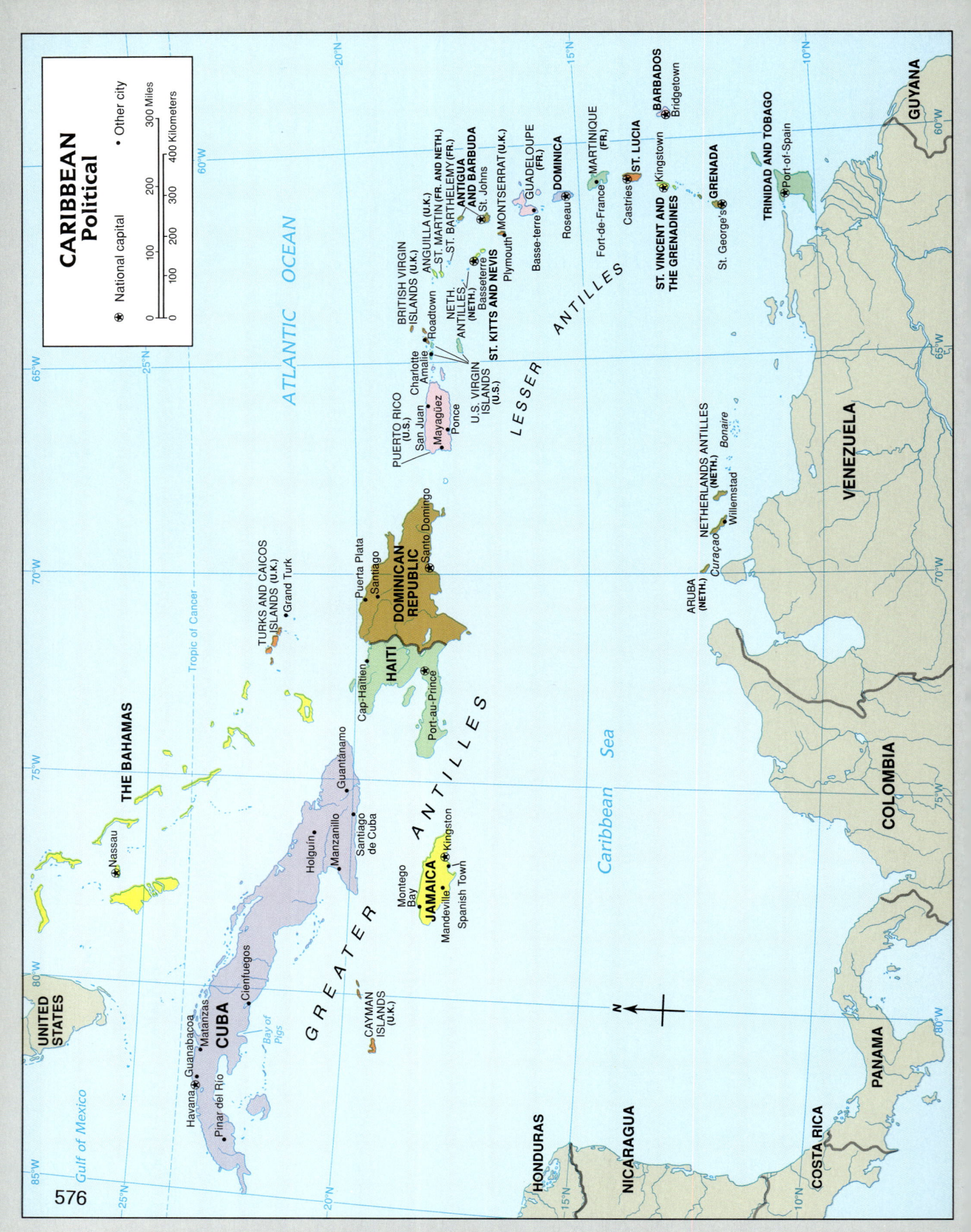

CARIBBEAN
Political

⊛ National capital   • Other city

| 0 | 100 | 200 | 300 Miles |
| 0 | 100 | 200 | 300 | 400 Kilometers |

ATLANTIC OCEAN

UNITED STATES

Gulf of Mexico

THE BAHAMAS

Nassau ⊛

Tropic of Cancer

TURKS AND CAICOS
ISLANDS (U.K.)
• Grand Turk

Havana ⊛
Guanabacoa
Matanzas
Pinar del Río
Cienfuegos
Bay of Pigs

CUBA

Holguín •
Manzanillo •
Santiago de Cuba •
Guantánamo

GREATER ANTILLES

CAYMAN ISLANDS (U.K.)

Montego Bay •
JAMAICA
Mandeville •
Spanish Town •
⊛ Kingston

Caribbean Sea

Puerta Plata •
Santiago •

DOMINICAN REPUBLIC

Santo Domingo ⊛

HAITI
Cap-Haïtien •
⊛ Port-au-Prince

PUERTO RICO (U.S.)
San Juan •
Mayagüez •
Ponce •

Charlotte Amalie
U.S. VIRGIN ISLANDS (U.S.)

BRITISH VIRGIN ISLANDS (U.K.)
Roadtown •

ANGUILLA (U.K.)
ST. MARTIN (FR. AND NETH.)
ST. BARTHELEMY (FR.)
ANTIGUA AND BARBUDA
• St. Johns

NETH. ANTILLES (NETH.)
Basseterre •
ST. KITTS AND NEVIS

Plymouth •
MONTSERRAT (U.K.)

GUADELOUPE (FR.)
Basse-terre •

DOMINICA
Roseau •

MARTINIQUE (FR.)
Fort-de-France •

ST. LUCIA
Castries ⊛

BARBADOS
Bridgetown ⊛

ST. VINCENT AND THE GRENADINES
⊛ Kingstown

GRENADA
St. George's ⊛

LESSER ANTILLES

TRINIDAD AND TOBAGO
Port-of-Spain ⊛

ARUBA (NETH.)

NETHERLANDS ANTILLES (NETH.)
Willemstad •
Curaçao
Bonaire

VENEZUELA

COLOMBIA

GUYANA

HONDURAS

NICARAGUA

COSTA RICA

PANAMA

576

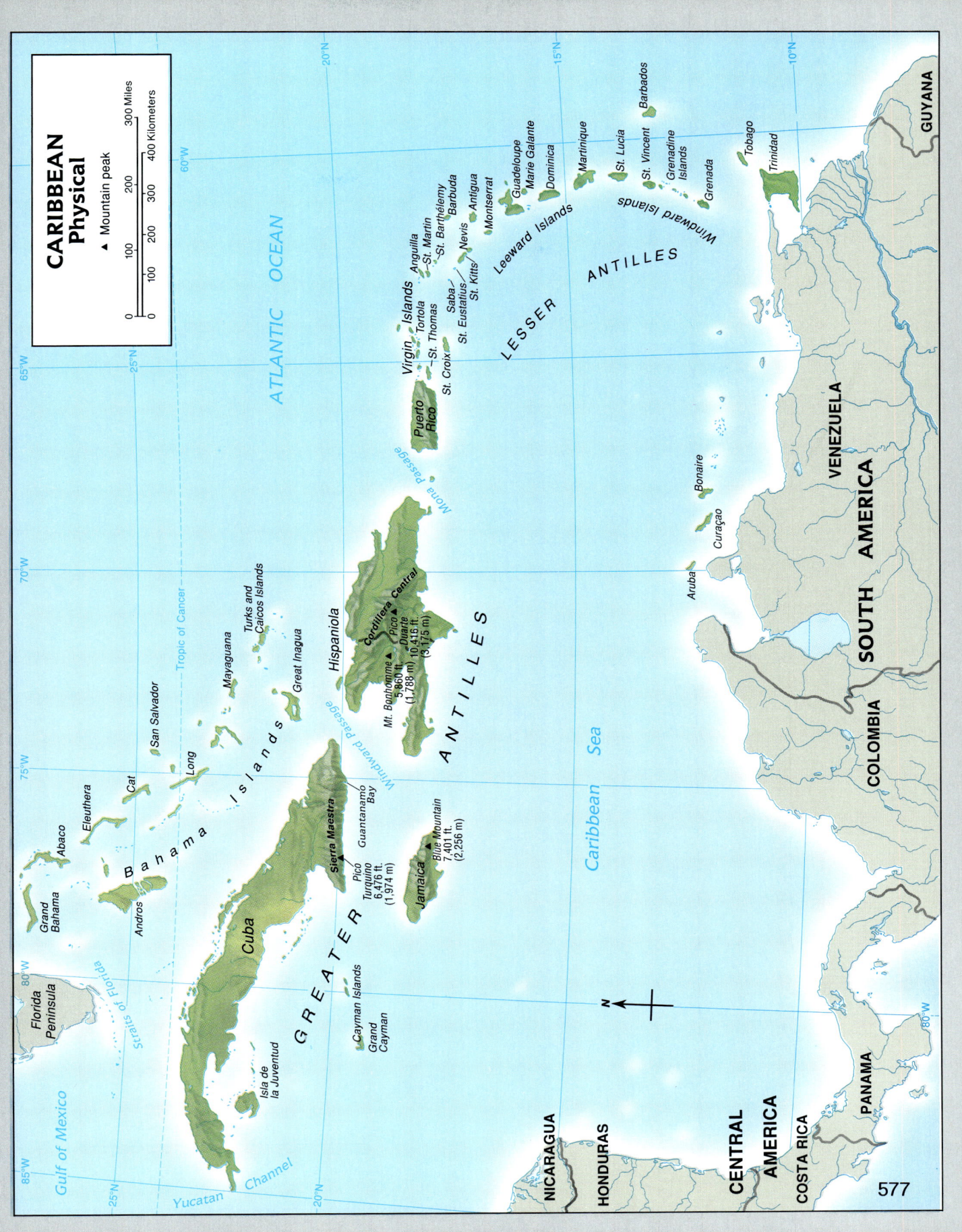

CARIBBEAN
Physical

▲ Mountain peak

300 Miles

400 Kilometers

ATLANTIC OCEAN

GUYANA

Barbados

Tobago
Trinidad

Marie Galante
Guadeloupe
Dominica
Martinique
St. Lucia
St. Vincent
Grenadine Islands
Grenada

Anguilla
St. Martin
St. Barthélemy
Barbuda
Antigua
Nevis
Montserrat
St. Kitts
St. Eustatius
Saba

Leeward Islands

Windward Islands

LESSER   ANTILLES

Virgin Islands
Tortola
St. Thomas
St. Croix

Puerto Rico

Mona Passage

Bonaire
Curaçao
Aruba

VENEZUELA

SOUTH AMERICA

COLOMBIA

Turks and
Caicos Islands

Mayaguana

Great Inagua

Hispaniola

Cordillera Central
Pico
Duarte
10,416 ft
(3,175 m) ▲

Mt. Bonhomme ▲
5,860 ft
(1,788 m)

GREATER   ANTILLES

Caribbean   Sea

San Salvador

Long

Cat

Eleuthera

Abaco

Grand
Bahama

Andros

Bahama   Islands

Tropic of Cancer

Sierra Maestra
Guantanamo
Bay

Windward Passage

Pico
Turquino
6,476 ft
(1,974 m)

Jamaica

Blue Mountain
7,401 ft
(2,256 m) ▲

Cuba

Cayman Islands
Grand
Cayman

Isla de
la Juventud

Florida
Peninsula

Straits of Florida

Gulf of Mexico

Yucatan Channel

NICARAGUA

HONDURAS

CENTRAL
AMERICA

COSTA RICA

PANAMA

N

577

Caribbean Sea

Central
America

80°W · 10°N

Barranquilla
Maracaibo
Valencia ● Caracas
VENEZUELA
Georgetown
Medellín
● Bogotá
Cali ●
COLOMBIA
GUYANA
Paramaribo
Cayenne
SURINAME
**FRENCH
GUIANA
(FR.)**

Gulf
of
Panama

Magdalena River

Orinoco River

Río Negro

Quito
ECUADOR
Equator · 0°
Guayaquil
Iquitos

Manaus
Amazon River
Belém

Tapajóz River
Xingu River

Trujillo
PERU
Callao ● Cuzco
Lima
Arequipa
*Lake
Titicaca*
● La Paz
BOLIVIA
● Sucre

B R A Z I L

Recife

● Brasília

Salvador
(Bahía)

Madeira River

São Francisco River

10°S

Belo
Horizonte

Antofagasta
Tucumán
PARAGUAY
● Asunción
Paraná River
São Paulo
Río de Janeiro

20°S · Tropic of Capricorn

Paraguay River

**PACIFIC
OCEAN**

**ATLANTIC
OCEAN**

Córdoba
Rosario
CHILE
Valparaíso
Santiago ●
ARGENTINA
Buenos
Aires
Concepción

Pôrto Alegre
URUGUAY
Montevideo
*Río de
la Plata*

30°S

Colorado River

Uruguay River

N

FALKLAND
ISLANDS
(U.K.)

Strait of
Magellan

Punta
Arenas

40°S

50°S

SOUTH AMERICA
Political

⊛ National capital · Other city

0 · 250 · 500 Miles
0 · 250 · 500 · 750 Kilometers

578

Caribbean Sea

Central America

Guajira Peninsula

Lake Maracaibo

Gulf of Panama

LLANOS

Orinoco River

River

GUIANA HIGHLANDS

Cauca

Magdalena

River

River

Equator

Japura

Río Negro

River

AMAZON

Amazon

River

Marajó Island

Gulf of Guayaquil

River

River

BASIN

River

River

Tapajóz River

River

Xingu

River

Parnaíba River

Cape Saõ Roque

Aguja Point

Marañon

Ucayali

Purus

Madeira

River

River

Araguaia River

Tocantins River

São Francisco River

ANDES MOUNTAINS

River

MATO GROSSO PLATEAU

BRAZILIAN HIGHLANDS

Lake Titicaca

Lake Poopó

ATACAMA DESERT

Paraguay River

GRAN CHACO

River

PACIFIC OCEAN

Tropic of Capricorn

Salado

River

Paraná

River

ATLANTIC OCEAN

ANDES MOUNTAINS

Uruguay River

Mt. Aconcagua ▲ 22,834 ft. (6,960 m)

PAMPAS

Río de la Plata

N

Colorado River

Blanca Bay

San Matías Gulf

Chiloé Island

PATAGONIA

Gulf of San Jorge

SOUTH AMERICA
Physical

Strait of Magellan

Falkland Islands (U.K.)

0   250   500 Miles
0   250   500   750 Kilometers

Tierra del Fuego

Cape Horn

579

DICTIONARY OF
GEOGRAPHIC TERMS

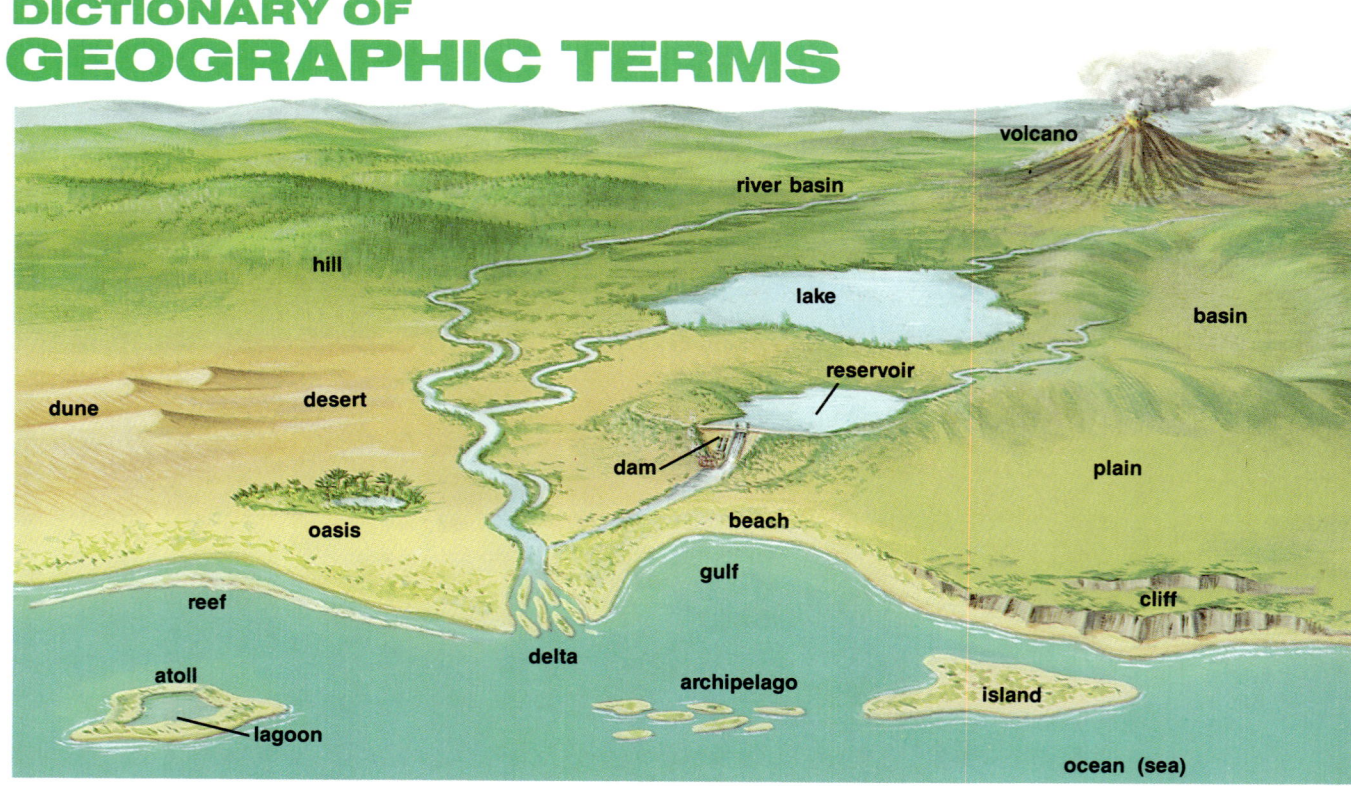

archipelago (är kə pel′ ə gō) A large group or chain of islands.

atoll (āt′ ôl) A ring-shaped coral island or string of islands, surrounding a lagoon.

basin (bā′ sin) An area of low-lying land surrounded by higher land. *See also* **river basin**.

bay (bā) Part of an ocean, sea, or lake, that extends into the land. A bay is usually smaller than a gulf.

beach (bēch) The gently sloping shore of an ocean or other body of water, especially that part covered by sand or pebbles.

butte (būt) A small, flat-topped hill. A butte is smaller than a plateau or a mesa.

canal (kə nal′) A waterway built to carry water for navigation or irrigation. Navigation canals usually connect two other bodies of water.

canyon (kan′ yən) A deep, narrow valley with steep sides.

cape (kāp) A projecting part of a coastline that extends into an ocean, sea, gulf, bay, or lake.

cliff (klif) A high, steep face of rock or earth.

coast (kōst) Land along an ocean or sea.

dam (dam) A wall built across a river to hold back the flowing water.

delta (del′ tə) Land formed at the mouth of a river by deposits of silt, sand, and pebbles.

desert (dez′ ərt) A very dry area where few plants grow.

dune (dün) A mound, hill, or ridge of sand that is heaped up by the wind.

fjord (fyôrd) A deep, narrow inlet of the sea between high, steep cliffs.

foothills (fut′ hilz) A hilly area at the base of a mountain range.

glacier (glā′ shər) A large sheet of ice that moves slowly over some land surface or down a valley.

gulf (gulf) Part of an ocean or sea that extends into the land. A gulf is usually larger than a bay.

harbor (här′ bər) A protected place along a shore where ships can safely anchor.

hill (hil) A rounded, raised landform, not as high as a mountain.

island (ī′ lənd) A body of land completely surrounded by water.

isthmus (is′ məs) A narrow strip of land bordered by water, that connects two larger bodies of land.

lagoon (lə gün′) A shallow body of water partly or completely enclosed within an atoll; a shallow body of sea water partly cut off from the sea by a narrow strip of land.

lake (lāk) A body of water completely surrounded by land.

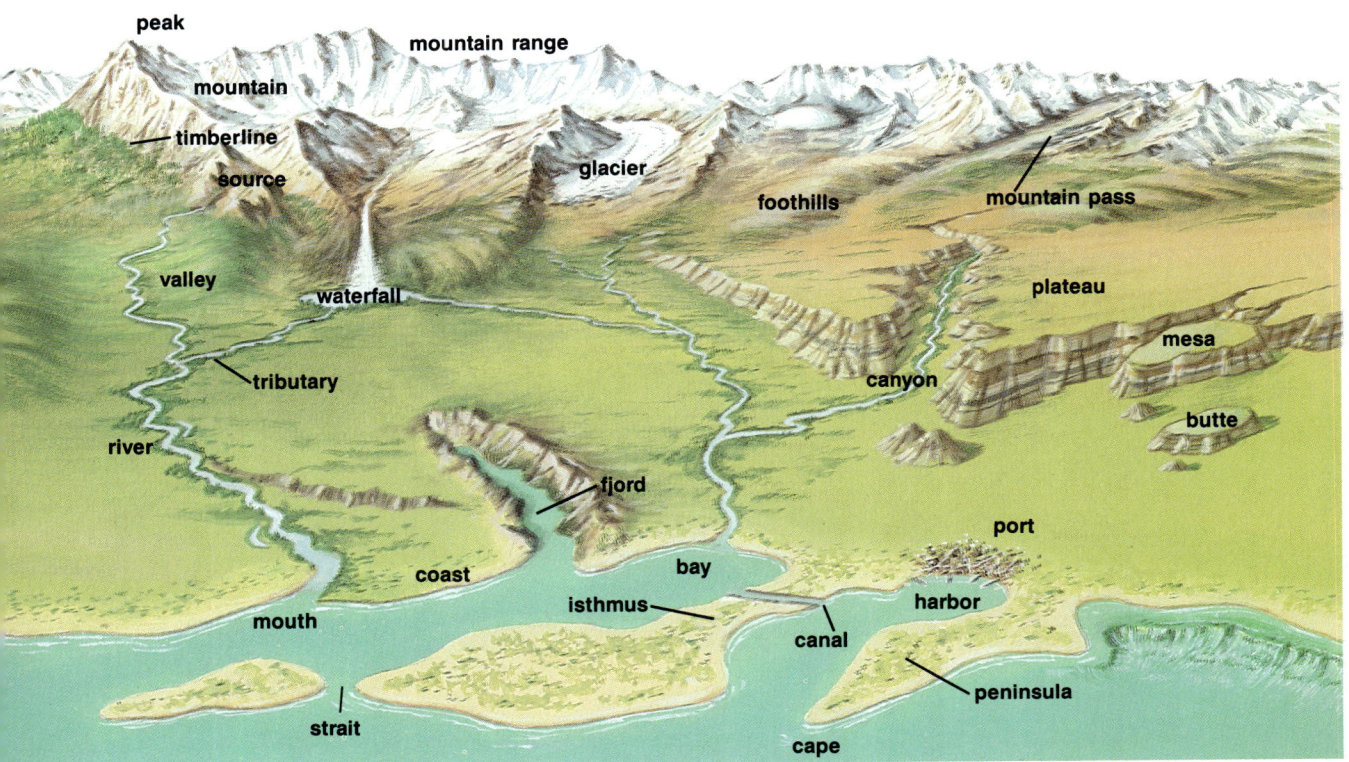

peak

mountain range

mountain

timberline

source

glacier

foothills

mountain pass

valley

waterfall

plateau

mesa

tributary

canyon

butte

river

fjord

port

coast

bay

harbor

mouth

isthmus

canal

peninsula

strait

cape

mesa (mā′ sə) A high, flat landform rising steeply above the surrounding land. A mesa is smaller than a plateau and larger than a butte.

mountain (mount′ ən) A high, rounded or pointed landform with steep sides, higher than a hill.

mountain pass (mount′ ən pas) An opening or gap through a mountain range.

mountain range (mount′ ən rānj) A row or chain of mountains.

mouth (mouth) The place where a river empties into another body of water.

oasis (ō ā′ sis) A place in the desert made fertile by a steady supply of water.

ocean (ō′ shən) One of the earth's four largest bodies of water. The four oceans are really a single connected body of salt water that covers about three fourths of the earth's surface.

peak (pēk) The pointed top of a mountain or hill.

peninsula (pə nin′ sə lə) A body of land nearly surrounded by water.

plain (plān) A large area of flat or nearly flat land.

plateau (pla tō′) A high, flat landform that rises steeply above the surrounding land. A plateau is larger than a mesa and a butte.

port (pôrt) A place where ships load and unload goods.

reef (rēf) A ridge of sand, rock, or coral that lies at or near the surface of a sea.

reservoir (rez′ ər vwär) A natural or artificial lake used to store water.

river (riv′ ər) A large stream of water that flows across the land and usually empties into a lake, ocean, or other river.

river basin (riv′ ər bās′ in) All the land drained by a river and its tributaries.

sea (sē) A large body of water partly or entirely surrounded by land; another word for *ocean*.

source (sôrs) The place where a river or stream begins.

strait (strāt) A narrow waterway or channel connecting two larger bodies of water.

timberline (tim′ bər līn) An imaginary line on mountains, above which trees do not grow.

tributary (trib′ yə ter ē) A river or stream that flows into a larger river or stream.

valley (val′ ē) An area of low land between hills or mountains.

volcano (vol kā′ nō) An opening in the earth through which lava, rock, gases, and ash are forced out.

waterfall (wô′ tər fôl) A flow of water falling from a high place to a lower place.

GAZETTEER

The Gazetteer is a geographical dictionary that will help you to pronounce and locate the places discussed in this book. Latitude and longitude are given for cities and some other places. The page number tells you where each place appears on a map.

PRONUNCIATION KEY

a	cap	êr	clear	oi	coin	ü	moon
ā	cake	hw	where	ôr	fork	ū	cute
ä	father	i	bib	ou	cow	ûr	term
är	car	ī	kite	sh	show	ə	about, taken,
âr	dare	ng	song	th	thin		pencil, apron,
ch	chain	o	top	th	those		helpful
e	hen	ō	rope	u	sun	ər	letter, dollar,
ē	me	ô	saw	ù	book		doctor

A

Acadia (ə kā′ dē ə) A former French colony in eastern Canada, now called the Maritime Provinces. (p. 125)

Alberta (al bûr′ tə) A province of Canada in the western part of the country. (p. 147)

Amazon Basin (am′ ə zon bā′ sin) The area drained by the Amazon River and its tributaries. (p. 442)

Amazon River (am′ ə zon riv′ ər) The longest river in South America and second-longest in the world. It drains half of South America and flows from the Andes Mountains across Brazil into the Atlantic Ocean. (p. 24)

Andes Mountains (an′ dēz moun′ tənz) The largest mountain system in the world. They extend along the west coast of South America. (p. 24)

Angel Falls (ān′ jəl fôlz) The world's highest waterfall, located in southeastern Venezuela; 6°N, 62°W. (p. 440)

Anglo-America (ang′ glō ə mer′ i kə) The culture region of the Western Hemisphere that was strongly influenced by England. Anglo-America includes Canada and the United States. (p. 49)

Antigua and Barbuda (an tē′ gə ənd bär bü′ də) An island nation including two of the Lesser Antilles. (p. 408)

Argentina (är jen tē′ nə) A country in southern South America. (p. 512)

Asunción (ä sün syōn′) The capital and largest city of Paraguay; 25°S, 57°W. (p. 512)

Atacama Desert (at ə käm′ ə dez′ ərt) A barren desert area of northern Chile that has many mineral resources. (p. 448)

Ayacucho (ī ə kü′ chō) A town in Peru; the site of the battle in 1824 where the last Spanish army in South America was defeated by Simón Bolívar's rebel forces; 14°S, 74°W. (p. 494)

B

Bahamas (bə hä′ məz) A group of islands located off the southeastern coast of Florida and north of Cuba and Hispaniola. (p. 382)

Baja California (bä′ hə kal ə fôr′ nyə) A peninsula that is part of northwestern Mexico. It is separated from the rest of Mexico by the Gulf of California. (p. 266)

Barbados (bär bā′ dōs) An island nation in the Lesser Antilles. (p. 408)

Basseterre (bäs târ′) The capital and largest city of St. Kitts and Nevis; 17°N, 63°W. (p. 19)

Bay of Fundy (bā əv fun′ dē) An inlet of the Atlantic Ocean in southeastern Canada. Located between New Brunswick and Nova Scotia, it is known for some of the world's highest tides. (p. 64)

Bay of Pigs (bā əv pigz) A bay on the southern shore of Cuba. It was the site of an attempted invasion by U.S.-trained Cubans who had been living in the United States. (p. 382)

Belize (be lēz') A country on the northeastern coast of Central America. (p. 352)

Belmopan (bel mō pän') The capital of Belize, located in the north-central part of the country; 17°N, 89°W. (p. 352)

Beringia (bə rin' jē ə) A sunken land bridge that once connected North America and Asia. It was located where the Bering Strait is today, between Alaska and the easternmost part of Russia. (p. 43)

Bogotá (bō' gə tä) The capital and largest city of Colombia; 4°N, 74°W. (p. 476)

Bolivia (bə liv' ē ə) A landlocked country in west-central South America. (p. 494)

Brasília (brə zēl' yə) The capital of Brazil, located in the east-central part of the country; 15°S, 47°W. (p. 532)

Brazil (brə zil') The largest country in South America, located in the northeastern part of the continent. (p. 532)

Bridgetown (brij' toun) The capital and largest city of Barbados; 13°N, 60°W. (p. 19)

British Columbia (brit' ish kə lum' bē ə) The westernmost province of Canada, located on the Pacific Ocean. (p. 143)

Buenos Aires (bwā' nəs ī' rəs) The capital and largest city of Argentina, located on the Río de la Plata; 34°S, 58°W. (p. 512)

C

Canada (kan' ə də) A country in northern North America bordering on the United States. Canada, the second-largest country in the world, is made up of ten provinces and two territories. (p. 64)

Canadian Shield (kə nā' dē ən shēld) A large plain that forms a horseshoe shape around Hudson Bay. The Canadian Shield was formed by glaciers during the Ice Age. (p. 64)

Canal Zone (kə nal' zōn) A ten-mile-wide (16-km-wide) strip of land in Panama, bordering the Panama Canal. It has been governed by the United States since 1903 and will be returned to Panama at the end of the twentieth century. (p. 346)

Caracas (kə rä' kəs) The capital and largest city of Venezuela; 10°N, 66°W. (p. 476)

Caribbean islands (kar ə bē' ən ī' ləndz) The archipelagoes, or groups of islands, located between North America and South America in the Caribbean Sea. (p. 19)

Castries (kas' trēz) The capital and largest city of St. Lucia; 14°N, 61°W. (p. 19)

Cayenne (kī en') The capital and largest city of French Guiana; 5°N, 52°W. (p. 476)

Central America (sen' trəl ə mer' i kə) A region that links North America and South America and separates the Pacific Ocean from the Caribbean Sea. It is part of North America and includes seven countries: Guatemala, Belize, El Salvador, Honduras, Nicaragua, Costa Rica, and Panama. (p. 21)

Central Plateau (sen' trəl pla tō') The high, broad plateau of central Mexico. It lies between the Eastern and Western Sierra Madres. (p. 266)

Chaco (chä' kō) A dry plain that extends across Argentina, Paraguay, and Bolivia. (p. 440)

Chile (chil' ē) A country in southwestern South America. (p. 494)

Coast Ranges (kōst rān' jəz) A group of mountains, lying along the Pacific Ocean and stretching from Alaska to California. (p. 65)

Colombia (kə lum' bē ə) A country in northwestern South America. (p. 476)

Copán (kō pän') An ancient Mayan city, located in the present-day country of Honduras; 15°N, 88°W. (p. 204)

Costa Rica (kos' tə rē' kə) A country in the southern part of Central America. (p. 352)

Cuba (kū' bə) A country on the largest and westernmost island of the Greater Antilles. (p. 382)

Cuzco (küs' kō) The capital of the ancient Incan Empire, located in present-day Peru; 14°S, 72°W. (p. 219)

D

Dominica (dom ə nē' kə) An island country in the Lesser Antilles. (p. 408)

Dominican Republic (də min' i kən ri pub' lik) A Caribbean country that occupies the eastern part of the island of Hispaniola. (p. 382)

E

Eastern Sierra Madre (ēs' tərn sē er' ə mä' drā) A mountain range that borders the Gulf of Mexico on the east coast of Mexico. (p. 266)

Ecuador (ek' wə dôr) A country in the northwestern part of South America. (p. 494)

El Salvador (el sal' və dôr) A country on the west coast of Central America. (p. 352)

F

Falkland Islands (fôk' lənd ī' ləndz) A group of islands in the southern Atlantic Ocean, east of southern Argentina. They are a British dependency, but Argentina also claims them and calls them the Malvinas. (p. 512)

GAZETTEER

583

French Guiana (french gē an′ ə) An overseas department of France, located in north-central South America. (p. 476)

G

Georgetown (jôrj′ toun) The capital and largest city of Guyana; 6°N, 58°W. (p. 476)

Gran Colombia (grän kə lum′ bē ə) A former country of northern South America that included the present-day countries of Colombia, Panama, Venezuela, and Ecuador. It lasted from 1819 to 1830. (p. 457)

Grand Banks (grand bangks) A shallow fishing area of the northern Atlantic Ocean, located southeast of the coast of Newfoundland. (p. 114)

Greater Antilles (grāt′ ər an til′ ēz) The four largest Caribbean islands: Cuba, Jamaica, Hispaniola, and Puerto Rico. (p. 382)

Great Lakes (grāt lāks) A group of the world's five largest freshwater lakes, located along the border between the United States and Canada. They include Lakes Superior, Michigan, Huron, Erie, and Ontario. (p. 24)

Greenland (grēn′ lənd) The world's largest island, lying northeast of the coast of North America and mostly within the Arctic Circle. (p. 19)

Grenada (gri nā′ də) An island nation of the Caribbean Sea. (p. 382)

Guatemala (gwä tə mä′ lə). A country in the northern part of Central America. (p. 352)

Guatemala City (gwä tə mä′ lə sit′ ē) The capital and largest city of Guatemala; 15°N, 91°W. (p. 352)

Guiana Highlands (gē an′ ə hī′ ləndz) A hilly and mountainous area in northern South America. It extends from eastern Venezuela across northern Brazil, Guyana, Suriname, and French Guiana. (p. 440)

Gulf Coastal Plain (gulf kōs′ təl plān) The largest lowland area in Mexico. It borders the Gulf of Mexico and includes the Yucatán Peninsula. (p. 266)

Gulf of California (gulf əv kal ə fôr′ nyə) An arm of the Pacific Ocean that separates Baja California from the rest of Mexico. (p. 266)

Gulf of Mexico (gulf əv mek′ si kō) A gulf that is connected with the Atlantic Ocean and the Caribbean Sea. It is bounded by the United States, Mexico, and Cuba. (p. 266)

Guyana (gī an′ ə) A country in north-central South America. (p. 476)

H

Haiti (hā′ tē) A Caribbean country that occupies the western part of the island of Hispaniola. (p. 382)

Havana (hə van′ ə) The capital, chief port, and largest city of Cuba; 23°N, 82°W. (p. 382)

Honduras (hon dúr′ əs) A country in northern Central America. (p. 352)

I

Interior Plains (in tîr′ ē ər plānz) A broad, flat region extending from the Arctic Ocean into the United States, located west of the Canadian Shield. (p. 64)

J

Jamaica (jə mā′ kə) A Caribbean island country that is one of the Greater Antilles. (p. 408)

K

Kingston (kingz′ tən) The capital and largest city of Jamaica; 18°N, 77°W. (p. 408)

Kingstown (kingz′ toun) The capital of St. Vincent and the Grenadines, located on the island of St. Vincent; 13°N, 61°W. (p. 408)

L

Lake Nicaragua (lāk nik ə rä′ gwə) The largest lake in Central America. It is located in the southern part of Nicaragua. (p. 326)

Lake Titicaca (lāk tit i kä′ kə) The largest lake in South America. It is located in the Andes Mountains between southeastern Peru and western Bolivia. (p. 440)

La Paz (lə päz′) A city in western Bolivia. It is the seat of the government and the administrative capital of the country as well as the country's largest city; 17°S, 68°W. (p. 494)

Latin America (lat′ in ə mer′ i kə) The culture region of the Western Hemisphere countries that lie south of the United States. The cultures of these lands were strongly influenced by Spain, Portugal, and France. (p. 49)

Lesser Antilles (les′ ər an til′ ēz) A chain of Caribbean islands that lie east and south of Puerto Rico and form the eastern boundary of the Caribbean Sea. (p. 382)

Lima (lē′ mə) The capital and largest city of Peru; 12°S, 77°W. (p. 494)

Llanos (yä′ nōs) A grassy plains area of South America, located between the Andes Mountains of Colombia and the Guiana Highlands. (p. 476)

Lower Canada (lō′ ər kan′ ə də) An English-speaking British colony established in 1791 in Canada. It is now the province of Ontario. (p. 127)

M

Machu Picchu (mäch′ ü pēk′ chü) An ancient Incan city in the Andes, located in present-day Peru; 13°S, 72°W. (p. 219)

Managua (mə nä′ gwə) The capital and largest city of Nicaragua; 12°N, 86°W. (p. 352)

Manitoba (man i tō′ bə) A province in south-central Canada. (p. 143)

Mexico (mek′ si kō) A country in southern North America, lying south of the 48 mainland United States and north of Central America. (p. 296)

Mexico City (mek′ si kō sit′ ē) The capital and largest city of Mexico, built over the site of the Aztec city of Tenochtitlán; 19°N, 99°W. (p. 296)

Middle America (mid′ əl ə mer′ i kə) The area that includes Mexico, Central America, and the Caribbean islands. (p. 21)

Montevideo (mon tə vi dā′ ō) The capital of Uruguay, located on the Río de la Plata; 35°S, 56°W. (p. 512)

Montreal (mon trē ôl′) The largest city in Canada, located in Quebec on the St. Lawrence River; 46°N, 74°W. (p. 125)

Mount Aconcagua (mount ak ən kä′ gwə) A mountain in the Andes, in western Argentina, the highest mountain in the Americas; 33°S, 70°W. (p. 24)

N

Nassau (nas′ ô) The capital and largest city of the Bahamas; 25°N, 77°W. (p. 408)

New Brunswick (nü brunz′ wik) A province of Canada in the eastern part of the country, formerly the western part of Nova Scotia. (p. 147)

Newfoundland (nü′ fənd lənd) An island of Canada that is off the east coast of mainland Canada. (p. 64)

New France (nü frans) A colony of France in North America from 1609 to 1763. (p. 121)

Nicaragua (nik ə rä′ gwə) A country in the middle part of Central America. (p. 352)

Northwest Territories (nôrth west′ ter′ i tôr ēz) A part of Canada in the northwestern part of the country. It is a territory and not a province. (p. 143)

O

Ontario (on târ′ ē ō) A province of Canada in the southeastern part of the country, north of the Great Lakes. (p. 154)

Oregon Country (ôr′ i gon kun′ trē) The area between California and Alaska that was claimed by both the United States and Great Britain until 1846. (p. 142)

Orinoco River (ôr ə nō′ kō riv′ ər) A large river in South America, rising in Colombia and flowing across Venezuela into the Atlantic Ocean. (p. 186)

Otavalo (ōt ə väl′ ō) A town in northeastern Ecuador where people make cloth, cloth goods, and other items in traditional designs; 0°N, 78°W. (p. 494)

Ottawa (ot′ ə wə) The capital of Canada located in the province of Ontario; 45°N, 76°W. (p. 154)

P

Pacific Rim (pə sif′ ik rim) The countries that border the Pacific Ocean. (p. 559)

Pampas (pam′ pəz) South America's vast, grassy, treeless plains that extend from the Atlantic Ocean to the Andes Mountains in Argentina and other countries. (p. 440)

Panama (pan′ ə mä) The southernmost country in Central America. (p. 352)

Panama City (pan′ ə mä sit′ ē) The capital and largest city of Panama; 9°N, 79°W. (p. 352)

Paraguay (par′ ə gwī) A country in south-central South America. (p. 512)

Paramaribo (par ə mar′ ə bō) The capital and largest city of Suriname; 6°N, 55°W. (p. 476)

Paraná River (par ə nä′ riv′ ər) A river in South America, flowing south through Brazil, Paraguay, and Argentina into the Río de la Plata. (p. 512)

Patagonia (pat ə gō′ nē ə) A region of plains and high plateaus in the southern part of South America between the Andes Mountains and the Atlantic Ocean. (p. 440)

Peru (pə rü′) A country in northwestern South America. (p. 494)

Port-au-Prince (pôrt ō prins′) The capital and largest city of Haiti; 18°N, 72° W. (p. 408)

Port-of-Spain (pôrt′ əv spān′) The capital and largest city of Trinidad and Tobago, 11°N, 61°W. (p. 408)

Puerto Rico (pwer′ tō rē′ kō) The easternmost island of the Greater Antilles. It is a commonwealth of the United States. (p. 384)

---

a cap; ā cake; ä father; är car; âr dare; ch chain; e hen; ē me; êr clear; hw where; i bib; ī kite; ng song; o top; ō rope; ô saw; oi coin; ôr fork; ou cow; sh show; th thin; <u>th</u> those; u sun; u̇ book; ü moon; ū cute; ûr term; ə about, taken, pencil, apron, helpful; ər letter, dollar, doctor

GAZETTEER

Q

Quebec (kwi bek′) Capital city of the province of Quebec, Canada's largest province; 46°N, 71°W. (p. 121)

Quito (kē′ tō) The capital city of Ecuador, located in the north-central part of the country; 0°, 79°W. (p. 494)

R

Red River (red riv′ ər) A settlement begun in 1811 in Canada at the place where the Red River joins the Assiniboine. (p. 142)

Rio de Janeiro (rē′ ō dā zhə när′ ō) A port city of southeastern Brazil, and a former capital of the country; 23°S, 43°W. (p. 466)

Río de la Plata (rē′ ō dā lä plä′ tə) The river system through which the Paraná and Uruguay rivers flow into the Atlantic Ocean. It is located on the southeastern coast of South America, between Uruguay and Argentina. (p. 186)

Rio Grande (rē′ ō grand) A river flowing from southwestern Colorado into the Gulf of Mexico and forming a border between the United States and Mexico. (p. 186)

Rocky Mountains (rok′ ē moun′ tənz) A mountain system of Canada and the United States, extending from northern Alaska to central New Mexico. (p. 65)

Roseau (rō zō′) The capital of Dominica; 15°N, 61°W. (p. 408)

S

St. George's (sānt jôr′ jiz) The capital and largest city of Grenada; 12°N, 62°W. (p. 19)

St. John's (sānt jonz) The capital and largest city of Antigua and Barbuda; 17°N, 62°W. (p. 19)

St. Kitts and Nevis (sānt kits′ ənd nē′ vis) An island nation in the Lesser Antilles made up of two islands, St. Kitts (also called St. Christopher) and Nevis. (p. 408)

St. Lawrence River (sānt lôr′ əns riv′ ər) A North American river that flows from Lake Ontario northeast into the Gulf of St. Lawrence. It is the chief outlet for the Great Lakes. (p. 66)

St. Lucia (sānt lü′ shə) An island nation in the Lesser Antilles. (p. 408)

St. Vincent and the Grenadines (sant vin′ sənt ənd thə gren′ ə dēnz) An island nation in the Lesser Antilles made up of the island of St. Vincent and the northern islands of the Grenadines. (p. 408)

San José (san hō zā′) The capital and largest city of Costa Rica; 10°N, 84°W. (p. 352)

San Juan (san hwän′) The capital and largest city of the Commonwealth of Puerto Rico; 19°N, 66°W. (p. 408)

San Salvador (san sal′ və dôr) The capital and largest city of El Salvador; 14°N, 89°W. (p. 352)

Santiago (san tē ä′ gō) The capital and largest city of Chile; 33°S, 71°W. (p. 494)

Santo Domingo (san′ tō də ming′ gō) The capital and largest city of the Dominican Republic; 19°N, 70°W. (p. 408)

São Paulo (sou pou′ lō) The largest city of Brazil, located in the southeastern part of the country; 23°S, 46°W. (p. 532)

Saskatchewan (sas kach′ ə won) A province of Canada, located in the western part of the country. (p. 147)

sertão (ser toun′) A dry inland region of northeastern Brazil. (p. 541)

Sonora Desert (sə nôr′ ə dez′ ərt) A desert that includes much of northern Mexico. (p. 266)

Strait of Magellan (strāt əv mə jel′ ən) A narrow waterway at the southern tip of South America. (p. 229)

Sucre (sü′ krā) The constitutional capital of Bolivia, located in the southern part of the country; 19°S, 65°W. (p. 494)

Suriname (sur′ ə näm) A country on the northeastern coast of South America. (p. 476)

T

Tegucigalpa (tə gü si gal′ pə) The capital and largest city of Honduras; 14°N, 87°W. (p. 352)

Tenochtitlán (te nôch tē tlän′) The capital of the ancient Aztec Empire, now the site of Mexico City; 19°N, 99°W. (p. 213)

Tierra del Fuego (tyer′ ə del fwā′ gō) A group of islands at the southern tip of South America. (p. 440)

Tikal (ti käl′) An ancient Mayan city, located in the present-day country of Guatemala; 17°N, 90°W. (p. 204)

Toronto (tə ron′ tō) The capital and largest city of the province of Ontario; 43°N, 79°W. (p. 154)

Trans-Amazon Highway (tranz am′ ə zon hī′ wā) A 3,350-mile (5,400-km) road running through the Amazon Basin. (p. 532)

Trinidad and Tobago (trin′ i dad ənd tə bā′ gō) A Caribbean country that includes the islands of Trinidad and Tobago. (p. 408)

Tumbes (tüm′ bās) An ancient Incan city at which Pizarro first saw evidence of the Incan Empire. It is located in present-day Peru; 4°S, 80°W. (p. 236)

GAZETTEER

U

Udirbi Park (ū dir′ bē pärk) A wilderness area and wildlife refuge set aside in Panama by the Cuna. (p. 352)

United States (ū nī′ tid stāts) A country mainly in North America consisting of fifty states, the District of Columbia, and several territories. (p. 19)

Upper Canada (up′ ər kan′ ə də) A French-speaking British colony established in 1791 in Canada. It is now the province of Quebec. (p. 127)

Uruguay (yùr′ ə gwī) A country on the southeastern coast of South America. (p. 512)

V

Venezuela (ven ə zwā′ lə) A country in northern South America, on the Caribbean. (p. 476)

Veracruz (ver ə krüz′) A coastal city of Mexico; 19°N, 96°W. (p. 271)

Viceroyalty of New Spain (vīs roi′ əl tē əv nü spān) The North American section of Spain's colonies in America, established as a governing district by the Spanish king in the 1500s. (p. 242)

Viceroyalty of Peru (vīs roi′ əl tē əv pə rü′) The South American section of Spanish America, established as a governing district by the Spanish king in the 1500s and later divided into three viceroyalties. (p. 242)

Villa El Salvador (vē′ yə el sal′ və dôr) A new town established by squatters on the outskirts of Lima, Peru; 12°S, 77°W. (p. 506)

W

Washington, D.C. (wô′ shing tən dē sē) The capital of the United States of America; 39°N, 77°W. (p. 19)

Western Sierra Madre (west′ ərn sē er′ ə mä′ drā) A mountain range that extends along the Pacific Ocean on the west coast of Mexico. (p. 266)

Y

Yucatán Peninsula (ū kə tan′ pə nin′ sə lə) A peninsula that includes southeastern Mexico and parts of Belize and Guatemala. It separates the Gulf of Mexico from the Caribbean Sea. (p. 266)

a cap; ā cake; ä father; är car; âr dare; ch chain; e hen; ē me; êr clear; hw where; i bib; ī kite; ng song; o top; ō rope; ô saw; oi coin; ôr fork; ou cow; sh show; th thin; th those; u sun; ù book; ü moon; ū cute; ûr term; ə about, taken, pencil, apron, helpful; ər letter, dollar, doctor

GAZETTEER

587

BIOGRAPHICAL DICTIONARY

This Biographical Dictionary will help you to identify and pronounce the names of the Key People discussed in this book. The page number tells you the page on which each person's name first appears in the text.

PRONUNCIATION KEY

a	cap	êr	clear	oi	coin	ü	moon
ā	cake	hw	where	ôr	fork	ū	cute
ä	father	i	bib	ou	cow	ûr	term
är	car	ī	kite	sh	show	ə	about, taken,
âr	dare	ng	song	th	thin		pencil, apron,
ch	chain	o	top	th	those		helpful
e	hen	ō	rope	u	sun	ər	letter, dollar,
ē	me	ô	saw	u̇	book		doctor

A

Alfonsín, Raúl (äl fōn sēn′, rä ül′), 1927– President of Argentina between 1983 and 1989 who believed in the principles of democracy. (p. 525)

Allegretti, Mary Helena (äl i gret′ ē, mä rē′ ə ā lā′ nə), 1948– Brazilian anthropologist who works to protect the way of life of the rubber tappers of the Amazon rain forest. (p. 549)

Allende, Salvador (ä yen′ dā, sal′ və dôr), 1908–1973 President of Chile between 1970 and 1973 who tried to bring socialism to Chile. (p. 469)

Amado, Jorge (ə mä′ dō, zhôr′ zhē), 1912– Well-known Brazilian writer whose many novels about life in Brazil include *Showdown* and *Gabriela, Clove and Cinnamon.* (p. 533)

Arias Sánchez, Oscar (ä′ ryäs sän′ ches, ōs′ cär), 1943– Became president of Costa Rica in 1986 and won the Nobel Peace Prize in 1987 for his regional peace plan to halt wars in Central America. (p. 347)

Atahualpa (ä tə wäl′ pə), 1502–1533 Incan ruler defeated by Spanish conquistador Francisco Pizarro in 1531. (p. 236)

B

Balboa, Vasco Núñez de (bal bō′ ə, väs′ kō nün′ yäs dä), 1475?–1517 Spanish explorer who reached the Pacific Ocean in 1513 by crossing the Isthmus of Panama. (p. 228)

Batista, Fulgencio (bə tēs′ tə, fu̇l hän′ syō), 1901–1973 Military dictator who took over Cuba in 1934. Batista was overthrown in 1958 by revolutionary forces led by Fidel Castro. (p. 421)

Batlle, José (bät′ yā, hō sä′), 1856–1929 President of Uruguay from 1903 to 1907 and again from 1911 to 1915. Batlle brought about many political and social reforms as president, and afterwards. (p. 468)

Betances, Ramon (be tän′ ses, rä mōn′), 1827–1898 Puerto Rican doctor who led an unsuccessful fight for independence in his homeland in 1868. (p. 399)

Betancourt, Rómulo (be tän kür′, rō′ mü lō), 1908– President of Venezuela from 1959 until 1964. He tried to improve the quality of life in Venezuela by investing oil profits in industry. (p. 487)

Bolívar, Simón (bō lē′ vär, sē mōn′), 1783–1830 Leader of the struggle for independence in South America. Known as "The Liberator," his armies freed Colombia, Venezuela, and Peru from Spanish rule. (p. 455)

Bonaparte, Napoleon (bō′ nə pärt, nə pō′ lē ən), 1769–1821 French military dictator and conqueror. (p. 455)

Bush, George (bu̇sh, jôrj), 1924– Became the forty-first President of the United States in 1989. (p. 347)

C

Cabot, John (kab′ ət, jon), 1450?–1498 Italian explorer working for England who reached Newfoundland in 1497. (p. 115)

Cabral, Pedro Álvares (kə bräl′, pā′ drō äl′ vär is), 1460?–1526? Portuguese navigator who reached the coast of Brazil in 1500. (p. 228)

BIOGRAPHICAL DICTIONARY

Cartier, Jacques (kär′ tyā, zhäk), 1491–1557 French explorer who searched for the Northwest Passage and reached the St. Lawrence River. Cartier started the city that became Montreal. (p. 116)

Castro, Fidel (käs′ trō, fē del′), 1926– Leader of the Cuban Revolution who has ruled Cuba since 1959. (p. 421)

Chamorro, Violeta (chä môr′ ō, vē ō lāt′ ə), 1929– Became president of Nicaragua in 1990. (p. 367)

Champlain, Samuel de (sham plān′, säm üel′ də), 1567–1635 French explorer known as the "Father of New France." Champlain established the city of Quebec in Canada in 1608. (p. 118)

Charles, Mary Eugenia (chärlz, mâr′ ē ü jē′ nē ə), 1919– Became prime minister of the Caribbean island of Dominica in 1980 and was elected for her third five-year term in 1990. (p. 402)

Collor de Mello, Fernando (kō lôr′ dä mel′ ō, fer nän dü), 1949– President of Brazil who was elected in 1989. (p. 549)

Columbus, Christopher (kə lum′ bəs, kris′ tə fər), 1451?–1506 Italian explorer, working for Spain, who sailed west from Europe in 1492 looking for Asia. Instead, he reached the Americas, opening up the Western Hemisphere to Europe. (p. 226)

Cortés, Hernando (kôr tez′, er nän′ dō), 1485–1547 Spanish conquistador who destroyed the Aztec Empire in 1521. (p. 232)

Cruz, Juana Inés de la (krüs, wän′ ä ē nās′ dä lä), 1651–1695 Spanish woman who became a nun after being refused entry to Mexico University, which only accepted men. She used the education provided by the church to become one of Mexico's greatest writers. (p. 247)

D

Dessalines, Jean-Jacques (de sä lēn′, zhän zhäk), 1758?–1806 Once held in slavery, Dessalines helped Haiti become the first colony in Latin America to gain its independence in 1803. (p. 397)

Díaz, Porfirio (dē′ äs, pôr fē′ ryō), 1830–1915 Ruled Mexico as a dictator from 1876 until 1911. (p. 287)

Durham, Earl of (dûr′ əm, ûrl əv), 1792–1840 British leader who wrote a report urging more self-government for the Canadian provinces. (p. 137)

Duvalier, François (dü väl yā′, frän swä′), 1907–1971 Haitian dictator who ruled from 1957 until his death in 1971. Duvalier used his special police force, the *Tonton Macoutes*, to terrorize any Haitians who dared opposed him. (p. 401)

Duvalier, Jean-Claude (dü väl yā′, zhän klod), 1951– Son of François Duvalier, he became dictator of Haiti after his father's death in 1971. He ruled with the same brutal methods as his father but was driven out of power in 1986. (p. 402)

E

Ericson, Leif (er′ ik sən, lēf), died 1020? Son of Eric the Red who landed in North America around the year 1000. Ericson named the land he explored Vinland. (p. 114)

Eric the Red (er′ ik <u>the</u> red), 950?–1000? Viking leader who explored Greenland around the year 980. (p. 114)

G

Gautier, Felisa Rincón de (gō tē yär′, fe lē′ sä rin kōn′ dä), 1897– Mayor of San Juan from 1946 to 1968 who helped win support for "Operation Bootstrap" in Puerto Rico. (p. 423)

Goethals, George W. (gō′ thəlz, jôrj), 1858–1928 United States engineer in charge of building the Panama Canal. (p. 345)

Gorgas, William (gôr′ gəs, wil′ yəm), 1854–1920 United States doctor whose work against yellow fever and malaria made possible the building of the Panama Canal. (p. 345)

H

Hidalgo, Miguel (e däl′ gō, mē gel′), 1753–1811 Mexican priest and leader of the Indian and mestizo revolt that started the Mexican War for Independence against Spain in 1810. (p. 277)

I

Iturbide, Agustín de (ē tür bē′ dä, ä gùs tēn′ dä), 1783–1824 First leader of Mexico after it won its independence from Spain in 1821. (p. 279)

J

João (zhwaù), 1769–1826 King of Portugal who fled to Brazil in 1808 after Napoleon Bonaparte sent troops into Portugal. (p. 462)

Juárez, Benito (hwä′ rez, be nē′ tō), 1806–1872 President of Mexico from 1858 to 1865 and again from 1867 to 1872. (p. 285)

K

Kahlo, Frida (kä′ lō, frē′ dä), 1907–1954 Mexican artist known especially for her self-portrait paintings. Kahlo was married to the artist Diego Rivera. (p. 310)

L

Las Casas, Bartolomé de (läs käs′ əs, bär tō lō mā′ də), 1474–1566 Spanish priest who worked to protect the rights of the Indians in New Spain. (p. 243)

M

Maceo, Antonio (mä sā′ ō, än tōn′ yō), 1845–1896 Cuban soldier who led Cuba's army in its fight for independence in 1868. (p. 400)

Mackenzie, Alexander (mə ken′ zē, al ig zan′ dər), 1764?–1820 First Canadian explorer to reach the western shore of North America by land. (p. 140)

Mackenzie, William Lyon (mə ken′ zē, wil′ yəm lī′ ən), 1795–1861 Canadian editor and political leader who set out to capture Toronto from the British in 1837. In his *Handbill for Rebellion*, Mackenzie called for Canadians to fight against British rule. (p. 136)

Madero, Francisco (ma de′ rō, frän sēs′ cō), 1873–1913 Champion of democracy who was president of Mexico from 1911 to 1913. (p. 287)

Magellan, Ferdinand (mə jel′ ən, fûr′ də nand), 1480?–1521 Portuguese explorer who led the first sea voyage around the world. (p. 228)

Manley, Norman (man′ lē, nôr′ mən), 1892–1969 Prime minister of Jamaica from 1953 to 1962. (p. 409)

Marina, Doña (mä rē′ nä, dōn′ yä), 1501–1550 Aztec princess who served as a guide and interpreter to Hernando Cortés during his conquest of Mexico. (p. 233)

Marley, Bob (mär′ lē, bob), 1945–1981 Jamaican musician who produced a new style of music called reggae. (p. 413)

Martí, José (mär tē′, hō sā′), 1853–1895 Cuban poet who was killed while fighting for Cuba's independence from Spain. (p. 400)

Maximilian (mak sə mil′ yən), 1832–1867 Austrian prince who was made Emperor of Mexico by the French in 1864. Maximilian was overthrown in 1867 after his French soldiers left Mexico. (p. 286)

McClung, Nellie (mə klung′, nel′ ē), 1873–1951 Canadian feminist who fought successfully for political and legal rights for Canadian women. (p. 148)

Moctezuma (mäk tə zü′ mə), 1480?–1520 Aztec ruler who was captured in 1519 and held prisoner until his death by the Spanish conquistador Hernando Cortés. (p. 233)

Monroe, James (mən rō′, jāmz), 1758–1831 Fifth President of the United States. In 1823 he stated that the United States would oppose attempts by European countries to intervene in the affairs of the Western Hemisphere. This policy became known as the Monroe Doctrine (p. 340)

Montcalm, Louis de (mänt kälm′, lwē də), 1712–1759 French general who died defending Quebec against the British in 1759. (p. 125)

Morelos, José (mō rā′ lōs, hō sā′), 1765–1815 Mexican leader in the revolution against Spain. (p. 279)

Muñoz Marín, Luis (mùn yōs′ mä rēn′, lù ēs′), 1898–1980 Governor of Puerto Rico from 1949 until 1965 who created the "Operation Bootstrap" program to diversify the economy. (p. 423)

N

Noriega, Manuel (nōr ē ā′ gä, män wel′), 1938– Dictator of Panama who was overthrown by the United States in 1989. (p. 347)

O

O'Higgins, Bernardo (ō hig′ ənz, ber när′ dō), 1778–1842 Creole soldier who, with the help of José de San Martín's troops, freed Chile from Spanish control. (p. 458)

Ortega, Daniel (ôr tä′ gə, dan yel′), 1945– A Sandinista leader of the Nicaraguan Revolution who governed Nicaragua from 1985 to 1990. (p. 367)

P

Papineau, Louis (pä′ pē nō, lwē), 1786–1871 French-Canadian leader who started a rebellion in 1837 against the British government in Lower Canada. (p. 136)

Paz, Octavio (päs, ok täv′ yō), 1914– Mexican poet and author who won the Nobel Prize for Literature in 1989. (p. 308)

Pedro I (pā′ drō), 1798–1834 Became the first emperor of an independent Brazil in 1822. After reigning for seven years, Pedro I was so unpopular with his subjects that he was forced to give up the throne to his son, Pedro II. (p. 463)

Pedro II (pā′ drō), 1825–1891 Emperor of Brazil who ended slavery in Brazil and tried to modernize his homeland. In 1889, after a revolt by the military and angry former slaveowners, Pedro II was forced to leave Brazil. (p. 463)

Pelé (pā lā′), 1940– Brazilian athlete considered to be the greatest soccer player of his time. Pelé was named Edson Arantes do Nascimento at birth but is known by his childhood nickname. (p. 535)

Pérez, Carlos Andrés (pā′ rās, kär′ lōs än drās′), 1922– President of Venezuela from 1974 to 1979, he promoted industry. Pérez started a second term as president in 1989. (p. 487)

Perón, Eva Marie (pə rōn′, ā′ vä mə rē′), 1919–1952 Popularly known as "Evita," she was active in running the government of Argentina during her husband's Juan Perón's first six years in power. (p. 523)

Perón, Juan Domingo (pə rōn', wän dō mēng' gō), 1895–1974 President of Argentina from 1946 until his overthrow by the military in 1955. Perón was again elected president in 1973 but died a year later. (p. 523)

Pinochet, Augusto (pē nō chā', ou gü' stō), 1915– Military leader who established a brutal dictatorship in Chile from 1973 until 1989. (p. 469)

Pizarro, Francisco (pi zär' ō, frän sēs' cō), 1471?–1541 Spanish conquistador who defeated the Incas in 1533. (p. 235)

Ponce de León, Juan (pons də lā ōn', wän), 1460?–1521 Spanish explorer who in 1513 reached the peninsula known today as Florida. (p. 228)

Reagan, Ronald (rā' gən, ro' nəld), 1911– Became the fortieth President of the United States in 1981 and held office until 1989. (p. 347)

Riel, Louis (rē el', lwē), 1844–1885 Leader of the métis of western Canada who helped start the "Red River Rising" in 1869. (p. 141)

Rivera, Diego (ri vâr ə, dyā' gō), 1886–1957 Mexican artist especially known for his dramatic mural paintings. Rivera was married to the artist Frida Kahlo. (p. 308)

Roosevelt, Theodore (rōz' velt, thē' ə dôr), 1858–1919 Became the twenty-sixth President of the United States in 1901 and held office until 1909. Roosevelt was responsible for the building of the Panama Canal. (p. 345)

Sandino, Augusto César (sän dē' nō, ou gü' stō sā' sär), 1895–1934 Nicaraguan leader who fought to remove United States Marines from his country during the 1930s. (p. 364)

San Martín, José de (san mär tēn', hō sā' dā), 1778–1850 Leader of the armies that freed Argentina and Chile from Spanish rule in 1818. (p. 457)

Santa Anna, Antonio López de (san' tə an' ə, an tō' nyō lō' päs dā), 1794–1876 Dictatorial ruler of Mexico. Santa Anna's troops fought unsuccessfully against the United States in the Mexican-American War. (p. 282)

Somoza, Anastasio (sōm ō' sä, än äs tä' syō), 1896–1956 President of Nicaragua who ruled as a dictator from 1936 to 1956. (p. 364)

Somoza, Anastasio "Tachito" (sōm ō' sä, än äs tä' syō tä che' tō), 1925–1980 Last member of the Somoza family to rule as a dictator in Nicaragua. (p. 365)

T

Toussaint L'Ouverture (tü sant' lü vər tür'), 1743–1803 Haitian soldier who fought for the independence of Haiti. (p. 396)

Tupac Amarú II (tü päk' äm är ü'), 1742?–1781 Mestizo leader in Peru who led an uprising against the Spanish in 1780. (p. 249)

V

Verrazano, Giovanni da (ver ə zän' ō, jō vän' nē dä), 1485?–1528 Italian explorer sailing for France who searched for the Northwest Passage. (p. 115)

Vespucci, Amerigo (ves pü' chē, äm ə rē' gō), 1454–1512 Italian explorer who realized that Christopher Columbus had reached a huge landmass previously unknown to Europeans. A German mapmaker named the new land America after Amerigo Vespucci. (p. 227)

Villa, Pancho (vē' ə, pän' chō), 1877?–1923 Mexican revolutionary who, with Emiliano Zapata, helped overthrow Porfirio Díaz in 1911. (p. 289)

W

Wolfe, James (wůlf, jāmz), 1727–1759 British general who led the capture of Quebec in 1759. (p. 125)

Y

Yrigoyen, Hipólito (ē rē gōy' ən, ē pō' lē tō), 1852–1933 President of Argentina from 1916 to 1922 and from 1928 to 1930. Yrigoyen often behaved more like a dictator than a president and was overthrown by the military in 1930. (p. 522)

Z

Zapata, Emiliano (sä pä' tə, ā mēl yän' ō), 1879–1919 Mexican revolutionary who, with Pancho Villa, helped overthrow Porfirio Díaz in 1911. (p. 289)

a cap; ā cake; ä father; är car; âr dare; ch chain; e hen; ē me; êr clear; hw where; i bib; ī kite; ng song; o top; ō rope; ô saw; oi coin; ôr fork; ou cow; sh show; th thin; <u>th</u> those; u sun; ů book; ü moon; ū cute; ûr term; ə about, taken, pencil, apron, helpful; ər letter, dollar, doctor

BIOGRAPHICAL DICTIONARY

GLOSSARY

This glossary will help you to pronounce and understand the meanings of the Key Vocabulary in this book. The page number at the end of the definition tells where the word first appears.

A

acid rain (as′ id rān) A form of pollution created when rain mixes with chemicals from the burning of fuels. (p. 75)

A.D. (ā dē) An abbreviation for *anno Domini,* Latin for "in the year of the Lord," used to indicate dates after the birth of Jesus. (p. 123)

altiplano (al ti plän′ ō) The high plain of South America, located in southern Peru and western Bolivia. (p. 441)

archaeology (är kē ol′ ə jē) The study of the way people lived in the past. (p. 42)

archipelago (är kə pel′ i gō) A group of islands. (p. 20)

artifact (är′ tə fakt) An object that was made by people, often by people of the past. (p. 42)

artisan (är′ tə zən) A person skilled in a particular craft; craftsperson. (p. 89)

astrolabe (as′ trə lāb) An instrument once used to measure the positions of stars, planets, and other heavenly bodies. (p. 226)

atlas (at′ ləs) A book of maps. (p. 343)

autonomy (ô ton′ ə mē) The right of self-government. (p. 402)

B

bar graph (bär graf) A chart that compares amounts by showing different sized bars. (p. 304)

barrio (bär′ ē ō) In Venezuela, a makeshift settlement on the edge of a city. (p. 480)

B.C. (bē sē) An abbreviation for "before Christ," used to indicate dates before the birth of Jesus. (p. 123)

bilingual (bī ling′ wəl) Having two officially recognized languages. (p. 149)

British North America Act (brit′ ish nôrth ə mer′ i kə akt) The law that made Canada an independent nation in 1867. (p. 138)

byline (bī′ līn) The printed name of the person who wrote a newspaper article. (p. 485)

C

call number (kôl num′ bər) A number and letter code that tells you where to find a book in the library. (p. 343)

campesino (käm pə sē′ nō) A poor farmer. (p. 359)

canal (kə nal′) A waterway built across land for boat travel, irrigation, or drainage. (p. 66)

caravel (kar′ ə vel) A small sailing ship developed in Portugal and Spain in the 1400s. (p. 226)

cardinal directions (kär′ də nəl di rek′ shənz) The four main directions: north, east, south, and west. (p. 9)

Carnaval (kär nä väl′) The Portuguese word for the period of celebration and merrymaking that comes just before Lent. Rio de Janeiro in Brazil is famous for its wild costumes, parades, and samba dancing during Carnaval. (p. 536)

cash crop (kash krop) A plant that is grown to be sold for money instead of for personal use. (p. 410)

cash economy (kash i kon′ ə mē) An economic system in which goods are exchanged for money. (p. 499)

caudillo (kou dē′ yō) A military dictator of nineteenth-century Latin America. (p. 341)

cause (kôz) An event that makes another event happen. (p. 166)

century (sen′ chə rē) A period of 100 years. (p. 122)

circle graph (sûr′ kəl graf) A circular chart that shows how large parts of something are in relation to each other, and to the whole. (p. 305)

civilization (siv ə lə zā′ shən) A culture that has developed systems of government, religion, and learning. (p. 203)

civil war (siv′ əl wôr) A war between two groups within one country. (p. 286)

classified ad (klas′ ə fīd ad) A short advertisement printed in small type and often placed in a newspaper by people who want to buy or sell something. (p. 484)

climate (klī′ mit) The weather patterns typical of an area over a long period of time. (p. 30)

climograph (klī′ mə graf) A graph that shows information about the temperature and precipitation of a place over a period of time. (p. 192)

colony (kol′ ə nē) A territory under the control of another, usually distant, country. (p. 118)

commercial farm (kə mûr′ shəl färm) A farm that raises crops and livestock for sale, not for the farmer's own use. (p. 302)

commonwealth (kom′ ən welth) The government of a nation or state. As a United States commonwealth, Puerto Rico has control over local affairs. (p. 425)

Commonwealth of Nations (kom′ ən welth əv nā′ shənz) An organization, including the United Kingdom and several independent nations that were once its colonies. Most Commonwealth nations accept the British monarch as their head. (p. 169)

communism (kom′ yə niz əm) A system of government in which the government controls the economy and the way of life. (p. 366)

community development (kə mū′ ni tē di vel′ əp mənt) Work done within a poor community to try to improve life there. (p. 549)

compass (kum′ pəs) An instrument that shows the direction of the magnetic north. (p. 226)

confederation (kən fed ə rā′ shən) A group of states or countries that join together for a common purpose. (p. 138)

conquistador (kon kēs′ tə dôr) A Spanish conqueror of Indian peoples in Central and South America during the 1500s. (p. 232)

continent (kon′ tə nənt) One of the seven large bodies of land on the earth. They are: North America, South America, Europe, Asia, Africa, Australia, and Antarctica. (p. 7)

contour interval (kon′ tûr in′ tər vəl) The difference in elevation between two contour lines on a contour map. (p. 335)

contour line (kon′ tûr līn) A line on a contour map that connects two areas of the same elevation. (p. 334)

contour map (kon tûr map) A map that shows differences in elevation. (p. 334)

Contra (kōn′ trä) One of the rebels who fought the Sandinista-led government of Nicaragua. (p. 366)

coral (kôr′ əl) A rocklike substance formed by skeletons of tiny sea animals. (p. 382)

coup (kü) A sudden overthrow of a government. (p. 342)

coureurs de bois (ku rûr′ də bwä) A French term meaning "woods runners" that refers to the early European fur trappers and fur traders in North America. (p. 119)

creole (krē′ ōl) A member of a Latin American social class made up of people who were born in the Americas and descended from the Spanish or Portuguese settlers. (p. 246)

culture (kul′ chər) The way of life of a people. (p. 48)

current (kûr′ ənt) A portion of water or air that flows continuously in approximately the same path. (p. 32)

custom (kus′ təm) A social habit or way of living of a group of people. (p. 49)

D

dateline (dāt′ līn) The line in a newspaper article that tells where and when the event took place or the article was written. (p. 485)

decade (dek′ ād) A period of ten years. (p. 122)

degree (di grē′) A unit of measurement indicating the distance between lines of latitude or lines of longitude. (p. 26)

GLOSSARY

593

democracy (di mok′ rə sē) A system of government in which the people rule. (p. 168)

developed economy (di vel′ əpt i kon′ ə mē) A system in which workers use a wide variety of resources in many different ways to produce a great many goods and services; a developed economy uses advanced methods, tools, and machines. (p. 164)

dictator (dik′ tā tər) A ruler with complete power and authority over a country. (p. 287)

dictionary (dik′ shə ner ē) A reference book that gives the meaning of words and tells how to pronounce them. (p. 343)

discrimination (di skrim ə nā′ shən) Unfair difference in treatment based on a person's color, race, or other differences. (p. 535)

distortion (di stôr′ shən) The shrinking, stretching, and changes in the shape and size of places that result when a globe is represented on the flat surface of a map. (p. 230)

distribution map (dis trə bū′ shən map) A map that shows how particular things are spread out in different parts of the world. (p. 13)

diversify (di vûr′ sə fī) To add variety to the economy; to grow or make many products. (p. 359)

Dominion (də min′ yən) A self-governing country under British rule. (p. 138)

E

editorial (ed i tôr′ ē əl) A newspaper article that gives the opinion of the editors. (p. 484)

effect (i fekt′) An event brought about by a cause. (p. 166)

ejido (ā hē′ dō) Government-owned farmland on which a group of farmers work together. (p. 301)

elevation (el ə vā′ shən) The height of land above sea level. (p. 23)

elevation map (el ə vā′ shən map) A physical map that uses color to show how high or low the land is. (p. 13)

emancipate (i man′ sə pāt) To set free. (p. 396)

emperor (em′ pər ər) A male ruler of an empire; often an absolute ruler. (p. 219)

empire (em′ pīr) A group of lands and people under the control of one government. (p. 213)

encomienda (en kō mē en′ də) A grant of Indians that the Spanish ruler made to colonists in Latin America. (p. 242)

encyclopedia (en sī klə pē′ dē ə) A book or series of books containing articles on many subjects. (p. 343)

environment (en vī′ rən mənt) All the land, water, plants, and animals found in an area. (p. 28)

equator (i kwā′ tər) An imaginary line around the earth halfway between the North Pole and the South Pole. The equator divides the earth into the Northern Hemisphere and the Southern Hemisphere. (p. 7)

estancia (es tän′ sē ə) A South American ranch. (p. 514)

estuary (es′ chü er ē) The mouth of a river, where the current meets the sea and the water is affected by tides. (p. 511)

ethnic group (eth′ nik grüp) A group of people who share a language, history, religion, and customs. (p. 154)

exile (eg′ zīl) To force a person to leave his or her country. (p. 400)

export (eks′ pôrt) Any item that is sent to another country for sale or trade. (p. 163)

extended family (ek stend′ id fam′ ə lē) A family that includes aunts, uncles, cousins, and grandparents as well as parents and children. (p. 297)

extinct (ek stingkt′) No longer in existence. (p. 36)

F

fact (fakt) A statement that can be proved to be true. (p. 208)

fault (fôlt) A crack in the earth's crust. (p. 325)

favela (fä vel′ ä) A slum in Brazil. (p. 547)

feature article (fē′ chər är′ ti kəl) A newspaper article about a person, issue, or event. (p. 484)

federal system (fed′ ər əl sis′ təm) A system of government in which the power is divided between the national government and the provincial government. (p. 168)

fjord (fyôrd) A deep, narrow inlet of the sea, bordered by steep cliffs. (p. 69)

foreign debt (fôr′ ən det) All the money a country owes to foreign banks and countries. (p. 488)

fossil fuel (fos′ əl fū′ əl) Any source of energy, such as coal, natural gas, and petroleum, that developed from the remains of plants and animals. (p. 272)

free trade (frē trād) The trading of goods without tariffs. (p. 170)

French and Indian War (french ənd in′ dē ən wôr) A war fought from 1754 to 1763 in North America between the French and their Indian allies and the British and their Indian allies. (p. 125)

G

gaucho (gou′ chō) A cowhand of the Pampas in South America. The original gauchos were descendants of Spanish outlaws and the Indians of the Pampas. (p. 518)

geography (jē og′ rə fē) The study of the earth and everything on it, including landforms, bodies of water, weather, plant and animal life, human life, and the effects of human activity on the earth. (p. 4)

glacier (glā′ shər) A thick sheet of slowly moving ice that covers part of the earth. (p. 42)

graph (graf) A chart or diagram that shows statistical information in a visual way. (p. 304)

great circle (grāt sûr kəl) Any circular line on the earth's surface that divides it into equal halves. (p. 268)

great-circle route (grāt sûr′ kəl rüt) The shortest route between any two places on the earth, often used by ships and airplanes. (p. 268)

grid (grid) A pattern of lines that cross each other, as latitude and longitude lines cross on a map. (p. 27)

guerrilla (gə ril′ ə) A fighter who makes hit-and-run raids on enemy positions but is usually not part of a regular army. (p. 470)

H

hacienda (hä sē en′ də) A large ranch or plantation in Latin America, often forming a self-sufficient community. (p. 247)

headline (hed′ līn) A phrase or sentence printed in large type at the beginning of a newspaper article. (p. 484)

hemisphere (hem′ i sfîr) Half of the earth, usually as divided at the equator or at the prime meridian. (p. 7)

hieroglyphics (hī ər ə glif′ iks) Ancient systems of writing that used symbols, signs, and pictures. (p. 204)

historical map (hi stôr′ i kəl map) A map that shows information about the past or shows where events took place. (p. 144)

history (his′ tə rē) The record of what happened in the past. (p. 41)

horizontal axis (hôr ə zont′ əl ak′ sis) The bottom line in the grid of a line or bar graph which identifies the information displayed above it. (p. 304)

Hudson's Bay Company (hud′ sənz bā kum′ pə nē) A British company that set up trading posts and explored along Hudson Bay. (p. 119)

humid (hū′ mid) Containing much water vapor; damp. (p. 271)

hydroelectric power (hī drō i lek′ trik pou′ ər) Electricity produced by the force of rapidly moving water. (p. 164)

I

Ice Age (īs āj) A long, cold period of time when glaciers covered much of the earth. (p. 42)

igloo (ig′ lü) An Inuit word for house, especially a dome-shaped house made of ice and snow. (p. 83)

immigrant (im′ i grənt) A person who moved to a new country to settle. (p. 132)

immigration (im i grā′ shən) The movement of people into a new country to make a permanent home there. (p. 153)

import (im′ pôrt) Any good that is brought into a country for sale or use. (p. 170)

industrialization (in dus′ trē ə li zā shən) Developing new manufacturing industries. (p. 515)

interdependent (in tər di pen′ dənt) The condition of depending on others. (p. 554)

intermediate directions (in tər mē′ dē it di rek′ shənz) The four directions between the cardinal directions. They are northeast, northwest, southeast, and southwest. (p. 9)

International Date Line (in tər nash′ ən əl dāt līn) An imaginary line that marks the boundary between one day and the next. The International Date Line runs north to south through the Pacific Ocean at about 180° longitude. (p. 444)

investor (in ves′ tər) A person who puts money into a project in the hope of making a profit. (p. 287)

irrigation (ir i gā′ shən) The watering of a dry land by means of canals, pipes, or streams. (p. 220)

isthmus (is′ məs) A narrow strip of land bordered by water that connects two larger areas of land. (p. 20)

a cap; ā cake; ä father; är car; âr dare; ch chain; e hen; ē me; êr clear; hw where; i bib; ī kite; ng song; o top; ō rope; ô saw; oi coin; ôr fork; ou cow; sh show; th thin; th those; u sun; u̇ book; ü moon; ū cute; ûr term; ə about, taken, pencil, apron, helpful; ər letter, dollar, doctor

GLOSSARY

Itaipu Dam (ē tī pü′ dam) A dam in Paraguay on the Paraná River. (p. 516)

K

kayak (kī′ ak) A small one-person boat made of sealskins stretched over a frame of whalebone or wood. (p. 83)

L

ladino (la dē′ nō) A Central American, usually of Indian or mestizo ancestry, who speaks Spanish and who adopts Latin American customs rather than following a traditional way of life. (p. 352)

landlocked (land′ lokt) Surrounded by land on all sides. (p. 493)

land reform (land ri fôrm′) A change in the pattern of ownership of land. (p. 301)

large-scale map (lärj′ skāl map) A map that shows more detail than a small-scale map by showing a smaller area. (p. 385)

latitude (lat′ i tüd) The distance north or south of the equator, expressed in degrees and shown as east-west lines on maps. (p. 26)

leeward (lē′ wərd) Located on islands or sides of islands that are sheltered from trade winds. (p. 387)

legacy (leg′ ə sē) The gifts a culture receives from earlier generations and passes on to future generations. (p. 156)

legislature (lej′ is lā chər) A government group that has the power to make or pass laws for a country or an area. (p. 135)

Lent (lent) The period of penitence observed in Christian churches during the forty days before Easter. (p. 536)

line graph (līn graf) A graph that uses a line or lines to show changes in amount over time. (p. 304)

literacy rate (lit′ ər ə sē rāt) The percentage of people who can read and write. (p. 512)

lock (lok) A kind of water elevator that moves boats to higher or lower levels. (p. 66)

long house (lông hous) A long, barrel-shaped building that is divided into sections and is sometimes shared by several families. (p. 86)

longitude (lon′ ji tüd) The distance east or west of the prime meridian, expressed in degrees, and shown as north-south lines on a map. (p. 26)

Loyalist (loi′ ə list) A North American colonist who remained loyal to Great Britain during the American Revolution. (p. 126)

M

map key (map kē) The part of a map that tells what the symbols stand for. (p. 11)

meridian (mə rid′ ē ən) Any line of longitude west or east of the prime meridian. Meridians meet at the North and South poles. (p. 27)

mesa (mā′ sə) A flat-topped hill or mountain with steep sides. (p. 442)

mestizo (mes tē′ zō) A person of mixed Indian and European ancestry. (p. 197)

métis (mā′ tēs) A descendant of French voyageurs and Indian women. (p. 141)

metropolitan area (met rə pol′ i tən âr′ ē ə) A large city and the suburbs and towns that surround it. (p. 198)

migration (mī grā′ shən) The movement of a group of people or animals from one place to another. (p. 42)

mineral (min′ ər əl) A natural substance, such as iron, gold, oil, or coal, that is dug out of the earth. (p. 34)

mission (mish′ ən) Land granted by the Spanish ruler to the Catholic Church in America to establish a religious community with a farm, living quarters, schools, churches, and workshops. (p. 243)

missionary (mish ə ner′ ē) A person sent by a church to spread its religion among nonbelievers. (p. 121)

monopoly (mə nop′ ə lē) The complete control over an area of trade and business. (p. 251)

Monroe Doctrine (mən rō′ dok′ trin) A statement of U.S. foreign policy, made in 1823, that said the United States would oppose any attempt by a European nation to gain control over any part of the Western Hemisphere. (p. 340)

mosaic (mō zā′ ik) A picture made up of many small pieces of stone, glass, or other material. (p. 153)

Mountie (moun′ tē) A member of the Royal Canadian Mounted Police, Canada's federal police force. (p. 142)

mulatto (mə lat′ ō) A person of mixed African and European ancestry. (p. 197)

myth (mith) A story about the gods, goddesses, heroes, and heroines of a group of people. (p. 95)

N

Nahuatl (nä′ wa təl) The language of the Aztecs, which is still spoken by Indian groups in Mexico and parts of Central America. (p. 295)

nationalize (nash′ ə nə līz) To place formerly private property under the control or ownership of the government. (p. 422)

natural resource (nach′ ər əl rē′ sôrs) Something found in nature that is useful to people. (p. 33)

navigable (nav′ i gə bəl) Deep and wide enough to allow boats or ships to travel. (p. 188)

news article (nüz är′ ti kəl) A newspaper article that tells facts about recent events in the community, nation, or world. (p. 484)

nomad (nō′ mad) A person who has no permanent home. (p. 42)

nonrenewable resource (non ri nü′ ə bəl rē′ sôrs) A natural resource, such as coal or iron, that can never be replaced once it is used. (p. 36)

North American Intervention (nôrth ə mer′ i kən in tər ven′ shən) The Mexican name for the war fought from 1846 to 1848 between Mexico and the United States; the Mexican-American War. (p. 283)

Northwest Passage (nôrth west′ pas′ ij) A water route connecting the Atlantic and Pacific oceans through northern North America. (p. 115)

O

opinion (ə pin′ yən) A personal view or belief. (p. 208)

Organization of American States (ôr gə nə zā′ shən əv ə mer′ i kən stāts) An organization including 28 nations of the Western Hemisphere; established to promote cooperation among its members. (p. 555)

P

parallel (par′ ə lel) Any line of latitude. Lines that are parallel never meet or cross. (p. 26)

patois (pat′ wä) A version of a language spoken in a region. (p. 477)

penal colony (pē′ nəl kol′ ə nē) A colony used as a prison. (p. 476)

peninsular (pe nēn sü lär′) A member of a Latin American social class made up of people who were born in Spain or Portugal. (p. 246)

peon (pē′ on) A name given to an Indian farm laborer who was forced to work on a hacienda to pay off a debt. (p. 248)

permafrost (pûr′ mə frôst) A permanently frozen layer of the earth found in arctic regions. (p. 74)

physical map (fiz′ i kəl map) A map that shows landforms and bodies of water. (p. 12)

plate tectonics (plāt tek ton′ iks) The study of the structure of large pieces, or plates, of the earth. (p. 18)

Platt Amendment (plat ə mend′ mənt) A section added to the Cuban constitution in 1902 by U.S politicians. It allowed U.S. troops to be sent to Cuba "for the preservation of Cuban independence." (p. 420)

polar climate (pō′ lər klī′ mit) The earth's coldest climate, like that found near the poles. (p. 31)

political map (pə lit′ i kəl map) A map that shows countries, capitals, and political boundaries. (p. 12)

pollution (pə lü′ shən) Damaging or dirtying the environment. (p. 35)

population density (pop yə lā′ shən den′ si tē) The number of people who live within a square mile or square kilometer of a given area. (p. 156)

portage (pôr′ tij) A land route between two bodies of water. (p. 120)

potlatch (pot′ lach) A feast at which a wealthy person gives away food and goods as a sign of weath and power. (p. 97)

precipitation (pri sip i tā′ shən) Any form of water, such as rain, hail, or snow, that falls to the earth. (p. 30)

prehistory (prē his′ tə rē) The study of the period in the past before the development of written records. (p. 41)

primary source (prī′ mer ē sôrs) A firsthand account written or prepared by someone who was present at an event. (p. 252)

prime meridian (prīm mə rid′ ē ən) The line of longitude that is marked 0° on a map of the world. East and west longitudes are measured from the prime meridian. (p. 8)

projection (prə jek′ shən) A way of showing the round earth on a flat surface. (p. 230)

province (prov′ ins) In early days, a place under British rule that was not part of Great Britain; today, a political division of a country. (p. 131)

pueblo joven (pwe′ blō hō′ bān) "Young town," an urban slum in Peru that often begins as a makeshift settlement. (p. 506)

pyramid (pir′ ə mid) A building with a square base and four triangular sides. (p. 204)

---

a cap; ā cake; ä father; är car; âr dare; ch chain; e hen; ē me; êr clear; hw where; i bib; ī kite; ng song; o top; ō rope; ô saw; oi coin; ôr fork; ou cow; sh show; th thin; <u>th</u> those; u sun; u̇ book; ü moon; ū cute; ûr term; ə about, taken, pencil, apron, helpful; ər letter, dollar, doctor

GLOSSARY

Q

Quebec Act (kwi bek′ akt) A 1774 British law that guaranteed French settlers the right to keep their own religion, language, and customs within Quebec. (p. 126)

R

racism (rā′ siz əm) The belief that one race is superior to another. (p. 408)

rain shadow (rān shad′ ō) An area that gets little rain because it is protected from rain-bearing winds. (p. 331)

rapids (rap′ idz) A part of a river with swiftly flowing water. (p. 66)

reasoned opinion (rē′ zənd ə pin′ yən) A personal belief that is supported by reasons or evidence. (p. 208)

rebellion (ri bel′ yən) An armed uprising or fight against the government. (p. 136)

recession (ri sesh′ ən) A period of slower business activity or growth. (p. 488)

reference (ref′ ər əns) Having to do with information to be referred to, as in a reference book; reference books include dictionaries and almanacs. (p. 343)

reform (ri fôrm′) A change made by a government to improve the lives of its people. (p. 285)

reggae (reg′ ā) A style of music that began in Jamaica. It combines elements of rock 'n' roll, blues, and calypso. (p. 413)

region (rē′ jən) An area with common features that set it apart from other areas. (p. 5)

relief (ri lēf′) A variation in elevation. (p. 335)

religion (ri lij′ ən) The way people worship the God or gods they believe in. (p. 51)

renewable resource (ri nü′ ə bəl rē′ sôrs) A natural resource that can replace or rebuild itself. (p. 35)

representative (rep ri zen′ tə tiv) A person who is chosen to act for others in making laws. (p. 168)

republic (ri pub′ lik) A form of government in which the power belongs to the citizens and the representatives they choose. (p. 281)

reserve (ri zûrv′) An area of land in Canada set aside for Indian use. (p. 155)

S

saga (sä′ gə) A type of story that originated in Viking Iceland and has been handed down through each generation. (p. 113)

samba (säm′ bə) Brazil's characteristic dance form. (p. 533)

Sandinista (sän də nēs′ tə) A follower of Augusto César Sandino, especially one who supported the establishment of a communist-based government in Nicaragua. (p. 364)

scale (skāl) The relative size of an object, such as a map, compared to the thing it represents. (p. 9)

secondary source (sek′ ən der ē sôrs) An account of an event written or prepared by using information from primary sources. (p. 252)

separatist (sep′ ər ə tist) A person who favors separating from a country or religious group. (p. 148)

service industry (sûr′ vis in′ də strē) A group of businesses in which the workers serve people by such activities as teaching, putting out fires, delivering mail, and so on. (p. 164)

shaman (shä′ mən) A religious leader who is considered able to influence the spirits that some people believe control the world. (p. 84)

slavery (slā′ və rē) The practice of making a person the property of another person. (p. 196)

small-scale map (smôl′ skāl map) A map that shows a large area of the earth in a small space. (p. 384)

social class (sō′ shəl klas) A rank of society in which the members share similar economic, educational, and social characteristics. (p. 246)

socialism (sō′ shə liz əm) An economic system under which all land, banks, factories, and large businesses are owned and controlled by the government, not by individuals. (p. 469)

society (sə sī′ i tē) A group of people bound together by a culture and purpose. (p. 49)

specialize (spesh′ ə līz) To concentrate on doing a particular kind of work. (p. 211)

squatter (skwot′ ər) A person who settles on land to which he or she has no legal right. (p. 504)

stampede (stam pēd′) A sudden scattering or headlong flight of a herd of frightened animals. (p. 91)

subsistence farmer (səb sis′ təns fär′ mər) A farmer who grows just enough to feed his or her family. (p. 302)

suffrage (suf′ rij) The right to vote. (p. 148)

summary (sum′ ə rē) A brief statement that tells the main idea in a piece of writing. (p. 403)

symbol (sim′ bəl) Anything that stands for something else. (p. 11)

T

tariff (tar′ if) A fee or tax placed on goods that are brought into a country. (p. 170)

temperate climate (tem′ pər it klī′ mit) The climate characteristic of the middle latitudes, marked by cool winters and warm summers. (p. 31)

tepee (tē′ pē) A cone-shaped tent made of skins stretched over tall poles. (p. 91)

terrace (ter′ is) One of a series of steplike levels of fields built into the sides of hills to provide flat land for farming. (p. 220)

terrorist (ter′ ər ist) A person who uses fear and violence to try to bring about change. (p. 470)

tierra caliente (tyer′ ə kä lyən′ tā) Latin America's hot region, found between sea level and 3,000 feet (900 m). (p. 189)

tierra fría (tyer′ ə frē′ ə) Latin America's cold region, found at elevations higher than 6,000 feet (1,800 m). (p. 189)

tierra templada (tyer′ ə tem plä′ də) Latin America's region of mild climate, found in middle elevations between 3,000 feet (900 m) and 6,000 feet (1,800 m). (p. 189)

timberline (tim′ bər līn) An imaginary line on mountains and in polar regions above which or north of which trees cannot grow. (p. 74)

time line (tīm līn) A diagram that shows the time and order in which important events took place. (p. 122)

time zone (tīm zōn) One of the 24 areas of time difference into which the earth is divided to compensate for the earth's rotation of 15° per hour. (p. 444)

topic sentence (top′ ik sen′ təns) One of the sentences that contain the main ideas in a piece of writing. (p. 403)

totem pole (tō′ təm pōl) A carved tree trunk showing the animals and other objects that have a special meaning for a family. (p. 95)

trade wind (trād wind) A wind that blows across the Atlantic Ocean west toward the Caribbean and brings a cooling breeze for most of the year. (p. 386)

tradition (trə dish′ ən) A custom or belief that is handed down from generation to generation. (p. 44)

transcontinental railroad (trans kon tə nen′ təl rāl′ rōd) A railroad that crosses a continent. (p. 142)

tributary (trib′ yə ter ē) A river or stream that flows into a larger body of water. (p. 23)

tribute (trib′ ūt) Goods, services, or money paid to a ruler or nation as a kind of tax. (p. 213)

tropical climate (trop′ i kəl klī′ mit) The climate of the tropics, or low latitudes, characterized by very warm temperatures and little temperature change over the year. (p. 30)

tropical rain forest (trop′ i kəl rān fôr′ ist) A warm, tropical area with high annual rainfall and many trees and other plants growing close together. (p. 189)

tundra (tun′ drə) A vast treeless plain in the northernmost parts of North America, Asia, and Europe. (p. 74)

V

value (val′ ū) A principle, standard, or ideal held by a person or group. (p. 50)

value judgment (val′ ū juj′ mənt) A type of opinion that shows how someone feels about a matter. (p. 208)

vegetation (vej i tā′ shən) Plant life. (p. 34)

vertical axis (vûr′ ti kəl ak′ sis) The outside left line in a line or bar graph, on which information is arranged in progression. (p. 304)

viceroyalty (vīs roi′ əl tē) One of the political divisions into which the Spanish and Portuguese divided Latin America. (p. 241)

voyageur (voi ə zhûr′) One of the French transporters in North America who carried furs and other goods in canoes between western trading posts and Quebec. (p. 120)

W

War of 1812 (wôr əv ā′ tēn twelv) The war between the United States and Great Britain that lasted from 1812 to 1815. (p. 134)

wigwam (wig′ wom) A small, domed house covered with strips of bark. (p. 86)

windward (wind′ wərd) Located on islands or sides of islands on which trade winds blow. (p. 387)

---

a cap; ā cake; ä father; är car; âr dare; ch chain; e hen; ē me; êr clear; hw where; i bib; ī kite; ng song; o top; ō rope; ô saw; oi coin; ôr fork; ou cow; sh show; th thin; th those; u sun; u̇ book; ü moon; ū cute; ûr term; ə about, taken, pencil, apron, helpful; ər letter, dollar, doctor

GLOSSARY

INDEX

Page references in italic type that follow an *m* indicate maps. Those following a *p* indicate photographs, artwork, or diagrams.

INDEX

INDEX

INDEX

INDEX

INDEX

INDEX

CREDITS

MAPS: R.R. Donnelly and Sons Company, Cartographic Services. CHARTS AND GRAPHS: Tom Cardamone Associates, Inc.

ILLUSTRATION CREDITS: Tom Cardamone: p. 246. **Cathy Diefendorf:** pp. 520, 521, 522, 523. **Allan Eitzen:** p. 52. **Joseph Forte:** pp. 43, 55, 128, 150, 238, 254, 292, 314, 348, 370, 404, 428, 472, 490, 508, 528, 550. **Howard Friedman:** pp. 580-581. **Lane Gregory:** pp. 418, 526. **Gershom Griffith:** p. 92. **Rudy Gutierrez:** pp. 354, 355, 356, 357. **Hank Iken:** pp. 18, 387. **Pam Johnson:** pp. 214, 215, 216, 217. **Steve Madson:** p. 87. **Jan Naimo Jones:** pp. 158, 159, 160, 161. **James Needham:** pp. 44, 45, 46, 47. **Jose Ortega:** pp. 414, 415, 416, 417. **Hima Pamoedjo:** pp. 172, 252-253. **Margaret Sanfilippo:** pp. 208, 368. **Dennis Schofield:** pp. 120, 220. **Blanche Sims:** pp. 166, 290. **Joel Snyder:** pp. 88-89, 105, 205, 212, 536, 537, 538, 539. **Robert Steele:** p. 534. **Susan Swan:** pp. 288, 330, 424. **Gary Undercuffler:** pp. 206, 248. **David Wenzel:** pp. 60-61, 108-109, 182-183, 260-261, 320-321, 376-377, 434-435. **Liliana Wilson:** pp. 310, 311, 312, 313. **Ashley Wolff:** pp. 98, 99, 100, 101.

PHOTOGRAPHY CREDITS
COVER: Front: Robert Frerck/The Stock Market. Back: Robert Frerck/Odyssey.

All photographs by The Macmillan/McGraw-Hill School Division (MMSD) except as noted below. **Table of Contents:** iii: T. James Mason/Black Star; M. Semeniuk/The Stock Market; B. Steve Satushek/The Image Bank. iv: T. Wolfgang Kaehler; M.T. The Granger Collection; M.B. The Granger Collection; B. Bjorn Bolstad/Peter Arnold, Inc. v: T. Loren McIntyre; M.T. D.D. Bryant/DDB Stock Photos; M.M. Robert Frerck/Odyssey; M.B. Laurie Platt Winfrey; B. Dan Budnik/Woodfin Camp & Assoc. vi: T. Loren McIntyre; M.T. Roy Morsch/The Stock Market; M.M. Luis Villota/The Stock Market; M.B. Bleibtreu/Sygma; B. Georges Ancona/International Stock Photography. vii: T. Steven Brown/The Stock Market; M.T. Richard Steedman/The Stock Market; M.B. Jana Schneider/The Image Bank; B. Loren McIntyre. viii: T. The Granger Collection; M.T. Carl Purcell; M.M. Robert Frerck/Odyssey; M.B. Luis Padilla/The Image Bank; B. Giuliano Colliva/The Image Bank. 4: George Gerster/COMSTOCK. 6: Ken Cavanagh/MMSD. **Chapter 1:** 16: James Mason/Black Star. 20: L. NASA; R. PHOTRI-LANDSAT. 23: Wolfgang Kaehler. 25: L. Fulvio Roiter/The Image Bank; R. Loren McIntyre/Woodfin Camp & Assoc. 31: David Brownell/The Image Bank. 32: Ed Robinson/Tom Stack & Assoc. 34: Luis Padilla/The Image Bank. 35: Andrea Pistolesi/The Image Bank. 37: Courtesy of Jeff Gibbs. **Chapter 2:** 40: Semeniuk/The Stock Market. 42: Courtesy of The Smithsonian Institution. 45: Dan Guravich/Photo Researchers. 47: L. Thor Larsen; R. Brian & Cherry Alexander. 51: L. Nick Nicholson/The Image Bank; R. Dennis Doran/West Stock. **Chapter 3:** 62: Steve Satushek/The Image Bank. 64-65: Bill Brooks/Masterfile. 67: Cameramann International. 68: T.L. Robert Frerck/Odyssey; B. Frank Whitney/The Image Bank. 68-69: T.R. Steve Satushek/The Image Bank. 69: R. Canapress Photo. 74: L. Albert Kuhnigk/Valan Photos. 74-75: Wolfgang Kaehler. 76: L. Thomas Kitchin/First Light, Toronto; R. Bill Brooks/Masterfile. **Chapter 4:** 80: Wolfgang Kaehler. 83: Momatiuk/Eastcott/Woodfin Camp & Assoc. 84: T.L. James Balog/Black Star; T.R. Wolfgang Kaehler; B.L. Werner Forman Archive. 86: "The Elk Hunter," by Bert Geer Phillips, Courtesy of The Anshutz Collection. 91: L. "Bison Hunters," by Logan/American Museum of Natural History (#VC1539-1); R. Museum of the American Indian/MMSD. 95: L. American Museum of Natural History (#32467); T.R. Museum of the American Indian/MMSD; B.R. AMNH (#19-1086). 96: American Museum of Natural History/MMSD. 97: L. By Permission of Readers' Digest Assoc.; R. Jose Azel/Woodfin Camp & Assoc. 99: Lawrence Migdale. 110: L. Brian Milne/First Light, Toronto; T.R. Eddie Hironaka/The Image Bank; M.R. Tom and Pat Leeson/West Stock; B.R. J.S.L./Stockphotos. **Chapter 5:** 112: The Granger Collection. 115: L. The Granger Collection; R. Michael Holford. 116: L. The Granger Collection; R. Lauros-Giraudon/Art Resources. 118: L.J. Eastcott/Y. Monatiuk/Valan Photos; R. The Granger Collection. 119: L. The Bettmann Archive; R. The Granger Collection. 126: L. The Bettmann Archive; R. The Granger Collection. 127: The Granger Collection. **Chapter 6:** 130: The Granger Collection. 132: The Bettmann Archive. 133: North Wind Picture Archive. 134: The Granger Collection. 136: McCord Museum of Canadian History. 137: Culver Pictures. 139: Courtesy of Nancy Pocock. 141: L. The Bettmann Archive; R. Michael Holford. 143: Royal Canadian Mounted Police. 144-145: National Archives of Canada. 148: Glenbow Archives, Calgary, Canada/The Image Bank. 149: L. Derek Caron/Masterfile; R. John De Vesser/Masterfile. **Chapter 7:** 152: Bjorn Bolstad/Peter Arnold, Inc. 155: T.L., B.R. Kennon Cooke/Valan Photos; T.R. Robert Frerck/Odyssey; B.L. Karen D. Rooney/Valan Photos. 156: Paul Von Baich/First Light, Toronto. 163: L. Alec Pytlowany/Masterfile; R. Gerard Vandystadt/Photo Researchers. 165: T. Thomas Kitchin/First Light, Toronto; B. Bill Brooks/Masterfile. 169: Carl Bigras/Valan Photos. 171: Mike Beedell/Miller COMSTOCK. 173: L. Johnathon Wenk/Black Star; R. Reuters/Bettmann. **Chapter 8:** 184: Loren McIntyre. 186-187: L. Robert Frerck/Woodfin Camp & Assoc. 187: R. Alon Reininger/Woodfin Camp & Assoc. 188: Loren McIntyre. 189: Gary Braasch/Woodfin Camp & Assoc. 190: L. Gary Braasch/Woodfin Camp & Assoc.; M. Wolfgang Kaehler; R. Loren McIntyre. 191: Tod Nissen. 196: T.L. Robert Frerck/Woodfin Camp & Assoc.; T.R., B.R. Robert Frerck/Odyssey; B.L. Albert Moldavy/Woodfin Camp & Assoc. 197: T. Robert Frerck/Woodfin Camp & Assoc.; B. Kenneth Garrett/Woodfin Camp & Assoc. 199: L. Kal Muller/Woodfin Camp & Assoc.; R. Robert Frerck/Woodfin Camp & Assoc. **Chapter 9:** 202: D. Donne Bryant/DDB Stock Photo. 206: Michael Holford/British Museum. 207: Robert Holland/DRK Photo. 211: L.D. Donne Bryant/DDB Stock Photo; R. Robert Frerck/Odyssey. 213: Robert Frerck/Odyssey. 219: Robert Frerck/The Stock Market. 221: Robert Frerck/Odyssey. **Chapter 10:** 224: Robert Frerck/Odyssey. 226: L. The Granger Collection; R. Painting by Rafael Monleon, Robert Frerck/Odyssey. 228: T. The Granger Collection; B. The Granger Collection. 233-236: The Granger Collection. 237: L. Robert Frerck/Odyssey; M., R. Loren McIntyre/Woodfin Camp & Assoc.; R. Loren McIntyre/Woodfin Camp & Assoc. **Chapter 11:** 240: Laurie Platt Winfrey. 243: Robert Frerck/Odyssey. 244: The Granger Collection. 247: Luis Villota/The Stock Market. 250: The Granger Collection. 262: T.L. Roy Morsch/The Stock Market; T.M. Werner Forman Archive; T.R. Tom Bean/The Stock Market; B.R. Daniel Berner/International Stock Photography; B.L. Carl Frank/Photo Researchers. 263: T.L. Luis Villota/The Stock Market; T.R. Luis Castaneda/The Image Bank; M. George Ancona/International Stock Photography; B. Luis S. Giner/The Stock Market. **Chapter 12:** 264: Dan Budnik/Woodfin Camp & Assoc. 266-267: Thomas Nes/The Stock Market. 272: Robert Frerck/Odyssey. 273: Kal Muller/Woodfin Camp & Assoc. **Chapter 13:** 276: Loren McIntyre. 278: R. Robert Frerck/Odyssey; L. E.R. Degginger/FPSA. 279: L., R. The Granger Collection. 280: L., R. Robert Frerck/Odyssey. 282: L. Laurie Platt Winfrey; R. The Granger Collection. 283: L., R. The Granger Collection. 286: Robert Frerck/Odyssey. 287: L. The Granger Collection; R. North Wind Picture Archives. 289: L. The Bettmann Archive; R. UPI/Bettmann. **Chapter 14:** 294: Roy Morsch/The Stock Market. 296-297: David Hiser/The Image Bank. 297: L. Suzanne L. Murphy/DDB Stock Photo; R. Barbara Cerva/DDB Stock Photo. 298: L. Stephanie Maze/Woodfin Camp & Assoc.; R. Eric Carle/Bruce Coleman. 299: Tod Nissen. 301: T. Randa Bishop/DPI; B. Stephanie Maze/Woodfin Camp & Assoc. 302: T.L. Robert Frerck/Tony Stone Worldwide; R. Randa Bishop/DPI; B.L. Byron Augustin/Tom Stack & Assoc. 303: L. Stephanie Maze/Woodfin Camp & Assoc.; R. Byron Augustin/Tom Stack & Assoc. 306-307: Christopher Morris/Black Star. 307: L. Harold Sund/The Image Bank; R. Faustine/The Image Bank. 308: T. Randa Bishop/DPI; B. David Hisek/The Image Bank. 309: L. Robert Frerck/The Stock Market; R. Victor Englebert/Odyssey. 310: "Self-Portrait" by Frida Kahlo, 1937/Hayden Harrera. **Chapter 15:** 324: Luis Villota/The Stock Market. 326: Hank Morgan/Rainbow. 327: L. John Cavanaugh/DDB Stock Photo; R. Janice Sheldon/Photo 20/20. 328: Robert Fried/DDB Stock Photo. 332: L. Jeff Foott/Bruce Coleman, Inc.; M. Peter Ward/Bruce Coleman, Inc.; R. Michael Fogden/Animals Animals. 333: Chip & Jill Isenhart/Tom Stack & Assoc. **Chapter 16:** 338: Bleibtreu/Sygma. 342: Paul Conkin/Monkmeyer Press Photos. 345: MMSD. 346: Robert Frerck/Odyssey. 347: Bleibtreu/Sygma. **Chapter 17:** 350: George Ancona/International Stock Photography. 353: T. Chip & Jill Eisenhart/Tom Stack & Assoc.; B. Jack Swenson/Tom Stack & Assoc. 359: L. Nicholas Devore III/Bruce Coleman, Inc.; R. Steve Worthup/Black Star. 360: DDB Stock Photos. 360-361: T. Richiardi/Allsport. 361: T.R. Byron Augustin/DDB Stock Photo; B.R. Robert Fried/DDB Stock Photo. 362: L., R. Robert Fried/DDB Stock Photo. 365: L. National Archive/Magnum Photos; R. Miami Herald. 366: L., R. Cindy Karp/Black Star. 367: L. Raimon/The Picture Cube; R. Reuters/Bettmann. **Chapter 18:** 380: Stephen Brown/The Stock Market. 383: L. David Burnett/Woodfin Camp & Assoc.; R. Jane Art Ltd./The Image Bank. 387: David J. Maenza/The Image Bank. 388-389: T. Gary A. Conner/DDB Stock Photo. 388: B.R. Giuliano Colliva/The Image Bank; L. Sipa Press. 389: M. Wayne Eastep/The Stock Market; R. Richard & Mary Magruder/The Image Bank. **Chapter 19:** 392: Richard Steedman/The Stock Market. 394: L., T.R., B.R. Pictures of Record; M. International Marine Publishing. 396: T.L., B., B.R. The Granger Collection; T.R. Robert Frerck/Woodfin Camp & Assoc. 397: T. The Granger Collection; B. Culver Pictures. 398: Courtesy of Ada Balcacer. 400: T. Culver Pictures; B. The Granger Collection. 401: L. Library of Congress/MMSD; R. The Granger Collection. 402: Randy O'Rourke/The Stock Market. **Chapter 20:** 406: Jana Schneider/The Image Bank. 409: Bob Strong/Sipa Press. 412: Werner J. Bertsch/Bruce Coleman, Inc. 413: L. Charles Steiner/Sygma; R. Mario Algaze/The Image Works. 421: T., B. The Bettmann Archive. 422: T. UPI/Bettmann; B. Bernard Gotfryd/Woodfin Camp & Assoc. 423: AP Photo. 425: Gabe Palmer/The Stock Market. 426: Nick Nickolson/The Image Bank; R.W. Bertsch/Bruce Coleman, Inc. **Chapter 21:** 438: Loren McIntyre. 441: T. Paolo Gori/The Image Bank; B. Alain Keler/Sygma. 443: T. Loren McIntyre; B. Wolfgang Kaehler. 447: L., R. Sygma. 449: L. Loren McIntyre/Black Star; R. Michael Fogden/DRK Photo. 450: L. Luis Castaneda/The Image Bank; R. John Maier, Jr./The Picture Group. **Chapter 22:** 454: The Granger Collection. 456: Owen Franken/Stock Boston. 458: The Bettmann Archive. 463: L., R. North Wind Picture Archives. 464: L. The Granger Collection; R. Culver Pictures. 467: L., R. North Wind Picture Archives. 468: Robert Frerck/Odyssey. 469: T.L. UPI/Bettmann; B.L. D. Goldberg/Sygma; B.R. Reuters/Bettmann. 470: L. Vera Lentz/Black Star; T.R. Christopher Morris/Black Star; B. Frederic Alban/Gamma-Liaison. 471: L. Susan Meiselas/Magnum Photos; R. Reuters/Bettmann. **Chapter 23:** 474: Carl Purcell. 477: David De Uries/Bruce Coleman, Inc. 479: L. Joan Klatcuro/DDB Stock Photo; R.R. Holleindre/Sygma. 480: R. Eric Millette/The Picture Cube; L.R. Perron/DDB Stock Photo. 481: Lee Kuhn/FPG International. 482: T. Alvez/FPG International. 483: T., B. Courtesy of Ray Schambach. 487: L. Rob Crandall/Stock, Boston; R. Sipa Press. 489: Alain Keler/Sygma. **Chapter 24:** 492: Robert Frerck/Odyssey. 495: L. Victor Englebert; R. Robert Frerck/Odyssey. 499: L. Victor Englebert; M. Victor Englebert/Photo Researchers; R. Loren McIntyre. 500: L. Loren McIntyre; R. Victor Englebert. 501: Luis Padilla/The Image Bank. 502: L. Loren McIntyre; R. Michael Graber. 503: T. Noble Proctor/Photo Researchers; B. Kathryn Shaw/Inter-American Foundation. 505: Carlos Goldin/DDB Stock Photo. 506: Victor Englebert. 507: L. Victor Englebert/Photo Researchers; R. Victor Englebert. **Chapter 25:** 510: Luis Padilla/The Image Bank. 513: Wallace Murray/DDB Stock Photo. 515: L. Gary Milburn/Tom Stack & Assoc.; R.N. Russel/Gamma-Liaison. 516: Loren McIntyre. 517: Carlos Goldin/DDB Stock Photo. 523: UPI/Bettmann. 524: Robert

Frerck/Odyssey. 525: Carrion/Sygma. **Chapter 26:** 530: Giuliano Colliva/The Image Bank. 533: L. Virginia Ferrero/DDB Stock Photos; R. Robert Fried/DDB Stock Photos. 535: L. Jean Anderson/The Stcck Market; R. Luis Villota/The Stock Market. 541: T. Alvez/FPG International. 542: L. Cameramann International. 542-543: Virginia Ferrero/DDB Stock Photos. 543: R. Haroldo & Flavia De Faria Castro/FPG International. 544: L. Bruno J. Zehnder/Peter Arnold, Inc., R. Toby Molenaar/The Image Bank. 547: T. Morton Beebe/The Image Bank; B. Robert Fried/DDB Stock Photos. 548: Virginia Ferrero/DDB Stock Photos. 549: SuperStock. **Chapter 27:** 554: L. Tony Craddock/Science Photo Library/Photo Researchers; R.J.L. Atlan/Sygma. 555: OAS. 556: T. Cynthia Rogers; B. David Finkel. 557: L. Dr. Richard Legeckis/Science Photo Library/Photo Researchers/T.R. McPhaden/NOAA/PMEL. B.R. Jan Robert Factor/Photo Researchers. 558: Bill Nation/The Picture Group. 560: Maria Taglienti/The Image Bank.

ACKNOWLEDGMENTS, continued from page ii

of Charles Scribner's Sons, an imprint of Macmillan Publishing Company. "Here" by Octavio Paz from NEW POETRY OF MEXICO selected, with notes by Octavio Paz, Ali Chumacero, Jose Emilio Pacheco, and Homero Aridjis. Bilingual edition edited by Mark Strand. Copyright © 1966 by Siglo XXL Editores, S. A. English translation copyright © 1970 by E. P. Dutton. Reprinted by permission of the publisher, Dutton, an imprint of New American Library, a division of Penguin Books USA Inc. Excerpts from "Flores del Volcan" and "Flowers from the Volcano" are reprinted from FLOWERS FROM THE VOLCANO by Claribel Alegría, translated by Carolyn Forché. Copyright © 1982 by Claribel Alegría and Carolyn Forché. Reprinted by permission of the University of Pittsburgh Press. Excerpt from "Wish Come True" (Chapter 1) of MINE FOR KEEPS by Jean Little. Copyright © 1962 by Jean Little. By permission of Little, Brown and Company and Little, Brown Canada. Excerpt from "Child of the Americas" in GETTING HOME ALIVE by Aurora Levins Morales and Rosario Morales. Copyright © 1986 by Aurora Levins Morales and Rosario Morales. Reprinted by permission of Firebrand Books, 141 The Commons, Ithaca, New York 14850. "My Bark Canoe" from The Botsford Collection of Folksongs, Vol. 1 by Florence Hudson Botsford. Copyright © 1930 (renewed) G. Schirmer, Inc. International Copyright secured. All rights reserved. Used by permission. "Mexican National Anthem" Words by Francisco González Bocanegra Music by Jaime Nunó. Translation by B. Romero. Versified by J. E. Hales. English words copyright J. B. Cramer & Co. Ltd. Used by permission. "Sweet Sugar Cane" from CANCIONES TIPICAS. Copyright 1941, copyright renewed 1968 by Silver Burdett Co. Used by permission of the publisher. "La Borinqueña" Words by Manuel Fernandez Jucas. Music by Felix Astol. English lyrics by Olga Paul. © 1957 EDWARD B. MARKS MUSIC COMPANY. Copyright renewed. Used by permission. All rights reserved. "Brazilian National Anthem" Words by Joaquim Osório Duque Estrada. Music by Francisco Manuel da Silva. Translation by Gastão Nothman. Versified by Sebastian Shaw. By permission of J. B. Cramer & Co. Ltd.

Howdy